ALABAMA
THE HISTORY OF
A DEEP SOUTH
STATE

ALABAMA

The History of a Deep South State

———

William Warren Rogers
Robert David Ward
Leah Rawls Atkins
Wayne Flynt

———

THE UNIVERSITY OF

ALABAMA

PRESS

Tuscaloosa and London

Publication of this book has been assisted by a generous gift from
The Kirkman and Elizabeth O'Neal Foundation, Inc.

Designed by Cameron Poulter

∞

The paper on which this book is printed
meets the minimum requirements of
American National Standard
for Information Science-Permanence of Paper
for Printed Library Materials,
ANSI Z39.48-1984.

Library of Congress Cataloging-in-Publication Data

Alabama : the history of a Deep South state / William Warren Rogers,
Robert David Ward, Leah Rawls Atkins, and Wayne Flynt
     p. cm.
Includes bibliographical references and index.
ISBN 0-8173-0712-5 (hard : alk. paper). —
ISBN 0-8173- 0714-1 (pbk. : alk. paper)
     1. Alabama—History
     F326.A553   1994
     976.1—dc20   93-27240

British Library Cataloguing-in-Publication Data available

3   4   5 / 99   98   97   96   95

This book is dedicated
to the memory of
M A L C O L M   C O O K   McMILLAN,
Alabama historian
(August 22, 1910–July 1, 1989)

Contents

Contents

Illustrations

Photographs or Drawings

Illustrations

Illustrations

Maps

Graphs

Preface

ALBERT BURTON MOORE published his *History of Alabama* in 1934, and it has remained the most comprehensive overall study of the state. A brief narrative history, *Alabama: A Place, a People, a Point of View,* by Daniel S. Gray in collaboration with J. Barton Starr, appeared in 1977. That same year Virginia Van der Veer Hamilton's useful and interpretative *Alabama, A Bicentennial History* was published. Statistical data and an outline of events through the nineteenth century are available in Lucille Griffith, ed., *Alabama: A Documentary History to 1900* (1972). The late Malcolm Cook McMillan of Auburn University, whose professional career was dedicated to the study of Alabama history, intended to revise Moore's book. While preparing the revision, he discovered that the appearance of many excellent scholarly articles and monographs on Alabama and the South, the increasing availability of original sources, and changing interpretations of history made a completely new and modern study necessary. His death in 1989 prevented Professor McMillan from writing the book. With the close collaboration and interest of Malcolm M. MacDonald, director of The University of Alabama Press, the four authors, who are students of Alabama history, researched and wrote the present volume.

By design the work makes no attempt to be a seamless study, but Professors Rogers and Ward served as general editors. The author or authors of each historical segment have written in his or her own style and presented individual interpretations and evaluations of events. Unifying threads of politics, religion, creative accomplishments, education, economics, geography and environment, military activities, race, and gender, of course, provide continuity. This volume is intended for general readers as well as for scholars and for use as a textbook in Alabama history. Besides providing a state history based on multiple primary and secondary sources, the purpose is also to explore and discuss topics that can be used as starting points for deeper and more detailed study. By offering interpretations of events and of people and their activities, the authors hope to stimulate thinking and inquiry that will agree with, qualify, or refute the positions they have taken.

This book could not have been produced without the prior work of many scholars and library and archival experts. A number of them have been kind enough to read parts of the manuscript and offer timely advice. The writers are in their debt. While taking responsibility for errors of fact and failure to include certain important topics, they would like especially to thank Kathryn E. Holland Braund, Edwin Bridges, Harriet E. Amos Doss, Robin Fabel, Elizabeth Fox-Genovese, Gene Geiger, Virginia Van der Veer Hamilton, Joseph H. Harrison, Wickham Henkels, Norwood A. Kerr, Jay Lamar, Joyce Lamont, Charlton Moseley, Jerry Oldshue, Robert Overstreet, Debbie Pendleton, Paul M. Pruitt, Jr., Robert R. Rea, William Warren Rogers, Jr., Serlester Williams, Beverly T. Denbow, and the staff of The University of Alabama Press.

Alabama: A Prospect

ALABAMA has played an important part in American history. It attracts attention and invites study. The state has in great abundance the perplexing paradoxes of the South and a number of its own idiosyncrasies. Anyone interested in Alabama's history can see at once the influence of geography. Resembling a rectangle that let itself get out of shape, Alabama is a north-south state. It stretches the better part of 415 miles from Ardmore on the Tennessee border to Bayou La Batre on the Gulf of Mexico. Going from east to west, a traveler would cross about 170 miles from Phenix City, anchored beside the Chattahoochee River, before reaching Isney, a matter of yards from Mississippi. Alabama is divided by nature into distinct sections that, overshading and overlapping at their edges, developed historically as separate political, economic, and cultural units. It is divided by law into sixty-seven counties (the first was Washington, organized June 4, 1800, and the last was Houston, established February 9, 1903).

By the 1840s a white yeoman farmer from Henry County in southeast Alabama's Wiregrass region (named for the tough original cover of grass) had much in common with his north Florida neighbors. He shared fewer mutual interests with the landed slaveholders of Marengo County in the Black Belt of south-central Alabama. There were similarities, of course, but the contrasts were prominent. That was true of other sections: the Tennessee Valley in the north, and below there the mountain and hill counties, then the piedmont and the Piney Woods to the southwest. Even at the county level, provincial pockets evolved—especially in the Appalachian regions where valleys, ridges, and plateaus separated communities, limiting communication and transportation.

A cursory glance at a map reveals a river system scarcely rivaled by any other state. The Tennessee River enters at the northeast corner and leaves by a northwest exit. In transit through Alabama it nourishes a valley well suited for agriculture, and its current has been harnessed for conservation and industrial production. The Coosa and the Tallapoosa rivers flow southeast through hills that suddenly change to flatlands

Alabama Counties

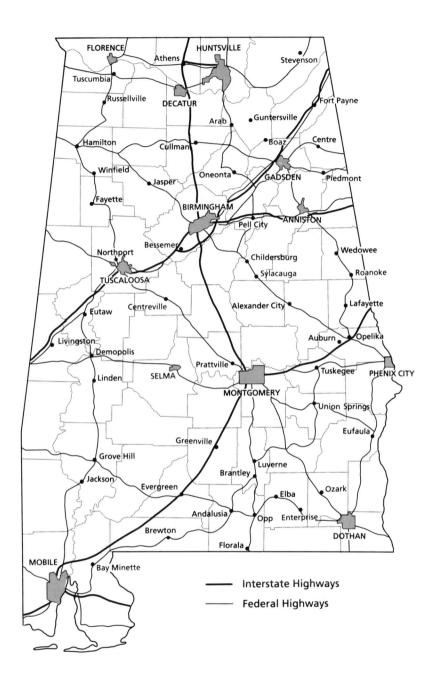

Federal and Interstate Highways in Alabama

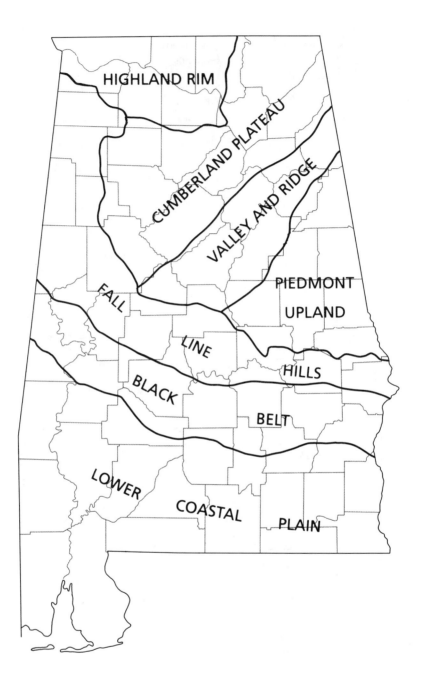

Physiographic Regions of Alabama

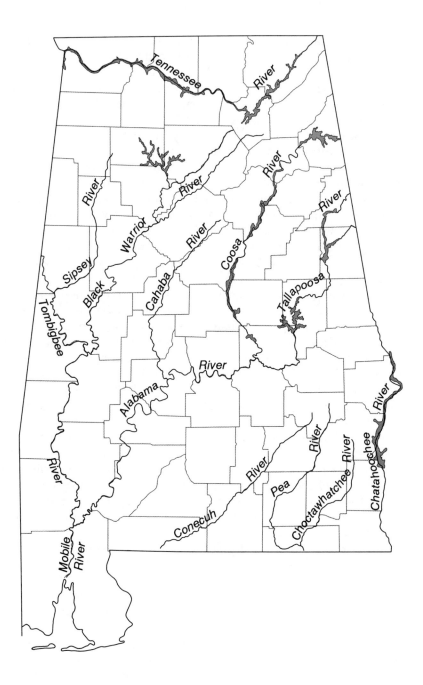

River Systems of Alabama

when the streams converge near Wetumpka and form the Alabama River. There the turbulence eases but remains steady as the Alabama meanders southwestward across the Black Belt, flows by Montgomery and Selma (where it is widened by the tributary Cahaba River), and drains what became a cotton kingdom in the antebellum period.

To the west and paralleling the Alabama's southern journey is the Tombigbee River. That broad waterway originates in Mississippi and courses south to intersect with the Black Warrior River. Originating in Alabama's central mountains, the Black Warrior has already outflanked Birmingham and passed by Tuscaloosa. At Demopolis the two waterways combine as the Tombigbee and continue south through the Piney Woods to a confluence with the Alabama north of Mobile. From there the waters divide to form a mix of land and water that includes the Mobile and Tensaw rivers, twisting and turning and forming the complex delta around Mobile Bay and the port that is Alabama's most historic city.

On the east the Chattahoochee River forms the common Alabama-Georgia boundary north of Phenix City and Columbus. It arrives there from the north Georgia mountains and at a fall line drops arrowlike to the corner of the two states and the northern demarcation of Florida. A few miles farther at Chattahoochee, Florida, it converges with the Flint River (headed southwest from above Albany, Georgia) to form the Apalachicola River and empty finally into Apalachicola Bay.

Early settlers found that much of Alabama's river system was navigable (only the major rivers have been mentioned), and by the late 1820s steamboats were carrying manufactured goods upstream and returning with cotton, hides, naval stores, and other agricultural produce. Peaking in the antebellum period, the rivers' commercial importance declined in the last half of the nineteenth and first decades of the twentieth centuries. Late in the twentieth century the rivers again became important for commerce and industry and as the source of hydroelectric power and recreational activities.

Forests of hardwoods and pines covered large portions of the state, and beneath the earth were extensive mineral deposits, including coal, iron ore, limestone, and marble. Much of the land yielded abundant crops, and the warm weather, long growing season, and plentiful rainfall created a profitable agrarian economy. Geography was and remains a major factor in Alabama history.

Beginning with prehistoric times and moving through the watershed of history that included the aboriginal inhabitants and succeeding peoples, Alabama became the home of distinct Indian tribes with complex cultures. Those encountered by European explorers and settlers were the Choctaw, Cherokee, Chickasaw, and, most powerful of all, the

Creek nation. The acquisition of Indian lands was sporadic and relentless, as though a patchwork quilt were being fashioned across the earth's surface. Determined but doomed resistance by the Indians resulted in warfare and sometimes peaceable cessions, usually forced and unfair. No part of the United States has a richer Indian history than Alabama. The state itself, as well as many counties, towns, rivers, and natural landmarks, bear resonant names taken from the Indian languages: Notasulga, Talladega, Etowah, Autauga, Cheaha, and Letohatchee, to name a few.

From the sixteenth century to the nineteenth, the future Alabama played a role in the game of European imperialism. In the name of mercantilism, the navies and armies of Spain, France, and England contended with each other for domination and possession. As the ultimate winner, a new nation—the United States—consolidated its position by creating the Mississippi Territory in 1798. Alabama was part of the territory. When Congress admitted Mississippi to the Union in 1817, Alabama became a separate territory. Growth was so rapid that it became the twenty-second state in 1819.

As Indian removal went forward and new lands were opened, settlers rushed in from Tennessee, Georgia, the Carolinas, and Virginia. Some were broadcloth planters who brought their slaves with them, but the majority were yeoman farmers with few if any chattels. In the next decades the frontier became more civilized, less raw at the edges— though the rate and extent of development and sophistication varied from place to place. Affluent Black Belt and Tennessee Valley slaveholders superimposed the plantation system, while independent farmers in those same and less fertile regions also earned their livelihood from the soil. Despite their legal status as property and their dominance by white owners, the slaves adapted to and altered the dominant culture around them and retained important elements of their African heritage. They almost equaled the white population by 1860 (there were 526,271 whites and 435,080 slaves). Besides the slaves, Alabama had 2,690 "free persons of color" on the eve of the Civil War. They were significant anachronisms in a society based on possessors, potential possessors, and the possessed.

Agriculture, primarily the growing of cotton, was the major source of Alabama's wealth before the Civil War. Yet the state was hardly a simple pastoral setting. It teemed with the complexities that come with the proximity of men and women engaged in the demands and dimensions of life. Religion, almost entirely Protestant, became important; education, not available to the mass of whites and denied to the blacks, was an instrument of power and advancement for those who acquired it; the presence and promise of railroads threatened to revolutionize transportation and economy; the perceived blessing and curse of slavery grew more intense as it became a moral as well as a political and economic question; embryonic evidence of industry suggested an alternative basis of wealth and employment; Mobile was the principal urban city, but the growth of Huntsville, Montgomery, and Tuscaloosa portended a change from agrarian dominance; politics became partisan and two-party as Democrats and Whigs competed, their causes presented with acrimony and intensity by talented and outspoken newspaper editors (not to mention letter writers identified and unidentified).

Nationalism was replaced by sectionalism as the debate over slavery intensified; by the 1850s one national crisis was exacerbated by another, and the national election of Abraham Lincoln caused Alabama to secede from the Union in January 1861. In February Alabama became a member of the Confederate States of America. Jefferson Davis was inaugurated president of the new nation at Montgomery on February 18. Montgomery served as the Confederate capital until May 21, 1861, when the seat of government was moved to Richmond, Virginia.

Although many Alabamians opposed the fire-eaters who touted the advantages of secession, once war came the populace gave important support. Besides agricultural supplies and weapons (Selma, with its state and Confederate arsenals, foundry, and navy yards, as well as privately owned factories, was a major manufacturing center for the tools of war), Alabama furnished enlisted men and officers who fought on all the major battlefields. Admiral Raphael Semmes commanded the *Alabama* with brilliance: the ship took sixty-nine prizes before being sunk. Within the state, Union raiders destroyed railroads and demoralized the countryside. The battle of Mobile Bay in 1864 was one of the important and stirring naval encounters in American history. Near the war's end Major General James H. Wilson led a cavalry raid south from northwest Alabama to capture Selma. His forces moved east to take Montgomery and continued across the Chattahoochee River to overrun Columbus, seize Macon, and end resistance in Georgia.

It was paradoxical that the Confederacy, whose philosophical underpinning was states' rights, fought a war whose success depended on centralized control. The subsequent lack of coordination, refusal to cooperate, and denial of civil and military responsibility extracted a heavy price. Despite initial patriotism, there was a strong element of Unionism in Alabama's Wiregrass and hill regions. Counties such as Winston and St. Clair not only had "layouts" (men who refused to serve in the army) but furnished significant numbers of soldiers who wore the Union blue. As defeats mounted and war-related economic problems worsened, Unionist sentiment grew. Defeat came in 1865 after four years of courageous struggle on the part of Alabamians and their fellow

Southerners. White Alabamians accepted the fact that slavery would end, but they still believed that Caucasians were the superior race. In spring 1865 both blacks and whites—with different expectations—braced for revolutionary changes that were sure to come.

Come they did. Acting under President Andrew Johnson's modification of Lincoln's moderate plan of Reconstruction, Alabama drafted a new constitution, ratified the Thirteenth Amendment, elected local, state, and national officers, and applied for readmission to the Union. All these things were accomplished without granting blacks the right to vote and with the imposition of black codes (special laws) that discriminated against the freedmen. The result was the defeat of Johnson by more vindicative Republican congressmen, known as radicals to defeated Southerners, and the installation of "Radical Reconstruction." Congressional Reconstruction included the imposition of military rule, new state constitutions that granted the franchise to blacks, denial of the franchise and the right to hold office to certain whites, and ratification of the Fourteenth Amendment. The Republican party was formed in Alabama and other Confederate states. Its components were white Northerners recently come South and dismissed as "carpetbaggers" by locals; native whites, considered traitors by their neighbors and branded as "scalawags"; and newly freed blacks who made up the foot soldiers of the Republican party.

The coalition took control of government at all levels and included the elected and the appointed. White Democrats denounced Radical Reconstruction as an orgy of corruption and misrule, bereft of anything positive. In fact, there was corruption, but there were also positive achievements. Nor were the Democrats without blame. By the time Republican hegemony ended in Alabama in 1874, the party (with all its faults) had produced an effective constitution in 1867–68, brought democracy to government, reformed the judiciary, provided for a public school system, and enacted (without the means to carry out) a broad program of social reform.

Throughout the years of Republican supremacy, the Democrats wooed former Whigs into their camp and demanded the restoration of white rule. That the fervid campaign had religious overtones was seen in the oft-used euphemism: Redemption. A minority of white Southerners fought back with violence. Members of the Ku Klux Klan and other night riders became a powerful force in the Black Belt and the Tennessee Valley. These terrorist organizations were not unknown in other sections. Reprisals and legislation by the federal government countered the Klan. Yet by the early 1870s corruption in the administration of President Ulysses S. Grant, a growing weariness among Northerners of Southern stories of outrage, and a desire to reap the harvests of industry and trade brought demands for change. In 1872 Congress passed the Amnesty Act, removing disabilities from all but the most prominent Confederate leaders. The symbolic measure was further evidence that the end of Radical Reconstruction was inevitable.

In state after state, including Alabama, white Southerners returned to political control, a vantage point that also assured them economic power. The new rulers were the old rulers—the Southern elite—plus young men coming of age in the 1880s. They called themselves Bourbon Democrats, the name deriving from the French royal house that was restored in 1815 following the defeat of Napoleon and the Congress of Vienna. Alabama's Bourbons—many of them Civil War veterans and heroes of the battle for redemption—preached economy, honesty in government, and white supremacy. They were fiscal conservatives who drafted a new constitution restricting state indebtedness. Blacks retained the right to vote, although how they voted was controlled by the Bourbons.

Beginning in the late 1870s north and north-central Alabama experienced an industrial boom. With Birmingham as the crown jewel, other cities—Anniston, Gadsden, Bessemer—combined to manufacture iron and steel and to produce specialized goods. Coal mines and other extractive industries yielded profits formerly unknown. The textile industry (of limited scope in the prewar era) made tentative but promising beginnings in Huntsville, the piedmont, and the Chattahoochee River Valley. Railroads, particularly the Louisville and Nashville, crisscrossed the state. Replacing cornfields with smokestacks was accomplished with local and outside capital. The Bourbons of the Black Belt retained power but made common cause (despite certain differences) with entrepreneurs of the burgeoning cities to enact legislation in harmony with the New South creed. That creed called for a balance between manufacturing and agriculture backed by legislation that either benefited business positively or, if logic indicated regulation that would lessen profits, was never passed.

Despite increasing economic diversification, most Alabamians continued to make their livelihood from the soil. The postwar decades brought bitter poverty to the poor white and black farmers. The crop lien and tenant farming system, intended as a temporary expedient, enslaved blacks and, as time passed, more and more whites. The majority of Alabama's farmers faced a cruel dilemma: production costs rose (fertilizer, equipment, jute bagging) and prices for farm products declined. The result was an increase in production to offset the drop in income. But each year surpluses piled up as profits merely broke even or turned to ascending, unpayable debt. The national economy was based on a deflationary monetary policy, and efforts by greenbackers and other advocates of inflation failed.

The Patrons of Husbandry (or Grange), a national farm organization, achieved some success with cooperatives and stores in the 1870s. In Alabama the Grange refused to enter politics because a third party would threaten Democratic solidarity. No one wanted, the Bourbons declared, a return to the misrule and corruption of Reconstruction. The Agricultural Wheel, a more militant farm organization, had limited success. Finally, the Farmers' Alliance spread across the South from Texas. By the 1880s it was entrenched in Alabama and offered salvation through a broad program of cooperative warehouses, stores, banks, insurance companies, and factories. The alliance demanded federal and state regulation of railroads and monopolies. Inflation and currency reform were also central, and the agrarian reformers devised the sub-treasury system whereby the federal government would guarantee farm prices and enlarge the money supply. Increasingly they advocated "free silver" to raise the amount of money in circulation and ease the burden of the debtor class.

When promises by Bourbon Democrats to pass proalliance laws proved to be no more than promises, Alabama alliancemen joined with other Southerners and midwesterners to form the People's party, also known as the Populist party. Its national ticket failed in 1892, but in Alabama the Populists won local and state elections and elected some congressmen. Reuben F. Kolb, an apostate Bourbon, was the most prominent Populist, although the party boasted a number of talented editors, writers, and politicians. Kolb would have been elected governor in 1892 and 1894 had there been a "free ballot and a fair count," but Democrats resorted to fraud and intimidation that equaled their efforts during Reconstruction.

After the election of 1896 the defeated Populists ceased to be a threat to Bourbon hegemony, yet their fusion with Republicans and organized labor and their appeal to black voters had been such a dangerous challenge that the Democrats determined to avoid future crises by removing the possibility of their recurrence. To do so they decided to use legal means to circumvent the Fifteenth Amendment that forbade voter discrimination on the basis of race. By employing a constitutional justification for disfranchisement that had nothing to do with race, they could banish blacks and poor whites from Alabama's election booths.

As the nation and the South entered the Progressive Age that lasted until World War I, Alabama's political leaders prepared to draft a constitution limiting progressivism to whites. In Alabama the Progressives claimed no close kin to the Populists, but they built on Populist reform traditions. The Progressives turned their attention to questions of railroad regulation, better government, upgraded education, and social welfare programs. Governor Braxton Bragg Comer typified Alabama progressivism, but it was a narrow reform movement at best—and at worst, it produced the constitution of 1901.

Delegates to the constitutional convention largely ignored the state's most pressing needs, but they accomplished their primary goal with devastating results. A complicated set of residence, literacy, property, taxation, and other requirements disfranchised almost all black voters. In time poor whites fell victim to the same restrictions.

The process was made complete with the adoption of a primary law. The measure limited participation in nominating elections of the Democratic party to whites. Nomination in the primary became tantamount to victory in the general election (the Republican vote was miniscule), and the Democrats were firmly in control. Their power remained absolute until 1944 when the United States Supreme Court ruled that primaries were an integral part of the election machinery. From that time forward, blacks raised the level of their struggle for voting rights to the crescendo of the civil rights movement.

The Alabama of the first half of the twentieth century was a state where whites ruled. Blacks remained a large minority with little improvement in their status as second-class citizens. The state was outside the mainstream of American life (and the mainstream was far from perfect), but some reforms were enacted during the Progressive Era, and determined efforts, such as eliminating the convict lease law, finally brought fruit in the late 1920s. The people struggled with the inadequacies of public education but benefited from advancements (free textbooks, increased pay, better-trained teachers) even when they fell short of actual needs. Social legislation was enacted grudgingly, but pressure was exerted, and various laws responded to human needs. Between the two world wars governors Thomas E. Kilby and Bibb Graves fought to apply the responsibilities and blessings of state government to the mass of Alabama citizens.

Yielding to few in their patriotism, Alabamians had offered themselves during the Spanish-American War (like soldiers from other states, they were not utilized), and they supported Woodrow Wilson and U.S. entry into World War I. They suffered through the 1920s, although a few prospered. The people struggled to cope with a century that offered them unprecedented creature comforts: automobiles, airplanes, movies, radio—wondrous new luxuries appeared today and became tomorrow's necessities. Modern was a word that produced fear as well as challenge.

The lists of well-to-do Alabamians dwindled to few during the Great Depression. But in that bleak time Alabama's politicians used their talents (and seniority) to become major figures in Franklin D. Roosevelt's New Deal. Senator Hugo L. Black, despite his earlier membership in the Ku Klux Klan, was appointed to the United States Supreme Court and became one of the nation's most distinguished justices. In Washington men such as House members Henry B. Steagall and John McDuffie, the Bankhead brothers (Congressman William B. Bankhead and Senator John Hollis Bankhead, Jr.), and Lister Hill, both a representative and a senator, were powerful men who left their names on important New Deal legislation. Various New Deal programs, not the least being the Tennessee Valley Authority (TVA), brought needed benefits and programs to Alabama that had permanent effects. The manufacture of hydroelectric power by the federal government served as a yardstick to regulate private utility companies.

With World War II came industrial prosperity, and some farmers made a profit for the first time in their lives. Alabamians marched, drove, sailed, and flew off to battle. Cities such as Mobile with its shipyards or Childersburg with its war plants were hard pressed to provide housing and public services. Women went to war as well; never before had they participated so vitally in factory work, and never before had they been so mobile and so independent. Anybody who wanted a job could have it— and at good pay. Alabama became a much more mobile society, and World War II wrought more fundamental changes than any period since the Civil War.

After 1945 Alabama entered the Atomic Age with more optimism than foreboding. Its citizens had helped win the war, and they hoped to enjoy the triumph by settling into decades of ongoing economic and social opportunity. More immediately they wanted to spend some of their savings for scarce, rationed, or nonexistent items such as cars, shoes, candy bars, refrigerators, vacuum cleaners, toasters, name-brand cigarettes, and beverages they had done without. No more victory gardens or scrap metal drives for them. Real sugar, dazzling white, would replace Karo syrup. Nylon stockings, not messy, runny "paint," would glamorize the legs of women.

Soon a new group of accumulated events came center stage. The cold war, the Korean War, the *Brown* decision of 1954, the civil rights struggle, the Vietnam War, rises and falls in employment and the standard of living, loss of personal identity and focus—all these and more lay ahead. In the postwar years men such as Lister Hill, Governor James E. Folsom, and U.S. Senator John Sparkman kept alive the tradition of liberalism that went back to Populism. Yet the civil rights movement (the Second Reconstruction) that began in the 1950s placed Alabama, perhaps more than any other state, squarely in the eye of the storm and squarely in the path of history. Among the many players in Alabama, where local events had international ramifications, none were more prominent, or more in contrast, than Governor George C. Wallace and the Reverend Dr. Martin Luther King, Jr.

And what of television, increased leisure time, pollution, the drug problem, the space age (Huntsville would play a vital part), rock and roll, country music (native son Hank Williams was highly successful and his influence has been enduring), secular challenges to traditional religion and concepts of morality (was media evangelism the answer?), and a thousand and one things compelling and trivial? How and why did the Solid Democratic South shift in national elections to a Solid Republican South and threaten to do so in state elections, and how permanent was the new arrangement? To what extent would race relations improve and to what extent had they improved? How, from beginning to present, did and does Alabama fit the national pattern? And what are the strengths and weaknesses of nonconformity? Does the state's past explain its present, and will that past serve as a guide for the future? The form and order of events need explanation and evaluation.

Once the home of aboriginal inhabitants, Alabama was claimed and occupied by European nations, later to become a permanent part of the United States. A cotton and slave state for more than half of the nineteenth century, Alabama declared its independence and joined another nation, the Confederate States of America, for its more than four-year history. The state assumed an uneasy and uncertain place in the nineteenth century's last thirty-five years. Its role in the twentieth century has been tumultuous but painfully predictable. This history, written in the last decade of that century, attempts to present, explain, and interpret the major events that occurred during Alabama's history and to do so in the larger context of the South and the nation.

PART ONE

From Early Times to the End of the Civil War

by
Leah Rawls Atkins

The dogtrot house was commonly built by Alabama settlers. When this photograph was taken about 1890, log dogtrot houses were still seen in the rural areas of the state. The uneven juncture of the roof indicated that the two cabins were built at different times. (Courtesy of the Alabama Department of Archives and History)

ONE

Native Peoples of Alabama

THE most violent confrontation between Europeans and native Americans occurred on a fall day in 1540 in what was to become Alabama. Hernando de Soto landed on the coast of Florida and moved inland.[1] His wanderings eventually led him into northeast Alabama. During his journey down the Coosa River he visited Mabila (Mauvilla), where the Indians enticed the Spaniards into a well-planned trap, an ambush that almost destroyed the expedition. De Soto's commissary wrote in his report, "We fought that day until nightfall, without a single Indian having surrendered to us."[2] Although three Spaniards made brief contact with Indians before de Soto's *entrada*, their accounts of these meetings are scanty. For de Soto's expedition four narratives exist, and all include descriptions and information about native Americans in Alabama. Thus, through their reports and diaries, the Spaniards traveling with de Soto ushered in the age of recorded Alabama history.

For information about the period before de Soto's arrival in Alabama, the historian must rely upon archaeology. Although archaeology reveals much, its dependence on a fragile physical record leaves many unanswered questions about the Indians. Generally, it is believed that the earliest inhabitants of North America crossed the Bering Strait from Siberia on a land bridge created when sea levels fell, perhaps around 50,000 B.C., although some postulate a more recent crossing. Probably hunting and gathering bands seeking the large mammals of the Ice Age, they were of a Mongoloid stock and likely bore a resemblance to the peoples of modern-day eastern Siberia. Gradually they moved south, reaching the tip of South America 10,000 years ago. In their migration they spread across North America. The warm climate, fertile soil, adequate rainfall, and abundant game in the forests and streams of the eastern woodlands particularly attracted them. From the Old World they brought fire and the ability to use it, and with them came their dogs, so important in Indian life.

In the Paleo-Indian stage, people traveled in groups of related kinsmen, hunting and foraging for food. Living a seminomadic life, they ate the

Indians often used animal skins as decoys or disguises when they hunted. (De Bry after Le Moyne. Courtesy of the Smithsonian Institution National Anthropological Archives, Bureau of American Ethnology Collection)

meat of large animals and gathered nuts, fruits, berries, and a wide range of plant foods in season. They chose shelters for living places that were close to water and food supplies, and they divided labor by gender and age, with the women caring for children and the shelter, making clothes, and gathering and cooking foods. Clothes were made from skins, and tools were fashioned from rocks, bones, teeth, shells, and wood. The men hunted and killed animals with spears tipped with stone points and probably caught fish with bone hooks or wicker traps. Meat may have been cooked over open fires and fish and river mussels baked in pits dug in the earth, lined and topped with hot coals. In order to carry or hold items, the people learned to weave baskets of reeds and vines. Paleo-Indians interred their dead with ritual and added worldly possessions to the grave, a practice that indicates belief in an afterlife.

Gradually the groups became seasonally sedentary and congregated in small independent communities. For thousands of years humans occasionally inhabited the Stanfield-Worley bluff shelter in Colbert County near Tuscumbia, the Flint Creek rock shelter in Morgan County, the Quad site near Decatur, and Russell Cave in Doran Cove near Bridgeport in Jackson County. At Russell Cave archaeologists have discovered many layers of cultural material. The occupants may have cleaned the living space by dumping fresh dirt and burying trash, or perhaps the stratum was created by a sedimentary process. The Stanfield-Worley shelter and the Flint Creek site are significant because they contain evidence of Paleo-Indians in their earliest cultural layers.[3]

The Archaic tradition developed approximately 8000 to 6000 B.C. as the earth warmed and as the large animals disappeared. The Indians became more dependent upon deer and smaller game and upon gathering nuts, berries, and plants. The use of an atlatl (a spear thrower) improved range and velocity, especially needed when hunting small game. Shellfish, although low in nutrients, was an easily obtained source of food, and various species of mussels and freshwater snails were steamed or eaten raw. Large shell middens dot the banks of Alabama rivers near shallow shoal areas where shellfish could be gathered effortlessly. As life became settled, such plants as squash, gourds, pumpkins, and sunflowers were domesticated and cultivated. The Indians built temporary dwellings of small trees and brush, and they fashioned ornaments of different designs. Copper was introduced, and some tools showed a fine workmanship.

The Gulf Formational stage is a recent division recommended by archaeologists to recognize significant ceramic developments in Indian culture. Three eras are suggested: early (2500–1200 B.C.), marked by the appearance of fiber-tempered pottery; middle (1200–500 B.C.), when sand or grit was used to temper the clay; and late (500–100 B.C.), when pottery vessels had podal supports and surfaces decorated with designs made by pressing wooden paddles marked with a pattern into wet clay. Gulf Formational cultures were located in river valleys and along the gulf coast, and trade between areas was evident. Artifacts from Gulf Formational cultures have been found in the Tennessee and Tombigbee valleys.

By 300 B.C. a new cultural stage developed in the east and spread to the south. Called the Woodland period, it lasted in Alabama until about A.D. 1000, but there was great regional variation in cultural changes throughout prehistory both in Alabama and in the Southeast in general. During this time the Indians constructed permanent houses, often square-shaped, of logs with mud walls and thatch roofs.[4] The bow and arrow appeared, and maize and squash were important cultivated foods. Family groups were identified with towns, and elaborate ceremonies became an important part of culture. Simple earthen mounds were raised over graves, and in time large earthworks were constructed as burial mounds.

In the Woodland era people learned to embellish their pottery with elaborate decorations, and designs became locally stylized. Motifs were usually symmetrical, marked with cords or fabric, stamped with a pattern, or etched with a sharp implement. Weaving was sophisticated both in the selection of fibers and in patterns and designs. Woven mats

5

were used for shoes, sleeping pallets, and vestments, and small shells were added as ornaments. Deer skins remained the primary material for clothing and blankets, but tanning methods improved. Although these people smoked tobacco, they did so usually only as part of a ceremony or ritual. The most intricate pipes were made from carved stone with a platform or were tubular pipes with human or animal images. Birds, turtles, frogs, and serpents were popular motifs, and freshwater pearls were often added to clothing.

Between A.D. 700 and 900 a new tradition dawned, perhaps with influences from Mesoamerica through trade or from migrations of tribes into Alabama. Called the Mississippian, this culture reached its height about A.D. 1300, some 200 years before Columbus's voyage of discovery. Agriculture was important, and settlements were located in river valleys where the soil was fertile and easily worked. Corn was the staple food of the Mississippian society. Ground into meal, baked into bread, boiled in water, and fried in oil, maize provided the sustenance of life for the Indians. The most important festival of the year was held in late summer and celebrated the ripening of the green corn.

Mound building was a significant part of Mississippian culture. Examples of Indian mounds abound in Alabama, especially in Mobile, Baldwin, Marengo, Clarke, and Washington counties, as well as other places. But Moundville, located on the banks of the Black Warrior River in Hale and Tuscaloosa counties, is Alabama's most significant mound complex. A bustling city of 3,000 people, one of the largest prehistoric communities discovered north of Mexico, surrounded the elaborate temple mound built on a plain high above the Black Warrior River (also called the Warrior River). Hundreds of people constructed the twenty rectangular- and round-shaped truncated pyramids by walking up a sloped ramp on one side to empty baskets filled with dirt on the top. After dumping the dirt, builders stomped and packed the earth with their feet, then returned to the bottom to gather more dirt. Arranged in a circle around a plaza, the mounds vary in size and height, with the tallest almost fifty-nine feet high and covering almost two acres. Such construction indicates a thriving culture directed by some central authority, a chiefdom with social integration, and a complex and organized society with a dense population and extensive productivity. The society produced adequate food and traded products great distances.[5]

Designs on pottery, shell, stone, and copper indicate that priests or medicine men wore special clothing and shawls of colorful feathers. They adorned themselves with gorgets (collars), bracelets, and earplugs, which have been found in burial sites. No doubt they were highly regarded in Mississippian society. Ritual was probably related to a fire-sun deity, the sun being the source of life and light, and fire being the

Usually known as the "rattlesnake disk," this artifact is the most famous piece of Alabama Indian art. It was found at the Moundville site by a farmer/landowner. This disk is Mississippian in age, made by the same culture that produced the flat-topped mounds and ornate pottery of the Moundville culture (about A.D. 1000–1450). (Courtesy of the Alabama Museum of Natural History)

earthly sacred representation of the sun. The Moundville Indians buried their dead with ceremony, often interring bodies under houses and including in the grave personal possessions for use in an afterlife. There are also examples of urn burials, especially of babies and small children. The graves in the temple mounds have produced a rich collection of artifacts, including embossed copper pendants, shell gorgets, engraved stone discs with notched edges, exquisite urns, and various types of pottery. Significantly, no European trade objects have been recovered from the mounds.

The finely made artifacts attest to the sophistication and complexity of the Mississippian culture. Favorite designs were the Greek cross, usually enclosed by a circle, the swastika with concentric circles around it, an open hand with an eye in the palm, the rattlesnake, a winged sun pierced with an arrow, and circles with scalloped or rayed edges. Human figures are depicted wearing elaborate hair crests, earplugs, bracelets, and necklaces. Faces are painted, usually with a nose-to-ear-mark, and feathers and beads are plaited into the hairpiece.[6]

Although the accounts of de Soto's journey describe Indian mounds at several villages, none describes Moundville, and it is generally conceded that the town at Moundville was abandoned by the time the Spanish arrived in the area. De Soto must have missed the site, probably unaware of its existence. In fact, despite careful evaluation of the four de Soto expedition accounts and extensive archaeological excavations in Alabama, no place in the state has been positively identified as a de Soto camping site. The route of de Soto, the location of the villages of Coosa and Atahachi, and the site of the battle of Mabila remain subject to speculation and disagreement among archaeologists, historians, and local chambers of commerce. Stories and legends abound, and although dozens of Alabamians through the years have whispered they know the secret, no one has ever come forward with conclusive evidence.

Twenty years after de Soto's expedition, men from the expedition of Tristán de Luna tried unsuccessfully to find the lands of Tascaluza and the province of Coosa that the de Soto narratives described. Jorge Cerón visited the area and wrote that the de Soto accounts of Coosa must be false for it was "of such an undesirable nature" that there was "no place where one may remain or erect a town."[7] The proof of de Soto's journey remains buried deep in the soils of Alabama.

Extensive migration of tribes occurred after de Soto visited, perhaps because of the epidemics that followed his *entrada*. This migration made it difficult when the European traders entered the Indian country in the next century to determine the location of tribes at the time of de Soto's expedition. By the seventeenth century the majority of native Americans living in what was to become Alabama were associated with four major Indian nations—Cherokee, Creek, Chickasaw, and Choctaw. Within these nations town names often provide a clue to the tribal composition of the larger "nations." Linguistic grouping would place the Cherokees in the Iroquoian language and the three other tribes in the Muskogean tongue, although within this group many languages were spoken.

The Cherokees occupied a vast domain covering the mountains of east Tennessee and north Georgia and extending into the northeastern corner of Alabama. The tribe probably originated in the Great Lakes region and migrated south but shared many customs and beliefs with its Muskogean neighbors. According to tribal legend the land of the Cherokees was given them by "the Great Spirit who is the father of the human family, and to whom the whole earth belongs."[8] They had lived in the mountains for hundreds of years when de Soto's army invaded their country.

When Scottish trader James Adair visited the area in 1735, he noted that the Cherokees cultivated hemp and grapes on the small patches of land suitable for planting in the mountains. He wrote that the swift and shallow rivers so close to villages were important as places for "purifying themselves" and for "fishing, fowling and killing of deer which come in the warm season" to eat the moss and tender grass on the banks of streams. The region, high in the mountains, was a healthy area where "the natives live commonly to a great age."[9]

Adair reported that war was important to Cherokee society, and the taking of scalps was considered a brave deed. Cherokee mothers taught their small boys to avenge insults and to endure hunger and pain without complaint. Those young warriors who did well in battle had titles bestowed upon them. William Fyffe described the Cherokee practice of older warriors "boasting of their exploits" with "such enthusiasm that the young are catch'd with it & eager to emulate them," an "excellent way to whet the courage of their youth."[10] When death was imminent, one observer noted that the Cherokee when tortured showed "an uncommon fortitude and resolution, and in the height of their misery will sing, dance, revile, and despise their tormentors till their strength and spirits fall."[11] Indians did not routinely torture prisoners but more often adopted them into the tribe or, by the eighteenth century, enslaved or sold them.

The major tribe of Mississippi, the Choctaw, extended into Alabama north of Mobile. A Choctaw tribal legend tells of a migration from the west when a sacred pole was placed upright in the ground at night. Each morning the people noted how the pole leaned and went in that direction, continuing to move eastward. One morning the pole remained straight, and there they stayed. The tall chief Tascaluza and the Indians de Soto met at Mabila were Choctaws. The Alabamas tribe, which gave its name to a river and a state, also migrated from the west and first lived with the Choctaws, then with the Creeks. The word *Alabama* comes from the Choctaw word that means "clearers of the thicket."[12]

The Choctaws hunted and fished but were also known as a farming people, raising beans, squash, melons, and pumpkins as well as corn. Houses were widely located and separated by cultivated fields. Choctaws were especially fond of playing stickball, a game in which the combatants wore a loincloth, a mane of horsehair dyed various colors, and a tail of white horsehair. In each hand the players carried a stick with a hoop racket on the end. The object was to scoop a hard deerskin ball into the hoop and to toss the ball through a goal at the end of the field without touching the ball. The games were rough and violent, and James Adair reported he saw players' arms and legs broken during a contest. The games were associated with Green Corn ceremonies and were played and attended with great enthusiasm, often with large wagers on the outcome.

The Choctaws were small of stature. They wore their hair long and

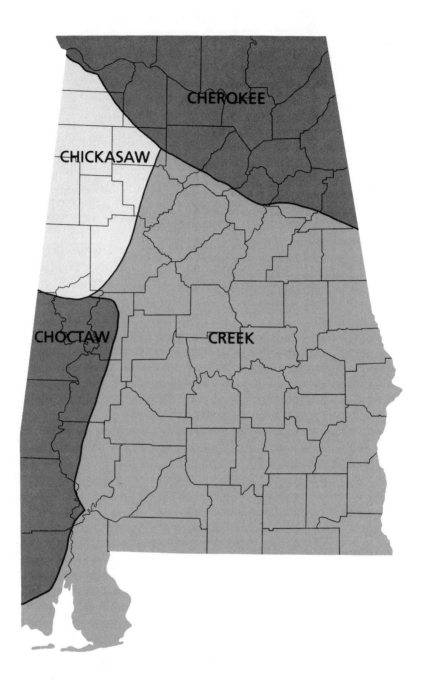

Distribution of Indian Tribes in Alabama

were called "Long Hairs" by other Indians or sometimes "Flatheads," after their custom of flattening their foreheads. To achieve this look, an infant's head was bound to a cradleboard and a slanted plank was pressed upon the soft cranium. The sloped frontal bone that resulted is evident on some of the skulls found interred at Moundville.

In addition to their appearance, Choctaws were known for their burial customs. William Bartram described the practice of placing the body on a high scaffold where the corpse, "lightly covered with a mantle," was to remain, "visited and protected by the friends and relations, until the flesh becomes putrid." Then "undertakers, who make it their business, carefully strip the flesh from the bones, wash and cleanse them," and pack them in an urn. They were stored in a community bonehouse until the house was full, and then a solemn funeral for all departed souls was held and the bones were interred in a common burial.[13]

The Choctaws benefited from trade with the French, with whom they allied in conflicts with the English. In the late eighteenth and early nineteenth centuries, they were quick to assimilate new farming methods; they planted European fruits and vegetables, cultivated cotton for spinning and weaving, and raised chickens for livestock. They were related to the Chickasaws but nevertheless were often at war with them. A tribal legend tells that physical separation of the tribes occurred after they moved across the "great waterway" (Mississippi River), became separated by a flood, and rains washed away all signs of the path taken by the Chickasaw. Touchy with one another in their new homes, the tribes' rivalry was inflamed by the Chickasaw alliance with the English.

The Chickasaws inhabited territory that covered portions of Tennessee and Kentucky, just touching Mississippi in the north and Alabama in a small area south of the Tennessee River. They were somewhat taller than the Choctaws, and their population was smaller. They relied less on farming, but like all tribes they gave women the responsibility of cultivating gardens. They were much more aggressive than the Choctaws, fierce fighters adept at surprise attacks. Jean-Baptiste Le Moyne de Bienville considered them "uncontestably the most brave of the continent."[14] They made great preparations for war, purified themselves, and painted their bodies red and black. During the attack they yelled and chanted an eerie cry that frightened their enemies. At least one historian has suggested the Chickasaw cry as the origin of the Rebel Yell used by Southern troops in the Civil War. During de Soto's *entrada* the fierce Chickasaws almost annihilated the Spanish by sneaking past the sentinels at night and striking without warning amid war cries and beating drums. Only one Spaniard was able to mount his horse, but he forgot to secure the girth and fell off "saddle and all" when he lunged at the first Indian. One de Soto account reported that "if the Indians had known how to follow up their victory, this would have been the last days of all the Christians of that army."[15] The Chickasaws killed fifty-nine of de Soto's horses, animals they feared, although two centuries later Chickasaws would have a reputation for horse breeding and fast ponies that helped in their surprise raids.

Chickasaw burial rituals were elaborate. They involved anointing the body with oil, painting the face red, dressing the corpse in fine clothes, and placing the body in a sitting position facing east in a grave dug in the floor of his house. Treasured possessions were placed in the grave and a eulogy was said. Burial was done only by relatives, who were then considered polluted by death and had to live apart and purify themselves by bathing. When epidemics wiped out entire families, bodies were left where they died, for there was no one to conduct the burials.

The Creeks were the largest and most significant Alabama Indian group, and they occupied most of the state. These Indians were named by the English for their affinity for establishing towns along the banks of creeks; they were actually a loose confederation of perhaps as many as seventeen separate tribes rather than a single tribe. Bartram in his accounts noted that the confederation of the Creeks was unusual. These groups banded together for protection after European epidemic diseases reduced tribal numbers. The Creeks controlled a vast frontier that was defended by scattered Creek towns whose names were later used to designate individual Indian groups within the confederation, hence the Eufaula and the Uchee (Yuchi). The Creeks were composed of two major divisions, the Upper and Lower Creeks. Okfuskee and Tuckabatchee, on the Tallapoosa River, and Little Tallassee, on the Coosa River, were major Upper Creek towns. The Lower Creeks lived along the Flint and Chattahoochee rivers. Cussita, near present-day Columbus, Georgia, and Coweta, south of present-day Phenix City, Alabama, were the two largest Lower Creek towns.

Towns were divided into peace (white) and war (red) towns with separate chiefs. Bartram noted that Coweta was "called the bloody town," where the "warriors assemble when a general war is proposed."[16] Meetings were held either on the town square or in the town house. David Taitt described the square at Tuckabatchee in 1772 as being "formed by four houses about forty feet in length" with openings in the front and seats of woven split cane.[17] When the Indian council convened, members took special seats assigned according to rank and function.

The Creeks followed the Muskogean tradition of adoption and readily assimilated Indian countrymen who came to trade and stayed to live. Many of the British traders from Charleston and the French garrisoned at Fort Toulouse fathered children by Creek mothers. Within two or three generations, these children assumed leadership roles in the Creek confederation, and many Creek chiefs carried English and Scottish names—McQueen, for example, and McGillivray, Weatherford, and McIntosh.

Although many social variations existed among tribes, the southeastern Indians shared a common culture, a tradition that was passed from generation to generation by story telling. Legends and myths were an important part of that culture. The myths explained things—the sources of water and fire, the formation of the earth, the origins of tribes. The legends told about migrations, long warfare, decisive battles, defeats and victories, times of abundance, famines, and epidemics. There were myths about monster turtles and huge snakes called Tie-snakes that were large enough to block a river or carry off a large animal. In some stories the rabbit, a favorite subject of Indian tales, was a trickster who outsmarted his enemies and fooled men. The Southern tribes also shared myths about great floods when the world was almost lost and stories about the corn woman who brought corn to the people. The Creeks, Chickasaws, and Choctaws shared a common migration legend of coming from "the land of the setting sun." In the Chickasaw version a dog led the people east. The long association between Indians and Africans on the frontier of the South resulted in a melding of folklore, and some stories appeared in both cultures.

In Indian culture women were responsible for food cultivation and preparation, taking care of the children, and producing clothing and household goods, such as pots and baskets, while men cleared land for planting, hunted, and constructed dwellings and public buildings. Men also held most of the public offices, both civil and military, and were largely responsible for the education of male children. Family groups and clans gave form to concepts of kinship; members supported each other and sought revenge for betrayals. Descent was matrilineal, and a woman's male relatives took responsibility for teaching her sons the ways of hunting and manhood. The Wind clan and the Bear clan were two important Creek clans.

Marriages were often arranged but never forced. If a young man was interested in wedding a girl, his courtship began indirectly. His mother's sister visited her mother's sister. A bowl of sofkee (hominy) was placed outside her house, and if she allowed the boy to come and eat from the bowl, she signified her willingness to marry him. But if she ran out and grabbed the bowl, she expressed her opposition indirectly without embarrassing him. Polygyny was often practiced by southeastern Indians but only with the first wife's consent. Otherwise, the husband faced charges of adultery, punishable by beating and mutilation at the hands of her kinsmen.

The Indians enjoyed playing games and loved to gamble, making large bets on the outcome of contests. In addition to stickball, chunkey (chungke) was a special favorite. It was played on a flat field by throwing sticks at rolling stones, with points scored by throwing the stick close to the stone. Adair described the playing poles as "about eight feet long, smooth, and tapering at each end, the points flat." The stones were "about two fingers broad at the edge, and two spans round." They were "rubbed smooth on the rocks" and "kept with the strictest religious care, from one generation to another, and are exempted from being buried with the dead. They belong to the town where they are used, and are carefully preserved."[18]

A number of Indian sports traditions have made their way into modern American society. A rough Indian ball game, played on a flat field with goals at each end and attended by enthusiastic cheering supporters, was a team sport not unlike modern football. Stickball bore a resemblance to lacrosse. An Indian fascination with high-stakes gambling on sports events and games of chance has not vanished from American life, and the ancestral Indian footraces, traditionally run on trading trails and open country and as contests between tribes, are now held on tracks in stadiums and on city streets. There is no evidence to show that Europeans brought these games to America. Observing the Pennsylvania Carlisle Indian School, John Steinbeck wrote that "for some twenty-odd years the Redmen raced across the stage of big-time football, leaving in their wake many a bewildered team . . . then vanished from the American sporting scene forever."[19]

When the native Americans gathered to play their ball games, they also included a time for dancing, which served social and religious purposes. Often named for animals, dances were accompanied by skin drums, gourd rattles, and cane flutes and by special songs and chants. Stomp dances often preceded major festivals, and they always took place at harvest-time ceremonies.

The Indian belief system was based upon a concept of three worlds: the Upper World, which was a perfect world above the sky vault; This World, which was a flat island hanging from the Upper World by four ropes and floating on the waters; and the Under World beneath the earth and the water, where chaos reigned. This World stood balanced between perfect order and disarray, an orderly place where rules applied. When bad things happened, the rules had been broken. In This World good would be rewarded and evil punished. The sun was associated with the Upper World and with sacred fire, and the moon was the sun's brother. There were three kinds of animals—birds, like the bald eagle that symbolized the peace and perfect order of the Upper World; four-footed animals, like the deer of This World; and vermin, epitomized by the rattlesnake, which was associated with the Under World. The Indians believed in ghosts, monsters, little people, spirits, and witches.[20]

Many illnesses were believed to be caused by animals who had been offended, so medicine men or prophets used magic, conjuring, and the medicinal properties of plants to achieve healing. The most valuable herbal medicine was made from the inner bark of a species of the willow, perhaps the gray willow. The bark, which contains some of the properties of aspirin, was soaked in cold water to make a tonic that was used for fever and malaria. The Indians also used poke root, sassafras, horsemint, peppermint, wild cherry bark, yellow root, and other herbs for medicinal purposes.

The southeastern belief system was based upon a concept of purity and pollution. Immoral acts would break the rules and threaten the well-being of the individual Indian as well as his/her people. A dark brew made from a species of holly (yaupon), common to the region but often transplanted by the Indians to be close at hand, played an important role in the purification ceremony. Called the black drink by Europeans, the Indian word meant "white drink," for white stood for purity, happiness, and social harmony. The holly leaves were picked, dried, then parched to make the active ingredient, caffeine, more soluble. The roasted leaves were placed in water and boiled, and the resulting beverage was strained and allowed to cool just enough to keep the tea from scalding the drinkers.

The caffeine in the concoction, which was consumed only by men, acted as a stimulant and a diuretic, increasing perspiration and thus purifying the body. Occasionally, the Alabama Indians added leaves or twigs from other plants or trees to the brew, and either these additives or the volume consumed may have caused the emetic reaction that sometimes occurred. It was ritually imbibed before council meetings, before going on raids or war parties, and during the Green Corn Ceremony.

The annual Green Corn Ceremony, the most important religious and recreational event of the year, brought people from near and far for the festivities, which lasted several days. Europeans called the ceremony the "busk," from its Creek name that meant "to fast." Fasting preceded the busk, a thanksgiving celebration for bountiful crops, that occurred from late July to early September after the last corn crop matured. In preparation for the ceremony, houses and garments were washed and cooking vessels cleaned. The old fire, thought impure, was extinguished, and a priest dressed in white started a new fire and announced that all transgressions (except murder) were forgiven. The men drank the black drink, and the dancing and games began. Only men participated in the ceremony, and guards stood watch to keep out the impure.

At Tuckabatchee special brass and copper plates that the Creeks be-

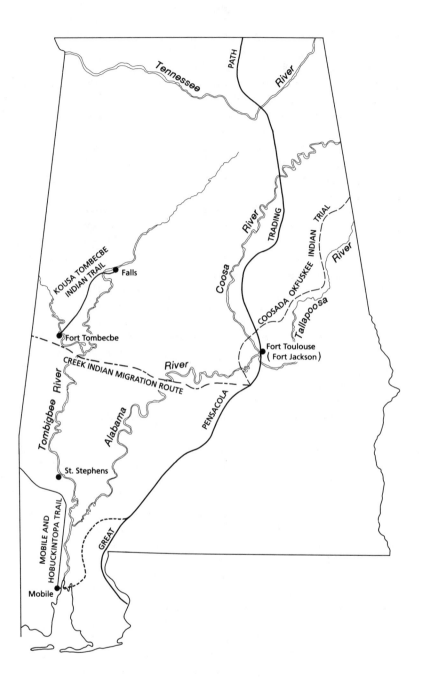

Indian Trails in Alabama

lieved were given to them by the Great Spirit were part of the Green Corn Ceremony. The brass was of European origin, and probably the copper was as well. Kept hidden during the year, the sacred objects were washed and displayed before the ceremony. Women were not allowed to touch or see them. The ceremony ended with participants covering themselves with white clay and then together washing in the nearest creek or stream. Symbolically, the old year had ended, society had been purified, and the new year had begun.[21]

The de Soto narratives indicate that the southeastern Indians were suffering from sicknesses and perhaps their population and power were already on the wane. America's native peoples possessed no natural immunity to diseases common in Europe for centuries, and casual contact with the Spanish along the gulf coast in the years before de Soto's *entrada* may already have taken a toll on the Alabama Indians. Smallpox was especially fatal, but measles, chicken pox, influenza, and diphtheria also ravaged the Indians of the Southeast following exposure to Europeans. The large expedition of de Soto, which covered such a vast area and lasted for so long, was devastating. His men had intimate contact with Indians in many villages, and they left not only mestizo progeny but also diseases that affected the people long after the Spanish were gone.

The effects of European diseases on native Americans included decimations of the population as whole villages succumbed to smallpox or another contagion. Villages became not only smaller but also fewer in number. Dual and mass burials became more common as necessity dictated changes in traditional burial patterns, and populations migrated, sometimes whole towns relocating in another area. The quality of cultural artifacts declined, and activities that required strong central leadership—such as building mounds and palisaded towns—ceased. When the European thrust of discovery turned to occupation and settlement, native American cultures lacked not only the technology to defend themselves but also vitality and strength of numbers.

European Exploration
and Colonization in Alabama

WHEN Christopher Columbus appeared at the Spanish court requesting support for a voyage of discovery, the monarchs, Ferdinand and Isabella, were eventually persuaded to turn their attention
beyond Spain's borders. With their backing, Columbus set sail. After a
ten-week western voyage across the Atlantic, he watched a flock of birds
"more varied in kind than any we had seen before and they were land
birds."[1] Finally, on October 11, 1492, a sailor called from the rigging,
"Tierra! Tierra!"[2] The Old World had reached the New.

Native Americans did not record how they received these strange pale
visitors from across the water, but Columbus concluded that they
thought he came from the sky. Other explorers confessed they took
advantage of the Indians' belief that the white man was divine and used
it to control them. Europeans reported native inhabitants bringing the
sick to be healed and making offerings to the Europeans. Soon, however,
native Americans not only learned that the newcomers were mortal but
also understood their motives. Even as they comprehended these revelations, they were rapidly seduced by the technology and material culture
the Europeans brought in their baggage.

Columbus made three more voyages to America. He was followed by
conquistadors who seized the wealth of the Aztec and Inca civilizations,
discovered the Pacific Ocean, and circumnavigated the globe. In 1513
Ponce de León sailed the western coast of *Pasqua de la Flores*, but a 1507
German map of the New World reproduced Mobile Bay in such detail
that it seems certain an unknown cartographer charted the Alabama
coast before the Spaniard.

In 1519 Alonzo de Piñeda sailed along the gulf coast and encountered
a number of bays and rivers, no doubt entering Mobile Bay. In his notes
he described a bay with a sizable Indian village on one shore and a large
deep river flowing into the bay. He reported that he sailed some eighteen
miles up the river and visited forty villages with a thriving Indian
culture. Piñeda's discovery has been identified as the Mississippi River,
but this may be incorrect, because the mouth of the Mississippi is too

marshy for habitation and his description in no way sounds like the delta. Piñeda spent several weeks in the area, repairing his ships and trading with the Indians before he sailed away.

In 1527 another Spanish conquistador, Pánfilo de Narváez, left Spain with a patent from Charles V to settle Florida. He sailed with a large, well-equipped expedition of 600 men, but the voyage was ill-fated. At a stop in Santo Domingo, a number of his men deserted, then a hurricane struck the ships off the coast of Cuba. After landing on the west coast of Florida, Narváez marched inland, alienated the Indians with cruel treatment, and suffered constant attacks. He then sent his supply ships west down the coast with orders to rendezvous with him—a tragic mistake, for he never saw them again.

When his food was almost gone, Narváez decided to build boats and sail toward Mexico to locate his supply ships. With great effort his men constructed five barges, and the 242 survivors embarked on a cruise westward along the beaches. The Spanish boats eventually entered Mobile Bay. It was probably there that they met several Indians in canoes, and a Greek carpenter named Teodoro and a black went with the Indians to find water. When the Indians returned without the two men, the Spanish argued with them. The treasurer of the expedition, Cabeza de Vaca, in his account of the affair recalled that more Indians arrived, including "five or six chiefs, who appeared to us to be most comely persons, and of more authority and condition than any we had hitherto seen." Cabeza de Vaca reported the men "wore the hair loose and very long, and were covered with robes of marten" with "inserted patches of fawn-colored fur."[3]

Narváez and his boat vanished at sea. Cabeza de Vaca and his slave Estebanico, with a few other survivors, stumbled ashore in Texas. They walked from one Indian village to another trying to find their way to Mexico. In March 1536, after wandering for eight years, Cabeza de Vaca and three others from the Narváez expedition came upon Spanish soldiers in western Mexico.

Cabeza de Vaca returned to Spain, where he learned that Charles V had appointed Hernando de Soto governor of Cuba and had given him a charter to conquer Florida. De Soto tried to persuade Cabeza de Vaca to join his expedition, but the veteran declined. Although no account details the conversations between the two men, Cabeza de Vaca was evidently evasive with de Soto about what he had found in Florida and shared little about his adventure. But Cabeza de Vaca's silence only whetted de Soto's appetite and convinced him that the Narváez survivor was hiding something.

Before de Soto embarked, Cabeza de Vaca presented Charles V with a grim report of his adventures along the gulf coast and Florida. His journal, published after de Soto's departure, had few specifics about Alabama, but his harrowing trip along the gulf coast contained the first description of native Americans in the future state.

Even had de Soto read Cabeza de Vaca's story before he left Spain, he probably would not have believed it. De Soto was an experienced conquistador who had distinguished himself as a captain with Hernando Pizarro in Peru. He returned to Spain a wealthy man and settled into the life of a gentleman, showing himself at court, spending "largely," and marrying well. Despite the unsuccessful adventures of Ponce de León and Narváez in Florida, de Soto was convinced that riches the likes of those discovered in Peru and Mexico existed in the interior. When de Soto announced his intentions, noblemen rushed to join him, many because of conversations with Cabeza de Vaca. De Soto recruited a variety of talents for his expedition—soldiers, blacksmiths, carpenters, shipbuilders, tailors, cobblers—in addition to nobles with nothing but money and a desire for more wealth. De Soto left Spain in seven ships fully loaded with food and supplies. He stopped in Cuba for fresh food and water, then sailed to Florida, landing somewhere near Tampa in May 1539. Four accounts recorded his expedition: the diary of de Soto's private secretary, Rodrigo Ranjel; the report to the king by the factor of the expedition, Hernandez de Biedma; the story related by a "Gentleman of Elvas"; and the narrative of Inca Garcilaso de la Vega, known as the Inca.

Soon after landing, de Soto encountered native Americans with memories of cruelties by other bearded white men, and de Soto's brutality only reinforced the remembrance. The Indians outnumbered the Spaniards, but the Europeans prevailed because they were heavily armed with pistols, long swords, lances, and daggers and because they wore metal helmets, thick quilted jackets, and shirts of mail. They rode horses, which gave them height and visual control of an area and allowed them to react quickly and move with great speed. The Indians had not seen horses before, and the animals both fascinated and frightened them. Native Americans soon learned that the strange invaders were looking for yellow metals and stones the Indians knew little about, and the quicker they were rid of them the better.

De Soto's excursion would have been a greater disaster if he had not been lucky and found an interpreter. Soon after landing, the Spanish brought several captured Indians into camp, but one proved to be a Spaniard, Juan Ortiz, who had been with the Narváez expedition. Ortiz had left Florida with the ships, but he returned to look for Narváez and was captured by the Indians, his life spared by a chief's daughter. Ortiz had lived with the Indians for twelve years and understood their language and customs, but he had not moved about and knew nothing of the country into which de Soto planned to venture.

To determine the exact path he traveled in his *entrada* (as the Spanish termed his journey) across the southeastern states, Congress established the De Soto Expedition Commission in 1935, and in 1939 it published speculations that seemed reasonable. In the years since then, fresh theories have been suggested based upon recent archaeological findings. So many different routes are proposed that the possible trail of de Soto looks like spaghetti spilled upon a map of the Southeast. Although the four chronicles of the expedition give details about many aspects of the journey, the topographical data are not specific enough, and time and distances traveled are too vague or contradictory for the route to be correlated to local terrain and plotted accurately on a map. Nonetheless, it is generally conceded that de Soto moved north up the Florida peninsula toward present-day Tallahassee, then north-northeast across Georgia and into the Carolinas. On these travels the only items of value de Soto found were some poor-quality freshwater pearls the Spanish stole from Indian graves. At some point, de Soto turned to the west and crossed the mountains into Tennessee, later following the valleys south into Georgia and Alabama.

One recent controversy over the de Soto trail concerns the location of de Soto's entrance into Alabama, critical in determining the approximate location of Mabila. The 1935 De Soto Commission placed the crossing near the Tennessee River at the northeast corner of Alabama. One opinion suggests that the sixteenth-century Indian village of Coosa was actually on the Coosawatte River near Carters, Georgia, and that de Soto moved into Alabama on the Coosa River and south to Talisi, which was located near Childersburg or perhaps at the junction of the Coosa and Tallapoosa rivers.[4] These views are opposed both by those who contend that Coosa was farther south in Cherokee County and by those who place Coosa, not Talisi, in Talladega County. The northeastern approach into Alabama might locate Mabila near the confluence of the Alabama and Cahaba rivers, rather than in southern Clarke County near the junction of the Alabama and Tombigbee rivers where it traditionally was held to be. Albert James Pickett in his history of Alabama, published in 1851, positioned Mabila on the north bank of the Alabama River at Choctaw Bluff.

Regardless of the location of these Indian villages, de Soto and his expedition entered Alabama in the northeast, followed the rivers, and visited a number of Indian towns. On the journey, the Spanish reported abundant food and thriving towns. They described Talisi as a large village on a great river surrounded by fields of corn. An Indian chief greeted de Soto at Talisi and delivered an invitation from Chief Tascaluza for de Soto to visit his province. De Soto accepted, and the Spanish traveled southwest to Atahachi, where they met Tascaluza. The Indian leader received the Spanish with ceremony. He was sitting on cushions with an Indian behind him waving "a fly-brush of plumes" to shelter him from the sun.[5] The imposing chief wore a "mantle of feathers down to his feet," had an appearance "full of dignity," and "wore a look of serenity." He was handsome, "muscular, lean, and symmetrical," an Indian so tall the Spanish "all considered him a giant." Although de Soto's cavalry tried to intimidate him by racing their horses closely, "their steeds leaping from side to side, and at times toward the Chief," Tascaluza never flinched and regarded them "with indifference."

De Soto talked with Tascaluza, and the Spaniard asked for food and men to carry his provisions and for women for his soldiers. Ranjel wrote that the Spanish desired the women for "servants and for their foul uses and lewdness, and that they had them baptized more on account of carnal intercourse with them than to teach them the faith." Tascaluza refused his requests, and de Soto took him hostage. Then the chief promised him bearers and whatever he needed, but only after they arrived at his village of Mabila. Taking Tascaluza with them, the Spanish pushed on, crossing over a great river on rafts. They visited Piachi, where they were shown the dagger of the Greek Teodoro and learned he was dead.

On the morning of October 18, 1540, the entourage entered Mabila, a village located on a plain above a wide river. The town was surrounded by a palisade, and inside were eighty large houses fronting a square. Tascaluza disappeared inside a house, and the Indians began to dance and sing while the Spanish grew more suspicious and uneasy. Suddenly, the Indians attacked, shooting arrows from the houses and forcing the Spanish to flee the village, leaving some of their horses behind. The Indians promptly killed the feared animals. De Soto rallied his men for a counterattack and set fire to the village. The battle, most of it hand-to-hand combat, lasted until nightfall. In his manuscript, the Inca claimed 11,000 Indians died; Biedma reported 5,000 killed; and the more reliable Ranjel related that the Spanish found 3,000 Indian bodies without counting the dead inside the burned village. The Gentleman of Elvas reported 2,500 dead. The Indian losses were probably fewer than any of these figures, but by any count they were extensive. Whether Tascaluza died or escaped was not discovered, but his town of Mabila and his Indians were destroyed.

Mabila was a costly victory for de Soto. Twenty-two Spaniards were killed and another twenty died later. Seven horses were dead and forty-eight others wounded. The freshwater pearls stolen from Cofitachique graves were lost, as were food, supplies, clothes, ornaments, and sacramental cups, wafers, and wine for the mass. The priests debated whether corn bread might be consecrated for the mass and decided it could not, so they observed a "dry mass." The Spanish remained at Mabila almost a month, healing their wounds. Ranjel tells of a Spanish knight of royal lineage worth two thousand ducats in Spain who was left "wearing a short garment of the blankets of that country, torn on the sides, his flesh showing, no hat, bare-headed, bare-footed, without hose or shoes, a buckler on his back, a sword without a shield, amidst heavy frosts and cold."

At Mabila, de Soto learned from an Indian that his Spanish ships waited for him at Ochuse (Pensacola), just as he had prearranged. But de Soto could not bear to end his expedition in failure. So he turned his army away from the Gulf of Mexico to the northwest, still seeking rich worlds to conquer. He crossed the Black Warrior River into a country where the natives were "easily secured" and where there was "an abundance of corn." The expedition moved into Mississippi, through Arkansas, then doubled back to the Mississippi River, where de Soto died of a fever near Natchez. The remnants of his army tried to reach Mexico through Texas, but the barren land forced them back to the Mississippi, where they constructed boats and escaped down the river.

De Soto's experience did not diminish the Spanish ambition to control Florida, for it was viewed as a protective lifeline to the riches of Mexico and the West Indies. King Philip II ordered his viceroy in Mexico, Don Luis de Velasco, to found a colony on the Gulf. In September 1558 Velasco sent Guido de las Bazáres with three ships to explore the coast. Bazáres rejected the Mississippi Delta as too soggy. He scouted Mobile Bay and was impressed with tall trees that could provide wood for repairing and building ships, a bay teeming with fish and oysters, and a land with plentiful game. A large river flowed into the harbor, and on the eastern shore Bazáres noted high red clay hills. He called it the Bay of Filipina, but his description so specifically describes Mobile Bay that it leaves little doubt where he was.[6]

Bazáres returned to Vera Cruz and made his report. Within a few months Don Tristán de Luna sailed for the gulf coast with 500 soldiers and more than 1,000 settlers, including women and children. He carried food, farm tools, seeds, horses, cattle, and other supplies to sustain a settlement until farmers could till the soil and produce adequate food. De Luna's group included a few veterans of de Soto's expedition and several Indians the de Soto survivors brought to Mexico. They recommended the rich province of Coosa as an ideal place for a Spanish town.

De Luna missed Ochuse the first time and stopped at Bazáres's Filipina Bay (Mobile) while his frigate looked for the deeper harbor. Informed that it was close, he unloaded his horses and sent them overland. Five days after de Luna landed at Ochuse, a hurricane blew in, sinking eight of his ships, destroying much of his food and equipment, and killing many of his people. To find food de Luna sent soldiers to locate Indian villages, where he knew corn would be growing. Hunger gripped the expedition, so he decided to move the colony to the village of Nanipacana on the Alabama River. The Indians there probably recalled stories of Mabila, and they burned their fields and fled with their maize before the full entourage arrived. The courage of the colony waned under threat of starvation, but scouting parties continued to search for Coosa and the thriving Indian villages and fertile fields de Soto had visited. They found only vast uninhabited areas where those villages had been. The changes that had occurred since de Soto's *entrada* were profound.

Demoralized, weak, and suffering from hunger, the men begged de Luna to return to Mexico "in order that we may not see ourselves perish and our wives and children die."[7] De Luna moved the colony to the coast, where they were rescued by a passing Spanish fleet headed to the east coast of Florida. Once more Spain had failed to settle on the Gulf. In 1565, four years later, they tried the Atlantic coast and established St. Augustine.

More than a century would pass before another European country attempted to colonize Alabama's bay or penetrate its wilderness rivers. By then the international power balance had shifted, and it was not the Spanish who came. The defeat of the Spanish Armada by the English sea dogs in 1588 symbolized the waning power of Spain, the country that had discovered the New World and dominated the Old with stolen gold.

If the sixteenth century found Spain at its zenith, the seventeenth century belonged to France. Ruled for seventy-two years by the great Sun King, Louis XIV, and served by brilliant ministers, France created an army that intimidated the Continent and a navy strong enough to support exploration and settlement in Canada. In 1608 the French flag flew in Quebec, and zealous Jesuit missionaries fanned out to convert the Indians. Many were martyred in the process. Father Jacques Marquette and Louis Joliet explored the Mississippi River, but it was Robert Cavalier, Sieur de La Salle, who floated down the river in 1682 and named the country for his king. Unfortunately, when he approached by the Gulf route, the islands and marshes of the delta hid the entrance, and he failed to locate the mouth of the waterway. On his trips La Salle was accompanied by Henri de Tonti, an Italian adventurer who sported an iron hand in place of the one he had lost fighting for France. A nearly legendary figure among the Indians, Tonti excited fascination and fear. Eventually he settled in Mobile, where his Indian experience proved invaluable to the French.

As French power on the European continent grew, so did England's control of America. English colonies were established at Jamestown, Virginia, in 1607 and at Plymouth, Massachusetts, in 1620. Despite high death rates in the early years, the colonies were eventually sustained by a flood of Scots, Irish, Welsh, and English who came seeking religious freedom, economic advancement, and refuge from British courts or from family difficulties. In the eighteenth century a high birthrate bolstered the English settlements that dotted the eastern seaboard. South Carolina was founded in 1670, its initial profits derived from Charleston traders who penetrated the Indian country into what became Alabama, bartering knives and goods for deer skins, animal pelts, and Indian slaves. Paris recognized that to counter the British and the Spanish at St. Augustine, and to protect Louisiana and the Mississippi River, France needed a fort on the Gulf of Mexico.

Hostility increased between France and England after William and Mary succeeded to the English throne in 1688. This shift in the European balance of power gave an urgency to French plans for a Gulf Coast settlement. If the French controlled Canada, the Mississippi River, the Ohio Valley, the Alabama River valleys, and the Gulf Coast, then the English were encircled and confined to the eastern seaboard. The stakes were high: control of vast reaches of land and the lucrative Indian fur trade. For more than a century, Alabama's wilderness was the scene of international intrigue as European powers pitted Indian tribes against one another, for the benefit of Paris and London.

The man responsible for "planting" the fleur-de-lis on the Gulf of Mexico was Pierre Le Moyne d'Iberville, a talented Canadian who appreciated the international powers at play. Born in Montreal, Iberville was one of eleven sons of a Frenchman who immigrated to Canada in 1641 and built a fortune through the fur trade. During King William's War, Iberville attacked the English in the Canadian area with such ferocity and success that he became a hero in the French court, where he enjoyed strong support. An experienced seaman comfortable leading the independent and rough Canadian fur trappers and woodsmen, Iberville was an excellent choice to lead a French settlement. Soon after King William's War ended, Iberville sailed from Brest with orders to establish a fort at the mouth of the Mississippi River. He carried soldiers and two hundred colonists, including a few women and children, and brought his twenty-one-year-old brother, Jean-Baptiste Le Moyne de Bienville, with him.

Bienville lived a long life, most of it on the Gulf Coast. An energetic man, he was a good organizer with a clear perception of his responsibilities. France governed its colonies as its crown ruled the nation—autocratically—and when Bienville served as governor, he ruled with authority. He inspired devoted loyalty from his followers and supported the Jesuits but was not above using them to his advantage. Bienville understood Indian culture, spoke several of their languages, and won Indian friendship and made alliances with them that he ratified by presenting them with European goods. Normally a kind and gentle man, he could be cruel. The men with whom he dealt learned to respect and fear him.

The Le Moyne brothers sailed into Pensacola Bay on January 27, 1699, and were surprised to find Spaniards who had arrived from Vera Cruz three months before. Sailing on, the French came to Mobile Point and cast anchor on January 31 at "the mouth of La Mobilla." The group scouted an island that Iberville named Massacre because of the large number of bones found there. Iberville explored the area and was pleased with what he discovered: "all kinds of trees, oaks, elm, ash, pines, and other trees I do not know, many creepers, sweet-smelling violets, and other yellow flowers."[8] From the top of an oak tree, Iberville saw brackish water flowing from a river into the bay. He did not detect the harbor on the northeast side of Massacre Island; determining the bay too shallow, he sailed on. He visited Biloxi, discovered the mouth of the Mississippi River on March 2, and traveled up the great waterway seeking a landing site. But the banks were low and marshy with snake-infested swamps, and he could not find a suitable location for a town. Iberville retraced his route to Biloxi and constructed a crude fort of squared logs. This site, Fort Maurepas, would be a base as he explored the coastal areas.

André Pénicaut, a carpenter who claimed to have arrived with Iberville, penned an interesting account of early Louisiana. He wrote that he was with the party that first scouted the "spot on high ground" near an Indian village some twenty miles up the Mobile River that Iberville eventually selected for his capital. The location placed the French closer to the Indians and closer to the English traders from the Carolinas where they could keep a watchful eye on them. Pénicaut noted that "illnesses were becoming frequent" in the summer heat at Fort Maurepas, making the move to higher ground urgent.[9] The French located a harbor on Massacre Island and called it Port Dauphin. They began moving men and materials from the Biloxi fort in 1702, off-loading the supplies at Port Dauphin, then transporting them in smaller boats up the river. Silt from Alabama rivers created shallow areas, and the entrance to the bay at Mobile Point was blocked by a treacherous and shifting bar that made navigation dangerous, especially in heavy swells.

Charles Levasseur, a skilled draftsman with knowledge of the Mobile area, designed and built the new fort at Twenty-seven Mile Bluff near present-day Mount Vernon. Levasseur constructed a square fort and placed cannon on each corner. Inside he designed buildings for soldiers and officers, a house used for a chapel, and a warehouse. Behind Fort Louis de la Louisiane, a village, commonly called La Mobile, was laid out in a grid pattern. Nicholas de La Salle, nephew to the earlier explorer, took a census in 1704 and reported a guardhouse, a forge, a gunsmith shop, and a kiln to make bricks. There were eighty one-story wooden houses, numerous farm animals, 180 men, twenty-seven families with ten children, and eleven Indian slave boys and girls.[10] Indian slaves were in great demand for labor to clear the land and till the fields. The Canadian rangers, *coureurs de bois,* avoided agricultural labor, and early settlers were often unfamiliar with farming. But Indian slaves proved physically and temperamentally unsuited to such hard work, and the importation of Africans soon began.

Communication between Mobile and Paris was tenuous, given the wars of the eighteenth century and Britain's control of the seas. Mobile once went three years without a supply ship from France, and local agriculture had to sustain the colony. Hunting and fishing often prevented starvation at the fort, and on occasion the French even resorted to purchasing food from the Spanish at Pensacola or Havana.

Although the Mobilian Indians near Fort Louis were friendly, other tribes, especially the Alabamas (in French, Alibamons), were not, and Indian attacks on the fort and ambushes of soldiers hunting or scouting were common. The French learned to be adept with their Indian diplomacy and had the advantage of Henri de Tonti, already a legend among the tribes. Bienville used entertainments and presents to purchase Indian loyalty as the French recruited allies against the English, stressing that the English took land and made war against the Indians. In 1700 the French signed an alliance with the Choctaws, a tribe Bienville estimated could send 8,000 warriors against the French and one the French must "cultivate the friendship" of and keep from "trading with the English."[11] Two years later the French were able to reconcile, at least temporarily, the Choctaws and the Chickasaws just before the resumption of Anglo-French hostilities.

In 1704 Fort Louis was running out of flour, but Bienville knew the *Pélican* was to arrive with supplies, more soldiers, and—what was especially anticipated—young women. Iberville had recommended to the Paris government that a hundred girls, "young and well-bred," be sent to Mobile to marry the Canadians, settle them down, and increase the population of Louisiana. Monseigneur Saint-Vallier, Bishop of Quebec, selected the girls from French orphanages and convents, and the group embarked from La Rochelle in April 1704. After a harrowing trip across the Atlantic and an unfortunate stop in Havana, where yellow fever invaded the ship, the *Pélican* arrived at Massacre Island, its passengers innocent of its pestilent cargo. Soon the feverish and sick began to die. There were not enough river barges in port to transport the passengers to the fort. But finally, the "twenty-three virtuous maidens" and their chaperones, "two gray nuns," arrived at Fort Louis, where they were greeted by stares of curious Canadians.[12] The women were exhausted from the voyage, gaunt from loss of weight, and many were feverish; their arrival was not "the glorious occasion that either the inhabitants of Mobile or the young women from Paris had envisioned."[13]

The women were given temporary housing while the courtship and negotiations for marriage began under the close supervision of the church. The young women were not prepared for the primitive environment of the wilderness. Although French customs had grown cruder under raw living conditions, the sense of hierarchy associated with rank, birth, and class so evident in French society remained in the social prejudices of the colony and prevented development of the cooperative spirit necessary for success in colonial adventures. The young women especially missed French bread and revolted against eating corn bread, a "Petticoat Insurrection" that "taxed Bienville's patience and ingenuity." Weddings soon brightened society, but yellow fever felled two suitors before they were married. These men may have been Charles Levasseur and Henri de Tonti, who died during the epidemic and were great losses to Bienville and Mobile. The French government continued to send women to Louisiana to boost the population. The "young ladies" of "virtuous raising" who arrived in 1728 brought their possessions in small trunks, called *cassettes,* and they were known as "*cassette* girls," a term sometimes applied to earlier as well as later arrivals.

The world was soon at war again, this time over the succession to the Spanish throne, a conflict called Queen Anne's War in America and one that again pitted England against Spain and France. After Iberville's death in 1706, Bienville, at the age of twenty-seven, became governor. Hostilities with England made Port Dauphin vulnerable. In 1710 an English privateer sailing from Jamaica captured the port, confiscated all the supplies, food, and deer skins stored there, looted the citizens, burned the houses, and sailed away. Fort Louis received the news, carried by canoe, several days later. The possibility of moving the fort closer to the bay and abandoning the exposed Port Dauphin was discussed. Then a flood came and assured the move.

In spring 1711 high water rushed into Fort Louis, causing soldiers and citizens to seek safety in trees. Bienville must have wondered about the Indian chief who told him the river had never flooded the site in his lifetime. Encouraged by his commissary Diron D'Artaguette, Bienville selected the place where the river meets the bay and surveyed a town. Soldiers and colonists began to dismantle houses and the fort and to move timbers and supplies back down the river. By the middle of 1712 the transfer was complete. Gradually, Old Mobile at Twenty-seven Mile Bluff reverted to wilderness.

When Queen Anne's War was over in 1713 France was left with a heavy national debt, which the expenses of Louisiana only increased. The crown convinced wealthy financier Antoine Crozat to lease the colony in return for a trade monopoly. Antoine de Lemothe Cadillac was sent to Mobile as governor. Cadillac persuaded Crozat that Louisiana had great potential for mines and could be profitable by increasing the fur trade. But English traders were penetrating the Creek country, and this encroachment concerned the French. To strengthen French presence in the area and to control the northern tributaries of the Mobile River, Paris considered a post "absolutely necessary in order to bring the savages into the interest of the French."[14] The Yamasee War (1715–16), an insurrection of the Yamasees and Creeks against the Charleston traders, presented an opportunity for the French. Bienville, using his knowledge of tribal dynamics, coaxed the Alabamas to the French cause by promising to locate a trading mission in the Creek country. The Alabamas Indians invited the French to build such a post at the confluence of the Coosa and Tallapoosa rivers. Paris insisted upon it.

In the summer of 1717 a French contingent under Lieutenant de La Tour Vitral had construction on Fort Toulouse well under way when an English party arrived in August carrying gifts and trade items for the Creeks. Surprised to find the French, the British government warned France that it was intruding on land claimed by Britain. Like a chess game, the British moved to check the French advance by establishing a trade mission on the upper Tallapoosa River at Okfuskee.

Fort Toulouse was intended only to facilitate the fur trade, never as a base for military operations against the Indians. The garrison had neither the manpower nor the fortifications to withstand a massive Indian attack. Surrounded by Creek Indian villages and by a small French farming community, Toulouse served as a bastion against the English so successfully that the old Scot trader James Adair called Toulouse that "dangerous Alabahma French garrison."[15] Scotsman William Bonar visited the Creek nation in 1756–57, spied on the French fort, and drew a map of the Indian villages. His "Draught (Draft) of the Creek nation" was decorated with vignettes of Indian life. When Jean-Bernard Bossu visited the fort in 1759, he was impressed with the Indians' fondness for the French and noted that the "Alabamas call their country the white land, or the land of peace," and "that trade can be carried on safely in Alabama territory."[16] But the success of Fort Toulouse depended upon supplies from Paris and support from Mobile, and French financial problems kept Toulouse and Louisiana underfunded.

During the interlude of peace, the French managed to make some improvements at Mobile. They renamed Massacre Island a less-threatening Ile Dauphine. The wooden fort at the new site on the river was bricked and named Fort Condé, but the town, the bay, and the river were always known as Mobile. In 1717 a hurricane washed ten feet of sand into the harbor at Port Dauphin, rendering it useless. Supplies had to be loaded directly from ships to smaller vessels and transported up the bay to the town. After five years Crozat perceived no prospect for any profit, so he relinquished his fifteen-year lease on the colony and Louisiana reverted to the crown.

France still wallowed in debt. The Duke de Orléans, regent for five-year-old Louis XV, was convinced by renegade Scottish gambler and promoter John Law that France's obligations could be wiped out by credit expansion and tax reform. A national bank would issue paper money backed by profits from colonial trade that would go to retire the French debt. His Western Company took over Louisiana, promoted expansion of the colony, and Bienville founded New Orleans in 1718 at a fine crescent on the Mississippi River.

Under Law's plan an economic boom began that spiraled out of control. The Western Company offered large land grants in Louisiana to prominent people, but the government required all immigrants to be Catholics. Thus, middle-class, hard-working French Huguenots immigrated to British colonies while Louisiana recruiters resorted to picking people from the streets of Paris to increase the population of the French colony. The Law years did bring some advances. The colony produced more of its food, although Mobile still had to import provisions, especially flour, and there was always a shortage of beef. New crops like oranges, figs, indigo, tobacco, and rice were introduced, and additional animals arrived. Unfortunately, many were slaughtered for food before stock growth could develop. Lumber, tar, and turpentine joined peltry as exports.

To clear the forests, cultivate the land, and work the wharves, Mobile needed labor, and there was never enough of it. The problem was solved by bringing in African slaves to work on the plantations and in the town. Bienville's adoption in 1724 of the *Code Noir,* a French West Indies slave code that gave greater protection to slaves than similar English codes, formalized the institution of slavery in Mobile. The French code forbade the separation of husbands and wives by sale; children under age fourteen could not be sold away from their mothers; and slaves were to be baptized Catholics. An economy dependent upon slavery became a significant feature of Mobile's development.

In 1729 the Natchez tribe's massacre of 250 whites at Fort Rosalie on the Mississippi River sent shock waves to Paris and discouraged French immigration. Mobile languished as only a garrison and trade center after the capital was moved to Biloxi in 1720 and to New Orleans in 1722. Law's speculative fever, known as the "Mississippi Bubble," finally burst, bringing down Law and many Frenchmen who had invested heavily in the scheme. In 1731 Louisiana again reverted to the king, and Bienville once more became governor.

The French retaliated for the Rosalie massacre by destroying the Natchez tribe, transporting captives to the West Indies as slaves and torturing others to death. Many survivors fled to the Chickasaws and Creeks and inflamed the Indians against the French—with British encouragement, of course. Bienville determined to move against the Chickasaws, and in 1736 he sent Captain Joseph Christophe de Lusser up the Tombigbee River to construct a fort and some cabins he could use as a base for his operation. With 550 soldiers, including 45 blacks "commanded by the brave free Simon," and 600 Choctaw Indians, the French looked impressive when they arrived at Fort Choiseul (but always called Fort Tombecbé). Unfortunately, this force was not enough to defeat the Chickasaws and their English supporters at the battle of Ackia, especially after Bienville's plans fell into the hands of the English. It was a disaster for the French.

By 1744 France was at war with Great Britain once more, this time over issues involving the Austrian succession. The Carolina and Georgia Indian traders might have attacked Mobile except that wilderness separated them. The peace signed in 1748 was little more than a truce. But before hostilities resumed, a significant reversal of alliances took place that was to change the course of Alabama history. In the Diplomatic Revolution, Great Britain allied with Prussia (instead of Austria) against France, Spain, and Austria. Under the new coalition the Prussian army, supplied by British manufactures, operated on the Continent, while the English navy controlled the seas. In America, British colonials greatly outnumbered the French, who had never caught the vision of a bold colonial expansion. France was decisively defeated in the French and Indian War (called the Seven Years War in Europe).

By the Peace of Paris (1763), France ceded Louisiana west of the Mississippi River to Spain and gave Canada and land east of the Mississippi to Great Britain, which ceded New Orleans to Spain and received Florida in return. French control of Mobile and Louisiana thus came to an inglorious end. Wrecked by wars, burdened by excessive debts, and maintaining an extravagant court, France's monarchy had never been successful in making Louisiana a priority, and its colonial support was weak and ineffective. Public attitudes never backed aggressive colonization, and governmental regulations were shortsighted. In sum, the French government failed to mobilize its material resources and lacked the moral force to maintain its colonial empire. The French colonists at Mobile felt betrayed at being delivered to the British, but they soon learned that Britain had the resources and the commitment that France did not.

The cession of Indian provinces in Alabama without any consultation angered the tribes, who distrusted the English even though they had learned that English trade goods were of better quality and of lower price than French goods. The peace of the Alabama wilderness was left in jeopardy. By the Proclamation of 1763, King George III hoped to buy time to solve the Indian problem on the frontier. The proclamation prohibited settlement beyond the Appalachian Mountains and south to the 31st parallel (later changed to 32° 28′). Florida was divided into two colonies: East Florida included the peninsula, and West Florida stretched from the Apalachicola and Chattahoochee rivers to the Mississippi River, including Mobile, with Pensacola as the capital. Englishmen were curious about the new colonies, particularly Mobile Bay, which was reported in imperialist propaganda to be "capable of containing the whole British navy."[17]

The French commander at Fort Condé, Pierre-Annibal DeVille, who waited for the arrival of British troops, hoped they would not come until the large Indian congress, scheduled to convene at Mobile on November 1, was over. The French planned to explain their departure from Louisiana and to present long overdue gifts to the Indians. But in October a British ship arrived off Mobile Bay. DeVille tried to delay the landing, but Major Robert Farmar insisted upon disembarking his men. On October 20, 1763, DeVille relinquished his command to Major Farmar, an American-born British army officer. The Union Jack fluttered over Mobile. Farmar sent Captain Thomas Ford up the Tombigbee to receive Fort Tombecbé, which the British named Fort York. Farmar was discouraged from sending redcoats to Fort Toulouse because of the hostility of the Creeks and the isolation of the fort. The French commander at Toulouse dumped cannon and powder in the Coosa River and abandoned the fort for Mobile.

The British were surely disappointed in what they found at Mobile, a small community of 350 people living in dilapidated housing under crude circumstances. Major Farmar found Fort Condé, renamed Fort Charlotte by the English, in poor condition. Weeds were growing over the ramparts, much of the wood was rotten, the hinges on the main gate were in disrepair, and the barracks were unfit for soldiers, yet no other accommodations were available. As soon as possible Farmar began renovating the fort, suggesting that the barracks be rebuilt with a second story to house the officers so they would not "be exposed to the inconvenience daily of being plundered by the savages, who have been ever used to come in and out as they pleased."[18]

The British felt uneasy with the large number of armed Indians congregating for the congress called by the French. Captain Lieutenant James Campbell, who arrived in Mobile with Farmar, wrote that 3,000

Indians were gathering in the town and were "daily fed at the French King's expense for three weeks." Campbell distrusted the French governor of New Orleans, Jean Jacques-Blaise D'Abbadie, and was "at a loss to divine his motive in taking so much pains to serve us." Major Farmar had no gifts comparable to those of the French, only "some trifles he picked from the merchants," which seemed to satisfy the Indians.[19] The British major disdained that "most disagreeable custom the French have introduced amongst the Indians . . . of giving them victuals and drink," but reluctantly he also did so.[20] When the Indians finally left Mobile, the English commander turned his attention to the French residents.

Farmar announced that Roman Catholicism would be tolerated and French property ownership respected, but the English language, the common law, and the Anglican church were officially installed. French citizens were given a reasonable time either to swear allegiance to Britain or sell their property and leave. Some departed for New Orleans, then learned that meant swearing loyalty to the Spanish crown, one despised even more than the English.

When Farmar arrived in Mobile his men were wearied from the Havana campaign and were suffering from scurvy. They had not recovered when the summer fevers came. In the months ahead the garrison fell ill from yellow fever, malaria, dysentery, typhus, and typhoid fever. So many died that Mobile became known as a "graveyard for Britons." When George Johnstone, governor of West Florida, arrived in Mobile, he complained that "the state of the town in filth, nastiness, & brushwood running over the houses is hardly to be credited." A Pensacola soldier observed that "no person that goes to Mobile, but may lay his account to have a very severe fever."[21] Shortages of medicine and medical personnel and no adequate hospital facility made matters worse. Not even a cleric was available to pray over those suffering illnesses or being buried.

Farmar ruled Mobile as military commander for one year until Governor Johnstone arrived and established civil government. Johnstone appointed a council and called for elections to an assembly, a new experience for French settlers. As governor, Johnstone foolishly and audaciously attempted to assert his authority over Major Farmar and the Mobile garrison. It was not long before the two men, both rather testy and confident of their authority, were embroiled in controversy. Johnstone had little respect for French residents of West Florida or for the new immigrants, whom he called "the refuse of the Jails of great Citys, and the overflowing Scum of the Empire."[22] Under the circumstances, he believed strong government was necessary.

The most pressing problem Governor Johnstone faced involved the Indians, and he knew little about the native peoples of the area. The

Creeks still did not trust the British, and London was determined to bring order and regulation to Indian trade. To help with the situation, Johnstone called on John Stuart, superintendent for Indian affairs in the southern district who had experience in the Indian country, and Chevalier Montault de Montbéraut, former commander of Fort Toulouse who was respected by the Indians and was a special friend to "the Mortar," a sagacious Creek chief of Okchai. Montbéraut was recruited because the British needed his Indian expertise and did not want him to move to New Orleans and join the Spanish. Montbéraut lived at Lisloy, a plantation west of Mobile where he farmed and raised cattle.

Montbéraut and Stuart arranged for several Indian congresses in Mobile and Pensacola where Johnstone met the tribes and pledged a British policy of peace, curtailment of liquor sales, regulation of trade, and creation of commissaries in the Indian country. The treaties brought a tenuous peace to the frontier, but Montbéraut's relationship with Johnstone and Stuart turned sour, and he appealed to King George III for satisfaction, leaving an interesting document detailing the arrangements.[23]

With the Indian problem temporarily solved, Johnstone turned his attention to other matters, especially the economic development of West Florida. He encouraged immigration and kept the council busy granting land at London's instructions of one hundred acres per head of household plus fifty more for each dependent. The production of food increased, and the colony became almost self-sufficient. On two projects he failed. Although he worked diligently to make the Iberville River navigable, thus allowing commerce to bypass Spanish New Orleans for Baton Rouge, it proved impractical and was abandoned. The governor wanted to establish trade with Spanish America, but London refused to relax the Navigation Acts that forbade it. Johnstone's advocacy of a war of annihilation against the Creeks frightened the ministry—Lord Shelburne called him "a Perfect Madman"—but Johnstone was already on his way to England on approved leave in February 1767 when his letter of dismissal was penned.[24] Lieutenant Governor Montfort Browne administered the government until Johnstone's replacement arrived. Browne was active in recruiting immigrants for the colony, especially Huguenots, when he was not engaged in furthering his own fortune. On March 16, 1767, John Eliot was appointed governor. A naval officer as was Johnstone, Eliot delayed his arrival in Pensacola until April 2, 1769. According to a petition to the Admiralty, Eliot arrived to "the great joy and satisfaction of all the inhabitants," who were pleased to be rid of Browne; however, one month later, Eliot hanged himself in his study, throwing "every thing into confusion."[25] Consequently, Browne resumed control until Elias Durnford was made lieutenant governor. An able administrator, Durnford served only a short time before Governor Peter Chester arrived in August 1770.

Governor Chester served for eleven years, until the Spanish from New Orleans captured Mobile and Pensacola during the American Revolution. Chester brought stability to the government but no end to the bickering and factionalism common in the administrations of other governors. Despite the problems of personality, British control brought sound colonial administration and a measure of self-government undreamed of under French rule. When discontent in the American colonies led to revolution, British West Florida became a haven for loyalists fleeing patriot forces. Large and isolated, the colony was inadequately defended, but the Americans only mounted one raid against the Gulf area. Although the residents were not happy with Chester's government, they did not follow the lead of the "immortal thirteen colonies" and join the rebellion. In 1779, when they petitioned King George III to complain that Governor Chester exercised "unwarrantable powers in various shapes in this infant colony," they did so within their understanding of the meaning of the imperial constitution.[26]

British rule in West Florida lasted only eighteen years, but in that time an elected assembly and appointed council were in place, giving the citizens of Mobile the experience of representative government. The Indians had remained fairly peaceful, and trade in peltry continued to be profitable and remained the number one West Florida export. Immigrants from the seaboard colonies and Great Britain were swelling the population and taking advantage of the generous land-grant policy. Although most were not experienced farmers and had difficulty locating crops that grew well in the soil and climate, by the end of British rule agriculture had moved the colony more toward self-sufficiency, and indigo, tobacco, cotton, and rice were exported along with timber products.

A historian who has studied the economy of British West Florida concluded that the promise of West Florida remained unfulfilled because it had a "persistent trade imbalance, high costs, and four shortages—of markets, of capital, of labor, and, above all, of time." But he noted that Great Britain valued West Florida not just for its economy but also for its harbors on the Gulf, so strategically placed near Spanish interests, and for its rivers that served as avenues into the Indian country.[27] Mobile, founded by the French and surrendered to the British, would undergo one more cultural change before it became part of the United States.

THREE

Creeks and Americans at War

WHEN thirteen of the seventeen British colonies of North America declared their independence from Great Britain in 1776, Alabama was a wilderness area claimed by Georgia from its sea-to-sea charter and by the most powerful Indian nation in the Southeast. Mobile and the southern portion of what was to become the state of Alabama were part of West Florida, which along with East Florida remained loyal to the crown. British subjects in the Indian country of Alabama, most of them Scotsmen, were far removed from the issues of the conflict and remained loyalists, and Mobile became a haven for refugees fleeing the successes of vengeful patriots in Georgia and South Carolina.

The British commander at Pensacola, General John Campbell, complained in 1779 that his troops, mainly composed of "Germans, condemned criminals and other species of gaol birds," were worn out and "the most unfit to be trusted."[1] London promised to strengthen Mobile's Fort Charlotte and Pensacola with troops from Jamaica but meanwhile urged the Gulf Coast towns to mount a "vigorous defense." James Willing's patriot raid down the Mississippi River struck fear in the hearts of citizens of Mobile, but it failed to rally any support for the American position. When a man appeared in the city with copies of the Declaration of Independence, considered contraband of war, he was imprisoned in Fort Charlotte. The situation changed dramatically in 1779 when Spain entered the war against Britain and especially after the ambitious and daring Spanish governor at New Orleans, Bernardo de Gálvez, began preparations to attack Mobile. General John Campbell concentrated on defending Pensacola, leaving Mobile to fend for itself under Lieutenant Governor Elias Durnford.

Gálvez sailed for Mobile in January 1780. His eleven ships contained supplies and 2,500 men, including Spanish soldiers, Louisiana militia Creole units, and companies of free blacks. Despite storms, which wrecked some of his ships, and problems crossing the bar into the bay, Gálvez landed at Choctaw Point, though amid such confusion he considered canceling the attack. Initial cannon blasts at the fort went unanswered, however, and Gálvez discovered the British were surprised and in far greater turmoil than he. The Spaniard estimated that Mobile could not muster 200 men.

Gálvez requested a surrender before he began serious shelling of Fort Charlotte, but Durnford refused, expecting reinforcements from Pensacola. During the bombardment several houses burned, at least one deliberately set afire by the British to obtain a clearer field for their cannons. After fourteen days the walls were breached. Campbell belatedly moved troops by land toward Tensaw, but there was no way to cross the bay and assist Mobile. His redcoat scouts reported a white flag raised over Fort Charlotte, then the Spanish banner flying. Campbell returned to Pensacola, which Gálvez captured the next year. Spain now controlled the Gulf Coast outlets for the Mississippi, Alabama, and Chattahoochee rivers, a situation that would prove intolerable for the new American nation.

The Spanish treated Mobile's citizens with generosity. Gálvez left José de Ezpeleta to enforce Spanish authority. Ezpeleta began by requiring citizens to swear loyalty to the Spanish king, making them promise "to behave" while they lived under his rule and be "good and loyal subjects of the Catholic monarch."[2] Although most of the citizens took the oath and adopted Catholicism, if only nominally, some sold their property and left for the United States or went up the river into Indian country. Property belonging to the British crown passed to the Spanish government, and vacant lands were granted to immigrants. Commandants had broad powers to settle disputes over property, certify sales, and punish crimes, but their rule was mild. Control by Spain served to confound further legal titles to lands that had already passed from French to British to Spanish law and were to transfer one more time to Mississippi territorial law.

After peace was made in 1783, Spanish strategy was to increase trade and population in West Florida and manipulate the Alabama Indians to Spain's advantage, using them as a buffer to discourage American settlements in the region. The Creeks, now the dominant Indians in the South, were reluctant to end their lucrative trade with the British, preferring English goods to Spanish ones. Most of the Creek trade out of Florida was accomplished through the Scottish firm of Panton, Forbes and Company, founded by William Panton, a Tory who fled Georgia during the American Revolution and who had received favorable treatment from the Spanish because of his friendship with a powerful Creek leader, Alexander McGillivray.

McGillivray's father, Lachlan McGillivray, arrived at Savannah, Georgia, in January 1736, a sixteen-year-old indentured servant to his cousin, John Mackintosh of Holme. The historian Albert James Pickett gave a romantic account of Lachlan's arrival in America with "a shilling in his pocket, a suit of clothes upon his back, a red head, a stout frame," and a cheerful disposition, contending he used a jackknife to swap for deer skins and thus entered the Charleston fur trade.[3]

On the Georgia frontier, McGillivray associated with young Indians. By 1741 he spoke enough Creek to be hired as an interpreter, and he left for the Creek country with James Bullock, receiving his license to trade from South Carolina three years later. By that time the Carolina traders had penetrated the Indian country so extensively that one observer reported to London that "they had fathered more than four hundred children," young Creeks and Cherokees who would grow up to be "influenced by the capitalistic values of their fathers and bound to their clans by the traditions of their mothers."[4] On one trip into Alabama McGillivray met Sehoy, the beautiful daughter of a Creek woman and a French soldier at Fort Toulouse, probably Captain Marchand de Courtel, who commanded the district. Sehoy was a member of the influential Wind clan, and McGillivray's relationship with her strengthened his position in the Creek nation.

McGillivray built a house at the falls of the Coosa River at Little Tallassee and planted an apple orchard that was still thriving decades later when John Pope visited the site. The Scottish trader and Sehoy had three children who lived to be adults: Jeannet, who married Louis Milfort; Sophia, who married Benjamin Durant; and Alexander, who was born in 1750. Although many traders had fleeting relationships with Indian women, Lachlan never took another wife.

From Little Tallassee McGillivray was a close observer of tribal dynamics in the area and kept the British government informed of frontier affairs. In 1751 he reported to William Pinckney, the South Carolina Indian commissioner, that the French had renovated Fort Toulouse and that it was strong and well supplied with soldiers, brandy, and a priest. Indeed, James Adair gave McGillivray credit for keeping the Creeks friendly to the English, especially during the conflicts with France. In the meantime, McGillivray traded English goods for deer skins, transporting the pelts from the backcountry to Augusta over a path that was "very bad Stoney and hilly." He raised rice, indigo, and corn and speculated in Georgia lands. Maintaining a residence in Augusta and later a plantation, Vale Royal, outside Savannah, he was elected to the Georgia General Assembly in 1768. When the colonies declared independence, he owned 11,190 acres and had parlayed his shilling and pocketknife into a small fortune.[5]

In 1773 McGillivray sent his son, then fourteen years old, to Charleston to be tutored under the direction of a cousin, Farquhar McGillivray. Young Alexander was in Charleston when the American

Revolution began and when his father, identified by Georgia patriots as one of the most important Tories, had property worth more than $100,000 confiscated. Lachlan McGillivray left for Scotland just before a price was placed upon his head by the Georgians, and Alexander went home to his mother's people at Little Tallassee, a young man hostile to the Americans, "too Scottish to be Creek and too Creek to be British."[6]

The young McGillivray farmed the fertile lands along the Coosa River as his father had, accumulating land and slaves. At least two of his several farms were superintended by white men. When John Pope visited him in 1791, he was building a "Log House embellished with dormer Windows" and enjoying his family, "two lovely Children, Alexander and Elizabeth," who "speak the English Tongue" well, and his wife, "a Model of Prudence and Discretion." McGillivray offered Pope good food, wine, and spirits and invited him to a "Ball-Match" between two townships. Sixty-two "alert young Fellows" played ball under the watchful eyes of "two old men, who are mutually chosen by the contending parties to decide all Controversies which may arise in the Course of the Game."[7]

In summer 1781 a group of Natchez loyalists visited McGillivray. When the Spanish took control of British West Florida, it included Natchez, and these people fled because they had revolted against Spanish rule. They were headed for Savannah through wild Indian country. Despite wandering (they were sometimes lost, trying to find the great trading paths of the Indians) and starvation, lack of water, and exhaustion, the band, which included women and small children, finally arrived at Little Tallassee. McGillivray gave them supplies and guides to the Flint River, and they eventually reached safety at Savannah.

For his loyalty to Great Britain, the English rewarded Alexander McGillivray and appointed him commissary for the Upper Creeks. In 1783 the Spanish governor at Pensacola wrote that McGillivray had "more influence among the Creek Nations than any other person" and that due to his persuasion the chiefs were "strongly opposed to the name of Americans" and would not attend the American congresses planned for Augusta and Savannah.[8] Because of McGillivray's friendship with William Panton, Spain allowed Panton to continue trading with England in return for a Spanish import-export tax.

The Peace of Paris (1783) ended the American Revolution and established the western boundary of the United States at the Mississippi River and the southern boundary at the thirty-first parallel. Spain contested this boundary and claimed territory to the line of 32° 28′. Georgia, by its sea-to-sea charter, claimed the Alabama-Mississippi area. Alexander McGillivray wrote that the Creeks felt betrayed by the British and being "divided between Spaniards and Americans is cruel and ungenerous."[9]

This disputed boundary was a significant foreign-policy issue that the new American nation had to address.

When George Washington was elected president of the United States, he moved to negotiate disputes between Georgia and the Southern Indians and to end the bloody Indian-white depredations on the frontier. Until then, Georgia had been alone in treating with the Indians. Federal commissioners tried to settle the disputes at a meeting at Rock Landing on the Oconee River in September 1789, but under McGillivray's leadership the Indians abruptly left the conference. Secretary of War Henry Knox wanted the approval of the Chickasaws and Choctaws to establish a fort at the Muscle Shoals. With "adequate force," Knox believed the post could be used "to intimidate the Creeks or to strike them with success."[10]

Searching for peace, President Washington in 1790 invited McGillivray and the Creek leadership to New York, where the group was entertained and eventually persuaded to cede Georgia land to the United States in the Treaty of New York. McGillivray was given the rank of brigadier general and a salary of $1,200 a year, with the Creek nation receiving an annuity of $1,500. The Creeks soon repudiated the treaty, primarily due to the manipulations of William Augustus Bowles, a British soldier and adventurer who had lived among the Creeks after the Revolution, and Baron Francisco de Carondelet, the Spanish governor of Louisiana.

In the next few years the Alabama region was the scene of constant machinations as the Spanish, British, and Americans vied for the loyalty of the Creeks. McGillivray negotiated a secret pact with the Spanish, who granted him the title of superintendent general of the Creek nation with a salary of $3,500. He was still a partner with William Panton, receiving subsidies from the British, and was generally recognized by the Creeks as their chief. Albert James Pickett wrote in his nineteenth-century history of Alabama that McGillivray "was almost unrivalled in intrigue," his conduct "was eminent for treachery, intrigue, and selfish aggrandizement," but he doubted if "Alabama has ever produced, or ever will produce, a man of greater ability." Drawing a comparison with the great French minister who was able sequentially to represent the Bourbon monarchy, the French revolutionists, and Napoleon, Pickett called McGillivray "the Talleyrand of Alabama."[11]

In May 1793 McGillivray confessed to James Seagrove, the American agent for the Creeks who resided on the Georgia coast because he was too fearful of the Indians to live nearby, that it was "no wonder the Indians are distracted, when they are tampered with on every side." He felt he was "a keeper of Bedlam, and nearly fit for an inhabitant."[12] When McGillivray died in 1793, he left a leadership void the Creeks

40

were never able to fill. The Georgia border continued to be the scene of Indian attacks: horses and cattle were run off, and houses were burned; fear was the common denominator. Into the vacuum stepped Benjamin Hawkins, North Carolina senator, friend of McGillivray, and Indian commissioner. President Washington asked Hawkins to sacrifice a few years of his life to try bringing civilization to the Indians. Hawkins traveled into Indian country to learn firsthand whether the Creeks would accept his policy of helping them learn about Anglo-American culture and improve their economic condition. Although it is true that Hawkins replaced McGillivray in influence, there was a difference: McGillivray sought to structure the Indians to protect their independence, while Hawkins perfected the tribal organization in order to control them.

Hawkins arrived in east Alabama in December 1796 and visited in the homes of white men like Richard Bailey, who with his Indian family had lived for forty years in the backcountry, farming and raising cattle and hogs with the help of seven slaves. Hawkins also called at the Durant and Weatherford homesteads on the banks of the Alabama River. Young William Weatherford, who was to become the famous Creek chief Red Eagle, was about fifteen years old. Hawkins returned to Georgia and established his agency on the Flint River, where he began to experiment with raising vegetables, peach trees, and strawberries; to train young Indian boys in the techniques of plowing, cattle raising, and farming; and to teach young girls the finer points of spinning and weaving.

American Indian relations were bound to international policy, especially so long as Spain controlled Florida and British firms dominated the Indian trade. Each side accused the other of intrigue with the Creeks. The disputed boundary area with Spanish Florida and the backcountry, much of it to become part of Alabama, was a land of conspiracies. President Washington sent Thomas Pinckney to Spain to negotiate free commerce on the Mississippi River to the Gulf. The treaty Pinckney signed in 1795, known as the Treaty of San Lorenzo, established the U.S. boundary at 31° latitude and provided that Spain would evacuate all forts north of that line. But no one in the Alabama-Tombigbee valleys was certain exactly where that line would fall.

Spain was confident that Fort San Esteban de Tombecbé, or St. Stephens, remained south of the border in Spanish West Florida. St. Stephens was constructed in 1789, not, as usually written, to guard Spanish West Florida against the Americans but rather to provide American settlers some protection from the Indians. Americans were rapidly settling along the Alabama rivers, taking advantage of Spain's generous land grants and promises of religious freedom and no taxes in return for oaths of loyalty to Spain.

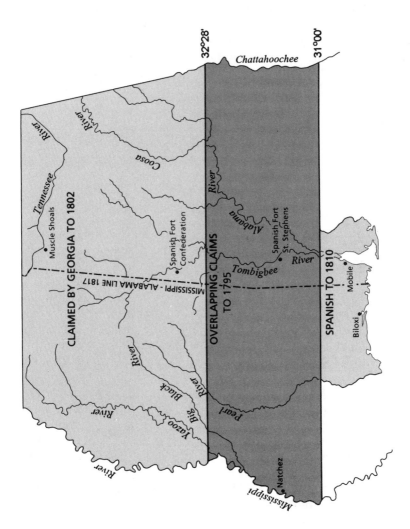

Mississippi Territory

In 1797 Andrew Ellicott, a Philadelphia engineer and surveyor general of the United States, was given responsibility for surveying the boundary, but Louisiana's governor Carondelet declined to cooperate and refused to order evacuation of the forts. The Spanish commander at Natchez provided assistance only after an angry American mob threatened him and took control of the town. Ellicott began his survey at the Mississippi River despite initial interferences from the Spanish and the Indians. North of Mobile a large stone was placed in 1799 to mark the 31° latitude. To secure safe passage for Ellicott's surveying crew east of the Alabama River, he and Hawkins met with the Creek chief Mad Dog at Miller's farm on the Conecuh River. The Creek informed them of Spanish intrigues against running the line and said the Spanish governor had a forked tongue, predicting he would not come to the meeting as scheduled, for "a man with two tongues can only speak to one at a time."[13] The governor was taken ill and did not attend.

Ellicott was slow in moving his party through the Lower Creek territory and did not heed Hawkins's advice to proceed during the "season of the Boos-ke-tah [busk], when all the discontented would be attending the ceremonies of the annual festival" in August. Hawkins was appalled that Ellicott's party was encumbered "with such unnecessary and useless baggage" as the "flat irons, alone, for the commissioners weigh 150 pounds and it takes four horses to move Mr. Ellicott's washerwoman."[14] Indian depredations near the Chattahoochee River forced the surveyors to retire before the surveying was completed, but the southern boundary of Mississippi and Alabama had been established.

United States jurisdiction over the disputed area was delayed not only by Spain's claims but also by Georgia's organization of the area into Bourbon County and by the state's 1789 sale of fifteen million acres to three "Yazoo" speculative land companies. President Washington revoked the sale as illegal, insisting on federal authority over the territory, but some speculators refused to comply. The Tennessee Company, led by Zachariah Cox, tried to establish control of lands at Muscle Shoals but was chased out by federal troops. Another speculator, James O'Fallon, an agent of the South Carolina Company, was arrested by federal authorities after he tried to implement a plan to drive the Spanish from Natchez, where the company's Yazoo land was located. Despite purchasing the lands at nearly give-away prices, the companies defaulted on payments to Georgia and the sales were canceled.

Six years later Georgia tried again. In the second Yazoo land sale, Georgia sold 21,500,000 acres, much of it in Alabama, for $500,000, or about 2¼ cents per acre. The speculative companies resold the land on credit for $1 per acre, leaving settlers with bogus titles. Eventually, some claims of bona fide Yazoo purchasers were satisfied by Georgia, while other claims were settled by Congress.

The federal government organized the Mississippi Territory in 1798 under the provisions of the Northwest Ordinance of 1787, although it was 1802 before Georgia gave up its claim to Alabama. President John Adams appointed Winthrop Sargent of Massachusetts as territorial governor. The government was organized at Natchez. The best land was located along the river, and the wealthiest population was clustered there. The next year, the capital was moved to Washington, a small town away from the Mississippi River that was selected to prevent undue Natchez influence. But the interests of the Alabama country were still underrepresented in the territorial government. A vast wilderness separated the area from Washington County, where settlers were surrounded by Indians and were uneasy over Spanish control of Mobile. To protect the area, the federal government constructed Fort Stoddert at Mount Vernon, north of Mobile.

A land cession by the Choctaws in 1805 relinquished more territory in the Tensaw basin, and cessions by the Chickasaw (in 1805) and the Cherokee (in 1806) opened up the Huntsville area. Survey of the lands was subject to the Land Ordinance of 1785. Townships of thirty-six square miles were surveyed off two east-west lines, the Huntsville Base Line and the St. Stephens Base Line, and two north-south lines, the St. Stephens Meridian and the Huntsville Meridian. Land was sold under the Land Law of 1800 as amended by the Land Act of 1804, which allowed settlers to purchase as little as 160 acres with payment in four installments. Land was first auctioned to the highest bidder: the remaining land sold at $2.00 an acre, or $1.64 an acre if the payment was in cash. The credit system was a mixed blessing. On one hand, it allowed the poor farmer to gain the otherwise unobtainable, while on the other it encouraged the speculation in land that contributed to the panic of 1819. A land office was opened at St. Stephens in 1803 and then at Huntsville in 1811.

Following the purchase of Louisiana from France in 1803 (Napoleon had pressured Spain into a secret treaty that returned the colony to France), President Thomas Jefferson considered a road between Washington, D.C., and New Orleans to be an "indispensable necessity." In 1805 the Creeks allowed the government to "forever hereafter have a right to a horse path, through the Creek country, from the Ocmulgee to Mobile."[15] The route would facilitate delivery of the U.S. mail, and it was surveyed, despite numerous problems, and cleared from Athens, Georgia, to Fort Stoddert. Under the threat of war with Great Britain in 1810, the road was widened, and settlers in increasing numbers used the road to reach the lands along the Tombigbee River—the 'Bigbee Valley—and the Tensaw country.

Unknown to President Jefferson, the ink was hardly dry on the Louisiana treaty before his vice-president, Aaron Burr of New York, was scheming with the Federalists for the secession of New England. Alexander Hamilton foiled the plot and provoked Burr into a duel that ended in Hamilton's death. Fleeing from justice, Burr encountered the "colorful bamboozler" General James Wilkinson, who commanded the American army in the West and was known as a "skillful and unscrupulous plotter." Burr's treachery turned to the west. He planned to rally the westerners and take West Florida, and perhaps Texas and Mexico, from Spain and some believed Louisiana from the United States as well. While Burr went overland, an armed flotilla was en route down the Mississippi River to New Orleans. Wilkinson, uneasy about the rumors circulating that identified him with the vice-president, betrayed the New Yorker. Burr discovered that President Jefferson had condemned his expedition and a warrant for his arrest was circulating.

Burr left the the Natchez area and fled toward Spanish Florida. On a moonlit night in February 1807, Nicholas Perkins, the local land agent, noticed two strangers passing through his tiny community of Wakefield in Washington County. They asked for directions to Major John Hinson's house, and Perkins became suspicious that one of the men might be Burr. He notified Lieutenant Edmund P. Gaines at Fort Stoddert. Burr was captured and held at the fort until he was transferred to Virginia, where he stood trial for treason. The still-controversial vice-president was acquitted. Stories of Burr's capture in Alabama were retold in the 'Bigbee Valley for years.

Settlers continued to flood down the Federal Road, which cut through Creek territory to the 'Bigbee settlements. Benjamin Hawkins reported in January 1811 that the road "is now crowded with travellers moving westward, for the safety of whose property at times I have some anxiety; yet I have had but two complaints during the fall and winter; two horses and some bells were stolen."[16] Meanwhile, relations between the United States and Great Britain became more strained. The British were at war with Napoleon, and their practice of boarding American ships and impressing seamen into the British navy was galling to the Americans. Rumors circulated on the frontier that the British were supplying arms to the Indians. The Congress elected in 1811 was filled with new faces, young men who grew to manhood on stories of patriotic gallantry against England during the Revolution. These young "War Hawks," led by Henry Clay of Kentucky, were determined not to back down from insult out of fear of confrontation. War with Britain seemed imminent, especially after militia attacked Prophet's Town on Tippecanoe Creek and found stores of arms made in Britain.

The great Shawnee chief Tecumseh was not at Tippecanoe that day, for he was in the South advocating a united stand against further white encroachment. He was encouraged by British agents in the Northwest who gambled that with a frontier in flames the United States could hardly mount an attack against the British in Canada. In turn, British agents promised to supply guns and powder to the Indians, although this was never the official policy of the London government. Tecumseh's entourage, composed of warriors from different tribes, was heavily armed with rifles, tomahawks, and scalping knives. In his appeal to the Chickasaw, he was foiled by the Colbert family, especially James, an interpreter who was an educated man "of unblemished character, three-fourths white."[17] Discouraged, Tecumseh departed for the Choctaws.

A Choctaw warrior described Tecumseh as wearing "two long crane feathers" on his head, "one white, the other dyed a brilliant red," the colors symbolizing peace and war.[18] Tecumseh's Indians were adorned with silver bands on their arms and silver gorgets and were painted alike in red war paint. Despite his great oratory, Tecumseh was not able to convince the Choctaws to fight the whites, for each argument was countered by Pushmataha, who insisted that the Choctaws were friends of the whites and that such a war would ruin their tribe. The Choctaws escorted Tecumseh's party to the edge of their territory and sent them toward the Creeks.

The Creeks felt squeezed between the Georgians and the growing Tombigbee settlements and resented white encroachments on their hunting grounds and living space. The confederation was fracturing because of old divisions, and it was on the verge of civil war over Hawkins's acculturation policies and the social and economic differences that had occurred within the tribe because of the extensive and lucrative deer-skin trade. Decades of intermarriage between Creeks and Europeans had produced a bilingual and bicultural people who were influenced by a market economy and who enjoyed the status that came with wealth. These Muskogee people lived as the Americans did—herding cattle, using African slaves to grow cotton, and raising food from barnyards, gardens, and orchards. Traditional tribal religious beliefs called for a sharing of property and wealth, but those Indians who had adopted the white man's ethic refused. Such life-styles offended the Muskogees' ancestral models of proper behavior.

Tecumseh arrived at Tuckabatchee during the annual council when some 5,000 white traders and Indian warriors and families gathered. His visit is clouded by time, legend, and conflicting accounts, but it seems he remained silent, playing a cat-and-mouse game, announcing he would speak, then refusing to do so. Benjamin Hawkins spoke on the first day, and Tecumseh waited until Hawkins grew impatient and left for his camp at Big Spring. Perhaps Hawkins felt poorly or, if Indian trader Sam Dale is to be believed, was overconfident of his ability to control the Creeks. In either case, after Hawkins left, Tecumseh and his party—naked except for a flap, their bodies painted black, and wearing such scowls on their faces that Dale recalled "they looked like a procession of devils"—came from Tecumseh's cabin. They sounded a war whoop that Dale called "a most diabolical yell."[19] Dale related that "everything was still as death: even the winds slept, and there was only the gentle rustle of the falling leaves." As Tecumseh began to talk, his eyes burned with a "supernatural lustre" during a speech in which he urged a war of annihilation against the whites. Hawkins, who was not there, later reported from information he gathered that Tecumseh's talk urged peace but incited war.

It is uncertain whether Tecumseh actually left a bunch of red sticks with the Southern Indians, sticks that were to be cast aside one by one until all were gone, at which time the tribes were to take the warpath in coordinated attacks across the frontier. But settlers at the time believed this story and called the Indians who took the warpath Red Sticks or Red Clubs because of the Indian tradition of showing a red war club in villages during hostilities.[20] Some doubt stories that Tecumseh, with information from Canadian astronomers, predicted a fiery comet, which appeared in the Southern sky soon after he left, or that he threatened to stomp his foot and destroy the houses at Tuckabatchee, which the Indians related to the earthquake that shook the Tallapoosa area the month after Tecumseh left. But George Stiggins, in his history of the Creeks written before 1836, said that Tecumseh threatened to "call forth his power and thereby make *the whole earth tremble*" and, when the earthquake came, the Indians and frontiersmen credited Tecumseh.[21]

There is agreement that Tecumseh and his Northwest Indian party taught the Creeks a new war dance, one tied to the prophetic movement. Through the songs and dances the Creek rebels tried to recapture their Muskogee aboriginal identity and gain the power to turn away from the white man's view of civilization. "Dancing this dance effectively socialized the prophets' visions," and those warriors who took up the fight against the whites in 1813 were those who performed the dance.[22] Paddy Walsh, an Indian boy adopted by a South Carolina loyalist, and Josiah Francis, known as "Crazy Medicine," were two leaders of the prophetic movement who led the hostile Creeks.

As the prophets increased their following among the Upper Creeks in 1812, depredations against whites grew. Several settlers were killed, and in May, Little Warrior's Creek band coming from the Northwest received incorrect information that war had started. They killed settlers on the Duck River in Tennessee and carried Martha Crawley as a hostage into Creek country, where she escaped and was rescued. Hawkins was able to convince the Creek council to punish the Indians responsible, and Little Warrior himself was murdered. Yet tension mounted on the Alabama frontier. Hawkins underestimated the strength of the Creek war party and the extent of the religious movement being led by the nativistic prophets who so bitterly resented Hawkins's program to acculturate them. The war party was strengthened by those who opposed Little Warrior's execution. In any case, Hawkins was too slow in reacting to the situation.

In April Congress again claimed Mobile. The governor of the Mississippi Territory immediately organized the area and appointed officials for the town. For one year Spanish soldiers occupied the fort but were too weak to drive the Americans from the city. In June the United States declared war on Great Britain, a conflict the nation was woefully unprepared to fight. The army was old and ill-trained and its equipment was obsolete. Nonetheless, attacks were planned on Canada from Detroit, Fort Niagara, and Lake Champlain.

With the American nation at war along the Canadian border, Red Stick Creeks besieged Big Warrior and the peaceful Creeks at Tuckabatchee, and at long last Hawkins requested troops. Relying upon the promises of British and Spanish agents to supply arms, Indians under the leadership of Peter McQueen, the prophet High Head Jim, and Josiah Francis sought powder and guns from Pensacola. The Spanish reluctantly gave powder and some supplies, but no guns. In July 1813, on the way home, the Indians were intercepted at Burnt Corn Creek by a militia group under Colonel James Caller of Washington County. The militia won the first round, but the Indians regrouped and attacked, sending Caller's forces into disarray and retreat. The victory heightened the morale of the Indians and increased the power of the prophets, who directed that all whites must be slain. The settlers finally realized they were in the middle of an Indian war, and families were ordered into hastily constructed forts for security.

One of those palisaded forts was around Sam Mims's house, which was located on Tensaw Lake off the Alabama River. The militia at the fort was under the command of Major Daniel Beasley, a Mississippi attorney who received his commission through politics. He had no military training, no experience with Indian warfare, and little common sense. His friend and the commander who had appointed him, Brigadier General Ferdinand L. Claiborne of the Mississippi territorial militia, visited Beasley at Fort Mims three weeks before the fatal Indian attack. Claiborne warned Beasley that he was "exceedingly exposed" and ordered him to "enroll every citizen that is willing to perform duty."[23] He told Beasley to build two additional blockhouses, strengthen the pickets, keep scouts on the move to detect Creeks, and respect his enemy. On August 13 a young boy sighted Indians near the fort, but Beasley rejected his account. Meanwhile, Claiborne continued to receive reports that the Creeks were planning an attack.

On the morning of the massacre at Fort Mims, Major Beasley wrote General Claiborne about a "false alarm" blamed on two slave boys who reported seeing "a great number of Indians Painted, running and hallooing" and on blacks sent home for supplies who reported that Indians had taken over the abandoned plantation and were "committing every Kind of Havoc."[24] Other blacks tending cattle near the stockade were flogged for falsely alarming the fort with stories about seeing Indians in war paint. That same day territorial judge Harry Toulmin wrote General Thomas Flournoy, commanding the regular army, that an escaped hostage told of a large body of Creeks headed toward Fort Mims. Toulmin and his family were crowded into the stockade at Mount Vernon, but he feared "a dreadful blow upon our Settlements, and a melancholy destruction of our population," a people so scattered and "so little accustomed to [Indian] warfare" that only a "feeble resistance" could be mounted.[25]

Just before the attack on Fort Mims, James Cornells rode up and shouted a warning through the open front gate, an alarm William Weatherford (known as Chief Red Eagle), who was hiding in the swamp with his warriors, heard clearly. Beasley ordered Cornells arrested, but he turned his horse and rode away. At noon on August 30, when lunch was being served, the Indians rushed the fort. Beasley had been so negligent that he could not close the stockade doors because sand had drifted against them. The Indians came in shooting the few firearms they had but also making good use of their tomahawks. They were not worried about dying because a prophet had used magic to keep them from harm. A number of blacks fought with the Red Sticks. Weatherford urged the warriors to spare women and children, but no quarter was given, and children and pregnant mothers were hacked apart just as the men were. Probably 250 were massacred or captured as slaves, although gossip and newspapers doubled and tripled that number.

Refugees gathered at Pierce's Mill about one mile away heard war whoops and firing from noon until four o'clock, but they were so few in number they could give no assistance to Fort Mims. The sky was black with vultures and a stench filled the air when a burial detail arrived three weeks later. The horrified Americans accomplished this task, interring 247 bodies, many of them of mixed Indian blood but including a few friendly Creeks. The attacking Indians lost more than 100 dead in the fight at Fort Mims, far more than the "three at most" promised by the prophets.[26] Several people made miraculous escapes from the doomed fort. A black woman named Hester was the first to reach Fort Stoddert with the news. Dr. Thomas G. Holmes made his way into the swamp and hid for days until he was rescued, while five other men fled into the woods. The most remarkable escape was made by the wife of Zachariah McGirth. Vicey McGirth and her seven daughters were captured by Sanota, a Creek boy she had raised. Sanota recognized her and took her and her daughters as "slaves" to his home. He protected them, and when he left for Horseshoe Bend, he sent them to Mobile where they were finally reunited with Zachariah, who had thought them all long dead.

Fear and hysteria swept the frontier. The Nashville *Clarion* reported that the massacre at Fort Mims had "supplied us with a pretext for dismemberment of [the Creek] country."[27] Although there were attacks on families living in isolated areas, the Indians were not able to follow up their victory. The Creeks had started a war almost totally unarmed, with no plans or strategy, and with poor leadership. In the long run, they could not win without British arms, which never came. As the alarm spread, four American armies converged on the Creeks: one from east Tennessee under John Cocke, one from Georgia under John Floyd, one from the Mississippi Territory under Ferdinand L. Claiborne, and one from west Tennessee under Andrew Jackson, who was on the verge of becoming a national hero.

When Tennessee governor Willie Blount ordered out the Tennessee Volunteer militia, Major General Andrew Jackson was still recuperating from wounds suffered in a fracas with Thomas Hart Benton and his brother Jesse. Jackson believed the Creeks were urged on by British agents, and he feared that the Spanish, who wanted back their control of Mobile, would assist the Indians in an attack on the city. He wrote John Coffee that he intended to exert all his "Industry to save Mobile" and was making preparations to move into Alabama as soon as he could travel.[28] Jackson established Fort Deposit and Fort Strother for supply bases and moved into the upper Coosa–Tallapoosa area. But he was frustrated by inadequate manpower, insufficient provisions for those he had, and the task of building supply roads through a wilderness.

In early November Jackson skirmished with the Indians at Tallaseehatchee, Talladega, and Hillabee. Meanwhile, on the Alabama River Sam Dale, James Smith, and Jeremiah Austill, in a small canoe paddled by a black man named Caesar, attacked a large war canoe carrying nine Indians. Militiamen and Indians on opposite banks cheered. The militia won, and Dale, Smith, and Austill became heroes, their tale of daring

McINTOSH,

William McIntosh, a Creek leader with some Scottish ancestry, lived in east Alabama. He supported the U.S. position and ceded territory to the American government in violation of Creek law. He was killed by his tribesmen for his betrayal. (Courtesy of the Alabama Department of Archives and History) bravery told to entertain frontier children on many a cold night; versions are still repeated in modern schoolrooms.

The Creeks gathered at the Holy Ground, a site of religious rituals on a high bank of the Alabama River. Although prophets sprinkled potions with magical powers to kill whites who entered, General Claiborne's army was not affected, and on December 23, 1813, they decimated the Indians. By legend William Weatherford jumped his horse off the bluff into the Alabama River to escape, but he probably rode down a side ravine and swam the river to safety.

On the Georgia border friendly Creeks under William McIntosh and Big Warrior defeated some Uchee Red Sticks and burned several villages. General Floyd and his Georgians built Fort Mitchell on the Chattahoochee and attacked and destroyed the village of Autosse on Calabee Creek. With provisions almost gone and the enlistments of his militia about to expire, Floyd returned to Fort Mitchell. Two months later he moved back into the Calabee area near Tuskegee, where he was attacked by a strong group of Creeks. Only jealousy among the Indian leaders, especially between William Weatherford and Paddy Walsh, prevented the Indian attack from being a complete rout of the militiamen. Following this conflict, Walsh, a natural orator who spoke many tribal tongues, told the Alabamas that "the Indians were unable to fight the white people with any success," and he urged that they "better go to Pensacola and be out of the way of harm until the nation could effect a peace."[29]

Jackson, too, was having trouble with expired enlistments, and rumors of short rations discouraged new volunteers. By the end of the year his army was disintegrating, but he refused to leave the field. With some new Volunteers he fought indecisive engagements against the Indians at Emuckfaw and Enitachopco, although some claimed the Tennesseans were victorious. Jackson knew the remaining Creeks were gathering at a major fortification inside a bend of the Tallapoosa River known as Tohopeka, or Horseshoe Bend, where one thousand warriors were under the leadership of Chief Menewa. The Indians had few arms and no leaders with any concept of military tactics. Jackson was determined to attack the village.

Reinforced by the Thirty-ninth Regiment, Jackson marched south from Fort Strother to Fort Williams, where a large group of friendly Creeks under William McIntosh joined him. With good intelligence of the terrain and fortifications, Jackson sent General John Coffee and his cavalry along with the Indians across the river bank at the rear of the Horseshoe to prevent any hostiles from escaping. Then Jackson attacked the Indians on March 27, 1814.

The Indians had constructed a thick brush and log fortification across the narrow area at the neck of the river's bend, and most of Jackson's casualties occurred in the fierce fighting and close combat at the breastwork. Major Lemuel P. Montgomery was "waving his hat and huzzaing" when he was hit in the head and died instantly. Sam Houston, a twenty-one-year-old Tennessee Volunteer, was wounded when a "barbed arrow struck deep" into his thigh when he stormed the barricade. He remembered that "Arrows, and spears, and balls were flying; swords and tomahawks were gleaming in the sun; and the whole Peninsula rang with the yell of the savage, and the groans of the dying."[30] Alexander McCulloch, who was across the river with Coffee during the battle, wrote his wife afterward that "the Tallapoosa might truly be called the River of blood for the water was so stained that at 10 Oclock at night it was very perceptibly bloody so much so that it could not be used." He believed that a thousand or more warriors had been killed and very few had escaped.[31] Houston recalled that when the sun went down that day, "it set over the ruin of the Creek Nation." Only a few hours earlier a thousand "brave savages had scowled on death," but now nothing could be seen but dense volumes of smoke "rising heavily over the corpses of painted warriors, and the burning ruins of their fortifications."[32]

Indeed, few Indians were able to flee the slaughter, and those who did hardly stopped before reaching the security of the Seminoles in Florida. The battle of Horseshoe Bend destroyed Creek power in Alabama and created the legend of Andrew Jackson. Jackson took his victorious troops to the site of old Fort Toulouse and constructed a stockade he named Fort Jackson. Defeated Indians came to submit to his terms. His most famous visitor was Chief Red Eagle, William Weatherford, who was not at the Horseshoe on the day of the battle. Legend surrounds Weatherford's sudden appearance at the fort and his personal surrender to Jackson, a brave act considering that militiamen were present who had lost relatives at Fort Mims and that the Tennesseans were not known for mercy.

The chiefs who signed the Treaty of Fort Jackson in August included only one Red Stick, but Creeks who had supported the U.S. forces were forced to give up lands covering almost half the state of Alabama. Despite reassurances and promises from the Americans, the tribes who had sided with the whites retained only the eastern portion of their territory. Within two decades they would be pushed even from this homeland. Andrew Jackson marched his Volunteers and frontier army to defend New Orleans from the British invasion. Although the War of 1812 ended in December 1814 by a treaty signed in Europe, news reached Americans only after Jackson had soundly thrashed the redcoats in Louisiana in January. Before the ink was dry on these treaties, whites, determined to squat and claim Creek lands, had begun a land rush into the territory.

FOUR

Land in the
Alabama Wilderness
Beckons

THE Creek War had caused a drastic decrease in the sale of public lands in Alabama and Mississippi. In 1812, 144,873 acres brought $299,904 into the federal treasury, while the next year only 30,261 acres were sold for $60,659. The defeat of the Creek Indians at Horseshoe Bend in 1814 brought peace to the Southwest frontier and caused "Alabama fever" to sweep the nation. Thousands of settlers began to migrate into the rich river valleys and carve farms from lands ceded by the Creeks. James Graham, writing from Lincoln County, North Carolina, observed that "The *Alabama Feaver* [sic] rages here with great violence and has carried off vast numbers of our Citizens. . . . There is no question that this *feaver* [sic] is contagious . . . for as soon as one neighbor visits another who has just returned from Alabama he immediately discovers the same symptoms which are exhibited by the one who has seen alluring Alabama."[1] Graham complained that "anxiety and confusion" reigned in his county as people were selling their farms to seek a "new home in the wide wild wilderness" of Alabama.[2]

In the decade before 1820 the population of Alabama increased more than 1,000 percent to 127,901, most of that growth coming after 1815. In 1830 the United States census counted a population of 309,527, a 142 percent increase, far greater than that for any other southwestern state.[3] Riding in wagons or on mules or horses, pushing or pulling a hogshead with all their worldly possessions, and even walking with gear upon their backs, settlers came from the piedmont regions of Georgia, South Carolina, North Carolina, and Virginia.

Those who flocked to Alabama were disillusioned with worn-out fields and poor economic conditions in the East and were attracted by cheap land from the Indian cessions, high cotton prices, and dreams of wealth. More fertile than the piedmont region of the seaboard South, Alabama also boasted navigable rivers to ship products destined for markets around the world. Some pioneers were small farmers who sold their eastern lands and used the profit as a stake to move west for a better life. A few were well-educated, prosperous planters who had served in Congress or state legislatures and who sold their holdings and moved to Alabama with substantial wealth. They all came with an unshakable confidence in the West.

In the older Southern states, plantation families, whose profits were being reduced by worn-out lands, encouraged younger sons to seek their fortunes and financed the move with slaves, farm animals, and supplies. A friend congratulated Bolling Hall for leaving Georgia and finding a place of "health, rich soil and cotton cultivation" where fine apple orchards and fig trees thrived in the same climate. He was "almost tempted to break off and follow" Hall to Alabama where "cotton flourishes & health abounds."[4]

For all the rich and wealthy who came west, the majority of settlers were poor men and their families who carried barely enough food to last until newly planted crops could reach harvest. Until then, they intended to live off the streams and forests. These families owned no slaves and had little chance of acquiring any. They would not gain vast lands or build grand mansions or accumulate the wealth that brought prestige and power. They were the yeoman farmers of Alabama whose lives were stories of survival and endurance and whose contributions to Alabama history were far greater than traditional accounts have stated.[5]

The Old Federal Road brought settlers down through Georgia into Alabama. First cut as a horse path after the purchase of Louisiana, it was widened in 1811 and improved as a wagon road. Settlers also came through Tennessee to follow the Huntsville–Tuscaloosa Road into the hill country of north Alabama. The continuous line of people, farm animals, wagons, and slaves meant that often travelers never left sight of one another. Only the profanity heard along the road kept one foreign visitor from comparing the movement to the biblical exodus. Although the Federal Road was dotted with taverns, forts, and stands to serve the travelers, the facilities were crude, the fare terrible, and the cost high. As late as 1831 Thomas Hamilton declared the Federal Road "to be positively, comparatively, and superlatively, the *very worst* I have ever traveled in the whole course of my peregrinations."[6]

Some travelers like Richard Breckenridge lost the path of the crude roads in north Alabama. Others literally bushwacked their way across the mountains, often hopelessly lost and searching for creeks and streams to follow toward rivers and known points. Breckenridge called northern Alabama "the most broken mountainous country I ever saw" and the one with the largest rattlesnakes.[7] Gideon Lincecum remembered an 1818 "roadless wilderness" full of deer, turkeys, and ducks as "the wildest, least trodden and tomahawk-marked country" he had ever explored. But he declared those six weeks on the road "the most delightful time I have ever spent in my life."[8] On the other hand, the

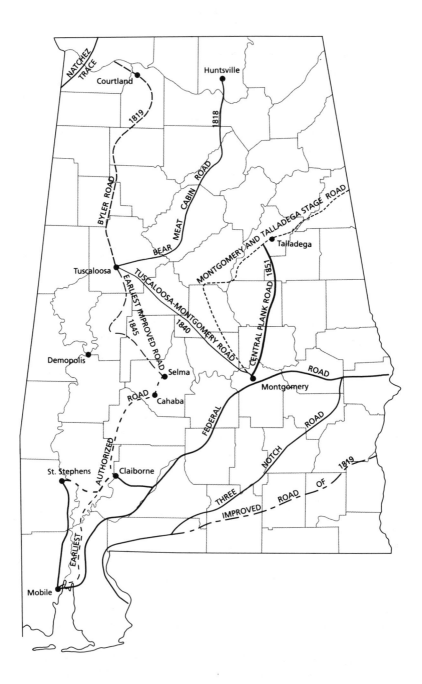

Early Roads in Alabama

Reverend John Owens, traveling from Virginia to Tuscaloosa in 1818, reported "sickness, upsets, breakages, and discouragements" to the point that he wished "he'd not been born." Infernal roads, straying horses, and rough, profane, and "shuffling" people made him declare that "the Devil turned loose."[9]

P. M. Goode described his trek into Alabama to James Asbury Tait in 1817 as unremarkable until he reached the Chattahoochee River, which was swollen by the winter rains. Twenty-two wagons and numerous other vehicles tried to cross with a hundred head of cattle and large droves of hogs. The livestock swam the river; the wagons were broken apart and sent across in canoes. It took two days to complete the crossing. Later the sheer number of travelers forced the party to wait a day to ford Line Creek. Goode considered the Federal Road "truly desperate."[10] Peggy Dow recalled that on the road she was "as much fatigued and worn out by travelling as ever I was in my life. I thought sometimes I should never stand it to get through the wilderness, but Providence gave me strength of body beyond what I could have expected."[11]

Conditions on the Alabama frontier were primitive, and food became a major concern as the influx of people continued. The *Niles' Weekly Register* reported in April 1817 that "The sudden and very numerous emigrations into the Alabama country threaten many with absolute starvation" unless food supplies arrived from other areas.[12] Along the Huntsville Road scarce corn sold for $4.00 a bushel.

The movement of people into Alabama was sizable enough to make the older states believe they were threatened with depopulation, which was one reason why they opposed a federal program of cheap western lands. In fact the Alabama migration began before government surveys were completed and before most of the land was available for sale. Early settlers were squatters on the public domain—or as one petition to the federal government called them, "Intruders on the Lands." Squatters selected the best land they could find. They preferred flat or gently rolling land with fertile soils and with springs or creeks for drinking water. They also sought access to navigable rivers and quickly staked the rich river-bottom lands. Squatters hoped to acquire title to their land when it was put on the market.

When the Choctaw lands were up for sale at St. Stephens in November 1815, the surveyor general warned the land register that trouble was brewing from "intruders who threaten with assassination any person who will dare to bid for the lands they, those Intruders, occupy." Squatters swarmed into the town, and during the sale government officials "were grossly insulted and the laws disregarded," despite the presence of the territorial marshal. But news that cotton was selling at twenty-five cents a pound in New Orleans stiffened the resolve of men with money to purchase good lands.[13]

If at all possible, men visited the area before they moved their families, scouting the land, making a selection, or purchasing surveyor's notes, which sold at a premium. This was an option most often allowed to the moderately well-off; the poor settler was lucky if he could make the trip to Alabama once. Often the wealthy brought slaves to help cut trees, clear land, fence fields, build crude cabins, and plant corn. They soon replaced the cabins with single-pen or double-pen log houses chinked with clay and heated by fireplaces with stone chimneys. Double-pen houses were connected by a roof, which made four-way ventilation possible, and were called "dog-trot" houses for the pets and other animals that wandered between the two rooms. Floors were made from either packed clay or puncheons (split logs placed in the mud with the flat side up). Sleeping quarters were built under the roof.

Williamson Hawkins was one typical pioneer. He served with the Tennessee Volunteers in Alabama during the Creek War and came back to the Jefferson County area in May 1815, bringing "all the supplies he could pack on one horse" and driving cattle before him. He cleared land in Jones Valley and planted a corn crop. Leaving a slave family to guard his improvements, he returned to Tennessee to move his family, women and children, white and black. The wagon was packed tightly with furniture, bedding, and clothes. Chickens traveled in baskets tied to the side and other farm animals trailed by ropes from the rear.[14] John Horry Dent at age twenty-one left a "fine and comfortable house" in South Carolina and "embarked in Wagons with the negroes leaving my dear Wife and little son to remain until I could go and return from the land of promise and provide for the negroes for that year" by making a good corn crop.[15]

Life on the frontier consisted of grinding and unremitting labor. Women and children worked in the fields hoeing, planting, and tending the fences and the animals. Wild animals could be dangerous, and many Alabama pioneer families had confrontations with bears, as Williamson Hawkins did when a bruin charged him into a yard fence. He survived by grabbing an axe from a woodpile and killing "the monster." There were no doctors, no clergy, and no teachers. Law enforcement was by individual might—or in some cases by vigilante action. In the early years there were no gristmills, sawmills, tanyards, or blacksmiths. If one wanted or needed something, self-labor was the unit of production. Clothing was often fashioned from skins and later from wool, cotton, or flax that had been spun, dyed, and woven by the women. Men constructed crude shoes from hides and repaired tools as best they could.

Corn, the basic staple, kept early frontier Alabamians alive. Eaten as

John Looney built this two-story dogtrot house in St. Clair County about 1820. Two-story and double-dogtrot houses were rare. Many dogtrot houses were improved as farms became more prosperous. (Courtesy of Robert Gamble)

ash cakes, corn pone, bread, and grits, it was supplemented by fresh game, fish, or a slaughtered hog from the family's droves that ran wild in the bush. The Lincecum family found plenty of food in the forest in 1818—deer, turkeys, ducks, wild grapes, and persimmons. When they camped along the Tombigbee River, Lincecum put out four hooks and his wife caught a twenty-five-pound blue catfish for dinner. The family that was fortunate enough to own a cow had milk, cheese, and butter, and honey or sorghum syrup provided a rare treat of sweetness. Sugar, white flour, and coffee were items of luxury. Sassafras tea, though good in its own right, proved an unsatisfactory substitute for coffee.

Alabama found no exception to man's ancient desire to find something to ferment and to drink. Persimmon beer, corn liquor, and peach or apple brandy eased the hard edges of reality and the aches and pains of living. Whiskey drinking was common on the frontier, and jugs of the precious liquid became a medium of exchange, often changing hands several times before the cork was lifted.

Life on the frontier was hard, drab, and confining, and neither men nor women had the social reinforcement, the leisure, or the opportunity to be creative or to express artistic personalities. Yet the women made lovely and useful piece quilts or crazy quilts and wove coverlets in such patterns as Lover's Knot and Whig Rose. They colored cotton and wool yarns with plant dyes—rattleweed for blue or partridge-berry for orange-red. Wildflowers, perhaps sweet shrubs, laurel, or honeysuckle, were transplanted close to the cabin and joined small herb gardens that provided both the seasonings for the kitchen and the medicines for the family. Women doctored the family and swapped treasured recipes for tonics and cures. Folklore recommended cobwebs, black pepper, and chimney soot to stop bleeding, snuff or tobacco for bee stings, and a tar rag around the neck to cure a sore throat. If these home remedies were not as effective as modern antibiotics, they were not as harmful as the purgatives, emetics, and bleeding practiced by the doctors of the "civilized" coastal towns. Many women gave birth to their children alone or with only the help of husbands, unless an older woman was in the household, sometimes a slave. Henry Watson reported that on the Alabama frontier "We have no women in this country who make it a business to nurse" but must "depend upon friends and relations or negroes."[16]

The isolation of families was intense, and women especially missed the kinship networks left behind. Neighbors were so distant that smoke from another house was rarely visible. The loneliness of everyday life made community events an irresistible attraction. House raisings, corn-shucking parties, and camp meetings brought distant neighbors together. The first missionaries, always at least ambivalent toward earthly pleasures, reported that there was little religion on the Alabama frontier. Settlers in Washington County were described as "grossly worldly and extremely wicked," and the Tennessee Valley was "destitute of spiritual instruction." Missionaries condemned "sinful propensities," profane speech, and fashionable amusements such as gambling, drinking whiskey, and dancing.[17] The urge to congregate made even funerals social occasions, although burials often were accomplished without the benefit of clergy. A memorial service was preached whenever a minister passed through the area, and during a single visit the divine might preach the funeral of the first wife, marry the man to his second wife, and christen children of the new marriage.

The Presbyterians probably were the first to use the camp meeting as a way to convert souls on the frontier, but a Methodist camp meeting took place at Woods Bluff as early as 1813. Notice of the time and place of camp meetings would slowly spread through a region. By the appointed day wagons and buggies filled with families had made their way to the campground, and hundreds of people camped for days while dozens of preachers exhorted by the light of the sun and moon. The services were emotional affairs with fiery preaching and much singing. Converted souls demonstrated their salvation by jerking movements or by falling down or rolling around. Not all who attended did so for religious reasons. Gamblers, con artists, prostitutes, and local ruffians congregated with the pious. Camp meetings were major social events. While the elders caught up on news and gossip, young people made friends and attended to the rituals of courting.

Land stood at the center of a pioneer's life, and camp meetings offered settlers an opportunity to exchange information. Always looking for good land, a settler was either squatting on a plot he hoped to make his own or was eyeing more land around the stake he had purchased. Land ensured future prosperity and possibly enormous wealth and social status. Its primacy gave the issues of federal land policy an overwhelming importance and ushered politics, faction, and special interests into frontier Alabama.

A number of Georgia politicians and men of affairs took a keen interest in the neighboring lands of Alabama. Chief among these figures was William Harris Crawford, first a senator from Georgia, later secretary of war, and then secretary of the treasury under President James Monroe. Crawford's home was in the Broad River area of Georgia where a close-knit group of Virginia families had immigrated following the American Revolution. Several sons and their young families, including Leroy Pope and John Williams Walker, acquired land in the Huntsville region in the land sales of 1809 and moved to Alabama in 1810. As a Georgia senator, Crawford represented the interests of his friends in Madison County, but when he moved into the cabinet, he came to depend on two other Broad River men, U.S. senators Charles Tait and William Wyatt Bibb of Georgia. John Williams Walker corresponded regularly with Tait and kept him fully informed about the political developments in Alabama. Tait was keenly interested because his son, James Asbury Tait, had moved his family to land he had purchased in south Alabama, and the senior Tait planned to join him.

True to his interest, Senator Tait pushed two crucial bills through Congress, one enabling Mississippi to form a state government and the other establishing the territory of Alabama. For his part, Crawford influenced the sale of the Indian cession lands by locating the first land office in Milledgeville, Georgia, which was convenient for Georgians but difficult for poor squatters in Alabama who had to travel to bid for their lands. Crawford made sure that his friend Alexander Pope was placed in charge of the office.[18]

While Crawford remained a Georgian, Tait and Bibb acquired land and moved to south Alabama. Bibb was appointed territorial governor and with his brother Thomas, Leroy Pope, and John Williams Walker constituted the "Georgia faction" (later called the Royal party or often identified with the Broad River of Georgia). For more than a decade this personal faction and economic group dominated Alabama politics.

Friends of the Georgia faction were in Milledgeville to purchase lands from the Creek cession when they were first auctioned on August 4, 1817. When a land office opened in Conecuh County the next year, small farmers acquired land at better prices, and squatters were often able to secure title to their homesteads. By 1819 yet another office operated in the new state capital at Cahaba (originally spelled Cahawba, the Choctaw word meaning "water above").

As people flooded into Alabama and acquired land, differences increased between the Alabama settlements along the Tombigbee River and in Madison County and the Mississippi settlements along the Mississippi River. In the early period, the western settlers who controlled the Mississippi territorial government were not responsive to the needs of the Alabama residents in the eastern part of the territory. As early as 1803 Alabama settlers began petitioning Congress to divide the territory, citing differences in customs, manners, and interests. "Nature," they wrote, "appears never to have designed the two countries to be under the same Government." Residents of the Tombigbee Valley complained that three hundred miles of "howling wilderness with its usual inhabitants of savages and beasts of prey" separated them from the capital of the territory and communication was difficult.[19] Alabama farmers sold their cotton through the port of Mobile, while western planters shipped their agricultural products down the Mississippi River to New Orleans. Many pioneers cited the territorial government's slow response to the Indian crisis in 1813 as a reason to bring the seat of government closer to the people of the Alabama–Tombigbee river valleys.

Mississippi politicians, with perhaps more greed than vision, supported admission to the Union as one state. But Alabama's fortunes advanced when its interests coincided with broader Southern strategies. Making two states out of the area would give the South more votes in the U.S. Senate and better protect Southern interests. Furthermore, with the huge migration into Alabama following the Creek War, Mississippians began to see merit in having two states. The burgeoning Alabama population now threatened to shift the locus of power to the east.

Several division lines were proposed. One suggestion, following the example of Tennessee, proposed an east-west line of demarcation. John Williams Walker, in a prescient mood, wrote to Charles Tait in January 1817, supporting such a division, "with a view of preventing as far as might be, any collisions of interests between the upper and lower country."[20] This proposal to separate the Tennessee Valley and north Alabama from the Tombigbee Valley and south Alabama was the first example of the sectionalism that would plague Alabama throughout its history.

Regional interests continued to change views and policies. When it became clear that the rapidly increasing population in the Tennessee Valley would give that area control of the new territory, north Alabama withdrew its objections to a north-south dividing line. That was the basis used when Georgia senator Charles Tait pushed the division of the Mississippi Territory in 1817. President Monroe appointed former Georgia senator William Wyatt Bibb as the new territorial governor of Alabama.

The enabling legislation temporarily located the capital of the new territory of Alabama at St. Stephens. In 1817 the town served as the county seat for Washington County and had a public square, hotels, a theater, a land office, the Tombeckbe Bank, a newspaper (the *Halcyon and Tombeckbe Advertiser*), and a school (Washington Academy). But there was no church. The itinerant Methodist preacher Lorenzo Dow visited the town in 1805 and described it as a godless place. One story told of a circuit-riding evangelist (some said it was Dow) who was thrown out of St. Stephens and cast adrift on the Tombigbee River. He shouted a curse upon the town that one day it would vanish, brick would not stand upon brick, and bats and owls would inhabit the place. With or without the benefit of curses, St. Stephens was deserted before the end of the nineteenth century.

In early summer 1817, French immigrants, Bonapartist exiles on their way to the White Bluff area of the Tombigbee, stopped at St. Stephens for several days. The settlers, led by Count Charles Lefebvre Desnouettes, had survived a perilous journey by sea from Philadelphia to Mobile. Boarding a government revenue cutter, they traveled up the river toward their land grants. During low-water time, St. Stephens was the head of ship navigation, and those proceeding north were forced to transfer to flatboats or barges that were poled by hand or pulled upriver. The French caused quite a stir on their arrival in St. Stephens, and they, in turn, probably suffered from severe culture shock as they experienced frontier conditions in Alabama.

Congress granted to the French four townships near the confluence of the Tombigbee and Warrior rivers. The French first called their town White Bluff and later Demopolis, a Greek word meaning city of the people. The French settlers began to clear the land, plant their vineyards and olive trees, and construct crude log cabins. But they were poorly prepared to endure the hard frontier life. The next year when the lands were officially surveyed by the government, the French learned they had cleared and improved land outside the townships of their grant. Many of the settlers moved away from Demopolis and founded Aigleville, south of the Warrior River, and later Arcola.

Grapes and olives did not thrive in the canebrake soils, and neither did the aristocrats and officers of Napoleon's army. The French had no experience with farming and spent too much money on hired hands. They lacked good drinking water, wagons, and teams and were plagued by squatters, high prices for provisions, and fevers. In later years tales were told of women in ball gowns planting corn and milking cows while their gentlemen cleared and plowed fields in their finest military uniforms. Although the settlement gave an exotic chapter to the history of Marengo County, and some of the French settlers remained and married into American families, most of the original settlers had abandoned the area for city life in Mobile or New Orleans by the late 1820s.

Soon after the French immigrants passed through St. Stephens, the town made plans to host the first territorial legislature, which had been called by Governor Bibb to meet January 19, 1818. Delegates would be those men who represented the Alabama region in the Mississippi territorial assembly. According to the Huntsville *Alabama Republican,* the representatives would find a prosperous town with increasing trade.

When the session of the Alabama General Assembly convened at the Douglass Hotel, there were few delegates to witness St. Stephens's hustle and bustle. Twelve members of the house and only one member of the senate were present. Senator James Titus of Madison County ran the upper chamber with great dispatch: he called the roll, made motions, voted on bills, and moved adjournment. The house was dominated by four representatives from Madison County—Clement C. Clay, Hugh McVay, Gabriel Moore, and John Williams Walker.

Walker was a man of great ability and was an influential leader, but the bill he introduced to confirm the charter of the renamed Huntsville Planters and Merchants Bank brought him no support from the average settler, who viewed banks as the agents of the upper classes, the holders of a money monopoly, and the instruments by which the rich grew richer. Walker's bill committed the Alabama Territory to accept the bank's notes and allowed the bank to expand by establishing new branches. Governor Bibb, breaking with Walker on this issue, vetoed the bill. He was concerned that the bank directors in Huntsville would exercise a disproportionate power over the commerce of the territory, and he doubted that Huntsville would ever develop into the economic center of the state.

But Walker was not to be stopped. He introduced another bill that was passed over the governor's objections. In addition, he supported repeal of the Mississippi Territorial Act Against Usury, a measure that allowed any interest rate agreed to in writing by both parties (with unstated rates limited to 8 percent). It was abundantly clear that the Georgia faction represented the interests of the creditors and that they were acting out the time-honored use of political power to protect their own interests at the expense of their constituents. This pro-creditor legislation became extremely unpopular with more democratic groups who proceeded to make private banks and public credit important political issues.[21]

Other measures that Walker supported proved more popular with the people. The militia was expanded, and the territorial government supplied provisions for the men. Walker supported Bibb's call for internal improvements and a commission to locate the best route for a road to connect the Tennessee River to the Warrior River at the Tuscaloosa falls. The legislature created thirteen new counties, defined boundaries of three judicial circuits, called for a territorial census, and chartered a school and another bank. In addition, the legislature approved two divorces and authorized the manumission of three slaves. The first slave granted freedom in Alabama was Rozetta, the female slave of a free black, Honore Colin of Mobile.[22] Before adjourning, the general assembly elected John Crowell as the first territorial delegate to Congress. Not a particularly impressive man, Crowell was nonetheless described as "an honest man, of plain good sense, of integrity, and good intentions."[23]

Probably the assembly's most significant step was the appointment of a commission to select a site for the state capital. The capital's location would influence economic development and land values, and both the Alabama–Cahaba River and Tombigbee–Warrior River contingents vied for it. The Tennessee Valley representatives realized the difficulties in locating the capital so far north, but they had a powerful swing vote and were courted by the other two factions. Before the next session of the legislature in November, the location of the capital became a major political issue.

The day before the territorial legislature adjourned, General Andrew Jackson left Tennessee to take charge of the war against the Seminole Indians. Although the conflict was concentrated in Florida, troops moved through and were quartered in Alabama, and a few skirmishes occurred in the territory. Considerable controversy raged over the "Florida affair" and Jackson's interpretation of his orders. But his conquest of St. Marks and Pensacola secured Alabama's southern border and heightened Jackson's hero status in the territory. The cession of Florida by Spain opened the possibility of Alabama gaining the panhandle area west of the Apalachicola River, a prospect, John Williams Walker wrote Charles Tait, that was "too obvious to be overlooked."[24]

Despite the Indian troubles in Florida, the immigration of settlers into the Alabama Territory continued unabated. By the time the territorial legislature assembled for its second session in November 1818, the population had surpassed the number required for admission to the Union. Walker, elected speaker of the house, prepared the petition for Alabama statehood and sent it to Senator Tait, who offered it to the upper house of Congress. With the newly completed census in hand, the general assembly began to apportion representation in the legislature so Congress could use this apportionment to allocate delegates to a constitutional convention.

Apportionment was the key to power. North Alabama supported representation based on white population only, rather than on a federal ratio that counted three-fifths of the black population. On a white-only basis, Madison County would be entitled to twice as many representatives as any other county. South Alabama was pacified by the passage of its amendment locating the permanent capital in the southern part of the territory at Cahaba, a location favored by Governor Bibb. In return Huntsville was made the temporary capital until Cahaba was laid out and a capitol constructed. These actions ended any hope that St. Stephens would be the capital of Alabama, and they rendered redundant the legislative commission's report that favored Tuscaloosa.

In an amazingly short time Alabama had moved through successive stages of cultural and political change. In a wilderness land in which Indians had roamed, white settlers and their slaves had built roads, cleared fields, and created homesteads and towns. Political developments had already illustrated conflicts that would continue to plague Alabama. Small farmers and planters had different views of banks and usury. More than geographical distance separated north Alabama from south Alabama, and apportionment of legislative seats was the means of protecting sectional and economic interests. After a brief territorial life, Alabama stood on the edge of statehood.

FIVE

The Early Years:
Defining the Issues

IN 1819 Huntsville was a bustling community of cotton planters located ten miles from the Tennessee River on a main road connecting north Alabama with the falls of the Warrior River at Tuscaloosa. The town grew around the big spring where John Hunt had settled about 1805. When the land was placed on the market four years later, Leroy Pope and his wealthy friends from the Broad River section of Georgia purchased the best. Anne Newport Royall, a Virginian writing from Huntsville in January 1818, described Pope as one of "the wealthiest men in the Territory," the land as "rich and beautiful," and Madison County as a place where the "appearance of wealth would baffle belief."[1] Big planters dominated the social and financial life of the area, but the vast majority of landowners in Madison County were small farmers from Tennessee. The ingredients for class conflict were in place from the beginning.

Plantations situated in the fertile valley around Huntsville produced abundant cotton. Wealth soon built a comfortable town. Anne Royall described "260 houses, principally built of brick," a bank, a courthouse, a market house, and twelve stores that faced a large square. She commented on the superior workmanship of the construction, "the best I have seen in all the states," noting that some houses were large three-story structures. There was no church, but the courthouse was used for worship services. She reported that the "citizens are gay, polite, and hospitable, and live in great splendor. Nothing like it in our country."[2]

On the eve of the opening of the state constitutional convention, Huntsville hospitality was tested on June 1, 1819, when an army lieutenant "unexpectedly arrived" with the news that a party including President James Monroe was entering the city. With no warning that the president was even in the area, the citizens of Huntsville hastily organized a welcome committee under Clement C. Clay. President Monroe was received with a flowery oration and an invitation to a public dinner the following evening. There was a flurry of activity as calls went out across the community for food and appropriate tableware.

The banquet, held in the assembly hall where five months later William Wyatt Bibb would be inaugurated governor of the state of Alabama, was attended by "more than one hundred of the most respectable citizens of Madison County." After dinner, "the cloth was removed," and twenty-one toasts, accompanied by "the discharge of cannon and appropriate songs," assured the president of the people's affection. Those attending toasted the Constitution, the memory of George Washington, and Major General Andrew Jackson ("He knows his duty to his country and performs it with energy and fidelity"). The next morning the president left for Nashville accompanied for some distance by his welcome party. Monroe stopped briefly to visit with John Williams Walker, who "mustered him a midday relish, a sort of second breakfast."[3]

As the temporary capital of the territory, Huntsville was the scene of the major steps to statehood. When President Monroe signed the Alabama enabling act on March 2, 1819, it was evident that Congress had dealt generously with the area, a credit to the influence of Georgia senator Charles Tait. Walker acknowledged this credit when he wrote to Tait, who planned to move from Georgia to his new plantation at Black's Bluff on the Alabama River, that "you have done your duty and I hope to see you a popular man in Alabama." The *Alabama Republican* claimed the act "embraces everything which the people of the territory could wish."[4]

In July 1819 the constitutional convention assembled in Huntsville and the delegates elected John Williams Walker as their president and John Campbell as secretary. Because it is easier for a large group to debate than to create, a committee of fifteen was appointed to draft the constitution. The committee included the convention's most talented members: four later became governors of Alabama, three went to Washington as senators, one became a federal Supreme Court justice, and one became the vice-president of the United States. The committee completed a constitution that was strongly influenced by the national document and the constitutions of other Southern states, especially Mississippi. The draft was rather liberal, but the convention, representing a frontier confidence in the common man and an even stronger belief in equality, amended it into a still more democratic instrument.

Although the committee's constitution included the federal ratio for apportioning representation in the state legislature, the convention rejected that in favor of a white population basis. Blacks, free or slaves, were not allowed to vote; the federal ratio would have given greater political power to areas with large slave populations. Annual elections and annual sessions of the legislature aimed to keep representatives closely in touch with their constituents. In line with postrevolutionary sentiments, and amplified by the experiences of the Mississippi Territory, great power was given to the legislature while the governor's prerogatives were limited. Governors were elected for two years and were restricted to two terms. The committee of fifteen recommended a gubernatorial veto with a two-thirds majority to override, but the convention allowed a veto only when the fraction was reduced to a simple majority. The constitution provided for a supreme court and circuit courts and allowed the legislature to establish other courts it deemed necessary. Judges would be elected by the legislature for life terms. The state was obliged to "encourage education" and to protect lands the federal government had donated to support schools.

Constitutions are usually the products of their time, and Alabamians were sharply aware of the land speculation and bank failures that marked the panic of 1819. Few who attended the convention were untouched by the disastrous fall in land prices, and the depression was one reason attacks upon perceived aristocracies and concentrated wealth, banks, and corporations became a distinctive style of Alabama politics. The constitutional delegates placed restrictions on banking, but they did allow the state to establish a bank if it owned two-fifths of the capital. In 1819 three private banks operated in Alabama: the Mobile Bank, the Tombeckbe Bank at St. Stephens, and the Planters and Merchants Bank at Huntsville. If the delegates could have read the future they might have reconsidered the question of a state bank. The pursuit of that policy had long and widespread effects and thrust the issue of banking into the heart of Alabama politics.

The Alabama constitution of 1819 was a liberal document for its time. It established universal white manhood suffrage without any property, tax-paying, or militia requirements for voting or for holding office. Among other Southern states, only Kentucky had such liberal provisions in 1819. The Alabama governor was elected by the people, not by the legislature, and the basis of apportionment was white. The bill of rights section on freedom of religion did not dictate any belief in God, as those in many of the older states did, and the provisions protecting slaves were unusual when compared to other Southern constitutions. Although slavery was sanctioned, the slaves were to be treated "with humanity" and provided with "necessary food and clothing," and owners were "to abstain from all injuries to them extending to life and limb." One who killed a slave would suffer the same punishment as if the offense had been "committed on a free white person," a clause limited only by deaths occurring during an insurrection.[5] Toward the close of the convention, Thomas Bibb and Israel Pickens tried but failed in an effort to give the legislature power to enfranchise free blacks.

Certain provisions did not make the constitution a step into the future. Although sheriffs were elected by the people, judges and most offices were appointed by the legislature. The most conservative feature of the constitution was one of the most fundamental: the document adopted at Huntsville on August 2, 1819, was never submitted to the people for ratification.

As soon as the convention completed its work, campaigning began for the elective offices. The first session of the General Assembly of Alabama, as the constitution styled the legislature, would be responsible for implementing the provision of government. A number of well-known political figures, among them John Williams Walker, Clement C. Clay, William Rufus King, Henry Chambers, Israel Pickens, and Henry Hitchcock, did not run for legislative seats. Their eyes were on appointive offices, most notably the two U.S. senate seats as well as the state judicial offices.

In the September elections territorial governor Bibb sought to continue in office; he was opposed by Marmaduke Williams of Tuscaloosa. Williams protested Bibb's methods in forcing the location of the capital at Cahaba in the face of the legislature's choice of Tuscaloosa. The issue failed to counteract Bibb's strength within the Georgia faction, and his personal reputation carried the election. The counties elected local leaders to the legislature, among them three veterans of the American Revolution (John Brown, Issac Welborn, and Anthony Winston) and Sam Dale and James Safford, participants in the Indian wars in Alabama.

The general assembly, which convened in Huntsville on October 25, was eventually attended by fifty-one representatives and twenty-two senators. As government organization proceeded, the assembly awaited word from Washington that statehood had been granted. James Dellett of Monroe County was elected speaker of the house, and Thomas Bibb, the governor's brother from Limestone County, was selected president of the senate, a position that made him the constitutional successor to the governorship. Governor Bibb sent the legislature a written message that stressed the need for education and internal improvements, and he observed that a good route connecting the Tennessee River with the Alabama River system would tie together the northern and southern parts of the state. Whether Bibb meant a water route or a road is not clear, although canal building was experiencing a boom following the construction of the Erie Canal in 1817. If the governor was thinking of a canal, he was vastly ahead of his time: the Tennessee-Tombigbee Waterway was completed in 1985, but the connection was made through the state of Mississippi.

Governor Bibb cautioned the legislators against factionalism and demagoguery and reminded them of their duty to enact general statutory revisions to make territorial law consonant with the new constitution.

He reported on the sale of lots in Cahaba and announced a deposit of $123,856 in the Planters and Merchants Bank to cover most of the cost of the capitol's ongoing construction.

Bibb urged the legislature to elect Alabama's two senators immediately so that national representation would be in place when the state was admitted to the Union. Important issues—including Missouri's petition for statehood, which had opened the festering issue of slavery—were to be decided. Alabama could provide two more votes for the South. To prevent sectional animosity within the state, it was understood that north Alabama would select one senator and south Alabama the other. In the face of rising resentment of its power and influence, the Georgia faction supported two of its own members for the positions: John Williams Walker for the north, and Charles Tait, who had moved from Georgia, for the south. Matters did not proceed as intended. State senators from south Alabama—who had no love for the Georgia faction—threw their support to William Rufus King and argued that Tait had not resided in Alabama long enough to merit the position. Although Tait wanted the senatorial appointment, he was unhappy over the "jealousy of Georgia influence." When he learned King wanted the position, he withdrew his name from consideration. Tait eventually was tendered a federal judgeship, and King and Walker were elected senators and proceeded to Washington.

William Rufus King served in the North Carolina state legislature, in Congress for three terms, and in American legations in Europe before buying land on the Alabama River and making his home in what is still known as King's Bend. An able politician, King represented those citizens most opposed to the Georgia faction. He served his state for twenty-nine years in the Senate, ending his career in the highest office ever held by an Alabamian—vice-president of the United States. But Walker's political career lasted only three years before ill health forced his resignation and return to Alabama. In Washington he was especially noted for his support of the Land Law of 1821, which provided relief for those who had made purchases on credit only to see the price of cotton plummet from twenty-five cents to ten cents a pound, making it impossible for them to finish paying for their land.

Before the general assembly began legislative business, General Andrew Jackson arrived in Huntsville to race his fine horses and to check on his property in north Alabama. Jackson's visit accentuated the growing alienation between the Georgia faction and the people of Alabama. The Washington leader of the Georgia faction, William Harris Crawford, was allied with Henry Clay against Jackson, but Old Hickory was immensely popular in the state. After the excitement of General Jackson's visit, the general assembly settled down to work and provided for the administration of school lands, created new counties, organized a state militia, and regulated the institution of slavery. Property taxes, licenses, and fees were established to support the state government, but the general assembly "adjourned without apportioning the legislature" in the constitutional time period.[6]

The legislators had returned to their homes before word reached Huntsville that on December 14, 1819, President Monroe had signed the resolution admitting Alabama to the Union as the twenty-second state. Friends wrote John Williams Walker in Washington calling the general assembly's session a "wise legislature" and describing its proceedings as an "appropriate production of an infant state."[7] John McKinley thought it was a *well informed & honest* legislature," but this verdict was not unanimous. Another correspondent hoped Walker "found a much wiser legislative body at Washington than the one [he] left in session at Huntsville."[8]

Governor Bibb thought the site he had selected at the confluence of the Alabama and Cahaba rivers was a perfect spot for Alabama's capital. Spanish accounts indicate there was an Indian town at the site, but by 1818 only a mound remained. The bluff on the west side was high, with springs and flatlands stretching to the backcountry. Here the capital would be laid out, and as the Huntsville *Alabama Republican* phrased it, a city would grow that would "vie with the largest inland towns in the country."[9]

Both rivers had clear channels for navigation by large boats, and the spot was centrally located and easily reached from other areas of the state. But this natural advantage was offset by the lingering resentment felt by legislators for Governor Bibb's choice of the site. When Bibb requested funds to build the capitol, the legislature appropriated only $10,000 for a temporary accommodation of the government. The governor was surely disappointed, but he pushed ahead with plans for the construction of the capitol and persuaded the federal government to increase the land donation for its support. The town was laid out into lots, which quickly sold at auction.

Governor Bibb did not live to see the completed brick capitol with its "imposing dome." Nor was he able to experience the bustling town of Cahaba with its hotels, boardinghouses, school, and two newspapers. Already weakened by tuberculosis, Bibb bruised his kidney in a "little injury" in September 1819. His health declined and he spent the first three months of 1820 in bed tormented by "as much pain . . . as ever fell to the lot of any man."[10] As Bibb lay sick and dying, Charles Tait wrote Senator Walker that Alabama would "again be exposed to great agitation and peril" if Bibb died. If he lived, Tait believed, his "talents and his conciliatory manners" would "silence the pretensions of little men and promote our general prosperity."[11] Bibb's injuries did not improve, and he died in July, leaving the capitol unfinished and the work of the state just beginning. Alabama lost a "man of commanding influence" whose support transcended sectional animosities, and Cahaba lost its strongest supporter.[12] Alabama's electorate were indeed soon agitated and at the next gubernatorial election threatened the "general prosperity" of the Georgia faction.

According to the Alabama constitution, the president of the state senate now succeeded to the governor's office. Bibb's younger brother, Thomas, would serve out the remaining eighteen months of the governor's term. Thomas Bibb was a planter-merchant who had moved to Alabama long before his brother, settling first in Madison County in 1811, then finally in Limestone County at Belle Mina. College-educated and popular, he understood the problems of his state, but he lacked his brother's political acumen.

The legislature met in Cahaba for the first time in the fall of 1820; it convened in the still-unfinished statehouse. After proper memorials to the deceased governor, including naming a county for him, the assembly began its business. The banking issue, which would reach enormous proportions, began with an act providing for a state bank with capital of two million dollars—one-half reserved for the state and one-half to be sold to the people. But this was an overly ambitious capitalization for a poor state and a poor people, and the stock was never sold. The assembly once more failed to pass a reapportionment act. The south Alabama faction was uneasy with Thomas Bibb and believed its interests would be best served if apportionment were delayed until after the next election. What the legislature would not face thus became the leading issue in the gubernatorial election.

Bibb, for his part, declined to be a candidate, and the Georgia faction supported Dr. Henry Chambers, a well-educated Virginian who had moved to Madison County in 1812 and established a medical practice. Chambers was opposed by Israel Pickens, who had once aligned with the Georgia faction. But Pickens, a shrewd and perceptive politician, recognized that the north Alabama members of the faction were too closely associated with the Planters and Merchants Bank. Under management of Leroy Pope, the bank had issued far too many notes, and Pope sometimes failed to distinguish his own money from the funds of the bank. Such poor banking practices were common in the South, and following the panic of 1819 Pope had been forced to suspend specie payments on June 16, 1820.

The banking crisis naturally provoked a storm of political repercussions. The issues were exacerbated—but the citizens were at least better informed—by the presence of first one newspaper and then another in

Huntsville. They provided a forum for the public to air its grievances and for the bank directors to defend their actions. As early as 1812 the *Madison Gazette* was published in Huntsville. In 1816 it merged with the *Alabama Republican,* which later became the *Southern Advocate and Huntsville Advertiser.* Edited by John Boardman 1819–1820 and published by Henry Adams during the period of 1820 to 1825, it was soon recognized as the organ of the aristocracy and bank interests in the area. Unsubstantiated but essentially correct rumors began to circulate about the Huntsville bank, and depositors began to withdraw their funds. In opposition to Pope, the bank, and the Georgia faction (now called the Royal party), the Huntsville *Democrat* began publishing in 1823. With a relentless attack on the Royal party, it helped to define the issues across the state.

This was the material that Israel Pickens used to his advantage as a candidate for governor in 1821. A former congressman from North Carolina, Pickens had moved to Alabama with his appointment as register of the land office in St. Stephens. A tall, thin man with great energy, he was a natural politician who had a keen understanding of finance. Arriving in Alabama with some wealth, he immediately won the confidence of merchants and developed a reputation for "bold" but "principled" actions.[13] He founded the Tombeckbe Bank in 1818 and directed it through the financially troubling perils of the panic of 1819 without suspending specie payments.

There was some irony in Pickens's new alignment with the forces of democracy and the common man. He was a banker, a wealthy man, attacking another banker and a great many wealthy men. In fact, in a spoof published in the St. Stephens *Halcyon and Tombeckbe Advertiser* Pickens was himself attacked as an exploiter. One verse of the piece, called "This is the Bank that Jack Built," went:

> *These are the Farmers, all poor and forlorn*
> *That sold to the Traders all shaven and shorn*
> *The Beef and the Butter, the Pork, and the Corn*
> *That were bought with the rags, all tatter'd and torn,*
> *That were issued as Money, Noon, Evening and Morn*
> *By the cunning Directors that manage the Men that own the*
> *Bank that Jack built.*[14]

The satire was a perfect reflection of the hostility toward corporate enterprise and the fear of monopoly that animated the small farmer on the frontier. Such distrust of business hampered economic development, but on the other hand, the banks of Alabama did not establish a track record of prudent management and the state singularly failed to demand it. The most unlettered farmers recognized that state government befriended the bankers and continued to do business with them. As an undeveloped but developing state, Alabama had very real financial problems. The fluctuation of cotton prices, the higher cost of purchasing goods in a protected market, and the lack of economic development and diversification contributed to the unsettled economic conditions that characterized the time.[15] Specie constantly flowed outward—to the federal government for land, to the seaboard states for slaves, and to the East and Europe for manufactured goods and supplies. An adequate and responsive credit system was an early problem that affected not only Alabama but the entire nation. And it was one of the last problems to be solved.

Pickens had spent years in the politics of North Carolina, and he appreciated the political value of being cast as the defender of the common man. His candidacy for governor raised a host of issues. John Williams Walker was so distressed at the prospect of Pickens's election that he offered to leave Washington and run for governor himself. But Henry Hitchcock wrote him that Henry Chambers was already committed, and Walker was thus probably saved "from the mortification of a defeat."[16] Pickens supporters were known as the "North Carolina faction," and they not only opposed the lingering Georgia influence but favored a state bank and reapportionment of the legislature.

By spring it was evident that Pickens would carry the late summer election, and the incumbents tried to control their expected losses. Governor Bibb, with the encouragement of north Alabama politicians, called for a special session of the legislature to consider apportionment before Pickens assumed office. Meeting in June, the two houses of the legislature had difficulty in agreeing, and Bibb vetoed the bill they finally passed. The veto prevailed, and once again the assembly had failed to reapportion the legislature. It was a last chance for the incumbents. In a gubernatorial contest as hot as the summer weather, Pickens defeated Chambers handily in August 1821.[17]

As the election of Pickens signified a change in the direction of Alabama politics, so too did the arrival of the *Harriet* at Cahaba two months after the election. Coming upriver from Mobile, the steamboat came around the bend with smoke belching and horn tooting. The *Harriet* was not the first steamboat to reach the city, for the *Tensas* had unloaded freight at Cahaba the previous year, but the *Harriet* drew crowds to the foot of Arch Street, and its arrival marked a significant step in the evolution of regularly scheduled steam traffic in Alabama. The first steamboat constructed in the state was probably the *Alabama,* built at St. Stephens in 1818. Its engine power proved inadequate against the river currents, and it steamed downstream to Mobile. The next year more powerful steamboats appeared on the Tombigbee River as far north as Demopolis, and traffic between St. Stephens and Mobile was common by 1820. The stronger flow of the Alabama River required even more powerful engines, and it was twelve months before the *Harriet* made its triumphal voyage to Cahaba; later it was the first steamboat to reach Montgomery. Steam-powered engines heralded a new day for river cities with exciting possibilities of receiving supplies and shipping crops by steamboat.

The citizens of Cahaba watching and cheering as the *Harriet* approached had every reason to consider whether the new mode of transportation would strengthen the town's claim as capital of Alabama. What benefited Cahaba would also encourage Montgomery, Wetumpka, and Tuscaloosa, all three farther upstream and more centrally located in the state. As it happened, it was not commercial rivalry or geographic location that determined the fate of Cahaba. Two occurrences combined to damage Cahaba's reputation beyond repair. Rains and unprecedented floods in the town in the summer and autumn of 1821 and 1822 were followed by an outbreak of "the bilious remitting fever," a disease Mobile physician Dr. Jabez Wiggins Heustis identified as yellow fever. Heustis blamed the fever on the heat, moisture, long rains, and flooded low areas, but he failed to connect these conditions with the breeding of the mosquitoes that actually carried and spread the disease.[18]

When the annual session of the assembly convened in rain-soaked Cahaba in late fall 1821, acting governor Thomas Bibb gave the legislature his final assessment of the issues the state faced. He identified the major crises as an empty state treasury and the pressing need to solve the banking and currency problems. Unfortunately, the handiest source of capital to fund a state bank would be the sale of the lands reserved for supporting a state university. Having outlined the size of the problems, Bibb then turned affairs over to Israel Pickens, who was inaugurated on November 9, 1821.

The correspondent for the *Alabama Republican,* observing affairs in Cahaba, reported that the Huntsville bank would be "roughly handled" by the Pickens administration to "compel her to resume specie payments." Pickens was indeed soon sparring with Leroy Pope of the Planters and Merchants Bank. Even after Pope had suspended specie payments, the state legislature allowed the acceptance of the bank's notes by the state treasury and, more specifically, allowed state treasury notes to be purchased with the greatly depreciated currency. Pickens was banker and economist enough to put an end to this unsound and partisan arrangement.

Turning toward implementation of his own ideas, Pickens had the legislature amend the 1820 act that created a university so that its funds could be invested. Pickens obviously wanted a state bank, but the legislature's version of that idea was a state bank controlled by the private bankers. Pickens vetoed the bill. In the next session of the legislature, the lawmakers again tried to pass a bill that failed to meet the governor's wishes. This time Pickens's supporters tabled the bill in the senate. The trustees of the university—which so far existed only on paper—had approved the investment of funds in a state bank.[19] The remaining problem, and the heart of the matter, was getting the legislature to pass an acceptable law. Pickens understood that his personal victory was not enough. The Georgia faction and the Huntsville bank's supporters (and they were essentially the same) had to be defeated in the legislative elections. In governments based upon separation of powers, effective government is the sum of its parts.

As the second year of Alabama statehood came to a close, many of the political and economic issues that would dominate the state's history for the next two centuries were identified. Sectional divisions between north and south Alabama over the location of the capital foretold sectional differences on a host of other issues. The question of how blacks would be counted to determine representation in the state legislature barely hid the far more complex issues of economic power and the use of government for its protection and advancement. The inability of the legislature to reapportion itself and stand above partisan motivations was to be repeated. Campaigns against wealth and aristocracy created statewide power bases, touching a responsive chord in the hearts of the common people. Crusades against vested interests and corporate monopolies rallied the little man to a cause. What was the proper role and influence of wealth? Should the minority of wealthy planters and bankers control the engine of government for their own purposes? Should and would a broader democracy prevail? Through the years these have been unanswered questions. The attempts at answers are the substance of Alabama's past.

SIX

The Early Years:
Confronting the Issues

THE second term of Israel Pickens marked a turn in the affairs of Alabama. With policies stated but not implemented—with a battle against the Royal party declared but not yet won—Pickens stood for reelection in 1823. The year before he had moved from Washington County to Greene County and was living on his plantation, Greenwood, two miles from Greensboro, "in the woods" but close to "good schools."[1] The move put him more squarely in the Black Belt, a tier of counties whose undulating terrain stretched across south-central Alabama. The name derived from its soil (dark, alluvial) and came to symbolize its population (slaves greatly outnumbered whites) and its culture (wealthy planters fashioned a plantation civilization, a cotton kingdom that was almost a state within a state). The Black Belt's political, economic, and ideological influence would have a deep and lasting impact on Alabama.

Once again Pickens was opposed by Henry Chambers, who represented the Broad River planters of the Georgia faction/Royal party. Senator William Kelly of Huntsville wrote Pickens, "The Royal party forms at this time too heavy a load for any man to carry" for "their friendship is as blasting as mildew." Kelly reported that although Chambers was trying to disassociate himself from the faction, he doubted that he could do so.[2] It was an accurate appraisal. Not only was Pickens victorious over Chambers a second time, but the governor's supporters won control of both houses of the legislature. Now power was added to policy, and it seemed certain that a state bank was in the offing.

Quietly, and with few to mourn it, the Georgia faction—but not the interests it represented—passed into memory. Weakened by the senatorial resignation of John Williams Walker in 1822 and his death early the following year, the faction was decimated by the elections of 1823. Although Chambers won election to the U.S. Senate in 1824, he died before taking his seat.

The year 1823 was notable also for the appearance of the Huntsville *Democrat,* edited by William B. Long, whose relentless and vitriolic attacks upon Leroy Pope and the Royal party warned small farmers of a conspiracy mounted by aristocratic forces. The charges, although ludicrous, reverberated across the state. Long alleged that the Huntsville bank could resume specie payments if it wished but did not in order to force small farmers to sell their acreage to the large planters. Fear spread across the land.[3]

The political demise of the Georgia faction was hardly noticed in the face of the excitement created by the dawning of a new force in Alabama politics. The emergence of Andrew Jackson as a symbol of democratic aspiration was the political manifestation of the affection and support that Alabamians had felt for the general since the Creek War. Jackson was a presidential candidate in 1824, and no one doubted he would carry Alabama's votes.

There were seeming contradictions in seeing Pickens and Jackson as leaders for the common man. Both were men of means, and in Tennessee Jackson was identified with the aristocratic element. Pickens was pledged to support a state bank, while Jackson later waged his greatest fight against the Bank of the United States. In the eyes of the theorists, a vast difference existed between private and state banking—and a difference in the banks they created. In Alabama the issue was clearly of private versus state banking. Pickens supported John Quincy Adams in 1824 and did not ride the early Jackson bandwagon; however, by championing the causes of the common man, he laid the groundwork for Jackson's democratic success in Alabama. In 1824 Jackson lost his presidential bid to John Quincy Adams, but corrupt bargain charges haunted Adams and his secretary of state Henry Clay and ensured Jackson's success four years later.

In 1824 the Alabama assembly wrote a bank bill that Governor Pickens signed into law. The state bank opened in Cahaba the next year with a capitalization of more than $200,000. Alabama did not have a treasury surplus to finance a bank, so if the bank were to be established the money would have to be borrowed. And borrowed it was. About one-half of the investment came from land designated for a university and from land granted by the federal government to finance internal improvements. The other half was provided by $100,000 of state bonds sold on the New York market. Perhaps it is stretching matters to refer to these designated public lands as "trust funds," but it is true that these worthy purposes were held hostage to the success of the state bank. The antibank Huntsville *Democrat* noted that the Bank of Alabama would begin operations with "the prayers and predictions of the Shylocks, the shavers, the skinflints and screwdrivers to the contrary notwithstanding." The *Niles' Weekly Register* responded, "Generally it is the business of banking which produces them."[4]

The Bank of Alabama would be governed by a president and a board of directors to be elected annually by a joint session of the state house and senate. This was the first major enterprise undertaken by the state, and it severely tested the ability of the legislature to oversee such a project. It did not augur well that "politics" in its narrowest and worst sense dominated the election of bank officers and that many legislators viewed the bank as an immense pork barrel waiting for their eager spoons.

The judgment that "private bankers and, as a rule, those who had means and an intelligent understanding of economic matters opposed the creation of a State bank"[5] mistakes the situation. The choice was not between well-managed and prudently administered private banks as opposed to a loosely run and poorly administered state bank. In the context of the times there were no guarantees that either type would be conducted in a safe and secure fashion or that the public interest would be served in either case. Private banking already had a poor record in Alabama, and with the speculative boom of the 1820s and 1830s that record grew even worse. Banking theory and banking practices were in their infancy, and the state did not have the mechanisms of administrative control in place to regulate and supervise large-scale enterprises. Its failure in bank management would be repeated in perhaps more disastrous fashion when it attempted to manage a prison system. Even if government regulation of private banking had been accepted in principle, it would have floundered on the shoals of naiveté, ignorance, and incompetence.

Governor Pickens did not intend to found a state bank that was destined for failure. The legislature was the nearest thing in government to the voice of the people, and the democracy of the common man was usually more offended by expertise than determined to use it. Nevertheless, the state bank started its operations in a conservative fashion, and the legislature, in hopes that protestations would help, multiplied the oaths of state bank officials to the point where they swore not even to think of evil. Because the Planters and Merchants Bank refused to resume specie payments, the Huntsville institution was closed by Governor Pickens on February 1, 1825.

A state bank was the major issue on the agenda of the Pickens forces. The other matter, equally real and symbolic, was the question of the reapportionment of the legislature. The Alabama River supporters of the capital location at Cahaba opposed any legislative apportionment under Governor Thomas Bibb. They knew the 1825 senate would reconsider the site of the capital, and they were determined to delay the apportionment as long as possible, hoping for a more generous representation for south Alabama. Under Pickens's leadership, the issue that proved so controversial in the called session of 1821 was decided with little note, but the Cahaba faction girded itself for the coming "seat of government" contest. As the end of his second term approached, Governor Pickens threw his support behind John Murphy to succeed him. Then he made plans to entertain the Marquis de Lafayette, who had accepted the governor's invitation to visit Alabama during his American tour.

Alabamians were isolated from the rest of the world, and communication was slow and difficult. Therefore the arrival in 1825 of such a dignitary as Lafayette had meaning beyond the responsibilities of hosting a French hero. His visit put ordinary citizens into touch with society beyond the state's borders and gave people an opportunity to identify with a broader world. His tour threw Alabamians into a frenzy of preparations, and the various entertainments painted an interesting portrait of Alabama society.

Arriving at the Chattahoochee River two days late, Lafayette met his Alabama escorts and plunged into the wilds of the Creek nation at Fort Mitchell. The French general was escorted across the river by "fifty Indian warriors, who were stripped naked and finely painted."[6] At Fort Mitchell the Indians entertained the sixty-eight-year-old hero with traditional Indian dances and war cries. The Frenchman was somewhat surprised by the primitive conditions, although during his travels down the Old Federal Road to Montgomery he was wined and dined with the best the inns had to offer. Lucas Tavern was "'done up' better than it will ever be again," and Thomas S. Woodward remembered the procession to Montgomery as such "a cavalcade never traveled that road before or since."[7] On April 3, 1825, with French horns announcing his arrival, Lafayette entered Montgomery and paused at two large tents decorated "with flowers and greenery" to greet the ladies of the city.[8] Three thousand people crowded the road before him and joined his entourage, following him into the town. Governor Pickens gave the welcome address on Goat Hill, but the ceremony was interrupted when Captain Thomas Carr, an old revolutionary war soldier, fell in a well and had to be hauled out. The next evening a grand ball was held in the Frenchman's honor, but he was so tired he left early.[9]

Lafayette then proceeded with the governor down the Alabama River to Cahaba.[10] At the capital a banquet was organized and a typical Alabama outdoor barbecue was attended by "all comers," including a few survivors of the French Vine and Olive Colony, who Lafayette's secretary judged were "not in a state of great prosperity."[11] Running late on his itinerary, the general rushed on to Mobile, where bells rang and cannons boomed when he touched the landing. Following another grand ball, Lafayette steamed toward New Orleans, leaving Alabama never quite the same. As long as memory lingered and then into the second and third generations, tales were told about Lafayette's visit to

Alabama—what people wore to the balls, where he slept, and upon what chairs he sat. One family even pointed with pride under their heirloom dining-room table to a cross that marked the place where Lafayette dined.

After reminiscences of General Lafayette's visit, the most talked about subject in Alabama was the possible removal of the state capital from Cahaba. North Alabama had never been satisfied with the capital's location in the south. Travel to Cahaba was difficult. From Huntsville travelers could take the Tuscaloosa Road through Jefferson County to the falls of the Warrior River. At Tuscaloosa they caught a keel- or flatboat going downriver to St. Stephens and then changed to a steamboat headed up the Alabama River to Cahaba. The overland route followed the Tuscaloosa Road to Elyton in Jefferson County, then took the trail south to Wilson's Hill (Montevallo) and the falls of the Cahaba River (Centreville). Here a traveler could take a flatboat to Cahaba or continue on the overland trail, which was well marked by 1825 but could boast few accommodations between the falls and the capital.

Besides the difficulty of reaching Cahaba, supporters of relocation pointed to the area's fevers and floods. Tales circulated of water so high that legislators were forced to row boats to enter second-story windows of the capitol. Yet the senate committee report on removal, which painted Cahaba in the worst possible light, failed to include the story.[12] The general assembly had the sole power to determine the question without the signature of the governor, and the votes in the house and senate clearly showed a division between the Warrior–Tombigbee river valleys and the Alabama–Cahaba river valleys. The western part of the state prevailed, and after considerable parliamentary maneuvering, Tuscaloosa was agreed upon as the new location. Cahaba continued to thrive as a river town for Dallas County, but when the county seat was moved to Selma, it began a slow decline. By the end of the nineteenth century, Cahaba had vanished; only the cemetery and a few structures remained of the once flourishing capital.

Before the vote was taken on the relocation site, the legislature certified Governor John Murphy's election with 12,511 votes cast. A North Carolinian, Murphy settled in Alabama in 1818 and was a delegate to the 1819 constitutional convention. He was elected governor twice (1825 and 1827), each time running without opposition. The void left by the destruction of the Royal party had not yet been filled by party or faction. Alabama become a territory and a state during the Era of Good Feelings, a time when the Federalist party no longer existed as an organization and factional conflict within the Republican party replaced traditional party politics. During the presidential election of 1824, a division between the supporters of John Quincy Adams and Henry Clay and those loyal to Andrew Jackson caused new parties to form. Members of the Clay-Adams faction were known as the National Republicans and the followers of Jackson first as Democratic Republicans, then just as Democrats. Alabama was strongly Jacksonian, and the Democratic party predominated throughout the antebellum period.

When Henry Chambers died in 1826 en route to Washington to take his place in the Senate, Israel Pickens made no secret of his interest in the seat. After settling some differences with Senator William Rufus King, Pickens obtained King's support, and Governor Murphy tendered the interim appointment, although this action violated the north-south understanding because both King and Pickens came from south Alabama. That the capital had been relocated farther north at Tuscaloosa may have eased the opposition to Pickens's appointment. State law required the Bank of Alabama to be located in the capital, so on May 23, 1826, bank president Andrew Pickens, brother of the governor, moved the bank's specie and paper notes, along with the state archives, from Cahaba to Tuscaloosa in five horse-drawn wagons escorted by ten armed men. The road was crude and rough, and travel was slow, but the valuable cargo reached Tuscaloosa without incident. The specie was placed in the vault that had already been constructed in the new bank building, on the north side of Broad Street across from the Bell Tavern.

The town of Tuscaloosa was situated on the shoals of the Black Warrior River at an Indian trail crossing. A Creek village at the headwaters was destroyed by Tennessee militia in October 1813. Three years later Richard Breckenridge described the falls "as handsome a situation for a town as I ever saw," with numerous excellent springs near the river.[13] By 1818 there was "a small log cabin village" at the falls when the Lincecum family arrived, and the next year the Alabama territorial legislature incorporated "Tuskaloosa."[14] When William Ely visited Tuscaloosa in 1820, he penned a vivid description in letters to his wife—taverns with roofs the rain poured through "literally in Streams," floors made from laying rough boards on the ground, people living in "dirty, small, Sod & mud Cabins."[15] The town was little changed when it became the capital and the legislature first assembled in 1826, holding sessions at the Bell Tavern. Architect William Nichols, an Englishman who immigrated to North Carolina at the turn of the century and then moved to Alabama, soon fashioned elegant buildings that rose amid the log cabins. He designed a capitol in the shape of a Greek cross and located it on the site selected by the legislature, Childress Hill. Although opposition continued from south Alabamians, who opposed appropriating money for a second capitol, the building was completed and the legislature met there in 1829. Nichols also designed the campus of the University of Alabama, placing a rotunda at the center. Tuscaloosa thus had two beautiful complexes of stylistically sophisticated architecture.

On the eve of the first legislative session in Tuscaloosa, Governor John Murphy received several pieces of bad news. First, Nicholas Biddle, president of the Bank of the United States, wrote him that despite the governor's objections, the BUS intended to locate a branch in Alabama.[16] Although the Alabama congressional delegation joined Murphy and requested the BUS not to open a branch in Mobile, the Mobile *Commercial Register* reported support for a branch bank. The port city needed more specie to back commercial transactions. Despite "some misgivings," the newspaper's opinion was that the BUS branch would occasion "no disadvantage to the state."[17] Governor Murphy contended that the Bank of Alabama would provide all the banking services the people of Mobile and the state required. Following such disturbing news, Governor Murphy learned that north Alabama newspapers were clamoring for the Bank of the United States to locate a branch in their region. Then Murphy discovered that Senator Israel Pickens, whom he expected to be his ally in any fight with Biddle and the BUS, had resigned from the Senate due to poor health and would not be considered for election to a full term. Pickens traveled to Cuba to try to restore his health, and there he died on April 24, 1827, leaving Murphy without the support of a popular leader who understood the intricacies of fiscal operations and banks better than any Alabama politician.

Because Pickens's senatorial appointment had violated the geographical gentleman's agreement, north Alabama newspapers immediately began to call for the election of one of their own. Ambitious men from the north began jockeying for position. Five men were considered, but the real race was between John McKinley, an attorney from Florence, and Clement C. Clay, a Huntsville lawyer and planter. In the early years, both had been identified with the Huntsville Planters and Merchants Bank and the Georgia faction, McKinley as an attorney for the bank and Clay as an original trustee and stockholder. But now traditional supporters switched sides, personality conflicts abounded, and even the Huntsville newspapers reversed their previous endorsements. The complicated machinations resulted in McKinley's narrow victory in the general assembly by a vote of 41–38. Charges and countercharges reverberated through the legislature and across north Alabama. One indirect result was a shoot-out on the streets of Huntsville between James White McClung and Huntsville *Democrat* editor Andrew Wills, who was killed.

McKinley and Clay played important political roles in Alabama and on the national scene for many years. Both were talented and ambitious men who were tuned to the changing political winds of the 1820s. Each was willing to adjust old alliances and previous positions to win office. McKinley was born in Virginia but with his parents moved to Kentucky where he grew to manhood and read law. He knew Henry Clay, who influenced his political attitudes. In 1811 during a Fourth of July celebration in Danville, Kentucky, McKinley was involved in a fight and left town in a hurry. He moved to Huntsville, opened a law practice, and worked with members of the Georgia faction. Later he married and moved to Florence. When Anne Royall visited him in 1821, she described McKinley as "a stout, fine looking man . . . of easy manners" and his home as containing "more taste and splendor" than she had ever seen.[18]

Clement C. (Comer) Clay and his son Clement Claiborne Clay, known as C. C. Clay, Jr., were significant political figures in Alabama for almost five decades. The elder Clay, like McKinley, was born in Virginia and moved west with his parents. The family settled in east Tennessee. Clay read law under Hugh Lawson White, a popular and able politician early associated with Andrew Jackson but who in 1836 joined the anti-Jackson forces and helped to found the Whig party. While visiting his sister in Madison County in 1810, Clay purchased land and moved there the next year. He served in the Alabama militia during the Creek War and soon became involved with Leroy Pope and the Planters and Merchants Bank. Clay's Georgia-faction connection helped secure his election by the legislature to a state judgeship and to chief justice in 1820. Although Clay tried to campaign in 1826 as a champion of the people, he had difficulty shaking his ties to the Huntsville aristocracy. Even though McKinley defeated Clay in the senatorial contest, Clay's political career was just beginning.[19]

John McKinley took his seat in Washington in December 1826, joining William Rufus King as an Alabama senator. The nation's politics were dominated by Andrew Jackson's fight with President John Quincy Adams and Secretary of State Henry Clay. Jackson's presidential campaign was already geared up and running, with the tariff question a part of it. As an agricultural state, Alabama opposed a tariff with rates designed to protect manufacturing interests that were concentrated in Northern states; however, some Alabamians were convinced that a protective tariff would encourage manufacturing to develop. Both Jackson and Henry Clay believed McKinley was favorable to their side. McKinley wrote Clay in 1823 that the Jackson "contagion" was spreading and later that, because of the influence of public opinion, he would have to support Clay "in the darkness."[20] McKinley was, at least publicly, in the Jacksonian camp. The tariff issue did not stir small farmers in Alabama because most of them did not understand the question anyway. They did comprehend the question of union. Governor Murphy read the general feeling correctly when he endorsed the constitutionality of the tariff and announced that Alabamians would not support the implica-

Dixon Hall Lewis was the leader of the early states' rights faction in Alabama. He was elected to Congress in 1828 and served seven terms until he resigned in 1844. He was appointed to the U.S. Senate that year and served until his death on October 25, 1848. (Courtesy of the William S. Hoole Special Collections, Gorgas Library, University of Alabama)

tions of South Carolina's nullification doctrine. Alabama would not interrupt the harmony of the Union over the tariff issue. But the nascent states' rights faction attacked Adams and Clay, using a theme that was later perfected to become the dominant theme of Alabama politics in the years before 1860.

Dixon Hall Lewis was the leader of Alabama's early states' rights faction. He read law under Judge Henry Hitchcock and began his political career in 1825 as a Lowndes County representative in the state legislature. A nephew of Bolling Hall, who was known for his strict Jeffersonian philosophy, Lewis declared his states' rights views while introducing a legislative resolution against the implied unconstitutional powers of the federal government. Although Lewis represented the interests of the large plantation-owning aristocracy and was originally a Crawford man, he soon understood the political necessity of supporting Jackson. Lewis was the man who presented the Alabama legislative resolution proposing Andrew Jackson for the presidency in 1827.

Two years later Lewis campaigned for Congress opposing federal aid to internal improvements, a surprising stand in a district dependent upon river commerce. Instead of confining his campaigning to landings and towns along the Alabama River, Lewis ventured into the backcountry. He rode in a wagon especially reinforced to sustain his 350 pounds, and he carried along a large chair to use when he stopped to visit because a normal chair could not accommodate his bulk. His size and his considerable oratorical talents drew a crowd wherever he traveled. On these forays Lewis preached that federal aid could only bring despotic federal control that would impinge upon the people's liberty. Although he entered the race late, Lewis won and continued to stress states' rights as a political concern long before the Alabama electorate accepted it as an issue.

Andrew Jackson carried Alabama on his march to the presidency in 1828, but those who opposed the general and supported the policies of Henry Clay were quietly coalescing into an opposition that later evolved into the Whig party. Many of these men were engaged in commercial operations, and they found the Jacksonian mistrust and downright hostility toward capital unsettling. Whiggish attitudes had a strong following in the large slaveholding areas of the southern Black Belt and the Tennessee Valley and among merchants in the towns, especially in Mobile.

Gabriel Moore of Huntsville was elected governor in 1829 without opposition. A native of North Carolina, Moore practiced law and was active in government from the first territorial legislature, when he was elected speaker of the house. He soon recognized the growing unpopularity of the Georgia faction and, like Clement C. Clay, disassociated himself from it early in his career. Moore was elected to Congress in 1822 when Alabama had only one congressional district, and he was reelected three times. During his last term Congress granted 400,000 acres of federal land to Alabama to support navigation improvements on the Tennessee River. Construction on a canal around Muscle Shoals began while Moore was governor and was completed in 1836. But the canal failed to serve the needs of north Alabama because it left several other shoals untouched. Only after completion of a railroad in the mid-1830s was the transportation of large quantities of cotton to market in New Orleans possible year round.

As his term drew to a close in 1831, Governor Moore challenged John McKinley for the senatorial position. McKinley had been criticized in Alabama for not voting to sustain President Jackson's veto of the Maysville Road bill and for his Kentucky ties to Henry Clay, which were suspect. McKinley received hostile letters from his state when the legislature was in session. He contemplated not standing for reelection, but he believed such a course would play into the hands of opponents led by Moore. The campaign was marred by deals and counterdeals. McKinley was the choice of Andrew Jackson. Governor Moore negotiated with the John C. Calhoun followers in the Alabama legislature, who wanted fewer Jackson supporters in the U.S. Senate. McKinley was defeated by Moore, who resigned his office as governor, leaving the president of the state senate, Samuel B. Moore, to serve out the remaining months of his term. Like most elections in these years, personalities and perceived offenses, real or unreal, swayed legislative votes and sides frequently changed.

The establishment in Mobile of a branch of the Bank of the United States exercised a restraining influence on paper currency in Alabama, exactly what the credit-hungry debtors of the state feared. Tensions increased between the state government and the bank. In his 1830 message Governor Moore asked the legislature to instruct the Alabama congressional delegation to vote against the national bank's charter when it came up for renewal. The measure passed the house but was tabled in the Alabama senate, where bank supporters and Whiggish interests were stronger. The charter of the Bank of the United States was to expire in 1836, and the Huntsville *Democrat*, which opposed the bank, suggested it should be located "in the middle of the Gulf of Mexico."[21] Henry Clay, who was seeking a campaign issue against Jackson for the presidential canvass in the fall, encouraged Nicholas Biddle to request recharter early. The recharter move began in January 1832 and ended with Jackson's veto of the bank bill in July. Congress was not able to override, and the question became a prime issue in the election. Senator William Rufus King wrote from Washington that

The Forks of Cypress, built in Lauderdale County near Florence by James Jackson about 1830, had a stunning colonnade that enclosed all four sides of the house. Jackson was a noted horsebreeder who had a private racetrack northeast of the house. Andrew Jackson often brought his horses to race there. (Courtesy of Dan Glenn)

Our protracted session is drawing to a close;—would to God I could say we have done what ought to be done. I have been in Congress long—I have witnessed great political excitement and strong devotion to party; but never have I witnessed such a departure from principle, to promote political objects, connected with the advancement of individual aspirants, as has characterized the proceedings of this session.[22]

Despite the rumblings of opposition to Jackson over the bank issue, Alabama remained strongly supportive of the president in the election of 1832. The Creek removal controversy that followed, however, ended Jackson's almost unanimous following in the state.

As Alabama filled with farms and plantations, white settlements pressed in upon lands still in Indian hands. People continued to travel down the Federal Road through the Creek territory in eastern Alabama, and land-hungry, unscrupulous white men coveted the Indian lands through which they passed. Indians retaliated against the encroachments, and an uneasy peace, frequently broken, settled in on the Alabama border. In Georgia the Indians regularly raided farms and stole livestock, especially from those living along the Florida line, and the federal government was urged to step in and solve the problem. One answer to the Indian question was removal—give the Indians western lands and remove them from Alabama and Georgia. Although the policy did not originate with Andrew Jackson, his administration enthusiastically negotiated additional agreements and directed the Indians west on the Trail of Tears. In 1825 William McIntosh met with federal commissioners and signed the Treaty of Indian Springs. The treaty violated the law passed the previous year at the Creek council meeting at Tuckabatchee that decreed death to any Creek who sold tribal lands. McIntosh's terms signed away lands in Georgia between the Flint and Chattahoochee rivers for $400,000 and a promise of like acreage west of the Mississippi. The enraged Creeks tried and convicted McIntosh in absentia, and a raiding party of two hundred Indians from Tuckabatchee and Okfuskee attacked McIntosh's home, a tavern at Lockchau Talofau. Led by Chief Menewa, the Indians allowed the white guests who were present to leave the house before burning it and shooting McIntosh.[23]

Such action did not seriously advance the Indian cause, and the government's policy was formalized in the Indian Removal Act of 1830. Federal agents began negotiations that resulted in the Treaty of Dancing Rabbit Creek with the Choctaws (1830), the Treaty of Cusseta with the Creeks (1832), and the Treaty of New Echota with the Cherokees (1835). For Alabama, the 1832 Creek cession brought on a political crisis, which came to a head in the administration of Governor John Gayle. A strong Jackson man, Gayle had been active in Alabama politics since territorial days, serving in the state legislature from Monroe County, then as justice of the state supreme court. He resigned to represent Greene County in the legislature and was speaker of the house when he joined Governor Samuel B. Moore, who was completing Gabriel Moore's term, and Nicholas Davis, a Limestone County planter, as a candidate in the 1831 election. The tariff was an issue, and Gayle's strong antinullification stand and pro-Jacksonian sentiments swept him into office.

The treaty with the Creeks allowed individual Indians the option of going west with the tribe or remaining in Alabama, in which case they could select a half section of land, 320 acres. Whites were to stay off the lands until the Indians harvested their crops and until surveys were completed and those Creeks who wished to remain selected their land. But Alabama did not wait. The legislature divided the Indian cession into counties and extended jurisdiction over it. The settlers did not wait either. Recognizing a grand land boom for what it was, whites rushed into the area. The Indians complained that "instead of our situation being relieved as was anticipated, we are distressed in ten-fold manner."[24] Many speculators and settlers purchased land allotments directly from Indians at absurdly low prices, had them certified by the United States Land Office, and moved onto the land. Conflicts between settlers and Indians increased. Federal troops at Fort Mitchell, though numerous, could not contain the violence and were unable to keep whites off the Indian land.

In late summer 1832 federal troops tried to dislodge whites at Irwinton (Eufaula) and burned the village. But the incident that exploded into a federal-state confrontation was the Hardeman Owens murder. Owens was one of the commissioners appointed to organize Russell County. He had a reputation as an "all-around villain," "a complete scoundrel" who was "blamed for a number of outrages around his home" on land he had acquired south of Fort Mitchell. He refused to move off it when ordered. Federal troops under the command of Jeremiah Austill, one of the heroes of the Alabama River canoe fight in the Creek War of 1812, went to Owens's homestead to dislodge him. Austill called Owens "one of the most daring men I ever met and one of the most dangerous."[25] Indians warned the troops that explosives were in the house. When confronted, Owens hastily departed out the rear door just before his cabin blew up. He was found in the woods, where he drew a pistol on a soldier who shot him "in self defense."[26] A Russell County grand jury returned a murder indictment against those responsible, but the commanding officer of Fort Mitchell prevented the sheriff from serving the warrant. The authority of the state of Alabama and the federal government met head-on. The emerging states' rights advocates had been toying with federal power versus states' rights, using the tariff and internal improvements as issues, but the people of Alabama had no immediate interest in such issues. Now the Indian lands question provided ample powder for the cannons of the states' rights faction.[27]

President Jackson, who had no reputation for pro-Indian policy, was determined to enforce his treaty and to evict all white squatters, but he surely was misinformed about the extent of settlement in the counties. Clement C. Clay wrote Jackson from Alabama, warning him that the situation was dangerous and "incalculable distress and injury, to many hundreds of our citizens, will be the consequence."[28] Governor Gayle felt betrayed because Secretary of War Lewis Cass had written to Senator Gabriel Moore that intruders who did not disturb the Indians would be allowed to remain as long as they did not interfere with the Indians' right to select land. Alabama's congressional delegation called on the president and defended the state's action, and Jackson sent Francis Scott Key to Alabama as a commissioner to negotiate the differences.

Key met with the soldiers at Fort Mitchell, and they agreed to appear for the trial. He talked with the surveyor, who convinced squatters that the Indian reservations did not include their improvements. The surveyor assured Key that his work would be completed by the time Jackson had set for all whites to be gone, thus making removal unnecessary and saving face for the president. At Tuscaloosa, Key met with Governor Gayle and tried to soften his hard feelings and to improve the federal government's relations with Alabama. He charmed Sarah Haynsworth Gayle and the children and reassured the governor. The soldier responsible for shooting Owens deserted the army and vanished, making a murder trial impossible. The immediate issues seemed resolved, but the affair had significant repercussions in Alabama politics. John Gayle moved away from Andrew Jackson and eventually joined the Whig party. In turning from Unionism toward a states' rights philosophy, Gayle helped strengthen the old Calhoun nullifiers and states' rights advocates in Alabama. Jackson's popularity in the state was tarnished. Alabama's former posture of strong support for the Union began to slip away as citizens expressed concern over the increase of federal powers. In particular, apprehension grew about what such an increase might mean for the owners of slaves and other citizens of Alabama should the growing agitation over the slavery issue continue unabated.

In the early years of statehood Alabama politicians had learned that to be elected they must persuade the people of their personal commitment to the interests and welfare of the common man. The agitation against the Royal party illustrated the importance of political appeals against wealth and privilege in a state where small farmers were in the majority. Later these campaigns took on the appearance of crusades to convince Alabamians that "through cooperative political action, they could command their destiny." Unfortunately, as one historian has noted, these crusades often diverted the energy of Alabamians "away from any effective agitation for substantial amelioration of their hard lot."[29]

SEVEN

The Cotton Kingdom

DURING the early decades of statehood, white and black Alabamians transformed the frontier into functioning communities. The white elite concentrated on building political and educational foundations, moving slowly away from frontier living conditions toward a society with stronger cultural resources. Lawyers and doctors established practices and teachers opened schools. Missionaries, circuit-riding evangelists, and camp meetings decreased as church buildings began to dot the rural countryside. Masonic and fraternal orders spread. Newspapers, sometimes two to a village, began printing. Sawmills and brick ovens allowed for more sophisticated construction of houses and stores, most built by black labor. Gristmills increased in rural areas, and bakeries appeared in towns. Mercantile establishments, small shops, and banks facilitated commercial enterprise. Bridges, ferries, roads, stagecoaches, and finally railroads improved transportation. All of this activity depended upon Alabama's economic development, which was founded upon the commercial cultivation of cotton.

A British visitor to Mobile in 1858 described the port as a city "where the people live in cotton houses and ride in cotton carriages. They buy cotton, sell cotton, think cotton, eat cotton, drink cotton, and dream cotton. They marry cotton wives, and unto them are born cotton children. In enumerating the charms of a fair widow, they begin by saying she makes so many bales of cotton. It is the great staple—the sum and substance of Alabama. It has made Mobile, and all its citizens."[1] This cotton kingdom was built upon the labor of black slaves.

The coexistence of white and black people in a biracial society formed a constant tension in Alabama's history, and regardless of persistent attempts to submerge it, race was never far from the surface of social, economic, and political life. The first blacks to arrive in America came to Virginia in 1619 aboard a Dutch ship and were worked initially as indentured servants. By 1660 Virginia law had changed for blacks, and they were held in permanent bondage. The institution of slavery was now a legal entity in America. From Louisiana as early as 1701, Bienville complained to the French government that he must have more laborers to till the land, especially the lands upriver from Mobile that were fertile but unhealthy. In 1721 a French ship of war, the *Africane,* arrived in Mobile with 120 blacks, only half the number that had embarked from Guinea in French West Africa. The *Marie* followed, landing with 338 slaves. Then the *Neride,* which sailed from Angola with a cargo of 350 human beings, arrived with only 238 alive.

Africans who became slaves in Alabama had origins mostly in the central grasslands or the coastal plains of the rain forest of West Africa. They came from agricultural tribes that enjoyed a rich variety of culture within decentralized societies that were ruled by kings. Extended families and kinship loyalties were strong and ancestors were revered. They believed in an afterlife. The tribes planted yams and vegetables and hunted for meat or raised sheep. They wove cloth and made baskets and pottery. Tribal warfare resulted in captured enemies becoming slaves, which were then sold to Europeans seeking labor, and they were transported across the ocean.

Mortality rates for blacks on the transatlantic passage were high. The trip was risky for sailor and passenger, but slaves were forced to travel in shallow shelves built below deck, and food and water were scarce, clothing inadequate, and exercise and fresh air meager. Cold seawater was pumped periodically across the shelves and the people to flush away human excrement. Along the waterfront taverns of the world, sailors told tales of being able to smell a slave ship several miles downwind.

The first destination of the slaves was most likely a Caribbean island where they were "seasoned" for a few years, taught French or English and how to work in gangs, and broken to the regime of slavery. For those blacks who survived the oceanic voyage and were shipped directly into Mobile, no comfort awaited them. They were sold to residents for $176, paid in three installments, a price established by the French Western Company, which controlled the commerce of the Louisiana colony. At Mobile many blacks were loaded on flat barges at the port and transported up the Alabama River for sale, while others were sold to owners of plantations along the eastern shore of Mobile Bay. Spanish, British, and Yankee slave traders followed the French in bringing slaves, and the black population of the Mobile area increased. At the time of the Declaration of Independence, slavery was legal and practiced in all the British colonies. But the ideals of the American Revolution made it difficult to justify enslavement. Gradually, slavery in the Northern states, where it was never entrenched and never used in large-scale commercial agriculture, was abolished by court decrees or statutes. Conscience and virtue came easily where slavery was not economically profitable.

Although Africans continued to arrive in Mobile until the international slave trade was outlawed in 1808, and some arrived illegally after that date, most slaves entering Alabama immigrated with their masters, following the usual pioneer routes into the area. Some slaves were brought by slave traders who purchased them from Virginia and Maryland owners or bought them in the slave markets of the East and then transported the chattels by ship to Mobile or less frequently walked them in coffles to Alabama.

Initially, labor was needed to clear the virgin forests, fence the fields, till the soil, and produce food. Later came the labor demands of commercial cultivation. Tobacco in Virginia and then rice and indigo in South Carolina were successful Southern commercial crops. In Georgia black-seed or long-staple cotton, grown after 1786, spread quickly along the islands and coastal areas to provide fiber to feed the never-ending demands of the English spinning and weaving machines. Although the outside of the black seed was slick and separated easily from the lint, the seeds still had to be removed by hand, and this was a slow process. The cultivation of long-staple cotton, also called sea-island cotton, did not expand into inland areas because the plants did not grow well away from the coast. As subsistence farmers pushed into the Southern piedmont, they searched for a commercial crop that would thrive in the red-clay soils and the rolling hills of the uplands, one that could be transported to market without spoiling in hot weather. They found it in Mexican or green-seed cotton. The sticky seed of this short-staple variety clung to the fibers, making removal by hand even slower and more difficult than separation of sea-island cotton.

The problem was solved in 1793 when Eli Whitney invented the cotton gin. A Yale graduate with mechanical skills, Whitney was tutoring on a Georgia plantation when he recognized the dilemma of separating seeds from short-staple cotton. Unaware that he, a Yankee, was creating a Southern monarch, Whitney devised a simple hand-cranked machine of rollers and spikes that could clean fifty pounds of lint a day. Whitney's invention made the production of cotton with slave labor enormously profitable, gave new life to human bondage in the South, and created a cotton-gin manufacturing industry that in Alabama would be dominated by New Englander Daniel Pratt and his gin factory at Prattville.

Cotton dominated the economy of Alabama. In 1828 Captain Basil Hall boarded the *Herald* at Montgomery for his trip to Mobile and found his ears "wearied with sound of Cotton! Cotton! Cotton!" At each landing the boat took on more cotton and new passengers whose first question was always, "What's cotton at?"[2] A visitor to Alabama in 1834 reported that "To sell cotton in order to buy negroes—to make more cotton to buy more negroes, 'ad infinitum,' is the aim and direct tendency of all the operations of the thorough going cotton planter: his whole soul is wrapped up in the pursuit."[3] Harriet Martineau explained that profit drove a planter to devote "every rod of his land to cotton-growing." She knew an Alabamian who "paid for his land and the maintenance of his slaves with the first crop and had a large sum over wherewith to buy more slaves and more land."[4]

Slavery thus became the indispensable component in the cotton kingdom in Alabama, intrinsically tied to the economic fortunes of the planters and representing the greatest dollar value in the portfolios of the wealthy and in the assets of the yeomen. The "peculiar institution," as Southerners called it to avoid using the word slavery, caused complicated social and cultural patterns to evolve and was a pervasive influence upon all aspects of Alabama society. Southern whites have been more comfortable with an interpretation that stressed a "kindly master" in a paternalistic system, somewhat like the plantation myth evident in John Pendleton Kennedy's romantic novel *Swallow Barn* (1832), which portrays the glamorous aristocratic life on a Virginia plantation. In Kennedy's picturesque treatment, the stereotypes appear—the kind and considerate master, the capable but submissive mistress, the thoughtless and frivolous belle, the contented and happy darky—all appear except the indolent trashy poor white, who presumably did not exist in Virginia. The plantation myth, perpetuated in literature from the early nineteenth century, reached its height in Margaret Mitchell's *Gone With the Wind* (1936).

Abolitionists were the first to establish a different interpretation, in its own way as one-sided as the romantic myth. Through the pages of William Lloyd Garrison's the *Liberator* (founded 1831), Theodore Dwight Weld's *American Slavery As It Is* (1839), and Harriet Beecher Stowe's *Uncle Tom's Cabin* (1852), the haughty and cruel master, the vicious and sadistic overseer, the shallow and indifferent mistress, and the proud and rebellious slave came vividly to life. Abolitionists and blacks pointed to the inherent sin of human bondage, the cruelties associated with discipline, the brutal treatment of runaways, and the degrading slave markets where humans were bought and sold and families divided. Historical evidence, most of it generated by white Southerners, exists to support some of both these interpretations, but it is clear that the slave-labor system was far from the plantation myth that pictured happy black folk singing melodious hymns while they plucked the white gold from the fields of Southern summer snow. Slave narratives, from the Fisk University collection or from interviews gathered by whites during a 1930s Federal Writers' Project (FWP), give eloquent testimony to the brutality of slavery.

Plantations in Alabama varied greatly in size and operations, but generally they were no larger than a man could walk in one hour from the slave cabins to the farthest cultivated field. Large planters often owned several plantations, living on one and employing overseers or sons to supervise the others. It is true that Alabama white men preferred to describe their agricultural units as plantations rather than as farms, but size was a factor in the distinction between the two. Social status and geography were also determining factors. Plantations might encompass 1,000 acres, with about one-third planted in cotton and the rest reserved for timber, pastureland, and gardens. In addition to the master's house, there were barns, sheds, animal pens, a smokehouse, a gin house, a blacksmith shop, and a spring- or well house. The slave quarters, a number of cabins grouped together, were some distance from the main residence. Jenny Proctor, born a slave in Alabama in 1850, described the slave houses on her plantation as "old ragged huts made out of poles and some of the cracks chinked up with mud and moss and some of them wasn't."[5] The one- or two-room log or rough-board cabins had a fireplace for heat or cooking. Wooden shutters kept out the bad weather. Furniture consisted of beds, a wooden box for clothes and blankets, a table, and several chairs. Bunks were sometimes nailed to the wall, and mattresses were stuffed with pine straw, corn shucks, or cotton. Small vegetable plots near the quarters were allotted to individual slaves. Their "patch" gardens increased the food available on the plantation and placed some of the burden of food production on the slaves. If the plantation had an absentee owner, or if it were large, there would be quarters for the overseer and his family.

The plantation tried to be self-sufficient, purchasing as little as possible. Supplies were usually ordered through the plantation's factor in Mobile who sold the cotton as an agent of the owner. Mercantile companies had difficulty getting established in inland towns because so much of the business was accomplished through factors in Mobile, New York, or Europe. Planters usually purchased yard goods, tools, and foods such as coffee, tea, flour, and sugar. New farm animals, especially mules, were acquired locally or from drovers moving south with herds from Missouri and Tennessee.

Clothing for slaves was ordered by the gross, muslin and calico for hot weather and linsey-woolsey for winter. Some masters dressed their slaves in homespun garments woven and sewn by the slaves. The English visitor Philip Henry Gosse was appalled by the thinly clad slave women he saw working in the fields, their "sordid rags" fluttering about them.[6] Children wore a "split-tailed shirt," called a "shirt iffen a boy wear it and call it a dress iffen the gal wear it."[7] Rough leather shoes were made by the plantation cobbler, or stiff brogans were bought in only two or three sizes. Both types rubbed blisters on the feet, one reason slaves went barefoot as much as possible. Cato, a slave in Ala-

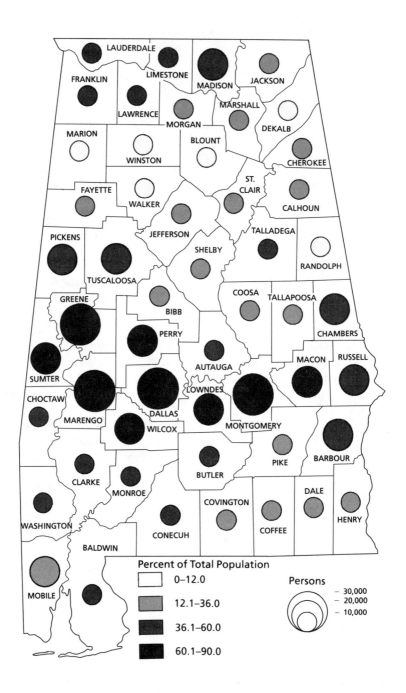

Black Population in 1860

bama, remembered how he cried when his master brought him "red russets from town" for he "didn't want to wear no rawhide shoes." House servants were given cast-off finery from the planter's family. Because he was a carriage driver, Cato recalled, he had "plenty of fine clothes, good woolen suits they spinned on the place, and doeskins and fine linens."[8]

Planters debated the best method of feeding slaves—whether to issue rations or to prepare food in a common kitchen. Large planters tended to issue rations, while small planters generally fed them together, usually from one kitchen where the planter's food was also prepared. Food was dished out on plates at mealtime, and no staples were issued to the slaves. When rations were allotted, they were normally distributed each week. On large plantations slave children were fed separately from their parents, often eating from troughs with their fingers. Slaves were given portions of pork and cornmeal, along with buttermilk, sweet potatoes, and sorghum. Meat was salt-cured and sometimes improperly preserved. The hot weather caused food to spoil quickly, and worms and flies were constant problems.

Slaves often supplemented their food rations by gardening and hunting. From gardens they provided greens, fresh corn, peas, and beans in season, and they gathered eggs from the chickens they raised. Occasionally slaves ate wild game, such as opossum, raccoon, birds, rabbits, and squirrels; fish from creeks and streams; and nuts and fruits. Ash cakes, corn pone, turnip greens, and pumpkins were other favorite foods, and flour biscuits were a rare luxury. Cooking was done in the cabins by the slaves each morning and evening. The noonday meal was delivered to the fields when, as Angie Garrett recalled in an FWP slave narrative, the mules and slaves would both be eating and resting. Because the work of the slave was hard, food was essential and was made available to most slaves, although certainly not in the quality or variety they desired. On many plantations the slaves were poorly fed. For Cato, a slave in Wilcox County, the "eating was good," but he knew plantations that "half-starved their Niggers," who were forced to "slip about" to other places "to piece out their meals."[9] Stealing food, especially chickens and hams, was a common reason slaves were punished.

Masters encouraged slaves to live in monogamous family units, convinced the system diminished male conflict over females, inspired fecundity, promoted tranquillity, discouraged running away, and followed God's law; however, slave marriages were not recognized by man's law. Slaves had to request permission from their owners to marry. Unions between slaves with different owners or living on separate plantations were not unheard of but were unusual. Children belonged to the mother's owner, and babies fathered by free men took the status of the mother. Although by 1852 Alabama law prohibited a child younger than ten from being sold separately from its mother, numerous separations occurred before and probably some after the law was enacted.

Frank Smith, who was born in Virginia, told an FWP interviewer that he was separated from his parents when he was four years old and they were sold off the plantation. Smith was sold again when he was fifteen to a man from Tennessee. A father could not prevent such a sale, nor the sale or sexual exploitation of his wife or children; however, a slave father was still the master of his household within the plantation. Men debased by slavery nonetheless took leadership roles in the quarters and in their own homes. The slave family and extended kin networks were important in child rearing. One study has suggested that masters preferred a matrifocal family with the mother as the central authority figure with responsibility for her children, a relationship that was ironically inconsistent with white patriarchal practice.

Within the slave family, stories and traditions were passed from one generation to another in the oral tradition of Africa. Children were nurtured, loved, and taught work patterns and work ethics. Family mores, crafts, folk tales, and religion were passed from one generation to another, and ways of avoiding punishment were shared. Parents taught their children how to resist without getting into trouble and how to get along with white people. Studies of the slaves living on Henry Watson's Greensboro plantation between 1843 and 1861 illustrate the continuity of family and kin groupings.[10] Despite enormous pressures and inherent weaknesses, the creation of a slave family was an act of faith and courage. Family networks of caring individuals buffered the depersonalization of slavery.

Religion was important in African culture, and Christianity, with its appeal to a God more powerful than any earthly master, was attractive to slaves and provided another buffer to human bondage. The promise of an afterlife, when worldly labors and burdens would be removed, was comforting. Masters encouraged their slaves to adopt religion, some because of a Christian mission to save souls, others because they were convinced that a religious slave was a more contented slave. Many owners took their slaves to their white churches, where the slaves sat in the balcony or in a separate section. Other planters directed church services on the plantation or invited white ministers to come and preach. Anthony Abercrombie's owner, James Abercrombie, allowed his slaves "to build a bresh arbor" on the plantation, and Lee Cato had his slaves build a church that "had a flo' and some seats" under a "roof of pine straw."[11]

In white sermons, Bible texts were highly selective. Verses that stressed the slaves' duty to obey their masters were emphasized, while the Christian concept of the brotherhood of man was omitted. Through decades of exposure, slaves developed their own brand of religion, a syncretism of their African heritage and their understanding of Christianity. The slave religion emphasized the Old Testament, especially the Hebrews' struggle against slavery and the flight from Egypt, with Moses leading his people out of the chains of bondage into the Promised Land. The African tradition of "danced religion" was evident. In slave prayer meetings (frequently called "praise meetings"), singing, rhythmical chants, swaying, shouting, hand clapping, and dancing rocked the quarters. Occasionally whites attended, but most times the prayer meetings were held in forests or in cabins where the windows and doors were draped with wet blankets to muffle the sounds of whispered chants and prayers. Black spirituals evolved as the most moving and well-known aspect of slave religion. Biblical stories in haunting melodies, such as "Go Down Moses" and "Mos' Done Toilin' Here," portrayed a God of hope for a suffering people. Black ministers developed a rhythmic preaching style. They were widely respected by the slaves and quietly moved between plantations, holding revivals and baptisms deep in the woods or sometimes joining white ministers, usually preaching at the end of the service. Old Ned in Harold Courlander's novel, *The African*, takes two young slave boys to a secret camp meeting, warning them that to be baptized they had to *"get the spirit. . . .* Not *some other* time . . . but *this* time!"*—for "it mought be a year or two 'fore they's another meetin' like this one."[12] Sarah Fitzpatrick, a house servant in Tuskegee, recalled that they "lack'ta shout a whole lot an' wid de white fo'ks al'round'em, dey couldn't shout jes' lack dey want to."[13]

Baptist pioneer leader Hosea Holcombe was aided by Daniel Davis's slave Job, who preached to large, mostly white congregations, first at Bethel Baptist Church and then in other churches across Jefferson County. Baylis E. Grace recalled hearing Job preach and described him as pious, devout, and eloquent. John Blackwell's slave Caesar was such a fine preacher that in 1829 a group of Montgomery pastors and laymen of the Alabama Baptist Association raised $625 and purchased him, and his trustees placed him at the James McLemore plantation. Caesar was a tall man with "a clear, musical voice, and graceful elocution" who often read from his Bible and preached to congregations of both blacks and whites at association meetings and at the First Baptist Church of Montgomery. If the audience became too excited, Caesar would stop and remark, "My brethren and sisters, when your cup is full, let it run over, but don't tilt it any."[14] Following the Virginia slave insurrection led by Nat Turner, a black preacher, Alabama planters cast a more suspicious eye on all black evangelists and supervised more carefully the religious gatherings of their slaves. By 1852 a state law required that whites be present during all religious services attended by slaves.

The work of bondsmen on plantations revolved around the production of cotton. Between the demands of the cotton crop—planting, chopping, picking, ginning, and baling, and then planting a new crop— the slaves mended fences, cut wood, turned the soil on new fields, built barns and additional slave cabins, cleaned and whitewashed the houses, and made brooms, shoes, candles, soap, and whatever else was needed on the plantation. Labor was assigned according to the skills, health, and talents of the slave. Most slaves were field hands, and both men and women toiled in the cotton fields. Older women, too feeble to work hard, were responsible for taking care of young children, who were usually not sent to the fields until age ten, although at least one planter dispatched children as young as five to be with their mothers while learning to work. Oliver Bell remembered his mother, a plow hand, taking him to the fields with her and leaving him under the shade of an oak tree where he sat all day with the tree as his nurse.

Children, if not sent to the fields, were assigned tasks around the house or the slave quarters, often under the supervision of the carriage driver or cook. Slave children gathered eggs, raked leaves, toted wood, fetched water, and swept floors. They looked after black babies and younger white children. They carded cotton while old women spun, and they shelled peas, milked cows, and carried messages around the plantation.

Frail and elderly bondsmen might be delegated to do odd jobs around the quarters or put to work spinning and weaving. Slaves served as carriage drivers, cooks, maids, nurses, and butlers for the master's family, while others had responsibility for the farm animals, the grounds, or vegetable or flower gardens. Skilled slaves—blacksmiths, carpenters, or brick masons—were involved in new construction or built churns, buckets, or furniture. Sometimes labor was accomplished by the "task system," where specific jobs were assigned for each work period, but most slaves labored in "gangs" from sunup to sundown with a rest period at midday, which was longer when the sun was hottest in the summertime. Each work gang was under the supervision of a driver, a slave who had responsibility for seeing that work was done. Work chants and melodious yells eased the boredom of forced labor.

On most plantations, slaves had Saturday evening and all day Sunday to spend time in the quarter washing clothes, cleaning their cabins, and cooking or down at the creek fishing or in the woods setting traps. But a former Alabama slave interviewed in 1910 recalled that he never saw rest, for the slaves would do "half-time work on Sunday pullin' fodder in the field for the mules an' cows."[15] When it rained, slaves were put to tasks inside while they waited for fair weather to return to work. When the crops were "laid by" in the summer, field hands "jubilated," singing and dancing into the night with extra portions of favorite foods. At Christmas women might be given new dresses and "head handkerchiefs," and the men could receive gifts—hats, knives, or little bottles of spirits—though some owners never gave any gifts. Some Saturday nights were spent dancing, singing, and watching the men wrestle. Corn shuckings were made into parties when neighboring slaves visited. Weddings and hog-killing time were other special occasions for celebrations.

Discipline was essential to a system of forced labor, and beating with a leather strap was the usual method of punishment. Oliver Bell of Sumter County remembered his mother being whipped by her master, who "made her pull her dress down 'roun' her waist en made her lay down cross de do' en he whooper her, en I 'members cryin' en Miss Becket said, 'go get dat boy er biskit.'"[16] Many masters preferred not to whip slaves but had drivers or overseers apply the lash. Other owners forbade whipping unless they were present, and some masters, like Lee Cato, prohibited it altogether.

Overseers usually rode horses and carried long whips with them into the fields. They often wore pistols to discourage insubordination. Occasionally, masters called on the local patrols to whip slaves who ran away or who were caught fighting. All adult white males in a community were required to serve on the patrol, a form of militia that theoretically rode the countryside at night to make sure no slaves were off the plantation without passes and no slave insurrection occurred. In practice the "patterollers," as the slaves called them, were out only occasionally, but with their hound dogs they were efficient in tracking down and capturing runaway slaves. If the slaves could outrun the patrol and get home first, they could avoid a whipping.

Slaves were punished for doing their work too slowly, for disobedience, for insolence, and for stealing. Jake Williams was whipped for staying out after his pass ran out, and Angie Garrett remembered an overseer whipping her with a leather strap for no real reason. Lucilla McCorkle, a minister's wife, severely whipped her slave before breakfast for "tardiness and apparent absence of mind."[17] A few plantations had small jails for disobedient slaves, but planters discovered prison was not a good solution for disciplining slaves who looked for ways to avoid labor. A slave who proved incorrigible was usually sold quickly before influencing other slaves on the plantation and before lash marks on the back, a tell-tale sign of a troublemaker, decreased his value at the slave market. But some owners were like the one Carrie Davis knew—a bad man whether the slaves behaved or not, who had regular days to "whip all de slaves."[18]

The demand for slave labor in Alabama promoted an active market for bondsmen, and the black population increased from 42,024 in 1820 to 342,884 by 1850. Part of the growth was due to a natural increase, which was encouraged by rewards to female slaves who delivered healthy babies. A lucrative slave trade accounted for the rest. Planters were uneasy about purchasing strange slaves, preferring to acquire slaves from the estates of neighbors and friends, but that source was not always sufficient to fill their needs and not always satisfactory. John Williams Walker purchased a slave in Tennessee only to discover when he arrived home "that the fellow had no toes to his feet." The seller had stuffed cotton in the toes of the man's shoes so Walker could not detect the deformity.[19] Some planters traveled to Virginia and Maryland to make personal selections there rather than deal with a slave trader. Bolling Hall corresponded with a South Carolina planter who sent him a list of slaves he had for sale. He divided the blacks into categories of "prime & healthy" and those getting old. One female was a "good midwife and plantation nurse." The planter wanted $725 cash per head, and he invited Hall to come and inspect them.[20]

Other planters had to turn to professional traders, who purchased slaves in the eastern markets and brought them by sea to Mobile or walked them to Alabama in coffles, taking five to seven weeks to reach the state. After the railroad connected Alabama to the upper South, many traders moved slaves by train. Slave trading increased in the autumn, when the weather was good and the planters had money from the sale of the cotton crop. The need for agricultural labor in Alabama and the high prices paid for chattels created a lively market for stolen slaves. Joshua Cox advertised in the Huntsville *Democrat* for a two-year-old Negro child taken from his Limestone County plantation by a white man, offering a $100 reward for return of the slave and a $200 reward for the thief.[21] The villain in Andrew Lytle's novel *The Long Night*, loosely based on historical events, was part of a "band of speculators" near Wetumpka who stole Negroes and farm animals. Samuel Murrell (also spelled Merril) led a notorious gang of robbers who stole slaves and robbed travelers along the trails of north Alabama.

Mobile was the state's largest slave-trade center. Slaves arrived by ship and departed by river packet with their new owners. The slave market in the port city was located on Royal Street and included housing for the slaves as well as auction blocks. Most inland towns had a place where slaves were bought and sold. The migratory slave trader advertised his slaves in the local newspapers, sold what he could, and moved on to another town. After Nat Turner's rebellion, Alabama enacted the 1832 anti-immigration law to stop traders from bringing Negroes involved in the insurrection into the state. Although Congress banned the international slave trade after 1808, there were occasional violations, and as late as 1859 blacks who spoke only African dialects were reported to be in Mobile. The last known shipment of Africans into Alabama occurred on the eve of the Civil War, when Tim Meaher's *Clotilde* arrived in Mobile with 116 survivors of a transatlantic voyage. The Africans were taken to John M. Dabney's plantation up the river from Mobile and hidden in a canebrake until they were sold.

The price of slaves in Alabama was dependent upon many factors. Second- and third-generation slaves, broken to slavery and able to speak English, brought more than new Africans, although some planters preferred the infusion of new blood into their slave lines. In the new areas in the Southwest, demand for slaves exceeded the ready market and drove the price up. Slaves with skills, such as blacksmiths, carpenters, and brick masons, were more valuable than common field hands. The use of slave labor in mining and industry was proving successful, and many planters hired out their slaves to townspeople or for industrial labor, thus bringing needed cash into the plantation account. Slaves with domestic experience and social graces, with reputations as good cooks, butlers, carriage drivers, or as leaders and good drivers, were in great demand and brought a high price. A prime field hand who sold for $350 in Washington, D.C., in 1800 would sell for $800 eight years later in Mobile.

While slave property was important to large slaveowners in the Black Belt, it was no less so for yeoman and poorer whites in the hill country. When Elias DeJarnette died in Jefferson County in 1824, his entire estate was probated at $1,896, with all but $70 consisting of a slave couple and four small children. In 1848 George James Roebuck swapped a 238-acre tract of land, now located in downtown Birmingham, for Judge William S. Mudd's thirty-five-year-old slave Lewis. The land was valued at $600. By 1860 the price of good field hands in Alabama peaked at $1,600, while a skilled slave might bring twice that amount. In 1860 Southerners owned about four million slaves valued at $2 billion.

With such a large investment of capital in labor, most owners took care that their slaves stayed healthy, but the nineteenth-century South was generally ignorant about medicine, health care, and sanitation, and many former slaves recalled being poorly cared for. Blankets were provided in winter, and new clothing was issued every fall. James Asbury Tait needed 800 yards of jersey and twilled woolen for "jackets and wrappers and breeches" for his slaves during the cold winter of 1836–37.[22] Owners believed it was better to make sure slaves stayed well rather than nurse sick ones. Agricultural journals of the period were filled with remedies and suggested medications for common slave ailments. The Alabama State Agricultural Society encouraged writers to submit articles detailing care and health management of slaves. Summer fevers, typhoid, yellow fever, malaria, and certainly cholera and smallpox were dreaded diseases for all Southerners, and pneumonia was a common cause of death in winter. To avoid illnesses, some planters insisted that slave cabins be torn down, moved, and rebuilt every three years so the accumulation of filth under the house would not cause unhealthy conditions.

Sick slaves preferred the care of fellow bondsmen and only accepted white doctoring as a last resort. Planters usually maintained a hospital, in reality little more than a specially equipped cabin set apart from the quarters. There sick slaves were taken and attended by a black nurse and the overseer as well as the planter and the mistress of the plantation. Mary Jane Battle had a room off her kitchen where she brought sick slaves, for it was too far from her house to the quarter to go to nurse them during the night. Dr. Robert J. Draughon of Claiborne deplored the planters' doctoring, what he called "domestic treatment," insisting that physicians could "save the subjects themselves much suffering."[23] To provide professional care, many planters had a contractual arrangement with local doctors who made routine visits to the plantation, came quickly in emergencies, and provided slaves with the same treatments given to the master's family. But some blacks, as well as whites, had more confidence in African herb doctors and were happier with less invasive procedures. Some slaves were swayed by old African superstitions, and voodoo practices remained common. The conjurer was the most feared man on the plantation as he went about casting spells, selling love potions, undoing the work of evil spirits, and curing illnesses.

Small planters directed their own farms, but large planters, or those men who owned several plantations, might employ an overseer or a son to manage some of their agricultural units. Maintaining quality management was often the bane of the planter's life. Good overseers, who were assigned primary responsibility for slave supervision and labor management on a daily basis, were hard to find and keep. William Wyatt Bibb wrote Charles Tait from his home at Coosada in 1818 that his private life was in disarray because of his political involvement and because "My overseer has been drunk most of his time, and suffered the grass & weeds to take the place of my corn."[24] James Asbury Tait counseled his children "never to have any trading or dealing with an overseer" and never to employ one "who will equalise himself with the Negro women. Besides the immorality of it, there are evils too numerous to be mentioned."[25] William Lowndes Yancey lost a small fortune in slave property when a disgruntled overseer poisoned a spring on his farm. Overseers had poor reputations with masters and were especially feared by slaves for their brutality.

Although slavery was primarily a plantation labor system, slave labor was successfully used in many Alabama industries. The Hobbs brothers used slave labor in their Fulton factory on Swann Creek in Limestone County. Slave labor operated the 100 looms and 3,000 spindles at the

Bell Factory, a cotton and woolen mill in Huntsville. Horace Ware trained slaves to work at the Shelby Iron Works, and Moses Stroup used slave labor at his Tannehill furnaces. Slaves mined coal at Hewell's Mines, owned by William L. Goold, a Scottish miner, and labored at the cotton presses in Mobile. Daniel Scott employed slaves as well as whites in his Scottsville textile mill in the 1840s. The Tallassee Factory, a textile mill producing osnaburg (a coarse heavy cloth of linen or cotton popular for work clothes), shirting, and sheeting, also utilized both slave and white labor when it opened in 1845, but by 1850 it had abandoned slave labor in favor of poor whites. On the other hand, Daniel Pratt first used white labor but by 1860 was utilizing more slave labor.

Plantation slaves were hired out in the winter to cut timber and build roads and railroads. The construction of the Muscle Shoals Canal used 500 to 600 blacks at $150 a year, not including clothing and medication. Newspapers were filled with advertisements requesting slaves for hire. The hiring of slaves frequently took place at county courthouses, and Huntsville, Mobile, Hayneville, and Lowndesboro were hiring centers. On rare occasions slaves with skills negotiated their own hire, although it was technically illegal for them to do so. Owners took a large percentage of their earnings, but slaves were allowed to keep some and occasionally were able to save enough to purchase their freedom. White labor opposed the practice of hiring slaves, objecting to competition from slave labor. This opposition was especially strong in Mobile, where about one-half of the city's free labor force were immigrants.

Slavery could not have existed without the sanction of law and extensive regulatory codes. The French code used in Mobile was replaced when the port became part of the Mississippi Territory. Alabama's slave code evolved with many statutory changes, most of them incorporated into the 1852 Alabama Code and some initiated through judicial interpretations. The Alabama Code contained two clauses that stand in significant juxtaposition: one confirmed the slave's status as property; the other acknowledged his or her status as person. Slaves had some protection under Alabama law, such as the right to trial by jury in capital cases, although the twelve white men who composed the jury often were slaveholders. Slaves also had the right to have court-appointed attorneys represent them. The law required that slaves must be treated "with humanity," provided "necessary food and clothing," and protected against injuries to "life and limb." Any person who maliciously killed a slave would be treated as though "an offense had been committed on a free white person" except in the "case of insurrection of such slave." These laws were difficult to enforce; when they were interpreted by judges and juries, many convictions were overturned in appeals to higher courts.[26]

Alabama laws restricted slaves in many ways and "defined slavery in a litany of rights denied," and those in charge of a slave were "to ensure that the slave not exercise the rights of a free person."[27] Testimony of a black, free or slave, against a white person was not admissible in court; however, slaves often testified as witnesses against other blacks and after 1841 took an oath in court just as any white witness did. Slaves could not own real property and could not acquire property by gift or will, although several Alabama planters found ways through careful instructions and requirements of their executors to pass assets to their mulatto children.

Edmund Townsend of Madison County left Elizabeth and Virginia, his two mulatto daughters, the bulk of his $500,000 estate and 195 slaves, but his will was not upheld when challenged in the court. When Edmund's brother Samuel died, he left instructions in his will that his executors were to transport the nine slaves he identified as his children to a free state and manumit them and provide money for their support.[28] His will was upheld, and the slaves were freed. Henry Stiles Atwood of Wilcox County left instructions for his executors to take care of his seven mulatto children by his slaves Candis and Mary, removing them to a free state, freeing them there, and providing funds for their support, provisions that also were upheld by the Alabama Supreme Court.

Under Alabama law slaves could not enter into contracts, lend money, rent any living quarters, own a horse or dog, keep hogs running loose, buy liquor, or leave the plantation without a written pass. Blacks were also forbidden to mix or sell medicines or to weigh cotton. It was illegal to teach a slave to read or write. When Nicholas Davis learned that James Fisher, his daughter's slave, was learning to write, he threatened to cut off Fisher's right hand.[29] Other masters were not so cruel. Many whites, like the owners of both Harriet Yancey and Maria Fearing, simply ignored the law and taught their slaves to read the Bible. When Professor Henry Tutwiler caught his seven-year-old daughter Julia playing school and teaching young slaves to read, he let her continue, wondering aloud what a judge would do with so young a criminal.

In general, Alabama law treated slaves as property rather than as persons with civil rights; however, the law gave slaves criminal status and listed the crimes and detailed the punishments for offenders. Crimes commonly committed by slaves were similar to those crimes committed by whites—assault, murder, rape, and larceny. Most small infractions, such as petty theft and brief episodes of running away, were handled within the plantation system, but crimes of murder, assault, rape, arson, and insurrection were taken to the state courts. When slaves committed murder, masters, overseers, and mistresses were most frequently the victims, and courts held that murder by slaves was not subject to degrees such as manslaughter. Anthony Abercrombie recalled a mean overseer who "got killed" down on the creek bank, and although the guilty party was never discovered, his master was convinced the field hands did it. Heywood Ford told a story about an overseer who was killed when a pack of hounds was sicced on him by a slave and his "red-bone possum and coon dog."[30] A Mount Meigs slave killed his owners in 1854 and "boasted of his deed" before he was burned alive by a vigilance committee.[31] Slaves who murdered other slaves might be lashed or could be executed, depending upon circumstances and testimony in court. When slaves were executed by the state, owners were compensated for one-half the slave's assessed value.

Slaves charged with or tried in court for crimes were not routinely convicted, and in many trials slaves were acquitted. There were a few examples of gubernatorial pardon of convicted slaves where there was serious question of guilt. In 1850 in Greene County several slaves belonging to Peter Hamilton beat him to death in his cotton field. The crime occurred after Hamilton rode up and said "they had not worked well" and he would take away their Fourth of July holiday. Of the four male workers in the field, only one, Jack, refused to hit his owner and was acquitted, but the presiding judge requested a gubernatorial pardon for the youngest slave, Bill, who he was convinced was not involved.[32] Violence was the most basic way to resist slavery, but slaves found numerous other ways to protest their circumstances. Planters frequently expressed exasperation at the slovenly work of slaves, their carelessness with tools, and their waste of food and grain, ways in which slaves easily fought their masters and opposed their enslavement.

Inciting a slave rebellion was considered the most severe crime. Although no slave insurrections occurred in Alabama, there were numerous rumors of slave unrest, and the white population lived in fear of a slave uprising. Charges of rape or attempted rape of white women caused an excited and passionate reaction in communities. In Washington County, a black man confessed to the murder and rape of Winnie Caller in 1827, and in Livingston a slave of James Thornton admitted to ravishing and murdering Thornton's fourteen-year-old daughter. Rape of black women by black men or by their white masters was not considered a crime. Sexual relations between the races, willingly or unwillingly, were not unusual in Alabama, although relations between white women and black men were rarely admitted.

Sexual relations between whites and blacks were probably more frequent than historical sources indicate. University of Alabama president Basil Manly was distressed at the misconduct of a number of students who induced Morgan, a slave belonging to a professor, to bring them a young slave girl whom the men "use in great numbers, nightly."[33]

While Lucius Verus Bierce was visiting Mooresville in 1823, he recorded in his journal a story about a local man so open in his liaison with a mulatto slave that he embarrassed his wife and scandalized Huntsville. Social pressure sided with his wife and forced the man to sell the girl in New Orleans.[34] Sarah Haynsworth Gayle, wife of Governor John Gayle, wrote of one such man: "His children and his son's children are their slaves, and probably, nay I think I heard, that his *child* and his *grand-child* have one mother?" Gayle was horrified by "those fathers whose beastly passions hurry to the bed of the slave do they feel no compunction when they see their blood sold, basely bartered like their horses? This sin is the leprosy of the earth nothing save the blood of the cross cleanses from it."[35] Mistresses who quickly recognized the master's familial traits in the slave children of neighboring plantations were blind to such traits in their own slaves.

Alabama's black population also included free blacks. Although the numbers were always small, they were looked upon with distrust by whites, who considered them a dangerous example in a slave society. Slaveowners attempted to limit contact between free blacks and their slaves. By the constitution of 1819, manumission was a right granted only by the legislature on petition; in its first session the Alabama legislature approved the manumission of seventeen slaves. Sometimes masters allowed slaves to purchase their freedom by selling the produce from their garden allotments or using some of the money they made from being hired out. Owners who freed slaves recognized a variety of reasons—for long years of meritorious service to a family or some heroic act or because the planter knew the slaves were his own children. After the Nat Turner rebellion, requests to the legislature for manumission decreased. Frequently planters freed slaves by wills or else provided for their comfort with yearly stipends and the right to occupy certain lands in perpetuity and the request they be allowed to live as though free.

Durant Hatch did not free his slave Jacob but charged his executor to settle Jacob on some portion of his land and allow him to "enjoy his own time under direction, control and protection of my executors."[36] In 1842 Richard G. Harrison's will set aside 960 acres for six of his slaves and left twenty-four other slaves to benefit the six, requiring that his executor give bond to ensure the will's provisions were carried out.[37] The growing threat from abolitionist propaganda influenced the Alabama legislature to prohibit manumission in 1860.

Mobile County had a large population of free blacks, many of whom were mulatto descendants of the Spanish and French. These Creole Negroes were well educated due to special provisions of Mobile law. They were prosperous merchants, barbers, blacksmiths, carpenters, draymen, and coachmen. Many were descendants of Pierre Chastang, who carried supplies for Andrew Jackson's troops during the War of 1812 and, when yellow fever spread in Mobile in 1819, cared for the sick and buried the dead. He was freed by popular subscription for these public services. When Chastang died in 1848, the *Alabama Planter* in Mobile lauded him as a "highly esteemed and respected" member of the community.[38] In 1850 Mobile had 41 percent of the state's free blacks.

Solomon Perteet, who operated a store in Tuscaloosa, was another well-known free black. When Sir Charles Lyell visited Tuscaloosa in 1846, he was amazed at Perteet's accumulation of wealth from his real estate transactions. James T. Rapier, the son of a free Negro woman and a planter from Huntsville, was sent by his father to Canada and Scotland for his education and later during Reconstruction represented Alabama in Congress. Many of Alabama's free blacks owned slaves. Seven Chastang families in Mobile owned twenty-seven slaves in 1850, and two other Mobile free blacks owned thirty slaves.

Horace King was one of the most famous free blacks in Alabama. A slave of South Carolina bridge contractor John Godwin, King supervised the construction of dozens of bridges in Alabama before and after he was manumitted by his owner with the approval of the Alabama legislature in 1846. While it was known that King worked on the Alabama capitol during construction in 1850–51, his responsibilities were not specified; however, he probably built the curving stairs. Restoration of the building in the late 1980s revealed that the bracing design that undergirded the stairs and connected them to the wall without any visible support was exactly the method King used to construct his bridges.

Alabama blacks made valuable contributions to the economic advancement of the state. Besides the state capitol, blacks constructed churches, large white-columned mansions, and brick city buildings. They built roads and bridges and laid railroad tracks. They not only picked cotton, they ginned and baled it, loaded it on drays, delivered it to the river wharves, and worked on steamboats that plied the inland waterways. Without the contributions of blacks, there would have been no cotton kingdom. Yet the price paid was high. When former slave Delia Garlic was interviewed in Montgomery in 1937, she offered to talk all day about the "awfulness" of slavery. "It's bad," she said, "to belong to folks dat own you soul an' body."[39]

Within a slave society blacks created a rich culture influenced by their African heritage. Although early historians believed little of Africa remained, recent studies have stressed the influences of African culture in the plantation quarters. From "dusk to dawn" slaves were not so carefully supervised by whites, and their time was their own. The slave family was strong, and extended families looked after children separated from their parents by sale or death. In the slave cabins, in the cleanly swept dirt streets of the quarters, and in the secluded "hushharbors" of the woods, slaves created a world of their own, secret from the master. In these private places blacks shared the trauma of bondage; worshiped, played, and danced together; developed self-esteem; and worked off hostility and aggression.

Between 1830 and 1860 the slave population in Alabama increased by 270.1 percent. The white population, numbering 526,271, expanded only 171 percent. In 1860 there were 437,271 slaves owned by 33,730 slaveowners, which was 6.4 percent of the white population, although probably one-third of white Alabama families included a slaveowner. There were only 1,687 large planters who owned more than fifty slaves. These planters controlled real estate that represented 29.6 percent of the value of all state property and owned assets that were 28.1 percent of Alabama's total wealth. Slave property was assessed per head with an ad valorem equation, and it was the revenue from the tax on this property that provided about one-third of the antebellum tax revenues of Alabama. Another third came from real estate taxes, mostly assessed against large cotton-growing plantations. Thus, before 1860 slavery drove the tax structure of Alabama, and directly or indirectly, paid most of the state's taxes. The tax burden fell heaviest on large planters, those best able to pay.

The South's peculiar institution hung as an albatross around the neck of Alabama and its people. With too much capital invested in labor and a labor system that was costly regardless of the need, commercial and industrial development was stifled. Investment diversity was thwarted by lack of capital. Economic advancement seemed to come easily from more land and slaves. Whites believed the labor of blacks could not be relied upon outside slavery, while abolition was inconceivable. White Alabamians thought they could not live in a state where all blacks were free. Yet in isolated rural areas white and black lives were frequently melded in familylike intensity. The irony of it was that so many humans—black and white—were able to live out their lives with honor and dignity within such a society.

EIGHT

Antebellum Society

ON the eve of the Civil War in 1860, Alabama planter Daniel R. Hundley published his interpretations of the class structure and social relations in the South. The dominant class was, of course, Hundley's "Southern Gentleman" of "faultless pedigree," although he thought the "Cotton Snobs" were more numerous. W. J. Cash in his classic 1941 work, *The Mind of the South*, challenged the legend of an antebellum South with a spreading plantation aristocracy. Cash suggested the frontier period was too near and time too limited for a true aristocracy to rise and rule before war came and ruined it all. This time constraint was certainly true for Alabama.[1] Yet the legend persisted, and no more so than in myths of the gentleman's mate, Hundley's "true-hearted daughter of the sunny South," a simple woman unaffected in manners, pure in speech and soul, and "ever blessed with an inborn grace and gentleness of spirit lovely to look upon." She was "A perfect woman, nobly planned, To warm, to comfort, and command."[2]

Despite the proverbial pedestal, white women in Alabama suffered under some of the same legal restrictions as free blacks and slaves. They, too, had no primary rights of citizenship and could neither vote nor serve on juries. Following the English common law, a married woman's possessions, including her personal clothes, were owned by her husband. Any real estate a married woman might inherit could be controlled by her husband, and he could sell it without her consent and appropriate the money for his own purposes. The editors of the reformist–free thought publication *Free Enquirer*, which was based in New York, noted in 1829 that "a married women belong[ed] to her matrimonial master, as in the case of any other slave."[3]

Ironically, Alabama—not New York, as often cited—was the first state in the nation where the legislature debated changing the common law property relationship between husband and wife. Enoch Parsons of Claiborne introduced a "ladies bill" in 1828, but it failed in the senate after opponents "questioned the wisdom of altering human and divine laws . . . God had vested in Adam and Moses."[4] Sally Wilson of Big Sandy,

Alabama, wrote to the *Free Enquirer* that she feared the Alabama legislature "in attempting to mend this miserable system" might create a worse one. For herself, she "had learned that it was a fearful thing for a female to get married."[5] Many Alabama women lost estates to pay their husbands' debts following the panic of 1837, and in 1840 the legislature provided for relief through individual petition. Swamped with such petitions, the legislature enacted Charles Gunter's bill in 1848 for separate women's estates. Yet two years later the legislature added restrictions that killed the reform impulse by preventing a married woman from controlling her estate unless she could prove that she had been abandoned by her husband or that "imbecility, intemperance, profligacy," or some other cause made him "unfit or incapable" of handling her estate.[6]

Antebellum Alabama society was male dominated, and there were more males in the state than females. Marriages came early to young women, often to girls of age thirteen or fourteen. Divorce was rare and required the approval of the state legislature. Husbands and fathers were the heads of their households. The wife's sphere was to obey, and in the words of Henry W. Hilliard, society expected "to see every man *manly,* and every woman *womanly.*"[7] A Southern man expected his Southern belle to be pious, modest, compassionate, quiet, and dainty, by nature self-denying and soft-spoken, a paragon of virtue. Once married, a woman was to be a submissive wife whose only reason for being was to amuse and serve her husband, bear his children, and train them in the ways they should go. Southern society decreed demanding rules for a genteel woman's behavior: she was to entertain graciously, receive callers, and return the calls promptly. She was to be chaste and pure, hiding any suggestion of pregnancy in public while enduring the pain of childbirth with silence. Many women chafed under the social restraints society placed upon them, noting in their diaries the similarity between women and slavery. Octavia Le Vert believed that "to be fettered and bound—yet seeming to be free" was worse than slavery. She wrote: "Talk about Bondage and Slavery! This is real bondage!"[8]

The Southern belle actually existed only in fiction and in the minds of most men and some women. Reality belied the myth, for women's household responsibilities and their obligations to their children (and if slaveholders, to their slaves) were heavy burdens. Circumstances often forced women into situations in which they had to assume total responsibility for their homes and their white and black families. If a husband were absent—away on business, off to war, or deceased—all the agricultural and business decisions were thrust into her hands. Sarah Haynsworth Gayle repeatedly had charge of her home when her husband was absent, but she was not comfortable with the task, once writing him

Octavia Walton Le Vert, who spoke several languages and had traveled in Europe, reigned over Mobile's antebellum society. She established a salon in her home and received guests every Monday. This portrait by Thomas Sully hangs at Oakleigh in Mobile. (Courtesy of the Historic Mobile Preservation Society)

in 1832: "Oh! come home, for mercy's sake, *what can* a *woman* do *without* her *husband?*"[9]

When Henry Watson of Greensboro traveled to Connecticut in 1848 following the death of his father, he left his wife, Sophy Peck Watson, in control of their town house and ten house servants, as well as a 990-acre plantation that an overseer managed at Newbern, a few miles south of Greensboro. Although Watson wrote home frequently and supported Sophy with advice and counsel, she alone had responsibility for operating her household and the plantation. The Watson overseer had little initiative and constantly promised Sophy more than he delivered. Throughout the summer Sophy visited the plantation often to make sure he did his job, and in her letters to her husband, she constantly requested information about farming techniques and once asked him about extra axletrees and the best method of trimming horses' hooves. In mid-July her overseer failed to see that the crops were hoed, and the fields were still "in the grass." During Watson's absence, several Negroes became ill, and Sophy nursed them as best she could with the help of her doctor. Yet three died during the long summer. Sophy wrote her husband, "I know things are not managed as they would be had you the direction and I doubt not you will find many things out of order when you come home and wish they had been done differently—but you must remember I did my best and that it is my first attempt."[10]

In the fiction and literature of plantation life, the mistress has been the primary focus of the writers. In the stories, aristocratic life has made the planter indolent and inert, while his Southern belle flits between the weak and fainting flirt and the steely woman burdened with the sweaty tasks of supervising a house, a kitchen, and a farm. Although Georgia produced the quintessential twentieth-century moonlight-and-magnolias novel of the antebellum South in *Gone With the Wind* (Margaret Mitchell [1936]), Alabama authors Lella Warren (*Foundation Stone* [1940]) and Margaret Walker (*Jubilee* [1966]) wrote more realistic accounts of antebellum Alabama based upon their family's experience from a white (Warren) and black (Walker) perspective. All three novels have strong female characters. Mitchell's Scarlett, a rebel, contrasts with Melanie, selfless and sweet. Warren's Gerta is a Yankee woman who provides strength for her husband, Yarbrough. Walker's Vyry, the daughter of her white master and his black mistress, is the strong force who keeps the white family together during the crises of illness, death, and war.

Despite the harsh realities of a woman's life, formal education for a young girl in antebellum Alabama did not include courses in plantation management. Daniel Hundley advised that Southern gentlemen educate their daughters at home. A daughter was taught to be a happy companion for her husband, taught the basic skills of reading, writing, and simple arithmetic and some appreciation for art and music. Israel Pickens wanted his daughter Julia to have her "reading & writing first attended to & after she writes well enough, arithmetic.—Till these are all completed, I do not want her to touch a pencil toward drawing, nor English grammar."[11] Daughters from wealthy homes were sent to female seminaries, which were little more than finishing schools, while middle class families might send their children to community one-teacher "blackberry academies." Advanced education for girls included subjects like poetry, literature, sewing, needlework, knitting, piano, and choral music. Young ladies were taught self-discipline, obedience to authority, poise, grace, good manners, spirituality, posture, and refinement. Reading, devotionals, chorus clubs, literary clubs, musical performances, declamation contests, and oral examinations were part of their school experience.

Contemporary educational theory suggested that higher learning was too taxing for women and could be physically detrimental, possibly resulting in brain fever. A typical view of women's education was held by Methodist minister Andrew A. Lipscomb, who was principal of Montgomery's Metropolitan Institute in 1850. He wrote that a woman "ought to be trained to tastefulness and mental activity, for the pleasures which they afford her—for the power which they give over her own feebleness, for the security which they yield against no small share of the ills of existence, and lastly for the peace and joy they so gently shed over her social relationships."[12] The Reverend William T. Hamilton of Mobile, speaking at the female seminary at Marion in 1845, denied that women were less capable of intellectual development or that a good education made a woman a sloppy housekeeper. He said a man was "blessed beyond ordinary mortals" if he married a well-educated woman who would be a more enjoyable companion.[13]

The donation of the sixteenth section of each township to support schools meant that some type of institute or academy was eventually established in most communities. The schools operated on both private and public funds. In 1823 the legislature divided administrative authority over local schools between three town commissioners and three district school trustees who were elected by local citizens. The commissioners had financial responsibility and managed the school lands, while the trustees ran the schools, hiring teachers, deciding tuition and admission policies, selecting textbooks, and approving curriculum. Monies for each school district varied according to the worth of the school lands. For instance, in Greene County the school land was located in "a most valuable section in this township" and was leased for considerable money.[14]

During the antebellum period the legislature chartered more than 250 academies, and according to the 1860 census, 206 academies were operating in Alabama with 400 teachers and 10,778 students enrolled. Many of these schools were similar to the one Philip Henry Gosse described in 1838. A young Englishman visiting Alabama, Gosse was hired by several fathers to teach their children, but other community families could include their children for a small fee. When Gosse began teaching, he had about 12 students in a school that was

a funny little place, built wholly of round, unhewn logs, notched at the end. . . . The desks are merely boards split, not sawn, out of pine logs, unhewn and unplaned, which slope from the walls and are supported by brackets. . . . A neat little desk, at which I write, and a chair on which I sit, are the only exceptions to the primitive rudeness of all our furniture, and the pupils are, mostly as rude as the house—real young hunters, who handle the long rifle with more ease and dexterity than the goosequill, and who are incomparably more at home in "twisting a rabbit," or "treeing a 'possum," than in conjugating a verb.[15]

The Greene Springs School for Boys became one of the most famous academies in Alabama. Opened in 1847 by Professor Henry Tutwiler, a former professor at LaGrange College and the University of Alabama, the school was located in Greene County near Havana (now in Hale County). Greene Springs occupied cottages and buildings of an old hotel at a favorite "watering place" and was soon recognized for the quality education Tutwiler provided. Later the school was noteworthy because Tutwiler allowed girls to enter, probably because his own precocious daughter Julia convinced him that females could also benefit from a classical education. The Valley Creek Academy, which was established at Summerfield in Dallas County in 1829, was another fine antebellum school. In 1841 it became part of Centenary Institute when the Methodists established a coeducational school. In the 1850s Centenary was educating some 300 students each year in separate buildings for male and female students located several blocks apart. Between 1855 and 1866 Summerfield was the residence of Bishop James O. Andrew, head of the Southern faction of the Methodist Episcopal Church, who frequently lectured in classes at Centenary.

Other typical schools were the Salem Male and Female Academy at Jonesboro, the Auburn Masonic Female Academy, and the Green Academy in Huntsville. In the 1830s the manual-labor school philosophy was popular in the nation, and the Presbyterian Manual Labor Institute of South Alabama at Marion and the Baptists' manual-labor school at Greensboro were examples in Alabama.

The most substantial progress in public education occurred in Mobile. There the direction of the schools was under the control of a board of school commissioners established by the legislature in 1826. This act recognized public education as a duty of the state. Mobile schools were supported by a dependable source of revenue, which came not only from the sixteenth-section lands but also from specified city fines and taxes. The construction in 1836 of Barton Academy, designed by famous architect Thomas James, was aided by $50,000 raised in a lottery. Yet despite the possibilities, the Mobile commissioners lacked vision in the early years and merely distributed funds to private and semipublic schools. Competition between private and public school supporters weakened the system until a polarizing referendum on the issue saw citizens speak resoundingly in favor of public education. Willis G. Clark, chairman of Mobile's new school board, surveyed northern school systems. He introduced a three-tier structure of primary, grammar, and high school grades. In 1852 Clark reopened Barton Academy, initiating what could be called the first real public school system in the state.

Educational reformers wanted to improve the quality of education in Alabama. They opposed locally controlled education, believing it "created a dismal instruction of mindless memorization and recitation." They advocated a more secure system of funding and were concerned over the crude buildings used for schools, described in an 1857 article in the *Alabama Educational Journal* as "actually unfit to shelter our dumb brutes."[16] As early as 1849 Governor Henry W. Collier of Tuscaloosa proposed, but the legislature rejected, establishing the office of state superintendent of education, which would have responsibility for supervising the education offered by local schools. In 1853 a general referendum was held on the issue of consolidating what was left of the sixteenth-section funds, the bulk of which were lost when the Bank of Alabama failed and was liquidated in the early 1840s. Wealthy Whig planters favored state-supported common schools, believing that ignorant people were poor citizens, while Democrats were more content with locally supported and locally controlled schools.

Inspired by the experiences in Mobile, Alexander Beaufort Meek, associate editor of the Mobile *Register* and chairman of the house committee on education, pushed through the Public School Act of 1854. Meek, a lawyer and native of South Carolina, was educated at the University of Alabama. He edited the Tuscaloosa *Flag of the Union* and the *Southron*, a literary journal. He was a poet and historian and a respected federal attorney for the southern district of Alabama. The Public School Act of 1854 established a state superintendent of education, and William F. Perry of Talladega was elected to the office. He introduced new courses into Alabama schools, including U.S. history and geography, and better textbooks like Webster's Blue-back Spelling Book and McGuffey's Readers. Perry also established the *Alabama Educational Journal* to communicate with the local schools, but it lasted only two years. Despite these advances, Alabama elementary schools offered such a rudimentary education that colleges and universities provided remedial or preliminary courses for entering freshmen.

There was no college in the territory when Alabama entered the Union in 1819. Although the enabling act provided public lands to support a state "seminary of learning," twelve years passed before the University of Alabama opened, "so great was the diversity of opinion" over selecting a location.[17] In the meantime, the Methodists opened LaGrange College in north Alabama in 1829, and the Catholics established Spring Hill College in Mobile in 1830. The need for an educated and trained clergy and a laity that could read the Bible spurred Christians to support denominational higher education. The Methodists founded Athens Female College in 1840 and the Tuskegee Female College, the Southern University at Greensboro, and the East Alabama Male College at Auburn in 1856. The Baptists created the Judson Female Institute at Marion in 1839, under president Milo P. Jewett. Howard College was organized in 1841 and opened the next year at Marion as the brother institution to Judson.

In 1827 the legislature finally agreed to establish the state university at the capital in Tuscaloosa, and classes began in 1831. Under President Alva Woods, a Harvard graduate who came to Alabama from the presidency of Transylvania University in Kentucky, the early faculty was outstanding. It included Henry Tutwiler; Thomas Manning, tutor of foreign languages; and John Fielding Wallace, professor of chemistry and natural history. Henry W. Hilliard, who was to become a congressman and Whig political leader, joined the faculty within a few months. The university opened with a campus composed of brick buildings: two large structures capable of accommodating one hundred students each, two professors' residences, a boardinghouse, a large hall with lecture rooms, and the Rotunda as the library. Of the original buildings, only Steward's Hall (one of the faculty residences, later known as the Gorgas House) survived the destruction in 1865 by Croxton's raiders. (The other three left by the raiders were not original.)

The early years at the university were difficult because President Woods's Harvard philosophy of rigid discipline did not fare well with young men raised in a frontier state. C. C. Clay, Jr., wrote his father about one incident in 1834 when President Woods responded to a rebellion and was greeted by boys who threw brickbats at him. Woods hastily retreated, and when the students began firing their pistols, he jumped out an open window with the students in hot pursuit. The president hid and the students could not find him so they "rocked his window."[18] The affair ended at one o'clock when the students went to bed.

120

Three years later, after the university board of trustees enacted a strict code of discipline with daily grade requirements, the students openly rebelled. They refused to sign good-conduct promises and give up their firearms. Most of the students enrolled at the university were suspended, and the faculty resigned. Woods was forced to step down and was replaced by Basil Manly, who restored order.

Until the 1850s there was no formal medical education in Alabama. Doctors received their schooling in the eastern states or abroad, or they were trained through apprenticeship. Sometimes the would-be physician just read a medical book and hung out his shingle announcing a practice. Doctors were needed because Alabama was particularly susceptible to summer fevers, especially yellow fever, which was epidemic in Mobile in 1819, 1837, and 1839. It was during the later epidemic that twelve Mobile men founded the "Can't Get Away Club" to collect money to provide care for victims. The club members nursed the sick and established a hospital in a hotel and a carriage house. An epidemic in 1853 killed one-tenth of the summer population of Mobile and left many orphans.

Montgomery suffered an epidemic in 1854, and the town was almost abandoned. Typhoid fever, malaria, and smallpox plagued the state. Because illness was particularly common in the state's largest urban area and so many outstanding doctors practiced in the city, Mobile doctors took a leadership role in the medical profession, founding first the Mobile Medical Society in 1841 and then the Alabama Medical Association in 1846. Dr. Josiah Clark Nott was one of the leaders. Nott received his education in South Carolina, New York, Philadelphia, and Paris. He became especially noted for his theory of a separate creation for black and white races.

Although there were several attempts to establish a medical college in Alabama, none was successful until Dr. Phillip Madison Shepard opened his Graefenberg Medical Institute at Dadeville in February 1852. No state money was involved, and Alabama made no attempt to regulate the school's instruction. Seven years later, following considerable effort, the legislature chartered the Medical College of Alabama, and it opened in Mobile under the direction of Dr. Nott and other prominent Mobile doctors.

Like medical education, legal education was also by apprenticeship. "Reading law" under a respected attorney was frequently part of the educational experiences of the gentry, even if standing before the court and taking the bar exam for licensing did not follow. Yet the exercise before a judge must not have been too difficult, for Lucius Verus Bierce studied law under De Sterne Houghton at Mooresville for five months in 1823 and was granted a license to practice by the supreme court. In 1845 the university announced the establishment of a law school, but it was not successful and was disbanded. Later it was moved to Montgomery and reopened in 1860, operating only one year before war came.

In a frontier state there was a desperate need for attorneys, men with the skills to defend the innocent and prosecute the guilty. Fraud and violence were common. Disputes over land, women, horses, cards, and slaves often degenerated into fistfights aided by knives, sticks, and teeth. Wills and deeds needed to be probated, and many counselors rode circuit, moving from one county courthouse to another. Although there were several local bench and bar groups, no state bar association was formed until after the Civil War. The legal fraternity made a significant contribution to state government and political leadership. Lawyers served in the legislature, as governor or judges, or held local offices, and they played an even more significant role in political party conventions.

Economic interests or political ambitions caused many lawyers to become directly or indirectly associated with early Alabama newspapers. The papers were supported in part by political or factional patronage, and with some advertisements and subscriptions they managed to survive. Politicians needed editorial support as much as editors needed financial support, and the most lucrative plum was a government contract for printing state documents. Lawyers frequently were the authors of long letters to the editor and sometimes, like Alexander Meek and Johnson Jones Hooper, served as editors. The earliest newspapers in the state were founded in the Mobile-Tombigbee area before Alabama became a state: the Mobile *Sentinel* (1811), the Mobile *Gazette* (1812), the St. Stephens *Halcyon* (1815), and the Blakeley *Sun and Alabama Advertiser* (1819). Eventually, the major Mobile newspaper evolved from a series of mergers to become the Mobile *Register*.

Huntsville was another early center of newspaper activity, and its editors were particularly noted for their vitriolic exchanges. The Huntsville *Alabama Republican* began publishing in 1816 and by 1819 was edited by John Boardman, who supported the John Quincy Adams-Henry Clay faction of the Republican party. His rival was William B. Long, editor of the Huntsville *Democrat* and a strong supporter of Andrew Jackson. Their exchanges became legendary. Long once called Boardman, a native of Connecticut, "the little gimble-mouthed Editor of the Yankee paper published in this place . . . the bow-wow-wow of the little creature who now growls from the Royal Manger"—a reference to the Royal party.[19] When schoolteacher Andrew Willis replaced Long, caustic comments increased—leading up to Willis's murder on a Huntsville street.

Tuscaloosa had a rich newspaper heritage that was especially significant while the city served as the capital. Papers published there included

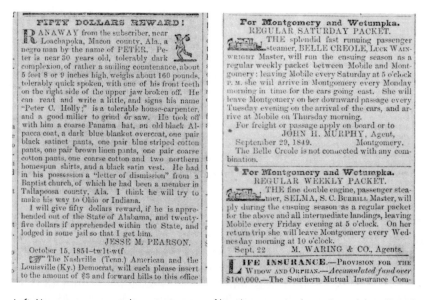

Left: Newspapers were an important means of locating runaway slaves. A careful reading of this advertisement for Peter, a thirty-year-old slave who ran away from his master in Macon County in 1851, tells much about slaves and slavery in Alabama. *Right:* By the late 1840s river and rail transportation connected Mobile and the Gulf to Montgomery, east Alabama, and the eastern seaboard, and the newspapers announced the regular schedules of steamers and railroads. (Courtesy of the Alabama Department of Archives and History)

the *Flag of the Union* (1823), *Alabama State Intelligencer* (1829), and the *Independent Monitor* (1836), whose most famous editor was Ryland Randolph, noted for his scathing attacks on Republicans, scalawags, and carpetbaggers during the Reconstruction period. Montgomery's newspaper tradition centered on the *Republican,* which became the *Alabama Journal,* a Whig paper, and on the Montgomery *Advertiser,* the Democratic organ.

Weekly or biweekly newspapers were established in most counties by 1860, and they provided important information and communication. Antebellum Alabama newspapers printed local news, congressional debates, political speeches, and legal announcements. Advertisements included slave sales, notices of runaway slaves and runaway wives, blurbs for traveling salesmen, merchant announcements of the arrival of goods, and ads for hotels and large mercantile establishments in nearby commercial towns. Letters to the editor, often signed with a nom de plume, presented dissertations on political and religious topics and personal or historical events. The papers listed unclaimed letters at the post office and included local and national obituaries and news from Europe and the capital cities of the East.

Less emphasis was placed on local news. Frequently, editorials from other newspapers were reprinted along with serialized fiction and British and American poetry. Favorite topics were romanticized fiction of the frontier South, melodramas, and the stories of medieval chivalry written by Sir Walter Scott. Humorous tales were also popular, like those of Johnson Jones Hooper and his picaresque character Captain Simon Suggs, who first made his appearance in Hooper's Lafayette *East Alabamian*. Many county newspapers were widely read across the state. The Eufaula *Spirit of the South* and William L. Yancey's Wetumpka *Argus* were examples of influential small town newspapers that shaped public opinion.

Other types of newspapers and journals were published in Alabama before the Civil War. The *Alabama Baptist* appeared in 1835, and several literary magazines were printed; the most well-known was probably the *Southron*, which published a few issues in Tuscaloosa in 1839. The *American Cotton Planter* was published in Montgomery from 1853 to 1861 and was one of the South's most widely read agricultural journals. The number of newspaper subscriptions increased in the 1850s, and many weekly newspapers changed to daily editions. The general prosperity of the decade, increased urban population, and interest in the growing sectional controversies promoted newspaper reading.

The success of the *Alabama Baptist* newspaper was not repeated by other denominations. In 1860 the Baptists were the largest denomination in Alabama, an achievement attributable to the evangelical spirit of the preachers, a democratic system of congregational governance, good organization through district associations, the use of camp meetings to promote evangelism and conversion, and adequate numbers of clergy through the use of lay ministers and bivocational preachers who farmed during the week and preached on Sunday. Although the call to preach took precedence over seminary training, the Baptists began establishing educational institutions in the 1830s to instruct their clergy and laity.

Adult baptism by total immersion was a key tenet of faith, with the ceremony being performed outdoors in creeks, ponds, and rivers, drawing large crowds of Baptists as well as non-Baptists. In fact, proximity to a stream of water was the primary basis in selecting the site of a rural Baptist church. Slaves often spoke with pride about being "deep water" Christians. Discipline was strict, and members were expelled for sexual misconduct, drinking, and gambling. A division occurred in the late 1830s over the question of the support of Christian missions, resulting in two groups—Missionary Baptists and Primitive Baptists.

But there was no division among Alabama Baptists on the question of slavery. When the national missions board refused to certify a slaveholder as a missionary in 1844, the Alabama Baptist State Convention sent a resolution to the general convention demanding assurance that slaveholders were equally eligible to be missionaries. The national board replied later that year that a slaveholder must divest himself of slave property before certification, for the board could never be a party to anything that might imply an approbation of slavery. Alabama Baptists moved with enthusiasm into the Southern Baptist Convention.

The first proclaimed Methodist preacher to minister to people on the Alabama frontier was Lorenzo Dow, who came in 1803. He employed the model of the "circuit riding" preacher who visited isolated communities, exhorting about damnation and declaring salvation, holding services and training Sunday school teachers, then moving on to other places. The horseback-riding preacher with his Bible and Methodist literature in his saddlebags was so common that many Methodists built small shed rooms on the sides of their front porches with bed and candle inside. The door of this "parson's room" stood ajar, ready for the preacher who appeared after the family had retired. Camp meetings and revivals were important occasions for conversion. The Methodist preacher condemned whiskey, wicked women, dancing, gambling, and defiling the Sabbath and called for individual sinners to repent their transgressions. Sermons, which lasted for hours, were interspersed with hymn singing that shook the loose leaves from the brush arbors. Methodists believed "sprinkling" with blessed water was sufficient for christening children, and the church was ruled by a hierarchy of bishops reflecting their episcopal heritage. In 1844 when the Methodist general conference ordered Georgia Bishop James O. Andrew to sell his slaves, Alabama Methodists supported the creation of the Methodist Episcopal Church, South.

The Presbytery of South Carolina sent missionaries to the Alabama frontier as early as 1817, but the Presbyterians with their Highland Scot and Scots-Irish heritage were not as numerous or as far-flung as the Baptists and Methodists. Because Presbyterian ministers were educated and seminary trained, it was impossible to find enough ordained clergy to service the growing population on the frontier. Thus, many traditional Scottish Presbyterians found their way into Baptist and Methodist congregations. Presbyterian ministers provided leadership in many ways, including the operation of private academies or in tutoring students. The first Presbyterian church in Alabama was established at Huntsville in 1818, and the denomination followed the Scots-Irish emigration to the small towns. Presbyterians were disciplined, hardworking, pious people who took their Calvinism seriously and were more likely to operate stores than plantations. Associate Reformed, Cumberland, and Old School Presbyterians were represented among Alabama's Presbyterian churches.

The Episcopal church, more aristocratic than the Presbyterian church,

Antebellum church architecture showed wide variations. *Above left:* The rural Missionary Baptist congregation in Orion built this simple clapboard church in 1858. Women and men entered separate doors and sat apart in the slip pews with a central divider. *Above right:* The Government Street Presbyterian Church in Mobile, constructed 1836–37, is an excellent example of fully matured Greek Revival style. *Lower left:* St. Luke's Episcopal Church in Jacksonville was completed in 1856. The board-and-batten Gothic design was popular for small rural Episcopal churches. *Lower right:* The Tuskegee Methodist Church was not completed until 1862 during the Civil War, and this fact may explain why one tower seems short and out of proportion. (Photos Courtesy of Robert Gamble)

was small in number but influential. Its membership was drawn from the wealthy planter classes, especially those who immigrated to Alabama from the Tidewater of Virginia and the seaboard South. The Episcopal church relied upon an ordained, educated, seminary-trained clergy and governed through a hierarchy, making it difficult for the church to follow its members as they pushed into the frontier. Although there was an Anglican church in Mobile during the British period, it fell into decline with the Spanish capture of the city during the American Revolution. Reestablishment came in 1822 when a frame church was built near old Fort Charlotte. The parish, the oldest in Alabama, erected Christ Church in an imposing Greek revival design in 1835.

By the late 1820s parishes were established in Tuscaloosa, Greensboro, Huntsville, and Montgomery, but they relied upon appropriations of the national church to help with expenses. When the Reverend Samuel S. Lewis visited Demopolis in 1833, he reported that there was "no church there of any kind," and he anticipated the people would support an Episcopal church if they could secure a clergyman.[20] In October 1832 Alabama was admitted as a diocese of the Episcopal church. The election of the Reverend Nicholas Hamner Cobbs as bishop in 1844 began a period of growth for the church. The enthusiastic Cobbs began organizing parishes, and soon tiny architecturally exquisite churches representing Ecclesiological Gothic style began appearing across the state. In the rural Black Belt areas, St. Andrew's Church (Prairieville, 1853), St. Luke's (Cahaba, 1852), and St. John's (Forkland, 1860) remain excellent examples of a style influenced by Richard Upjohn's *Rural Architecture* (1852).

The oldest Christian denomination in Alabama was the Catholic church, which arrived with the French settlers in the Gulf Coast and was strengthened during the Spanish control of Mobile between 1780 and 1813. Composed first of French and Spanish Creoles, the church was large and influential in Mobile until the American conquest resulted in an influx of Protestants. Under the leadership of Bishop Michael Portier, the Catholic community built Spring Hill College and the Cathedral of the Immaculate Conception (begun 1833). The parish of St. Vincent de Paul was established in 1847 to serve the large number of Irish Catholics who arrived in the 1840s, and by 1860 the Irish had supplanted the Creoles as the largest ethnic group in the church. The tradition of religious toleration in Mobile was temporarily interrupted by the anti-Catholicism of the Know-Nothing or Native American party in the mid-1850s. The Know-Nothings pressured the city into removing the Sisters of Charity from management of the City Hospital, but the nuns soon had their own Catholic hospital, the new Providence Hospital established by Bishop Portier. Anti-Catholicism prevailed in Mobile for several years, then subsided.

Mobile was also the entry point for most of the Jews who immigrated to Alabama in the antebellum period. The New Orleans merchant firm of Samuel Israel, Alexander Solomons, and Joseph de Palacios acquired property in Mobile in 1763 to facilitate their commercial dealings with the British garrison. Philip Phillips, elected to Congress in 1853, was a prominent Jewish attorney who represented the Bank of Mobile. Jewish immigration increased after 1830. Many began as peddlers, walking with knapsacks of merchandise on their backs, supplying the needs of rural households. Later they established stores and banks in the towns. In Demopolis Isaac Marx founded the Marx Banking Company and in Camden Daniel W. Bloch was a planter and merchant whose brother Morris settled in Selma. Although the Mobile Jewish community established a temple in 1844, other Jewish congregations date from the post–Civil War era. Before the organization of congregations, some Jews joined the Christian community around them and, like prominent Mobile physician Dr. Solomon Mordecai who married a Methodist, adopted the Christian faith.

Printing religious tracts, fraternal-organization publications, association records, and government documents was an important source of income for Alabama's printers, but little money was to be gained from publishing belles lettres. The demands of the frontier were too arduous for people to have much time to contemplate and write. What was written had practical uses of informing or educating. Such a work was Henry Hitchcock's manual for Alabama justices of the peace published in 1822, the book accorded the honor of being the first to be printed in Alabama. There was also Dr. Jabez Wiggins Heustis's 1825 medical work on the fevers in Cahaba in 1822–23. *The Lost Virgin of the South* (1833), a story of a white girl adopted by friendly Cherokee Indians during the Creek War, written under a pseudonym and poorly printed in Courtland, is usually credited with being the first novel published in the state. The wealthy preferred to import their books, often ordering them from the Mobile Dauphin Street shop of S. H. Goetzel and Company or from local merchants. Classic literary works, such as those by Shakespeare, Cervantes, and John Bunyan, were popular, but it was the literature of the late romantic movement that most inspired the South—the poetry of Byron, Burns, Keats, Shelley, Coleridge, and Wordsworth and especially the romantic historical novels of Sir Walter Scott.

Alabamians took Sir Walter to heart. Scott's descriptions of manor houses, serfs, and chivalry made it easy for planters or their ladies to think of their world in terms of a medieval aristocracy. Virginia Tunstall Clay remembered that her Uncle Tom Tunstall's reading Scott aloud instilled in her "a pride of family." Scott's romances were favorites of Sarah Gayle.[21] Mark Twain claimed that Scott drove Southerners crazy and that the "Sir Walter disease" was responsible for making every Southern gentleman a Major or Colonel and for creating the Southern love for "bogus decorations" and love of rank and caste.[22]

Daniel Hundley pointed to the Southern middle classes' "love of titles, bestowed without regard to any sort of military service." Every other man, said Hundley, was either "Captain, or Co-lo-nel, or Knight at arms."[23] The 1865 novel by University of Alabama professor and Alabama congressman Henry W. Hilliard, *De Vane: A Story of Plebeians and Patricians*, adapted *Ivanhoe* to college life on the grounds of the University of Virginia. There is a hint that the novel is somewhat autobiographical. Following Scott's lead, *De Vane* has an emphasis upon "the cult of manners, the cult of woman, the cult of the gallant knight, the loyalty to caste" in a Virginia locale. The hero's horse is even named "Ivanhoe." In Scott's *Waverley Novels* Scottish clansmen fight English Saxons, and soon Southerners saw themselves as "brave and noble Norman knights" doing battle against Yankees who became "churlish Saxons."[24] They even began utilizing Scott's use of an archaic Scottish term, "Southron," which Scotsmen used with contempt to describe Englishmen. A literary journal named the *Southron* was established in Tuscaloosa in 1839.

While Hilliard was a professor at the university, he influenced many young men to take up creative pens. A number of Alabamians enjoyed writing poetry—contemporary newspapers were filled with local verse—and two received wide recognition: William Russell Smith and Alexander Beaufort Meek, attorneys who dabbled in politics and poetry. Smith, who recorded the debates in the secessionist convention in 1860, wrote *College Musings: or Twigs from Parnassus* while a student at the university in Tuscaloosa. Later he published *The Uses of Solitude*. Meek is best remembered for his epic poem *The Red Eagle* (1855), a romantic treatment of William Weatherford's life. Later he published a collection of poems entitled *Songs and Poetry of the South*. "The Mocking-Bird" was one of Meek's most popular poems, although "Balaklava," inspired by an incident in the Crimean War, was even more frequently reprinted. He edited the *Southron* during its lifetime of only a few issues.

Jeremiah Clemens was another Hilliard student. A lawyer and a cousin of Mark Twain, Clemens wrote two novels, *Bernard Lile: An Historical-Romance Embracing the Period of the Texas Revolution and the Mexican War* (1856) and *Mustang Gray* (1858). Neither was especially well received nationally, but the second novel sold well in the South. In 1860 he published *The Rivals*, whose plot concentrated on the animosity between Alexander Hamilton and Aaron Burr. His best and final novel was *Tobias Wilson: A Tale of the Great Rebellion* (1865). It described the first years of the Civil War in the South and the terrible injustices done to Union supporters and antisecessionists in north Alabama. Sometimes drawing on his own experiences, Clemens filled his historical novels with romantic adventure and fast-paced action.

Alabama's most popular novelists were two women, Augusta Jane Evans and Caroline Lee Hentz. Although neither was born in Alabama, both lived in the state for extended periods. Hentz, a native of Massachusetts, moved with her husband, a schoolteacher, to Florence, Alabama, in 1835. She later lived in Tuscaloosa and Tuskegee, then left the state for Georgia and Florida. Her several novels, all set in the plantation South, were stories with romantic twists, violence, and fast action, and they sold well. Her female characters were usually wealthy and secure women, but the diary Hentz kept during her second year in Alabama reveals her personally to have been a hardworking mother. She administered the boarding department and taught in her husband's school.

Augusta Jane Evans was Alabama's most widely read antebellum writer. Born in Columbus, Georgia, she moved with her family first to Texas and then to Mobile, where she began her literary career at the age of fifteen with *Inez: A Tale of the Alamo.* Her 1859 novel *Beulah* became a best seller and was financially rewarding. *St. Elmo* (1866) was her most popular novel, but *Macaria: or, Altars of Sacrifice* (1864) was such a brilliant defense of the Southern cause that Union commanders forbade their soldiers to read the work while on occupation duty during Reconstruction. While Hentz emphasized action and violence in her fiction, Evans portrayed internal conflicts between characters. Her heroines began in poverty and married wealth. Her virtuous, zealous, and soul-searching women guided men to the altars of Christianity. Evans believed that woman's place was in the home rocking the cradle and nursing the sick. Yet her characters as well as her own life suggested an independence and strength of character that belied the submissive and fainting Southern belle. Through her literary career Evans sought a wider world for her talents than the restrictive life of a belle.

But it was not flowery romantic adventure, the highly emotional and exciting fiction of writers like Evans, Hentz, and Clemens, that twentieth-century literary critics and scholars recognized as Alabama's major contribution to American literature. What they cited was the realistic humor of the Old Southwest, the picaresque tales of the frontier with their rogues, scoundrels, skinflints, and con artists, their men on the make, looking for easy ways to fashion a fortune. The first in Alabama to follow the path blazed by Augustus Baldwin Longstreet in Georgia in the early 1830s was Johnson Jones Hooper. He was a transplanted North Carolinian who settled in Lafayette, practiced law, and edited the *East Alabamian.* "Jonce" Hooper published "Taking the Census in Alabama" in his newspaper sometime in the summer of 1843, and it was reprinted by William T. Porter, editor of the New York *Spirit of the*

Times. Hooper's talent was immediately recognized by Porter, who encouraged Hooper to write more.

In 1844 Hooper's most infamous character, Captain Simon Suggs, made his appearance in the newspaper. In 1845 *Some Adventures of Captain Simon Suggs* was published in Philadelphia. Suggs's ethical system was based upon the aphorism "It is good to be shifty in a new country." The redoubtable Suggs conned con men, swindled city slickers and speculators, and even tricked his own father out of a horse.[25] For Suggs, books "aint fitten for nothin' but jist to give to children goin' to school, to keep 'em outen mischief," and he believed that "Book larning spiles a man ef he's got mother-wit, and ef he aint got that, it don't do him no good."[26] Combining clever dialect and ready wit with an understanding of the natural peculiarities and experiences of isolated rural folk, Hooper created characters in a genre that amused antebellum Americans North and South. Much of Hooper's own experiences and his Whig philosophy permeated his writings. Hooper satirized social values and religious camp meetings and often made slaves the brunt of his humor. Throughout his work Hooper suggested the contrasts between the disciplined eastern world of his childhood and a society just emerging from the freedom and lawlessness of the frontier.

Joseph Glover Baldwin followed his friend Jonce Hooper in writing humorous stories. A lawyer and journalist like Hooper, Baldwin was a Virginian who traveled west to Mississippi, then established a law practice first in Gainesville and later in Livingston, Alabama. But Baldwin's sketches differed from Hooper's. He did not rely upon backwoods speech oddities, and his sketches were more sophisticated and contained numerous literary allusions. Baldwin's pieces were not written for newspapers, but beginning in 1852 they were published in the South's leading literary journal, the *Southern Literary Messenger.*

In 1853 *The Flush Times of Alabama and Mississippi* appeared. Baldwin was more concerned than Hooper with the historical significance of his satire, and he clearly wrote for a more literate audience. In one essay Baldwin introduced Colonel Simon Suggs, Jr., the fictional son of his friend Hooper's fabled character and an even more sophisticated rogue and swindler than his father. Suggs, Jr., was a man who perfected the chasing of buxom women and easy dollars. But there were more sober essays in the collection, such as his biographical studies of Francis S. Lyon and Sargent S. Prentiss. Baldwin's next book, *Party Leaders,* was a collection of biographical essays on prominent figures, but it never reached the popularity of *The Flush Times.* Baldwin left Alabama for California in 1854, where he became a prominent attorney and a justice of the California Supreme Court.

John Gorman Barr, a contemporary of Hooper and Baldwin, was a less well-known writer of Old Southwest humor, probably because he never published a collection of his writings. His work appeared between 1855 and 1857 in Porter's *Spirit of the Times* under the pseudonym "Omega." Born in North Carolina, Barr traveled with his widowed mother to Tuscaloosa in 1835. He attended the University of Alabama, where he left a record as a brilliant student, later working as a tutor and reading law. He raised a company of volunteers to fight in the Mexican War, then returned to Tuscaloosa to become part of the city's bright young literary group, which included Alexander Beaufort Meek, William Russell Smith, and Professor Frederick A. P. Barnard. Barr entered politics and was elected to the legislature. Although he does not have the reputation of Hooper and Baldwin, Barr gave a vivid literary portrait of life in Tuscaloosa and western Alabama, a portrait drawn with keen wit.

Three other nationally published, still-remembered Old Southwest humorists also lived in Alabama for various periods of their lives— Kittrell J. Warren, Harden E. Taliaferro, and George Washington Harris. Harris was especially admired for his creation of a notorious scoundrel named Sut Lovingood. These writers of Old Southwest humor often portrayed people who were known generally as crackers and whose culture frequently was of Celtic origin.

The writer who made the most significant historical contribution to Alabama was Albert James Pickett. In 1851 he published the first history of the state. Pickett was a wealthy Autauga County planter who had immigrated to Alabama in 1818 and developed an early interest in local history. He prepared himself by reading history books and by corresponding with the state's early political leaders, many of whom he interviewed personally. He wrote letters to the editors of state newspapers, requesting primary sources, and he ordered translations of materials from European archives dealing with the French and Spanish periods. For many years Pickett's *History of Alabama, and Incidentally of Georgia and Mississippi, from the Earliest Period* was the only history of the state. When it appeared there were lively reviews in state newspapers and some disagreement with his facts, especially when he dealt with events in the memory of many citizens. Pickett ended his book with the early years of statehood. Although his account is dated, neglects much of north Alabama, and is uneven in quality, it is still a valuable work.

If Pickett is the father of Alabama history, the grand dame of Alabama antebellum culture and society was Octavia Walton Le Vert. Born in Augusta, Georgia, Le Vert moved with her parents to Mobile and married a prominent physician. She was well educated and spoke several languages, conversing in French with Lafayette on his visit to Mobile in 1825. She spent the years 1853–55 in Europe, where she was entertained by the social elite. Returning to Mobile, she wrote *Souvenirs of Travel*, a work Alabamians, and others, read with excitement. Following the French, Madame Le Vert established a salon in her home, receiving guests on Monday beginning at eleven o'clock in the morning and continuing through the evening. Writers, artists, teachers, politicians, foreign visitors, actors, and celebrities of all sorts gathered to discuss literature, the fine arts, politics, history, and philosophy.

Madame Le Vert fulfilled her wifely duty by delivering five children in ten years, but she chafed under society's restrictive view of women, writing: "I am a woman and her lot is never to rise. Why should I strive in the paths of learning? Who will ever appreciate them? Who will ever praise them?"[27] Although her writings today are little remembered, she is. At one time she had the widest international following of any Alabamian, and her salon was influential in setting the cultural tone for Mobile.

Mobile, the oldest city in the state, was also in 1860 the largest urban area, with 29,258 people compared to Montgomery's 8,843, Tuscaloosa's 3,989, and Selma's 3,177. With its French and Spanish heritage, the city became the cultural center of Alabama, a status Mobile held with pride. On the eve of the Civil War, most Alabamians lived on isolated farms, in rural communities, or in small towns. Because it was the port for the shipment of most of the state's cotton, Alabamians had special reasons to visit the city. A trip to Mobile was a rare privilege enjoyed by few but dreamed about by many. In 1835 the actor Tyrone Power found in Mobile "the best appointed hotel in the Southern country and society congenial and amiable." He was amazed, however, at the coarse clothes and "humble wooden dwellings" of the Alabama planters and of the violence he found in their society. One night Power learned that a supposed minor distraction in a dress box during one of his performances was actually a man being stabbed to death.[28]

Many planters scheduled their honeymoons in Mobile during the winter season, reserving rooms at the Battle House after it opened in 1852. When Joseph Holt Ingraham visited the Battle House he noted its only "drawback as Irish servants" for "Southerners do not know exactly how to address servants of their own color."[29] Besides Alabama planters, Mobile attracted a large number of foreign and Northern tourists and businessmen. Those who came to Mobile, whether for business or pleasure, were significant to the city's economy, and every effort was made to provide proper entertainments. The operation of a theater featuring national touring companies was an important part of social life. Noah Miller Ludlow's theater, the Mobile, was constructed in 1824 and in 1826 offered the first performance of *Macbeth* in Alabama. Although several theaters were lost to fire, Mobile offered at least one theater during the antebellum period. One of the most famous was James Caldwell's Royal Street Theater, which burned in 1860.

Theaters charged patrons twenty-five cents to one dollar to see plays, minstrels, operas, concerts, and ballets. Magicians, aerial performances, gymnasts, and jugglers shared the stage with trained animals. Visits to Mobile by Tom Thumb, Siamese twins, and a ventriloquist especially intrigued the city during the antebellum period. More intellectual performances included lectures on the courts of George III and George IV by the English novelist William M. Thackeray.

Huntsville and Montgomery had theaters that attracted national touring companies. Edwin Booth, Louis Tasistro, Tyrone Power, and the exotic Lola Montez all appeared on Alabama stages. Smaller communities developed their own amateur thespian groups and either used academy stages or adapted other facilities for performances. The Camden Thespian Society was formed in 1846, and Benjamin Fitzpatrick starred in the Montgomery Thespian Society's performance of *Julius Caesar* at the Montgomery Hotel.

Artistic expression, like drama, was difficult to pursue in a frontier society. Portrait painters from the North came south in the winter, traveling through Huntsville to Tuscaloosa, Montgomery, and Mobile. Sometimes they stayed with planters for several weeks in order to paint family members, then moved on to other plantations. Often they advertised in local newspapers.

One of Alabama's best-known portrait painters was Nicola Marschall, a German who arrived in Mobile in 1849. Marschall taught art, music, and French at Judson and painted planter portraits across the Black Belt. Caroline Hentz's husband, Dr. Nicholas Marcellus Hentz, a Frenchman, was recognized for his exquisite miniatures, and William Frye, originally from Bohemia, painted both landscapes and portraits in his studio in Huntsville. Edward Troye, known for his paintings of horses, kept a studio on Bienville Square and taught at Spring Hill College. John James Audubon worked in Mobile for a while, and the hummingbird that appeared in his *Birds of America* was painted in the city.

George Cooke, a native of Maryland who studied art in Europe, was the favorite artist of Daniel Pratt, who owned many of Cooke's paintings and provided a studio and gallery for him in New Orleans. Cooke painted portraits of Pratt and his wife and children on a visit to Prattville. Following his death in New Orleans, Cooke was buried in the Pratt family cemetery in Alabama. Wealthy Alabamians commissioned portraits to strengthen family pride and achieve a sense of immortality. Yeomen and the poor passed to their reward without leaving any record of what they looked like until the camera made portraits affordable to many people. When Emily Moore's daughter Bettie died, her mother lamented that although she had a lock of her hair, she wished she had a likeness to remember her by. She wrote her sister, "have all of your children taken, you will not regret it if they were to die."[30]

Music was a different story. Because the voice was free, the ballads and songs of England, Scotland, and Ireland warmed the cold nights on the Alabama frontier, and emotional hymns reverberated through camp meetings, brush arbors, and small churches. Music from the dulcimer, fiddle, guitar, and banjo kept the feet moving at planned or impromptu dances. Miles E. Tarver, a Yankee traveling salesman, attended a singing at Ashville at the Hodges's home where three girls under eleven years of age "sang many beautiful parts with great correctness and beauty keeping perfect time."[31] Pianos were expensive luxuries and for many years were uncommon outside Mobile, but by 1860 music lessons were an important part of the curriculum in the better schools for girls. Even some original music was scored in the state. Professor Charles Andrews, who taught music at the Wilcox Female Academy, composed "The Camden Grand Polka" and "Alabama's Sunny Clime."

The antebellum cotton kingdom in Alabama was a society of contrasts. In the salons of Mobile urban sophistication reigned, as foreigners and Northern-born citizens did business with country planters. On Royal Street a gentleman might challenge an equal to a duel, while a block away along the river wharf men might engage in a bowie-knife fight or an eye-gouging contest. Gambling, drinking, and dancing were common, despite hell-raising preachers and brush arbor revivals. The satin and lace dresses of belles were unknown in cabins, where women wore homespun shifts. The aristocratic medieval world of Sir Walter Scott was the literature of the parlor, though humor from the lives of yeoman farmers formed the tales recounted in the newspapers. Yet illiteracy was still common, and free public schools enrolled fewer than 15 percent of white children in 1860. In 1842 Mary Betts Lewis wrote from Huntsville to her sister, who was studying in Paris, warning that "You will recollect, my wanderer, that if you live, a change must come 'o'er the spirit of your dream' and you in spite of travel, in defiance of all the allurements of Paris and a finished education, you must again become a backwoods woman! And only so far would I recommend to you to looking into the future."[32]

Cotton crops were the way to wealth in the Black Belt, while small farmers in the Wiregrass and the hill country looked to corn harvests to sustain the family. Alabama was a society with a strong commitment to freedom yet dominated by slavery. Despite the contrasts and despite sectional or class differences, strong ties bound white Alabamians together: a fierce independence, a shared Southern identity, and an uneasiness over the presence of large numbers of black bondsmen in their community.

NINE

Party Politics and States' Rights

W HEN John Gayle became governor in 1831, Alabama was enjoying "the flush times." A period of economic prosperity sent cotton prices up and settlers continued to flood into the state. The Democratic party with its commitment to the Union and to Jacksonian democracy dominated politics. Alabama was strongly opposed to the protective tariff—every member of the state's congressional delegation voted against the Tariff of 1828—and there was a powerful core of Nullifiers under the leadership of Dixon Hall Lewis. But there was no widespread support for South Carolina's nullification of the tariff. In November 1832, in the heat of the controversy, Governor Gayle shared with the general assembly his opinion that should a state adopt nullification "she will have to abandon the Union, or return to it with feelings of disappointment and humiliation. . . . As sure as it shall succeed, its triumphs will be stained with fraternal blood, and the proudest of its trophies will be the destruction of constitutional liberty."[1] Ironically, within three decades Alabama moved from the strong nationalism of the Jacksonian period to supporting a states' rights position that led to secession.

In 1832 most Alabamians sided with President Jackson in his fight against the Bank of the United States. Opposition to concentrated wealth and power was an Alabama political characteristic with a long tradition. States' rights advocates insisted that the bank was unconstitutional anyway, and fears lingered that the BUS might compete unfairly with the Bank of Alabama. Few tears were shed when the "monster" was slain by Old Hickory. But the national bank was not the issue in the state that it was elsewhere, and it was the controversy over the removal of the Creek Indians and control of the land in the Creek cession that caused the brilliance of Jackson's leadership to dim and the cause of states' rights to increase in popularity.

The Creek affair moved Gayle away from Jackson to a states' rights position. Yet the governor and his followers were careful to stress the differences between a state nullifying a federal law (such as the tariff) and a state assuming authority over its own territory (as Alabama did in the Creek controversy). Land was a frontier people's most important possession, and Alabamians perceived their state as protecting its citizens' right to settle on the lands in the Indian cession. In the legislative elections before the Creek affair, the Nullifiers—as they were called by their opponents—held 25 percent of the seats in the general assembly. Six months later a new states' rights coalition formed as men shifted to support Gayle or converted to positions more hostile to federal power. Alarmed, Jackson's supporters tried to rally the Gayle men back into the fold. The legislative breakdown was about evenly divided between the Nullifiers (30 percent), the Gayle-Jackson supporters, who were as yet unwilling to break completely with the president (25 percent), and the "whole-hog Jackson men" (45 percent).[2]

President Jackson let it be known that Martin Van Buren was his choice for his successor. As an alternative to Van Buren, Judge Hugh Lawson White of Tennessee coalesced the opposition to Jackson. In South Carolina, the Nullifiers who opposed Jackson took the appellation "Whigs," condemning Jackson's supporters as "Tories." *Whig* was first a generic term applied to all those who opposed Jackson and Jacksonian democracy, and it was some time before the apparatus of a party organization developed. But by 1834 the Whig party was the popular vehicle to oppose Jackson. Nationally, the party was a strange combination of John C. Calhoun with his Nullifiers and states' rights advocates and the John Quincy Adams—Henry Clay faction, which supported a strong central government, a national bank, a protective tariff, and internal improvements.

In Alabama the Whigs rose to power on the Creek affair as a states' rights issue. The men who entered the new political alliance that emerged in Alabama from the legislative sessions of 1834 were, not surprisingly, from the cotton-producing areas of the state. Different economic interests in south and north Alabama resulted in different political attitudes, differences between the cotton kingdom with its international ties and market economy and the more isolated and self-sufficient corn-growing hill-country farmers. The Whigs' support for an active government and the party's strength among large planters convinced yeoman voters that the Whig party was one with the wealthy aristocracy, the traditional villain of Alabama politics. An attempt by the new coalition to unseat William Rufus King, senior senator and a Jackson man, failed. No candidate would openly oppose King, although King's rival, Dixon Hall Lewis, just happened to be in Tuscaloosa when the legislative vote was scheduled. The division of the Democratic party into a Jackson-King-Unionist faction and a Lewis—states' rights group was evident.

Clement C. Clay, former state supreme court chief justice and congressman since 1828, was nominated to run for governor. Clay supported Jackson and opposed the probank forces when he was in the House of Representatives. For Clay, the gubernatorial campaign was a challenge because he had to make certain he was not drawn into national politics during the Alabama canvass. Clay was in the middle because Judge White, his old legal preceptor, was leading the opposition to Jackson.

Only at the last minute did the anti-Jackson party find a candidate to oppose Clay: General Enoch Parsons. The political ineptitude of Parsons was revealed when he rode into Tuscaloosa, stumbled into a Methodist oration, and suddenly at the conclusion "starts up and gives the sober congregation, more numerous in females [who could not vote] than males, an address announcing himself a candidate for Governor."[3] Clay easily defeated Parsons's token effort. The Jacksonians were concerned by the strong opposition they encountered in the general assembly. Before the presidential election they called for a Democratic party convention to nominate an electoral slate for Jackson's choice of Van Buren as his successor. The first state party convention in Alabama met in Tuscaloosa in December 1835 and endorsed Van Buren for president; Clay joined the support for the "Little Magician" only after he was elected governor. Van Buren won Alabama's electoral vote, but by the end of the decade the opposition to Jackson had clearly evolved into the Whig party. Alabama became a two-party state, although no Whig ever won a statewide election.

During his term as governor, Clay stressed education and internal improvements, but his administration was dominated by two events—the Creek War of 1836, a consequence of the Creek removal, and the panic of 1837, the economic whirlwind that chased the flush times from Alabama. The removal of the Creek Indians from eastern Alabama was not accomplished peacefully, and violence continued in the Indian lands. Bands of young braves roamed, stealing cows and burning houses and barns. Through confusion and lack of communication, federal forces were not available to quell the disturbances, so Clay called out the state militia. Eventually, several thousand militiamen tracked down the hostile Indians, and the last Indian battle in Alabama was fought in 1837 at Hobdy's Bridge on the Pea River. Two years later the tribes were gone, leaving behind individual Indians, a heritage of Indian place names, arrowheads and broken pottery buried beneath the leaves and ceremonial mounds, and burial grounds and abandoned town sites. For generations Indian tales and legends were repeated, and Indian blood coursed through the veins of many Alabamians.

The second major event of Clay's term, the panic of 1837, brought hard times to the state. Initiated by international factors, including large silver imports and increased British interest rates, the national economic depression was fueled by a combination of policies and events—alone none of them were good, but combined they spelled disaster for the economy. Jackson's fight against the Bank of the United States shook up banks and the monied interests, and his destruction of the BUS left the government and the country without a stabilizing fiscal agency. Speculation ran wild during the boom of the early 1830s. It was fed by an inflated paper currency, a condition that Jackson abruptly ended with his Specie Circular of July 1836, which limited the acceptance of federal land payments to specie—gold or silver. The specie circular effectively applied the brakes to the flush times in Alabama and forced the price of land, cotton, and slaves downward.

Mobile felt the recession first when factors and merchants stopped payments to their clients and creditors, although the Bank of Mobile brought stability to the city's financial dealings and was recognized across the state for its sound banking practices. In the financial crisis, the Tuscaloosa state bank president removed his bank's collection bills from the Mobile branch of the Alabama state bank and transferred them "to the private Bank of Mobile, indicating that, when the chips were down, the state bank administrators knew which banks were solvent."[4] The Bank of Alabama tried to ease the stringent currency conditions but could not. When the legislature met in June 1837, its solution was to compel the banks to increase circulation (already too inflated) and to defer specie payments. These moves only exacerbated the crisis. Alabama banks tried to obtain specie in Cuba and in New Orleans, where they found prospects for procuring it "gloomy," but specie had to be acquired "on some terms, as our stock . . . is diminishing from 2 to 4000 dollars daily."[5]

Meanwhile, Senator Gabriel Moore had offended the state's Jacksonians by his criticism of the president, by his move toward states' rights, and by his support of the abortive attempt to unseat William Rufus King. The legislature instructed him to resign. Moore ignored the request and served out his term. To succeed Moore, the legislature elected Democrat John McKinley, who had been in the Senate from 1821 to 1831. Before McKinley took his seat, President Van Buren appointed him to the Supreme Court, the first Alabamian to serve as a justice.

In his fifteen years on the high court, McKinley wrote only eighteen majority opinions and several concurring and dissenting ones. But in three of his first circuit court cases, McKinley's decisions (based upon a strong states' rights philosophy) shocked the commercial community. Regarding one of the cases, Justice Joseph Story wrote Charles Sumner in Massachusetts that

My brother, McKinley, has recently made a most sweeping decision in the Circuit Court of Alabama which has frightened half the lawyers and all the corporations of the

139

country out of their proprieties. He has held that a corporation created in one state has no power to contract (or, it would seem, even to act) in any other state, either directly or by an agent. So banks, insurance companies, manufacturing companies, etc., have no capacity to take or discount notes in another State, or to underwrite policies or to buy or sell goods. The cases in which he made these decisions have gone to the Supreme Court. [6]

During appeal the three cases were combined for Supreme Court hearings. After extensive arguments, the Court reversed McKinley's decisions. Chief Justice Roger B. Taney wrote the majority opinion, and McKinley penned a polite dissent defending his earlier stand. McKinley's move to the federal bench gave the legislature a Senate vacancy to fill in 1837. Governor Clay, the popular choice, was selected and he resigned as governor. Hugh McVay, who had moved from Madison to Lauderdale County in 1818, was the presiding officer of the state senate, and he took over the reins of power in Tuscaloosa, while Clay made plans to be in Washington for the special September session.

In the early years of the Van Buren presidency, the schism in the Alabama Democratic party healed as the states' rights faction approved of Van Buren's subtreasury system and seemed less threatened by the New Yorker's leadership than they had been by Jackson's. In the gubernatorial election of 1837, Democratic candidate Arthur P. Bagby defeated anti–Van Buren candidate Samuel W. Oliver. The Democratic margin of victory was reduced because the Whigs became more organized, drew such leaders as Oliver, John Gayle, James Dellet, and Arthur F. Hopkins into the party, and held state conventions in 1839 and 1840.

Arthur Bagby was governor during the hardest times of the economic depression. In spring 1837, John McKinley wrote Andrew Jackson from New Orleans that most of the cotton houses had failed and "no cotton can be sold here at present—scarcely at any price." [7] McKinley, like most Alabamians, was desperately short of cash and could find no way to acquire any. Banks had suspended specie payments, real estate values had plummeted, manufactured goods could not be sold, and commercial transactions almost ceased. Most of the speculation of the flush times was accomplished on borrowed money. When the bottom fell out of the real estate market, the inflated debts remained but could not be paid by the debtors nor collected by creditors. Philip Phillips, an attorney who arrived in Mobile from Charleston in 1835, speculated in land with his $5,000 inheritance, then borrowed another $25,000, and lost it all. The shortage of currency seriously hurt urban families because they often had no money to buy food. The city of Mobile defaulted on its bonded indebtedness because taxes could not be collected and assessments fell. Citizens who usually went to the mountains to avoid the summer heat in Mobile stayed home because they had no funds for travel.

Governor Bagby recognized that the Bank of Alabama contributed to the economic crisis and that the state banks were a major problem. He was not alone in his concern. For years political leaders had voiced apprehension over the operation of the state banks. The Bank of Alabama had been founded by Israel Pickens in a crusade to rid the state of the aristocratic Georgia faction and corrupt private banks. To many voters, the state bank symbolized democracy, and politicians criticizing the bank did so at peril to their offices. Accurate information on the financial condition of the main bank (at Tuscaloosa) and its branches was impossible to obtain. Although in 1834 the bank reported such enormous profits that the legislature abolished taxes, in truth the bank was not in the healthy condition it seemed to be, and there was serious trouble with its management.

The legislature elected the president and board of directors of the Tuscaloosa bank annually, and with the creation of branch banks in Montgomery, Mobile, Huntsville, and Decatur, at least seventy bank offices might be filled. Candidates were not lacking, and before a legislative vote the city of Tuscaloosa and the capitol's halls would be crowded with men seeking votes. Good cigars, oysters, fine liquors, and brandy were provided the legislators. In one of Johnson Jones Hooper's stories, Simon Suggs shared a mail coach to Tuscaloosa with a bank-director candidate who mistakenly assumed that Suggs was a legislator, though Suggs coyly denied it. Nevertheless, he conned the candidate out of a twenty-dollar bribe to influence the directorship election in his behalf, an occurrence Alabamians believed happened frequently.

Following the directorship elections, some legislators negotiated loans from the banks, although not as excessively as the antibank faction charged. Most of the directors were honest and capable men, but the incompetent and dishonest were sometimes elected. The state bank was created to aid planters and provide indispensable capital and a circulating currency for a rapidly growing state with an expanding economy. The bank obliged, but with reckless management and overextended loans. One study suggests that the bank's loans were actually sound; it was the panic that made them uncollectible. In *The Flush Times of Alabama and Mississippi*, Joseph Glover Baldwin wrote, "The State banks were issuing their bills by the sheet, like a patent steam printing-press *its* issues; and no other showing was asked of the applicant for the loan than an authentication of his great distress for money." Baldwin noted that the banks: "chartered on a specie basis, did a flourishing business on the promissory notes of the individual stockholders ingeniously substituted in lieu of cash. They issued ten for one, the *one* being fictitious."[8]

In extremely shaky condition for years, the Bank of Alabama managed to survive only because the economic boom continued, because of legislative inertia, and because it had little competition from private banks and citizens remained convinced that a private banking system was even more evil than the state one. Warnings sounded in newspapers and in the legislature were ignored. Despite the concern of governors, strong support for the state bank maintained the status quo. Monies designated as bank profits were funneled into supporting state government, but the panic of 1837 caused a run on state banks in the spring, and they were forced to suspend specie payments. Governor Bagby succeeded in coaxing the legislature into passing a law requiring each bank to have two audits a year, an interim one and a final report to be delivered to the governor, not the legislature. Although Bagby pressed for reform, little was accomplished, and the question of bank reform became the key issue in the gubernatorial election of 1841.

The Alabama Whigs hoped to build upon the strength shown in the 1840 presidential election. The Whig nominee for president, William Henry Harrison, ran his "log cabin" and "hard cider" campaign and made the Whig ticket attractive in Alabama. To counteract the challenge, the Democratic press began reporting wild Whig excesses: Mobile Whigs were arrested for "riotous and disorderly conduct"; General Harrison was a "Federalist of the Reign of Terror stripe"; and Arthur F. Hopkins was accused of corresponding with a notorious abolitionist.[9] The Democrats portrayed the Whigs as the broadcloth party of aristocracy and wealth, despite the "log cabin" campaign rhetoric. The Huntsville *Democrat* challenged the voters of north Alabama to "forget not who are your opponents" and to respond by going to the polls if they were "opposed to odious distinctions between rich and poor" and the privileges of a favorite few, at the expense of the many. The newspaper urged north Alabama men to "rally from the coves, the valleys, the plains, and the hills."[10]

Alabama's electoral vote went to Van Buren, but Harrison was elected president. In Alabama the vote was markedly sectional. The Democrats were able to associate Harrison with abolitionist sentiments, and he lost some Whig votes and failed to carry any county north of the Black Belt. Five northern counties—DeKalb, St. Clair, Marshall, Madison, and Jackson—gave Van Buren more than his statewide margin of victory, a situation one Whig newspaper called "party despotism."[11] The Whigs were never able to carry the state in a presidential election, although they lost by only 5 percent in 1840 and 1 percent in 1848. Nor were they able to elect a Whig governor or win a joint ballot in the legislature; but twice, in 1849 and 1851, they captured a majority in the state senate. The Whig party dominated certain sections of the state, however, and was able to hold two congressional seats from 1829 to 1843, with the exception of the general-ticket election that was contrived by the Democrats to counter the sectional strength of the Whig party.

Traditional interpretations of the Whigs as a broadcloth party of wealthy slaveowners have been challenged as simplistic. Economic factors alone do not seem to account for party alignment. Alabama Whigs were more likely to grow cotton than corn, to be older men and those of Northern birth, and to own slaves. But slave ownership alone was not the determining factor either, for many of the larger slaveowners were Democrats. Whigs were more likely to come "from those whom environment, access to information, and temperament inclined toward an awareness of a way of life beyond their horizons of space and time," while Democrats "were more likely to come from those preoccupied with the way of life of their immediate place and time."[12]

To destroy the Whig base, the Democrats introduced a bill that required all candidates to run state-at-large elections on a general-ticket system for congressional representatives. Democratic nominees, who could not carry their Whig districts, would be elected because of the large Democratic majorities in northern Alabama. Governor Bagby called for the legislation, and Nathaniel Terry introduced the bill in the senate, admitting that its effect would protect Dixon Hall Lewis from the Whig majority in Montgomery. The Whigs in the legislature used every parliamentary maneuver available to kill the bill, but it became law in January 1841. Amid cries of tyranny, charges of a usurpation of power by the solidly Democratic northern counties, and accusations that the law violated political principle, the Whigs demanded a popular referendum.

Before that could be accomplished, President Harrison called a special session of Congress to meet in May. Because the terms of Alabama congressmen had expired in March, and the new election was not scheduled until August, Governor Bagby convened the legislature to approve a special election to be conducted under the general-ticket provisions. In the May contest, all the Democratic candidates won, results the Tuscaloosa *Independent Monitor* called "so foul a conspiracy against popular rights."[13] As planned, the margin of victory was provided by the five strongly Democratic northern counties.

When the general assembly passed the special election bill, it included a rider that gave the voters an opportunity in the August gubernatorial election to express their opinion on the general-ticket system. The Whig candidate for governor, James White McClung, announced his opposition to state-at-large elections. Throughout the campaign, Whig newspapers vehemently condemned the general ticket. And in the election enough Democratic voters agreed, their disapproval tabulated in an early use of the popular referendum. In 1841 at the next session, the legislature repealed the general ticket, and congressional district elections resumed. The Tuscaloosa *Independent Monitor* called the three Democratic congressmen elected under the general-ticket scheme "notorious smugglees from Alabama" who had obtained their seats by proscription and tyranny. The newspaper demanded the "immediate surrender of trusts" they could not hold "with honor or decency."[14]

The Democratic candidate for governor, Benjamin Fitzpatrick, was too popular and the party too strong to be affected by a general-ticket scheme backlash. Fitzpatrick made the bank an issue in his campaign and assured voters that: "I have never borrowed a dollar from a bank, neither was I ever president or director of one. I am a tiller of the earth and look to that as the only source of prosperity and wealth."[15] Fitzpatrick was elected, and in his inaugural address he gave a typical Jacksonian view of government, proclaiming: "that in the practical administration of all government, economy is one of the highest of public virtues. The essence of modern oppression is taxation. The measure of popular liberty may be found in the amount of money which is taken from the people to support the government; when the amount is increased beyond the requirement of a rigid economy, the government becomes profligate and oppressive."[16] He was well aware that ending the state bank's responsibility to finance state government would mean an increase in taxes, a responsibility Alabamians were reluctant to assume.

Bank reformers were elected to the legislature, and the more the legislature investigated the bank, the worse were the scandals they uncovered. One exposed scheme involved several members of the legislature who conspired "to swindle the banks and rob the people" by issuing false bills of exchange. The legislature revealed individual legislators' bank debts. While these loans may have been sound initially, despite any legislative influence or political pressure, the panic of 1837 had rendered them worthless, and the appearance of corruption doomed the bank. The Whigs advocated selling bank stock to raise more capital and employing more experienced managers to serve the needs of commerce, rather than just agriculture. Democratic leaders first assumed that reform could save the bank and it could still benefit the people; however, the hill-country Democrats soon insisted that the concentration of capital within the banking structure was "intrinsically corrupting" and they favored liquidation.[17]

Governor Fitzpatrick failed to achieve the reform he wanted because the friends of the bank opposed changes and stymied the legislature's efforts. During summer 1842 a frustrated Fitzpatrick discussed the bank with Henry Goldthwaite and John A. Campbell during the session of the supreme court. Campbell agreed to stand for the legislature and lead the banking-reform measures. At the next session, Campbell served as chair of the house committee on the state bank, and his voluminous reports detailing debts that were irrecoverable shocked the state. The concentration of economic power in the state banks and the corruption that followed the abuse of that power was not to be forgotten by the electorate.

Campbell recommended complete reform and the immediate liquidation of the branch banks at Mobile and Decatur, warning the legislature that if it faltered the "character of the State will be degraded to the level of its currency," a condition "to which our gloomiest forebodings have not yet descended."[18] The legislature ordered the branch banks liquidated, placed restrictions upon the main bank at Tuscaloosa, and gave the governor power to investigate expenses and initiate suits to recover illegal disbursements. A tax law was passed to take the burden of supporting the state government from the bank. Liquidation of the banks had to be accomplished slowly to prevent further loss and damage. When the bank charter expired on January 1, 1845, Governor Fitzpatrick opposed any renewal.

Yet the institution's supporters still did not give up their fight to preserve the Bank of Alabama. When the Democratic convention was held in Tuscaloosa in 1845, the Warrior and Tombigbee rivers were so low that boats had difficulty reaching the capital, and delegates were detained on the river. The friends of the bank in the convention rushed through the nomination of Nathaniel Terry, a strong bank supporter and one of the legislators who owed the bank a large amount of money. The Democratic bank reformers responded by persuading Joshua L. Martin to oppose Terry as an independent candidate on a bank-reform platform. The Whigs nominated no candidate but watched the fight within the Democratic party and voted for Martin, who won.

As the election results spread, a crowd of Terry supporters gathered at the Tuscaloosa post office. When "the door was thrown open and the news proclaimed," one observer "questioned whether a cannon charged with grape, and fired along the pavement, could have cleared it much sooner."[19] Martin's election sealed the fate of the bank, and early in 1846 the legislature appointed a commission headed by Francis S. Lyon to regulate the bank's affairs, collect as many debts as possible, and move toward liquidation. Lyon by all accounts performed yeoman service. Baldwin in his sketch of Lyon in *The Flush Times of Alabama and Mississippi* wrote: "The State trembled on the verge of Repudiation; if the assets of the banks were lost, the honor of the State was gone. The road through the Bank operations was like the road through Hounslow heath, every step a robbery. . . . [Lyon] succeeded wonderfully. He kept untarnished the honor of the State. He restored its solvency, and, clothed with such vast trusts, . . . he discharged them with a fidelity which can neither be exaggerated nor denied."[20]

The legislative session of 1842–43 not only initiated bank reform but also changed the way congressional districts were apportioned. Alabama's congressional representation was increased from five to seven as a result of the 1840 census. The congressional districts would have to be redrawn and reapportioned. The U.S. Constitution required that in apportioning representation, three-fifths of a state's slave population would be counted in determining population for representation purposes. South Alabama, with its large slave population, received a greater proportional representation than the predominately white areas in north Alabama's hill country. Because the general-ticket election act had been repealed, the Democrats now planned to weaken the Whigs by substituting a white basis of apportionment for the usual federal ratio. David Hubbard of Lawrence County introduced the resolution in the house, and after heated debate it passed both houses on a party division. There was reason to question the law's constitutionality, and concern was expressed that such a move might encourage Northern politicians to advocate changing the federal ratio to a white basis, thus reducing the voting strength of the South in the House of Representatives. Even so, the white basis of apportionment remained.

Felix Grundy McConnell was one of those Alabama legislators who showed no shame in advocating a gerrymander of the congressional districts "to the best advantage of the Democratic party."[21] He also pioneered a demagogic style that frequently appears in Alabama politics. A tall, muscular, and rough-hewn Tennessee native with almost no formal education, McConnell was elected to the legislature from Talladega in 1838. In 1843 he was sent to the state senate. He had a magnetic personality and a quick wit reenforced by frequent sips from a whiskey bottle. McConnell had a flare for the dramatic, especially when it might garner him votes, and stories about him circulated through his district and in Tuscaloosa. One such tale had him on the road meeting a poor family lamenting over their dead horse because plowing time was upon them. McConnell quickly jumped from his horse, gave the animal with a flourish to the family, threw his saddle on his back, and began the twenty-mile walk to town. The story secured hundreds of votes for McConnell among the common folk of his district. In 1842 the Tuscaloosa Methodist Church sponsored a temperance lecture during the legislative session, probably to discourage the rowdy drinking that accompanied the conclaves. A Polish military officer was delivering the main address when McConnell wandered in, probably warm with spirits. At the conclusion, McConnell surprised the audience by standing, confessing his addiction to whiskey, and offering to be the first person to join the proposed temperance society. The Tuscaloosa *Independent Monitor* reported that seventy-five or eighty followed McConnell in taking the pledge.

Although McConnell's antics embarrassed the Democratic party, he was unbeatable in his county. McConnell took advantage of the new congressional apportionment and ran for Congress from the seventh district, a mountainous area of small farmers who voted Democratic.

They sent McConnell to Washington. The capital was dumbfounded by McConnell, and the House of Representatives often broke into gales of laughter at his loud aside comments. Early in his first session, during a heated argument over parliamentary procedure, there were shrill calls for the speaker to bring "the gentleman from New York to order," whereupon McConnell's booming voice was heard: "I have never seen him in order yet, and I have been here three weeks."[22] After the annexation of Texas, McConnell introduced a resolution to annex Ireland to the United States so the Irish could be freed from the tyranny of British rule.

The Alabama Democratic leadership, nonplussed by McConnell's behavior, outmaneuvered his supporters at the district nominating convention, and the nomination went to Samuel F. Rice instead. But McConnell insisted that as the incumbent he was already chosen by the people, and he campaigned as an independent, a man-of-the-people who was denied the nomination by slick, probank politicians in a rigged convention. It was a political battle the "bloody seventh" district long remembered. Judge John W. Vandiver recalled four decades later that the election was one of the most exciting campaigns ever witnessed in east Alabama, "a rough and tumble contest which brought out people by the acre."[23] McConnell won.

When McConnell returned to Congress, he introduced a bill for the federal government to donate, rather than sell, acreage in the public domain to actual settlers who would live on the land and farm it. Other congressional representatives of the poor in the Southern highlands and piney woods advocated similar ideas, but McConnell was the first to introduce a measure that later became known as a homestead bill. McConnell illustrates that during these years Alabama, as one historian has suggested, was not a rising aristocracy but the opposite. After 1832 voters elected men more poorly educated than those in the decade before and voted incumbents out of office more quickly. The electorate was more offended by "intellectual pretensions" than in the first decade of statehood.[24] McConnell's demagogic posture, his appeals to the common man, his campaigns against wealth and privilege, and his support of legislation popular with the poor was a political style perfected by other Alabama politicians as a way to achieve office and power.

Alabamians discussed two significant issues during the early 1840s— the desirability of moving from annual to biennial legislative sessions and the need to move the capital from Tuscaloosa to a more central location. Both changes required constitutional amendments. Biennial sessions were thought less expensive, and something could be said for keeping the legislature in a state of adjournment. South Alabama had never been happy with the location of the capital at Tuscaloosa, but north Alabama was. The population center of the state had shifted after the Creek lands were opened in eastern Alabama, and the wealth of the state was concentrated in the commercial activities around the cities of Selma, Montgomery, Wetumpka, and Mobile. The flow of water in the Warrior River was erratic and travel to Tuscaloosa from the south was not dependable. From the north the Huntsville Road was a slower and rougher ride, but it was more reliable even with rains, swollen creeks, and knee-deep mud than traveling up the river.

Newspapers debated the issue. Several editors pointed to the expense of constructing a new capitol, while others noted the deteriorating condition of the present structure. The Tuscaloosa *Independent Monitor* admitted that Montgomery was a fast-growing, booming town but insisted that the "wagons, drays, and auctions, the fruit of active commerce," would actually distract the legislators and interfere with state business.[25] One editor suggested that the capitol be constructed on wheels so every part of the state could enjoy having it for a time. Businessmen in Montgomery offered to raise $75,000 to cover the cost of building a domed capitol.

The people responded in referendums on both issues by approving biennial sessions by an overwhelming majority (55,819 to 5,167) and agreeing to move the capital by a comfortable margin (33,798 to 27,320). Following considerable skirmishing, the legislature ratified both changes in one resolution. Later the two houses joined together in the house chamber and voted on exactly where the capital would be relocated. After sixteen ballots Montgomery won.

The city of Montgomery selected a spot back from the bluff, a rolling hill with a fine view of the river. On this land Andrew Dexter's goats grazed, and it was called Goat Hill by local residents. The folklore of later generations that "the hill received its name from the creatures legislating within the capitol, rather than from those that grazed the slopes," was not true. The city deeded Goat Hill to the state, and construction began immediately. The capitol was designed by Stephen D. Button in a "lush rendition of the Greek revival" that made use of Corinthian columns on the portico.[26] The building was finished and ready to receive the 113 boxes of state records and documents when they arrived by wagon from Tuscaloosa in November. The legislature convened in the new facility on December 6, 1847. William Garrett, secretary of state, recalled the crowds that packed the city and attended the opening session, and he remembered that the candidates for state jobs "were as thick as blackbirds in a fresh plowed field in Spring." The scene was repeated at the opening of every Alabama legislature.[27]

Unfortunately, the new capitol did not stand long. Fire broke out in the attic above the house chamber in the early afternoon of December 14,

1849. Both houses were in session. The senate quickly adjourned, but the house was in such panic and confusion that the members dashed from the room carrying what they could out the door. Public documents and records were saved from the basement and second floors, but the state library on the third floor, with its valuable collection of historical works, maps, books, and manuscript journals, was lost. The next day citizens offered the general assembly temporary accommodations, and the legislature met on Monday in the sanctuary of the Methodist church. The burning of the capitol renewed talk of moving the capital again, but the legislature appropriated funds to rebuild on the foundations that remained. For the legislature and for Montgomery, the commitment to the capital was a permanent one, but in the early 1870s James R. Powell, a legislator when the general assembly voted to move the capital from Tuscaloosa in 1846 and a founder of Birmingham in 1871, had a large square block surveyed on a knoll at the top of Twentieth Street in the "Magic City." Powell named it Capitol Park. He promised that one day the capital of Alabama would be moved to Birmingham. The fact that it never was moved influenced the course of Alabama history.

Jacksonian democracy left white Alabamians with a strong sense of individualism and a determination to preserve their freedom and independence. The Jacksonian generation believed that hard work brought virtue and that corruption was the result of education and wealth. Enlightened leadership, which the revolutionary generation of Southerners provided the nation, was now suspect in Alabama. The devotion to Union had survived the challenge of nullification on the tariff issue, but the early states' rights supporters were strengthened by the Creek cession controversy, and the ground was fertile for sowing the seeds of "Southern rights." The rise of the Whig party invited Alabamians to adopt a broad national philosophy and support policies that would diversify the productive power and enhance the commercial and manufacturing aspects of the state's economy; however, the Whigs were geographically concentrated, they supported the principles that were suspect among the yeoman voters who controlled statewide elections, and they never had the widespread support necessary to lead the state.

The nation's manifest destiny to settle the continent to the Pacific Ocean caused the South to make the extension of slave territory a Southern priority. With the cost of slaves and land rising, many non-slaveholders saw no possibility of moving into the planter class and emigrated in the decade before the Civil War. In the Black Belt the planter class grew stronger. A study of Dallas County shows that more than 67 percent of white males over age ten who were living there in 1850 had left by 1860. As slaves became more numerous and slave ownership more concentrated, it was evident that the protection of slavery in Alabama was dependent upon the nonslaveholders who controlled the ballot box. To make the hill-country yeomen loyal to slavery, despite their usual fear and hostility toward the planter class, would take extraordinary efforts. One way to encourage their support was to remind them that the taxes paid on slaves represented almost one-third of state revenues. The small farmer–yeoman class was mostly illiterate, lived in isolated areas, and could be swayed most effectively by oral arguments. A man who was perhaps Alabama's greatest orator, a man committed to the interests of the yeoman, to the preservation and extension of slavery, and to Southern nationalism, stood ready to assume leadership.

TEN

Yancey and the Alabama Platform

BETWEEN 1830 and 1860, hundreds of land-hungry Alabamians, ever dreaming of the riches of the West, moved to Texas. At first emigrants wrote "Gone to Texas" on the doors of their cabins, but by the mid-1850s "G.T.T." would explain everything. The Texas census of 1860 put Alabama second only to Tennessee in providing settlers for the Lone Star state. The United States had abandoned Texas for Florida in the 1819 treaty with Spain. Later Mexico won its independence and granted Texas land to Stephen Austin, and by 1835, 30,000 people—many of them from Alabama—had taken up residence. In time the settlers had disagreements with the Mexican government over slavery, but cultural and religious differences became increasingly important. Friction ultimately grew into a revolution when Texans under Sam Houston declared their independence.

In spring 1836 Santa Anna, commanding 6,000 troops, moved north. At San Antonio he met 200 Texans under the leadership of Colonel William B. Travis, an Alabamian from Conecuh County. Travis heroically refused to surrender or retreat, and he died along with his friends Jim Bowie and Davy Crockett. Many adventure-loving Alabama men rushed to Texas to "Remember the Alamo!" before the chance for glory was gone. Sam Houston, with Santa Anna following him, retreated toward the American border while President Andrew Jackson reinforced the U.S. Army in nearby Louisiana. At San Jacinto, Houston suddenly turned on the Mexicans, defeated them, and won independence for Texas. His victory was cheered across Alabama and sparked even more emigration to the Lone Star state. Four years later, in 1840, Houston courted and married Margaret Lea of Marion, Alabama.

Alabamians favored allowing Texas to join the Union because it would add two Southern votes in the Senate. But abolitionists were adamant against the annexation of more slave territory. During the presidential campaign of 1844, James K. Polk, leading the proexpansion Democrats, defeated Henry Clay, who had attempted to avoid the issue. Lame-duck president John Tyler pushed annexation through a joint congressional resolution before Polk assumed the presidency. Mexico objected, claiming the United States had annexed its territory. After Polk ordered American troops to move across the Nueces River, the Mexicans attacked. Alabama responded by sending hundreds of volunteer soldiers. The Mexican War, a training ground for many Americans who lived to fight in the Civil War, accelerated the sectional conflict, complicated the political party scene, and hastened the rise of Alabama's William L. Yancey.

Yancey first was an advocate of Southern rights within the Union. Essentially, he supported the South's right to maintain the institution of slavery without interference from the federal government and Southerners' right to carry slave property into the federal territories. These were the main tenets of "Southern rights." One historian has asserted that "without Yancey's brilliant oratory and indefatigable labors there would have been no secession, no Southern Confederacy."[1] That is perhaps too much responsibility to place on Yancey, but in any event, it was Yancey who wrote the Alabama Platform upon which the Democratic party eventually divided in 1860, and it was he who led the Alabama walkout at the Charleston Democratic convention that year. Furthermore, fully one year before the 1860 presidential election, Yancey pushed for an Alabama secession convention, should circumstances threaten the state.

William Lowndes Yancey was born in South Carolina and reared in Georgia until his widowed mother married Nathan Sidney S. Beman, a Northern Presbyterian minister who was teaching school in Georgia. Beman somehow acquired control of the small Yancey family trust, sold three slaves, probably pocketed the money, and moved his family to Troy, New York. Beman had violent fights with Yancey's mother. From the age of seven, Yancey coped with an explosive atmosphere in his family, a foreign North, and a hypocritical, mean-spirited stepfather who pontificated extreme repentance and radical abolitionism both in his church and in his home. Once, the abolitionist Charles G. Finney preached at a revival at Beman's church, and Yancey probably was there to hear it. Later when Yancey harangued against Yankees and abolitionists, he likely had his stepfather in mind. But despite family problems, Beman saw that his stepson was well educated at Williams College. Northern newspapers later claimed Yancey was suspended for "tossing a pickle barrel through the window of a Methodist meeting house," a never-proved tale.[2]

With the disputes between Beman and his mother becoming ever more acrimonious, Yancey shook the Northern soil from his feet and went south to study law in Sparta, Georgia, then moved to South Carolina to the office of Unionist Benjamin F. Perry. For a while Yancey edited the Greenville *Mountaineer*, an antinullification Unionist paper.

Left: William Lowndes Yancey, newspaper editor, politician, and orator, was the leader of the fire-eaters, those men who wanted secession and an independent Southern nation. *Right:* Governor Thomas Hill Watts, who was working in the Confederate government in Richmond in 1863, was elected after Southern armies were defeated at Gettysburg and Vicksburg. A peace democrat and a reconstructionist at heart, he worked hard to defend the state from invasion and lobbied for its interests in Richmond. (Photos Courtesy of the Alabama Department of Archives and History)

Perry recalled that Yancey was a man of "genius & talents, a man of impulse and feeling; but not a wise & sagacious man in politics."[3]

In 1835 Yancey married Sarah Caroline Earle, daughter of a wealthy South Carolina planter, and the next year moved to Alabama, where he settled on a plantation near Cahaba and became editor of the Cahaba *Democrat* and practiced law. In 1838 on a trip to South Carolina, Yancey lost his temper in a quarrel with his wife's uncle and pulled a concealed pistol and shot him. At his murder trial Yancey claimed self-defense, and his attorney made much of the custom of carrying pistols in the Southwest and Yancey's recent dangerous journey through Indian territory. He was convicted of manslaughter, fined, and sentenced to one year in prison; the governor commuted the sentence after three months. The following year Yancey's slaves were poisoned, many fatally. The affair was blamed on "a vulgar feud" between his overseer and another overseer on a neighboring plantation.[4] Yancey sold what he could, left Cahaba, and moved to Wetumpka to edit the *Argus* with his brother.

Yancey began his political career in 1841 as a member of the Alabama house of representatives and two years later was elected to the state senate. Yancey entered the Alabama General Assembly as a reform candidate pledged to bank reform, public school education, revisions in the penal code, and prison reform. He opposed planter domination and favored apportioning congressional districts on a white-population basis, internal improvements at state expense, and, perhaps because of his mother's experiences, the right of a married woman to control her property. Yancey's views were not always consistent; his advocacy of slavery as a positive good did not square with his opposition to apportionment based upon slave population, but both are understandable if viewed in light of his opposition to the Whigs and the wealthy and his support for yeoman farmers.

In 1844 Yancey was elected to Congress on a platform of "a strict and rigid construction of the federal Constitution," and he repudiated his former Unionism.[5] Yancey's temper led to an illegal but comical bloodless duel with North Carolina congressman Thomas L. Clingman. Because Alabama law prohibited officeholders from dueling, Yancey's friends introduced a special bill in the legislature to exempt him, and it became law over Governor Joshua L. Martin's veto. Suddenly, in July 1846, Yancey resigned from Congress, citing personal and financial reasons. It was ironic that upon his departure he denounced the entire Pennsylvania delegation "with one brilliant exception, Mr. Wilmot."[6] The next month, David Wilmot slipped a rider onto an appropriations bill that simply stated that slavery would never exist in any territory gained from Mexico. Twice the Wilmot Proviso passed the House, but Southern opposition defeated it in the Senate. The proviso marked a renewal of the slavery controversy, and as the dispute moved the South toward a break with the Union, Yancey played a major role in making certain there were no solutions or permanent compromises along the way.

During these years, Yancey cooperated closely with Dixon Hall Lewis, who had entered Congress in March 1829 and had won reelection over all candidates the Union Democrats and Whigs put against him. The Wetumpka *Argus* called Lewis "a shrewd, sensible, well informed, practical man and one of the best business men in the House." Despite a reputation as an excellent orator, Lewis rarely spoke in the House. In April 1844 Governor Fitzpatrick appointed Lewis (his brother-in-law) to William Rufus King's Senate seat after King accepted President John Tyler's appointment as the nation's minister to France.

In the Senate Lewis supported the nomination of James K. Polk and continued to oppose the tariff. In 1845, becoming more suspicious of Polk on the tariff issue, he wrote Yancey and proposed a plan to make the tariff the central issue for *"unwhigging"* the Democratic party and for convincing the Democrats they should not "like whipt spaniels, lick the hand which smites, though it be the hand of a Democrat."[7] Lewis detailed how the South's press could be rallied to the cause and could help mold public opinion. Lewis and Yancey continued to correspond, and the stout congressman had a strong influence on Yancey.

In 1847 the Democrats called a convention and, bypassing incumbent Governor Martin, who had been elected on an independent Democratic ticket, nominated Congressman Reuben Chapman for governor. Martin planned to challenge Chapman at the polls, but when the Whigs nominated Nicholas Davis of Limestone County, a popular planter who had served in the legislature for many years as a Democrat, Martin withdrew. Despite Davis's popularity, he could not garner enough votes to defeat Chapman. A Virginian by birth, Chapman was a planter who practiced law in Huntsville. Following his inauguration, Chapman held an elegant public reception in Montgomery that set the standard for inaugural entertainments for years to come. The Democrats controlled both houses of the legislature, but the Whigs elected former governor John Gayle to Congress from the Mobile district and reelected Henry Hilliard in the Montgomery district.

When William Rufus King returned from his diplomatic post in France, he wanted to return to the Senate. He set his sights on Lewis's Senate seat, which was to be decided in December 1847. The Whigs refused to sit back and allow the contest to be fought by two Democrats. They nominated Whig leader Arthur F. Hopkins. President Polk and his secretary of state, James Buchanan, an intimate friend of King, supported King's election. On the first ballot the votes stood Lewis 50, King 34, and Hopkins 48. For seventeen ballots Lewis gained votes while King lost, but the Whigs refused to throw their support to either Democratic candidate and stayed with Hopkins. On the eighteenth ballot King withdrew to avoid being defeated, and Lewis was reelected.

The strongly contested struggle was probably the most significant senatorial election in the antebellum period. It pitted the Unionists— called "Hunkers" by their south Alabama opponents, who equated them with the blindly loyalist faction in New York state politics—against the states' rights group, called by their north Alabama opponents the "Chivalry." To capture enough Hunker votes to win the seat, Lewis was forced to pledge support for the national Democratic party. Lewis was supported by his brothers-in-law, John A. Elmore (law partner of Yancey) and former governor Benjamin Fitzpatrick. The King faction labeled the family group the "Montgomery Regency," but other politicians from the Montgomery area were part of this force that became a power in state politics in the next decade. King regained a Senate seat when Polk tendered Arthur Bagby a diplomatic appointment to Russia and Governor Chapman appointed King to replace Bagby in the Senate. Although both senators were from south Alabama, King was a Unionist and suited north Alabama.

The Democrats met in Montgomery in February 1848 to select delegates to the summer national convention. The meeting was divided between the Hunkers of north Alabama, who wanted a Union man nominated, perhaps James Buchanan, and the south Alabama Democrats, who preferred a states' rights man. The Union faction intended to make Nathaniel Terry chairman and, through his control of committee appointments and the gavel, ensure "the nomination of electors and delegates of the 'purest water.'"[8] But the south Alabama faction gained control of the convention with an adroit move by John Erwin that made Leroy Pope Walker chairman.

With south Alabama men in control, the convention struggled to adopt a position statement that would not offend Northern Democrats, who favored a squatter sovereignty platform with Lewis Cass as the nominee. During the debates and while the document was being amended, Yancey spoke eloquently. He favored a resolution that the federal government had a duty to protect slavery in the territories and that slaveowners had the right to take their slave property into the territories without interference. The concept contradicted Cass's idea of popular sovereignty and set the Alabama party on a collision course with the national party. Yancey's resolution also called for Alabama's delegates to the Democratic National Convention to refrain from voting for any presidential candidate who would not pledge to support his proposals, which were soon known as the Alabama Platform.

At the Baltimore convention in late May 1848, Cass was nominated on a Democratic platform that remained silent on slavery. Yet Cass's personal support of popular sovereignty was well known. John A. Winston held the Alabama delegation in check during the convention, and when Cass was nominated they did not leave as instructed. Yancey and one supporter adhered to the directions of the state party that adopted the Alabama Platform, and they walked out of the convention, refusing to endorse Cass. In 1848 Yancey departed the Democratic convention virtually alone; twelve years later he would take all the Alabama delegation and the lower South with him and destroy the unity of the Democratic party.

Those Alabama Democrats who stayed in the 1848 convention in violation of their instructions published a defense of their actions and denounced Yancey. Yancey defended himself. He felt betrayed by party politics and considered forming a Southern Rights party. He requested the support of Dixon Hall Lewis because, Yancey wrote, "I occupy the ground marked out for me *by you*—Let us know at once, and candidly, your views."[9] But Lewis refused to support Yancey, encouraging him instead to seek control of the Democratic party. Lewis doubted that Yancey "could carry a single County in the State" on a third-party ticket.[10] Lewis was far more attuned to the attitudes in Alabama and much more realistic in his appraisal of the political situation than Yancey. A decade later Yancey would use Lewis's recommendation.

In the election of 1848, many Alabama Democrats preferred the Whig candidate, General Zachary Taylor, who was a slaveholder marketed by the Whigs as a "national candidate" who could appeal to all and who could heal sectional wounds. The voter turnout in Alabama was low, apathy was widespread, and Cass carried the state by a slim majority (31,173 to 30,482); however, Taylor was elected as the second Whig president. The organization of the Free Soil party by New York Democrats and abolitionist Whigs rid the Democrats and the Whigs of the most militant abolitionist and anti-Southern factions, encouraging Alabamians to remain in the national parties. Dixon Hall Lewis's health was failing, which was no surprise with his weight between 420 and 500 pounds. A friend of George S. Houston suggested that "Old Dick will die of his fat belly by the next session," and he did.[11] Lewis's death in October 1848 left Yancey heir to the extreme states' rights faction in Alabama. While Lewis had been a veteran of Washington politics who recognized the necessity of compromise and understood the realities of national politics, Yancey marched to the tune of a different drummer. His goal was not accommodation but an independent Southern nation. Although it would be three years before the term *fire-eater* was used to describe those who advocated an independent Southern nation, Yancey was already a recognized leader of Southern radicals.

The sectional issues that surfaced during the Mexican War became more tense during summer and fall 1848. The great Kentucky Whig Henry Clay spoke of compromise. John C. Calhoun insisted there could be none. Clay contended that Congress had the right to limit slavery in the territories. Calhoun denied it. The future of the territories of New Mexico and Utah hung in the balance as the debates continued, but Calhoun's health was rapidly declining. On December 23, 1848, he called a meeting of the Southern representatives and senators in the Senate chamber. He presented a draft of an "Address of the Southern Delegates in Congress to their Constituents," which warned of the crisis the South faced. If the North could control slavery in the territories, the address declared, it could also abolish slavery and enfranchise the blacks. For three weeks the wording of the address was debated and was especially opposed by the Whigs. Finally, in January it was signed by forty-eight Southerners.

Calhoun's address stirred Alabamians to attend mass meetings and to support resolutions, and Governor Chapman advocated calling a Southern convention to discuss the South's crisis in the Union. Congressman George S. Houston of Athens refused to sign Calhoun's address, and when he returned to Alabama he attempted to rally north Alabama's opposition to the disunion sentiment of the address, but he failed. He had misjudged the attitudes of his constituents and discovered support for Calhoun everywhere. Houston was forced to defend his own record, and soon after his return he wrote Howell Cobb of Georgia that he found *"very general discontent"* among his friends because he did not sign Calhoun's address.[12] Houston had hopes of being elected to the Senate but decided not to stand for reelection to the House because of the climate of opinion. His old political enemy David Hubbard entered the campaign. The elections of 1849 were important not only because of the national issues but also because the legislature would elect two senators.

Governor Chapman decided to forget the normal formality of a second-term nomination and called for a state convention. Although Yancey supported Chapman's renomination, he failed to secure it. After balloting for two days, the Democrats nominated Henry W. Collier of Tuscaloosa, chief justice of the Alabama Supreme Court and respected in every part of the state because of his years on the bench. At the Montgomery convention resolutions of censure were introduced against the Alabama congressmen who failed to sign the Calhoun address, resolutions aimed more at defeating Henry W. Hilliard than Houston, who was not running. After the convention Houston wrote Howell Cobb that "Alabama is gone, 'hook and line'" for the Calhoun men. Houston regretted not running because he believed he could have won. "My district is lost," he wrote Cobb, "and a rabid Calhoun man, an old nullifier and an enemy of mine, will be elected."[13]

The Whigs did not oppose the Democratic nominee Collier. In the legislative elections, the Whigs secured a majority of one in the senate. The session was marked by the burning of the capitol, and Judge Collier's inauguration had to take place at the Methodist church. Benjamin Fitzpatrick was appointed to fill the Senate seat left vacant by Lewis's death, but he later was defeated by Jeremiah Clemens for the balance of the unexpired term. William Rufus King, who occupied the second seat, was elected in a close ballot over Arthur F. Hopkins.

In the congressional elections the Democrats won except in Mobile and Montgomery. In the Montgomery district, the spirited contest was between two Whigs, Henry W. Hilliard, who was running for reelection, and his challenger James L. Pugh. The internecine contest was called "The War of the Roses." Pugh was supported by the Eufaula Regency, a Calhoun–states' rights group. Yancey campaigned for Pugh, and he and Hilliard confronted each other so much on the hustings that some people must have believed it was a Yancey-Hilliard contest. Pugh attacked Hilliard's record in Congress, but Hilliard defended his record and succeeded in being reelected. Houston wrote Howell Cobb that the Chivalry "are now most gloriously rebuked" and that Williamson R. W.

Cobb had won by one thousand votes in north Alabama even though the "[Calhoun] address men ran at [him] very hard."[14]

Williamson R. W. Cobb was a Unionist congressman who dismayed the states' rights faction. A Tennessee native of Bellefontaine in Jackson County, Cobb entered the state legislature in 1844 and perfected a demagogic style of campaigning. In the legislature he supported a measure to exempt family household items—dishes, forks, plates, and a coffee pot—from sale under execution and used this act as a stepping-stone to Congress. He campaigned among the poor in the mountains, appealing to the common folk, going about chewing on a corn pone or an onion. Cobb even sang songs, rattling tinware to keep time. In 1847 he ran for Congress and defeated two opponents, then beat Jeremiah Clemens in 1849. Cobb was able to defeat the best men the Huntsville aristocracy could send against him, and he maintained the loyalty of his constituents, keeping them firmly in the Unionist camp until the eve of the Civil War.

President Zachary Taylor had hardly settled into the White House before all the sectional issues predicted by Calhoun thundered at his door. Gold had been discovered north of San Francisco at Sutter's Mill, and the great gold rush of 1849 began. As the population of California increased, pressure built for admission as a free state. In Alabama the gold rush was important because many Alabamians participated, providing the expertise gained from years of gold-mining activities in east Alabama. Gold was discovered in the Alabama Creek lands in the 1830s and was soon mined in several areas remembered by such names as Goldville, Gold Hill, Silver Hill, and Goldberg.

The largest mine of the Alabama gold rush of 1835–36 was at Arbacoochee, a Cleburne County community that numbered 5,000 in 1845. The boom town boasted hotels, stores, barrooms, mining-equipment stores, a racetrack, houses, and tents. The mine employed 500 men, most of them working alluvial deposits, hand panning through sand and gravel and later employing a rocker-box or washer to shake the soil, which left the heavier gold in the bottom of the pan. Still later the miners developed the sluice trough. Other Alabama gold-boom towns were Chulafinee, Kemp Mountain, and Pinetucky. Mines with the colorful names of Birdsong, Log Pitts, and Hog Mountain were located in the Goldville district of northern Tallapoosa County, while the Blue Hill and Silver Hill mines were to the south along the Devil's Backbone near Blue Creek.

One of the best-known mines, Dutch Bend, was on the bank of Hillabee Creek and belonged to a German who worked the mine for many years and melted his gold into one-ounce bars. The federal mint reported that gold ore worth $376,000 was sent from Alabama between 1830 and 1860, but that was not a full indication of the total amount produced. When word of the discovery of gold at Sutter's Mill reached Alabama, most miners had abandoned the poor Alabama deposits and many were already searching for the rich veins of California, probably taking with them local gold bars to finance their western adventure. Although some of the Alabama mines were worked off and on into the twentieth century, gold mining was more a romantic interlude in the mining history of the state than a significant economic activity.

The 1849 gold rush made statehood for California imperative. Statehood without slavery was petitioned for, but if granted would destroy the delicate balance of free and slave states. The balance had been maintained since Alabama entered the Union in 1819. Disputes over the boundary of Texas, the status of slavery in the New Mexico and Utah territories, the abolition of the slave trade in the District of Columbia, and a stronger federal fugitive-slave law were issues being contested. Henry Clay presented eight resolutions designed to compromise the issues. Calhoun opposed them, but Daniel Webster spoke for compromise. As the crisis grew, Calhoun convinced Mississippi senator Henry S. Foote to call a general Southern convention to meet in June in Nashville to discuss building a united front to defend the South's rights within the Union.

Governor Collier supported the convention, and as the congressional debates on the Compromise of 1850 grew more serious, the Alabama legislature selected delegates. Both Henry Hilliard, the Unionist leader, and William L. Yancey, the Southern rights leader, opposed the gathering, but for different reasons. Hilliard thought it would offend the North and make compromise more difficult, while Yancey believed some conservative plan might actually be successful and secession could be avoided, which would thwart his plans for an independent Southern nation. No plan was acceptable to all political factions in Alabama. The Unionists insisted that some act of aggression must occur to justify disunion. In contrast, the Southern rights men wanted immediate secession and insisted that aggression had already occurred. Before the convention could meet, John C. Calhoun died in Washington, leaving a leadership vacuum for the Southern rights advocates in Congress and across the South.

The Nashville convention adjourned with little accomplished. Throughout the early summer the political climate remained as hot as the weather. President Taylor was opposed to some aspects of the Compromise of 1850, but when he died suddenly in July, Millard Fillmore, who had presided over the Senate during the debates and favored the compromise, assumed the presidency. In August Yancey joined Robert Barnwell Rhett at a Southern rights meeting in Macon, Georgia, where he urged the South to prepare for war because "the argument is exhausted and we must stand to our arms."[15] One critic observed that the "godlike Rhett and his adjutant Yancey preached most eloquently in behalf of treason."[16] By September the compromise legislation was enacted, and Congress adjourned. Alabamians generally supported the compromise and were relieved that a crisis had been averted. The issue was momentarily defused, and when the second session of the Nashville convention met in November, Alabama sent only eight delegates. The convention fizzled and was dismissed with a parting condemnation of the Compromise of 1850.

The compromise was the main issue during the Alabama elections of 1851. The state was divided between the radicals who wanted secession and the conservatives who supported compromise. The conservatives wanted to protect the South's position within the nation, but they firmly believed there was not yet justification for disrupting the Union. Southern radicals were stronger in settled areas with larger populations, near towns with access to a newspaper. The more radical Southern rights advocates were around Cahaba, Montgomery, and Eufaula, with Mobile and the Coosa Valley two other strongholds of Southern rights supporters. Yancey-organized groups across the state held a Southern rights convention in Montgomery. The rhetoric was strong, causing Whig Unionist Howell Rose of Coosa County to call the secessionists "fire-eaters," a name that stuck.[17] Many of the leaders of the movement had never before been active in politics. Following an attack on his character, Senator Clemens charged that the disunionists were "a wretched minority," men without character "until they crawled into a Southern Rights Association and fancied that *treason* gave respectability to villainy."[18]

Moving to counter the Southern Rights Association, the Unionists began Union Clubs and met in a convention to endorse conservative candidates. Party lines were blurred on the compromise issue, with each contingent having a mixture of strange bedfellows. Radical secessionists Yancey and Samuel F. Rice were joined by moderates Benjamin Fitzpatrick and former Unionist William Rufus King in the Southern rights group. The Unionists proposed B. G. Shields for governor, and although the Southern rights faction opposed Governor Collier earlier for not calling a state convention to consider secession, by election time they favored him. The Unionists agreed to the "Georgia Platform," which favored the compromise, but they insisted that the compromise be fully observed and warned the North not to make future aggressions against the South. Collier, the cautious conservative, was reelected for a second term, the legislature was controlled by Unionists, and Alabama accepted the compromise.

In the congressional races the bitter contest was in the Montgomery district, where Hilliard announced his retirement from Congress and supported James Abercrombie for his seat. Abercrombie, acclaimed the wealthiest man in south Alabama, had strong family ties to the Montgomery Regency. John Cochran, a Eufaula lawyer, was the Southern rights candidate, and Yancey campaigned for him. Contemporaries pointed to the contest as featuring the finest display of oratory in Alabama political history. Although Hilliard and Yancey had met many times in debate, it was this campaign that most Alabamians would remember.

Large crowds came to listen to the two men and their candidates. In his speeches Yancey declared that the South had been totally defeated by the Compromise of 1850 and that secession was the only course open, while Cochran urged Alabamians to stop buying Northern goods. Hilliard and Abercrombie warned against piecemeal secession, which they believed would destroy the unity of the South. At political rallies the public was urged not to do business with any man who was not for Southern rights. Indicating their general support for compromise, the people of Montgomery's congressional district, Whigs and Union Democrats, elected Abercrombie.

The Unionists won five congressional seats, losing only Mobile and Wetumpka. The elections of 1851 battered the secessionists. Alabama was not yet ready for the ultimate step of secession, but the radicals anticipated that the compromise could not last. Auburn's Southern rights leader, William F. Samford, commented, "This day hangs like an avalanche over our heads; a brief hour of stillness and sunshine is to be succeeded by an earthquake."[19]

The legislature of 1851 convened in the new capitol, and Governor Collier was inaugurated in the house chamber. The fight over the compromise had shattered the parties in Alabama. Johnson Jones Hooper said the Whig party was "as dead as a mackerel."[20] Governor Collier quietly began to reorganize the Democratic party. By the time the party convened to select delegates to the national convention, the Democrats controlled the legislature and the party was strong. In February 1852 the legislature redrew the state senatorial districts and further reduced Whig power. The national Democrats' nomination of William Rufus King for vice-president in 1852 and the appointment the next year of John A. Campbell to the Supreme Court strengthened the party, while state Whigs were increasingly embarrassed by the vocal bursts and strength of the abolitionist element in their national party.

The Whig nomination of a man considered soft on the Fugitive Slave Law, the haughty General Winfield Scott, forced many Alabamians to stay home or vote for the Democratic ticket of Franklin Pierce for president and Senator King for vice-president. They ran on a platform that insisted upon the finality of the Compromise of 1850. Yancey and the fire-eaters had nominated a third pair, George M. Troup of Georgia and John A. Quitman of Mississippi, but it was a futile move. Pierce carried Alabama with 26,881 votes to Scott's 16,038. Troup polled only 2,174. Almost 23,000 more men voted in the congressional elections the previous year, indicating that many were dissatisfied with all three candidates and stayed away from the polls.

Vice-President King now held the highest office ever entrusted to an Alabamian, but he did not live to preside over the Senate. Poor health sent him to Cuba, and a special act of Congress allowed him to take his oath of office on March 4, 1853. When his condition deteriorated, he sailed for Mobile, hoping to reach home before he died. His death came at his plantation at King's Bend on April 18, 1853. King's election had left a vacancy in the U.S. Senate, and his death created a void in Alabama's political leadership. The state lost a strong Jacksonian and a committed Unionist. A younger generation of politicians was moving to the front, and they had a different political philosophy.

As King passed from the Washington scene, another Alabamian moved to the capital to make his mark. On the recommendation of two justices, President Pierce appointed John A. Campbell to the Supreme Court. Born in Georgia, educated at Franklin College (later the University of Georgia) and the U.S. Military Academy, Campbell studied law and was admitted to the bar at the age of eighteen. He moved to Alabama and began a law practice first in Montgomery and later Mobile, where he became expert in untangling land titles. He often argued cases before the state supreme court. As a justice, Campbell's opinions on the high court reflected his states' rights view and his Jeffersonian emphasis upon individual rights over governmental restrictions.

The gubernatorial election of 1853 introduced several candidates and new issues. State support for internal improvements and education and the desirability of limiting the sale and consumption of alcohol were injected into the campaign. John A. Winston of Sumter County was a popular Democratic choice for governor. He was a Southern rights man who opposed state aid for internal improvements. Winston's opposition came from north Alabama Unionists who, along with railroad and commercial interests, favored public appropriations for internal improvements. Thomas A. Walker had strong support in north Alabama, and the Montgomery Regency hoped to nominate and elect Congressman S. W. Harris governor so they could send Bolling Hall to Congress in his stead. Winston's supporters persevered, and on the eighth ballot he was nominated by acclamation, although Union Democrats still feared he was too close to the Montgomery Regency.

The Whigs met in convention and nominated Richard Wilde Walker

C. C. Clay, Jr., of Huntsville *(left)*, along with Benjamin Fitzpatrick, served as U.S. Senators in 1861. They both resigned their seats and returned home following Alabama's secession. Virginia Tunstall Clay *(right)*, wife of U.S. Senator C. C. Clay, Jr., was the belle of Washington society while her husband was serving in the capital. She was a strong supporter of the South and left a voluminous collection of letters that are important in studying Alabama antebellum history. (Photos Courtesy of the Huntsville Public Library)

of Lauderdale County. In the classic Whig tradition, Walker advocated better education, state aid for internal improvements, and more commerce and manufacturing. Poor health forced him out of the race, and in the election the Whigs scattered their ballots between hill-country lawyer William S. Earnest of Jefferson County and A. Q. Nicks of Talladega County. Secession was not an issue, and as voters returned to the fold of their previous party allegiance, the Democratic victory was complete.

In the congressional elections the Democrats won six seats, losing only the Montgomery district, where the Whig incumbent James Abercrombie was reelected despite a strong contest by Tuskegee lawyer David Clopton. Three campaigns were particularly significant. S. W. Harris managed to survive a well-financed plan to nominate Bolling Hall of the Montgomery Regency, and then Harris defeated his Whig opponent. Philip Phillips won in the Mobile district by advocating the federal river and harbor improvements that were strongly supported in the port city. Phillips was to play an important role the next year in the Kansas-Nebraska maneuvers in the House of Representatives.

In the Huntsville district, C. C. Clay, Jr., answered the call of the Huntsville leadership and challenged the popular Union Democrat Williamson R. W. Cobb. Clay was beaten, leaving Cobb's undefeated record intact. He had rattled his tinware and crockery across north Alabama, rallying the small farmers and the poor by latching onto the homestead bill, introduced into Congress by Talladegan Felix Grundy McConnell in 1846. In his campaigning Cobb sang a song that began, "Uncle Sam is rich enough to give us all a farm," followed by verse after verse of items the poor might dream of owning. Against Cobb's performance Clay, with his Southern rights background and planter reputation, had no chance. Besides, Clay's wife, Virginia, noted, "He can't sing!"[21] Although Clay outwardly took defeat at the hands of such a demagogue with grace, he deeply resented his defeat. Clay wrote Bolling Hall that he felt he had "been beaten by an ass for the H. of Rep." and that Cobb could "always command the vote of those who can't or don't read against any lawyer, townsman, or state-rights man,—each of whom is regarded as a suspicious character."[22]

John A. Winston held the distinction of being the first Alabama governor born in the state. His family had moved from Tennessee to Madison County, where Winston was born in 1812. In the early 1830s he purchased land in Sumter County, established a plantation, and was elected to the legislature in 1839. Later, he operated a commission house in Mobile. A Democrat with strong states' rights views, he was skilled at political manipulation and never forgave anyone who opposed him. He was cynical, vindictive, and willing to deal for political favors. In 1847 when he realized his wife was having a romance with his friend and legislative colleague, Dr. Sidney S. Perry, he shot Perry, successfully claiming "justifiable homicide," and divorced his wife.[23]

Winston particularly disliked William L. Yancey because of their bitter disagreement at the Baltimore convention in 1848. In his first address to the legislature, Winston expounded his states' rights political creed. He approved of lending any treasury surplus to railroad companies, with "adequate security," but he absolutely opposed any expenditures for internal improvements until the state was out of debt. He strongly favored "a judicious system of popular education" and supported the Education Act of 1854 introduced by Alexander Beaufort Meek.

Two U.S. senators were to be chosen by the legislature that certified Winston's election. Benjamin Fitzpatrick was elected to serve King's unexpired term. Senator Jeremiah Clemens's term expired in March, and this position was normally held by a north Alabamian. C. C. Clay, Jr., had a plan. Son of a governor and senator, Clay served as his father's personal secretary for many years. He represented Madison County in the legislature, practiced before the Alabama Supreme Court (which brought him to the capital frequently), and was active in party politics.

As a presidential elector in 1853, Clay used the capitol meeting to visit with the Montgomery Regency. Later he wrote Bolling Hall that he considered the greatest threat to come not from the Whigs but from Union Democrats who would join with the Whigs to prevent a states' rights Democrat from being elected. Clay insisted that Williamson R. W. Cobb's political power in north Alabama had to be broken. Clemens was too thick with the Whigs, and he and Cobb were too closely affiliated. Clay then stated why he deserved to be considered for the Senate seat: he was a Southern rights man, and he had worked loyally for the Democratic party. He had a strong following in north Alabama, but his election to the Senate depended upon the support of his south Alabama friends. The legislative elections went exactly according to Clay's plan. He was elected to succeed Clemens. On the train to Washington that winter, Senator Fitzpatrick presented Williamson R. W. Cobb to Virginia Clay, who received him coolly and in their exchange chided him about beating her husband in the congressional race. Cobb retorted, "You ought to feel obliged to me. For I made your husband a Senator!"[24]

Before Winston's administration, the governor's power to veto was rarely used; when it was invoked, it was justified by reasons of flawed construction of the bill or questions about its constitutionality. Traditionally, the veto was not used in cases of differences of opinion or disagreements in policy with the legislature. Governor Winston earned the sobriquet "the Veto Governor" by wielding the executive privilege so many times, mostly on bills providing state aid to railroads. He believed that railroad development should be by private investment and that the state was in too much debt (from the failure of the state bank) to incur more bonded obligations. Of the few bills the legislature managed to pass over his veto, one was a $400,000 loan to the Mobile and Ohio Railroad, a small amount considering that the city of Mobile provided $1,100,000 and the federal government supplied federal land grants. The legislature disliked the governor's sarcastic and often high-handed manner and resented his unrelenting determination to protect the state treasury, noting that neighboring states were pushing forward and developing more railroad transportation facilities. Governor Winston also vetoed a bill that would have provided $150,000 to complete the construction of the state insane hospital at Tuscaloosa.

In 1854 the Montgomery *Alabama Journal* led a move to have the white basis of apportionment changed to the federal ratio or mixed basis. Alabama was the only Southern state to use the white basis in determining congressional districts rather than the constitutional ratio, which counted three-fifths of the slaves. The white basis gave north Alabama a political advantage, but south Alabama legislators who supported a black basis or federal ratio quoted John C. Calhoun that the white basis was "the entering wedge of abolitionism."[25] The debate ended with a close senate vote defeating the bill. The Whigs and south Alabama voted for the measure, and the Democrats and north Alabama voted against it. Following the decision, Democrats redrew the congressional districts to their advantage, gerrymandering the central Black Belt counties to ensure greater Democratic control.

Alabamians followed the congressional debates on the Nebraska bill with great interest. Seeking Southern support for the organization of the Nebraska Territory, Senator Stephen A. Douglas of Illinois introduced an amended bill that was silent on the question of slavery and followed the wording of the 1850 Utah and New Mexico bills. Later, Alabama congressman Philip Phillips and Kentucky senator Archibald Dixon persuaded Douglas to include language that explicitly repealed the 1820 Missouri Compromise, which would have prohibited slavery north of the 36° 30' line. Douglas also divided the area into two territories—Nebraska and Kansas. A lengthy and acrimonious debate ensued in Congress, with free-soil senators Charles Sumner, William H. Seward, and Salmon P. Chase leading the opposition.

Douglas's introduction of the notion of popular sovereignty—which allowed the people of a territory to determine the status of slavery—violated the Southern principle that Congress had no right to prohibit an owner from taking his slave property into any national territory. On the other hand, the repeal of the Missouri Compromise opened the possibility that the South could settle Kansas and petition for statehood as a slave state. The Democratic press in Alabama generally opposed Douglas's proposed popular sovereignty, and Alabama Whigs were embarrassed by the abolitionist stands of the Northern members of their party. Weakened by the debates over the Compromise of 1850 and the secession movement that followed, the Whigs were incapable of surviving the Kansas-Nebraska fight. Being pushed to accept a Southern rights creed, they were not yet ready to move into the Democratic party. Many Whigs welcomed the appearance of the American party, more commonly known as the Know-Nothing party, which entered Alabama politics in 1854.

The enormous immigration into the Northern states by the Irish and Germans in the 1840s and 1850s stirred an antiforeign movement. Most of the Irish were Roman Catholics, a church still considered alien to many American Protestants. The Supreme Order of the Star-Spangled Banner, organized by the most extreme nativists in 1849, grew into the American party. An organization with signs, special handshakes, and oaths, the party swore its members to secrecy. When asked about the order, a member replied, "I know nothing." In Alabama the foreign-born and Catholic population was concentrated in the Mobile area, but the party attracted a statewide following. The Democrats considered it a Whig plot and opposed its secrecy as un-American. In Montgomery and Mobile the party elected mayors in 1854 and held a convention to organize for the 1855 state elections. It attracted men who opposed Governor Winston (and his vetoes of state aid to internal improvements) and old Whigs like Johnson Jones Hooper, who edited the American party organ, the Montgomery *Mail.*

In summer 1855 the party nominated George D. Shortridge of Shelby County on a nativist platform that included federal noninterference with slavery. The campaign speeches and debates were bitter. Ministers urged their congregations to vote the American ticket. The American party press made the mistake of attacking the Primitive Baptists (who were opposed to secret organizations), sending them all straight into the Democratic party, where they may have made the difference in the election. The party reached its peak in early summer, but by election time the Democrats and Governor Winston were in control, although both parties stationed watchers in Mobile to detect fraud at the polls. The election passed without the violence feared, and Winston began a second term. In the congressional races, the regular Democrats elected five congressmen. A Know-Nothing candidate, James A. Stallworth, won from the Mobile district, and William Russell Smith, a Democratic convert to the American party, took the Tuscaloosa district with Whig support.

The passage of the Kansas-Nebraska Act caused Northerners, who wished to make certain the two territories became free-soil states, to organize an emigration campaign. The New England Emigrant Aid Company sent settlers into Kansas carrying Sharps rifles, called "Beecher's Bibles." To counter the free-soilers, proslavery emigrant-aid societies were organized in Missouri, and the Southern states were urged to send settlers. Conflict over land claims and confrontations between free-soilers and proslavery men turned the territory into "Bleeding Kansas." In August 1855 Henry D. Clayton of Barbour County took his wife, Victoria, and some 100 potential settlers to Kansas. Victoria Clayton was surprised by the violence and lawlessness of the Kansas frontier. After settling the men on land, procuring supplies for them, and exacting promises "to cast their votes for the interest, as we then thought, of our beloved South," the Claytons returned to Alabama.[26] In November 1855 a Eufaula lawyer, Jefferson Buford, advertised for prospective Kansas immigrants to join him for a trip west in February 1856. Rendezvous points were established at Columbus, Georgia, Montgomery, and Mobile, and eventually 500 men traveled west to Kansas. Many of the men carried Bibles given to them by Dr. Isaac T. Tichenor of the Montgomery First Baptist Church, who pronounced them better for bringing out brotherly love than the Sharps rifles recommended by the Reverend Henry Ward Beecher.

The abolitionist crusade continued to amaze and alienate Alabamians. Harriet Beecher Stowe's 1852 novel, *Uncle Tom's Cabin*, with its searing portrayal of the terrible inhumanity of slavery, swept the North and stirred hearts that had been untouched by the pleas of abolitionists. John Brown's massacre of proslavery settlers along Pottawatomie Creek in Kansas stunned the state. Then the violence entered the hallowed halls of Congress in May 1856, when Congressman Preston Brooks responded physically to Senator Charles Sumner's bitter verbal attack on South Carolina senator A. P. Butler. Brooks assaulted Sumner with a cane, beating him about the head and neck.

Potentially the most dangerous political threat to Alabama was the coalescence of a ragtag group of free-soilers, abolitionists, disgruntled Whigs, unhappy Democrats, Know-Nothings, and other opponents of the Kansas-Nebraska Act. The Republican party they formed blew out of the West with religious zeal, determined to stop the spread of slavery, a position that stood squarely against Yancey's Alabama Platform. The Republicans also advocated such policies as federal aid to railroads, enactment of a homestead law, land grants to support agricultural and mechanical colleges, and a high protective tariff—all programs that were anathema to white Southerners. In both North and South new voices and younger men assumed leadership roles with agendas that had no room for compromise. At the same time that the Republican party was spreading in the North, the two-party system in Alabama was dying. Unionism remained strong in north Alabama, but most politicians scurried to join the cause of Southern rights.

In the ten years before 1855, William L. Yancey had been a central figure in Alabama politics, serving one term in Congress but retiring because of his disillusionment with political parties. He then moved to the role of "outside agitator," advocating a party based upon Southern principles and Southern rights. Yancey saw clearly the issue of federal power to dictate the type of property a citizen might own and how average Alabamians would perceive such an act as tyrannical and despotic and a violation of their concept of freedom. Yancey conceived the Alabama Platform as a way to unite the South, but Unionism was too strong and the death of John C. Calhoun and the failure of the Nashville convention assured the success of the Compromise of 1850. William Rufus King's death in 1853 left a void in the Jacksonian-Unionist camp in Alabama, one that neither Houston, Clemens, or Cobb could fill. The Kansas-Nebraska Act unleashed an abolitionist free-soil backlash that destroyed the Whig party. Yancey's dream of a Southern nation seemed more probable; his waiting was coming to an end.

ELEVEN

The Secession Crisis

IN fall 1855 the continued violence in Kansas concerned Alabamians, as did the surprising successes of Republican party candidates in northeastern and midwestern congressional elections. When the Thirty-fourth Congress convened in December 1855, Republicans composed 45 percent of the House of Representatives. Sectionalism was aggravated when the House speakership contest took two months and 133 ballots before a Republican was elected. Fledgling Republicans hoped Kansas would explode while all eyes were on the fall presidential elections. In the summer, Alabama planter John Horry Dent wrote a Northern relative of his wife that under the present political conditions, the South surely must secede from "a Union with the North, or give up all pretensions to honour and self-respect." If Northerners doubted it, they "little understand the Southern Character. . . . No Sir, we will quit the Union so soon as you elect a Black Republican President, cost what it may in blood or treasure."[1]

By the end of the year, both the Whig party and the American party had lost favor with the people of Alabama. To voters, the Democratic party seemed the only viable alternative, but it was rife with factional divisions—including States' Rights Democrats, Union Democrats, and former Whigs. At an organizational meeting in Montgomery in January 1856, William L. Yancey adopted Dixon Lewis's recommendation that he work to control the Democratic party rather than agitate for a Southern party. Yancey now insisted that the protection of the South could only be assured through the national Democratic party. The state Democrats adopted Yancey's 1848 Alabama Platform, which denied popular sovereignty and insisted that the federal government had a constitutional obligation to protect slave property in the territories.

Before the Democratic party met to select a candidate, proslavery settlers were massacred in Kansas and the Sumner-Brooks attack occurred in the Senate chamber, both escalating the sectional crisis. When the convention opened in Cincinnati, many delegates considered incumbent Democratic president Franklin Pierce too weak to defeat the

Republicans. Thomas Hubbard Hobbs, a member of the Alabama delegation, explained that Alabama "voted first for Pierce, & then for Douglas because we wished the next contest to be decided on the sole issue of the Kansas bill," but the Alabama delegates were "satisfied" with the nomination of James Buchanan.[2] The former Pennsylvania senator had been a close personal friend of the late William Rufus King, and he had many friends in Alabama.

The 1856 presidential campaign was especially significant in north Alabama where Yancey took to the stump to defend President Pierce and support Buchanan; Jeremiah Clemens attacked the Democratic party, Pierce, and Buchanan; and Henry W. Hilliard supported Fillmore and the American party ticket. Yancey's discussion of Southern rights issues in north Alabama, where Unionism was strong, helped that section better understand how south Alabama viewed the crisis. For many citizens of the Tennessee Valley, it was their first occasion to hear Yancey speak. The presidential election was significant because it alerted Alabama moderates and Unionists to the growing strength of the Republican party in the North and convinced them that Republicans would not compromise or cooperate with the South. The proslavery decision of the Supreme Court in the 1857 Dred Scott case (with Justice John A. Campbell of Alabama concurring) only temporarily allayed such fears.

Following the election of Buchanan, there was no state party to oppose the Alabama Democratic party in the gubernatorial election, but there were plenty of Democratic candidates who wanted Governor Winston's responsibilities. William F. Samford of Macon County and former congressman David Hubbard from Lawrence County represented the most extreme Southern rights position. John Cochran of Eufaula had a long record of Southern rights activities, while Andrew B. Moore of Perry County and John E. Moore of Florence were more moderate. After three days and twenty-six ballots, the 230 delegates agreed on Judge Andrew Barry Moore, and he was unopposed when he was elected in summer 1857.

As Governor Winston's second term drew to a close, he considered challenging the reelection of C. C. Clay, Jr., to the U.S. Senate. When his message to the legislature included a reapportionment law based upon the federal ratio (instead of the white basis), it was immediately interpreted as a ploy to gain Black Belt support for his candidacy. North Alabama already viewed Winston's ambition with suspicion, because Clay's seat was the north Alabama one, while the legislature opposed Winston because of his vetoes and his opposition to state aid to railroads. State aid for railroad construction was a popular concept in the 1850s, but throughout his two terms Governor Winston believed the state could not "without violation of principle, take money from the people to lend to corporations, monopolies or individuals."[3] When the legislature refused to heed his warning, Winston ultimately vetoed thirty-six bills. Although the legislature overrode twenty-seven, the governor, through technicalities and various means, frustrated the legislature's wishes, and no state money went to support internal improvements during Winston's second term.

In 1853 the Montgomery *Advertiser* had cautioned against "too much distrust of companies," but two years later it warned that corporations backed by money and talented men would accomplish their goals by "fair or foul means" and in doing so would "debauch the public morals, corrupt legislation, undermine the freedom of the press, and disarm opposition either by bribery or by strong and overawing denunciations." The *Advertiser* anticipated that the "'mania' for railroads" would soon vanish and the state would be saved from investing in "a hundred ill digested and unneeded railways."[4] Although by the end of his term in 1857 Winston had some popular support among the voters, the legislature defeated his senatorial bid. William Garrett, a former speaker of the house, noted that on the state-aid issue "the moral heroism of the occasion" was with the governor, as he "contended single-handed against a formidable majority in both houses of the Legislature."[5]

One interpretation notes the significance of the state aid to railroads crisis in undermining the confidence the masses had in the state legislature. The public viewed the Alabama lawmakers as yielding "the welfare of the state to the needs of corporations." It is ironic that when Alabama went to war within a few years, the "welfare of the state" was imperiled by the paucity of railroads connecting areas without navigable waters. The confrontation between the governor and the legislature strengthened "immeasurably the citizenry's sense that its liberty was imperiled." According to this analysis, the controversy advanced the fortunes of those who claimed "to know the precise nature of the danger and to be able to deal with it" and set the stage for the climax of secession.[6]

Yancey was the leader of the faction that had most to gain, and in spring 1858 he had an opportunity to influence representatives from throughout the South who were in Montgomery to attend the Southern Commercial Convention. Beginning in the 1830s, commercial conventions provided a forum for an exchange of agricultural information and for supporting a more diversified economy, encouraging manufacturing, and promoting railroad expansion. Unfortunately, the conventions were often sidetracked by political topics and as a result were generally unsuccessful in achieving their goals. The South—and Alabama—failed to appreciate that many economic problems were deeply rooted in social patterns, a slave-labor system, and staple crop agriculture.

When the Montgomery convention opened, Yancey gave an eloquent plea in support of resuming the African trade and turned the convention into a debate upon Southern rights and secession. Edmund Ruffin, who was in the Virginia delegation, was impressed by Yancey's eloquence and power as a speaker but noted that "he is so fluent that he does not know when to stop." Before returning to Virginia, Ruffin had occasion to visit with Yancey at the Exchange Hotel. The old agricultural reformer suggested that Fourth of July celebrations should be used to capture the popular imagination of the South, with Yancey tying Southern independence and the South's revolution to the American cause against the British.[7]

The Alabama planters who gathered in Montgomery for the commercial convention were enjoying a prosperous economy. The panic of 1857 had little effect upon cotton, and prices remained high throughout the 1850s, reaching 13.5 cents in 1857. Alabama cotton production almost doubled between 1850 and 1860, with about half of the cotton produced in the Black Belt. The Tennessee Valley planted more grains and diversified its crops, and cotton production increased very little. But the Wiregrass, the southwest, and the hill counties showed a cotton production growth of more than 200 percent between 1850 and 1860. In Blount, Walker, Winston, and Covington counties the increase topped 300 percent, indicating that farmers in these regions were moving into a market economy with cash-crop production.[8]

Much of the success of Alabama's improved agricultural production may be traced to Dr. Noah B. Cloud, a Macon and Montgomery County planter and agricultural reformer. A South Carolina native and Philadelphia-trained physician, Cloud was a scientific farmer who read widely, conducted experiments on his land, and kept extensive records of his yields. Cloud believed that the South invested too much of its resources in land and labor and failed to maintain the fertility of the soil. He advocated applying abundant fertilizer—guano, cottonseed, barnyard manure, leaves, table food scraps, and pine straw—to enrich the soil and increase the yield. He thought that fields should fallow the year before planting cotton, and crops should be diversified and rotated. Better seeds should be planted, and picking, ginning, and bailing should be accomplished with more care.

Cloud promoted his ideas through letters and, after 1853, through his journal the *Cotton Planter*. Four years later Cloud combined the *Cotton Planter* with another agricultural newspaper, the *Soil of the South*, and the journal became the *American Cotton Planter and Soil of the South*. Cloud advocated the production of additional livestock on farms, the planting of vineyards and orchards, and the use of more melons, peas, and beans to supplement plantation food. He supported state and local agricultural societies, planters' conventions, exhibitions, and cattle shows. County and state fairs became important social events in rural Alabama as well as a forum for the exchange of agricultural information.

During the Civil War there was a shortage of food for families in north Alabama with absent soldier-fathers, and few provisions could be sent to Confederate troops. But for Cloud's agricultural leadership in the 1850s, the starvation in Alabama could have been worse. His contributions were often overlooked by his contemporaries because of his politics. When Southern rights was orthodoxy, Cloud was a Unionist; in the decade after the war, he supported the Republican party, was branded a scalawag, and served an unhappy term as state superintendent of education. In the Reconstruction period Cloud continued to support industrial development, and he encouraged immigration into Alabama.

Cloud's activities and the agricultural reform movement played a role in increasing the value of improved farmland in Alabama from $64,323,224 in 1850 to $175,824,622 in 1860. Acreage under cultivation rose from just over four million acres in 1850 to more than six million acres ten years later. Alabama ranked second nationally in cotton production in 1860, but war conditions and the blockade of Southern ports shifted the emphasis from cotton to food production.

Although the antebellum commercial conventions always addressed the lack of Southern manufactures, only minimal progress was made in promoting industry and manufacturing in Alabama during the decade before war came in 1861. Those who advocated secession seemed oblivious to the possibility that independence might have to be won by force of arms. The existence of minerals in the north Alabama hill country was known by the early settlers, but it was not appreciated and was little exploited. When the English geologist Sir Charles Lyell visited the state in 1846, he shocked the Black Belt planters by announcing that although their soil was rich, the wealth of Alabama was in the hill country. This assessment was reinforced by Professor Michael Toumey of the University of Alabama, who was appointed the first state geologist two years after Lyell's visit. Yet in 1859 when the state legislature was considering a railroad route through the section, south Alabama planter interests opposed, and Judge Thomas A. Walker of Calhoun County, who was involved with the Tennessee and Selma Railroad Company, castigated the hill country "as so poor that a buzzard would have to carry provisions on his back or starve to death on his passage."[9]

The most successful and widely recognized industrialist in antebellum Alabama had long appreciated the potential of the mineral district. Daniel Pratt, a native of New Hampshire, was an apprenticed carpenter who traveled South, learned about gin manufacturing in Clinton, Georgia, from Samuel Griswold, then in 1833 moved to Alabama. Pratt established a gin factory north of Montgomery on Autauga Creek. Later, he acquired 2,000 acres north along the creek and created a complete company town patterned after those he remembered in New England. He constructed houses and churches for his workers and named his village Prattville. He appreciated the value of education and built a good school for the children. By 1846 the community was almost self-sufficient. The town had its own grist- and flour mills, stores, blacksmith, tin and printing shops, and a sawmill. In 1851 *De Bow's Review* described a village of 800 people with thirty-five houses, noting a communitywide prohibition against the sale of spirits.

In his extensive factory operations, Pratt employed both white and slave labor. In the beginning he was committed to poor white labor. He articulated a goal of wishing to dignify labor in the South and "give the laboring class an opportunity of not only making an independent living, but to train up workmen who could give dignity to labor."[10] But by the 1850s, with white labor proving unsatisfactory and the secessionists attacking his Northern birth and loyalty to the South, Pratt invested heavily in slaves and began to use them in his factories. Pratt's 2,800 spindles and 100 looms produced 2,000 bales of osnaburg a year. The woolen mill made kersey, a coarse ribbed woolen cloth used for coats and work clothes. Pratt's fabric was not accepted in the local market until his superintendent, Gardner Hale, devised a scheme to stamp the material with a foreign name and ship it to New York and then back to Alabama. After the merchandise was accepted by buyers in Montgomery, Hale and Pratt announced the hoax. Another Pratt factory produced windows, doors, and blinds. The industrial village also fabricated metal products and manufactured carriages, and one unit built bridges designed by Pratt, who also financed plank roads.

Despite his diversified investments, Pratt's fortune was based primarily upon the manufacture and sale of high-quality cotton gins. In 1859, of total income of $681,637, almost one-third came from his gin manufacturing. His operations were streamlined and extensive, located in a large three-story building with an elevator. By 1860 he was producing 1,500 gins each year and employing several hundred workers. That year Alabama was the leading manufacturer of gins in the nation, and Pratt produced about one-fourth of the gins made in the state. He imported Sheffield sheet steel from England for the saws of his gin, but from the beginning of his operations in Alabama, he purchased homemade iron from Shelby and Bibb County ironmakers for the gin castings. Pratt's foundry worked 100 tons of pig iron a year.

Pratt encouraged Alabama planters to diversify their holdings and invest in manufacturing. Through his friendship with Noah B. Cloud, in the columns of Cloud's *American Cotton Planter,* and by his letters to

Alabama newspapers, Pratt extolled the virtues of manufacturing. In 1847 he insisted that $50,000 invested in manufacturing would return a greater profit than the same amount put into agriculture, noting that farming wore out the land while industrial investment created permanent wealth. In 1849 Pratt warned that industrial development was retarded by Alabama's attitude toward banks and by bank policies that limited credit to agricultural investments. He declared that banks were necessary evils, for manufacturing could not prosper without them. Although Pratt had some support in Alabama, he was opposed by many and was warned to confine himself to manufacturing cotton goods. In 1850 Pratt helped write the Autauga Southern Rights Union resolutions, which stated that Alabama must encourage manufacturers in case the state ever needed to protect itself.

Pratt's contribution to his adopted state was extensive and long range. His contacts with the early iron industry in Alabama, especially with Horace Ware and his Shelby Iron Company, and his knowledge and appreciation of the riches of the mineral district to the north of Prattville caused Pratt to purchase large tracts of mineral lands. The capital he accumulated from his gin factory, combined with his inclination to save and invest, allowed Pratt to amass one of the largest Alabama fortunes of the period, one with excellent cash flow. With family and business associates living in New England, Pratt must have maintained wide investments and bank accounts in the North, for his personal wealth survived the Civil War. His knowledge of the mineral district and his commitment to developing Alabama's industrial potential led him to risk capital in the Birmingham district. Through his own involvement and the business activities of his son-in-law, Henry Fairchild DeBardeleben, who had married Pratt's only child, Ellen, Pratt played a leading role in establishing the iron industry in Alabama by purchasing homemade pig iron for his gins and, after the war, by investing his capital in potentially lucrative, but risky, New South ventures.

The cry for increased manufacturing was buttressed by Southern nationalism, which preached economic independence from the North. Besides Daniel Pratt's mill, other textile mills developed in Alabama. The Swift Creek mill near Autaugaville, with 3,500 spindles, 100 looms, and forty workers' houses in a mill village, represented a $100,000 investment in 1849. The factory produced osnaburg, sheeting, thread, and yarn and at first employed mostly women. The Bell Factory in Huntsville, the Globe Factory in Florence, and the Decatur Factory were running 5,500 spindles in 1850. In 1858 Martin Weakley and Company in Florence operated 23,000 spindles. Daniel Scott's Tuscaloosa Manufacturing Company in Bibb County was the center of an extensive textile mill operation running 25,000 spindles and 50 looms. The mills of

Marks and Barnett and the looms located at Tallassee Falls both thrived. Jones M. Gunn operated a mill in Dallas County on steam power and ran 1,152 spindles. In 1865 he was selling osnaburg for Confederate uniforms for $1 to $4 a yard. Montgomery, Mobile, and DeKalb counties had a few small manufacturers. In 1860 Alabama had fourteen textile mills producing cloth goods worth more than $1 million and employing more than 1,300 people. But industrial development in the decade progressed more slowly than its promoters wished. Certainly the unstable banking system, the general distrust of corporations, and an inadequate transportation system where there were no navigable rivers discouraged manufacturing and industrial investments in Alabama.

By the late 1850s the state was covered with a system of roads, somewhat improved, and a few turnpikes and plank roads. The roads linked county courthouses with crossroad villages, towns with river landings, and cities with the backcountry. Stagecoaches ran regular routes, carrying mail, passengers, and small merchandise. More bridges made fording Alabama's numerous creeks easier than it had been for the early settlers, and ferries were available at major river crossings. The preferred method of transportation, the steamboat, was satisfactory, but much of the state was not blessed with navigable rivers. The iron horse was the answer.

In Alabama railroad routes were initially surveyed to facilitate but not supplant river transportation. The Tuscumbia Railway Company was chartered by the legislature in 1830, and its two-mile road when completed in 1832 was one of the earliest railroads in the nation. Financed by wealthy Tennessee Valley planters concerned with marketing their cotton in New Orleans, the rail line avoided only part of the Muscle Shoals on the Tennessee River, and economically it was a disaster. Equipment was inadequate, the train kept no regular schedule, and the iron rails were too light and began to sag. Often the steam engine would not run and mules pulled the cars. By 1834 the railway stretched forty-six miles from Tuscumbia to Decatur, avoiding all the shoals. In 1847 the road was sold and eventually became part of the Memphis and Charleston Railroad.

The second railway in Alabama, the Montgomery Railroad Company, chartered in 1832, was also financed by planters. The route would connect Montgomery with the cotton-growing areas of east Alabama and west Georgia and the Chattahoochee River at West Point. The railroad would cross the Creek country, running north of the Old Federal Road. Construction money was raised in Montgomery and Mobile, where the merchants and cotton factors expected windfall profits from increased trade. Abner McGehee, a wealthy planter and part of the Broad River group of settlers who contributed so much to the development of Alabama towns and commerce, was the moving force behind the railroad. McGehee's uncle, John B. Scott, and Scott's son-in-law, Charles T. Pollard, joined in the venture. McGehee's nephew, Frank M. Gilmer, later was a leader in the South and North Railroad.

These planters were interested in railroads for more than shipping cotton. They anticipated commercial advances and profit from a rail connection to Montgomery. Scott used slave labor to grade the roads only after the lay-by season, and this policy slowed construction. Indian unrest in the Creek country, the panic of 1837, and shortages of capital also delayed completion of the road. In 1840 Pollard convinced the legislature to provide a loan of $1,200,000 to the company. In that year, Alabama citizens, discouraged by the slow pace of railroad development, approved more road construction. Disgusted with an attitude he considered backward, the editor of *De Bow's Review* rebuked Alabama: "God may have given you coal and iron sufficient to work the spindles and navies of the world, but they will sleep in your everlasting hills until the trumpet of Gabriel shall sound unless you can do something better than build turnpikes."[11]

Undaunted by Alabamians' lack of confidence in railroads, Pollard continued construction on the Montgomery–West Point line that reached Franklin by the end of 1840. But it was seven more years before tracks ran to Auburn and eleven years before trains entered West Point. Sir Charles Lyell rode the West Point line on his visit in 1846, describing cars with benches and a center aisle. Young boys entered the train at each stop to sell apples and biscuits, jumping off at the last moment, but he judged them not in danger because the cars never traveled more than fifteen miles an hour. When Thomas Hubbard Hobbs left his home in Athens in 1855 bound for the opening of the Alabama legislature in Montgomery, he was able to travel the Memphis and Charleston to Chattanooga, the Western and Atlantic to Atlanta, and finally the West Point line to Montgomery.

Mobile took a positive stand on railroad construction as a way to foster urban commercial growth. Businessmen, ever sensitive to competition from New Orleans, recognized the need to find new markets, and plans were developed in 1847 for a rail line to reach from Mobile to the Ohio River. When Stephen A. Douglas visited Mobile in 1849, railroad investors discussed with him the need for federal aid to construct the line. Although the Alabama congressional delegation was generally opposed to federal aid to railroads, William Rufus King supported the plan and agreed to rally Southern approval behind Douglas's Illinois Central Railroad in return for the latter's inclusion of the Mobile and Ohio.

Mobile residents were so certain that a railroad connection to the Midwest would mean prosperity that they approved a special railroad tax to help finance construction. But Governor Winston, who was opposed to state aid, thwarted all efforts of the state legislature to provide support. Capitalists' British loans were finally secured to complete the line, and by 1861 tracks were in use from Mobile to Columbus, Kentucky. In advertisements, the Mobile and Ohio Railroad stressed the safety of travel by railroad compared with the dangerous voyages down the Mississippi on steamboats that caught fire and often sank. Cotton and produce once bound for New Orleans now went by rail to Mobile, but not in the quantity Mobilians anticipated.

The need to connect the Tennessee River with the Alabama River was the reason behind the 1836 charter of the Selma and Tennessee Railroad. When the plan was revived in 1850, the name was changed to the Alabama and Tennessee Rivers Railroad. By 1853 the line reached from Selma to Montevallo and by 1861 was completed through Talladega to Blue Mountain (Anniston). The railroad linked the Coosa Valley cotton farmers with Selma and river portage to Mobile. Although the line failed to reach its destination of Gunter's Landing on the Tennessee River before war stopped construction, the rail line to Montevallo and the spur built during the war to Brock's Gap were important because they carried iron from the Shades Valley furnaces to the Confederate Naval Ordnance Works at Selma. The Alabama and City of Montgomery Railroad Company, which was chartered in 1836 to construct a road connecting Montgomery with Mobile and Pensacola, had a difficult time until it was taken over by Charles Pollard, president of the Montgomery and West Point Railroad, in 1853. By 1860 the road reached Pollard on the Florida line.

Railroad construction in the North was far ahead of Alabama's accomplishments in the 1850s. An extensive network of railroads crossed the Allegheny Mountains and bound the Midwest to the Northeast. Produce from the American heartland, once sent by river packet to New Orleans, now traveled on iron rails to Buffalo and New York City. The close economic ties of the upper and lower Mississippi Valley were loosened, and the South stood alone as the sectional crisis grew. Much of Alabama remained isolated, untouched by navigable water or iron rails, despite 743 miles of track completed by 1860.

Yet considering the problems, Alabama was fortunate to complete construction of so many miles. Small farmers distrusted corporations. Railroad building was difficult for a state where wealth was measured by cotton production and surplus capital was traditionally invested in land and slaves. Without a stable banking system, and despite a governor who had popular support for his adamant opposition to state aid for private corporations, railroad building and industrial development made surprising progress. A historian who has studied nineteenth-century

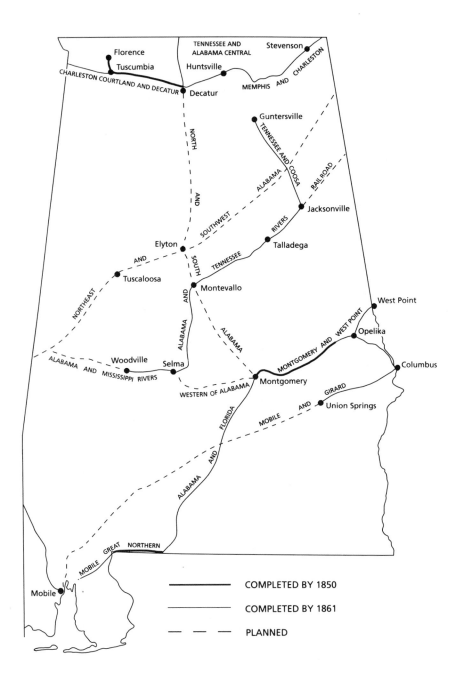

Railroads in Alabama, 1861

TENNESSEE AND
ALABAMA CENTRAL

Stevenson

Florence

Tuscumbia

CHARLESTON COURTLAND AND DECATUR

Huntsville

MEMPHIS AND CHARLESTON

Decatur

NORTH AND

Guntersville

TENNESSEE AND COOSA

ALABAMA

SOUTHWEST

RAIL ROAD

Jacksonville

RIVERS

Elyton

Talladega

TENNESSEE

AND

NORTHEAST

Tuscaloosa

SOUTH

AND

Montevallo

ALABAMA

ALABAMA

West Point

Opelika

MONTGOMERY AND WEST POINT

Columbus

ALABAMA AND MISSISSIPPI RIVERS

Woodville

Selma

WESTERN OF ALABAMA

Montgomery

GIRARD

MOBILE AND

Union Springs

FLORIDA

ALABAMA AND

MOBILE GREAT NORTHERN

Mobile

COMPLETED BY 1850

COMPLETED BY 1861

PLANNED

development in Alabama contends that "much of Alabama's elite—including planters—favored a modern economy well before the war," that "the distinction between the planters and the bourgeoisie has been overdrawn for Alabama," and that it was insufficient capital and inadequate public and private credit and "not ideological opposition to industrialization that limited economic development."[12]

The man responsible for making the most of Alabama's economic resources was Governor Andrew Barry Moore, who was destined to lead Alabama during the critical period of secession, independence, and the early months of the Confederacy. A native of South Carolina, Moore followed his father west to Marion in Perry County when he was eighteen years old. He taught school, then practiced law, and was elected to the state legislature as a Democrat. His political career was hampered by his support for the white basis of apportionment (opposed by his Black Belt constituency) and by the great Whig strength in Perry County. A tall, well-built man, Moore opposed secession and was often in the Union Democratic camp. Because the Democratic party had no opposition, Moore's reelection in 1859 was challenged by the Yancey faction. William F. Samford, described as "one of the most aggressive secessionists in the state," ran on an "Independent Southern Rights" ticket but was overwhelmingly defeated.[13] Most Alabamians still looked to the national Democratic party to defend Southern rights.

Moore directed a variety of state welfare programs during his two administrations: the hospital for the insane at Tuscaloosa opened under the direction of Dr. Peter Bryce, the school for the blind at Talladega began operations, and state support for education was increased. But Moore is more remembered for his leadership in the secession crisis and during the first year of war. A moderate, Moore resisted Southern rights activists who tried to push him on a more radical course. John Brown's raid at Harper's Ferry, Virginia, in October 1859 caused Governor Moore to reevaluate his position, and he encouraged the legislature to strengthen the state militia. Volunteer units organized by counties were supported by an appropriation of $200,000. The legislature also chartered the Southern Firearms Company to supply the Alabama militia with arms. Before adjourning, the legislature passed a resolution in February instructing the governor to call an election should a Republican party candidate be elected president during the fall elections.[14]

In January 1860 the state Democratic party met to elect delegates to the national convention scheduled to gather in Charleston, South Carolina, in April. A "grim sort of quietude and determinism" prevailed. There was a struggle to gain control of the party between the Yancey forces and conservatives under the leadership of John Forsyth, editor of the Mobile *Register,* who supported Stephen A. Douglas's nomination. A young John Tyler Morgan chaired the credentials committee, and he confirmed Yancey delegates. With his uncompromising position, Yancey won control of the convention. The Alabama delegates were instructed to abide by the Alabama Platform and withdraw from the Democratic convention if the protection of slave property in the territories was not included in the Democratic platform. The party sent a stellar delegation to Charleston that included such leaders as Yancey, Francis S. Lyon, John A. Winston, Reuben Chapman, Leroy Pope Walker, and Alexander Beaufort Meek.

The convention assembled on April 23 in Charleston—of all Southern cities, the strongest citadel of the fire-eaters. The city was overcrowded, and accommodations and food were expensive. Northern delegates were amazed by the passion for Southern rights they observed in the people of Charleston and by the united determination to defend the South that permeated the Southern delegations. Northerners were also shocked by the hostility they found for Northern interests. While the convention waited four days for the report of the platform committee, all eyes were on William L. Yancey, who sat quietly in his seat. Northern journalists speculated whether Yancey could really lead the South out of the Democratic party.

Two platform reports were finally presented to the convention: the majority report, favorable to the South, and the minority report, supporting Douglas's popular sovereignty. When the issue went to the floor for debate, Yancey rose to speak for the South, and ladies in the gallery threw flowers. Brushing aside a tear, Yancey insisted on federal protection of slave property in the territories—his Alabama Platform. With his oratory and his position, he took the galleries and the crowds outside in the streets. His every word was met with thunderous applause. But he could not sway Northern delegates, and he did not have the votes on the convention floor to force the Alabama Platform on the Democratic party. After the ballot was announced, Leroy Pope Walker read a protest, and the Alabama delegation rose and walked slowly from the convention. Other Deep South states followed. The convention, in shock, adjourned without a nomination, agreeing to meet again in early summer.

By midsummer four candidates were campaigning for the presidency: Stephen A. Douglas, nominated on a Northern Democratic ticket favoring popular sovereignty; John C. Breckinridge, nominated by Southern Democrats on the Alabama Platform; John Bell, nominated by a group of Whigs on the Constitutional Union ticket with a compromise platform; and Abraham Lincoln, nominated by the Republican party, with a platform that would prohibit slavery in the territories.

Yancey toured the North speaking for Breckinridge, and Douglas campaigned in Alabama. Neither was successful. Northern states went for

Lincoln, and Douglas carried only five Alabama counties: Mobile in the south and Lauderdale, Lawrence, Madison, and Marshall in the Tennessee Valley. The former Whig John Bell won five counties also, including Greene and Macon in the Black Belt, Butler in the red clay counties, and Covington in the Wiregrass. Breckinridge swept the rest of the state. Although the anti-Breckinridge newspapers charged Yancey with dividing the Democratic party and assuring a Republican victory, a careful tabulation of Republican votes by states proved Lincoln would have won over any combination of his opponents.

The election of Lincoln and the strong secessionist attitudes presented problems for staunch Unionists. For two Northern-born planters, the crisis was especially difficult. William P. Gould, a rich Whig planter in the Black Belt, expected John Bell to win. After he recognized Lincoln's election as inevitable, he realized he would have to change his views or "stand alone." Henry Watson returned to his home in Greensboro from a Northern visit before Christmas 1860 to an electrified political climate. He cautioned delay, hoping for some compromise, but soon "ceased to expect that Reason will resume her sway."[15] In north Alabama there was talk of forming a new state, to be called Nickajack, composed of the Alabama, Georgia, and Tennessee areas that opposed secession. When secession came, Winston County threatened to secede from Alabama and form "the Free State of Winston."

Governor Moore was determined to wait for the presidential electors to cast their votes before responding to the legislature's resolution to call for elections to a secession convention. But he announced that he would issue the summons on December 24. Candidates began organizing immediately. Yancey and his followers were known as "straight-out secessionists" and advocated immediate secession. They were opposed by the "cooperationists," who favored withdrawing from the Union in cooperation with other Southern states; by others who would rather cooperate but ultimately would favor secession; by Unionists who wished to have the North address Southern grievances; and by those ultra-Unionists who were adamantly opposed to secession.[16]

The campaign was spirited. Yancey spoke for immediate secession, insisting that war would not come. The election results followed the traditional sectional division within the state. North Alabama elected cooperationist candidates, and south Alabama supported immediate secessionists. The only exceptions were Calhoun County (voting with the south) and Conecuh County (electing cooperationists). The issue of secession was never submitted to the people, but by the election of convention delegates, the voters spoke and the immediate secessionists won a slim majority (54–46) of delegates. The popular vote was 35,693 for immediate secessionist candidates and 28,181 for cooperationists.

The delegates who gathered in Montgomery for the opening of the secession convention were experienced politicians, middle-aged men who were mostly lawyers and planters. Seventy-nine of the 100 members owned slaves, and the typical delegate was worth about $35,000. Secessionists were slightly more affluent than cooperationists because the sections they represented were the wealthy cotton-growing areas of south and central Alabama.[17]

In Montgomery the public houses were filled with people, and excitement rippled through the crowded streets as the delegates arrived. Every man was present when the convention assembled in the chambers of the house of representatives on January 7. Although the cooperationists still hoped to win control of the convention, the election of the secessionist William M. Brooks as permanent chairman foretold the outcome. On the first day the galleries were filled and the commotion was so loud that the convention decided to bar visitors from the hall. After vigorous debate and despite delaying tactics, the vote on the ordinance of secession was taken on January 11, and Alabama became a "free, sovereign, and independent state."[18] North Alabama cooperationists tried to have the secession ordinance submitted to the people for ratification, but south Alabama secessionists opposed, insisting that the election to the convention was a referendum and that the urgency of the situation would not allow time for an election. Seven cooperationists bowed to the inevitable and voted for secession. The ballot was 61 for and 39 against.

Just before the secession vote was taken by the convention, within sight of the capitol, the Episcopal bishop of Alabama, Nicholas Hamner Cobbs, was stricken by a fatal stroke. An opponent of secession, which he believed could not be accomplished peacefully, Cobbs had openly prayed that "if it was God's will" he be spared the anguish of living to see Alabama secede. He did not. Jeremiah Clemens, author of the minority report against secession, wrote his Huntsville friend George W. Neal on the night of January 11 that secession "was celebrated today by the firing of cannon and ringing of bells. Tonight bonfires are blazing, speeches are being made, music is swelling on the air, and every conceivable demonstration of joy and enthusiasm is everywhere being made." Clemens could not restrain his tears when the American flag was lowered and the new flag of Alabama, made by the ladies of Montgomery, was raised. He warned Neal that he envisioned "storms that are gathering," and he could "not see how we are to pass through them."[19]

The causes of secession have long been analyzed and debated. White Alabamians, steeped in the doctrines of individualism, freedom, and Jacksonian democracy, yet yoked to the institution of slavery, which denied freedom, were painfully aware of the consequences of a loss of freedom.[20] White Alabamians certainly felt threatened by a Republican party opposed to the protection of slave property in the territories and influenced by militants whose stated goal was the abolition of slavery.

The monetary loss of slave property—some $200 to $300 million of Alabama capital—was just as unthinkable to slaveholders who owned one or two slaves as it was to large planters who had fortunes invested. The destruction of a controlled and dependable labor system concerned both groups, but the issue of race was a significant factor, too. The editor of the Montgomery *Mail* acknowledged this significance when he wrote: "In the struggle for maintaining the ascendancy of our race in the South—our home—we see no chance for victory but in withdrawing from the Union. To remain in the Union is to lose all that white men hold dear in government. We vote to go out." Daniel Hundley wrote in December 1860 that it would not be the rich slaveholders who would suffer, for they had the means "speedily to take themselves and their fortunes out of a country once more delivered over to barbarism and besotted ignorance of Central Africa." The nonslaveholders and poorer whites would "suffer most" from emancipation of blacks that would "disfigure the whole fair face of this prosperous, smiling, and happy Southern land."[21] Alabamians interpreted coercion by the federal government on the issue of slavery a violation of individual rights. It was the right of self-determination they advocated, a Southern nation created through secession, which they believed was a state's constitutional right. But they were well aware that the right to own slaves lurked behind the shibboleth of Southern rights.

Patriotic parades and celebrations radiated from Montgomery as news of Alabama's secession spread across the land. When the ordinance was finally enrolled, some delegates who voted against secession signed it to present a united front. When Brooks dismissed the convention, he looked back on the grievances the South believed it suffered in the Union and predicted that "come what may, sink or swim, live or die, survive or perish, Alabama will never enter its ill-fated portals; no, *never-never-never.*"[22]

TWELVE

At War with the Union

ALABAMIANS hoped that secession could be accomplished peacefully and that the North would not try to use military force to coerce an independent South. The state was in poor condition to fight a war. Despite the iron ore and coal deposits in the mineral district, there were few iron furnaces and no railroads into the hill country. In fact, vast areas of the state were isolated without river or rail transportation and without telegraphic communication. Banks were weak and had little specie accumulation. Most of the manufactured goods—plows, tools, sewing needles, buttons, nails, woolen materials, machinery parts— were supplied by Northern or foreign industries. Planters relied upon imported flour, sugar, coffee, textiles, and especially salt to preserve meats, and mules were regularly purchased from Missouri and Tennessee. Although small farms were more self-sustaining, their production of food depended upon white male labor that soon would be absent, gone to defend the South.

The state was vulnerable to invasion, its river systems providing highways for naval assault. Mobile Bay, defended by Forts Morgan and Gaines, could be blockaded, preventing cotton from being exported and imported supplies from reaching citizens or the military. Governor Moore was aware of the state's exposure and was concerned that hostilities would force Alabama to defend itself. In summer and fall 1860 the governor had agents in New England to purchase guns and ammunition for the state's militia. In July Ben McCulloch was unsuccessful in procuring rifles from Colonel Samuel Colt in Hartford, Connecticut, but Colonel James R. Powell managed to acquire rifles and pistols a few months later from the Ames Manufacturing Company of Chicopee, Massachusetts, and from the Tredegar Iron Works in Richmond. At one point Powell telegraphed Governor Moore from New York that such frantic buying of weapons was occurring in the city there were "no guns at any price" except on order.

Moore knew he needed all the specie presently in the state to purchase arms, and following the election of Lincoln he pressured state banks to stop redeeming notes with specie. He estimated the state would require $1 million to finance munitions. Three banks complied with the governor's request before the legislature mandated the suspension of specie by statute in February 1861. Saying he needed to stay informed, Moore sent commissioners to other Southern states to advise and consult with him about their circumstances, but the real purpose was to encourage the states to join Alabama in secession.

On January 3, 1861, Governor Moore activated six companies of the Volunteer Corps of Alabama, which had been created the previous year. The next day, in a daring move justified as necessary to secure peaceful secession, Moore ordered the state troops to seize federal installations in Alabama before the state seceded. By January 5, Fort Morgan, Fort Gaines, and the United States Arsenal at Mount Vernon were controlled by Alabama. The governor hastened to inform President James Buchanan of the action he took "to avoid and not to provoke hostilities between the State and Federal Government."[1] Moore was convinced the secession convention would take Alabama out of the Union, and Alabama would be a sovereign and independent republic no longer subject to the United States government. Immediate secessionists praised the governor's decision, but some cooperationists, like William S. Earnest of Jefferson County, believed the governor committed treason because Alabama was still in the Union.

By the end of January a spirit of unity had decreased opposition to secession. In some areas of the hill country there were even bursts of a martial spirit. In Elyton ladies fashioned blue cockades from cotton bolls, and at the Jefferson County courthouse homemade cannons sounded when news arrived of the secession of each Southern state. The state militia, legally composed of all male citizens but traditionally little more than a paper or ceremonial group, was reorganized and began to drill across the state. Volunteer companies were raised in every community; however, a shortage of arms required that men supply their own weapons and horses. Many wealthy leaders raised companies and furnished arms from their own resources. Daniel Pratt equipped the poorer members of the Prattville Dragoons with horses and weapons, and Joel E. Matthews of Selma contributed $15,000 to outfit local soldiers.

The secession convention gave Governor Moore the power to create an army for the defense of the state on January 19, 1861, and he promptly ordered the countryside scoured for arms. He sent J. W. Echols to purchase food for the army, made Duff Green quartermaster general of the state, and appointed George T. Goldthwaite adjutant general. The governor's quick response to secession made Alabama more prepared for independence and for defending itself than any other Southern state.

Florida had been unable to secure control of Fort Pickens at Pensacola, and Moore sent Alabama troops to assist. He believed that "the safety of the seceding states of the Gulf" was not secure while Fort Pickens remained in federal control. The First Alabama Regiment of Volunteers was in camp at Fort Barrancas, Florida, by the first of April 1861. Among the regiment were local companies with such colorful names as the Eufaula Pioneers, the Wilcox True Blues, the Tallapoosa Rifles, the Rough and Ready Pioneers, and the Red Eagles. A young volunteer, Edward Young McMorris, estimated that 35 percent of the recruits were under twenty-five years of age. The Eufaula volunteers established a handwritten camp newspaper, the *Pioneer Banner,* to send news to sweethearts left behind. Consisting of poetry, letters, and accounts of life in camp, it anticipated glories soon to be won and illustrated the typical romantic attitude toward the conflict. But McMorris's memoir was tempered by experience. He recalled the constant marches, "trudging along at drill through deep sand beneath a burning sun," stale-smelling barracks, arbors made of seaweed, rations of beef and baker's bread, and a hospital filled with men sick from measles, malaria, and typhoid fever.[2] Governor Moore was frustrated that an Alabama military leader was not able to take charge of the troops at Pensacola. Florida's commander, William H. Chase, who had constructed Fort Pickens when he was in the army, was slow to act and lost any early opportunity to seize the stronghold. After two months of service Alabama paid the regiment in specie, one of the few times specie was paid to Southern soldiers during the war.

In the critical period when Alabama was not in the Union but before the formation of the Confederacy, the secession convention assumed extensive powers, and probably unconstitutional ones, but the times were exceptional. The Alabama constitution had to be revised to reflect the elimination of federal control. Although there were differences of opinion about the extent of the convention's power and just how authority should be shared between the state legislature and "the convention of the people," all agreed on the necessity of dealing expeditiously with constitutional issues. The convention remained in session two months. Myriad details needed attention: drawing up new mail contracts, repealing statutes or constitutional provisions referring to Alabama's status in the Union, assuming ownership and control of the public lands within the state, establishing a valid currency, and clarifying the position of judicial officers. The convention also debated the African slave trade and refused to reopen it. After the formation of the Confederacy, the convention made Alabama part of the new nation and ratified the Confederate constitution. North Alabama representatives, still troubled that the issue of secession was not submitted to a vote of the people, argued that there should be a referendum on the Confederate constitution and the revisions to the Alabama constitution. But the convention declined, asserting that time was crucial and that the original constitution in Alabama was adopted by convention vote.[3]

During the critical days of January, before the secession vote, the convention was in close contact with Alabama's congressional delegation. Congressmen James L. Pugh and J. L. M. Curry arrived in Montgomery the day before the ballot and informed the convention that there could be no compromise short of accepting Lincoln's election. They counseled secession and predicted no hostilities. When news that Alabama had seceded reached Washington, D.C., the state's delegation met and determined to withdraw together on January 21, but Williamson R. W. Cobb refused to cooperate. Ever the Unionist, Cobb had made an impassioned plea for "gentlemen to come forward and endeavor to save the country," but his hope for compromise was now gone. Cobb remained in Congress until January 30, then delivered a long farewell address to the House, beseeching his "northern friends . . . to save the country."[4] When Cobb ran for the Confederate congress in 1861, he was defeated, but in 1863, with the glory of war fading, he was elected on a wave of antiwar sentiment.

Alabama's two senators played different roles after leaving Washington. C. C. Clay, Jr., a strong secessionist, became actively involved with the Confederate government, serving in the Senate and on a secret mission to Canada, where he planned a daring Confederate raid into Vermont. Benjamin Fitzpatrick, who opposed secession, retreated to his plantation near Wetumpka.

While the secession convention was meeting, Alabama responded to South Carolina's suggestion and invited representatives of the seceding states to Montgomery to discuss the formation of a Confederate government. The Alabama capital was centrally located with good rail connections to the east and was the home of secessionist leader William L. Yancey. The invitation was accepted, and the Confederate congress convened in the Alabama senate chambers on February 4, though opposition to Yancey in the Alabama convention denied him a place in the Alabama delegation. Six states were present: South Carolina, Georgia, Mississippi, Florida, Louisiana, and Alabama. Texas delegates arrived later.

Talk on the streets and discussion in the congress immediately centered on the selection of an executive officer for the new government. Yancey, who probably did more than any man to create the Southern nation, was not seriously considered, but there was some sentiment for South Carolina's fire-eater, Robert Barnwell Rhett. Georgia's Howell Cobb, Robert Toombs, and Alexander Stephens stood ready to serve. The honor went instead to Jefferson Davis—planter, U.S. Military Academy

Montgomery citizens witnessed the inauguration of Jefferson Davis as president of the Confederate States of America in front of the Alabama capitol, February 18, 1861. (Courtesy of the Alabama Department of Archives and History)

graduate, veteran of the Mexican War, former secretary of war, and U.S. senator from Mississippi. Despite the later controversy surrounding his leadership, Davis was an excellent choice given the options. When he was notified of his election, he was at his plantation, Brierfield, on the Mississippi River.

The route Davis took to Montgomery illustrated a serious problem the South and Alabama faced during the war: an inadequate transportation system and the near impossibility of moving troops and supplies through some areas. Davis traveled to Vicksburg by river, then by railroad to Jackson. Because there was no rail connection between Meridian and Montgomery, he took the railroad north to Grand Junction, then boarded the Memphis and Charleston Railroad and went across north Alabama to Chattanooga. From there he traveled south to Atlanta and southwest to West Point. At the Alabama border, Davis was met by a welcoming party and boarded a special car, complete with a four-poster bed, provided by the Montgomery and West Point Railroad.[5] Davis's arrival in Montgomery was hailed with artillery salutes. At the Exchange Hotel a crowd waited in the street, and Davis greeted it briefly, then retired. The throng called for Yancey. The Alabama fire-eater delivered a short address remembered for the words that, with Davis, "the man and the hour have met."[6]

Two years before the Confederate congress gathered, an English visitor described Montgomery as a "pleasant town" where "everyone looks clean and well off, schools and churches bright and white as new pennies. Children polite and pleasant."[7] Although Montgomery was a major river port and a commercial center, by most standards it was only a quiet little town when it became the "cradle of the Confederacy." Its 1860 population of 8,843 people was nearly equally divided between blacks and whites. In the three months the city served as the meeting place of the Confederate congress, the population almost doubled. United States military officers and enlisted men with Southern backgrounds gathered in the city to request commissions in the Confederate army. Office seekers and ambitious men crowded the city. Contractors wishing to build for the government, salesmen hawking their wares, and arms dealers all came seeking profits. Thomas Cooper DeLeon described the clamor of lobbyists and contractors "now gathered to gorge upon" the new nation. He wrote that by the hundreds they flocked, "blinking bleared eyes at any chance. . . . Busy and active at all hours, the lobby of the Exchange, when the crowd and the noise rose to the flood at night, smacked no little of pandemonium."[8]

William Howard Russell, a reporter for the London *Times*, was one of many newspaper correspondents who came to Montgomery. Fresh from his brilliant coverage of the Crimean War, Russell was critical of the capital city. He complained that his hotel room was filthy (full of flies and fleas), the weather hot, and the only cold water in the Alabama River. Food was served him from dirty plates on a "vile table-cloth," and the menu listed "as many odd dishes" as he ever saw, including "oyster-plants, 'possums, raccoons, frogs, and . . . toads." His diary included scathing descriptions and denunciations of slavery.[9] Another diarist preceded Russell to the capital. Mary Chesnut, the wife of former South Carolina senator James Chesnut, Jr., learned to reply when asked how she liked Montgomery: "Charming—I find it charming." Yet she protested in her diary about the flies and mosquitoes and felt that "a want of neatness and a want of good things to eat did drive us away."[10]

Despite overcrowded conditions that strained the entire community, Montgomery strove to be a gracious capital for the new nation, and many Alabamians played important roles in the government of the Confederacy. President Davis appointed Leroy Pope Walker secretary of war, but Walker resigned before the end of the year. Johnson Jones Hooper, creator of Simon Suggs and editor of the Montgomery *Mail,* became secretary of the Confederate congress and served until his death in Richmond in 1862. Henry Hotze accepted an assignment to direct Confederate propaganda in Europe. Hotze was born in Switzerland and was on the staff of the Mobile *Register* before the war. He served with the Mobile Cadets on the Virginia front for three months before being sent to London in 1862 as the Confederate commercial agent. Hotze was to promote the Confederacy, and he submitted articles to the principal British newspapers and in May established the *Index,* a weekly newspaper designed to influence public opinion.

As winter turned to spring, the Montgomery weather grew warmer and the hotels more crowded. Fears of impending illness made the Confederate congress apprehensive. When R. M. T. Hunter of Virginia passed "the marbleyards going to the capitol," he surveyed the tombstones and moaned that he would surely sicken and die in Montgomery.[11] The secession of Virginia provided an opportunity to move the capital. Virginia had prestige and industrial and agricultural resources, and a Virginia capital might influence the border states. A location so near Washington would bring the government closer to anticipated battlefields and make it easier to communicate with the generals. In May 1861 the Confederate government abandoned Montgomery and moved to Richmond. The change made the Virginia front more significant and diminished the importance of the western campaigns, where the war was to be lost.

Southerners hoped there would be no hostilities, but at the same time they prepared to defend the new nation. Abraham Lincoln remained silent on secession. North and South, the people waited for his inaugural address on March 4, 1861. He minced no words. Lincoln proclaimed the Union to be perpetual, older than the Constitution, and separation impossible. He placed the issue of civil war in the hands of his dissatisfied countrymen and reaffirmed the oath he had just taken to "preserve, protect and defend" the government of the United States. Meanwhile, in Montgomery the new national flag of the Confederacy, the stars and bars, probably the one designed by Marion's Nicola Marschall, was being raised at the Alabama capitol, precisely timed to symbolize defiance.

War was coming. But when and where? On March 31, Howell Cobb wrote his wife from Mobile that the port looked more like a military barracks than a commercial city. Fort Pickens at Pensacola, Fort Taylor at Key West, and Fort Sumter in Charleston's harbor were the coastal fortifications still in Union hands. The South demanded their evacuation. John Forsyth, editor of the Mobile *Register,* was part of the Confederate delegation sent to Washington to secure peaceful secession, but Secretary of State William H. Seward refused to receive the group. During these crucial days negotiations instead began between Seward and Alabama's justice John A. Campbell, who was initially inclined to resign his Supreme Court seat following Alabama's secession but remained on the Court at the urging of his colleagues. Campbell was caught in the middle trying to mediate the crisis. Seward assured him Fort Sumter would be evacuated, but Lincoln later took a firm stand and ordered a relief expedition. Campbell accused Seward and the administration of "systematic duplicity" in the negotiations and placed the blame of hostilities on the "equivocating conduct of the Administration."[12]

When the Confederate government became convinced that Fort Sumter would not be evacuated and Lincoln intended to resupply it, the decision was made to force the issue. Following a meeting of the Confederate cabinet in Montgomery, Secretary of War Leroy Pope Walker of Huntsville telegraphed General Pierre G. T. Beauregard to demand the fort's evacuation and, if refused, "to reduce it."[13] The Confederate bombardment began on April 12, and on April 15 Lincoln called the militia into service to enforce federal laws. Alabama's hopes for peaceful secession were shattered. Thomas Cooper DeLeon observed that the news of Sumter was received in Montgomery "like a thunder clap upon the most skeptical, that there was to be war after all!"[14]

A number of Alabamians took leadership roles in the Confederate military. Lieutenant General James Longstreet, although South Carolina-born and Georgia-reared, was living with his mother in Alabama when he was appointed to the U.S. Military Academy at West Point. One of Robert E. Lee's most reliable lieutenants in the Army of Northern Virginia, he was Alabama's most prominent general until he became a scapegoat for the Confederate defeat at Gettysburg and thus was blamed by some for the South's eventual failure to win independence. In the years after the war, Lee was deified and Longstreet vilified.

Major generals from Alabama included John H. Forney, who was teaching at the U.S. Military Academy in 1860 and later fought in Virginia and in the western theater at Vicksburg; Henry D. Clayton of Eufaula and Opelika, who commanded a regiment in Braxton Bragg's Kentucky campaign and took part in the battles around Chattanooga, Atlanta, and in east Tennessee; Jones M. Withers of Huntsville and Mobile, who was assigned to the defenses of Mobile, commanded troops at Shiloh, and was with General Kirby Smith in Kentucky; and Robert E. Rodes, a Virginian who was in Alabama working on the Great Southern Railroad when secession came. He raised the Warrior Guards, who were sent to Pensacola by Governor Moore, and later commanded troops at

Manassas in 1861 and the major battles of the Virginia theater. He was killed at the battle of Winchester in 1864.

Alabama commissioned thirty-six brigadier generals. Nine of these were U.S. Military Academy graduates, and ten were killed in battle. They commanded Alabama troops in virtually every major campaign. Among the better known generals were Edmund W. Pettus, Charles M. Shelley, Philip D. Roddey, Edward Asbury O'Neal, Pinkney D. Bowles, and Archibald Gracie, Jr., who was killed at Petersburg in 1864. Alabama had its own special idols, and as the war receded into history, the heroes became more numerous and their heroic deeds more valiant. After 1865 honorable service to the South and courage under fire were basic credentials for election to political offices. William C. Oates was one example. He lost his right arm near Petersburg in 1864 and was elected to Congress seven times and won a controversial race for governor in 1894.

John Pelham was one of Alabama's favorite heroes, but one who failed to survive the war. A native of Calhoun County, Pelham was a student at the U.S. Military Academy when the war began and earned his military reputation while in charge of J. E. B. Stuart's horse artillery in Stonewall Jackson's corps. Pelham could always be depended upon to have his guns at the right place, to aim them well, and to pour rapid fire upon the enemy. During the battle of Fredericksburg, General Lee praised Pelham's courage and in his report of the battle referred to him as the "gallant" Pelham, a name that stuck. A tall young man with blue eyes that "could see right through you," the Gallant Pelham was a flirt who blushed easily and laughed quickly, who loved to dance and court girls near his campsites. He fell mortally wounded at the battle of Kelly's Ford on March 17, 1863, and it was said that a half-dozen Virginia belles went into mourning. He was only twenty-four years old.

The Alabama Brigade, composed of Alabama regiments, was one of the most famous brigades in Lee's Army of Northern Virginia. The group built a reputation for fierce fighting at Seven Pines and at Salem Church routed the federals. Birkett D. Fry and Cadmus M. Wilcox led two groups of the brigade in General George E. Pickett's charge on the Union lines at Cemetery Ridge. The Alabama Brigade suffered 781 casualties in two days of fighting at Gettysburg. Alabama losses at Gettysburg were 1,750 dead plus others captured or wounded. John Caldwell Calhoun Sanders of Tuscaloosa led the brigade after Wilcox was promoted. Sanders was fatally wounded in 1864 while he commanded the Alabama Brigade in fighting south of Petersburg, Virginia. He was twenty-four years old.

Alabama's Raphael Semmes became the Confederate naval hero for all the South. Following a thirty-five-year naval career, Semmes moved to Mobile in 1849 to practice law. In February 1861 he was commissioned a commander in the Confederate navy, and five months later, after converting a steam packet into a commerce raider, he sailed the CSS *Sumter* to attack Northern commercial shipping. The *Sumter* captured eighteen ships in the next six months before being blockaded at Gibraltar. Semmes then took command of an English-built raider, the CSS *Alabama,* a ship as "fast as the wind" that Semmes sailed all over the world, terrorizing U.S. merchant vessels.

Josiah Gorgas, a Pennsylvania native who adopted Alabama when he married Amelia Gayle, daughter of former governor John Gayle, made significant contributions to the Southern cause as chief of ordnance for the Confederacy. Gorgas immediately recognized the need to procure Confederate arms abroad and sent University of Alabama chemistry professor Caleb Huse to Europe. Huse, a U.S. Military Academy graduate knowledgeable about foreign ordnance, made excellent selections. Gorgas noted with pride that Huse managed with little funds to purchase a fine supply of munitions and to run his department into nearly a half million sterling debt.

Gorgas was a master at improvisation, and he forced industrialization on the South. He was a competent administrator with a keen ability to judge men. For instance, he placed William LeRoy Broun, later president of the college at Auburn, in charge of the Richmond Arsenal, which was converted to weapons production. Gorgas, a wizard of logistics, produced miracles. Probably the greatest testament to his success was that although the Confederate army was often short of food, dressed in rags, and barefoot, a lack of munitions was never the reason it lost a battle.

To protect arms manufactures and position them closer to the army, Gorgas dispersed factories across the South. He appreciated Alabama's interior location and was familiar with the mineral district of the state. Investment in Alabama's industrial resources, neglected before 1860, was stimulated by the emergencies of war. Following the fall of New Orleans in 1862, the Mount Vernon Arsenal was moved to Selma and became the first of three major Confederate installations in the city. The Selma Arsenal made ammunition. The Selma Naval Ordnance Works manufactured artillery and, under Commander Catesby ap Roger Jones and George Peacock, produced a cannon every five days. The Confederate Naval Yard built ships and was noted for launching the CSS *Tennessee* in 1863 to defend Mobile Bay.

Selma's Confederate Nitre Works had responsibility for procuring niter from nearby limestone caves. When supplies were low, the agent in charge advertised in the Selma *Sentinel* for ladies to save the contents of their chamber pots—urine, a rich source of nitrogen to make gunpowder. Besides the government facilities, there were many small private arms plants in Selma. At the war's peak, perhaps as many as 10,000 workers were employed in Selma factories making munitions for the Confederacy. The long list of buildings and equipment destroyed by the Union raid on Selma in 1865 was an impressive testimony to the industrial complex operating there at the end of the war.

Selma became an important manufacturing center because the city had river and rail transportation, because the plantations in the area produced abundant food for workers, and because Selma had rail access to the iron ore and furnaces in the mineral district. Fifteen Alabama furnaces, most of them blown in after 1861, provided pig iron for the Confederacy. Five furnaces—Brierfield in Bibb County, Shelby in Shelby County, Tannehill in Tuscaloosa County, and Oxmoor and Irondale in Jefferson County—produced together more than ninety tons of pig iron a day. Horace Ware's Shelby Iron Company was reorganized and expanded but had difficulty dealing with the Confederate government while trying to maintain company assets. The Red Mountain Iron and Coal Company, formed by Frank M. Gilmer and John T. Milner, constructed extensive iron operations at Oxmoor. With support from the Richmond government, the company built a rail spur from Montevallo into the mineral district but only as far as Shades Mountain. The company was not able to secure enough blasting powder to cut through the sixty feet of solid rock it encountered there. Thus, pig iron was transported by ox-drawn wagons down Shades Valley to reach the railhead at Brock's Gap, then it was shipped to Selma on the Alabama and Tennessee Rivers Railroad.

Toward the end of the war, with the naval blockade secure, one authority estimated that the Selma Arsenal was producing one-half of the cannon and two-thirds of the ammunition utilized by the Confederacy. After 1863, except for captured federal supplies, Selma and the Tredegar Iron Works at Richmond were the only Confederate sources for ammunition. Confederate general Dabney H. Maury praised the Brooke guns made in Selma for the defense of Mobile, and when Union general James H. Wilson destroyed the Selma installations in 1865, they were described as the best in existence.

Alabama also produced the world's first submarine. Two men arrived in Mobile in 1862, fleeing the Union occupation of New Orleans and bringing with them plans for a submarine. They had constructed a vessel but sank it as the federals closed in on the city. In Mobile they built a second submarine. Many citizens hoped this strange invention would help break the naval blockade, but the craft sank during trials because someone left a hatch open. A third ship was assembled and named the *Hunley* after one of the investors in the project. The ship was made of wood, was thirty feet long, and had a conning tower with an air shaft. It was propelled by the crew turning cranks connected to a propeller. Mobile Bay proved too shallow for the craft to maneuver a torpedo under vessels, so it was dismantled and hauled to Charleston, South Carolina. Under cover of a dark evening on February 17, 1864, the *Hunley* successfully destroyed a warship but never returned to port, its fate still a mystery. Although the *Hunley* was only an interesting footnote during the Civil War, within fifty years submarines became an important part of naval warfare.

Of all the significant resources that Alabama gave to the Confederate cause, manpower was the most important. By the time Alabama men marched off to war, they were fighting for Southern independence in the spirit of the American Revolution, not to preserve property in slavery, which most of them did not own anyway. Alabamians believed the war would be over before the first frost fell, and men initially volunteered for short periods. By October Governor Moore announced that 27,000 Alabamians were enrolled in twenty-eight regiments of infantry and one cavalry regiment. Records do not exist to determine accurately how many Alabama men served in the military during the war, but good estimates can be made. The total Alabama white male population in 1860 was 270,190, and of that number some 127,000 would become eligible for military duty during the four years of war. Colonel W. H. Fowler, who was in charge of army records, estimated that 120,000 white Alabamians fought for the Confederacy at one time or another; he reported in 1865 that Alabama sent more men into military service, and the men represented a greater percent of the state's population, than any other Southern state. But the total number of white Alabamians who served in the Confederate military is cautiously estimated as about 90,000 to 100,000.[15]

Alabama also supplied troops to the Union army. Some 2,700 whites from the hill country of northwest Alabama, a center of disloyalty for the Confederacy, fought for the Union. The First Alabama Cavalry, U.S.A., was recruited from these "Tories of the hills" in 1862 by Joseph Palmer. The regiment fought well in several engagements and its knowledge of the terrain and roads in north Alabama proved invaluable to the Union cavalry. Portions of the group were in Union colonel Abel D. Streight's 1863 raid into Alabama, and General William Tecumseh Sherman selected the unit as his "headquarters escort" during his march through Georgia.

Perhaps as many as 10,000 Alabama blacks from the Tennessee Valley plantations enlisted during Union occupation of north Alabama and served with Northern regiments. John Smith, a Selma slave, served with both armies. He went off to war with his master, who was killed near Blue Mountain. Smith then joined Union troops and was with General

James H. Wilson when he captured Selma.[16] There were many slaves in the field with Confederate troops, and some actually fought, although they usually took care of horses and equipment, cooked meals, hauled supplies, washed clothes, and carried the wounded or dead from the battlefields. Many blacks, free and slave, assisted the war effort in nonmilitary ways. Slaves built defensive installations, especially those around Mobile. They graded roads, constructed railroads, drove supply wagons, and labored in iron foundries and munitions industries. The service of slaves was involuntary, their labor impressed from their masters. The Richmond government discussed raising black troops, and blacks were recruited in February 1865, but none saw combat. The Alabama legislature granted Mobile's free blacks permission to enlist for the defense of the city in 1862, and early in 1865 John Tyler Morgan received permission to raise black troops for Confederate service. But by then it was too late.

The early Confederate mustering-in services were festive occasions. Men of the upper class arrived for duty with two suits, one a full-dress uniform, perhaps of fancy "heavy gray cassimere, trimmed with blue, three rows of bottons in front of coat, and red plumes tipped with white." The other suit was fatigues for everyday wear.[17] Slaveholders brought servants, wagons loaded with provisions, tents, blankets, and furniture. They rode fine-blooded horses and carried splendid swords and pistols. Mary A. H. Gay remembered watching the Selma Magnolia Cadets muster in: "wealthy, cultured young gentlemen voluntarily turning their backs upon the luxuries and endearments of affluent homes" to accept "the privations and hardships of warfare."[18]

In the first year of war, wives sometimes accompanied their husbands to their duty posts. Henry Hotze recalled a dinner party on the Virginia front in 1862 when two wives from Mobile (who were temporarily living in Norfolk) joined the men for dinner. Linens hid a board table, and china, silver, and wine were brought from town. Black cooks prepared the food. The presence of the women made it a grand party, though Hotze observed that the men might soon need them as nurses. When battles began or the armies moved, the women were left behind and all surplus baggage was abandoned or lost.

The middle class and the poor did not have it so well. They came to muster wearing whatever clothes they had, bringing a change in a sack over their shoulders. Some were later given uniforms, but as the war continued, these wore out and were rarely replaced. Food and clothes from home kept the army in the field. Benjamin Franklin Jackson wrote to his wife, Matilda, saying he received the shoes and socks she sent and "was very proud to get them for I was barefooted or nearly so." He asked her for an old wool quilt, "if you have any for I have not got any blanket nor cant get any, so I fare bad of a cold night."[19] Thomas T. Bigbee of Pondtown in Dale County was near Chattanooga in November 1863 when he wrote his wife: "I need a sute of close . . . I recon send my jacket . . . I want my pants linde it is gitting mity cold up here."[20] Harden Cochrane of Tuscaloosa complained of the "exorbitant prices" in the field and expressed appreciation for the socks, newspapers, books, and "drawers" delivered to him by neighbors.[21] In January 1864, 180 men of the Fifty-ninth Alabama were without shoes.

Life in the army was hard. William Jemison Mims wrote his wife, Kate, in Jefferson County that he had "felt the fatigues, hungars & thirsts incident to forced marches," and he had to "eat bread without beef & beef without bread & some meals have been passed without either." Benjamin Franklin Jackson complained to his wife that he had "really suffered for lack of bread" and a "small pone of corn bread" cost two dollars. The cold weather in Virginia bothered Turner Vaughan the most. It was May, and he was sleeping on snow with only one blanket over him when he wrote his father that "what I have to endure here if attempted at home would kill me in less than a week."[22] Isaac J. Rogers of Franklin County camped at Fort Henry in February 1862 with "no Sheltering whatever not so much as a Blanket" and endured long nights of rain, sleet, and snow with the Twenty-seventh Alabama Infantry.[23]

Southern soldiers often resorted to pillaging the dead for shoes, coats, belts, and pants to survive the cold. Tents and blankets were especially in short supply, and Confederates were pleased to capture Northern shipments of medicines, food, and clothing, as well as weapons and powder. W. E. Preston of the Thirty-third Alabama recalled that after the battle of Stones River the Confederates took Springfield rifles from the battlefield, traded "our cedar canteens" for good cloth-covered tin U.S. canteens, and picked up blankets, good black hats, blue overcoats, and shelter tents.[24]

Because Alabama companies were recruited from the same area, the men had often grown up together and many were kin by marriage or birth. Often the community would send a wagon loaded with food, clothes, and supplies for the company, along with letters from home, pencils, ink, and paper to write back. Letters from the front were frequently hand delivered by furloughed men returning home. William Jemison Mims sent a letter to Kate from the trenches near Petersburg in March 1865, writing: "although I dare say this poor convalescent will have some 200 miles to walk and about as many letters to pack as an old U.S. Mail Coach ought to undertake still I cannot resist the inclination to add this one to his load."[25]

Because the men in each company knew each other so well, fatalities were hard on the men and harder still on the families at home. Samuel

King Vann wrote from the trenches near Atlanta to his sweetheart at Cedar Grove, "O! how awful 'tis to see friends falling about me."[26] Six weeks later Vann's company came home on furlough to Old Mount Pinson and he wrote: "It seemed almost like peace was made to see our old Co. come marching home at the same time, though it makes me feel bad to think about how many marched off with the Co. that did not march back with us. O! tis awful to think how many noble-hearted brave men have fallen since our Co. left here." Of the one hundred men who mustered in 1861, only nine were left. New recruits brought the company up to twenty-four.[27]

One-fourth of the one million Southern men who fought in the Confederate army died of wounds or disease. The Confederates lost 24 percent of the men engaged at Shiloh and 30 percent of those who fought at Gettysburg. The Twenty-second Alabama lost 55 percent of its soldiers in an attack on Horseshoe Ridge. The high casualty ratio was due to fighting tactics—frontal assaults and two-line formations—repeating rifles, inadequate doctors and medical services, and lack of medicines.

Although Catholic sisters operated a hospital in Mobile before the war, nursing as a profession had not developed in Alabama. Southern women always nursed family, neighbors, and slaves but never strange men. The war changed this social standard, and hospitals staffed by "respectable ladies" of the community were established all over the state. The women of Montgomery opened a three-story hospital on Commerce Street, and a hospital was opened in Sumter County in the old Female Academy and soon expanded into a nearby warehouse and hotel. Fannie A. Beers, a nurse at Buckner Hospital at Gainesville, found deplorable conditions after Shiloh: men suffering from gangrenous wounds, scurvy, and fevers; crowded conditions and inadequate medicines and supplies; and governmental red tape that prevented any improvement. The Sisters of Charity operated St. Mary's Hospital in Montgomery and Providence Hospital in Mobile, and when they ran short of medicines, they smuggled drugs from Northern-occupied New Orleans. The Sisters of Mercy moved their hospital after the fall of Vicksburg to Shelby Springs. Dormitories at Howard College in Marion and Old Main Hall at the men's college in Auburn were both used as military hospitals.

Although most Alabama women stayed home to nurse the sick and wounded, others went to the army, opening hospitals close to battlefields. When it was evident that a great conflict would be fought in Virginia in late spring 1861, Juliet Opie Hopkins of Mobile traveled to Virginia and with her own money opened a hospital for Alabama soldiers. Her work was supported first by donations from citizens and soldiers' families and then by the state of Alabama. During the course of the war she supervised several facilities for Alabama soldiers in Virginia and was wounded twice at the battle of Seven Pines while moving soldiers from the field. Her hospitals were well run and staffed by Alabama women who joined Mrs. Hopkins to nurse the sick and wounded. In September 1862 Governor Moore expressed his gratitude for her "great personal sacrifice and indefatigable labor in behalf of our gallant soldiers."[28] To honor Juliet Hopkins, two denominations of Alabama Confederate bills displayed her picture.

Kate Cumming was twenty-eight years old when she left Mobile with twenty-four other women for the Shiloh battlefield. For three years she kept a journal as she nursed soldiers of the Army of Tennessee. "Nothing," she wrote on her first visit to the wards, "that I had ever heard or read had given me the faintest idea of the horrors witnessed here." She noted men "mutilated in every imaginable way, lying on the floor, just as they were taken from the battle-field."[29] For days Cumming did not undress or sleep as she comforted men dying so quickly all around her that she never had time to know their names.

With death as a constant companion, religion played a comforting role in the lives of soldiers. Many Alabama ministers became chaplains and went off to war with large numbers of their congregations. Presbyterian minister William D. Chadick of Jackson County joined the Fourth Alabama and became known as the "fighting parson" during the battle of Manassas. Isaac T. Tichenor, pastor of Montgomery's First Baptist Church, was with the Seventeenth Alabama Regiment at Shiloh, where he preached a sermon before going into battle at eleven-thirty on a Sunday morning. Tichenor earned a reputation as a sharpshooter and fought with "unsurpassed bravery" when he was not preaching. Baptist minister N. D. Renfroe of Jacksonville was killed at the battle of Fredericksburg. His brother, J. J. D. Renfroe, who was pastor of a Talladega church and served in the Tenth Alabama Regiment, was probably Alabama's most widely known chaplain.

Although a religious feeling was always present in the camps and efforts to discourage gambling and drinking were constant, in 1863 and 1864 an evangelical awakening swept through the Southern armies. In the western theater preachers and chaplains no doubt exaggerated when they claimed to have baptized 150,000 soldiers, but thousands of conversions did occur. Probably on the Virginia front 10 percent of Lee's army were converted in the "Great Revival" in fall 1863. J. J. D. Renfroe gave sermons throughout the Army of Northern Virginia following the defeat at Gettysburg and baptized men in an icy pond near Petersburg. Renfroe recalled preaching to hundreds of men, building arbors for revivals, holding prayer meetings in the trenches and Bible classes when shells were flying overhead. The Confederate government supported the religious spirit, and President Davis announced special days for fasting and prayer. Thousands of Bibles were smuggled from the North and from England, surviving a blockade run to reach soldiers at the front.

When the war was over, revivals affected Alabama churches, which swelled with converts, but the defeat of Southern armies defending a cause white Southerners considered righteous presented a theological dilemma. One Alabama Baptist association resolved in 1862 that the war "inaugurated by our enemies must be regarded as a providential visitation upon us on account of our sins" but after heated debate added, "Though entirely just on our part."[30]

THIRTEEN

The Home Front

WOMEN greeted the news of the secession of Alabama initially as their men did—some with enthusiasm, some with opposition, others with heavy hearts—but generally the fervor of Southern nationalism swept the state. Men volunteered for military duty and left their communities amid parades, waving flags, and martial music. Southern romanticism reached a peak as warriors became the subjects of hero worship. Girls and women began collecting small portraits, autographs, and locks of hair of favorite soldiers or generals. The darkly handsome Pierre G. T. Beauregard, the brave Stonewall Jackson, and the daring Nathan Bedford Forrest were popular heroes in Alabama. Before the romance faded and the cruel realities of war became obvious, even the most credulous patriots realized that the "fairer portion of humanity" would bear a heavy burden when war came. Sarah Espy of Cherokee County, already a widow, was living on a small farm with her children when she heard that Lincoln intended to coerce the seceding states. She wrote in her diary March 19, 1861, "I fear our happy days are all gone."[1]

Women supported the war effort immediately by sewing militia and Confederate uniforms and, when cloth was gone, spinning and weaving more yardage. They wove fabrics of wool and cotton thread, and when their men suffered on the Virginia fronts during the cold winters, wool was in great demand. Parthenia A. Hague recalled that "every household now became a miniature factory," and women made all kinds of materials, "cloth in stripes broad and narrow, and in checks wide and small," muslins and jeans cloth as well as plain fabric.[2] Younger women were taught by older women who remembered techniques from the pioneer days of their youth. Women organized Ladies Aid Societies in towns and most counties and stitched bags to be filled with sand for fortifications. Sewing clothing and knitting socks for soldiers became almost a cottage industry. To raise money for the war, women sponsored bazaars and raffles, put on concerts and plays, and held dancing parties and balls. Martha Jane Hatter of Greensboro made two beautiful quilts that were auctioned to raise money for ships. Because the purchaser returned the "gunboat quilts," they were auctioned several times. Women worked in textile mills producing fabric for the army and in arms industries such as the Selma Arsenal, where nimble fingers used to the embroidery needle rolled and assembled cartridges.

But women, who were not allowed to vote, took no part in the gubernatorial elections scheduled for August 1861. The secession crisis, the organization of the Confederate government, and the beginning of war exhausted Alabamians so much that there was little interest in a political campaign. Newspapers across the state suggested candidates— Thomas H. Watts of Montgomery, John E. Moore of Florence, Robert Jemison, Jr., of Tuscaloosa, Thomas J. Judge of Montgomery, and John Gill Shorter of Eufaula. Shorter, a Democrat, strong Yanceyite, and member of the Eufaula Regency, was the most popular choice. He was serving in the Confederate congress in Richmond. Jemison and Judge had no statewide base and withdrew. Moore pulled out of the race, bitterly blasting south Alabama's control of state politics and insisting it was north Alabama's turn to have a governor.

Watts, a former Whig, campaigned while Shorter stayed in Richmond. Both tried to avoid divisive issues because there was a war to be won. As expected, Watts ran well in the Black Belt and old Whig strongholds, while Shorter carried his east Alabama home area and the strongly Democratic vote of north Alabama. Shorter defeated Watts by almost 10,000 votes. Thus, in one of those great ironies so common in Alabama politics, Shorter, a states' rights secessionist, was elected governor by the Democratic votes of north Alabama Unionists.

The geographical mix of Shorter's vote made it difficult for him to rally support behind his leadership and Alabama's war effort. His political strength lay in sections most opposed to the war. At his inauguration he challenged Alabamians to endure all burdens as the state fought for "the sacred right of self-government, inherited from our fathers."[3] Later he confessed that at the time he had no idea how severe those burdens and hardships would be. Shorter's election followed in the aftermath of the South's victory at First Manassas, but within twelve months the high hopes of the Confederate cause would be crumbling in retreats.

Shorter faced numerous problems—supplying soldiers for the Confederate army and for the state militia, defending the state from invasions north and south, supporting unpopular Confederate measures such as the conscription law, supplying food for Alabama troops at the front, and delivering salt and food to their wives, children, widows, and orphans at home. Shorter recognized the significance of industrial production of war materials and home manufacturing, and he encouraged both to win the war. He was sustained by a confidence in his own ability and a belief in the Southern cause, an "inward approval" that nurtured a self-righteousness and impaired his political instincts.

The Northern plan of battle—to capture Richmond, blockade the Southern ports, control the Mississippi River, and invade the lower South—kept the fighting away from Alabama during the first year of the war. But the fall of Fort Henry on the Tennessee River in February 1862 allowed federal gunboats to sail up the river to Florence. With the Confederate defeat at Shiloh, the Tennessee Valley was open to Union troops. General O. M. Mitchell captured Huntsville on April 11, 1862. A Fourth Ohio Cavalry trooper remembered that "such a clatter never before awoke the echoes among those Alabama hills," while in town a warning spread that "the turnpike is black with the Yankees," their horses' hoofbeats heard from "a mile off."[4] The Union forces captured fifteen locomotives plus passenger, box, and platform cars; telegraphic equipment; and 200 prisoners.

On May 2 Colonel John Basil Turchin led his blue-coated Eighth Brigade into Athens, a quiet little town west of Huntsville. Turchin was a Russian immigrant and veteran of the Crimean War with different ideas about spoils of war and plunder. Turchin turned his troops loose to pillage and loot. General Mitchell blamed Turchin for the breakdown in discipline and was shocked by the atrocities that occurred. Mitchell condemned the "lawless vagabonds" who perpetrated rape, robbery, and arson in Union uniforms. Northern general Don Carlos Buell called the sack of Athens "a case of undisputed atrocity." Although Mitchell and Buell had Turchin arrested and tried before a court-martial, where he was found guilty, Mrs. Turchin traveled to Washington, D.C., to plead her husband's case before the president. Lincoln granted Turchin a presidential pardon and a promotion.

Federal occupation and fighting in north Alabama sent refugees fleeing to the south. For those who stayed, many of them women with their men in Confederate service, life was difficult. Mary Cook Chadick was shocked when General Mitchell "complained that the ladies of Huntsville have given his officers the 'cold shoulder' by not having received them into the social circle!" After soldiers arrested two women for having a Confederate flag, Mitchell issued a general order admonishing women "to go home and behave yourselves."[5] The women refused. They smuggled letters, news, and information to Confederate soldiers hiding in the hills and harassed the Yankees as best they could. They brought food and blankets to Southerners imprisoned by the federals, moved the wounded into private houses, and resisted having their homes commandeered to billet soldiers. They learned to exist without dependable black labor, as slaves were encouraged by the army to leave plantations and homes and assert their independence. The sack of

Athens and the occupation of federal troops diminished Union support in the Tennessee Valley. Many prominent planters and Confederates (all those who could) had already left for safer places and had taken their valuables with them.

In April 1862, with the South surrounded by federal troops, the Confederate government passed a conscription law requiring three years of military service for all able-bodied white males ages eighteen to thirty-five. The conscription law allowed a man to pay for a substitute, an immigrant or male younger or older than the law required. The rich could afford to hire substitutes, the poor could not. Some men became adept at being substitutes, deserting often so they might collect from another man and reenlist. In September the law was amended to exempt planters and overseers who supervised twenty or more slaves. These provisions gave planters an advantage and led to charges that it was "a rich man's war and a poor man's fight."

As their men volunteered for military service, and later as conscription agents scoured the hills and hollows for able-bodied males, women sent their sons off as they came of age. In Cherokee County Sarah Espy wrote in her diary that her youngest son, Virgil, had enlisted: "I had hoped to keep my last one a little longer, but it seems he must go too, and encounter all the evils of camp-life." She looked back to 1860 when she was "surrounded by a happy family; now all is threatened desolation." If she could have known then what four years of war would bring, "reason would have left me."[6]

All across the state females became heads of households with the responsibilities of caring for their families, houses, animals, and farms. For the first time, many wives were required to keep plantation record books and handle money, deciding how it would be spent or, in its absence, figuring ways to barter for their needs. Nancy E. Barrow of Chambers County wrote her husband, James, in Virginia in 1864 that she had "a great many cares on my mind" for the ground was too wet to plow. Using an interesting selection of personal pronouns, she told him, "I will now inform you that my stock are all alive," and "I have four young [calves]." She wept when she went to church without him; and before closing, Nancy wrote, "My dear old man you have no idea how anxious I am to see you again one time more."[7]

Some planters, especially those with small numbers of slaves, trusted their black people as family, but as the war progressed, as troops occupied the northern part of the state, and after Lincoln decreed emancipation, distrust set in. Despite Alabama law, many women were forced by necessity to supervise their slaves alone, without a white man on the premises. For many, this was a frightening situation. Jane Brasfield of Greene County wrote the governor, asking that her son be allowed to come home because her slaves were "now pretty much at the mercy of their own will." Mary Fitzpatrick of Wetumpka, unable to manage their slaves, begged her husband to return.[8] An invalid, Hattie Motley of Autauga County, wrote of "monstrous woes unheard of except in the excited brain of some hypochondriac novel-writer." She was surrounded by plantations where there was no supervision of slaves, and she lived in fear after a slave raped the daughter of a neighbor.[9] Susanna Clay wrote her son Clement from Huntsville that "we cannot exert any authority" over the slaves and that his Negroes were as "free as ours."[10]

Soldiers often blamed conditions at home when requesting an exemption. J. W. Hill told Governor Shorter that he needed to go home: his mother and two younger sisters were alone on his plantation with seventy slaves who were not working. Hill wrote that he "was one among the first that volunteered my services for the defense of our country, and served my time out at Ft. Morgan." Someone noted on the letter that the secretary of war refuses to "discharge any man able to do duty."[11]

Slaveholding women had drivers and field hands to continue the work of the plantation and produce food, but white women of the mountains, the hill country, and the Wiregrass did not, and it fell to them and their children to produce what they would eat. When war began, crops were in the ground and many were already harvested before the men went off to fight, but by spring 1862 women were having trouble getting crops planted. Most poor farmers plowed with oxen, animals that were difficult for women and children to handle.

Shelby was one example of a county almost depopulated of men. Laurence M. Jones warned Governor Shorter that there were 300 men left in Shelby from an 1860 male population of 1,600. Jones begged the governor to stop the once-a-week militia drillings so the men who remained could stay home and "make all the corn" they could. Come spring planting, he predicted, there would be "300 females" in Shelby "at handles of the plow."[12] In March 1862 M. L. Stansel wrote from Pickens County that Shorter's call for 400 troops "almost literally depopulated the county of men." There were not enough men left for overseers; in the county's poorer parts, if the men left, "their little farms must remain wholly uncultivated during the year."[13] In Coosa County raising 800 men translated into 15,000 acres uncultivated. By April 1862 Alabama had furnished 17 percent of its white males. Two years later the number of Alabama soldiers exceeded the state's voting population.

Communication between armies on the move and the home front was always difficult and slow, but letters flowed, many written by barely literate men and women struggling to correspond. James B. Daniel was a twenty-one-year-old farmer from Chambers County when he enlisted in 1862. He wrote his wife, Mattie, from Virginia that he had "not received nary letter from you," although he "wrote five or six to you and have got nearly plum out of heart. I don't think you cear wether I hear from you or note but I will keep a looking for one."[14] Elias Davis wrote his brother-in-law in Jefferson County: "You can't imagine how I am troubled at the condition of my family, but it is out of my power to have things otherwise."[15] Sometimes it took two months for a letter from Alabama to reach the army in Virginia. When Sarah Wood asked her husband to come home to Coosa County, he replied: "I am not vexed for you to ask me to come home . . . that is a natural consequence. and if I live I expect to come as soon as I can honerably . . . dont become dishartened for we are in a glorious cause, fighting for our fiersides and those we left behind."[16]

Men wanted to stay informed about conditions at home, and their letters were filled with questions. Husbands sent specific instructions and advice, urging wives to raise as much food as possible, to save money and barter for what they needed, to keep someone spinning and weaving all the time, to look after the stock and make sure the smoke-house was kept locked. They recommended when to slaughter hogs and how many. They advised as to how much molasses to make and which fields to plant in corn. Wives were told to hire out the slaves when they could and to defer judgment on agricultural decisions to trusted slaves who knew best about the crops. Women were warned to keep the fences repaired, to secure the corncrib, to save all the food they could, and not to spend any money. Ben Crumly cautioned his wife, Arabella, "to be as saving of your corn and fodder as you can for I am afraid the time is near at hand when corn can't be bought."[17] Food supplies were threatened by a severe shortage of salt, which was necessary to preserve meats, and some families were forced to dig up the dirt floors of smokehouses to retrieve salt that had been deposited there for decades.

Wives left alone with young children and a hard-scrabble farm could not have survived without kinship networks and good neighbors. Many families had agreements that one son or brother would stay home and look after all the families through the war. Adam McCain warned Governor Shorter that he must have an exemption because he had two brothers, three brothers-in-law, and two nephews off in the war, and he was looking after five women, seventeen children, and fifty Negroes. Some women took their children and went home to their parents or moved in with other relatives. Often the accommodations were not satisfactory, and wives complained to their husbands. But many women had no place to take their families.

Food became more scarce and, even when available, the inflated wartime prices were beyond the reach of the poor, who suffered most. The cost of flour rose from $40 a barrel in 1862 to $300 in 1864. Shoes that sold for $25 in 1862 cost $150 a pair two years later. Inflation also reflected a lack of confidence in Confederate currency. Local relief associations were organized, and military aid societies began helping indigent families as well as soldiers in the field. County governments established relief committees to provide aid, merchants offered credit, planters sold food below cost, and neighbors helped widows, orphans, and soldiers' families. Ministers often served on county indigent relief committees. They reminded their congregations that charity was blessed, and churches shared with their members in need and assumed responsibility for children orphaned by war.

Although droughts plagued Alabama during the war years, food was available in south Alabama during most of the conflict. Even so, Alabama's inadequate transportation system made it impossible to convey food to the northern hill country and Wiregrass where people were starving. Black Belt planters were often visited by poor women carrying sacks over their shoulders looking for food. These "corn women" would scour the picked-over fields, fill their bags, and walk home. Sometimes planters gave them corn from good supplies.

Private efforts of the community and the county governments could not satisfy the need. State aid to indigent soldiers' families began in 1861 and was coordinated through the probate judges' offices and the county commissions. As the system developed, the probate offices surveyed needs and compiled lists of the truly indigent. In the last two years of the war at least one-fourth of the white population of the state was dependent upon aid. In 1863 twenty-nine counties reported that more than one-third of their families were receiving aid as indigent soldiers' families. In 1864 Shelby County had 66 percent of its families destitute, and Mobile County requested aid for 7,020 persons. Reports from the counties are incomplete, but state and county aid to the indigent families of soldiers during the war exceeded $12 million, not including private philanthropy and church work.

Drugs and medicines were in shorter supply than food. Alabama had failed to develop a pharmaceutical industry before the war, and the blockade cut off supplies of such drugs as morphine, calomel, and quinine. Even whiskey was difficult to find. Governor Shorter had stopped the distillation of spirits to save grain for food—against considerable opposition in areas where the right to make liquor was often held dearer than Southern independence. Women cultivated gardens of medicinal herbs and even grew poppies to make opium for laudanum. Their own health, never good from pregnancies and childbirth complications, often broke under the burdens of heavy work loads, poor food, the stress of managing alone, the strain of nursing soldiers, and the grief of mourning loved ones who died of disease and battle wounds.

As the wails of woe and sorrow from home were reflected more and more in letters to the combatants, and as their own situation in the army deteriorated, soldiers' desertion rates increased. The Talladega *Democratic Watchtower* reported on September 16, 1863, that deserters were brought home by "the cries of mothers, sisters, wives, daughters," and the Richmond, Virginia, *Whig* agreed. In 1864 the newspaper observed: "The want of food with their families at home is the cause of over half the desertions."[18] The Alabama counties with the highest desertion rates were located in the poorer sections, the hilly and mountainous regions south of the Tennessee Valley and the southeastern Wiregrass, areas where support for the war was never strong. When the War Department reported 50,000 to 100,000 men evading service and 40,000 to 50,000 without leave, the general in charge of conscription in Alabama estimated that there were "from 8,000 to 10,000 deserters and tory conscripts in the mountains of north Alabama, many of whom had deserted the second, third, and fourth (some of them) time." He concluded that there were "so many that shooting them appears to be out of the question."[19]

Many of the men avoiding conscription were "mossbacks," who vowed to stay in the hills until moss grew on their backs. Some of them formed gangs, riding together, stealing, looting, and spreading fear. Bush Jones wrote Governor Shorter from the trenches near Chattanooga that his home county, St. Clair, was "infested by a band of traitors and deserters, enemies to our country and its cause who are pillaging, robbing, harassing, and intimidating the families of loyal citizens and soldiers." On the other hand, that same month soldiers stationed at Pollard wrote the governor to complain that Confederate cavalry riding in Barbour County to look for deserters were arresting aged fathers, killing stock, confiscating food, looting stores, and plundering houses.[20] Joseph G. Sanders of Dale County fought on both sides. Mustered into a Georgia Confederate regiment early in the war, he later deserted and joined the Union army in Florida. As a lieutenant in the First Florida Cavalry, he became known as an infamous bushwhacker who raided the Wiregrass.

Despite these problems, the war pressed on. North Alabama was relatively quiet until spring 1863 when Colonel Abel D. Streight cut across the state on a Union raid from Eastport, Mississippi, to Rome, Georgia. His goal was to sever Braxton Bragg's supply line from Atlanta and destroy the cannon foundry and the Western and Atlanta machine shops at Rome. Federal general William S. Rosecrans approved Streight's plan, which called for a body of two thousand men to move rapidly across north Alabama and reach Rome before Confederate general Nathan Bedford Forrest, who was in Tennessee, found out they were there. The daring raid relied on surprise and rapid execution. Federals around Tuscumbia were to hold the attention of the Confederates while

Streight slipped away. Problems developed for the federals after a short-age of horses forced the army to supply Streight with mules. Many of the mules came down with distemper, and a large number escaped into the countryside, probably stampeded by Confederate cavalrymen. To com-pound Streight's problems, most of his men were infantry with no riding skills, and many of the mules were young and unbroken.

Despite his predicament, Streight and his mule-back army—called the "Jackass Cavalry"—were on the move by the third week of April 1863. Riding with Streight to guide the bluecoats were two companies of north Alabama Unionists from the First Alabama Union Cavalry. From East-port, Streight rode to Tuscumbia, then south to Russellville, Mount Hope, and Moulton, traveling deep into Alabama. It was raining hard, and the roads were almost impassable.

General Forrest finally was alerted to the Union raid when a Tuscum-bia citizen informed him that two thousand soldiers had just passed through Mount Hope. Forrest moved south. At Day's Gap the Confede-rate leader caught up with the federals, his scouts reporting that at daybreak "in one mighty effort nearly two thousand mules braying in far-reaching and penetrating chorus set the echoes in vibration among the Alabama mountains."[21] Streight was shocked by Forrest's attack on his rear guard. For the next three days the two armies fought a desperate running battle across north Alabama as both forces dashed toward Rome, the men hardly stopping to sleep or eat between skirmishes.

During the ride, Forrest's reputation as a "wizard of the saddle" was secured, an Alabama heroine and a hero were created, and stories originated that became folklore. At Blountsville, Streight rode directly into the town's May Day celebration, where all the best horses and mules from the countryside were gathered with their owners. Carriages and wagons were filled with hams, fried chicken, and picnic fare, but the exhausted bluecoats hardly had time to eat the food and confiscate the animals before Forrest was hot on their trail again. Near Gadsden the federal troops burned the bridge over Black Creek, but Forrest was able to continue his rapid pursuit after sixteen-year-old Emma Sansom showed him a shallow ford. While the Union troops were searching for a ferry on the west side of the Coosa River, John A. Wisdom spied them from the opposite bank. Concluding that the federal soldiers were headed for Rome, Georgia, Wisdom began a remarkable sixty-seven-mile ride to Rome, changing horses five times and reaching the town in eight hours. In Paul Revere style, he warned, "The Yankees are coming."

Meanwhile, Streight's troopers, riding wearily on a moonless night, became lost in a labyrinth of wagon roads and trails in a cut-over forest area near Gaylesville. Streight recalled that despite every exertion he could make, "the command became separated and scattered into several

Left: Emma Sansom showed Gen. Nathan Bedford Forrest a ford over Black Creek on the road between Blountsville and Gadsden as Forrest and his Confederate troops chased Union Col. A. D. Streight and his cavalry across north Alabama, April 19–May 3, 1863. *Right:* Nathan Bedford Forrest opposed secession but joined the Confederate army as a private in June 1861. With no military training or experience, he rose to prominence on his natural instincts for warfare. (Photos Courtesy of the Alabama Department of Archives and History)

squads, traveling in different directions."[22] Sarah Epsy wrote in her diary that her Cherokee County neighbor reported Yankees in her yard in large numbers and that they "had taken their horses and were very insolent—this is dreadful." The next day she commented that the "Yanks ran wild and were so hotly pursued they could not tarry long in this vicinity. They took every mule Mr. Finley had."[23] When dawn came, the bluecoats, weary, weak, and confused, stumbled upon the Lawrence plantation, where many fell asleep before they could eat. But soon Forrest's men, who had slept while the federals staggered lost in the woods, began another attack.

Streight had no idea how few men Forrest had, but the Confederate general knew Streight outmanned him three to one. Forrest sent an officer of his staff to Streight and demanded his surrender to stop the bloodshed. Streight agreed to parley only with Forrest. While meeting with Streight under the truce, Forrest had his guns pulled and had his men march over the crest of a hill behind him but passing in view of the Union colonel, then circle down out of sight and move up again. Forrest talked while Streight counted, and then the Union officer conferred with his commanders and assessed the situation. Streight's ammunition was wet and "worthless," his "horses and mules in a desperate condition," his men were "overcome with fatigue and loss of sleep," and he was "confronted by fully three times our number, in the heart of the enemy's country."[24] Fearful that the Alabama Unionists riding with him would be treated as traitors, Streight insisted that all his men be held as prisoners of war. Forrest agreed, and Streight presented Forrest with his sword and surrendered about 1,700 men to Forrest's cavalry of less than 500. When the Union colonel discovered he had been duped, he angrily demanded that Forrest return his sword, but the Southern leader refused.

The invasion of the state by Northern troops made Governor John Gill Shorter more unpopular. He began his term with the support of the people and was elected by a strong vote in north Alabama. But intrusion by the enemy and occupation of north Alabama cities, the defeat of the Confederate armies in Kentucky, Tennessee, and Maryland, the conscription act, heavy taxes, and widespread destitution caused his popularity to plummet and attitudes toward the war and the Confederate government to change. At midsummer the news of the fall of Vicksburg and the defeat at Gettysburg did not help the morale problems in Alabama.

Shorter had served ably as governor, but he faced insurmountable problems. Because of the war, party politics had ceased and candid debate was stifled. Shorter defended his administration of the state and blamed the shortages of arms and manpower on the Confederate government's refusal to make the defense of Alabama a priority. North Alabama was decimated by the war and bitter because so little had been done to protect the region. In the months before the gubernatorial election, soldiers demanded the right to vote, but committees of the house and senate determined that an amendment to the residency clause of the constitution of 1861 would be necessary, and this change could not be accomplished before the election. The decision to refuse to allow Confederate soldiers to vote was controversial, and its effect undoubtedly hurt Shorter. Thomas H. Watts was a reluctant candidate who said he would accept the governorship if the people elected him, but he would not canvass for the office. He stayed in Richmond during the campaign, tending to his duties as attorney general of the Confederacy. With Watts remaining in Richmond, Shorter preferred to keep politicking on a low key.

Opposition in north Alabama to the war resulted in a formidable peace movement by Reconstructionists, those convinced the Confederacy could not win and should quit fighting and return to the Union. Despite Watts's support for the war, leaders of the north Alabama "peace party" were drawn to him, and he was at heart a Reconstructionist.

Confederate disasters at Gettysburg and Vicksburg during the summer increased support for an end to the war. The strength of secret peace societies among the poor in the hill countries and the Wiregrass made it a class movement. To Yancey's close friend James H. Stewart, by early summer it was obvious that Yancey "had abandoned all hope of achieving the independence so much desired; and he *wanted to die, did die,* from sheer disappointment, overwhelmed with grief from the crisis he knew was inevitable."[25] The fire-eater passed away at his plantation house near Montgomery on July 27, 1863. The legislature elected in August 1863 contained men of the Peace party. Their influence sent antisecessionist Robert Jemison to fill Yancey's senate seat. C. C. Clay, Jr., the other Alabama Confederate senator, was defeated by Richard Wilde Walker, a moderate.

The Whig party benefited from the backlash against the secessionists of 1861 and gained in the August 1863 elections. Watts, a former Unionist Whig, easily defeated Shorter by a vote of 28,221 to 9,664. Shorter believed he was defeated "for holding up the state to its high resolves and crowding the people to the performance of their duty."[26] The *Clarke County Journal* explained that Shorter lost over such issues as "impressing your Negroes for defense," "the calling up of every able-bodied man for service," "the salt question and the liquor question," and "peace prices in war time."[27]

Watts returned to Alabama following the election to face as governor the same mounting problems that had plagued Shorter—shortages of food and salt, constant demands for more soldiers, increased desertion, the need to enforce conscription, and scarcities of medicines and such consumer items as thread, sewing needles, and even cotton yarn. There was a scarcity of farm animals and tools, and wartime inflation and speculation continued to send prices sky-high. Although Watts cooperated with the Confederacy, he took an independent attitude toward Jefferson Davis and the Richmond government. He prosecuted the war with staunch vigor but at the same time defended the state rights of Alabama. He especially was irritated by Confederate enrolling officers who conscripted his militia officers, and he was supported by the legislature, which set a fine and prison sentence for conscript officers who forced into service any militia exempted by the governor. Watts needed a militia to defend the state during Union invasions.

The Confederate rout of Abel Streight's raid was followed by another short invasion in October 1863 by the First Alabama Union Cavalry under George E. Spencer. Moving south from federal camps near Corinth, Mississippi, Spencer's Tory forces were turned back north of Jasper. At the time north Alabama's defense was in the hands of Philip D. Roddey. His small cavalry force occasionally rode with both Joe Wheeler

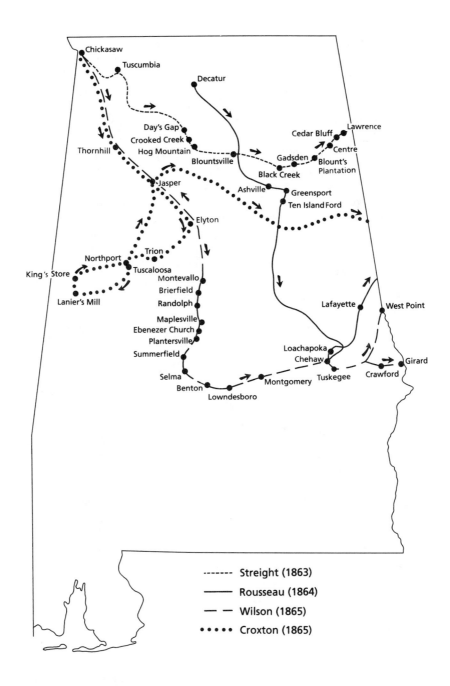

Chickasaw
Tuscumbia
Decatur
Lawrence
Day's Gap
Cedar Bluff
Crooked Creek
Centre
Hog Mountain
Gadsden
Thornhill
Blountsville
Blount's Plantation
Black Creek
Jasper
Ashville
Greensport
Ten Island Ford
Elyton
Trion
Northport
King's Store
Tuscaloosa
Montevallo
Brierfield
Lanier's Mill
Randolph
Maplesville
Lafayette
West Point
Ebenezer Church
Plantersville
Summerfield
Loachapoka
Chehaw
Girard
Selma
Tuskegee
Crawford
Benton
Montgomery
Lowndesboro

------- Streight (1863)
——— Rousseau (1864)
— — Wilson (1865)
• • • • Croxton (1865)

Union Raids into Alabama during the Civil War

and Nathan Bedford Forrest. But by 1864 Roddey's forces were depleted and the defenses of Alabama were spread thin, while the enemy was growing stronger and more audacious. Despite pleas from citizens and testimony to the significant Confederate iron and manufacturing resources in the area, the Richmond government sent no aid because it had none to send, and the Alabama legislature refused to provide a coordinated defense.

In spring 1864 William T. Sherman began his push south from Chattanooga. He was determined to stop the flow of supplies to the Confederate army before him, and he ordered Lovell H. Rousseau to take 2,500 cavalry from Decatur, Alabama, and cut the rail line supplying Atlanta. He directed Rousseau to move quickly and not risk getting delayed, to destroy the tracks of the Montgomery and West Point Railroad near Opelika, and then to join him near Marietta, Georgia. General A. J. Smith was to occupy Forrest near Tupelo, Mississippi, and Sherman promised to keep Joseph E. Johnston "fully employed" to give Rousseau time. General Rousseau was told not to take any wagons but to pack some horses. He was to "travel early and late in the day, but rest at midday and midnight." Sherman cautioned his general to do his work thoroughly, burning the railroad ties in piles, heating the iron rails in the middle, and twisting them when red hot so they could not be used again.[28]

Rousseau left Decatur on July 10, crossed Sand Mountain, and passed through Blountsville. At Ashville the cavalry found plenty of corn and oats for the horses and kept the blacksmiths busy putting new shoes on the mounts. After crossing the Coosa River and routing a small group of Confederates, Rousseau reached Talladega. He found a store of supplies and food, which he confiscated. He destroyed two gun factories, railroad cars, and the depot. After feigning an attack on the Coosa River bridge of the Alabama and Tennessee Rivers Railroad, Rousseau continued south toward his objective. His troops had difficulty crossing the Tallapoosa River at Stowe's Ferry but then marched through Dadeville straight to Loachapoka. Just before the arrival of the bluecoats, a southbound train passed that carried Confederate general Braxton Bragg to Montgomery, a lost prize for the raiders.

After a few hours of rest, the soldiers began their work of destroying the tracks. The cross-ties were made of pitch pine and burned quickly into a fire hot enough to weaken the rails so they could be twisted. Rousseau sent detachments north to Auburn and Opelika and south to Notasulga, destroying the tracks as they moved. A long line of fires sent black smoke billowing for miles down the track. At Loachapoka nearby houses were barely saved when the wind caught and spread the fire.

Rousseau's raid went virtually unopposed. The few militiamen in the

Opelika area were ineffective, the Confederate soldiers at Auburn were wounded and too sick to help, and the train of soldiers sent from Montgomery (which included cadets from the University of Alabama) engaged the Union troops briefly at Chehaw Station before retreating. The bluecoats confiscated or burned supplies at Opelika and Columbus, Georgia, before turning north toward Lafayette on their way to Marietta. The raid destroyed thirty miles of track, and despite heroic efforts by the local residents who marshaled wagons, drays, and labor to move supplies from Notasulga to the other side of Opelika, the interruption of supplies occurred at a critical time in the defense of Atlanta and proved devastating to the Confederacy.

While General Rousseau's cavalry was moving south through Alabama, there were indications that the Union navy blockading Mobile Bay might be ready to take the offensive and try to enter the harbor. The ship channel between Dauphin Island (defended by Fort Gaines) and Mobile Point (defended by Fort Morgan) was narrow and mined with torpedoes (the term used for submerged mines). The Confederates had begun building Fort Powell to defend Grant's Pass, but it remained unfinished. Mobile was an important port for blockade runners taking out cotton to exchange for munitions, medicines, and gunpowder. Many Mobile captains engaged in blockade running, whether out of loyalty for the cause or for the large profits to be made. They operated fast, low-silhouetted ships to escape the naval warships guarding the bay. After the fall of New Orleans in April 1862, the federal fleet was strengthened and the run through the blockade became more difficult—requiring audacity, daring tactics, and imagination but also increasing profits. The blockade was not secure until 1864.

In September 1862 the CSS *Florida* suddenly arrived in Mobile. A Confederate raider constructed in England, the ship was commanded by John N. Moffitt, who was bringing it into Confederate waters for the first time. Although Moffitt was not able to use his guns and was undermanned, he tricked the federal blockaders at the bay channel by flying a British flag as a *ruse de guerre* and managed to enter the harbor with moderate damage to his ship. The *Florida* underwent repairs and outfitting, while the crew recovered from yellow fever and Moffitt recruited additional numbers. Despite the quarantine, citizens came to see the sleek, low-lying vessel being repaired in the Montrose shipyards. Four months later the *Florida* was ready to sail and again challenged the Northern fleet off Mobile Bay and succeeded in reaching the open sea. In its career the *Florida* captured thirty-eight ships and with its tenders (supply ships) twenty-two more. The raider captured or destroyed United States commerce worth more than $4 million.

As Mobilians followed the successes of the *Florida,* they paid even greater attention to another commerce raider commanded by Mobile's Raphael Semmes. Constructed in Liverpool as the *Enrica,* the ship sailed out of England while Union spies watched. Semmes took command on August 24, 1862, while the craft was anchored off the coast of Wales. He commissioned the ship *Alabama* and raised the Confederate flag. During the next two years the *Alabama* attacked Northern merchant vessels all over the world, capturing sixty-nine vessels and cargo worth $5.1 million.

When the *Alabama* engaged the USS *Hatteras* off Galveston in 1863 and sank the federal warship, the event was headline news all over the world. The *Alabama*'s successes caused insurance rates to skyrocket. But the end came when the *Alabama,* caught in a French port, was challenged by the USS *Kearsarge* off the coast of Cherbourg. News of the impending battle spread across Europe by telegraph, and some 15,000 people gathered along the shore, on rooftops, and in yachts and fishing boats after Semmes announced he would sail on Sunday, June 18, 1864. The *Kearsarge* had superior guns, fresh powder, and a newly installed chain cable hung vertically over the center of each side, which meant the ship was partially ironclad, a fact unknown to Semmes. The *Kearsarge* was too strong for the *Alabama.* Semmes sent the ship's funds ashore, and the South's most successful raider steamed out to the challenge, past thousands of people. The *Alabama* was escorted by the French ironclad frigate *Couronne,* which was to keep the battle outside France's three-mile limit. The Confederate ship passed close to the French liner *Napoleon,* and the Southerners were surprised to see its crew cheering from the riggings and to hear its band playing "Dixie."

The battle began some seven miles off the coast, and the *Alabama* fought bravely for two hours before receiving a fatal blow. The London *Times* commented that the "quick and cunning craft that raced so swiftly and roamed the deep so long" had found a fitting grave in the Norman waters.[29] Going down in battle was more appropriate than having the *Alabama* rot at anchor in a foreign port or worse still, captured. Semmes was plucked from the sea by an English yachtsman, much to the chagrin of the United States Navy.

When news of the *Alabama*'s sinking reached Mobile, the citizens were carefully watching the buildup of federal naval power in the Gulf beyond Mobile Point. Admiral David G. Farragut had planned to enter the bay after he took New Orleans but was delayed by Washington's priority of first controlling the Mississippi River. While his flagship *Hartford* was being refurbished at the Brooklyn Navy Yard at Christmastime 1863, Farragut learned from a spy that a giant ironclad had been constructed to defend Mobile. Knowing that Confederate admiral Franklin Buchanan, commander of the *Virginia* during its battle with the *Monitor* and an expert on ironclad warfare, was in charge of the Mobile defenses, Farragut made haste to ready the *Hartford* to sail south. He need not have hurried. The *Tennessee*, towed from Selma for its final outfitting, could not then cross the shallow Dog River Bar into the bay. Admiral Buchanan fumed: "I am doing all I can to get the *Tennessee* over the bar. . . . What folly to build vessels up our rivers which cannot cross the bars at the mouths. . . . [The *Tennessee*] will have to go nearly twenty miles down the Bay before she will be in water sufficient to float her."[30]

It was summer before the *Tennessee* managed to cross the bar. Soon Farragut, aboard a gunship in the Mississippi Sound, spied the ship cruising the waters of the bay. The *Tennessee* was the strongest ship ever built to that time, its sides covered with six-inch iron plates over twenty-four inches of oak and pine planks. With its six Brooke cannons mounted on pivots, Farragut described the ship as formidable-looking. But unknown to Farragut, the *Tennessee* had two fatal flaws: slow engines salvaged from a riverboat and steering chains outside the armored deck.

Although Washington had not supplied Farragut with all he requested, he began the battle of Mobile Bay on the morning of August 5, 1864, with fourteen wooden ships, four ironclads, 2,700 men, and 197 guns. Confederate forces faced him with the *Tennessee* and three wooden ships, 427 men, and 22 guns. The 40 guns of Fort Morgan and 16 at Fort Gaines, along with torpedoes beside the narrow channel, would with luck make up the difference. The federal ironclad *Tecumseh* fired the first shot, and the battle commenced with the guns of Fort Morgan blazing from Mobile Point as the federal fleet came through the channel two abreast. The *Tecumseh* was the first ship sunk, probably by a torpedo. The smoke made it impossible to see clearly. The *Brooklyn* halted and began backing up, and the rest of the fleet stalled. Farragut, tied to the main-mast rigging of the *Hartford*, saw disaster at hand, and despite the torpedoes, in desperation as much as bravery, gave his famous order: "Damn the torpedoes! Go Ahead!" (Often quoted as "Damn the torpedoes! Full speed ahead!")[31]

Within three hours the federal fleet was in the bay and the three wooden Confederate ships were out of the battle. The *Tennessee*, left alone to fight, continued to cause Farragut consternation, and he ordered the ironclad rammed. Surrounded by enemy ships, the *Tennessee* had gun shutters jammed, steam about gone, and steering chain severed, when it hoisted a white flag. The great battle of Mobile Bay was over. The city girded itself for impending assault and occupation, knowing its land defenses and available manpower were unequal to the task. But the federal forces overestimated the fortifications and were content to control the bay and its forts and bide their time.

In fall 1864 Alabamians harvested their late summer crops and picked whatever cotton had been planted. The Confederacy was faltering or was in full retreat on all fronts. Atlanta fell in September. In November Lincoln and his Union party defeated the Peace Democrats. General Ulysses S. Grant was tightening his noose around Richmond, and Lee's army sat behind its Petersburg entrenchments. To finish off the war, Grant proposed sending another cavalry raid deep into Alabama to destroy the Selma munitions works, which continued to supply the arms for resistance in the west. He selected General James H. Wilson, who gathered a large cavalry force north of the Tennessee River.

In February the Alabama governor warned citizens of impending invasions from both Mobile Bay and north Alabama and called on the state's sixteen- and seventeen-year-olds to defend Alabama, for "subjugation means the confiscation of your property."[32] Wilson was delayed by poor weather, but finally on March 22, 1865, he managed to ferry 13,480 cavalrymen with their arms and horses across a rain-swollen Tennessee River. Wilson hoped that Confederate general Forrest would remain in Mississippi and that his raiders could move quickly through Alabama. He divided his men and took three different roads toward Jasper. Resting briefly, he sent General Emory Upton on to capture Elyton, destroy the iron furnaces in Shades Valley, and hold the Cahaba River crossing. The bluecoats met almost no resistance.

Wilson himself left Jasper with the rest of the troopers after daylight on March 30 and arrived in Elyton at one o'clock in the afternoon. He ate lunch at Judge William S. Mudd's house, "The Grove" (now Arlington), and learned from Mudd, who had just returned from Tuscaloosa, that no Confederate troops were in the vicinity. Wilson ordered the military school there burned, and John T. Croxton's First Brigade was detached and sent south. Above Tuscaloosa Croxton made a difficult crossing of the Warrior River with some loss of life. The city should not have been surprised by his entrance from the northwest, for earlier in the day bodies dressed in blue uniforms were spotted floating under the Tuscaloosa bridge. University cadets and local militia could not stop the bluecoats, and the federal forces began to burn the buildings of the University of Alabama. After the fires, only the president's mansion, the observatory, the Gorgas home (the only structure from the original campus), and ironically, the one true military building on campus, the small round guardhouse, were standing.

Wilson moved south toward Selma with little opposition until he reached Montevallo, where he defeated a small group of Forrest's cavalry. The "wizard of the saddle" had run out of men and horses, and all he could manage was to slow the Union advance. Forrest retreated to Selma to find the fortifications manned only by skeleton forces and the city stripped of anything that might benefit the federal troops. Although everybody who could walk was ordered to the breastworks, manpower was insufficient to defend the city. Unknown to Forrest, Wilson had been supplied with detailed plans of the fortifications. The attack began on April 2, and in short order a parapet was taken. The stars and stripes were soon flying above Selma again, and Wilson's raiders began the destruction they came to do, burning all the Confederate and private manufacturing facilities that had sustained the Confederacy for so long. The list compiled for General Wilson by General E. F. Winslow of property destroyed included twenty-four buildings of the Selma Arsenal, five large buildings of the Confederate Naval Ordnance Works, eighteen buildings of the Confederate Nitre Works, five buildings of the Selma Iron Works, and numerous other private factories and foundries.

As the federal troops burned Selma, Union prisoners were leaving Castle Morgan, the infamous Confederate prison at nearby Cahaba. The rains that had delayed and then plagued Wilson caused the Cahaba and Alabama rivers to overflow their banks and flood the prison stockade. Prisoners floated around, clinging to pieces of wood, or crawled to the top of sheds or upper bunks. Most of the prisoners were exchanged through Vicksburg, some 1,000 of them boarding the ill-fated *Sultana* for the trip north. The voyage ended eight miles above Memphis when the *Sultana's* boilers exploded and the boat burned and sank in the middle of the Mississippi River with great loss of life.

Meanwhile, General Forrest could do nothing to stop Wilson's raiders. He retreated to Gainesville and established a headquarters, while General Wilson moved toward the cradle of the Confederacy. News of the destruction of Tuscaloosa and Selma by Wilson's raid, as well as stories about the addition of a black regiment, reached Montgomery before the Union troops arrived. Governor Watts and state officials quickly departed for Union Springs, taking with them government documents, specie, and all the valuables they could carry. A new capital was to be established at Eufaula.

While Confederates were burning cotton warehouses and supplies in Montgomery to keep them from the enemy, a small group of Southern soldiers was preparing to defend Fort Blakeley from imminent attack by Federal troops. Some 400 battle-weary veterans from Missouri Confederate units were in fortifications along the banks of the Tensaw River and were supported by 2,000 Alabama reserves, some untested University of Alabama cadets. Although Confederate spirits were high, no chance existed that the small number of soldiers could stop a Union advance that included 45,000 men, some of them ex-slaves from Mississippi and Alabama. On April 9, the very day that Robert E. Lee surrendered his Army of Northern Virginia to General Grant, the attack began. The bluecoats soon breached the defenses, and in hand-to-hand combat, with vision limited by gunsmoke and dust, confusion reigned. Some Confederates tried to surrender, some Union troops went out of control, and the result was slaughter. When the sun set that day over Mobile Bay, Confederate dreams were dashed forever.

Three days later General James Wilson arrived in Montgomery. The militia refused the governor's call to defend the city, and the bluecoats began a systematic burning of foundries, rolling mills, niter works, riverboats, and railroad cars. Dense smoke covered the sky for days. In south Alabama General Richard Taylor surrendered the soldiers in his Department of the West to General E. R. S. Canby at Citronelle on May 4, 1865. The capitulation included General Dabney H. Maury's troops at Mobile and General Forrest's cavalry. Rumors circulated that Forrest would refuse to surrender his forces, but when General Taylor ordered him to do so, he complied.

The four-year war was over. Alabama society had collapsed under the strain of wartime conditions. Specie had vanished, spent for military supplies and food or secretly buried for its safety. Barter replaced inflated paper currency. Many schools and churches were closed, and probably one-fourth of the newspapers ceased publication. Cotton was piled on plantations or stored and would be burned by invading armies or confiscated as matériel of war. The slave-labor system had completely broken down in areas invaded by Northern armies. Slaves left the plantations, many following the bluecoated soldiers on the road to freedom. Women watched the dusty roads clogged with returning Confederate soldiers, hoping to see the familiar figure of a loved one. Yet before Alabamians could consider the meaning of defeat and speculate on the future, immediate needs for food and shelter had to be faced. For those who endured, the process of survival continued. Rebuilding fortunes remained only a dream. The smoke of burning buildings had not yet dissipated when the Civil War, a term used even by Jefferson Davis, began its passage from reality into the mists of myth. Within two decades it emerged as the War Between the States, the name the South preferred, believing it recognized the right of secession and the sovereignty of the Confederacy. But this name, too, ironically implied a conflict between the Northern and Southern states within a compact of the union.

PART TWO

From 1865
through 1920
by
William Warren Rogers and
Robert David Ward

Alabama House of Representatives in 1892. The House was the scene of acrimonious political battles between the Bourbon Democrats and the Populists. (Courtesy of the Alabama Department of Archives and History)

FOURTEEN

Reconstruction:
The Second Beginning

O N December 14, 1819, Alabama was admitted to the Union. Alabamians born in that year were only forty-two years old when their state seceded and joined the Confederacy. Yet some of them had children old enough to fight and die in the four years of warfare. In two brief generations Alabama had been settled, and its population had grown eightfold. Adopting and then adapting the social practices of its parent states (most notably Georgia and South Carolina), Alabama was building its own identity from the challenges of a rich and varied environment.

Throughout the 1830s and 1840s the state moved through years of growth and change, of innovation and reform. Then in the 1850s the heavy hand of slavery tightened its grip and slowly squeezed out the alternatives of accommodation to change and receptivity to new ideas. Under the increasing barrage of attack and criticism, Fortress Alabama dug a moat of isolation. On January 11, 1861, with the vote for secession, the castle door was closed and bolted. Alabama and its neighbors entered a new age of brief triumph and ultimate disaster.

When organized resistance ended in spring 1865, the old order seemed smashed to pieces by the blows of war. Slavery was gone, government no longer operated, and the social fabric was ripped and torn to the point of dissolution. Now, once again, Alabama stood poised on a new frontier; now, for the second time, society was in the making. It is one thing to bring a primitive order out of the wilderness, but it is quite another to fashion and weave a far more complex web of institutions. This time, change would be the product of defeat instead of hope and expectation, and the initial plans for the future would be drawn by the victors.

Reconstruction took the existing ingredients of Alabama life and shuffled them and dealt them out again to match a vision that was itself incomplete and unfinished. The old planter class, weakened materially for a while, had a flawed and challenged claim to leadership. The huge majority of small farmers survived but now were sunk from merely being poor to being utterly impoverished—and often they hated the planter architects of their misfortune. And there were the blacks cast adrift as pawns and sacrifices to the interests and enmities of others and struggling to find some substance to the promises and the laws of freedom.

The war changed Alabama life; it added industry and the entrepreneur to the social mix. But as externals changed, the old verities and the old arrangements stayed the same. Alabama accepted the war's political verdict but rejected its social judgment. It built a postbellum society in the incredible likeness of what had gone before. It did not accept the idea or the law that blacks were free and equal and independent citizens. And in fact the nation had not accepted it. Radical Republicans might for a time win their Northern neighbors' votes for a program to force democratic forms on a "sinful" South. Yet those same leaders did not force the questions of implementation and enforcement of racial democracy at home. That failure cost them the moral equity of successful leadership and with it any chance of changing the South.

Reconstruction in Alabama was a laboratory of social ferment, a vast experiment in action, inaction, and reaction. It revealed the volatility of minds and hearts. Here was a sharp picture of group behavior that succeeding generations would inspect from different angles and with different interpretations.

The Civil War ended with a tumultuous series of events. On April 4, 1865, President Lincoln made his second inaugural address and asked the nation "to do all which may achieve and cherish a just and lasting peace." Only five days later General Robert E. Lee surrendered to General Ulysses S. Grant at Appomattox Courthouse, and in another five days Lincoln lay dead from an assassin's bullet. On April 26 General Joseph E. Johnston surrendered to General William T. Sherman in North Carolina, and on May 4 General E. R. S. Canby, at Citronelle, Alabama, accepted the surrender of the last Confederate forces east of the Mississippi. Jefferson Davis was captured by Union troops in Georgia on May 10. The war was over.

What followed was a bitter time of turmoil and confusion for the South and for Alabama. The shooting stopped, but it was replaced by an uncertain peace. There was no treaty—how could there be if, as the North insisted, there had been no Southern nation? The white citizens of the state, often less than united before the war, were more fractured and divided than before.

Some Alabamians had invested their entire stock of emotional loyalty in the Confederate cause. For these men and women defeat was far too bitter to endure at the scene of their past triumphs. They joined other recruits for the exile colonies that moved to Brazil or Mexico, or they went west to build a new life in a new place. As fanatics of a cause, they were a distinct minority. Their adventure as expatriates was largely quixotic—expenses, poor land, and the alien environment assailed them—and most of them ultimately returned.

The majority of the planter and professional classes who supported secession and war came home from the army or from wartime duties. Most had lost heavily, not simply in money and property but in the status of leadership. They were the authors of misery, the leaders who had failed. It was this group, in Northern eyes, that bore the burden of secession and treason. They had hopes of recovering some degree of prosperity, although for the moment political leadership seemed to have passed them by.

Another group from the old ruling class whose material fortunes suffered just as much faced a different future. They were the conservatives of 1860, men of wealth and position who opposed secession but supported the Confederacy with varying degrees of loyalty and drive. They had a better claim to preferment on the relative scale of loyalty to the Union. Yet few of them could have taken the "iron-clad" oath required of federal officeholders.

Like their leaders, the rank and file of white Alabamians split along the lines of ideology and interest. The majority were swept up in the course of events and willingly or under coercion supported the Confederacy. Many, particularly from the hill counties of north Alabama, opposed the war, evaded conscription, or deserted from the army. They were hounded and persecuted by their conforming neighbors or by Confederate officials. If there were Confederates bitter in defeat, the Alabama Unionists were a group bitter in victory—and hopeful of righting the wrongs they had suffered during the fighting.

Whatever the effects of the war on white Alabamians, however altered their condition or changed their status, the most cataclysmic changes came to blacks. Almost one-half of the state's people were slaves in 1861; almost one-half of the people became free in 1865. The new freedom lacked definition, it lacked content, but it seemed to turn the old society on its head. For the blacks it was a time for jubilation, for release, for confusion—and for cares and worries about the future.

These were the people who remained after the four-year reign of death and destruction. Alabama received both in good measure. The hostilities were so disruptive that the record of how many Alabamians enlisted in the army and how many were killed is confused and misleading. Some scholars have contended that 90,000 enlisted in the Confederate or Union armies, while others report 122,000 enlistments. Both figures seem high when measured against census figures: men age fifteen to sixty numbered 126,587 in 1860, and the greatest span for

Confederate conscription ages was seventeen to fifty. Provisional Governor Lewis E. Parsons announced that Alabama suffered 34,000 killed or died of wounds with another 35,000 disabled. A little later Governor Robert M. Patton put the number dead at 40,000. Historians have argued over a plausible number, but none has denied that Alabama lost heavily in the fighting. Counting may indicate the size of loss, but there are no adequate measures for what even one life can mean.

When the subject of loss is not life but property, statistics become less sensitive. It is a story endlessly told of a devastated South, a region penalized into the future by Yankee pillaging and destruction. Alabama's damage was real. The state suffered severely from the planned destruction carried out by both sides and by foraging troops, again from both sides, as they lived off the land. In keeping with the illogic of war, north Alabama—the area of few slaves, vocal in opposition to secession, and strong in Unionism—fared the worse. The troops of both armies surged back and forth across it, while the Black Belt, home of the planter and secessionist spirit, was almost untouched.

In 1865, as General James H. Wilson left north Alabama for his celebrated raid through the state's center, he reported: "The entire valley of the Tennessee having been devastated by two years of warfare was quite as destitute of any supplies as the hill country south of it. In all directions, for a hundred and twenty miles, there was almost complete destitution."[1] Huntsville was occupied several times. Decatur, Tuscumbia, and Athens suffered severe damage. The wartime level of destruction and the fight for survival intensified the bitterness of Reconstruction. In 1865 Governor Parsons appointed Marcus H. Cruikshank as the state's commissioner of relief for the destitute, and Cruikshank visited neighboring states to seek aid.

Across Alabama miles of railroad track were destroyed and many depots burned. Sixteen of Alabama's seventeen blast furnaces were put out of production. There was heavy damage in Tuscaloosa (all but four buildings of the University of Alabama were burned) and even heavier in Selma, where the fighting was fierce and the huge Confederate arsenal was destroyed. Montgomery lost three steamboats, a foundry, a rolling mill, and 97,000 bales of cotton burned by retreating Confederates. Union troopers spared the state penitentiary at Wetumpka and contented themselves with bringing emancipation to the prisoners.

Alabama's railroads were hurt far more by a defeat that destroyed their financial structure than by a bending of their rails. It is hard to argue that the destruction of the blast furnaces delayed the coming of the iron industry. Yet the war brought crippling amendments to the Alabama economy. It was not from Union property destruction but from the emancipation of the slaves that Alabama lost at least $200 million of capital investment. The state's currency system was destroyed, as were most financial investments. Debts owed by the Confederacy were gone forever, and personal debts were largely uncollectible.

Alabama agriculture was left in a shambles of loss and confusion. The plantation system based on slave labor was gone, leaving only a vast uncertainty as to what might replace it. The small farmer class, diminished in manpower, in many cases had lost what few assets it had started with. Fields were abandoned; destruction and lack of attention ruined improvements; equipment was broken or missing. Livestock losses were so severe that even by 1870 levels were below those of 1860. Worms, insects, and parasites were present in telling numbers but had to diet on poor crops in 1865. There was a shortage of seeds for 1866.

Clarke County, south of the Black Belt and off the track of invading armies, offered an example of the war's effects. In 1860 it had 901 farms; by 1870 there were only 751. Its tilled acres went from 99,000 to 61,000, its cotton crop declined by one-third, and its food products slipped below the levels of 1860. "Work as our people may," an east Alabama editor later despaired, "do what they can—pray and work, yet they fail. . . . And we ask, involuntarily, is the South abandoned, that the very earth doth mock us!"[2]

Federal troops occupied Alabama's cities and many of the small towns, and their presence contributed both to what passed for order and government and to violence and depredation. The soldiers' job was made more difficult as many blacks, in a perfect test of freedom, left their plantations and flocked to the towns and cities. Destitute whites and blacks had to be fed and basic public health measures had to be enforced. General George H. Thomas, in an order that affected north Alabama, decreed that sheriffs, judges, commissioners, and justices of the peace were to continue in office and enforce the laws existing prior to secession. There was no general policy of military government to guide the soldiers. They referred major issues to the War Department for instructions. Such was the fate of a petition signed by numerous Alabamians asking General Frederick Steele to set in motion the procedure for restoring Alabama to the Union. There was no answer to their request.

To the trouble caused by marauding troops and deserters from both sides, Alabamians furnished their own domestic violence. Particularly in central and north Alabama, wartime repression of Unionists was answered by attacks on former Confederates and raids and counterraids. The patriotic image of united Alabamians strong in their solidarity for states' rights and secession was the creation of a later time, a myth of the "Lost Cause." There was a large measure of loyalty, but there was never unanimity.

Alabamians, whether defeated Confederates or stalwart Unionists, had reason to wonder about their future and what their role would be. Lincoln based his ideas of Reconstruction on the charitable foundation of the future loyalty of Confederates. He offered a pardon to Confederate supporters who would take an oath to support the Constitution and the Union. When the newly loyal group equaled one-tenth of the voters of 1860, a state could elect officials, establish its government, abolish slavery, and receive presidential recognition of its return to the Union.

The North's war aims in 1865 went beyond the simple restoration of the Union that existed in 1861. Lincoln himself had been forced to move on to include emancipation. The radicals of his own party opposed the easy return of the planter leadership and the oligarchic society it represented. The Radical Republicans' Wade-Davis bill of 1864 rejected Lincoln's forgiving hopes of future loyalty and based its new electorate in the South on wartime behavior. No one who had voluntarily borne arms against the United States and no one who had held state or Confederate office could vote or run as a delegate to a state convention. When a majority of white males had taken an oath of allegiance, the pure-at-heart Unionists were to frame a constitution, prohibit slavery, and repudiate the Confederate debt. Lincoln killed the Wade-Davis bill with a pocket veto, while telling Southerners they could follow its program if they wished. And here on ambiguity the matter rested as the war ended and Lincoln vanished from the scene.

President Andrew Johnson of Tennessee was a close neighbor to Alabama and at one in background and belief with the Unionists there. Johnson spoke menacingly of punishing treason as a crime, but in the months from April to December 1865, when Congress again came into session, he adopted policies almost as lenient as those of Lincoln. To the earlier bases of pardon Johnson specified that those with taxable property over $20,000 (and other special cases) must apply to him for exoneration. Except for wealthy planters, Johnson was accepting an electorate based on future loyalty.

One by one President Johnson issued proclamations that named provisional governors and laid out the process of reconstituting each state. Alabama's turn came on June 21, 1865. Johnson appointed Lewis E. Parsons of Talladega as the provisional governor; no more moderate figure than Parsons existed among the state's hostile factions.

Born in New York in 1817, Parsons was the grandson of Jonathan Edwards, the prophet of New England's "Great Awakening." He studied law in Pennsylvania and New York and settled in Talladega in 1840. Parsons was a staunch Whig, a distinguished lawyer, and a pillar of the community. By 1860, searching for a political home, he was a Douglas Democrat. He opposed secession but represented his county in the legislature in 1863. Never an agitator, Parsons was openly conservative. As a contemporary noted, "He has manifestly been a Union man, without disguise, though offering no fractious opposition to the majority."[3] He now assumed a difficult job.

Only a week after Parsons was appointed governor, the War Department reorganized its military departments. Alabama was included in the Military Division of the Tennessee under General George H. Thomas. The command of the Department of Alabama went to General Charles R. Woods, who had led the expedition to resupply Fort Sumter in 1861 and who had been with Sherman on his march to the sea.

By the terms of President Johnson's proclamation, existing laws in Alabama, except those pertaining to slavery, were kept in force. Governor Parsons could (and he largely did) leave the former Confederate state officials in office as he guided the political process toward statehood. The first step was to establish an electorate of "loyal" voters. At least 120 army officers toured the state, administering the oath "to support, protect, and defend the Constitution of the United States." The work went slowly until the commanding officer ruled that all eligible voters must take the oath. At least 50,000 Alabamians did so—a major reduction from the 90,000 who had voted in 1860. A few more voters were added as President Johnson issued pardons to excluded classes (up to 1868, Johnson pardoned 1,456 Alabamians, including 72 affluent women).

On August 31, 1865, approximately 56,000 voters elected delegates to the constitutional convention. Of the ninety-nine delegates, a majority were over fifty years old. The thirty-three lawyers and forty-two farmers were joined by six doctors, nine merchants, two teachers, and seven ministers. Forty-five of the delegates had been Whigs. But the major split in the convention was not by age, or occupation, or previous political orientation. The delegates have been classified as sixty-three "conservatives" and thirty-six north Alabama "anti-Confederates." Another division could include the thirty delegates representing "black counties" and the sixty-nine supporting the interests of "white counties." Whether that split prevailed depended on the issue being addressed.

There were major concerns, some to be decided in substance, others only in form. A long wrangle concerned repealing the Ordinance of Secession without implying that anyone had been wrong in the first place. The issue was finally decided with a declaration, without editorial comment, that the ordinance was "null and void." After good faith and legitimacy were duly praised, the state's war debt was declared void by a vote of 60 to 19.

The orientation of some delegates was revealed by talk of not abolishing slavery until the courts determined the constitutionality of wartime actions. Common sense prevailed by a vote of 89 to 3: the convention declared that inasmuch as slavery had been destroyed it could not exist in the state.

Turning its attention to the electorate and representation, the convention walked among the basic issues of Reconstruction. It provided for a census in 1866. Then, using those current numbers, state senators and representatives would be apportioned on the basis of the white population. The provision was a solid foundation for the Huntsville *Advocate's* assertion that "this is a white man's government and a white man's state."[4] There was nothing new in the approach or in the split it represented between small farmer interests and the planters. In 1843 Alabama had passed a measure abolishing the three-fifths rule (counting three-fifths of the slaves for purposes of representation) to the fervid protests and opposition of the Black Belt's planters and politicians. Now, in 1865, the convention took exactly the same action. There were thirty Black Belt votes against the measure because it would lessen their representation in the state legislature.

Without positively addressing the issue of full political rights for blacks, the convention managed to answer the matter with a sharp negative. It voted unanimously to table a petition from blacks in Mobile asking for the right to vote. Here, early in Reconstruction, was the hard core of an issue that inflamed and illuminated Alabama politics for the next forty years. The equation was complex in alternatives but simple to state. If the blacks did not vote, if there was a white basis of representation, the northern and southeastern white counties would control state government in their own interest. If the blacks were ever allowed to vote, the consequences branched in complexity. Would they vote from narrow economic interests or broader political concerns? If the former bondsmen voted Republican and if the poor whites voted the same, they would have overwhelming power in the state. If blacks could be persuaded to follow the lead of their former Black Belt masters, then that white minority would hold power in its hands. This was the basic political equation in Alabama until 1901, and it operated in a host of transient solutions and arrangements. By a vote of 61 to 25 the convention approved its handiwork. The constitution, over the strong opposition of the Unionists, went into effect without a referendum by the people. The first step was completed. The second phase of government creation was at hand.

The new constitution was not immediately implemented, but elections were held in November 1865 for governor, legislators, and state and county officials. No gubernatorial candidate claimed south Alabama as his home. Robert M. Patton was from Lauderdale County on the Tennessee line; William Russell Smith lived in Tuscaloosa County; and Michael J. Bulger was the closest to the Black Belt in Tallapoosa County. If the planters were not directly represented by the candidates, the Unionists of north Alabama felt utterly betrayed. They had no immediate objection to white government. They were concerned about *which* whites were in control. Patton, Smith, and Bulger—like Governor Parsons—were men who had opposed secession, but once secession was accomplished, they had accepted Alabama's new status. Thus, in Unionist eyes they had supported the war. Governor Parsons, moreover, had retained many of the state's Confederate officials. The Unionists saw the same old power structure still in domination.

Patton won the election with a strong showing over Bulger and Smith, and the way seemed clear for him and the legislature to assume their duties. Although the legislature met on November 20, Governor-elect Patton had to wait another month to take his office. With President Johnson's approval he was inaugurated on December 13. Parsons was not relieved as provisional governor until December 18, and he actually turned over his office on December 20. In the meanwhile, the legislature, following Johnson's wishes, made Alabama the twenty-seventh state to ratify the Thirteenth Amendment abolishing slavery. The vote was counted for ratification, and the vote was not thrown out when it later became plain that Alabama was not back in the Union after all.

Such contradictions were proof that affairs were on the march in a larger arena than Alabama. The broader ramifications became more clear when Alabama's two new senators and six representatives—along with those of the other former Confederate states—were refused their seats in Congress. Thaddeus Stevens, the Radical Republican leader in the House, introduced a resolution creating the Joint Committee of Fifteen on Reconstruction to investigate conditions in the Southern states. His view of the Johnson-approved governments was sharply stated. He proposed no recognition of those he called "whitewashed rebels." Earlier Stevens had declared: "To Congress alone belongs the power of Reconstruction, of giving law to the vanquished."[5] The maneuvers of Stevens and like-minded congressmen boded ill for the president's plan for Reconstruction and therefore for the fledgling administration of Governor Patton in Alabama.

To many Northerners the trouble with Johnson's plan was basic: it had not changed anything. Unrepentant rebels still held sway in the South, loyal Unionists were proscribed, and the black man merely exchanged one form of slavery for another and remained at best only half a citizen. This view raised the question of what the war was supposed to have accomplished. If it had been intended to reconstitute the South in the image of a more democratic North, or to place political power in the hands of the loyal common man (and all of this was full of strained images), then plainly it had failed. And nowhere was that failure more manifest than in the first months of black freedom.

When the arrival of federal troops brought an end to slavery, the newly emancipated blacks discovered that at least in spirit they had a friend at court. On March 3, 1865, Congress established the Bureau of Refugees, Freedmen, and Abandoned Lands. The Freedmen's Bureau was armed with a broad mandate of responsibility over all matters relating to the former slaves. Its role in the process of Reconstruction was controversial at the time and has been controversial among historians ever since. Was it a bumbling bureaucracy whose works were completely swept away? Did it perform a notable if imperfect job in protecting blacks in their rights? Were its aims and purposes the victim of white intransigence on the one hand and less than strong Radical Republican support on the other? In Alabama the Freedmen's Bureau reflected many contradictory images and the picture that emerged was never clear of distortion.

The organization was formed as an agency of the War Department under General Oliver Otis Howard. During the first years its assistant commissioners, who supervised entire states, and their agents were army officers—and later often former army officers. General Howard moved into an area that was new and untried, unprecedented in its problems of directing a former slave society toward freedom, and fraught with endless obstacles of attitude and self-interest. In form the bureau was centralized in Washington (and Howard was not a free agent to do whatever he pleased), but its policies were acted out on the state and county levels.

As his assistant commissioner in Alabama, Howard appointed the young General Wager Swayne, who was destined to be his longest serving state official. After 1866 Swayne was both assistant commissioner and the district military commander. Swayne was a lawyer by training, one among thousands of civilians swept up in the war who made their mark as soldiers. He lost a leg and gained a Congressional Medal of Honor. No armchair soldier, Swayne was appointed to the Alabama position while still convalescing from his amputation. He moved into the command post at Montgomery in August 1865.

The Freedmen's Bureau was active in the areas of justice, labor, education, relief, medical aid, and, after black suffrage was granted in 1867, political education. And it was in two of these often overlapping jurisdictions that General Swayne made his first moves.

As the blacks moved away from their legal status as bondsmen, they found no category to define their new existence. No longer slaves, were they not entitled to the same legal status, the same rights and privileges possessed by whites? The question of status was the heart of the matter because it did not follow that Southern whites, forced to abandon slavery, were willing to welcome the new freedmen as equals. Their new status was a blank slate, and General Swayne immediately picked up the chalk and began to write.

Under military occupation, Alabama laws enacted prior to January 11, 1861 (except for those pertaining to slavery), were in force, and the old judges still sat. The situation caused Swayne a problem. The old laws did not permit black testimony in white trials—a basic tenet for a slave society that was founded on inequality and the anathema of having a black testify against a white.

In Washington General Howard had already addressed the question. Meeting with his assistant commissioners in May (Swayne had not yet been appointed), Howard issued a circular authorizing them to try cases involving blacks in bureau courts if the civil courts were not functioning or refused to allow black testimony. Howard's circular seemed to establish a liberal policy. President Johnson approved because he wanted to create an image of black rights adequately protected and to advance the argument of admitting the Southern states immediately to the Union.

Most of the assistant commissioners, realizing that blacks would not receive fair trials in the civil courts, tried to handle black cases in their own bureau courts. In Alabama General Swayne followed his own procedures. First, he asked Governor Parsons to order the removal of blacks' disabilities under the law and, specifically, to give them the right to testify. Parsons responded that such an order was "politically inexpedient" because it would excite hard-line whites and hurt the chances for a moderate constitutional convention.

Swayne immediately took action. He announced that henceforth Alabama judicial officers would be considered bureau agents for the administration of justice. They were to try cases involving blacks with no distinctions on racial grounds. If a judge refused or continued to deny blacks equal justice, he would lose his bureau appointment and martial law could be instituted in his district.

Swayne was correct that equal justice should be made a part of the state courts if it was to exist at all. But to judge equality on the narrow basis of allowing black testimony was a dangerous gamble. His temporary suspension of a few judges and his three uses of bureau courts did not guarantee black equality before the law. It was simply too easy to allow black testimony and then ignore it. Most Alabama judges accepted their unwanted commissions. Governor Parsons now urged compliance, and the constitutional convention enacted an ordinance requiring judges to serve as bureau agents. Not sure that blacks would obtain legal equality from white judges and juries, Swayne said, "I wish I could pay an agent in every county to watch over these courts."[6]

Swayne took immediate action in another area of critical importance. Widespread poverty and suffering and heavy demands on the bureau to prevent starvation emphasized the question of black labor. The large numbers of blacks who had left their plantations for the cities gave credence to white fears (shared by General Swayne) that the former chattels might refuse to work. There was the attendant attitude that a free-labor system was impossible because blacks would not work without coercion. Nothing better illustrated the confusion of the time and the absence of considered plans than the question of a new labor system.

In the so-called second confiscation act, passed by Congress in 1862, the property of all officers of the late Confederacy was liable to immediate confiscation by the federal government. Moreover, the property of all persons supporting rebellion could be forfeited on sixty days' notice. Even as punishment for treason, the act was draconian, and it raised issues beyond punishment and vengeance.

By 1865 Thaddeus Stevens was working hard to implement the law and confiscate the estates of former Confederates. Stevens saw at least 394 million acres of Southern land under federal ownership, and he advocated giving every adult black man 40 acres of the seized property. The rest would be sold to pay the war debt and military pensions and to compensate Unionists for their losses. It was a radical plan, a bold stroke that would have slashed the fabric of Southern life in two directions.

Stevens's plan would have grievously weakened the class of Southern planters. Many of them, even without confiscation, were forced to sell a part or all of their lands after the war. But the transactions most often substituted new planters for the old. The majority kept their property by instituting the tenant farming system. Large landowners suffered a serious illness, but their class was far from dead.

In the other direction, land given to blacks would not have produced a racial utopia, but it would have shifted the overwhelming balance of economic power. There would still have been large white landowners. There was no guarantee that all the blacks would keep their small farms, and many former slaves would have remained as landless farm laborers. Yet allowing thousands of blacks an independence denied them without land of their own would have moved the scale of social forces.

It was a plan that might have been. It did not strengthen Stevens's case to ride the coattails of confiscation. The idea was hurt by being linked with punishment, and it directly assaulted the temple where the rights of private property were kept. A more feasible and acceptable stroke would have been to *purchase* Southern land for distribution to whites and blacks. The postwar market was flooded with cheap land. Equity aside, distribution of small farms to blacks had more to recommend it as social policy than compensation for slaveowners—which also failed.

In some instances Alabama blacks managed to acquire land and keep it under a host of pressures. But there was little "abandoned land" to give them in the state, and their ability to buy land was most often stymied by inexperience, poor credit, and no cash. The Southern Homestead Act of 1866 provided little land for Alabama blacks. There were

6,732,058 acres of public land in Alabama (20.7 percent of the entire state), but of the 16,284 homestead applications, only 6,293 titles were actually issued. The amount of land taken amounted to 720,773 acres, but most of it was totally unsuited to farming. According to the Mobile *Daily Advertiser and Register,* no tract of land was available where a farmer "would not starve and be taxed to death in three weeks."[7]

There was no comparison between the political freedom possible (for it was never guaranteed) for the small landowners and that of black field hands on plantations who were carried into town on election day to vote the way their employers directed. Ultimately, the majority of blacks were consumed by the same prewar pattern of Southern agriculture where dozens and sometimes hundreds built the income of the large landowner. One Dallas County white man remarked: "The nigger is going to be made a serf, sure as you live. Planters will have an understanding among themselves: 'You won't hire my niggers and I won't hire yours.' Then what's left to them?"[8] As the years went by, the small white farmer was also sucked into the whirlpool of tenant farming and the crop lien system and was smashed against the rocks of economic inequality.

General Swayne in 1865 contemplated not the future but the hard, implacable present. Swayne's priorities were to disabuse Alabama blacks that they would receive free land. His message to the freedmen was to "hope for nothing, but go to work and behave yourselves."[9] The sentiment paralleled that of Governor Patton: "the Negro must be made to realize that freedom does not mean idleness and vagrancy."[10] On August 30, 1865, Swayne announced his labor policy. Blacks and their employers would sign contracts (in writing if for longer than one month), and the contracts required approval by the bureau. That agency would not set wage levels (in practice, pay varied from ten to twelve dollars a month for male field hands and six to ten dollars for women). Food, shelter, and medical help were the employers' obligations, and costs for the unemployed members of a family were deducted from the employee's pay. In an almost cashless society, money wages were soon discontinued. The standard contract awarded the black man a share of the crop according to how much of the expenses he paid.

Swayne considered the contract-labor system as a temporary expedient to get blacks back to work. He saw the real regulators as those basic market forces of the blacks' need to eat and the planters' need for labor. Admitting that without protection the black worker could not bargain equitably with the planter, Swayne insisted that the contract system need not long remain. As a result the bureau exercised some protection for the blacks for a time. Yet the system either allowed the blacks to be defrauded and thrown off the land or defrauded into debt that bound them as strongly as the shackles of slavery. The suggestion that Swayne's contracts were a prelude to collective bargaining ignores the fact that they were almost never the result of either collective action or free bargaining. Growing cotton on large plantations could be more efficient than on small farms and economic pressure forced a continuation of the plantation system, but to gain efficiency at the expense of the degradation of the labor force was a dubious bargain.

With white fears of a black "strike" allayed, further action on the labor front came from the constitutional convention and the legislature that followed it. To many whites the contract system under bureau supervision did not produce the requisite control of black labor—and certainly not the broader social control that slavery had allowed. Such flaws could be eliminated by remedial legislation.

The constitutional convention of 1865 failed to make blacks equal before the law. Instead, it advised the legislature to pass laws protecting blacks in "the full enjoyment of their rights, person, and property and guard them and the state from all evil that might arise from their sudden emancipation."[11] The legislature, coming into session on November 20, 1865, emphasized the latter clause. A bill was passed that would have forced blacks to accept labor contracts (Swayne called it "a rival of slavery"), but Governor Patton, aware of hostile reactions in the North, refused to accept it.

When the legislature reconvened on January 15, 1866, it enacted laws—which collectively became the Alabama black code—to regulate the labor condition and conduct of blacks. Compared to the regulations in other Southern states, the Alabama laws were moderate—a comparison that afforded little benefit to blacks. Defining a vagrant as a runaway, common drunkard, "stubborn servant," or "any person who habitually neglects his employment," the vagrancy law dealt with the labor problem. Anyone convicted of vagrancy could be fined $50 (an unusually large sum). If unable to pay, the person could be confined to jail or after three days of public advertisement be hired out for as long as six months until the fine was paid. An apprentice law followed and provided that all orphans, or children whose parents refused to support them, could be put into custody of a suitable person. If the child had been a slave, the former master was given custody. A runaway apprentice was a vagrant. To complete the realities of control, pistols were taxed at $2 and bowie knives at $3—unlikely sums for a black to pay.

In their language the Alabama laws applied to black and white alike, and it was claimed that the vagrancy act was modeled on that of Massachusetts. In fact, the laws were aimed at blacks alone. This early, in matters of race, Alabama legislators began the process of obscuring reality. It was not necessary for laws to spell out discrimination to be discriminatory. Enforcement could apply the law exactly where legislative motive had intended.

In sum, President Johnson's plan of Reconstruction allowed the white conservatives to return to power. Their immediate use of the law emphasized a determination to deny legal and social equality to blacks and to control their labor effectively. It also emphasized a blindness to the meaning of the war and an inability to see themselves as others saw them. The attitudinal defeat of the Confederacy, if ever real at all, lasted for the briefest of times. This mindset was the South's contribution to the downfall of the Johnson governments and the coming of Radical Reconstruction.

Before the Freedmen's Bureau is removed from center stage, other aspects of its work require notice. It distributed rations to thousands of blacks and whites in the "starving time" of 1865–66. It set up "home colonies" as clearinghouses for black labor and as support for those who could not work. It established hospitals at Mobile, Montgomery, Demopolis, Selma, Huntsville, Talladega, and Garland (in Butler County). With assistance from the Pittsburgh Freedman's Aid Society and the Northwestern Aid Society of Chicago, the bureau opened schools for blacks. The bureau also helped the American Missionary Association establish Talladega College to train black teachers.

Despite the good works, the bureau's efforts have been faulted as too little and lacking in a hard appraisal of the situation. Attempts at relief were not efficiently administered, but it is insensitive to dismiss them by charging that the agency only acted because the need was so great. That the bureau could have done more should not obscure its positive accomplishments.

In the area of black education the critics have a stronger case. Initially there was animosity by whites to any education for the freedmen. Black schools were burned and teachers terrorized. Even by 1867, when bureau officials congratulated themselves on growing white support, they overlooked the real situation. Black education in Southern hands was acceptable. If education could emancipate and free, it could also enslave and control. It was always a question of what people were taught—and by whom.

The Freedmen's Bureau helped. At first it was a bulwark against starvation for blacks and whites. Its educational efforts were full of promise but empty of long-term benefit. Its guardianship of blacks in their transition to free labor, however well motivated, had cutting limitations. The bureau operated within the social and economic concepts of the time, and it operated in an untried area of administration. It supported the system of labor contracts and attempted to protect blacks against unscrupulous planters. Yet the bureau did not break the pattern that left most blacks in the same role they had held in slavery. That was why the war, in fundamentals, seemed to make such little difference in Southern life.

Radical or congressional Reconstruction has been usually considered as imposed from outside, the product of certain congressmen in their test of will and policy with President Johnson. Although the decisions came from Washington, there was a much stronger interaction between state and national levels than supposed. As noted, the Alabama Unionists were increasingly dissatisfied with presidential Reconstruction. Their old Confederate enemies were still lodged in office. Relief supplies often did not get to them. They complained of discrimination by the courts, and they became even more inclined to take up arms to even the score. The Unionists of Alabama began to organize; their vehicle was the Union League.

The league was a secret organization started in the North to support the war effort. Now it came South and began to enroll first white Unionists and later blacks. With perhaps a thousand members in December 1865, the league grew rapidly and fed on the dissatisfaction of hard times and the hostility toward the Johnson government. In 1866 Alabama Unionist leaders went to Washington to discuss home affairs with Republican congressmen. They emphasized the error of giving political power to opponents of secession rather than to those who had been loyal Unionists throughout the war. With Union League organization, the north Alabamians contested conservative control (with mixed success in local elections). Political activity demonstrated their weakness. Despite probable majorities in Fayette, Marion, Walker, and Winston counties, the Unionists were a distinct minority in the state. In 1867 they numbered between ten and fifteen thousand—at most only one-fifth of the state electorate.

With the rise of Radical Republican strength in the North and the growing certainty that Congress would adopt its own Reconstruction plan, the Alabama Unionists had to confront a basic question. If Congress ordained black suffrage, and if the Republicans could control black votes, the Unionists could become the majority party in Alabama. The fact that conservative Black Belt leaders were moving toward at least a qualified black suffrage demanded thought. While the Unionists had been and remained antiplanter, they were also antiblack. They were as racist as their Black Belt cousins. They wanted the black votes that could put them in power, but they did not want the social equality that might go with it. They opted for black suffrage, but there was always tension in the party. The South was on the threshold of Radical Reconstruction, and in Alabama the Unionists were a vital part of a complex power struggle that affected every aspect of society.

FIFTEEN

_____

Radical Reconstruction

IN Washington the Radical Republican movement gathered momentum. On April 9, 1866, Congress passed the Civil Rights Act over President Johnson's veto. The measure was an obvious rebuttal to the Southern black codes. It provided that persons born in the United States were citizens and that such persons "of every race and color" had the right to give evidence in the courts, hold property, and receive equal benefit of the laws. Denial of a person's equal rights was punishable by fine and imprisonment on conviction in federal court. Strict enforcement would have produced full dockets in Alabama and the South.

In their victory over Johnson the sponsors of the Civil Rights Act were unsure of its constitutionality. It seemed necessary to incorporate its major provisions in the Constitution, and the result was the proposed Fourteenth Amendment. The amendment prohibited the states from denying any person life, liberty, or property without due process of law. Although it defined citizenship to include blacks, there was no specific requirement for black suffrage. Instead it promised to reduce the representation of any state denying the right to vote—and that could have included some Northern states.

The Fourteenth Amendment went to the states for their consideration. Every Southern state except Tennessee refused to ratify it. The Alabama legislature acted in concert, although without the last-minute advice of President Johnson it might have approved the amendment as a measure of necessity.

The Radical Republicans' motives and methods directly affected Alabama. On March 2, 1867, the first of the four major Reconstruction acts was passed. It divided the ten "unreconstructed" states into five military districts commanded by army generals. The commander in the Third Military District (Florida, Georgia, and Alabama) could use civil government if he wished or ignore it if he chose. He could make arrests and conduct trials. Obviously the Southern states were heading back under military government. The political future was also spelled out. With blacks voting, elections would be held for a constitutional convention.

Former Confederate leaders disfranchised by the proposed Fourteenth Amendment could not vote in the election. The convention had to write exactly these suffrage requirements into the new constitution. When the document was approved, and when the Alabama legislature ratified the Fourteenth Amendment, then Congress would decide if the state was entitled to representation in Washington.

The act of March 2 outlined the plan, but it was almost silent on the procedure to be followed. Congress spelled out the process in the act of March 23, 1867. The military government was authorized to register the voters and hold an election for a convention. It took a third act (July 19, 1867) to deal with the "true intent and meaning" of the first two. The military was superior to the civil governments. Indeed, the latter were "not legal." Voter registration boards could decide if a man had voluntarily supported the Confederacy. The measure would have been the last of the national Reconstruction acts had it not been for events in Alabama.

As soon as the act of March 2 was passed and before Major General John Pope took command of the Third Military District (with Wager Swayne still commanding in Alabama), the soon-to-be-enfranchised blacks began to organize. On March 4 in Mobile, Lawrence Berry of the African Methodist Episcopal Zion Church and E. C. Branch, publisher of the Mobile *Nationalist,* called a meeting to organize a political society. More meetings followed to spread the word of black political activism. Born in Alabama and educated in Canada, James T. Rapier presided over a meeting of blacks in Florence to nominate a voting registrar for Lauderdale County. With a promise to "enter upon the discharge of our new obligations with a sincere desire to promote peace, harmony, and union," the meeting nominated his father, John H. Rapier, Sr., for the position.[1]

All over the state similar meetings went on—in Madison and Morgan counties, at Kingston in Autauga County, at Tuskegee, Montgomery, Selma, Hayneville, and Bluffton. Many of the meetings were attended by blacks and whites, and both often shared the speaker's platform. In the other political camp in these early days the conservative whites still hoped to control the black vote. Even so, their stated belief that white voters should lead "the inferior colored race" offered few inducements for blacks to sign up as Democrats.[2] On May 14, 1867, an unlikely public forum was held in Montgomery. United States senator Henry Wilson of Massachusetts, a thorough-going Radical Republican, stood on the capitol steps and debated James H. Clanton, chairman of the State Democratic Executive Committee of Alabama. Both men appealed to the former slaves for their votes. Clanton emphasized a common background and the Southern whites' long friendship with blacks.

Such political congeniality was short-lived. On the night of May 14 in Mobile, when hundreds of blacks assembled to hear a speech by William D. "Pig Iron" Kelley of Pennsylvania, a group of white men fired at the crowd. In Greensboro, in the Black Belt, a white storekeeper shot and killed the black registrar of Hale County after an argument. Increasingly, white Democrats moved away from accommodation or even serious political dialogue with black and white Republicans. They defined the state as white men's country and made race their salient weapon. It stayed that way for almost one hundred years.

For their part, the Alabama Unionists began propagandizing among the blacks. Their effort to publicize the Republican party was marked by factionalism and ideological disagreement. There were "moderate" Unionists who were reluctant to accept the Republican label, and there were radicals who strongly supported congressional Reconstruction. White yeomen of the hill counties often favored the confiscation and distribution of rebel property even when they were troubled by racial cooperation.

On June 4–5, 1867, delegates met in Montgomery for the first convention of the Alabama Republican party. It was not entirely a demonstration of unity. Once the convention opened, heated debate followed a motion to seat federal judge Richard Busteed. The jurist was a Republican, but he had spoken publicly against black suffrage. The argument was between those who believed that all support should be accepted and those who saw black suffrage as a test of party loyalty. Finally, on the morning of the second day, the delegates voted (148–25) against seating Busteed and belatedly got around to preparing a platform.

The convention unanimously stated its support for congressional Reconstruction and the Fourteenth Amendment. The delegates pledged to work for free speech, a free press, public education, and an end to racial discrimination. Unanimity for the platform concealed conservative Republican unhappiness with the radicals. The seeds of discord between native-born Unionists (the "scalawags" in the tainted terminology of the Democrats) and the blacks and the late-arriving whites (the "carpetbaggers") could already be discerned.

By this time General Pope, after some differences of opinion with President Johnson, was ready to begin the process of voter registration. Three-man boards with one black member were established for the forty-four registration districts. Now there were two parallel themes in what occurred. The first was the necessity of informing the blacks of their new rights and getting them to register. Black leaders and white Republicans, already working hard, were joined (and sometimes they were one and the same) by agents of the Freedmen's Bureau. That the

243

bureau agents were often politically partisan was inherent in the situation. It defied logic that blacks would have voted Democratic under any circumstances. The other theme—the issue and outcome of the disfranchisement of white voters—rapidly took matters into the realm of mathematics.

In 1870 Alabama had 521,384 whites and 475,510 blacks. When registration in 1867 was complete the figures showed that 61,295 whites and 104,418 blacks had registered. If whites had registered in proportion to their total population at the same rate of black registrations, 114,704 would have qualified to vote. Whatever the debatable assumptions, perhaps as many as 53,409 whites did not register—either because they made no effort to register or because they were rejected and disfranchised for wartime activity. No records were kept of how many whites were disfranchised. The standard Southern explanation for the triumph of Radical Reconstruction was that black majorities were created by the deliberate disfranchisement of white majorities. Alabama was the only Southern state where registration numbers suggest that disfranchisement would have accomplished this end. But it is difficult to believe that some 50,000 whites were disfranchised in Alabama. More likely, while disfranchisement cut into the strength of the Democrats, whites became a voter minority because they refused to register to vote.

Having established an electorate, General Pope next called an election for voters to decide whether they wanted to have a constitutional convention and, if so, who their delegates would be. Alabama was the guinea pig in the process, and what happened in the state attracted national attention. Pope set October 1–4, 1867, as the dates for the election.

For the first time in the state's history, black men went to the polls to vote. The outcome was overwhelmingly clear: of the 95,866 votes cast, 90,283 (71,730 blacks and 18,553 whites) favored a convention and voted on delegates, while 5,583 (assumed to be whites) voiced their opposition. The Reconstruction act of March 23 specified that a convention would be called (1) provided a majority of those voting approved and (2) if the majority vote was a majority of the total number of *registered* voters. Because a majority of the registered voters was 82,857, there were votes to spare to satisfy the requirement.

The results also showed that 32,788 registered blacks did not vote, nor did 37,159 whites. Perhaps coercion explained the black nonvote, while apathy accounted for the white no-shows. But while the election was still continuing (October 2), at least one Democratic editor was already planning a way to thwart Radical Republican moves. He urged whites to register and then not vote and thus prevent a majority. The strategy would be tried later on the issue of ratification.

The result of delegate selection was everything the Radicals could have wished. Of the 100 delegates, 96 were Republicans, including 18 blacks. The overwhelming majority momentarily hid the divisive forces at work among the party factions. Those were put on display when the convention opened in Montgomery on November 5.

Native-born white Republicans were usually radical on political and economic issues but not on matters of racial equality. Their stand was a reminder that Reconstruction involved more issues than the glaring one of black rights. Daniel H. Bingham, a native New Yorker and the oldest, most vindictive and powerful delegate, explained the situation to Thaddeus Stevens. The convention, according to Bingham, while not averse to issues concerning blacks, also wanted to advance the interests of white Unionists. Bingham, who shared Stevens's proscriptive views, wanted to restrict suffrage beyond the requirement of the Reconstruction acts. In that way the north Alabama Republicans could control public affairs. Yet the Black Belt counties with their white minorities allowed the blacks and their white allies to be lenient on the issue of disfranchisement. They simply did not need it. But the white Republicans of the hill counties had to have strong Confederate disfranchisement to give them majority control.

When the convention opened, the native white delegates vigorously pushed their program. They spoke of making support of the Reconstruction acts a prerequisite for voting. They wanted immediate action by General Pope to expel the incumbents in civil offices (he refused), and they pushed hard for debt relief. But they were swimming hard against the tide. The word came down from Washington—from Horace Greeley and Senator Henry Wilson, and it was reinforced by Generals Pope and Swayne—that moderation should be the watchword. Alabama was a test case of Reconstruction, and the national radicals wanted no extremist embarrassments that might alienate Northern opinion. Under external pressure the convention turned away from major efforts at disfranchisement—and from extreme ideas of debt relief and land distribution.

If the native white element lost heavily in the convention, so too did the blacks. While the convention voted down (54–23) amendments that would have segregated public facilities, there was no affirmative statement on social equality for blacks. The assumed necessity for moderation won the day.

What the new instrument of government did not win was a unified party. By the time the constitution was complete, almost one-third of the native white Republicans were opposed to it. When Republican nominations produced an all-white slate headed by William Hugh Smith, a conservative on the race issue, blacks protested the party's conservative orientation. Perhaps, considering their disparate parts, the Republicans were incapable of achieving political unity. But their conservative turn at the convention narrowed the differences between the parties and focused attention on racial issues and civil rights as the outstanding political questions. So the Republicans marched out in disordered array to give battle for their new constitution and for the election of new state officials. There was outright desertion of the party by large numbers of native whites, and there was discontent and murmuring in the ranks by the blacks.

Little noticed amid the political tumult over the constitution was the nonpartisan provision that guaranteed property rights of women. Actually the convention gave constitutional support to statutory protection for women's property rights enacted in Alabama before the Civil War. Neither the prior legislation or the constitutional guarantees were motivated by a pure desire to reform an inequitable system. The real reasons were chivalry (which if misplaced was at least idealistic), family self-interest, and hard times. Even so, the Alabama constitution (as well as the constitutions of Florida and Texas) forbade men to sell their homesteads without the consent of their wives. Women were launched on the road to legal equality in property rights, but nothing was done about the more controversial issue of political participation.

What was important to the voters—exclusively men—was whether the Republicans would get the constitution adopted or whether the Democrats would block ratification. As has been seen, the Democrats had reason for optimism. Their Republican opponents were suffering from divisive tensions, and it now seemed possible to stymie the radical program. The Democratic plan was to make no nominations for offices; the leaders pinned their hopes on obstruction. The call went out to register and then refuse to vote. That would prevent the vote cast from equaling one-half of the registered voters and thus would defeat the constitution. There was nothing technically wrong with the strategy, but there was reason to wonder what the results might produce. By the end of December 1867, white registration stood at 72,748 (it had been 61,295 the previous October), and by February 1, 1868, it had risen to probably 75,000 whites. Black registrations by the same date were down to 95,000 (from 104,418 in October). At least 85,000 persons had to vote for the election to be valid. Democratic strategy needed not only whites but thousands of blacks to stay away from the polls.

The elections began on February 4, just as a severe storm swept through the state. Military authorities extended the voting time through February 8, but all election officials were not informed, and counties voted for varying lengths of time. The results as reported by General George G. Meade (who had replaced General Pope) showed that 70,812 citizens voted for the constitution and 1,005 opposed it—a total vote of 71,817. Blacks voted for the constitution 62,089 to 105. Whites supported it 5,802 to 900. (Race was not recorded for 2,921 voters.) The Democrats accomplished exactly what they had planned. Out of a white registration of 75,000 only 6,702 voted; from a registration of 95,000 blacks only 62,194 went to the polls. Even after General Meade made corrections for counties that did not vote at all and for those where blatant fraud was found, the vote was still 8,114 votes short of a majority. With the same Republican white vote that approved the convention, the constitution would have been ratified.

General Meade pondered the reasons for the vote and drew some reasonable conclusions. There was vigorous opposition by the Democrats, "who by social ostracism and through business relations influenced many white votes, and by discharging and refusing employment, intimidated colored voters." There were the "merits of the constitution itself," and opposition to the candidates for office. Meade made an unheeded recommendation: call another convention to revise the constitution.[3]

Alabama was an embarrassing case for the Radical Republicans, and they moved to solve the problem. On March 11, 1868, the fourth Reconstruction act was passed. Ratification of a state constitution, it stated, "shall be decided by a majority of the votes actually cast." With the Senate delayed by the impeachment trial of President Johnson, Congress moved to admit Georgia, Louisiana, North Carolina, South Carolina, and Alabama to the Union. Alabama was in and out of the bill as it made its way through the legislative process, but it was in it when Congress passed the measure and sent it to President Johnson. He vetoed it after pointing out that the Alabama constitution had been rejected by the people under the rules laid down by Congress. Johnson was overridden once again. Now Alabama could put its new governmental apparatus into effect: the legislature could convene, ratify the Fourteenth Amendment, and in Washington the congressional delegation would be sworn in. On July 25, 1868, Alabama's two senators took their seats.

A new set of men now sat in Washington and Montgomery and spoke for Alabama. Its two United States senators were George E. Spencer (who served until March 3, 1879) and Willard Warner. Born in New York, Spencer attended college, practiced law, and held public office in Iowa. He joined the Union army, helped organize the First Alabama Union Cavalry, and moved to the state in 1865. His colleague (until 1871) was a native of Ohio. Warner was a college graduate who served in his state's legislature. He moved to Alabama in 1867 and was also a Union army veteran.

Of the six-man House delegation—Francis W. Kellogg, Charles W.

Above left: James T. Rapier, educated in Canada, represented the Second Congressional District and was one of three black Alabamians to serve in the national House of Representatives during Reconstruction. *Above right:* George E. Spencer, former Union officer whose background was New York and Iowa, was elected as a Republican to the U.S. Senate in 1868. *Lower left:* George Smith Houston was elected governor in 1874 in a pivotal election to return the Democratic party to power. *Lower right:* J. L. M. Curry, Baptist minister, college president, professor, author, legislator, and Congressman, was also director of the Peabody Fund for Education. (Photos Courtesy of the Alabama Department of Archives and History)

Buckley, Benjamin W. Norris, Charles W. Pierce, John B. Callis, and Thomas Haughey—five were Republicans. Four of them (Buckley, Norris, Pierce, and Callis) had been Freedmen's Bureau agents. Unlike the other five delegates, Dr. Haughey was a longtime resident of Alabama, moving to the state in 1841. In the remaining years of Reconstruction the majority of Alabama's Republican delegation were native born. The number of Conservative Democrats constantly increased. From one member in the first group, they added one more in the next Congress and three in the following one. There was little to choose from between Republican and Democratic congressmen in either education or political experience. From 1868 to 1874 four out of five congressmen served only one term, testimony to the volatile nature of Alabama politics. The best record was that of Republican Charles Hays, a former slaveowner and a Confederate veteran, who served four consecutive terms with the support of Black Belt voters. A touch of humor and irony was provided by the Conservative Democrats who spoke about the iniquities of "scalawags" and "carpetbaggers" but found nothing wrong with Congressman Charles W. Pierce. He was born in New York and did not come to Alabama until the end of the war. Congressman Pierce was a Democrat.

William Hugh Smith was Alabama's new governor. Born in 1828 in Georgia, he came to Alabama with his parents, who settled in Randolph County in 1839. He received "an academic education," read law, and was admitted to the bar in 1850. Smith represented Randolph County in the legislature from 1855 to 1859. His record was straight from the mold of the Southern planter-lawyer-politician, but his political sentiments were those of north Alabama. A Douglas Democrat in 1860, he opposed secession. Smith was narrowly defeated for the provisional Confederate congress, and in 1862 he crossed over into federal lines for the duration of the war. It was also charged that he "entered Confederate service and later deserted." Losing appointment to Parsons as provisional governor, he served briefly as a judge. In 1867 Smith was named by General Pope as superintendent of voter registration. His were the virtues and the defects of a classic north Alabama Unionist. He was variously described as a man "of no executive ability . . . and in few respects a fit person to be governor" and as a man "temperate," "prudent," "forbearing and humane."[4]

Smith had ability, but his accumulated prejudices were ill-suited to the situation. He had no sympathy for the black men whose votes put him in office. He distrusted the radicals who controlled the black vote. Smith's own faction of the party was too small to direct affairs and too small to afford a firm political base.

The composition of the first legislature demonstrated that political power had moved into new hands. The senate's thirty-two Republicans included one black. There was only one Democrat. In the house there were ninety-four Republicans, twenty-six of whom were black, and three Democrats. In matters of race it was the first legislature in Alabama that remotely approached equity in representation.

Early American reform movements, and sometimes the political parties they fostered, tended to be one-shot, single-issue attempts to challenge the status quo. Founded on preventing the spread of slavery, the Republican party was pushed by events toward abolitionism and, at least in its Southern policy, to political equality for blacks. Except for such measures as the Homestead Act, the Republican party never transcended its conservative economic constituency and thus relinquished its role as a spokesman for the common man. The party had no hard theoretical position, save in rhetoric, that placed it on the issues of the day or that committed it to a social vision of the future. In Alabama the Republicans sometimes professed a sort of pragmatic populism made up of poor white economic demands and black hopes for equality. But they never agreed on practical implementation or did battle for economic and social reform. Reconstruction in Alabama was a revolution that increasingly lost its cause and became an exercise in holding power.

The tortuous turns of Reconstruction politics necessitate compression, but the story includes Alabama's senators, George E. Spencer and Willard Warner. Spencer had the immodest ambition of controlling all federal patronage in the state, a desire that automatically put him in competition with Warner. There was further animosity between radical Spencer and native son Governor Smith. The governor was at odds with the "carpetbagger"-black faction of the party, and, with Ku Klux Klan activities on the increase, he refused to call for the federal troops that Senator Spencer wanted.

Spencer's strategy spoke eloquently to his standing as a champion of chicanery. He hoped to defeat Smith for renomination in 1870 and allow the election of a Democratic legislature that would refuse to reelect Senator Warner. Then in 1872 he would need a Republican legislature to ensure his own reelection and deliver a Republican vote for the presidency.

In important particulars, the performance went as rehearsed. Spencer failed to defeat Governor Smith's bid for renomination, but in the process James T. Rapier was nominated for secretary of state. North Alabamians were angered that a black was nominated for a state office. On the other hand, the Spencer group threatened to support Robert Burns Lindsay, the Democratic nominee for governor. The Republican coalition was subjected to its own internal strains and to the rising tide of violence associated with the Ku Klux Klan. Founded in Pulaski, Tennessee, in

1866, the Klan, with its bizarre costumes and its program of intimidation, spread into Alabama.

The Klan's instrument was violence, its goal to spread fear and apprehension that would weaken the Republicans in votes and cripple their leadership. Its victims were blacks (particularly politically active blacks), Union Leaguers, Freedmen's Bureau officials, and Northern white teachers in black schools. Whippings were the standard Klan punishment, but as the election of 1870 drew near, murders were committed with increasing frequency. The Klan killed five blacks and the Canadian schoolteacher at Cross Plains in Calhoun County and murdered the white solicitor and several blacks in Greene County. There were further killings in Sumter County, where Stephen S. Renfroe (the future sheriff) led the Klan in a campaign designed to scare blacks away from the polls.

The Klan was a powerful political weapon, and it was technically true that the Democratic party did not formally endorse the paramilitary order. On the other hand, the party did not repudiate the Klan and profited immensely from its activities. It cuts through the petty legalisms of the matter to remember that Klan members were Democrats.

The Republicans took the preventive measures that were available. They established one voting day in November for all of the elections in 1870 to facilitate the stationing of federal troops in strategic areas. Even then it was much easier to catch criminals after the fact (as difficult as that could be) than to prevent the commission of a crime. The political campaign of 1870 was climaxed by an attack on a Republican rally in Eutaw, the Greene County seat. The meeting was attacked, gunfire broke out, and blood was shed. With that note of violence reverberating through the state, the election took place. Robert B. Lindsay, the Democratic candidate, defeated Governor Smith by a margin of only 1,409 votes (76,977 to 75,568). A normal Republican vote (as of 1868) in Sumter and Greene counties would have carried the election for Smith. Klan violence elected a Democratic governor and a Democratic legislature that in turn named the Democrat George T. Goldthwaite to the U.S. Senate. Willard Warner, as will be seen, returned to his work of building an iron furnace, and Senator Spencer, in a strange chain of events, had won his version of a victory.

Klan violence may have worked too well. There was a strong public and political reaction in the North, and Congress passed the Ku Klux Klan Act of April 20, 1871. The result was increased use of troops, arrests, and jail sentences for those convicted of "kluxing." Congress also established the Joint Select Committee on the Condition of Affairs in the Late Insurrection States, and it took testimony in Washington and in Alabama. Some Democrats were already repelled by Klan enormities, while others realized that their continuation might provoke additional wrath (and intervention) from Washington. The result was that extremists like Ryland Randolph fell out of favor, local Klans were disbanded, and by the end of 1871 the order was almost dead in Alabama.

In 1872, with federal troops present at the polling places, David P. Lewis, a native Southern white Republican, was elected governor over Thomas H. Herndon (with no blacks nominated for cabinet offices). Sumter and Greene counties once again returned their usual Republican majorities. The same election put control of the legislature in doubt. From November 1872 to March 1873, there were *two* legislatures—one Republican, one Democratic. Under a complex compromise engineered by George H. Williams, Grant's attorney general, the radicals constituted a majority in a single legislature. Spencer was reelected, but his black followers were the losers. They were exploited, manipulated, and routinely betrayed—less by the Democrats than by the only party that promised them help and support.

Bad memories hang heavy over Alabama's Reconstruction period, in part the product of endless Democratic stories, in part the reflection of undoubted fact. Republican corruption cannot be rationalized with the argument that stronger men than some of the radicals have succumbed to power and temptation. Dishonesty cannot be excused by the fact that a postwar loosening of public morality runs like a bad refrain through American history. The radicals did not invent the view that government was a private trough instead of a public trust. Nor did the view stop with them. But what they did or allowed to be done, magnified by the cries of Democratic self-interest, tends to obscure the positive achievements of the period.

Corruption of legislatures occurs when there is money to be protected or money to be made. During Reconstruction there was money to be made from railroads—from their financing, their construction, and sometimes even from their operation. Much of the fraud was associated with railroads, and it was compounded by poor bookkeeping or by no bookkeeping at all. The state's level of public management had always been low. Even before the war the larger projects of state government—the bank and the penitentiary—were marked by a naive lack of control or accounting. The war produced a higher level of managerial expertise—but not in those who now wielded power and kept the books.

Traditionally, American civic boosters have responded to talk of improved transportation for their locales. The canal, the plank road, and then the railroad each provided visions of great wealth waiting to pour into a lucky area. Such dreams fueled the investments of the gullible, including millions of individuals and dozens of governments. More calm analysis might have restored proportion. Construction between two points in a region devoid of anything worth shipping from and to cannot expect to generate wealth. Nor can it fail to produce bankrupt railroads. A railroad built into a domain of potential value can stimulate development and population growth. The result can be a dangerous race between market expansion and railroad revenue.

In 1860 the state had eleven railroads spanning 743 miles and costing $17,591,188. By 1867 most of the war damage to the rails had been repaired, and the siren song of prosperity was heard in poverty-stricken Alabama. With agriculture depressed and still lacking meaningful industrial growth (the mineral belt developed later), Alabama had no critical need for extensive railroad building. At issue was not a matter of calm market appraisal: it was a matter of money.

Before the war the state flirted with underwriting railroad construction but repealed its acts before any funds were expended. On February 19, 1867, the Democrat-controlled legislature, in an unfortunate move, authorized the governor to endorse the first mortgage bonds of any railroad at the rate of $12,000 a mile when it had built twenty miles of new road. In return for making the railroad's bonds a state obligation (which would help their sale), the governor could name two directors to sit on its board. The Democrats were overthrown, but their railroad act was not allowed to die.

In August and September 1868, the radical legislature passed laws reviving the 1867 act and changing its terms. Now endorsements would be made at $16,000 a mile in five-mile increments, and that included track laid twenty miles past state boundaries. The next year Governor Smith pointed out the dangers of a law that applied to all railroads. He warned that the statute would promote the construction of roads where no market could sustain them, and he recommended limiting state aid to specific cases. The unheeding legislature passed another law similar to the first. Now added were the paper safeguards of requiring proof that a five-mile segment had been built and having the company detail its use of bond money. Endorsement was a first lien on the road by the state, and if a company defaulted on its bonds the state could seize the road. The intentions were good, but they had little to do with what happened.

With good cause various scholars have illustrated the state's railroad scandals with the case of the Alabama and Chattanooga Railroad. After paying $200,000 (apparently in bribes to state politicians) for its state charter, the company moved to recoup its investment. Governor Smith, in what has passed as merely a case of inept bookkeeping, endorsed bonds worth $4,720,000 for the company. Only 240 miles of track were ever completed (entitling the company to $768,000), and only 154 of those were in the correct state (Alabama). Returning to its cornucopia of wealth, and with wholesale bribery of the legislature, the company got $2,000,000 in state bonds with its property as security. Most of the bonanza was used to build a hotel and opera house in Chattanooga, Tennessee. Under such management the Alabama and Chattanooga proceeded into bankruptcy and could not pay the interest on its bonds. The state paid the interest and seized the road and tried to operate it. The state then bought the road at a bankruptcy sale for $312,000 (was it buying its own railroad?), only to be reversed by state and federal courts. The state ended up paying the first mortgage holders $1,000,000 to take the line back in order "to be out of the business."[5]

To a lesser extent the same machinations were repeated with the South and North Alabama Railroad, the East Alabama and Cincinnati, the Selma and Gulf, the Mobile and Alabama, the Montgomery and Eufaula, and others. In addition to state support, counties and cities also issued bonds, leading to the famous "strangulated" counties that went into bankruptcy. Viewed with perspective, it was a sorry story of human gullibility, unregulated entrepreneurs, and dishonest politicians. The taxpayers were the victims.

Where railroad fraud showed an unhappy present and a mortgaged future, another area of state activity held the crucial promise of a better life for all Alabamians. Organized efforts at education had started with two private schools—Washington Academy in Mobile in 1811 and Green Academy in Huntsville in 1812. Throughout the antebellum period Mobile led the state in the quality of its schools and in making education a public duty instead of a private venture. Between 1820 and 1860 more than 250 private academies were chartered by the legislature. While the Alabama constitution of 1819 pledged that education would "forever be encouraged," and the legislature in 1823 created county "School Commissioners," no system of public education existed until 1854. That year an act appropriated state funds, and counties were authorized to collect school taxes on real and personal property. William F. Perry, a teacher from Talladega, was chosen by the legislature as the first state superintendent of education.

The new system had difficulties and drawbacks but real gains were made in the face of public apathy and insufficient funds before the coming of the war almost destroyed the endeavor. In 1860, 61,751 students (slightly over one-half of those eligible) attended the 1,903 public schools for instruction by the state's 2,038 teachers. Blacks were prevented by law from being educated—the finest commentary possible on the enlightening and emancipating values of knowledge and awareness. In March 1865, state superintendent of education John B. Taylor reported to Governor Thomas H. Watts that "it is impossible to approximate the conditions of public schools within the State."[6] It was time to start all over again.

Efforts by the Freedmen's Bureau to foster black education and the resulting difficulties have been noted. One historian of the period explained—with a racism made no more palatable by its honesty—that the education of blacks by their former owners "would be a step towards securing control over the negro race by the best native whites, who have always believed and will always believe that the negro should be controlled by them."[7] That point was negated by Alabama's constitution of 1868, which was not framed by the "best native whites." What the document provided for public education was a solid mark in its favor.

The constitution did not specify separate school systems for whites and blacks—a displeasing point to the north Alabama Republicans. The State Board of Education, made up of two elected members from each of Alabama's six congressional districts, decreed that separate schools should be provided if parents were unwilling for their children to attend unsegregated classes. The action was an accurate reflection of native white attitudes, but it began the long and painful attempt by a poor state to operate two systems of public education on funds inadequate for one. The constitution provided that the schools would receive one-fifth of the state revenue plus the proceeds from the poll tax, other special taxes, and the income from school lands.

The most curious aspect of the Reconstruction school system (modeled after that of Iowa) was the enormous power given to the State Board of Education. Its regulations had the force of law; it could overrule the governor's objections; and while the legislature could repeal the board's acts, it could not pass its own. The board's most positive achievements were its efforts to guarantee public education for blacks at every level of state funding. Alabama's system of public education was segregated, but funds were apportioned according to the school population. Not until 1891 did the state change its formula and allow township authorities to apportion funds as they deemed "just and equitable."[8] That action ended any pretense of a school system that was "separate but equal."

Under more organized and determined leadership the board might have achieved more, but its members were often split and indecisive. Peyton Finley of Montgomery County sat as the only black member of the board. The organization was expensive and inefficient, and it challenged traditional concepts of separation of powers.

The first superintendent of public instruction under the new constitution was Dr. Noah B. Cloud. A prewar editor well known for advocating scientific agriculture, he was unfairly described as "a man without character, without education, and entirely without administrative ability."[9] Cloud lacked the force of personality and leadership the position demanded, but he struggled to put the system into operation. In the area of black education he presided over a demanding effort with the assistance of the Freedmen's Bureau and the missionary associations. The results were uneven. For blacks and whites the larger towns had the best schools with more funds and better-qualified teachers. In comparison to rural counties and villages, the towns had a higher degree of social control and a concentration of administrative expertise. The extreme individuality produced by expansive rural living often produced great personalities but rarely models of unified group action.

Considering the confusion of the times, an impressive start—whether judged by gender or by race—had been made in 1870. The superintendent of public instruction claimed that the state's 1,355 white and 490 black schools enrolled 229,139 whites and 157,918 blacks. The federal census of 1870 credited the state with more public schools and far fewer students. According to the census, Alabama had 2,173 male and 835 female teachers.

Superintendent Cloud faced all the problems attendant to a new organization. He encountered additional difficulties with the Mobile school system, which guarded its independence, and he faced the more basic opposition of whites who viewed black education as a danger to society. With education came ideas and expanded horizons that might tempt blacks to look beyond the boundaries of the cotton field. Such attitudes, in part, were responsible for the changes that occurred in the black schools.

The first teachers in the black schools had been the representatives of the charitable and missionary associations who came to the South after 1865. Particularly in the rural areas they encountered bitter opposition from the native whites. Some whites were opposed to all black education; others feared the effects of exposing blacks to "Freedmen's Readers" and "Freedmen's Histories" that taught an un-Southern version of social realities. White reaction fueled the drive to secure native white teachers for blacks. If the trend lessened white antagonism, it signally failed to improve black schools. One historian tersely concluded that "Negro schools served as dumping grounds for the rejects from white institutions."[10]

Inevitably the question of higher education for blacks was raised. With segregation already operating on the primary level, it was natural to establish black normal schools, and their basic function was to train teachers. As they began to graduate teachers, placement became a major question. Plainly they were not going to be hired to teach white children. Blacks realized that segregated schools might endure far into the future, and with every passing year more and more black teachers were available. First in the cities, then finally statewide, black teachers for black schools became the norm.

There were two normal schools for blacks. One was the Marion Normal School and University for Colored Students. Located in the Black Belt, the school was originally called the Lincoln Normal School and was headed by W. B. Patterson, a white man. Later, in 1889, the school was moved to Montgomery and in the twentieth century became Alabama State University. William Hooper Councill, born a slave in North Carolina, headed the other black normal school at Huntsville. Under Councill, who became a Democrat and adroitly worked to advance his institution, the normal school, under the influence of Tuskegee Institute, added an industrial program. In the 1890s the school, profiting from Councill's leadership and political ties, became Alabama's agricultural and mechanical college for blacks.

White higher education, if relatively better supported, had an equally difficult time. In 1873 the legislature provided for the establishment of a white normal school at Florence, largely to assuage the town's disappointment at losing its bid for the land-grant college. In 1872 the state had accepted the terms of the Morrill Act of 1862 and after problems with geography, religion, public relations, and race awarded the college to the little town of Auburn. The University of Alabama had been left with its heritage and little else. Most of its buildings had been destroyed by Union raiders in 1865, and when it tried to resume instruction in 1868 its professors and its students were intimidated by the local Ku Klux Klan. Not until the term of 1871–72 did the university successfully resume operations.

Through the administration of Dr. Cloud, past the two years of Joseph Hodgson, the Democrat who defeated Cloud in 1870, and into the term of Republican Joseph Speed (1872–74), the Alabama school system ground itself into bankruptcy. The legislature did not appropriate the required funds, the system was plagued with mismanagement and outright fraud, and the teachers were paid in state notes of doubtful value. Even under Speed, who was respected by Democrats, a legislative committee concluded that "there was a want of system . . . as must necessarily keep . . . [the department] in inextricable confusion."[11]

When Democrats launched their major effort to reclaim state government, their point of attack was the waste, inefficiency, fraud, and scandal that permeated Republican administrations. They were correct. Corruption existed, and it despoiled almost every area of state operations. It ranged from the leasing of state prisoners for railroad construction that resulted in barbarous exploitation and mass deaths to the stealing of school funds by the sons of Superintendent Cloud.

If such factors played a role in Republican defeat—contributing to the failure of the party's programs and furnishing ammunition to Conservative Democrats—it was the outward display of a more serious inner weakness. Alabama Republicans were tragically divided, and it was race that lay at the heart of the division. Had the former slave been a landowner, it might have been easier to transcend prejudice and forge a viable alliance of black and white. The future showed that common interest and common effort were possible even as it demonstrated the limitations and difficulties of collaboration.

Reconstruction in Alabama might have combined the forces that called for change, for repairing past evils, for building some better future where many more would be allowed to share the bounty and the benefits of society. Present for a while and in varying degrees were the slogans and the parades, the visions and the hopes for change. Unfortunately, expectations for reconstructing an embedded culture, even the attempts to make inroads on it, lay far beyond the skills and the understanding of the Alabama Republicans of the Reconstruction era. What came after them endured for a very long time.

SIXTEEN

The Bourbon Oligarchy
and the New Old South

POWER groups seek to control government in order to shape a culture that protects their interests and recognizes their superior position. This was a major theme of Reconstruction as Republicans and Democrats fought their political battles. The Republican party dabbled with a new order for the South—most clearly seen in its efforts to make the black man a full-fledged participant in Southern society. The Democrats obstructed that program and tried to gain power for themselves.

Even equality at the ballot box does not guarantee a government of pure democracy. The many vote and the few rule with greater or lesser degrees of responsibility. Without strong offsetting social canons, laws and policies tend to conform to the weight of wealth, the power of prestige, and on rare occasions, the influence of intellect. Because the radical program left the majority of blacks in the status of less-than-independent wage earners and then of sharecroppers, it perpetuated economic control in a planter class. To a further extent the Republicans failed to protect fully the right to vote and to ensure fair elections. These defeats doomed their political reforms to failure.

It was hardly surprising, and perhaps even natural, that the catastrophic Southern defeat in the Civil War was rapidly reinterpreted as a victorious triumph of spirit and principle. Southern orators, novelists, and historians almost immediately began to construct a story of happy slaves and kindly masters and to explain how this social Eden was destroyed by rabid abolitionists and radical reconstructionists. The extremes of this view—John Witherspoon DuBose's historical treatment of Reconstruction in Alabama is a good example—portrayed Southern leaders as wise, humane, and brave in contrast to the self-serving and dishonest "aliens" who corrupted Southern life and society with their democratic views of equality for blacks and whites.

The myth of the Lost Cause opened with a picture of the beneficent life that slavery had brought. Next, the myth created an uncritical gospel of heroic sacrifice by Confederate soldiers and composed a litany of the indignities suffered under the "invading army." The triumphal climax came when Southerners gained redemption under the banner of the Democratic party and reclaimed the promised land.

Thus did myth avoid and preclude a hard appraisement of the recent past. There was rarely a public admission, and never a consensus, that slavery was a vicious system of exploitation; almost never was there recognition that secession and war had produced not only heroes but an appalling and wasteful loss of life; and only as a doctrine of dissent was there a stated belief that the future rightly belonged to efforts toward a more perfect democracy—and not at all to the claims of a counterfeit cotton aristocracy. The myth of the Lost Cause and an Old South that never was became self-perpetuating. In the South and in Alabama, whites—always with exceptions and degrees of intensity, certitude, and conviction—built a regional identity based on pride, prejudice, and an abiding sense of persecution.

By 1874, almost ten years since the end of the war, Northern passions had begun to cool, and with the changed attitudes went the hope of making the South over in another image. The administration of Governor David P. Lewis was coming to an end. The planter-dominated Democratic party surveyed the scene and developed its agenda. Individual Democrats might desire election for the prestige and power that came with public office, but the party was playing for the higher stakes of social control. It wanted laws to safeguard property, to cut state expenditures, and to reduce taxes. Above all else the party, as servant of its conservative leaders, wanted legislation to protect their economic arrangements and provide them with a disciplined labor force.

The Conservative Democrats wanted blacks effectively tied to the land and therefore to the white landlords. Enacting the program depended on a Democratic victory in 1874. Tactical and strategic maneuvers vital to cleansing the Republican stables at Montgomery (and making secure the sixty-five county courthouses) called for careful planning.

The problems confronting Alabama Republicans in 1874 were displayed by the party's trauma in the closing months of Governor Lewis's term. With an almost evenly divided legislature, Lewis found it impossible to produce a constructive program. The state teetered on the edge of bankruptcy, and the panic of 1873 threatened to destroy all economic gains. In the midst of such travail the black legislators in the house and senate produced a legislative crisis. They made a major effort to pass legislation abolishing racial segregation on public carriers and in public schools. The plan would have given meaningful implementation to the often proclaimed principles of the party, but it touched the rawest nerve of Alabama Republicans.

Although the Democrats helped weaken the bill in the senate, they were able to sit back in amusement and anticipation as the Republicans tried not to tear their party apart. To support black civil rights actively would alienate the party's white north Alabama constituency—and Governor Lewis and other Republican leaders were strongly committed to appeasing that minority faction. The blacks, a majority of the party, lacked the legislative strength to pass the law. Native white Republicans dominated state politics by using black votes and returning little to them. Alabama Republicans of Northern birth, notably Senator Spencer, used those same black votes to gain federal influence and the lucrative patronage of federal jobs. The blacks fared no better at their hands. In the struggle over integrating public carriers and schools, a shaky "unity" was maintained only because the Republicans failed to take definitive action on civil rights in the legislature. The house accepted a weak substitute; the senate approved a different version—and the legislature adjourned having done nothing at all.

As civil rights legislation stirred racial prejudice in state debate, a similar proposal on the national level further influenced the course of Alabama politics. In December 1873 Senator Charles Sumner of Massachusetts introduced a national civil rights bill. Sumner, the martyr of the abolitionist cause after his beating in 1856 by Representative Preston Brooks of South Carolina, would have outlawed racial discrimination in public carriers and at theaters and hotels. Black exclusion from juries would have been forbidden. For Alabama Democrats the rancorous debate in Congress was the ideal accompaniment for their campaign. The old charges—the warnings against the evil "scalawags" and "carpetbaggers," the awful nature of "Negro rule," governmental incompetence, corruption, and debt—could be repeated and given new life. The Republicans could be portrayed as the party of racial equality: They stood for racially mixed schools and for whites and blacks sharing trains and hotels.

Could anyone doubt that it would all lead to "mongrelization" of the races? These were not newly discovered Democratic views, but in earlier elections the Democrats had held back from an open white-versus-black fight. In part, Conservative Democrats had feared further federal intervention, and they had hoped to avoid the total alienation of Black Belt labor. Experience now decreed that Democratic control of black voters would have to come in different ways. It was impossible to alienate the already alienated, and there was a supreme prize to be won in another quarter.

Democratic leaders calculated that an election run on extremist issues—white survival, civilization versus barbarism—would force a racial polarization at the ballot box. White planters of the Black Belt and the Tennessee Valley and small farmers of south Alabama would be joined by the small farmer–Unionist element of north Alabama. The latter group, usually the foes of Black Belt planter interests, would now forget their historic grievances, forsake their Republican aberrations, and join their white brothers in a seamless alliance of racial solidarity. It was the Democratic formula for "home rule," for "redemption," for the victory that would allow its interests to succeed.

Every advantage needed to be exploited, and with their candidate for governor they brought man and plan together. The party nominated George S. Houston of north Alabama—over the opposition of some Democrats whose principles were drawn too tightly to leave room for maneuver. Houston was born in Tennessee and came to Alabama when he was ten years old. After studying law in Kentucky, Houston returned and served in the state legislature. Moving to Athens in Limestone County, he served in the national House of Representatives for most of the 1840s and 1850s. It was Houston's orientation after 1860 that made him a perfect candidate for the Democrats in 1874. Houston supported Douglas in 1861, opposed secession, and sat out the war at home. In 1865 he was a U.S. senator-elect under Johnson's ill-fated plan of Reconstruction. He was the classic Unionist. Houston's geographical and philosophical assets guaranteed the Democrats strong support from north Alabama. They had the proper candidate to fit their campaign strategy.

Faced with the imminent defection of white voters in north Alabama, the Republicans were beset with a growing restiveness from black supporters. In June black political leaders held a convention in Montgomery. The delegates knew that militant demands for civil rights would alienate white voters. Yet blacks demanded a larger share of party nominations, and they declared their support for Sumner's civil rights bill. They denounced Governor Lewis and two of the white Republican congressmen.

The disintegration of the Alabama Republican party continued with a nominating convention held on August 20, 1874. With former governor Lewis E. Parsons presiding and serving as chairman of the platform committee, native whites were firmly in control. The selection of delegates had been gerrymandered to give the Black Belt counties, with 65 percent of the Republican voters, only 47 percent of the delegates. As could be expected, black Republicans got almost nothing for which they had asked.

The convention issued a strong declaration in favor of political and civil equality for all men but refused to endorse nondiscrimination in schools and public carriers. Lewis was renominated for governor, and only one non-Southern white man was named for a state executive office. Four out of five nominees for chancellors, ten out of eleven candidates for circuit judgeships, and all the nominees for the state supreme court were native whites. Reorganization of the state executive committee resulted in an unequal division between the white factions. The blacks got one member.

Matters were marginally better in the district conventions that nominated the congressional candidates (the state convention had renominated the two native white incumbents who held congressmen-at-large seats). The former slave Jeremiah Haralson was the nominee of the first district, and James T. Rapier, the black incumbent, sought reelection in the second. A native white was selected in the third, and the redoubtable Charles Hays—the only Alabama white congressman to support Sumner's civil rights bill—gained renomination in the fourth district. Beset by a tardy realism, the Republicans did not even bother to nominate candidates for the fifth and sixth districts.

The campaign was waged with unequaled fury and was fought out on two levels. Democratic speakers and editors issued sulfuric tirades against miscreant "scalawags" and "carpetbaggers." There were constant reports that blacks were arming and drilling in the swamps preparatory to mass burnings and massacres. Over and beyond everything else was the constant racial litany. "There are but two parties now in the field," one editor declared, "the negro party and the white man's party. There is no middle ground between the two—to one or the other, every man must belong. He that isn't for us is against us. . . . Nigger or no nigger is the question."[1]

Democratic campaign speeches and editorials were at least directed to some part of the mind. Another approach was to a variety of physical violence and the fear that it engendered. In the style begun by the Ku Klux Klan, and now continued by the White League and the White Men's Association, masked and unmasked riders whipped and beat and intimidated. Black Republican leaders were attacked. Republican meetings were disrupted, and at least two of their spokesmen were killed. Even if the responsibilities of federal authorities had been defined, and even if there had been a strong effort to enforce the law, 679 federal troops scattered in thirty locations in twenty-two counties would have been inadequate. On election day in Opelika there was effective control, but in Eufaula and Mobile there was a travesty of justice. In those two cities there was an open season on popular passions, and orderly, legally conducted voting was notably absent.

An era ended on November 3, 1874. On the issue of race alone the Democrats would have won, but they added the certitude of violence and fraud. Riots assured the party of carrying Barbour and Mobile counties. Elsewhere ballots were destroyed or stolen or thrown out on bogus technicalities. White Georgians crossed the Chattahoochee River to lend support at the ballot box. Years later Hilary A. Herbert (an Alabama congressman and secretary of the navy in Grover Cleveland's cabinet) admitted that the Democrats had assured victory by fradulent voting and counting. A congressional committee, inspired to investigate by Congressman Hays, concluded that there was fraud on both sides.

The general pattern of Democratic voting closely followed the plan of campaign. Houston's 107,118 votes came from north Alabama (except Winston and Talladega counties) and from the Wiregrass and Piney Woods areas to the south. Even counties with heavy black populations such as Pickens, Choctaw, Clarke, Monroe, Barbour, and Lee voted (or were counted) Democratic. Lewis had a respectable vote of 93,934, most of it from the Black Belt.

The Democrats proclaimed the redemption of the state ("Glory! Glory! Glory!" one ecstatic editor announced), and the future confirmed the effective demise of the Republicans.[2] Still, there were anomalies in the victory. The thirty-three blacks elected to the state house and senate were a larger delegation than in the heyday of Reconstruction. Nor was it a complete rout for other Republicans. Charles Hays and James T. Rapier were reelected to Congress, and the Republicans won two chancellorships and five county circuit court judgeships. But the future was bleak. The Democratic legislature gerrymandered congressional districts to destroy black majorities, and the Republicans' own internal conflicts completed the process. For three decades they were a party of federal officeholders, existing on patronage and largess, and real state organization was abandoned. After 1900, in north Alabama, the party's ranks were swelled as Populists turned Republican. At least for a time this swing brought Republican control to some county governments plus the election of state representatives and a few congressmen.

With state government firmly in their hands, the Democrats began to change Republican policies and dismantle their political mechanisms, replacing them with a new structure that would guarantee Democratic interests. This was the period of Bourbon Reconstruction. There was much to do, and some time elapsed before the new edifice was complete. The Conservative Democrats were entering an eighteen-year reign that would have no serious challenge. The party had achieved its definition of "redemption," but the word *Bourbon* rather than *Redeemer* became a more frequent synonym for Democrats. Just as the House of Bourbon was restored in France after the defeat of Napoleon, so were white conservative Alabamians returned to power in 1874. A white Alabamian could be a Bourbon without being a reactionary, but the connotation of Bourbonism was never in doubt. Republicans used the word in its pejorative sense, but to those who proudly wore the label it meant honesty and efficiency in government—and adherence to white supremacy.

The state debt was a vital question for the Houston administration. It was an issue so fundamental that political parties declined to discuss its ramifications in public. Some Conservative Democrats had opposed Houston's nomination because he was against repudiation of the Reconstruction debt. The Democratic platform had begged the question by pledging the repayment of the debt "justly owed by the state." There was merit in the Democrats' charge that much of the Republican-generated debt was the product of fraud and corruption (the railroad bonds were a case in point). But another consideration caused some conservatives to stir uneasily. What if Alabama repudiated most of its debt? Would such action discourage investment in the state and scare off buyers for Alabama securities? Even a debt that reeked of illegality was still a debt. Men of property, concerned with what was owed to them, were never sure that only "bad" debts would be repudiated. It was a sensitive question.

With legislative approval, Governor Houston in December 1874 established a commission to recommend adjustments to the state debt. Houston named two men to serve with him, and his choices established a triumvirate of the state's richest individuals. The two were Tristam B. Bethea of Mobile and Montgomery and Levi W. Lawler of Talladega. With innocence and truth it was said of Bethea that "the renown of his great wealth, and success as a planter, and his skill in accumulation, gave much force to his character."[3] Lawler had national financial connections and "great business qualities." He belonged "to the old commercial house of Baker & Lawler and Company in Mobile."[4] The range of the trio's investments is not known, but Houston and Lawler had been directors of railroads in competition with the infamous Alabama and Chattanooga.

After a year of investigation the commissioners rendered their report, and it was approved by the legislature. The settlement was a collection of compromises, but in sum it reduced state indebtedness from $30 million to $12.5 million. While some of the railroad bonds were totally repudiated, the bondholders of the Alabama and Chattanooga gave up their old bonds and received $1 million in new ones and 500,000 acres of valuable mineral lands. The full story of debt settlement remains to be told.

Another matter closely connected with the problems of debt and taxes was high on the imperative list of most Bourbon Democrats. To them the hated 1868 Republican constitution had to be scrapped and a new one substituted before the stain of Reconstruction could be erased. Still, there were some Democratic doubts. Black Belt party stalwarts feared that a constitutional convention might alter population as the criterion for apportionment and take away the blacks' right to vote. Hardly altruistic, their fears were those of a local minority that planned to control black votes. But across the state Democratic voices demanded a new constitution.

When the Democratic legislature convened in December 1874, Governor Houston appointed a committee to consider the question of a constitutional convention. It reported affirmatively, and the legislature decreed that in early August 1875 an election would decide at the same time whether the voters wanted a convention and who the delegates would be.

Under the direction of Walter Lawrence Bragg, chairman of the State Democratic Executive Committee and manager of Houston's victory in 1874, the Democrats opened the campaign. Once again they drew the color line in basic black and white. When not declaiming on the evils of "black rule," their speakers demanded a reorganization of state government and limitations on the public debt.

The Republicans, on the way down but not totally out, were in agreement in their opposition to a new constitution. Their factions were not united in what to do about it. The native-born whites counseled Republicans to vote against a convention and to refuse to vote on delegates—the political equivalent of a spoiled child who will not play. The white latecomers and their black allies, under the leadership of Representative Datus E. Coon (a former Iowa newspaperman and Union general), argued for a vigorous campaign to elect delegates and control the convention.

The Democrats denounced the iniquities of race and Reconstruction, and the Republicans countered with the theme that with a convention "all the results of the war are to be reversed. . . , and a system of human slavery is to be again established."[5] The people voted on August 3, 1875, with 77,763 in favor of a convention and 59,928 opposed. There would be eighty Democratic delegates, twelve Republicans (four of whom were blacks), and seven "independents."

When the delegates gathered at Montgomery in September it was clear that the old state leadership had returned. Leroy Pope Walker (lawyer, former circuit judge, Confederate secretary of war, and brigadier general in the Confederate army) was elected president of the convention. Joining him were Rufus W. Cobb (lawyer, Civil War veteran, state senator, future governor), Edward A. O'Neal (lawyer, legislator, secessionist, Confederate brigadier general, Bourbon, future governor), William C. Oates (teacher, lawyer, editor, one-armed hero of the Civil War, legislator, future congressman, and future governor), William J. Samford (planter, lawyer, Confederate veteran and prisoner of war, and future congressman, state senator, and governor), and James L. Pugh (lawyer, prewar congressman, Confederate veteran, Confederate congressman, future U.S. senator). More than half of the delegates were attorneys, and a number were Confederate veterans.

There was unity in the party name of Democrat, even of Bourbon, but beyond the nomenclature were disparate interests and conflicting viewpoints. Historians still debate the substance and the nuances of whether the Black Belt planters were at war or as one with the rising industrial-commercial interests of north Alabama. The constitution that emerged in 1875 can be read as a Black Belt victory. The prohibition against internal improvements, for example, was apparently an agrarian triumph over the forces of commerce. In fact, the Democrats had made political capital for years on Republican railroad subsidies, although they were guilty of the same practices. Opposition to state support of internal improvements was an integral part of Democratic ideology.

With most of the work done in caucus by the Democrats, the committees reported to the convention and a constitution was assembled. Its bill of rights proclaimed that "established fact" declared against secession from the Union (although a majority report had defended it), that foreigners had the same rights as native-born citizens (immigration was encouraged), and that there could be neither educational nor property qualifications for voting or holding office. In a little-noticed provision, voters had to cast their ballot in the beat (precinct) where they resided. The Fifteenth Amendment was there for all to see. Neither the state nor its counties and municipalities could lend money or credit for internal improvements to individuals or corporations; lotteries were forbidden; and local and special legislation was restricted. In a provision designed to forestall federal intervention, the times for federal and state elections were separated. The office of lieutenant governor was abolished, all state executive officers would serve two-year terms, and the governor, whose power was generally reduced, was given an item veto of appropriations.

In keeping with Democratic promises of frugality, there were provisions for lowering the salaries of judges and executive officials (once lowered they could then be increased). State taxation was limited to 7.5 mills on the dollar and counties and cities would have to get by with .5 percent. Even worse, the constitution provided that after five years the state tax limit would decline an additional 2.5 mills. Agrarian forces talked of a complete repudiation of the state debt, but, as noted, the matter was left to the debt commission to decide. That was surely a victory for the commercial interests.

In the area of education the controversial semilegislative State Board of Education was abolished. There would be an elected state superintendent of education, separate schools for whites and blacks, and much less money appropriated for education. The Democrats opted for decentralization in control of educational affairs. For that they would pay the price in inefficiency and a lowering of already inadequate educational standards.

Following a campaign for ratification, the people voted. The Democrats gave formal recognition to the tenets of Bourbonism: retrenchment, reform, and white dominance. On November 16, 1875, the voters ratified the constitution by a vote of 85,662 to 29,217. The Democrats were triumphant. The Republicans almost immediately indulged in suicidal moves of further party destruction. No one doubted—certainly not blacks—that Alabama was a white man's state.

Why had the Republicans failed? They lacked the extensive public voice of the Democrats and the ability to defend their cause and spread the word. Democratic newspapers sharply outnumbered their Republican rivals and almost always followed far more belligerent editorial stances. Democratic papers such as the Tuscaloosa *Independent Monitor,* edited by the brilliant but unreconstructed and embittered Ryland Randolph, or the Eutaw *Whig and Observer,* or the Marion *Commonwealth,* or the influential Montgomery *Mail* routinely endorsed violence against Republicans. Transcending what the Republican party in Alabama did to itself—the factionalism, the greed and ambition, the inept administration—failure came because the Democrats successfully portrayed it as the party of the black man. Most white Alabamians, including the planter-hating Unionists, looked on the former slaves as an inferior race. They saw Republicans as the unscrupulous manipulators of black voters, a foreign element, an alien party, a constant reminder of defeat and humiliation.

Without doubt some white Democrats accepted the principle that a democracy has to guarantee all its citizens the right to participate in government. Yet such persons collided with reality. Their fears said that universal political equality threatened their own political dominance and created the potential for social and economic equality, which was unacceptable to the white decision makers in Alabama. So the Bourbon Democrats prospered politically and maintained their domination of state government.

Houston served two terms and was succeeded by Rufus W. Cobb of Shelby County in 1878. In 1882 Edward A. O'Neal was elected governor and served until 1886. By this time the winds of change were slowly building, and the political and economic system erected by the Bourbons began to feel the threatening tremors of dissent.

These decades of Bourbon rule left an impress on Alabama institutions that penalized Alabamians into the next century. This was particularly true of the ceilings placed on taxation and the parsimonious support for public education. Under the laws of 1877 and 1879 the state superintendent of education appointed county superintendents (they became elective in the 1880s) who in turn named superintendents for townships. From the beginning, black schools were inferior to white, due initially to implementation of educational policies and not to the wording of the law. Until 1891 school funds were distributed on the number of students by race—an equitable division of the inadequate funds. Black school terms consistently ran for fewer months than whites, and teachers' salaries favored white men in a descending curve of race and gender. With the law of 1891 township authorities could apportion to each school whatever they might "deem just and equitable." This was an invitation to abuse and it had predictable results: white schools got more money, black schools got less. What actual influence did it have? In 1900 Alabama had 104,883 whites age ten years or older who were illiterate, while 338,605 blacks were in that category. In the Black Belt's Greene County there were 131 white and 9,711 black illiterates. In neighboring Dallas County there were 278 whites and 22,079 blacks who could neither read nor write.

Money, fairly or inequitably expended, was the sticking point of educational growth and advance. No one experienced the lack of money for education—personally and institutionally—more than Alabama's teachers. The Alabama Education Association (founded in 1856, revived in 1871, and reformed in 1881) and the Alabama State Teachers Association (organized in 1882 and responsive to the leadership of Booker T. Washington) represented the interests of white and black teachers, respectively. Both organizations supported the legislation of the 1880s that created school districts and gave them the power of local taxation. This legislation might have broken the straitjacket of tax ceilings, but the Alabama Supreme Court ruled such laws unconstitutional. Any special tax for education had to remain within the five-mill limitation. Huntsville legislator Oscar R. Hundley proposed a bill to permit school districts to levy special taxes, but it was defeated in 1888. The effort to pass the "Hundley amendment" to change the constitution was narrowly defeated in 1894. There was irony aplenty when the Alabama Education Association, stung by the defeat of the Hundley amendment, added its voice in 1896 to the chorus demanding a new constitution. That would be the ultimate Pandora's box of troubles.

Alabama was an overwhelmingly rural, agricultural state before the Civil War, and it remained predominately rural into the twentieth century. That fact alone was a major influence on the life of its people and a major determinant of its social and political institutions. It was the form and nature of Alabama's agricultural system that determined the distribution of wealth, decided the status of rich and poor, apportioned power and influence, and created the economic groups that competed for advancement and protection.

With the end of the war Alabamians did not immediately arrive at a substitute for slavery, nor did any of the alternatives ever achieve universal support. But a system was hammered out that organized labor and established the credit necessary in the woeful absence of capital in the postwar years.

Cotton remained the state's great cash crop, but its production brought dramatic changes from antebellum patterns. State cotton production did not equal the 1860 level for the next thirty years. The nine Black Belt counties with the largest cotton production in 1860 produced an average of only 63 percent of that amount in 1890. Conversely, twenty-one counties in the northern and southern sections had cotton crops in 1890 that averaged 46 percent larger than those of 1860. The cultivation of cotton became a much more evenly distributed occupation in the postwar years. Yet white counties (hill and Wiregrass) whose agricultural economies were self-sufficient before 1860 were so short of capital that they switched in the New South to market systems. Even so, the democratization of involvement did not signify growing wealth and broad economic independence in the white counties.

In the early years of Reconstruction, Black Belt planters fumbled blindly in the grabbag of labor alternatives. The labor contract insisted on by the Freedmen's Bureau could take two forms: a wage system or a share system. More was involved than whether a man was paid a weekly or monthly wage or whether he took a share of the crop at harvesttime. For the black man the form of a labor contract also determined whether he would work in a "gang," as he had as a slave, or whether he would farm his own parcel as a family unit. The choice was not clear cut for either the black who furnished the labor or the planter who owned the land. Some planters preferred the wage system with its direct but short-term control of labor. Others liked the share system with its greater labor incentives and its longer-term security. Blacks often preferred the share system with its less stringent control and greater freedom.

No referendums or surveys measured the rival systems, and the evidence of preference is divided. Historians have offered numerous explanations. One thesis holds that blacks "forced" the planters to go to the share system—that planters were figuratively dragged into sharecropping, protesting as they went. Other scholars contend that for at least ten years planters and blacks felt and tested their way and that most found sharecropping, if not the "best" system, then at least the best they could manage. The conclusion that the freedmen overwhelmingly preferred the share system is open to challenge. A black labor convention held in Montgomery in 1873 voted to abandon sharecropping and go to annual wages payable monthly.

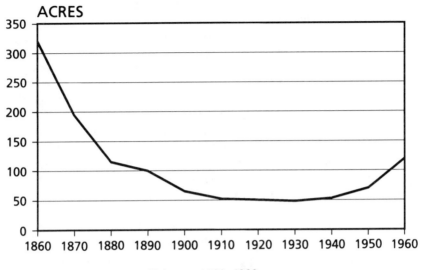

ACRES

Average Size of Farms in Alabama, 1860–1960

In truth, reality in Alabama had nothing to do with academic investigations after the fact. Was a wage system even possible? Was sufficient currency in circulation in Alabama—and available to the planters—to support the payment of money wages? There was an unknown amount of specie, but it was unlikely that planters either had enough specie or were willing to pay wages with it. Most specie was hoarded. There were national bank notes that were introduced to Southerners when the war was over. In 1869 the state of Massachusetts had five times the national bank note circulation of the entire South. Bridgeport, Connecticut, had more than Texas, Alabama, and North and South Carolina combined. Alabama could not have sustained a wage system with that paper currency. Greenbacks remained a possibility (even when state banks were reestablished, their notes were taxed at 10 percent). In 1865–66 the New York financial press estimated that $100 million in greenbacks poured into the South. Estimates in 1868–69 suggested that $50 million was being hoarded there. Hoarding might have been necessary in the absence of banks, but it remains equally unclear that those funds were in the South or in planters' hands.

In Alabama it was not possible to underwrite a wage system even for the Black Belt counties and certainly not for the entire state. A wage system would have necessitated an enormous mortgage debt by landowners to raise wage and operating expenses, and land values were far too low to raise much. Or, ironically, it might have made the landowner a credit slave to the crop lien system as he pledged his crops for capital. Instead, sharecropping supported by the crop lien system for tenants became the characteristic pattern for the state.

Capital lies at the beginning and the continuance of industrial and agricultural enterprise. Individuals either have enough or make enough to finance matters themselves, or they sell shares in the undertaking, or they borrow funds in the hope of repayment and then independence. Only in theory were these alternatives open to Southern landowners and laborers. The facts argued a narrower range of options. Most blacks (and an increasing number of white farmers) had only their labor to offer. They lacked the funds to pay rent for land, to buy a mule and implements, and to keep themselves and their families alive while they tried to make a crop. They only had the problematical value of the crop they hoped to make.

The crop lien was the laborer's commodity futures market. From a local merchant or from the landowner himself the laborer got an advance, sometimes only in seed and supplies, sometimes at least a part in cash. In return he gave the merchant or planter a lien on the crop, a claim against the crop to satisfy the debt. The lender kept the books and did the figuring, and while he did not charge interest he accomplished the same profit-making enterprise with enormous markups. When the year was over and the crop was made, lender and borrower settled up. If the settling was done by the landowner, he took his share for rent, and he took his profit for supplies. A merchant would charge only for supplies. As the system operated, most tenants fell into a pattern of debt that narrowed the opportunities and the options even more.

Sharecropping was subject to a variety of terms that turned on what was furnished by tenant and by landlord. The crop lien that underwrote the system depended on the law and its assignment of priorities. If one man furnished the land and another the supplies, who had first call on the crop to reclaim his money? And what were the rights of the tenant? Did he have a lien on the crop as well? Laws rarely benefited poor farmers, although matters did not start off too badly in 1866. The legislature's crop lien law gave "any person" the right to collect for advances made to plant a crop. Liens for supplies and for rent had equal status.

During the 1870s amendments strengthened the landlord's claim on his tenant's crops over that of the merchant. That priority, neo-Marxist interpreters insist, clearly defined class warfare between merchant and planter. Many Black Belt landowners wanted exclusive control over their black labor—and the double profit that came from renting the land and loaning for the supplies. But matters were more complicated than that. In 1876 the Alabama senate repealed the lien law, although repeal failed in the house. There were rising attacks on the crop lien, not least by those who realized that it bound the farmer to cash-crop cotton production.

The effort at repeal was generally opposed by the merchants but also by the small farmers and tenants. As the Seale *Russell Register* pointed out in 1876, "there is not one man in five hundred now who can carry on a cash business."[6] Some large planters favored changes in the law to prevent difficulties between merchants and planters. The truth was that in Black Belt and hill counties the move of the planters into merchant operations was matched by the merchants who bought land, assumed mortgages, and became planters themselves.

Scholars differ on what it all meant. One historian contends that the swapping of roles "soon developed common interests."[7] Another insists that "it makes a great deal of difference whether merchants became landlords or planters became merchants."[8] The latter concept concerns "class" and dooms the merchant to wander through his store and count his money in less than patrician manner. Thus, the rise of "merchant-planters" in white counties was not a "merger of social classes, because there had been no planter class in the hills."[9] That generalization is true only to the extent that in 1860 a hill county like Shelby had far fewer planters than a Black Belt county such as Dallas, or to apply the same time and criterion to the black county of Wilcox and the white county of St. Clair.

Even so, in 1860 Shelby County had 438 slaveholders who owned 3,622 chattels (32 owned between 20 and 30 slaves, 4 between 70 and 100, and 1 between 100 and 200). In St. Clair County 257 slaveowners held human property numbered at 1,768 (4 owned between 70 and 100 slaves). To possess any slaves put a person in a special category. The hill counties did have planters in the antebellum period, and they were an elite.

Further attacks on the crop lien system came in the early 1880s. But what could replace it? The Republican radicals, attempting to protect the poor from losing everything through foreclosure, established exemptions of $1,000 for personal property and $2,000 for real property. The legislation provided protection from creditors, but it could prevent one from even getting a creditor—from using a mortgage to secure credit. No one was likely to loan money when exemptions prevented its collection. The Democratic answer was the 1875 constitution: a prospective debtor could waive his exemptions. In effect, exemptions had fostered the crop lien system; now the waiver of exemption allowed the mortgage of property as a feasible credit source. Propertyless white and black agricultural laborers still seemed left out because they had no property to mortgage. They had the lien laws.

273

The fate of the crop lien law was one of turns and twists. Under the Bourbons four lien laws favored the landlord first, then the merchant, and the tenant least of all. Then a law of 1885 repealed the law in all but twenty-three counties. The next year two laws reenacted the lien in twelve counties, and in 1887 two more counties were returned to its requirements. Down to the turn of the century other laws repealed and reapplied the crop lien in different counties.

In Alabama's sharecropping agricultural system, landlords and merchants had more mutual than opposing interests. In fact, as landlord-merchants and merchant-landlords their differences were difficult to discern. In late-nineteenth-century Alabama neither landlords nor merchants would have qualified for the upper echelons of Gilded Age wealth and society. But in the impoverished world of black and white share-croppers—the majority of Alabama farmers—everything was relative.

As the Bourbons worked to put their earthly home in order, so too did Alabamians pick up the pieces and try to build the institutions of their spiritual domain. The coming of the Civil War had fragmented the national unity of many Protestant denominations, and with the end of the war and the demise of slavery Southern churches split into white and black congregations. With racial separation as a cardinal principle in the white social philosophy, unsegregated churches had little chance of survival. The establishment of black churches was a manifestation as well of newly gained freedom, and they provided unity, leadership, and inspiration—they were a central organizing agency—for the black community.

The census of 1870 did not differentiate between white and black churches (although separation was already a fact), but its figures suggest that religion was perhaps an even stronger force than it had been in 1860. In that last of the prewar years 1,875 churches in the state held property valued at $1,930,499. By 1870 the number had grown to 2,095, and, surprisingly, property value had increased to $2,414,515. The Methodists led the way with the most churches, followed by the regular Baptists, the Presbyterians, Episcopalians, Roman Catholics, and two Jewish synagogues. The next two decades saw continued growth, with the evangelical churches (a strong emphasis on the Bible and informal worship) growing the most rapidly. The Baptists, black and white, supplanted the Methodists as the largest denomination. In 1890 Alabama had 559,171 church members, of whom 46.2 percent were Baptists and 43.4 percent were Methodists.

As the product of society, churches showed the prevalence of earthly values. The social status of Southern churches went up in direct correlation with the required intermediaries and ceremonies in the process of salvation—and was in inverse ratio with the noise generated on the trip.

This formula placed mainstream evangelical churches such as the Baptists and especially the Pentecostal groups on the lower social rungs while elevating the ceremonial but restrained Episcopalians (and to some degree the Presbyterians) to the top of the pyramid. Perhaps the poor, unnoticed in this life, raised a joyful noise unto the Lord to prevent being overlooked when it really counted.

Different churches had distinctive characteristics. Baptists made quarreling with each other a virtue and saw their frequent splits and new churches as a mark of their vitality. Presbyterians were known for the educational attainments of their ministers, and Episcopalians, small in number, were often people of wealth and achievement. Yet among the evangelical churches doctrinal differences were usually minor. Most subscribed to variations on the theme of a personal God and Savior. The generalization that the South's, as well as Alabama's, religious thrust was Protestant, conservative, and with an emphasis on "old-time religion" is valid. It is equally true that fundamentalism was not all pervasive, although social welfare issues may have been narrowly construed. It is hard to imagine a more "this worldly" but still "safe" reform than the prohibition movement.

Despite the inroads of manufacturing and industry, Alabama was a rural state of small towns. The various churches offered social as well as spiritual comfort to isolated and often economically depressed citizens. For most Alabamians their churches were an integral part of life. There were homecomings, dinners on the grounds, revivals and emotional revivalists, hymn singings, baptisms, choir practices, and vacation Bible schools. Most Southern ministers, in keeping with their congregations, were grossly underpaid (with a little cash supplemented with quantities of food), and ministers' wives bore a heavy burden of social responsibility and humanitarian relief. At the very least, most Southerners wanted a preacher to marry them and bury them, a practical translation of their belief that the church was necessary to their existence.

By 1906 growth had continued. Alabama ranked eighteenth in the nation in population, but in proportion of church members (824,209) it was in eighth position. Alabama's black church members (397,178) put them second in the nation. As might be expected, Alabama did not fare well relative to the value of church property. A major occupation of many Alabama congregations was the struggle to repair church buildings or build new edifices. Clearing a church from debt was the occasion for a special service and a ceremonial burning of the mortgage. By this time new religious groups—the Lutherans, Congregationalists, and Latter-Day Saints—had entered the Alabama census listings. Baptists and Methodists still led in total membership (the Baptists had increased to 53 percent of the total; the Methodists had declined to 31 percent), but there was a surprise even for Alabamians in the rankings. Third place, with 6 percent of the religious population, was now held by the Catholics. It was a hidden group insofar as its membership was geographically concentrated (Jefferson, Mobile, and Montgomery counties had the largest number) and it had no churches in thirty-eight of the sixty-seven counties. Even more limited territorially were the Jewish congregations with the "big city" counties of Jefferson, Montgomery, and Mobile again leading the list.

Ten years later the earlier trends still continued and some new ones had emerged. The Sunday school movement was still expanding, and women still joined churches in greater numbers than men. But now there was the growing presence of Pentecostal churches among blacks and whites—Churches of God General Assembly, Pentecostal Church of the Nazarene, and Pentecostal Holiness Church. These premillennial groups spread rapidly among the depressed sharecroppers and textile and other industrial workers. The dynamics of holiness fundamentalism were acted out with emotional displays and speaking in tongues— efforts to make immediate and real the surety of an eternal reward.

The Southerners' religion rarely led them to question the status quo or demand change. Religious values were interpreted in the context of social realities. With exceptions, churches and ministers who had earlier decided that the Bible sanctioned slavery tended to ignore segregation, industrial exploitation, or political corruption. There was, however, another side to the matter. It is at least possible that the runaway success of denominations such as the Baptists lay directly in the fact that they furnished an open forum, at least in religious matters, in an otherwise almost closed society. In the religious sphere every person was equal. If the social verities were beyond debate or discussion, it was always open season on matters of predestination, the evils (or beneficence) of foreign missions, varieties of baptism, or the use of wine or unfermented grape juice in the communion service. Each person was his or her own judge and authority. It was a circumscribed but real flowering of independence and individualism blooming at random in the formal garden of conformity. In religion as nowhere else in Alabama life, democracy was a vital force and its diversity was its strength.

SEVENTEEN

The Agricultural Alternative and the Rise of Industry

IT seemed that Alabama had found a way to take the past with it into the future, and some Alabamians were prepared to live forever with their new version of 1850. But an idealized past and a rationalized present, while they may provoke intense loyalties, are only temporary bulwarks against the forces of time and change.

And change came to Alabama in the Bourbon decades. It did not come in the rich lands of the Black Belt. It came instead in the areas where poor whites struggled for a living, where both planters and blacks were few. It came to north Alabama with mines and mills, with coal and iron. Where cotton built a different culture in the South—an aberrational society—industry spoke of national norms and common values. But Alabama avoided the mainstream currents. When change occurred it often seemed that the state had carried out an industrial revolution according to its own design and specifications.

The recipe for industrialization was not one of specific proportions meticulously weighed out. Certain ingredients were required, but the mix was subject to endless variation, and the result varied from superb creation to utter ruin. Cooks and societies have their failures. For heavy industry there must be raw materials in sufficient quantity and quality. There must be transportation to take men and products to the points of process. Labor, from highly skilled to primitive, must be available. And deep within it all is the leaven that stirs the matter into action: there must be capital and management to drive the disparate parts and establish procedure, process, and production. How long such building takes is subject to each part and combination. But it must take place within an established social and political framework, and that framework can run the spectrum from granting unrestricted welcome and material aid to guarded hostility that sours optimism, destroys profit, and impedes industrial endeavor.

Far more than contiguous Georgia, infinitely more than neighboring Mississippi, and ultimately surpassing bordering Tennessee, Alabama became the South's center for coal and iron production. The consequences were profound. Alabama moved from a technological base exemplified by a mule-drawn wagon and cotton chopped with a hoe to the blast furnace, coke ovens, and the electrification of coal mines. At the same time, and for a long time, the state had sharecropping and the crop lien system and the modern labor union. Incongruously there was kinship here, even if the relationship was mostly unknown and unacknowledged. In Alabama it was not a process of ending the old and starting the new. Instead, the old was kept and the new was added. Old social values and old ways of doing things lived persistently with modern technology. Dreams of the past and hopes for the future were inextricably entangled. Such relationships produced a culture of complex richness—and perhaps the ultimate social tensions.

The first person to discover coal in Alabama was probably some early Indian who noticed the black, flaky rocks that outcropped along the Coosa, the Cahaba, and the Warrior rivers. One campfire accidentally built among such rocks would have provided the data for discovery. There is no record of the Indians deliberately mining coal, but there are suggestions that white settlers in 1815 dug it and burned it in the future Shelby and Bibb counties.

Here was industry in embryo. The raw material was there, but there was no knowledge of large-scale mining techniques, no labor collected to perform the work, no capital seeking multiplication, and no transportation except the rivers to haul coal to the points of demand. By 1856 some of the inadequacies had been reduced. In that year the Alabama Coal Mining Company "began the first regular, systematic, underground mining" near Montevallo.[1] Three years later the company installed a steam engine for haulage, and it employed Joseph Squire, an Englishman, to manage the works. If Alabama were to create memorials to its industrial pioneers, Joseph Squire would merit one of the first. Squire could run coal mines with practical efficiency, but he left his most enduring mark with his exploration of the Alabama coalfields—a work that made fortunes for the capitalists who listened to him.

The demands of the Civil War stimulated Alabama coal mining and produced an expansion of its primitive iron industry. Alabama's seven blast furnaces in 1861 increased to sixteen in 1865. They lay in a rough semicircle east and south of present-day Birmingham. The furnaces exploited the brown hematite ore, and they were based on charcoal technology. The Civil War destroyed the iron furnaces but not the iron industry. It reduced available capital and temporarily disrupted railroad transportation, but little time elapsed between the Confederate defeat and the return of iron production.

In Jefferson County the Irondale furnace was back in blast by late 1865 under the direction of its wartime manager. Financed by a group of

Brierfield Iron Works operated in Bibb County before the Civil War and resumed short-lived production by 1867 under the control of Southern capitalists. (Courtesy of the Alabama Department of Archives and History)

Cincinnati, Ohio, investors, it survived until 1873. The Brierfield furnaces in Bibb County were acquired by a group of Southern investors, including Josiah Gorgas, the former head of Confederate ordnance. Production resumed in 1867 and with changes of ownership continued until the panic of 1873. The Brierfield works lacked sufficient capital and suffered from difficulties in management. The Cornwall furnace in Cherokee County was back in operation in 1867, the joint venture of the Noble brothers (the founders of Anniston) and three Illinois investors. It was out of operation by 1875, but Cornwall furnace was more than replaced by former Republican senator Willard Warner's Tecumseh Iron Company. The most durable of the iron companies was the Shelby Iron Company, which had strong New York and Connecticut investors (who had a controlling interest), used experienced managers, and profited from its access to both the Selma, Rome, and Dalton Railroad and the Louisville and Nashville (the South and North Alabama Railroad).

What happened next in the hitherto abbreviated industrialization of Alabama was a tangled web of interest, snake-oil promotion schemes, and solid technical experiment. At least as early as 1869 the juxtaposition of iron ore, coal, and limestone had been noted around the village of Elyton in Jefferson County. Endless editorials mentioned the valuable

279

minerals as being "locked in the bowels of the earth." In 1871 Colonel James R. Powell's Elyton Land Company laid out the city blocks and lots of Birmingham. But visions of giant cities with teeming thousands mining coal and feeding the furnaces of a major iron industry grew faint in 1873. The economic panic of that year and resulting distress destroyed Alabama's tenuous markets and closed its furnaces.

Over and beyond a financial depression that affected the whole country, the Alabama promoters had a basic problem. In the best of times it was difficult to make a profit by using brown hematite ore and charcoal. The ore had a relatively low iron content, and charcoal production quickly razed the surrounding forests. There was some truth in the Pittsburgh jibe that "those fools down in Alabama are shipping us ferruginous sandstone and calling it iron ore."[2] Nor was coal mining in a state of progressive development. While the switch by railroads from wood to coal produced a market, the cost of shipping coal prevented demands from the local domestic market and the carriers from creating a boom.

Threatened investment proved a powerful incentive to action. The Birmingham investors and speculators were in critical straits as Elyton Land Company stock hovered around seventeen cents on the dollar. To the rescue came the 1870s version of research and development. The matter started, quite unintentionally, with the Eureka Mining Company and its young manager, Henry F. DeBardeleben. The ward and then the son-in-law of Daniel Pratt, Alabama's premier entrepreneur, DeBardeleben was learning the hard way about mining coal and making iron at the old Oxmoor furnaces. "I failed to make good," he said later, and he resigned his position.[3] The furnaces shut down, and DeBardeleben gathered his forces for a fresh assault on fame and fortune.

The Eureka Mining Company now became the Eureka Mining and Transportation Company of Alabama. Both its name and its liberal corporation charter were more resounding than its balance sheet and its prospects. But it did have one asset of major value: its new manager was Levin S. Goodrich, not only a practical iron maker, as befitted the grandson of Daniel Hillman (founder in 1830 of the Old Tannehill furnace), but a man interested in putting the business on a scientific basis. Using chemical analysis of his ores, Goodrich wanted to push ahead with experiments to produce pig iron with coke instead of charcoal. The company's directors had no quarrel with progress but a great fear of its price. With a debt of $240,000, they made a public offer of their furnaces to anyone willing to experiment with profitable iron production.

More than the Eureka company was at stake. If coal mining and iron production failed in the Birmingham area it would be the death of investment in the Elyton Land Company, in Jefferson County land, the South and North Alabama Railroad, and the expansion of the Louisville and Nashville into Alabama. The impending economic debacle forced new managerial efforts. The upshot was the organization of the Cooperative Experimental Coke and Iron Company with Levin Goodrich as its superintendent. There was work on coke furnaces, the conversion to hot blast, and an examination of possible coals for coking. And on February 28, 1876, coke pig iron of good quality was made.

What had been a tenuous potential for industrial growth became a reality. One editor proclaimed that the future lay in the "great thinking world of ingenious contrivances."[4] Another journalist noted that "where today the wary fox has his home, where there is nothing now to break the stillness save the 'gee-haw' of the solitary ploughman, the voice of steam will be heard."[5] Hyperbole can be accurate. In 1870 Jefferson County had a population of 12,345. By 1880 it was 23,272, and by 1890 it had grown to 88,501. Alabama mined 13,000 tons of coal in 1870. In 1892 the figure was 5,500,000 tons valued at $5,788,898. In parallel growth, Alabama's pig iron production was 11,000 tons in 1872, 800,000 tons by 1890, and over 1,000,000 tons by 1900.

Hard times and precarious profits caused a welter of company reorganization in the early years. It was no less a labyrinthian chain as the 1880s brought growth and prosperity, and Alabama capitalists danced through the intricate steps toward consolidation and monopoly. Along the many lines that were followed, none was more interesting than the career of Henry F. DeBardeleben, the self-confessed failure as manager of the Eureka Mining Company.

DeBardeleben, as noted, had his father-in-law, or at least his wife's inheritance, to finance his business career. Daniel Pratt's Red Mountain Iron and Coal Company, in addition to coal mines and the Oxmoor furnaces, owned 5,600 acres of mineral land. After Pratt's death, DeBardeleben sold this interest on Red Mountain for $160,000 and soon had the ubiquitous Joseph Squire scouting through the coal lands and buying choice acreage. In 1878, with Truman H. Aldrich and James W. Sloss, DeBardeleben established the Pratt Coal and Coke Company. The operation was preeminently successful, although DeBardeleben never worked well with his equals. In 1881 Sloss and Aldrich withdrew, and DeBardeleben reigned supreme over Alabama's largest coal company.

While operating the Pratt company and setting up additional coal and iron companies, DeBardeleben, at the age of forty-one, experienced a rare crisis in confidence. Apparently convinced that he had tuberculosis, he sold his interest in the Pratt company for $600,000 to a syndicate headed by Enoch Ensley. DeBardeleben left for Mexico. While he was either recuperating or discovering that nothing was wrong with him,

Ensley was busy selling Pratt interests to the Tennessee Coal, Iron and Railroad Company.

By 1885 DeBardeleben was not only back in Birmingham but deeply enmeshed in developing his 30,000 acres of land around Blue Creek and Red Mountain. He contributed the land and a group of English and South Carolina investors contributed the money to organize the DeBardeleben Coal and Iron Company and the Bessemer Land Improvement Company. The first company had the job of mining coal and making iron; the second was charged with promoting the new city of Bessemer. As the fledgling town's aptly named newspaper, the Bessemer *Pig*, announced, "The boom is at hand."[6]

All the stir soon produced the classic problems associated with two large frogs in one small puddle. DeBardeleben competed against the Tennessee company with a vengeance, and by 1890 James Bowron, the treasurer of TCI, observed that DeBardeleben was cutting prices and fighting TCI in every possible way. Competition was supposed to be the lifeblood of capitalism, but in fact, to any rational capitalist, it was a lamentable way to run a railroad—or a mine, or a blast furnace. Because it was always better to cooperate and make more money than to compete and make less, something had to be done.

And done it was. In 1892 TCI invented $8 million of stock and swapped it for all of the DeBardeleben stock. With the possibilities of painless invention established, TCI issued another $3 million in stock and acquired Truman Aldrich's Cahaba Coal Mining Company. By such flights of imagination TCI became the largest coal and iron company in Alabama and the third largest in the nation.

Predictably, DeBardeleben, now first vice-president of TCI, was neither satisfied nor satiated. The robber baron psychology—the drive to win, to dominate—burned brighter than ever. In 1893 he tried to corner TCI stock. In six weeks he lost from $750,000 to $2,500,000, and he lost his investment in TCI. When DeBardeleben died in 1910, his estate was valued at $84,000. He was a classic entrepreneur of the Gilded Age, a master of self-promotion, prodigal with his schemes and visions, stingy with his labor force, and narrow in his social conscience. Unlike Andrew Carnegie, DeBardeleben built no libraries.

By 1890 there was capital in Alabama to finance industrial development. There was an extensive railroad network to serve the northern part of the state. Replacing the host of flamboyant entrepreneurs, staid and calculating businessmen organized and managed the enterprises. And, of course, there was a labor force that set the explosives in the mines and loaded the cars with coal, and charged the furnaces and dug the iron ore. Who were these men and what was the shape and nature of their world?

The census takers of 1890 produced interesting data on the composition of Alabama's mining labor force. Alabama labor was divided into four parts—three of them were as free as society and economics allowed, and the fourth, if not slave, was at least captive. The numbers said that 34.9 percent were native-born whites, and most of them were Alabamians only a bare step removed from the trials and tribulations of tenant farming. Pay that took the form of cash (even scrip) in hand, no matter how incommensurate with the labor that produced it, was preferable to the inexorable debt that came with sharecropping. The second group, larger than might be imagined, was foreign born. These made up 18.7 percent of the mining work force and were largely immigrants from England, Scotland, Ireland, Holland, and Italy. Since the days of Reconstruction Alabama had made tentative efforts to promote a foreign labor force. For complicated reasons, both Republicans (who saw political advantages) and Democrats (who wanted less dependence on black laborers) promoted immigration. One Alabama newspaper offered an invitation to "every athletic Northman, every brawny immigrant from the Emerald Isle, or continental Europe."[7] The reality of even a token immigration—for Alabama, with all its furnaces, was no melting pot—caused bitterness and discord. When foreign miners came as individuals a smooth assimilation was possible. When they were brought in by mining companies through labor brokers, they were a challenge to native miners who vowed that "they are not going to take our places in the mines. We came here first and propose to stay."[8]

Blacks easily outnumbered native whites as the largest single group of coal miners. They constituted 46.2 percent of the labor force. Here again race divided common interest and fragmented a common effort. While many black miners supported unionization and were the staunchest of allies, there was an inexhaustible supply of new black labor, which mine owners used as a club and a weapon. The large number of available workers made it hard to preach the doctrine of labor solidarity. Given their first alternative to the rural life of growing cotton, Alabama black men were not inclined to dictate the terms of their employment.

The fourth group of miners was made up of state and county convicts who were hired out to the coal companies. Although small numbers worked for farmers and turpentine companies, by far the largest proportion was sent to the mines. Convict labor had the strongest effect on mining in the state, and its use revealed much about the policies of the Bourbons. Convict leasing evolved, but greed was always the common denominator.

In 1839 the Alabama legislature, in a notable act of contemporary reform, authorized the building of a penitentiary. It was completed in 1841. By 1846 the state had compiled a dismal record of poor administration and rising debts, and the legislature began the practice of leasing the penitentiary to private individuals who used prison labor for manufacturing ventures. Leasing was dramatically terminated in 1862 when the lessee, Dr. Ambrose Burrows, received an ax blow to the head, and the state directly administered the penitentiary (and made a profit) for the rest of the war. Reconstruction brought the black codes and forced labor for vagrancy. Even when the discriminatory codes were abandoned, hard labor for the county remained. Criminals serving felony sentences were sent to the state penitentiary. Those convicted of misdemeanors went to the county jail and on to lessees to work out their fines and court costs.

In convict leasing there was little to choose, except in matters of scale, between probusiness Republicans and supposedly proagriculture Bourbon Democrats. Governor Robert M. Patton started the process of leasing state prisoners outside the penitentiary, and the system was brought to fruition by Warden John Hollis Bankhead; Governor Rufus W. Cobb opposed Bankhead's plans, but he favored leasing. Bankhead housed the prisoners at the mines in prisons built by the favored coal companies. No political faction in the state's history did more for industry than the Bourbons, and in spite of their protestations of honesty no group profited more from unethical deals and exploitation.

Convict leasing corrupted the legal system with its "arrests on order," and it viciously discriminated against blacks who were its chief target. Leasing corrupted prison administration with endless cases of fraud and collusion with the coal companies. And it corrupted the labor market by giving companies a guaranteed labor force immune to union organization and strikes.

Free miners lived far above the scale of the convicts—a reminder that poverty and deprivation are relative terms. Most of the miners rented company houses, and they made their purchases at the company store. They were usually paid in scrip, and in the early days they were subject to company weighmen and company records for an account of their production. They had to pay for the dynamite used in blasting and for their tools. A strike in 1880 at Coketon disclosed that the miners were paying for labor to push the cars from the main slope (the strike was broken by bringing in 100 convicts). Wage rates of $1.00 a ton and 80 cents a ton in 1879 and 50 cents and then 47.5 cents a ton in 1882 (the company wanted to pay 45 cents) correctly suggested that the typical miner did indeed "owe his soul to the company store."

The heady promises by the acolytes of industrialization—the New South advocates of fortune and progress—were unintelligible to Alabama's coal miners. They performed back-breaking labor in the most dangerous circumstances and received pittances for their reward. If misery were competitive, what was the answer to the conundrum of who was better off: the oppressed and exploited industrial workers or the slave in the cotton field? If an answer existed, it may be that one system had a far greater potential for change. That advantage might mean nothing to an individual at any given time, but to a great many people over a much longer time it could mean some replica of progress, some greater chance through the diversification of opportunities. Industrialization ultimately built a major urban area in Alabama. That development brought problems of its own, but it slowly crumbled and consumed the desiccated fossils of the past.

While native Alabamians played a role in the early iron industry, the growth and consolidation in iron and coal tended inexorably toward the establishment of a "colonial industry." In 1900 the ruling Tennessee Coal and Iron Company had 210,000 shares of stock outstanding. Ninety-one percent of the stock was owned by New Yorkers as against .3 percent by Alabamians. When TCI was acquired by United States Steel in 1907, new capital and management were infused into the company. Even so, the new arrangement removed control even further away, and it subjected Alabama interests to the primary concerns of Pittsburgh.

Southerners boiled with indignation at a picture of the exploiting Yankee holding back Southern growth and progress. It was cheaper to produce iron in Birmingham than Pittsburgh, but after 1907 even a Birmingham customer for TCI steel paid the Pittsburgh price plus the nonexistent freight charge from Pittsburgh to Birmingham (after 1909 one paid the $3.00 a ton "Birmingham differential"). Robbing Alabama of its competitive advantage may have retarded growth. But even most Alabamians failed to realize the size of their iron and steel industry. As early as 1880 Alabama's iron production was the fourth largest in the nation; by 1900 Birmingham exported three-fourths of all pig iron shipped from the United States, and its cast iron pipe industry produced 35 percent of the nation's total output.

While the growth of coal and iron production was the most dramatic aspect of Alabama's agricultural alternative, it was not the only area of major industrial endeavor. Before the Civil War there were Southern stalwarts who argued the rationality of putting cotton textile mills where the cotton grew. While Southern funds for investment were limited, a start was made by 1860. Alabama had fourteen textile mills with an average capitalization of $94,000 (average capitalization of mills in 1900 was $375,443). Most of these mills were small operations with an average work force of ninety-four. Following the patterns of employment set in England and then New England, Alabama's textile labor force in 1860 was 59 percent female.

The war's effects on this embryo industry were reflected in the decline

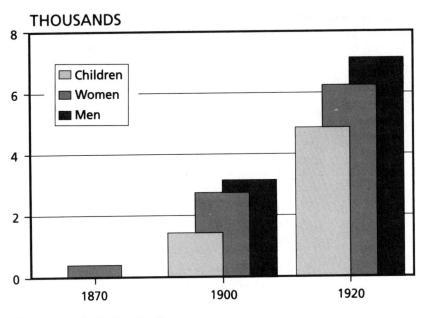

THOUSANDS

Employment in Cotton Textiles

of cotton mill labor in Alabama from its total of 1,312 in 1860 to 744 by 1870. During the next thirty years there was at first slow and steady growth followed by a terrific spurt in mill building (1880 is the traditional date for the beginning of rapid growth). In 1890 Alabama had thirteen textile mills with a total capitalization of $2,853,015 and an employment of 2,088. Only ten years later there were thirty-one mills capitalized at $11,638,757 with 8,332 workers (38 percent men, 33 percent women, 29 percent children under sixteen years of age).

With the exception of larger cities such as Birmingham, Anniston, and Huntsville, most of the state's textile mills were located in smaller towns—in Autaugaville, Prattville, Tallassee, Lanett, Langdale, Alexander City, and Sylacauga. Textile mills were promoted with a religious fervor that preached economic salvation with the coming of industry. Towns vied with each other as the site of a textile mill, and civic boosters made an art of self-extolment. In fact, this competition was effect rather than cause. More and more textile mills were built in the South—and in Alabama—and existing mills were enlarged because, as the Twelfth Census of 1900 put it, "the return upon investment in Southern cotton mills has greatly exceeded that upon factories in the North."[9] While there were economies to be derived from raw material shipping costs, the major Southern attraction was cheap labor. That was, and it remains to the present, an abiding factor in Southern economic development. The economic equation for investment in 1880 was yielding an average return of more than 20 percent, a return made sweeter by the state law of 1897 that exempted anyone who invested $50,000 in a textile mill from all state, county, and municipal taxes for ten years.

As will be seen later, the rise of the textile industry had repercussions all its own. An extremely paternalistic industry, it did not immediately lead to the formation of labor unions, as happened in iron and coal. It produced its own shocks and disorders among the established ways. The textile industry was the state's first major endeavor open to women, and it stood at the very center of the controversy over child labor, the bellwether of Alabama reformers for the next decades.

Industrialization was a mixed blessing in Alabama, as it was in most places. It favored some and it harmed others. It offered job alternatives to a bankrupt tenant class while often denying a meaningful rise in economic status or an improvement in the quality of life. No adequate social micrometer exists to measure the infinitely small gradations in the human condition. There are certainly times and situations when one more piece of corn bread on the plate can be taken as a reason for thanksgiving.

If industrialization did not break the Bourbon hegemony in Alabama, it challenged it from top to bottom. Nonagricultural capitalism produced a new group of social movers with their own interests to push and protect, and it produced a new class of workers who chafed as uneasily as the tenant farmers under a system that seemed to grind their life away. As the 1880s moved along there were shocks and tremors and portents in Alabama of challenge and change. And when it came, and even with its outcome, it was one of Alabama's finest hours.

EIGHTEEN

New Winds and Old Voices

As industrialization's version of progress slowly encroached on the mineral belt, Alabama's farmers remained on a treadmill of poor cotton prices, little profit, usurious interest rates, and a sharply deflationary money supply. At the bottom of the economic spectrum, the small farmer was lucky to stay even in life and was almost precluded from advancement.

Nowhere did the status quo seem so fixed as in the political control of the Democratic party. It sat in monolithic dominance, rarely challenged by the tattered remnants of Republicanism. The Bourbons did not generally lead the choir in stanzas of praise to industry and the New South. Yet they were content to accommodate those voices of fellow conservatives and men of property provided they did not challenge vested interests and the political power that protected them. If mining coal was a different economic life for a black man than chopping cotton, it posed no automatic threat to the social arrangement. The mine owner was as determined to hire his labor at the cheapest prices and control his laborer's life as was the Black Belt cotton planter. Industrialization produced new avenues of protest for white and black, but those were not roads opened by the owners and the operators. They sought to block and obstruct the routes to reform.

The mechanics of Democratic party control were simple and effective. The party controlled every aspect and avenue of nomination and election to public office. Nominations were awarded by the leadership to safe and loyal candidates by party caucus. Democrats registered the voters, kept the voting lists, conducted the elections, and after counting the ballots, announced the winners. In the Black Belt counties Democrats did something else: in election after election those counties with overwhelming black populations voted strongly for Democratic candidates. Had blacks deserted the Republican party and made common cause with their landlords? No, but they were either intimidated against voting at all, or they were physically taken to the polls by white landowners and required to vote for the Democratic candidates.

Basic to the party's rationale for existence was the shibboleth of white supremacy. Fearful that disagreements between white men might open the door for "black government," the Bourbons sat heavily on relevant public debate. Their campaigns were conducted on the increasingly irrelevant issues of how they had redeemed the state and of economy in government. Issues that might have formed the texture of Alabama debate—agricultural policy, taxation, finance and money matters, railroad regulation, and education—were seen as dangerously divisive. Because white men often did not agree on such matters, their discussion tended to magnify class distinctions. They were best cloaked in silence. The more disagreement that found its way to the surface, the stronger grew the pressure to qualify the black's right to vote or to disfranchise him entirely. The Bourbon formula was to exercise the prerequisites and rewards of the class structure, deny class in public debate, and attack dissenters as wild radicals if they raised class interests and questions.

Inevitably, even in an oligarchy, people disagree. Those disagreements are sharpened by economic disparity and by hard times, by slights and wrongs and injustice. There were all of those in Alabama, and only the rigidities and fears of race explain why the voices of protest were so long delayed. Nowhere was submission by silence more true than in agriculture. It is instructive to consider the plight of the American farmer after the Civil War. Certain economic facts of life formed the stage on which the political struggles for reform were acted out.

The Homestead Act of 1862 and the generous grants of land to railroads produced an enormous flow of population to the West. There were 2,044,077 farms in the United States in 1860. By 1910 there were 6,361,502, which meant that in fifty years more than twice as many farmers settled on the land than in the nation's previous three hundred years. The immense amount of land brought under cultivation would by itself have greatly increased production. But the expansion was magnified by a labor shortage that placed a premium on invention and use of farm machinery. The actual contribution of machinery gives flavor to the facts. It took sixty-one hours of labor in 1830 to produce twenty bushels of wheat and only three hours by 1896 to produce the same amount. The result would have been an incredible American success story if demand had increased hand in hand with production. But it did not. Production rose more than 150 percent from 1870 to 1900, while population rose by 100 percent. Nor did foreign demand increase to take up the slack. Exports of wheat held steady after 1885. The opening of the Suez Canal in 1869 lowered the price of Indian cotton to Europe's textile industry, increased competition with American cotton, and reduced the profits of both.

The massive overexpansion of western production—coupled with severe drought conditions that saddled farmers with debts they could not pay—accounted for farm protest in that region. While the South and Alabama did not experience the same expansion of settlement, their farmers suffered from similar woes and common foes. The price of cotton (in gold) was thirty cents a pound in 1866, eight cents in 1878, and seven cents by 1894. While the invention of the tie binder, bundle carrier, and reaper lowered the cost of wheat production (and increased farm debt), no corresponding inventions aided the cotton farmer. The major costs of growing cotton were labor costs, and the prudent planter tried to cut those costs to the bone. When these economies reached the point of irreducibility, and when the price of cotton fell, the Southern squeeze became a panic.

The manufactured goods bought by farmers were made by industries that increasingly shrank in the number of competitive units as they increased in volume of production. Monopoly, or more usually oligopoly, was taking command. Foreign competition that might have reduced prices was stifled by the high tariffs of the Republicans. Adding devastation to disaster, and emphasizing who used the government for their own interests, were the deflationary monetary policies. They increased the purchasing power of the dollar, rewarding those who had money and penalizing those who did not. Such was the system that more and more farmers wanted to modify in their own interest. The order of things needed to be changed.

In Alabama the door to change was guarded by the Bourbons. And who was knocking on that door? The Republicans—vilified, attacked, ostracized, and defeated—were divided, but not proportionately, into two factions. The "Lily Whites" filled federal offices in the state with their few adherents, while the "Black and Tans" were exploited in their party as they were in society. The Republicans, first led by Arthur Bingham and then by Dr. Robert A. Moseley, Jr., had a tenuous existence. From time to time the party fielded candidates (most often in congressional elections), but its real power lay in playing fusion politics with other anti-Bourbon groups. The splits and strains were clearly displayed when the Republicans gathered in Birmingham in 1889 to take the pulse of the party. They met in *three* conventions: the Lily Whites (who wanted to throw the blacks out of the party); the Black and Tans with some whites under Moseley; and a convention of blacks under John Gee, who correctly protested their treatment at every level of American society. Advertised confusion was hardly the stuff of threat and peril to the Bourbons.

Far more insidious and threatening in theory were the Independents. They were much more than the "spurious spawn of dying Radicalism."[1] Some composed the flotsam of earlier hopes, the jetsam of dead ends and defunct crusades. Many were men who had been Democrats in good standing, men who had occupied the inner sanctum of Bourbon power and control. R. H. Powell was from Union Springs (Bullock County) in the deep reaches of the Black Belt. Powell was a safe member of the Bourbon hierarchy and president of the Alabama Press Association. But he deserted the arbiters of respectability and became an Independent. His crisis of conscience (and that of many like him) was not over the substance of Bourbon beliefs. It was a question of methods, procedures, and process.

Powell believed that power obtained by less than democratic methods was power wrongfully held. The Independents, true to their name, made temporary and shifting political alliances on the local level. Most stood for less caucus control ("courthouse ring" rule was denounced), for a greater involvement of the citizens in government, for debtor relief, and for election law reform.

Geographically the Independents (and the Greenbackers) were strongest in the hill counties of north Alabama. They resented state government run by and in the interest of Black Belt planters and urban industrialists. Independents were not antiblack, but they made little effort to organize or enlist the black voter. They furnished troops for later fights, but as Independents they remained fragmented and separated, and while their efforts failed, they were no less grand and no less hopeless.

While almost any group was more organized than the Independents, the Greenbackers, at least on the national level, were a party with a hard and specific program for the ills of the day. Inflation through the issuance of greenbacks might have been debatable, but the party was correct in advocating inflation to cope with the catastrophic panic of 1873. In Alabama it was sometimes difficult to tell a Greenbacker from an Independent—or from a disgruntled Democrat. William M. Lowe of Huntsville was the state's leading Greenback party spokesman. While Lowe protested his Democratic loyalty in 1876, he ran as a Greenback candidate for Congress in 1878 and won.

The status of a political party in Alabama could be gauged by the extent of its newspaper support. The Greenback party was not without a journalistic voice. The Montgomery *Workingman's Advocate* and the Courtland *Wide Awake Sentinel* were avowedly Greenback, and the black Mobile *Gazette* supported Lowe and other Greenback candidates.

In 1880 the Greenbackers, with Independents in attendance, met in Montgomery determined to storm the Bourbon battlements. Strongly dominated by north Alabama, the convention nominated the Reverend James M. Pickens of Lawrence County for governor. The party denounced the Bourbon-supported convict lease system, advocated equitable taxation and better schools, and promised help for the "misrepresented, ring-ruled, caucus-ridden, tax-burdened people of the whole state."[2] Although the Republicans endorsed the Greenback ticket, blacks did not vote heavily in the August election. Pickens received 92,000 fewer votes than the Democratic standard bearer, Rufus W. Cobb.

The Greenbackers regrouped in 1882 and nominated James L. Sheffield of Marshall County for governor. Once again the Republicans, in an ideological nightmare of contradictions, endorsed the Greenback candidate. The black Republican majority opposed fusion, but the party leaders paid no attention. Sheffield's votes were almost entirely from north Alabama, but that fact made his 31 percent of the vote a telling blow at the Bourbon facade of white solidarity.

The Democrats were less than amused at the Greenback assault. Alabama's U.S. senator James L. Pugh put it pointedly but privately in a letter. Pugh wrote: "Independentism means radicalism in the form in which it has persecuted, oppressed and impoverished the white people of the South. For good or evil the Negroes of the South must be governed by the white people."[3] The senator's statement was Democratic truth and Bourbon gospel.

Whatever Democratic fears, an eventual Greenback victory was not the stuff of destiny. William M. Lowe, the soul of the party, died in 1882, and attempts to establish a coalition People's Anti-Bourbon party went nowhere. Most Alabamians who voted for Lowe or Pickens or Sheffield were not partisans of Greenback monetary utopias anyway. What most really wanted was to democratize the Democratic party; economic policy and economic conditions were not yet at center stage. But what would happen if the triggers of human behavior were reversed? What if a political movement was based on want and need, on the realization that when one man profited too much one hundred men had to suffer? What if such a political movement swept through the people of the state? It was a chilling thought for Bourbon leaders given to introspection.

What classes and what interests would form the basis for a popular movement? Certainly the agrarians would be included, but agricultural groups ran the gamut from major planters to small farmers and the marginal wage earners. There was no one agricultural interest; there were layers of farmer interests. That structure made working together difficult and fragmented agriculture into the complexities of self-interest. Beyond the farmers was the rural proletariat of the mines and mills. Theoretically that group would be easier to organize and no less zealous in seeking political power to protect itself. Blacks were economic members of both these groups. If they were made active partners, farmers and laborers would be an irresistible force. If they were left outside, or if their voting power was split, reform would rest on chance and happenstance.

Usage tends to confirm belief, and the usual concept of the "Farmer's Revolt" and the "Agrarian Uprising" is that of embattled farmers standing alone in their quest for reform. In some states that scenario was close to actuality. It was not so in Alabama, where farmer grievances grew hand in hand with the awakening of Alabama labor. Each group turned to organization at almost the same time for different but connected reasons. Farm protests and labor strikes were parallel events, and when the majority farmers turned to politics the workers were at their side. In part the alliance was a natural carry-over of class values and attitudes. Most Alabama workers were still fresh from the farm, and they went right on living in a rural environment. But even lacking this common denominator the result would have been the same. The farmer-labor combination at one end reflected the Bourbon–big business coalition at the other. The question was always who controlled government in its own interest, never one that asked who the Bourbons would side with in a labor dispute.

The labor movement in Alabama, as already noted, centered among the coal miners. They were the largest labor occupation, and the nature of their work and the abuses of the operators were the fuses to an explosion. Miners had little or no experience with organization (most of that expertise came from foreign or Northern immigrants), and they faced extreme operator intolerance. Their movement began with the smallest of steps. A strike is testimony to collective action, and early strikes occurred without the base of a general union. In 1879 miners at two companies went on strike to protest wage reductions of 20 percent. The miners lost the strike. The next year a strike at Coketon saw miners protest having to pay to have the coal hauled out of the mine. How the company broke the strike was a grim dress rehearsal for the future. The operators moved one hundred state convicts into the mine and fired the strikers. That was that. There should be little wonder that the convict lease system (integral to the Bourbon-industrialist philosophy) became a major target for labor and farmer hostility.

A rising curve of strikes occurred throughout the 1880s. Many were products of the Knights of Labor, who came into the state with the new decade. The Knights had secret membership in local assemblies, but where Knight activity can be identified, it speaks of militant labor action and a surprising number of successful strikes. Still, most strikes were lost because the owners brought in foreign labor or, more often, blacks to break the strike. That weapon, coupled with convict labor, made it difficult to reduce production enough to put pressure on a company for a settlement. In 1885 miners met in Birmingham to organize the miners' Anti-Convict League and Union of Alabama, which was hailed by a local editor as "the first effort toward making a systematic war on the use of convicts in competition with free labor in the state."[4] As political consciousness came to the farmers, it came as well to the coal miners.

By 1886 the Knights were declining in membership (the national leadership was following a less militant no-strike policy). In 1888 the miners met in Birmingham to draw up a statewide pay scale and establish a state union. The result was a State Federation of Miners, and numerous strikes indicated the federation's determination to stop the constant wage reductions.

The culmination of the first period of labor organizing in Alabama came in 1894 and was part of a full-scale reform movement that swept the state. At that point farmers had strong political support from the miners, and the influence of organized-labor issues was reflected in the platforms of the agrarians. The combination was embryonic in terms of later decades, and, as ultimately happened, it failed in political action. But it remains as a classic example of farmer-labor collaboration, the old foundation of American mass reform. Labor's role will be seen again, but it was in agriculture that the first moves of organization occurred. The steps were not political organization except in the broadest terms. The foundation of group consciousness first had to be established.

Farmer solidarity came to Alabama with the National Grange of the Patrons of Husbandry, founded in 1867 by Oliver H. Kelley and six other employees of the U.S. Department of Agriculture. The Grange was a social and educational organization, dedicated to farmer unity, pride, and prosperity. It spread into the Midwest, but its acceptance in the South—beset with a siege psychology since the days of slavery—was delayed. Alabama Democrats at first suspected that the Grange was "Yankee humbug," while Republicans were afraid that it represented a new Ku Klux Klan. It was neither one nor the other.

In 1872, under the leadership of Evander McIver Law, a Tuskegee planter, the Grange began to spread in Alabama. By 1877 it claimed a membership of 14,440. It signed up small farmers, but Grange leadership, exemplified by Law and by the first grandmaster, William H. Chambers, came from men of property and standing. The Grange proclaimed its mission "to reform and elevate . . . agriculture, by making it independent and profitable, and its followers intelligent and prosperous."[5] The Patrons (or Grangers) sought a renaissance for themselves and their fellow farmers. While nonpolitical, the order favored governmental reform by electing farmers instead of lawyers and merchants to public office.

The Grange was a giant social group. It brought farmers together in picnics and barbecues and singing sessions. It was one of the first national orders to admit women to membership; the offices of "Flora," "Pomona," and "Ceres" in each Grange were held by women. They were no less dedicated than the men. Reacting to the panic of 1873, the women of Cherokee County resolved to practice strict economy and "purchase for dress material nothing dearer than calico or homespun."[6] In Marengo County the women members of Orville Grange No. 226 voted to practice "retrenchment in our household matters."[7] Gatherings of the Patrons offered something for everyone. Grange lecturers advocated crop diversification and the wage system, as if such problems could be solved by an act of will. The Alabama Grange established several grammar and high schools that emphasized scientific agriculture. It may not have been typical, but the Mountain Grange High School in Morgan County was notable for classes in Greek, Latin, astronomy, and chemistry. The Grange was a staunch defender and promoter of the land-grant college for whites at Auburn.

Larger Granges had libraries, and farmers followed their order's affairs in the *Alabama Grange*, in archetypical Bourbon Robert McKee's Selma *Southern Argus*, in the Montgomery *Southern Plantation*, or in the *Farm Journal*, edited by Chambers. Many of the state's weekly newspapers regularly ran Grange columns.

The Grange saw the farmer as the exploited victim of a distribution system where middlemen tacked their profits onto prices. According to the national leadership, farmers should set up cooperative stores to break the merchant monopoly. But Alabama Grangers were wary of large business ventures, and Grandmaster Chambers was opposed to farmers trying to play the role of merchants. In fact, large planters, backed by the crop lien system, had profitably been playing that role for a decade. Some cooperative ventures were started but were quickly run out of business by merchants who undersold them. That tactic brought prices down, but it provided the briefest period of relief. More successful was the official Grange riverboat that plied the Tombigbee and Black Warrior rivers and lowered the price of shipping cotton.

The famous Granger laws of the western states that brought railroad regulation were not duplicated in Alabama. The Alabama railroad commission, established in 1881 and given less than adequate power to fix rates, was not the product of Granger agitation and influence. The *Southern Plantation* took no stand on regulation, McKee in the *Southern Argus* opposed it, and the second state convention tabled resolutions for rate reduction. True to that orientation, Alabama's Patrons of Husbandry did not follow the national body into more radical avenues in the 1890s.

The Grange in Alabama counted few substantive triumphs, but its effect was more than minimal. The Grange influenced men. For many farmers it gave an introductory experience in collective action, it interpreted a common interest, it brought understanding of how business worked and why agriculture suffered. In that sense the Grangers were a far more insidious threat to the Bourbons than the vocal opponents who attacked them. The Grange was a sponsor of "organized thinking"—always a dangerous activity, a first step in efforts to improve the human condition.

The Independents in Alabama politics, opposed to Democratic party procedures, were largely silent on class and economic issues. Alabama Greenbackers were less than happy with their party's monetary views. The Grange, while organizing farmers and suggesting economic changes, avoided the pitfalls and the realities of politics. Next in the sequence of stepping-stones that led to the far shore of open and avowed revolt was the organization known as the Agricultural Wheel. Organized in 1882 at W. T. McBee's schoolhouse (eight miles from Des Arc, Arkansas), the Wheel has often been submerged and overshadowed by the more famous Farmers' Alliance with which it merged. Even though the Alabama Wheel condemned political action, enough of it occurred to suggest that the Wheel had rolled another revolution down the road.

By 1886 several local Wheels had been organized in north Alabama—the home, until the civil rights movement of the 1960s, of every major protest movement in the state's history. The *Alabama State Wheel* was being published in Franklin County to spread the word, and the word seemed much the same as the gospel according to the Grange. The Wheel advocated cooperative manufactures and followed the practice of naming a local storekeeper as "Wheel Merchant" and trading only with him.

Aided by its geographic concentration of strength, the Alabama Wheel held its first state convention in January 1887. Members listened as national Wheel grand lecturer R. H. Morehead extolled the order's bright future. That August delegates met again and decided to pay salaries to their state officers. In January 1888 fifty delegates arrived in Moulton in Lawrence County. According to a local editor, they celebrated the Wheel's success so energetically that "we have not seen so much drunkenness in our usually quiet town in years."[8] Perhaps with business still unattended to, another convention was held in August 1888. The delegates represented something less than 4,000 members, all concentrated in Tennessee Valley counties except for an oasis to the south made up of Hale County and its solid Black Belt neighbor of Perry County. By August 1889 the Wheel claimed 75,000 members, a more than liberal estimate.

The Wheel took a strong stand against excessive railroad rates, condemned the Louisville and Nashville Railroad, and called for legislative action on the issue. Grass-roots sentiment could be gauged by the resolution of a local Wheel: "the time has come for the laboring classes to lay down all political prejudices and rise above lines, and demand of our representatives a strict account of their political actions."[9]

This was the talk of activists, and they found a kindred and more advanced spirit in editor R. G. Malone, who took over the *State Wheel* in 1887. Malone, an advocate of Henry George's single-tax idea, endorsed the platform of the National Labor party, which was organized in Cincinnati in 1887. Surely few Alabamians in that year would have joined Malone in his advocacy of the confiscation and redistribution of all land. He was the stormy petrel of Wheel affairs. Malone carried on a vituperative press war with the Democratic Moulton *Advertiser,* was censured by his own organization, and then was fired as editor for his "communistic doctrines."[10]

Malone was not alone in pushing the commonality of farmers and laborers and urging them to unite in a political party. J. J. Woodall of Morgan County, a veteran of the Independent and Greenback parties and now a Wheeler, championed the movement. In September 1887 Woodall and others met in Birmingham to form the state Union Labor party. Blacks were among the one hundred delegates who condemned national banks and the convict lease system and who named J. J. Jefferies of the Knights of Labor as permanent chairman. The Bourbon reaction was perfectly expressed by the Moulton *Advertiser:* "the scum of creation was there—anarchists, socialists and communists."[11]

The Alabama Wheel was given to splits and divisions and was not at all embarrassed to display its problems to the public. The Lawrence County Wheel decided in 1888 to take direct political action and run a slate of county candidates. The Lawrence Wheelers were well aware that with 28 percent of their population black they needed as many of those votes as possible. The national Wheel had allowed blacks to establish separate Wheels, and the whites now invited black members to attend their meetings—and sit in silence in segregated seats. It was at least a quiet beginning, but the rest of the affair was one of noisy acrimony.

The Moulton *Advertiser,* convinced that most Wheel members were Democrats, supported and praised the initial actions. But when the Wheel named only four Democrats among twelve candidates, the *Advertiser* recoiled in horror and attacked the proceedings. The *State Wheel,* under a new editor whose views seemed identical to Malone's, roiled the waters with a fiery editorial that spoke of farmers getting their rights "through blood up to the bridle bits."[12] The county Wheel then met and repudiated the *State Wheel,* the state president suspended the Lawrence County Wheel, and everyone ended up furious with everyone else.

It may have been for the best when merger talks were held between the Wheel and the Farmers' Alliance. The latter was a force already larger and surely better organized. In 1889 the Wheel ceased to exist, leaving, at least in theory, a more unified farm movement.

Between the heyday of Republican rule during Reconstruction and the demise of the Wheel, Alabama had already experienced more political turmoil and tensions, more social unrest and unease than in all of its previous history. Among the reasons were national transitions and influences as industry grew and values and aspirations changed. It was plain to some, and not difficult to show to others, that the promises of prosperity through industrialization were overdrawn and often false. While rampant capitalism could be and was defended as the natural order of things, it was difficult to defend on grounds of justice, humanity, or moral equity.

When the view—ranging from conviction to mere stirrings of doubt—spread that government was not representative, that the political process had been hijacked by the rich and the privileged, then the troops to fill the ranks of protest movements could be mobilized. Always and everywhere in the nation was the standing contradiction waiting for someone to use it: the professed theory of a democratic government responsive to the issues and interests of the majority as opposed to the stark reality of political leaders who colluded with the exploiters.

To be rural, even to be uneducated, bore no relation to intelligence. A small farmer in rough and rocky Bibb County could easily equate his own narrow world of experience to broader theories and explanations. He knew firsthand the exorbitant cost of credit. Year after year he learned that the harder he worked and the more he grew the less he made. Knowing all about debt, he was an authority on the absence of money. If he left his land (or if he lost it) and went into the coal mines to support his family, he quickly discovered a second act of the same play—with the same unhappy ending. In the middle of poverty, farm movements spread and grew like a flash of fire. Even in their conservative phases they offered some shared emotional security—the company that misery is supposed to love.

The Farmers' Alliance, the culminating crown of the agrarian organizations, had an humble beginning in Texas in the 1870s as a farmers' protective association against horse thieves and cattle rustlers. After varying vicissitudes the order broadened its message and sent out disciples to spread the new word. The word fell on fertile soil in Alabama. In March 1887 the state's first alliance was formed at Beech Grove in Madison County. Limestone, Jackson, and Marshall counties soon had alliances, and the movement spread. By the close of summer Shelby County had 1,300 members, and a strong organization had developed in neighboring Bibb County. A plethora of preachers worked in alliance vineyards, and there was often an evangelical spirit, a revival atmosphere, to the organizational proceedings. The new order had a particular appeal to Baptist ministers. Quite often the alliance simply co-opted the membership of the local Grange or Wheel, the members figuratively marching en masse to the new movement.

One newspaper editor stressed the universal appeal of the alliance: it "admits to membership farmers, farmer laborers, mechanics, doctors, ministers of the gospel, ladies and boys of sixteen."[13] In fact, it was limited to farmers. Only later, when politics swirled in the air, were Citizens' Alliances formed to enlist the city types.

After an abortive effort at creating a state organization, the Farmers' Alliance tried the loyalties of its new members by holding a state convention in cool but inaccessible Cave Spring in Madison County. More than three thousand delegates made the trip in August 1887. They elected Samuel M. Adams of Bibb County (an ordained Baptist preacher and the speaker of the state house of representatives) as the alliance state president and voted to affiliate with the national order.

The alliance spread throughout Alabama, entering areas where earlier organizations had found barren ground. Strong organizations could be found in the Piney Woods and the Wiregrass. Montgomery County had an alliance by 1889, as did Conecuh, Barbour, and Wilcox counties as well. But even at flood tide the alliance was at its weakest in the Black Belt. There the large landowners (often absentee owners) were as likely to be agricultural investors as true farmers. Many were professional men or merchants or politicians who operated with predominately black tenant farmers and who discouraged the alliance. Some alliances admitted blacks, but they were neither numerous nor particularly successful. The separate black alliance, however, was another matter.

Texas, that breeding ground of discontent and farmers' movements, was the home of what came to be called the Colored Farmers' National Alliance and Co-operative Union. It grew with rapidity, and by 1891 its white founder, General R. M. Humphrey, claimed a membership of 1,200,000. Humphrey appointed another white man, Harry G. McCall, as superintendent for Alabama.

McCall would not strike the modern mind as a crusader for racial equality. Yet when attacked by the Montgomery *Advertiser* for coordinating the organization of black alliances, McCall replied that he had helped them "with the assistance of better men and Democrats than anybody connected with *The Advertiser*."[14] The alliance was supported by black farmers, and by 1889 McCall claimed a membership of 50,000. Butler County had thirteen Colored Alliances, and Montgomery County had six. In general its economic activities paralleled those of the white alliance, although on a smaller scale. Some conservative white alliancemen did not approve of the black organizations, but others helped and supported the black movement.

Why did the alliance find such instant popularity with white and black farmers? Nothing was really new, but it was expressed with greater clarity and with a greater zeal. One advocate explained that "it has gone before the public with its principles clearly defined, its mission being to free the farmers from the oppression of debt, restore the country to a cash basis, to bring prosperity to the farming interest and happiness to the farmer's home."[15] Dr. C. E. Jones amplified the sentiments by asking why farmers should be "menials and paupers, to be driven by monopolies . . . like cattle and swine?" Farmers were being used and manipulated, but by pulling together they would conquer the "adversaries who threaten to oppress us."[16]

The alliance's phenomenal success forced a consideration of its political implications. Democratic editors (given to constant paranoia) began to murmur their misgivings. With the alliance barely founded, one editor worried that it would enter politics and "cause very annoying complications in the black belt next summer."[17] By 1889, with 125,000 members, the alliance was a force in public life even as it proclaimed its nonpolitical character. Whatever the dabblings of the Wheel in Union Labor party ideas, the alliance was broadly assumed to be composed of Democrats. In the early years it did not seem contradictory to hear Senator John Tyler Morgan (Confederate general and quintessential Bourbon) praise the alliance and its works.

A simplistic view of the alliancemen (and the Populists) has them rising in protest of capitalism and industrialization. That picture conjures up bucolic hayseeds rushing about and orating on the lost agricultural Garden of Eden that now must be regained. The clock would be turned back to the sylvan era of Jeffersonian democracy, and the pure and virtuous farmers would vanquish industry and reinherit the Earth. In fact, the alliance did not seek to destroy capitalism or industry. It wanted a place at the trough for the farmers, which meant that a great many already fat interests would have to be shouldered aside. The alliance program was infinitely broader than the view afforded by looking over plow handles at the backside of a mule. If the program had succeeded, it would have shaped the future in a far different way.

The first thrust of the alliance came in the area of business organization. The program was similar to the Grange and the Wheel, but it planned more broadly, attempted much more, and was more successful. Only when the alliance's efforts at economic salvation were weakening would its full energies be turned to political solutions.

When the Alabama Farmers' Alliance launched its economic attack on its nominated forces of darkness, one vested interest fared surprisingly well. For most agrarian groups in most places the word *railroad* was a trigger to diatribe and attack. But not in Alabama. Although an alliance-sponsored bill in 1890 would have increased the state railroad commission's powers, the order made the proper motions of support but no real protest as the Louisville and Nashville had the bill killed in legislative committee. The farmers were simply not incensed over the sins of the railroads. At least in part this stance was the result of the shrewd and thoughtful policies of the Louisville and Nashville. That railroad—so easy to cast as ogre and villain—made sure that it shipped agricultural commodities to fairs and conventions at reduced rates. Delegates to farm organization meetings always received reduced fares, and Reuben F. Kolb, Alabama's commissioner of agriculture, was kept as a friend and sympathetic supporter. The L&N saw to it that alliance business enterprises got the best of rates. There *were* men who knew how to run a railroad.

If the railroads escaped the full brunt of agrarian anger, other enterprises did not. Price increases earned an automatic citation for sin. Perhaps the saddest part of the alliance program lay in the efforts of its members to decrease expenses. Spartan vows were made to eliminate luxuries and purchase only necessary items, to use less sugar and coffee and tobacco, and to "guard against everything that has a tendency to extravagance."[18]

Alliance business ventures were started all over the state. A favorite form of endeavor was the cooperative association with a constitution, board of directors, and manager. Shares were sold to raise capital, and all purchasers shared in the profits. Some county alliances used the Wheel technique of designating an official merchant. The storekeeper would lower his prices to the barest minimum, and the alliance would guarantee him a much larger volume of business. Particularly dear to the alliance heart was the warehouse. It was a simpler operation than a mercantile establishment and often made an important difference in the storage costs paid on cotton. Aware of the business problems experienced by the Grange, the alliance tried to lay careful plans and hire good supervisors for its exchanges and warehouses.

Independent economic operations by the alliance saved the farmers money and threatened existing business establishments. While not typical, what happened in Dothan illustrated the local wars of interest. The "Queen City of the Wiregrass" was a sawmill community known as Poplar Head in 1858, acquired a post office in 1871, and became the bustling village of Dothan in 1885 by virtue of its location on the Alabama Midland Railroad. When the alliance established a warehouse in Dothan, merchants, warehouse operators, and bankers banded together to levy a fifty-dollar tax on the operation. The alliance counterattacked by moving its warehouse outside the city limits. The city council then placed a tax on cotton hauled through the town. This escalation led to threats and harsh words and ended in a gunfight that left one wounded and two dead.

There was no end to alliance plans and ventures. There was a fertilizer company at Clayton, a cottonseed oil mill at Union Springs, and a large bank at Selma. There were plans, but no implementation, for the East Alabama Manufacturing Company to produce bagging and for a manufacturing company capitalized at $125,000 in Butler County. The largest of the alliance enterprises was the state exchange. The plan was for the exchange to act as the central purchasing agent for all alliances in the state. It would make huge cash purchases and resell to the local groups without the intervention of the dreaded middleman. In September 1888 officers and directors were chosen and plans made to locate the exchange in Birmingham. Second thoughts produced a contest for the location; it would go to the town that made the best offer. The exchange was incorporated in 1889, and its $250,000 of capital stock was to be sold to alliances throughout the state; the county alliances would own the corporation.

Several towns competed fiercely to gain the exchange, and immense confusion occurred as to how it would operate. While Selma, Florence, Anniston, Eufaula, Sheffield, Birmingham, and Montgomery made their offers, George F. Gaither, the operation's secretary, tried to explain that the exchange was a purchasing agent, not the state's largest store. It would fill orders from its member alliances, but it would not stock goods. Under the terms of its liberal charter, a cotton bagging factory, an implement and plow factory, a cottonseed mill, and a textile mill were also planned. Birmingham seemingly won the contest for location, but Montgomery ended up as the home of the state exchange.

When the exchange opened for business in fall 1889, two matters quickly became clear. Its agents immediately moved into the cotton market, buying cotton from the farmers, sending small purchases on to Montgomery, and shipping lots over one hundred bales straight to Liverpool. This may have been good business, but it went far beyond the purchasing of supplies. It greatly complicated the business by dealing directly with individuals rather than with member alliances. The exchange reported that it did $100,000 in business in 1889 and $140,000 in 1890. The figures spoke well for its volume but said nothing of its assets and liabilities. A cotton factory was purchased for $15,000 in 1889, additional machinery was acquired, and efforts were made to produce cotton bagging to free farmers from the monopolistic prices of the infamous jute-bagging trust. The factory produced cotton bagging, but the product was judged too weak for wrapping, and in 1890 the plant was closed and the machinery sold.

With all the fanfare, with all the bright hopes and optimistic reports, the state exchange and many other alliance businesses failed or were failing by the end of 1891. They failed from poor or shifting management and from sharp competition by the merchants; and they failed because they tried to build far too big and much too fast. Aside from the short-lived savings some farmers may have received, the alliance clearly won only one fight on the economic front: the major effort against the jute-bagging trust. It was important as an economic victory, and it played a role in moving the alliance toward political action.

In 1888 the jute manufacturers raised their prices and thus increased the pressure on the cost-conscious farmers. A great hue and cry was raised, and the alliance made immediate plans to wrap their cotton bales in cotton bagging. Resolutions were passed that threatened to expel any farmer using the iniquitous jute; a Southern convention in Birmingham voted in favor of cotton bagging; and Southern agricultural commissioners, including Alabama's Reuben F. Kolb, endorsed the action. Difficulties arose when English cotton merchants did not like cotton bagging and declined to stock both types for repair. Political repercussions came when news of English displeasure arrived in the columns of the Montgomery *Advertiser*. The revelation occurred in August 1889, just as the Alabama Farmers' Alliance prepared to open its state convention in Auburn.

The *Advertiser*, under William Wallace Screws, was bedrock conservative (reactionary, to its foes) in its approach to social and political questions. The paper's stance had made it a potent force in the Democratic party. Screws, an articulate Bourbon, mistrusted the alliance and saw the possibilities for embarrassment. He followed up his announcement of English opposition to cotton bagging with interviews of Montgomery wholesalers. Stocked with jute bagging they could not sell, the merchants piously reported that farmers could not afford to suffer losses "in order to fight a trust."[19] The alliance delegates at Auburn were furious over what they correctly saw as an attack by the *Advertiser*. They drafted and adopted resolutions censuring the newspaper in terms such as "utter contempt" and "monopolists or their advocates."[20]

Screws immediately counterattacked as the outraged innocent, and other newspapers chose sides and added to the uproar. It was Screws who turned the matter to political questions. He claimed that the alliance was being used for personal advancement—a thinly veiled attack on Commissioner Kolb, the overwhelming choice for governor in a poll taken at the Auburn convention. Screws was a master at journalistic infighting and the promotion of the irrelevant. He launched a hunt for the authors of the alliance resolutions, and they were duly identified with further charges and countercharges.

The upshot was that the jute companies gave in to farmer pressure and lowered their prices, and the alliance and the *Advertiser* became dedicated and deadly enemies. Even without the jute issue the failure of the alliance economic program would have forced its leaders into political waters. What the farmer could not do for himself would have to be done with the authority and energies of government.

The Wheel had rolled into murky waters in 1887 with its efforts to launch a labor party, and in 1888 the alliance appeared to be similarly caught. In March, seventy delegates arrived in Montgomery for a labor convention; they included members but not necessarily representatives of the Knights of Labor, the Wheel, and the Farmers' Alliance. Blacks were well represented and, although seated separately, took an active part in the proceedings.

The convention established the "Labor Party of the State of Alabama" and adopted a platform that favored higher wages, better highways, changes in the convict lease system, and government ownership of companies in communications and transportation. Some county alliances condemned the convention and declared the alliance's neutrality in the political process. In Chilton County the chairman of the local Republican executive committee invited alliance members to attend the Republican county convention. Even the threat of political action was a sensitive matter, and Alabama Farmers' Alliance president Samuel Adams issued an open letter of clarification. He declared that forming a labor party was a dubious course and that the Democratic party offered the best route to agricultural relief. Adams was careful to note that individual alliance members were free to join the political party of their choice.

Adams did not state the obvious, but his followers acted on it. If the ruling Democratic party offered the best chance to advance agrarian interests, then the alliance should seize control and use it to the hilt. Alliance speakers began reminding their audiences that farmers *were* the Democratic party. Alliances in Bibb and Shelby counties dominated their county Democratic conventions and named the candidates. Separate political parties were not the only threat to Bourbon hegemony. The Farmers' Alliance was on the march.

NINETEEN
———

The Defeat of Reform

POLITICS was the major source of public entertainment in Alabama, and the show opened early in 1889 with the anticipated identification and appraisement of candidates. Commissioner of Agriculture Reuben F. Kolb got the early notices and the strong reviews. Kolb was a native of strategically placed Barbour County (a large physical and cultural area that had characteristics of the Black Belt and the Wiregrass regions). While the Farmers' Alliance was Kolb's obvious base of strength, he also had strong labor support in north Alabama. Kolb moved about the state speaking to alliance meetings—an effective means of campaigning while remaining unannounced. If Kolb was circumspect about his ambitions, he shared podiums with speakers eager to work in a "Kolb for Governor" campaign.

While the Alabama press debated the merits of possible candidates, the Alabama Farmers' Alliance sent its delegates (including Kolb) to a national convention in St. Louis. The proceedings made clear that the Southerners preferred to stay within the folds of the Democratic party and maintain the secrecy of their alliance membership. No fusion with the Knights of Labor took place, although the two organizations agreed on a joint program for reform legislation: the St. Louis platform or demands. Of particular pertinence to Alabamians was the pledge to "support for office only such men as can be depended upon to enact these principles into . . . law, uninfluenced by party caucus."[1]

If the convention produced no formal union of the Southern and Northern alliances or with labor unions, its platform introduced the famous subtreasury plan. It was prepared by a committee headed by C. W. Macune, editor of the alliance's *National Economist,* published in Washington, D.C., which was also headquarters for the Southern Farmers' Alliance. The plan (perfected and given more prominence at the Ocala, Florida, convention in 1890) seemed simple. It was one of those ideas that had occurred to few before its publication but became obvious to all after they heard it.

The subtreasury plan called for the federal government to build a warehouse or grain elevator in every county that produced agricultural products worth at least $500,000 a year. The farmer was still free to sell his crops on the market (the glut of harvest always depressed the price that he received), but now he would have an alternative: he could take his produce to the subtreasury warehouse. The warehouse would store the crop and give the farmer a certificate of deposit. The deposited crop would be security for a loan to the farmer equal to 80 percent of its current value, payable in legal tender at an interest rate of 1 percent. If the farmer did not redeem his crop during the year, the warehouse would sell it to the highest bidder. But if the price rose during the year, the farmer could still sell his certificate of deposit (he would receive the difference between the certificate price and the new selling price), and the buyer would collect the crop by paying the subtreasury the certificate price.

The subtreasury plan would have been a sharp turn in policy, beginning with direct government intervention in the marketing process and proceeding to the issue of periodically inflating the currency on a vast scale. It was innovative and creative, and whether workable or not, it was considerably ahead of its time. The plan was not the first scheme to provide a farmer with a commodity basis of credit—the wretched crop lien system did that—but it attempted to solve the peculiar and destructive operation of farm credit and agricultural marketing. The idea was hotly debated and vigorously attacked by conservatives, and it was effectively killed in Congress. But in its time the subtreasury plan stood as a single desert flower amid the general aridity of ideas.

The Alabama delegates returned from St. Louis to the cries of the Montgomery *Advertiser* demanding that Kolb explain his stand on the St. Louis demands. Kolb's answer was to announce formally his candidacy for governor—although he later explained that the Alabama delegation had not approved the resolution on the party caucus. Kolb took a conservative stand on preserving the Democratic party, and alliance newspapers denied any threat to white supremacy. The *Advertiser* was not convinced. All it needed was a candidate to run against Kolb.

The newspaper found its man in the person of Thomas G. Jones, a Civil War veteran and adjutant general of the Alabama militia. Three other candidates joined the race, a situation that guaranteed a split vote when the state Democratic convention met in May 1890. Kolb was the only candidate who had statewide appeal and support, but there were early indications that his opponents had conferred on their mutual interest in a "stop Kolb" movement. The *Advertiser* did yeoman work in agitating the issue of Kolb's railroad passes, and Kolb waited too long in requesting an audit of his accounts. There was a drumfire of charges that the alliance was intent on forming a third party. But as I. L. Brock of the

Centre *Cherokee Sentinel* explained, the alliance might control the party, "take it from the hands of the tricksters and bosses that now manipulate it," and "why should we not?"[2]

Many newspapers such as Brock's were founded to champion the alliance, and they were becoming increasingly political. Once the Populist party was formed, the alliance newspapers were joined by new journals whose sole purpose was political persuasion. They all came to be known as the "reform press," and, with capable editors, they were relentless in their attacks on Bourbon newspapers.

For the alliance to seize control through established procedures meant overcoming opponents who made the rules. The Democratic executive committee, under the chairmanship of Henry Clay Tompkins (a Kolb adversary), set the number of delegates in time-honored, self-serving fashion. Delegates were apportioned on the basis of the last vote for governor. Black Belt counties showed huge majorities for Democratic candidates. On the basis of the blacks who were voted Democratic, the white minority received disproportionate representation. No black could sit in the Democratic convention. Controlling and manipulating votes not only won elections but kept control of the party machinery as well.

County convention fights took place all over the state as alliance forces attempted to name Kolb delegates. Splits occurred, and rival delegations were named in many counties. In Kolb's home county of Barbour the contesting factions had at each other with the weapons of convenience—knives, stove wood, and umbrellas.

When the state convention opened in Montgomery on May 28, 1890, one thing was clear: 264 votes were required for a majority and nomination. Kolb led each of his opponents, but it was not known if he had a majority. He did not. A vote on a report from the credentials committee showed 235 Kolb votes to his various opponents' 276. When the voting for the nomination began, Kolb stayed near 237 votes for ballot after ballot. After three days and thirty-three ballots, matters were still stalled, and the managers of the anti-Kolb candidates met in high council. In a perverse but pragmatic decision, they determined that because Jones was the weakest candidate in his ability to control his delegates (if Jones withdrew, most of his votes would go to Kolb), the other candidates would drop out and throw their votes to Jones. On the fourth day and the thirty-fourth ballot, Jones received 269 votes and Kolb got 256.

Kolb lost the nomination, but the alliance did not entirely lose the contest. Kolb loyally campaigned for Jones, who easily beat his Republican rival in the August election. Alliance candidates won a majority of seats in the house of representatives and were strong in the senate. When the legislature met in November, a plan to elect Kolb to the U.S. Senate failed, but alliancemen were not disheartened. The order was strong and still growing, and it had already given the Democratic party a powerful shock. The alliance, convinced that right ultimately triumphs and that the justice of a cause governs its success, prepared for future battles.

That future intruded with overwhelming speed. The catalyst for the progression of affairs was the Ocala convention in December 1890. Dedicated (and curious) reformers descended on the small town in central Florida. Present were delegates from the Northern Farmers' Alliance, the Southern Farmers' Alliance, the Colored Alliance, and the Knights of Labor. There was a great deal of talk about forming a third party in open attack on their opponents (the Republicans in the West, the Democrats in the South). The Southern delegates were still not prepared to go that far, but they endorsed the subtreasury plan and a series of alliance demands. The Ocala platform—especially the subtreasury plan—was made party gospel.

In Alabama alliance president Adams announced that the demands were a test of party loyalty—if a member did not support them he would be suspended. Congressman William C. Oates (with the backing of the Montgomery *Advertiser*) asked the State Democratic Executive Committee to defrock all Democrats who *did* accept the demands. The committee was not yet willing to force the issue, but Ocala was the turning point in party divergence.

In May 1891 a third party convention was held in Cincinnati, and it took the momentous step of forming the People's or Populist party. Few Southerners were in attendance, and in Alabama Kolb and his lieutenants still saw value in a conservative course. When the Alabama Farmers' Alliance met in Brundidge two months later (an exuberant gathering of 8,000 who drank 10,000 "pounds" of beer and ate 5,000 pounds of pork and an unbelievable 80,000 pounds of bread), the delegates pledged their support to Ocala but voted against forming a third party.

People come in assorted types and temperaments, and the alliance was true to the human condition. If it numbered those who feared to leave the Democratic party, it contained others who spoke of the solid South and fears of black supremacy as "such rot."[3] Pressure mounted on the alliance for independent action. The Geneva County Alliance attacked the Democrats and the Republicans and declared for the People's party. The Marshall County Alliance stopped a bare step short of that action.

As 1892 approached, Alabama politics—never strong on calm and rational debate—became a wild three-ring circus. In a significant move, the alliance created Citizens' Alliances to broaden its political base. Governor Jones was burned in effigy in Athens, with help from alliance leader Hector D. Lane, whom Jones, not realizing his complicity, appointed to succeed Kolb as commissioner of agriculture pending the election of 1892. Kolb refused to leave his office until the state supreme court ruled against him. The legislature (strongly influenced by its alliance membership) redrew the map of congressional districts and gerrymandered the Black Belt counties in an effort to reduce the black majorities that always came up Democratic.

It was clear to most politicians that either a third party or a Democratic split would make a free black vote a priceless commodity. Black political power was a possibility because it might decide the winner. If held captive by either side (and no one really believed that blacks would freely vote with the Bourbons), it would once again determine the balance of power. Some alliancemen feared a split in the Democratic party; they reacted to the repetitive warning chant of "black rule" and saw white supremacy trembling in the balance. No simple division occurred along the lines of modern liberalism and conservatism—as confusing and inexact as that split still remains. Alabama's agrarian-labor movement was a teeming, somewhat inchoate, contradictory, hurly-burly avalanche for change.

Orthodox Democrats argued that by party practice Governor Jones was entitled to a second term, but few Alabamians believed that Kolb would not run again in 1892. The only question was what party name would be on his ticket. As late as April 1892, Kolb announced that he would accept an honest decision by the state convention, that he was a Democrat, and that all alliancemen should be Democrats. At the same time, the People's party was growing in the state, not least through the feverish and brilliant work of the young Joseph C. "the Evangel" Manning.

With the State Democratic Executive Committee deciding which contested county delegations would initially be seated in the state convention (and county committees had the same power), it seemed certain that Jones had more delegates than Kolb. Even when Kolb supporters captured a county convention, that victory was not decisive. In Dale County the convention elected seventy delegates for Kolb and thirty for Jones. The Jones supporters left the convention, convened on their own, and elected a solid slate for the governor.

The outraged editor of the Selma *Mirror* rhetorically asked, "will Kolb . . . submit to such ruling and be swindled and counted out by such rascality?"[4] Kolb himself answered: "Such a course will force two state conventions and two—nominations—and I will be the nominee of the simon pure Jeffersonian Democracy, and Jones the nominee of the machine Democracy."[5] And that, "simon pure" or not, was exactly what happened.

When the state convention opened on June 8, an uncompromising

Left: Reuben F. Kolb, agricultural commissioner, was prominent in the Farmers' Alliance and was a Populist leader who ran for governor in the bitter campaigns of 1892 and 1894. *Right:* Thomas G. Jones was a Civil War veteran and a Bourbon leader who was elected governor in 1890 and succeeded himself in the controversial election of 1892. (Photos Courtesy of the Alabama Department of Archives and History)

State Democratic Executive Committee turned down several Kolb proposals, including one to hold a primary to nominate candidates for state offices. The "Jeffersonian Democrats" then met in their own convention and nominated Kolb for governor. Kolb gave a fiery speech of acceptance: "You need better schools and better roads. We should demand the abolition of the present convict system. We should send men to the Legislature who . . . would secure and enforce a fair ballot and an honest count."[6] The platform was a full collection of the reforms of the day, including the free coinage of silver and a federal income tax. While the party's future nominations were to be decided by statewide primaries with voting restricted to white voters, the party pledged itself to the protection of black rights and encouragement and aid so that "through the means of kindness, a better understanding and more satisfactory condition may exist between the races."[7]

The Bourbons, with the renomination of Jones complete in their own convention, countered with a pledge to pass election laws "as will better secure the government of the State in the hands of the intelligent and virtuous."[8] The message was clear to all. The Democratic press surpassed itself with vituperative attacks on the "nigger rights section" of the Jeffersonian platform.[9] The question of whether allowing blacks to vote jeopardized white supremacy was the stuff of propaganda and bombast.

The immediate reality was how the black man would vote and how he would be voted.

During the campaign both parties sought the black vote. The Democrats came out little better than arguing that Kolb's record against blacks was worse than Jones's. Kolb made a telling point by citing Democratic intentions of upholding white supremacy with an elite group of voters. Peyton G. Bowman, a major Jeffersonian leader, made a direct appeal for black support. "Let the colored man," said Bowman, "stand up for his race and vote for a free ballot and civil liberty."[10]

It takes a free ballot to preserve one, but the ballot was not free in the election of August 1892. The final and official count was Jones, 126,959 and Kolb, 115,524—a Jones victory by 11,435 votes. Where did those votes come from? Outside the Black Belt counties Kolb won over Jones by 15,399 votes. The Black Belt vote elected Jones to another term, and the votes of blacks did it. In the fifteen Black Belt counties that he carried, Jones had 30,217 more votes than Kolb. Ballots for Kolb were thrown out on a host of charges, and blacks were voted for Jones. Democrats made little effort to cover up blatant examples of fraud. Robert McKee, the conscience of the Bourbon oligarchy, admitted to a Jeffersonian opponent that "it is demonstrable to the dullest understanding that you have with you . . . a majority of the white voters of the state."[11] Chappell Cory of Birmingham, with no love for Kolb, wrote to Governor Jones that fraud was so rampant that the "only question is, what proportion will endorse it?"[12]

Short of rebellion it did not matter what proportion endorsed it. Alabama had no laws or constitutional provision that allowed an election challenge. There was much talk and outraged protest by the Jeffersonians, but that did not stop Governor Jones from beginning his rocky and troubled second term. The reformers were not cast down. As one put it: "The voice of the people—both white and black—has been stifled. We are coolly asked what we propose to do about it. We believe that right will ultimately prevail, and that the common sense of all intelligent men will come to see the enormity of this crime in its true light."[13]

Neither the Bourbons nor the Jeffersonians and Populists were quiet or lethargic during the next two years. Illustrating the tangled web of politics and policy were the efforts of the Bourbons to call a constitutional convention or, failing that, to pass the Sayre election law. Following the dubious role model of Mississippi, many Bourbons in 1890 had favored a new constitution to disfranchise the blacks with educational and property qualifications for voting. That thousands of poor whites would also be disfranchised was not a matter for alarm. As the Evergreen *Star* put it, "the only safety to our free institutions is in a denial of the ballot to the ignorant of all races."[14] In spite of such appeals, the time was not right to cause a division within the party. Postponement, however, did not mean forgetfulness.

What was stymied through constitutional change could still be accomplished through legislation. First, the Democrats struck down an attempt to pass an election contest law. Then they enacted the Sayre election law (named for its author, A. D. Sayre of Montgomery). Purposely complicated (it had forty-eight sections), the law stipulated that the prospective voter must register in May in his home precinct. Registrars would be appointed by the governor, and they would name their assistants. The requirement of a May registration at the farmers' busy season was bad enough, yet the real possibilities for election control came in the power of registrars and election officials to add and subtract names from the registration lists and fill out the ballots of illiterate voters. No poll observers could come closer than within fifty feet of a ballot box, and the keenest-eyed Jeffersonian might have trouble spotting fraud at that distance. The Sayre law, said one reformer, was "conceived in iniquity, born in sin and [is] the child of the devil."[15]

After their defeat in 1892, Jeffersonian Democrats practiced a racism born of frustration. In a move that forgot reform principles, the Jeffersonians suggested a white party primary for April 1894 to select a new executive committee and nominate state officers. Both sides would be allowed to have poll observers. As one Jeffersonian leader explained, "the purpose is to maintain white supremacy, and to have a ticket selected where only white men will vote."[16] Although it sounded like their own pronouncements, the State Democratic Executive Committee rejected the overture. The Democratic press piously issued such thoughts as "give us an honest colored democrat every time, in preference to a renegade or a bolter."[17] The Populists, who had not been party to the proferred compromise, intensified their attacks on the Democrats and wondered why the Jeffersonians were still lingering.

In the meantime, Kolb toured the county picnics that showcased political rallies. That he had the energy to make so many speeches was equaled by his stomach's capacity to digest so much barbecue. Kolb was available for 1894, although he believed that the election would be a repeat of 1892. There was a scattering of opposition to Kolb in Jeffersonian ranks because Kolb was not radical enough. In truth, the Jeffersonians had long overstayed their welcome in the Democratic party, and their efforts at compromise were more embarrassing than productive.

The Democratic front-runner to succeed Governor Jones was the amputeed Civil War veteran William C. Oates of Henry County. He was an ultraconservative and a consistent one: he hated the alliance, opposed government ownership of the railroads, objected to the free coinage of silver, and strongly endorsed President Grover Cleveland. As one Jeffersonian put it, "your valiant one-armed hero can work the veteran racket more adroitly and successfully than any fellow of the stars and bars who shows a scar or empty sleeve as a passport to office."[18]

Political maneuvering and infighting before the election reached a fever pitch of excitement. One day's charges and countercharges were almost immediately covered up by the next day's revelations and rebuttals. The "reform press" put its full assortment of feisty editors into play. While they roused the faithful to action, sometimes their individualism strained party unity. A good example was James M. Whitehead, editor of the Populist Greenville *Living Truth*. Having lost a leg at Cold Harbor, Whitehead was unimpressed with Oates's empty sleeve. He was a fierce debater, a rabid Populist, and an ardent lover of his own ideas. Dissent was in his blood. As a fellow editor said, if Whitehead went to heaven, "he would soon get out of joint there and raise his objections to the arrangement."[19] It all made for the most colorful, antagonistic, no-holds-barred struggle in the state's history.

The Jeffersonians and the Populists held their conventions at the same time in February 1894. Meeting separately and then together, they nominated Kolb. The platform was the usual plea for a free and honest vote and the free coinage of silver plus a classic plank of doubletalk advocating either a protective tariff for revenue or a revenue tariff for protection. The latter offering was designed to ease the strain of Republican collaboration. A series of planks addressed labor problems with due emphasis on the plight of the coal miners. The farmer-labor alliance was clear. Although editor Whitehead attacked Jeffersonian separatism, Kolb remained convinced that it was the best route to follow. So the contest was conducted by two campaign managers, with William H. Skaggs (an articulate editor-politician-philosopher from Talladega) acting as coordinator.

If the reformers wanted to dramatize the plight of labor and what they considered the arrogant power of the ruling class, they could have done no better than the actual course of events. In April 1894 almost eight thousand Alabama miners went on strike against the coal companies. Short of slave labor, it was difficult to imagine a more exploitative system than the coal industry. Miners' wages, always pitifully low, were now reduced even further in the vise of economic depression. The miners were cheated on the coal they mined, cheated on the rents they were charged, cheated at the company store, and summarily fired at the hint of complaint or union activity.

State and county convicts continued to work during the strike, allowing the companies to maintain a reduced production. Although miners threatened to release the convicts, the real trouble came as the companies began to import strikebreakers (predominately blacks). Predictably, violence occurred against people and property, and miners constantly clashed with the hundreds of company "special deputies." Governor Jones had no compunctions against heeding the requests of his coal company supporters for state troops. The strike was broken, but it raised political and class consciousness to even greater heights, and it cemented the farmer-labor tie with moral and physical support.

The Democrats, with the reformers safely removed from the party, now instituted party primaries and even allowed representation at their convention to be based on county population. After a sharp fight with Joseph F. Johnston of Birmingham, Oates was nominated. Johnston, a banker who supported free silver, was more liberal than Oates, and he now raised the cry of fraud and attacked the "unreliable and unprincipled" Montgomery *Advertiser.*[20] Oates had opposed both the Hatch Act (federal money for agricultural experimentation) and the Blair bill (federal money for public education). It was not, he said, in the best interests of the state to educate children beyond the primary grades. Experience showed that whites and blacks "if educated beyond this point" declined "ever to work another day in the sun."[21]

Aligned against Oates and the Democrats were the Jeffersonians, the Populists, and most of the Republicans. In this strange amalgam of farmers, coal miners, federal officeholders, and blacks, no one doubted that the black man was a crucial ingredient. While both sides sought favor with the black voter, the Jeffersonians argued that it would be better if blacks did not vote at all. In theory—and it was in error—an uncast ballot could not be fraudulently counted. The reformers could easily win if they got the black vote and still win if the Democrats could not steal it. Facing that fact, Dr. Robert A. Moseley, Jr., the leader of the Republican "Black and Tans," issued a notice advising blacks in fifteen Black Belt counties not to register or vote in the election. It was an ominous forecast when one Democratic editor in the Black Belt openly justified fraud because "the extremity of the situation demanded it."[22] Oates refused to join Kolb in a public statement asking election managers to be impartial.

There were differences in detail between the elections of 1892 and 1894, but they were bound together by the cement of corruption. Fewer Alabamians voted in 1894, and Oates defeated Kolb 111,875 to 83,292. Where Jones in 1892 had carried fifteen Black Belt counties by huge majorities, Oates in 1894 carried seventeen by even greater margins. Kolb had held his 1892 strength, and he gained votes in the coal mining counties.

There were fears of violence and cries for revolution in Alabama, but short of final extremes the defeated candidates could do nothing. In

Washington congressional candidates of Republican persuasion received the attention of the House of Representatives, and its investigations displayed the magnitude and the mechanism of fraud. In Dallas County in the Black Belt, almost all of the blacks were Republicans, and they did not register. No matter. They were counted as Democratic votes along with the long dead or otherwise departed.

The Jeffersonians met in convention and assured themselves that Kolb had been rightfully elected. They voted not to establish a rival state government, and they finally left the halfway house of Jeffersonian democracy and joined the People's party. On inauguration day Kolb and other reform candidates held their own ceremony. After their oaths were taken, they marched up Dexter Avenue to the state capitol. The Montgomery Mounted Rifles, the Blues (state militia companies), and the city police were on hand to quell anticipated violence. Kolb conferred with Governor Jones, who refused him permission to speak anywhere on the capitol grounds. Kolb mounted a wagon across the street and gave his speech. He insisted that he was the rightful governor, but he cautioned against violence and only suggested that his followers refuse to pay taxes. Kolb was trapped in situation and circumstance.

For the nation the rhythm of reform reached its apogee in 1896. In Alabama that point—almost invisible to the participants—had come and gone in 1894. It was not that quietness descended or that the fight slackened, but for many Alabamians the sharp edges of belief began to lose their surety. Too many years of rhetoric, conflicting personalities, false trails of hope, and bitter defeat wore thin some of their conviction and certitude.

In 1895 "Governor" Kolb, as he styled himself, asked the legislature to pass an election contest law, and somewhat surprisingly it did. The law might help the future, but it gave no opportunity for Kolb to put the past on trial. And it was the future where hope still flickered. The major issue in Populist ranks was whether to fuse with the Republicans in 1896. Fusion had been accomplished on the local level for county officials and national offices, but the state ticket had never been divided. Adams opposed fusion, and Manning split hairs in favor of "cooperation." Kolb entered the argument with attacks on Republican representative William F. Aldrich, who was busy voting for sound money. The Populists were at last face to face with the fact that their program was in direct opposition to Republican policies, while at home their shared enmity for the Democrats pulled them together.

It was one thing to argue party purity, as Kolb now did, and quite another to explain how the Populists, defeated in two elections with Republican support, could win in a third without that help. That was the position of Albert T. Goodwyn, the longtime Populist leader from

Elmore County. In July 1895 the People's party gathered in convention at Birmingham to air its differences and heal its wounds. It was decided that only the state convention could decide on fusion and that the nominee for governor had to be "an avowed Populist."[23] Republicans were thanked for their past help, and their future cooperation was invited.

The Populist peace conference did not stop the arguments. Kolb continued to oppose fusion, but while he retained the symbolism of leadership, more militant Populists were raising their voices against him. Perhaps Kolb realized that his leadership was slipping. In July 1895 he announced that he would not be a candidate for governor in 1896, thus opening the way for new voices and new leaders.

There was stress and strain in all the parties, including the Democrats who now faced the rising tide of free silver mania that threatened a massive party attack on their own president. Alabama's Bourbon leaders did not have to look far to find free silver dissidents. It was instructive that the Birmingham *Daily State,* established to forward Joseph F. Johnston's candidacy for governor, became one of the loudest voices for the free coinage of silver.

Democratic party proceedings showed that anyone could play with fusion. With Johnston advocating free silver, the hard-core Bourbons pushed the candidacy of Mobile's Richard H. Clarke, U.S. congressman from the First Congressional District. But the state executive committee was pro-Johnston, and it issued a call inviting "all conservative voters, irrespective of past political associations or differences," to take part in the selection of delegates to the state convention.[24] The invitation was bitterly opposed by the conservatives. They branded Johnston a Populist who supported silver, attacked President Cleveland, and opposed Democratic election practices.

The tirades were accurate, and they suggested that Johnston was the most dangerous of candidates to face the Populists. By stealing Populist issues Johnston was stealing their votes. He blurred the lines between reactionary and reformer, and he made it likely that some old Jeffersonians would now come back home. When the Democratic primary was held in April 1896, Johnston had an easy win over Clarke. The state convention nominated Johnston, but it also recalled the party to its mission: "It is our purpose to maintain a government in this State, fair and just to all under control of the white men of Alabama."[25]

The Populists, still acting as their own worst enemies by continuing the fusion debate, moved to nominate a candidate for governor. With Kolb off the field, his opponent on fusion, Albert T. Goodwyn, was viewed as the strongest and most appealing of the candidates. The Populists and the Republicans held their conventions in Montgomery at the same time, creating an obvious opportunity for some degree of fusion. However, dissident groups of Populists and Republicans opposed it, each side claiming that they would lose party "identity."

The truth was that all of American political life was in flux and movement, and Alabamians were pushed and pulled by events at home and in the nation. William Wallace Screws of the Montgomery *Advertiser* had left the cloistered offices of the kingmaker and sought the Democratic nomination for the Second Congressional District seat. But when the hated Johnston won the party nomination for governor and the Democrats came out for free silver and nominated William Jennings Bryan for president, Screws withdrew from the race. It was a superb moment for the Populists. As one editor wrote, Screws, "once advertised to eat populists like sardines and crackers," turned out to be a "humbug— or better still, a doodlebug."[26]

In the end fusion won the day. The Populists nominated Goodwyn for governor, and the slate included three Republicans. The platform stood firm for free silver and a free ballot and a fair count. Several counties had problems with fusion, but even the national Republican nomination of William McKinley on a gold platform did not break the Alabama marriage of convenience.

In the campaign the Populists made an all-out effort to capture the black vote. As the Tuscaloosa *Journal* put it, "the Negroes well know that it is to the People's Party of Alabama that they must look for the continued enjoyment of those rights guaranteed them by the constitution."[27] Such statements infuriated solid Democrats, and their party ran strongly on its traditional appeals for white supremacy.

And what were the results? Johnston was elected governor with 128,541 votes to Goodwyn's 89,290. Johnston swept the Black Belt counties—the litmus test for fraud—but he also ran strongly in northern counties. He would have won by a narrow margin if the Black Belt votes had all been thrown out. Various postmortems concluded that the Populists lost because of fusion, but in the specific examples of Joseph C. Manning and Samuel M. Adams, they lost bids for the state legislature when county Populists refused to cooperate with Republicans. Johnston was a strong candidate for 1896. He seduced Populist votes on the silver issue even as the Democrats stirred the racial pot and won votes on old fears. Goodwyn was an able man and a strong candidate, but for the farmers he was not Reuben F. Kolb.

Their spirit assailed by friction and division, the Populists fared badly in the national election. Kolb's Birmingham *People's Weekly Tribune* came out for the Democratic ticket of Bryan and Arthur Sewall of Maine. The endorsement earned Kolb the ire of those who supported the Populist ticket of Bryan and Tom Watson of Georgia. Kolb and his followers, said one furious writer, "milked the reform movement for all there was in it, and like hogs, have now returned to their wallow."[28] Even as Kolb came home to the Democratic party, its ultraconservatives left it for the Gold Democrats. The ticket of Bryan and Sewall carried Alabama, but party loyalty became a scarce commodity. When the dust settled and McKinley entered the White House, Populists divided on divergent paths. Some went over to the Republicans, who out of necessity opposed the Bourbons. Others returned to the Democrats, rationalizing that Bryan was the great hope of reform. And a few stayed exactly where they were and fought the fight for reform on the county level well into the opening decade of the new century.

Contemporaries and modern scholars have argued over the significance of the Populist upheaval and what it meant. Eight years of reform agitation clearly demonstrated that the movement's institutionalized view of race was different from that of the Democrats. Everyone knew it then, and it caused a vast amount of trouble. Populists saw and understood and often spoke on how race had been used to exploit and manipulate. No one who understood that fact still held the same old views. Populists nearly always failed to meet later standards of racial liberalism. So did nearly all of the later Progressives and nearly all of the New Dealers. Did Populists have only their conspiracy theories? No Populist of those days need have felt embarrassment because he had no plans to change the world. The Populists did not advocate cataclysmic change. They wanted to retain large parts of capitalism's "competitive" aspects. So did Progressives and New Dealers and every main-line reform movement in American history.

Of course the Populists wanted political power. Rational discourse exercised on entrenched power groups rarely brings about change. However flawed, populism was a genuine reform movement. The same cannot be said of the period of progressivism that followed. What later took the stage in Alabama and called itself the Progressive movement was little more than the changing of the guard in the Democratic party. Johnston was a sign of this change, the coming to power of the manufacturers and the bankers, the redistribution of power so that once again the dog could wag the tail.

The Alabama movement for reform was always ahead of many of its leaders, and a conservative Kolb never exploited the dynamic potential for change. And what about the Democrats? They practiced and endorsed fraud in 1892 and 1894—and less so in 1896—from the same antidemocratic stance they had assumed in the years of Reconstruction. For them the end justified the means, even if the means debased the political process. Majority rule was made a mockery, and the will of the people was denied. Many of the Bourbons did not believe in democracy any more than the old planter "aristocracy" had. They kept themselves in power because they considered themselves an "elite," constituting, as they said, the "virtuous and the intelligent."

Were the Populists, as their critics claimed, "merely provincial"?[29] Populism remains as the only American reform movement to be founded firmly and broadly at the local level. Thousands of Progressive clubs never dotted the nation; New Deal study groups never pored over the National Industrial Recovery Act. But thousands of alliances and People's party meetings were held where the subtreasury plan was dissected and debated, where the mechanism of money was discussed and examined. Populism went on in everyday life; it was lived by its participants; it was as real as the country school where meetings were held, as real as the local newspaper, and as real as poverty and debt— and hope and aspiration.

Far more than any reform movement before or since, populism came from the ground up. Other crusades usually waved flags emblazoned with slogans and mouthed impassioned rhetoric, but none educated its followers so thoroughly in the complexities of economic life. How many contemporary Americans can speak with informed knowledge on how their monetary system works? The Populists knew how theirs worked and who benefited from it. In Alabama the movement went beyond the problems of the farmer and concerned itself with the new life of industrial labor. It was a farmer-labor coalition in Alabama, and it correctly identified the persons and the problems and the policies with which labor reformers still had to deal.

Populism failed, and because it failed the same poverty continued and an "elite" still ruled, and the blacks sank even further into the deadend of segregation and disfranchisement. It is the Populist claim to our attention that, in spite of everything, a true and native people's crusade almost succeeded.

TWENTY

Politics, Education,
and the "Splendid Little War"

LOOKING back on the administration of Joseph F. Johnston—chosen as Alabama's thirtieth civilian governor in 1896—historians have almost unanimously seen his years as the stepping-stones of transition that bind the Populist revolt to the later Progressive period. Johnston took the reformers' issues, especially the demand for free silver, and used them to appeal to Populists and Jeffersonians and lure them back into the Democratic party. Put more generically, he sought the support of north Alabama voters. Johnston's background as a Birmingham industrialist, businessman, and banker seemed to be an irresistible link to a progressive future.

Even so, matters were more complicated than the simple transition school of thought suggests. Johnston worked hard to take the splintered factions of Alabama political life and assemble them in a new coalition. The old ruling combination was the constantly reassessed but mutually beneficial alliance of Black Belt planters and Birmingham coal and iron capitalists. The planters' influence came in their organizational control of the Democratic party, while their power rested on the ability to win any state election by manipulating the black vote. The industrialists usually played a quieter role in the coalition (but with great rewards) in part because they lacked either a real or manufactured constituency that could guarantee success at the polls.

Johnston lost his bid for the governorship in 1894 to the conservative alliance. In 1896 he defeated Richard H. Clarke of Mobile, who had Black Belt support, and went on to win the general election. He had produced his own constituency, if only temporarily, and it marked a shift from south to north, from planter to businessman. While accurately reflecting the realities of economic power, the combination was unstable, and it failed to last in the face of racial politics.

There was ambivalence, a constant tension of conflicting aims and interests in the record of the Johnston years. His business orientation and relationships were clear. As his private secretary Johnston named Chappell Cory, the former secretary of the Birmingham Commercial

Club established in 1893 by businessman Braxton Bragg Comer and Rufus Rhodes of the Birmingham *News*. Sydenham B. Trapp became the new president of the Board of Convict Inspectors; Trapp had been Comer's partner in the wholesale grain business in Anniston before Comer moved to Birmingham. The North Alabama Old Friends Association was in session.

The issue of convict leasing reveals the problems inherent in appraising Governor Johnston. One historian accorded Johnston praise as the "sponsor" of a bill introduced in the senate by Dr. Russell M. Cunningham "to abolish the noxious convict leasing system."[1] In fact, Johnston's statement to the legislature on leasing showed less commitment to reform than evidenced by the conservative Governor Oates. Johnston did not recommend abolishing leasing but only suggested that such a goal be held "steadily in view." He recommended giving the Board of Convict Inspectors greater authority "to hire convicts either publicly or privately."[2] Cunningham's bill would have abolished the county leasing of convicts, not state leasing. The bill, reinforced by the disclosures of a legislative investigating committee, passed the senate and deadlocked with a strong prolease bill in the house.

It was plain to all Alabamians that no change could be made in convict leasing without some other place to send the prisoners (previous inspectors attempted to create alternatives with farms and textile mills). Yet Sydenham Trapp recommended that the mill at Speigner be sold (Trapp later closed it, and the mill was leased to a private company) and that convicts on the state farms be leased out. Both Tennessee Coal and Iron Company and Sloss Iron and Steel (Johnston's old corporation) received new five-year convict lease contracts at a substantial savings over the previous four-year rates. These contracts, and later ones, were marked with gross irregularities in granting and in revenue collection. Trapp excused the illegalities with the defense that "it was all done with the sanction of the Governor."[3] None of this maneuvering showed Johnston's commitment to reform nor did it mark him as even a "proto-progressive."

In other areas the evidence is less damaging to Johnston, though it may still fail to sustain his image. Of much concern to Jefferson County businessmen, the Birmingham Commercial Club, and textile manufacturer Braxton Bragg Comer was the issue of railroad rates. Although it was established early, Alabama's railroad commission had always lacked statutory authority for effective rate regulation. What powers it possessed had been effectively controlled by packing the commission with friends of the railroads. Alabama Populists had taken a surprisingly generous view of railroad iniquities and high rates. Thus the attack on the railroads devolved on the businessmen who as manufacturers, processors, or retailers saw their profit margins compressed as railroad profits expanded. The issue was real enough, and in later years Governor Comer made it the linchpin of what passed for Alabama progressivism.

Johnston's annual message to the legislature recommended additional powers and broader jurisdiction to the railroad commission, but it lacked the priority standing that the Comer group desired. Nevertheless a railroad bill was introduced that would give the commission (in line with Georgia's practice) the power to set rates rather than to respond to company changes. The bill passed the senate, but in the house the railroads brought out their lobbyists. Under the leadership of Representative A. A. Wiley, an attorney for the Atlantic Coastline, the bill was defeated. In 1898 Johnston once again recommended action, but his request did not even rise to the level of legislative action. Where Comer and his friends were involved in businesses sensitive to freight rates, Johnston had served (some would have said still served) the interests of coal and iron where railroads were prime customers and close allies.

Nothing was closer to Johnston's image as an efficient businessman-governor than state finance. He began his term in a cloud of charges and countercharges on the size of the state deficit. Whatever the true amount, the issue of state revenue called into question thorny issues: not simply equitable assessments, but the nature of state taxes themselves.

The vast majority of Alabamians were poor people. They had not shared in the profits of cotton cultivation or in the wealth derived from mining coal and making iron and steel. Their taxes were heavily tilted toward property, and often property was the only thing of value that they owned. Those who made the laws and set the taxes and established the assessments were either large property owners or their spokesmen. They controlled state government, and they controlled county government, and they opposed paying taxes commensurate with their wealth. While not attempting to shift the tax burden away from property, they successfully shifted a fair share away from *their* property. This ploy accentuated the already low tax ceilings mandated by the constitution even though a greatly increased level of revenue was desperately needed if Alabama was ever to start the laborious process of raising its quality of life to even national averages.

Governor Johnston's answer to state deficits was to decrease state expenditures while trying to increase the level of tax assessments to bring in more revenue. Assessment of property was the job of county tax assessors, and, statewide, their performance had been woeful. Granting inaccuracies, there was a basic problem when the Bureau of the Census found taxable property in Alabama in 1890 of $604,241,859 while for the same year the tax assessors could find only $258,979,578 as a tax base. All taxpayers may have profited from low valuations, but the large owners gained a disproportionate reduction in their taxes and wanted to maintain it.

Earlier governors had raised the problem of assessments, and now Johnston tried his hand. In 1897 the legislature defied the Black Belt press and passed a law allowing the governor to appoint a state tax commissioner. He was given authority to name a commissioner for each county. This measure was not as centralizing as it seemed. The state officers did not replace the county assessors; they operated parallel to them with the jobs of assessing property that had escaped taxation and collecting unpaid back taxes. If logic raised doubts about curing one inefficient operation by creating another layer of government, the test came down to the final results. After one year of operation, in 1898, assessment of real and personal property was $9,048,365 higher than the previous year. What sounded like progress was not enough to close the gap. In 1890, 57 percent of property values had escaped taxation. Ten years later, and despite all the efforts, 65 percent of property went unassessed.

Johnston continued the trend—it was one of necessity rather than philosophy—toward a slow centralization of state financial control. He was not aided by a perverse legislature that specifically denied the examiner of public accounts power to require a uniform system of accounting for all state and county offices. One observer accurately concluded that "Alabama's financial system was based upon a simple agrarian society and was ill equipped to meet the demands of a complex industrial state." It was equally correct that "the chief objective of Governor Johnston in trying to achieve stability and efficiency was to reduce taxes, not increase the services of the state."[4]

The realities of an inequitable tax structure and low state revenues inexorably showed up in the level of support for social services. During the years of Bourbon rule the paucity of support was excused or justified by a philosophy that denied all but a hard core of governmental responsibility. Even those areas of support, including the universally shared need for education, received minimal levels of funding.

As already noted, the public school system suffered a major setback with the passage of the law in 1891 allowing township officials arbitrarily to apportion school funds. By 1900 the benchmarks of public education (number of schools, enrollment, term lengths, and pay scales) had not yet reached the extremes of racial imbalance, but they were well on the way. For both races public education was limited mainly to ungraded schools. While many towns and cities had high schools, not until 1907 did the legislature provide for a high school in every county. The prosperous cities of Alabama soon had the state's best schools, the product of an elevated regard for education and extraordinary efforts at

Young black students at Big Zion school, ca. 1900 (Courtesy of the Alabama Department of Archives and History)

financial support. In 1900 monthly salaries for white teachers in the cities averaged $56 compared with $24 a month in the rural counties. The cities paid for their schools "through tuition payments, the meager state funds, bond issues, and appropriations from their city councils."[5]

Alabama's educational leaders, painfully aware of the state's national ranking, realized that only extraordinary efforts could change the educational truism of "once behind always behind." What could be done for Alabama? In 1896 the Alabama Education Association, stymied in its efforts to increase tax revenue by legislation, appointed a committee to press for a new constitution. This committee was headed by Dr. John Herbert Phillips, Birmingham's superintendent of city schools. The "Phillips report" called for a state board of education, higher qualifications for superintendents, the allocation of a fixed percentage of state revenue to education (and its more equitable distribution), higher certification requirements for teachers and higher salaries, and the establishment of school districts with local taxing power.

The AEA, along with the rest of the state, received a new constitution in 1901, but the motives and results of this change would have little to do with the agenda of the educators. It was a sharp defeat, but the cause of public education did not die. Men such as State Superintendent of Education John William Abercrombie, Dr. J. L. M. Curry, and Edgar Gardner Murphy—with the aid of the teachers' associations, the Alabama Industrial and Commercial Association, the Alabama Federation of Women's Clubs, and organized labor—kept up the pressure for change. And improvements were made. School districts were redrawn using population centers and natural boundaries, a state textbook commission decreed uniform textbooks, minimum school calendars were set, and county superintendents felt the standardization of duties and qualifications.

Despite all the trappings of better organization, the differences in white and black schools were widening. In 1908 the total value of all the equipment in Alabama schools was only $262,218. The black share of that was $21,825. Of the 383 public school libraries, students in black schools had access to 25. Further advances in Alabama education would occur by the end of the First World War, and further sobering statistics would surface. In 1921 Alabama spent a considerably smaller percentage of its total revenue for public schools than it had in 1913.

To speak of public education, even on the primary and secondary level, may distort the picture of education in Alabama. Throughout these years the state had a bewildering array of high schools, academies, and institutes spanning the educational spectrum from primary grades to college-level courses. Particularly in the earlier decades no clear dividing line existed between many of the "colleges" and what could be considered secondary education. There was a confused mix of private, public, black, white, male, female, and coeducational schools, and even the line between public and private was blurred by the legislative penchant for allowing private schools to receive public funds.

While statistics rarely speak directly to quality, they indicate the size and shape of a particular subject. If higher education in Alabama was judged by the number of colleges founded from 1865 to 1920, it would qualify the state as an educational leader. In those years the legislature either chartered or rechartered fifty-eight colleges. With at least twenty other colleges founded or operating, an Alabama student had a theoretical choice of seventy-eight colleges to attend, ranging from the University of Alabama to White Sulphur Springs College, Eutaw Female College, or even the Polytechnic College and Ladies Institute of Cullman. It seems clear that many of these colleges either never opened or operated for short periods of time. Still, there was an incredible diversity of offerings and surely a wide disparity in standards and quality.

Over the years some private colleges grew and prospered, some gained state support and public status, and some public colleges grew and changed in role and status. Names changed, colleges moved from one town to another, and many failed and closed their doors forever. Out of the struggles of success and failure the still-varied, but much-refined, modern structure of higher education emerged.

The oldest of the private colleges—and that usually meant church-

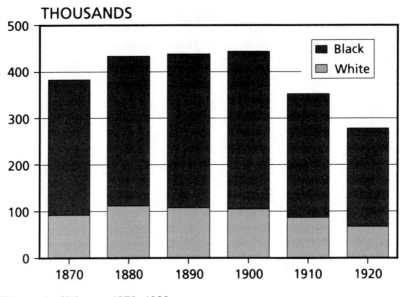

THOUSANDS

Illiteracy in Alabama, 1870–1920

sponsored—was Spring Hill in Mobile. It was the second college established in Alabama (its cornerstone was laid on July 4, 1830) and the first permanent Catholic college in the South. Placed under the jurisdiction of the Jesuits of Lyon, France, in 1847, it established and maintained a solid reputation for academic performance. For the Protestant denominations the words of the Methodist Reverend Archelaus H. Mitchell in 1854 might well have constituted their marching orders. "We need institutions," he said, "that are not afraid to declare themselves full upon the side of God and religion."[6] From Southern University founded at Greensboro in 1856, and the North Alabama Conference College (Owenton College) established near Birmingham in 1898, the Methodists created the unified Birmingham-Southern College in 1918. In 1854 the Methodists founded Tuskegee Female College, moved it to Montgomery in 1909 and renamed it Women's College of Alabama, and made it Huntingdon College in 1935.

The Baptists were equally active. After participating in an interdenominational school in 1836, local Baptists at Marion founded Judson Female Institute in 1838. Milo P. Jewett, its president until 1855, went on to become a prominent founder of Vassar College. Judson survived the Civil War (the Baptist-sponsored Alabama Central Female College in Montgomery, founded in 1857, was a wartime casualty) and continued its chosen role in the education of white women. What became Samford University had a particularly convoluted journey. In 1832 the Alabama

State Baptist Convention made its plans for a seminary for indigent young men called to the ministry. As a result the Greene County Institute (near Greensboro) was founded and operated until the panic of 1837 forced it to close. It was surprisingly strong in science instruction and possessed its own exquisitely made Alvan Clarke refracting telescope. The Baptists tried again with the founding of Howard College at Marion in 1841. Its building (formerly used by Judson) burned in 1844, and its new building burned in 1854. Closed during the war, it reopened in 1865. In 1886, suffering from the almost standard financial difficulties, the college was moved to East Lake in Birmingham, and in 1957 Howard College moved again, this time to a new campus in Birmingham's Shades Valley. In 1965 the school's name was changed to Samford University.

The private black colleges of necessity lacked a prewar tradition. The oldest of these institutions was Talladega College, begun as a school in 1865 by William Savery and Thomas Tarrant, both former slaves, and enlarged into a college in 1867 with help from the American Missionary Association and the Freedmen's Bureau. Miles College was founded in 1908 by the Alabama Conference of the Colored Methodist Episcopal Church, the fruit of earlier schools at Docena and Thomasville. Under the aegis of the Alabama Colored Baptist State Convention, the Alabama Normal and Theological School was opened in 1878 at Selma. At first operating as a junior college (with elementary and high school training as well), Selma University became a four-year institution in 1885. Oakwood College in Huntsville, supported by the Seventh-Day Adventist Church, began its life in 1896 as the Oakwood Industrial School and became a senior college in 1943. Present-day Stillman College in Tuscaloosa began in 1874 as a training school for black ministers. A high school and junior college for many years, it began a four-year program in 1949.

Fires that destroyed their buildings and unremitting fiscal stringency that threatened foreclosure were the prevailing motifs of the private colleges. But the public institutions had their own varied origins and their own travails. A major motive in the establishment of state colleges lay in the necessity to train teachers for the public school system. Education—as history proved—always produced the need for further education. From that pragmatic motive came the "normal school" (meaning of "regular" or "standard" instruction). The first in Alabama, and the first in the South, was the State Normal College located at Florence in 1872. The Methodists had founded LaGrange College in 1829; it became Florence Wesleyan University in 1855; and that institution was deeded to the state in 1873. It became the prototype of later normal colleges, remitting tuition fees to those students who agreed to teach for two years. In 1929 it became Teacher's College of Florence; in 1957 the name was changed to Florence State College; in 1968 it progressed to Florence State University; and in 1974 it reached its apogee as the University of North Alabama.

A similar journey awaited the normal colleges of Jacksonville, Livingston, and Troy. The Jacksonville school, founded in 1883, had antecedents in the Jacksonville Male Academy (1836), the Jacksonville Female Academy (1837), and Calhoun College (1869). In 1929 Jacksonville State Normal School became Jacksonville State Teachers College; by 1957 it had moved to Jacksonville State College; and in 1966 it was made Jacksonville State University. Livingston Female Academy and Normal School was also founded in 1883, and it was endowed with the drive and ability of Alabama's premier woman educator and reformer, Julia Strudwick Tutwiler. In 1887 a white coeducational normal school was established at Troy, and it grew and enlarged its role to become Troy State University in 1968.

Educational theory was divided in those Victorian days on the merits and benefits of coeducational endeavor. Although there was a strong trend of women being admitted to former all-male schools, legislators were not convinced that exclusively female colleges were anachronisms. The female college was a standard fixture on the Alabama scene—as witness the long life of Athens Female College, first Baptist, then Methodist, and a state institution in 1976. The growing belief that if women did not teach, they could at least profit from practical training, gave birth in 1896 to the Alabama Girls Industrial School at Montevallo. Here too the push and pull of institutional evolution proceeded apace. In 1923 the school dropped its high school work and became Alabama College, the State College for Women. It completed the sequence of growth by becoming coeducational in 1956, and in 1969 its name was changed to the University of Montevallo.

Whether the initial impetus came from the need for teachers or from the desire for female institutions, very few of Alabama's efforts at higher education were the result of planning or the coordinated assessment of need. Colleges were located in towns in response to political bargains and effective boosterism; they were supported at varying levels of inadequacy; and they grew in fits and starts in step with a natural rhythm of population and enrollment. In the long run political apportionment of educational opportunity can produce a rough equity in geographic distribution—and it did for Alabama. But politics rarely takes the comprehensive view. Legislatures act far better than they plan, and the result in higher education is most often almost identical competing institutions within hierarchies of financial support. Social institutions tend to multiply in size and complexity, and educational institutions are no exception.

It has been suggested that a one-room schoolhouse dealing with the Three R's, if given money enough, will inexorably grow to a giant campus with hundreds of buildings and offerings ranging from beginning cosmetology to doctorates in nuclear physics. There is, in short, no such thing as a satisfied educator or a completed educational system.

In Alabama, as in the rest of the South, the problems of educational support were compounded by the decision to establish parallel institutions for whites and blacks. The parallelism was flawed, but some efforts were made. Over the weekend, on December 6 and 9, 1873, the legislature created two black normal schools. Saturday's action established a state normal school and university at Marion, while on the following Tuesday an institution was created that opened as the Huntsville Normal and Industrial School in 1875. The Marion institution would take over the Lincoln Normal School and receive $2,000 a year in state funds. Its purpose was clearly stated: it would provide "for the liberal education of the colored race" in the same fashion "as is already provided for the education of the white race in our university and colleges."[7] In 1887 an act was passed with the seeming intention of making the school the "University of Alabama for Blacks." But only two years later matters took a different turn; now the school was to be known as the State Normal School for Colored Students, and its board of trustees located it in Montgomery. It too went through the stages of metamorphosis, moving from State Teachers College to Alabama State College for Negroes and then to Alabama State College. In 1969 it became Alabama State University.

The Huntsville school opened its doors with sixty-five students and two teachers, but it had the incomparable advantage of having William H. Councill as its first president. Councill, born a slave in North Carolina and educated in a Freedmen's Bureau school, moved to Alabama and entered the volatile world of Reconstruction politics. His good relations with white politicians gained him the presidency of the Huntsville school—and rewards for his school as well. When the Morrill Act of 1890 promised annual appropriations to land-grant colleges, Booker T. Washington of Tuskegee Institute proposed that the black schools at Huntsville, Tuskegee, and Montgomery divide the black share in equitable fashion. But when it was decided that only one black college in a state could receive the funds, Councill was the winner of the competition (Tuskegee gained land-grant status in 1899). By 1948, after several changes of name, the institution at Huntsville became Alabama Agricultural and Mechanical College.

The most famous among the black colleges was without a doubt Tuskegee Institute (it held a variety of names before its present appellation of Tuskegee University). While it received an annual state appropri-

Left: Born a slave in Virginia, Booker T. Washington was the founder of Tuskegee Institute and president until his death in 1915. He became the single most influential black man in the nation. *Right:* George Washington Carver, a native of Missouri, gained prominence as a scientist at Tuskegee Institute for his research developing commercial uses for native products such as peanuts, sweet potatoes, cotton, and pecans. (Photos Courtesy of the Alabama Department of Archives and History)

ation, it had endowments and donations from many sources, and it was not technically a "state" school. All through the decades around the turn of the century, when the white-black relationship plunged to its lowest depths, the soul of Tuskegee and the internationally recognized voice of American blacks was Booker T. Washington. Tuskegee stressed vocational and industrial training, and perhaps the perfect combination in education was the basic research performed by George Washington Carver and the dedicated agricultural extension work of Thomas Monroe Campbell. One man discovered; the other spread the word.

Booker T. Washington, born a slave in Virginia in 1856, was an exceptional man who came to exercise national influence, as well as control of the Republican party in Alabama, and to stand as a controversial figure in black affairs. In race relations Washington preached the doctrine of accommodation. In a famous speech at the Atlanta Cotton States and International Exposition in 1895, he enunciated his "Atlanta compromise." Blacks should strive for economic independence, he said, and accept, at least for the time being, their political isolation and social proscription. More militant black leaders saw Washington as an "Uncle Tom," supinely surrendering the black man's civil rights. Washington was a realist in a bitter time. It now seems clearer that political rights—however much they are justified and rightfully due to every citizen—are no cure-all or panacea for the social and economic problems of minority *or* majority groups. Washington was a conservative in racial matters, but his advice was not in error.

Where the second Morrill Act had benefited Councill's college in Huntsville, the first Morrill Act in 1862 was the very reason for the existence of what ultimately became Auburn University. That act provided for a gift to applying states of 30,000 acres of public land for each member of its congressional delegation—a beneficence that would bestow 240,000 acres on Alabama. The year 1862 was less than auspicious for Confederate states to gain federal largess, and it was not until 1869 that Alabama belatedly (and racing against a deadline) made application for its grant. The proceeds of the gift were to be used to establish a college that offered courses in agriculture, engineering, and military training—a practical American antidote to classical education.

Alabama's neighbors offered little guidance by their actions. On one side Mississippi set up a separate land-grant college, while on the other Georgia designated its state university to receive its funds and perform the functions. The Alabama State Board of Education (led by Peyton Finley, its only black member), Governor Patton, and the champions of the University of Alabama, argued—with practical wisdom—that Tuscaloosa should be the home of Morrill money. Inasmuch as none of the funds could be expended on buildings, this argument made eminently good sense, although modern readers will note that it would have rendered future Alabama–Auburn football games impossible. Next, Florence offered the facilities of Florence Wesleyan University, and the little town of Auburn countered with an offer of the land and buildings of the Methodist Alabama Male College. As the legislature considered the matter (November 1871–February 1872), Elyton (now part of Birmingham) and Talladega advanced their claims. The issue of race was added to the argument over location. Holland Thompson, a black member of the legislature from Montgomery, pointed out the inequity in placing all the Morrill funds in a white institution. Attempts to gain an integrated school, to build two schools, or withhold funds for a future black school all failed. In the end Auburn won the battle of location. It made the best offer, and its lobbying forces were the most effective.

Underfunded from its inception (Alabama, until 1883, was the only state that did not supplement Morrill funds), the Auburn institution began its life under the leadership of Isaac T. Tichenor. In its offerings the letter of the Morrill Act was observed, but the school's major emphasis was literary and classical. In 1882 Dr. William LeRoy Broun put the college on a path of science and technological training. Engineering courses were expanded, but the liberal arts were not abandoned. Broun was succeeded by Dr. Charles C. Thach, who served until 1920.

The child of federal munificence, Auburn continued to profit from national educational policy. Funds for agricultural research came with the passage of the Hatch Act in 1887; the Morrill Act of 1890 provided annual funds; the Smith-Lever Act of 1914 supported demonstration and extension work; and in 1917 the Smith-Hughes Act appropriated money to train vocational agriculture teachers.

The handling of the Smith-Lever funds affords a telling example of educational politics—and of the almost automatic exclusion of blacks from positions of supervision and control. When the act was passed in 1914 (it was a natural extension of the Morrill acts of 1862 and 1890), Alabama's governor was Emmet O'Neal. If legislatures were not in session, governors were empowered to designate the college or colleges to administer the funds. Acting under this authority, Governor O'Neal conferred with Dr. Charles C. Thach, president of Alabama Polytechnic Institute (Auburn's name since 1899). It was agreed that Auburn would receive and allocate Smith-Lever funds. This agreement did not mean that Alabama A&M and Tuskegee would not receive any federal monies, but it did mean that they would be dependent upon Auburn.

The matter might have ended had not Booker T. Washington actively sought an independent share for Tuskegee. O'Neal was now between two fires, and pursuant to Washington's request he appointed a special committee (all whites, including Commissioner of Agriculture and Industries Reuben F. Kolb) to visit Tuskegee and make a report. Kolb's committee, apparently unaware of the O'Neal-Thach agreement, recommended that 30 percent of Smith-Lever funds be divided equally between Tuskegee and Alabama A&M. President Walter S. Buchanan of A&M mounted his own spirited campaign (with black and white supporters). All of this activity was classic stuff for a primer on the mismanagement of an issue. O'Neal finally made it clear that Auburn would handle the funds, and the legislature approved the decision.

From the beginning the Smith-Lever Act had a positive effect that grew with the passing years. Governor O'Neal was not insensitive to black needs, but he ignored the pride and sense of participation that black schools would have experienced if they had been allowed a role. For him, and for the state legislature, it was not so much a case of justice denied as it was one of justice uncomprehended.

In the early years Auburn students wore uniforms of cadet gray (they cost $19), tuition was free, and the total expense for an "economical student" was within $200 a year.[8] In 1892 three women were admitted to the junior class, and all three graduated in 1894. Dr. George Petrie, Auburn's pioneer historian, was the first coach of the football team in

1892, although its most famous coach was John W. Heisman, who served from 1895 to 1899. As the college grew it more nearly resembled a university that offered the benefit of Morrill Act requirements. Nevertheless it remained Alabama Polytechnic Institute until 1960, when title and fact came together as Auburn University.

How the University of Alabama at Tuscaloosa fell victim to the scourge of war as most of its buildings went up in smoke has already been described. The immediate years of peace also were not a time for solid growth and development at the "Capstone."

The physical loss of its buildings turned out to be the smallest of the university's problems. A new building was constructed during 1867–68 (Centre Building, later Woods Hall), but at that juncture Reconstruction politics came to the fore. The Radical Republican constitution in 1867 had abolished the university board of trustees and substituted an elected board of regents. The Republicans attempted to make the university another sinecure for the party faithful and its ideology conform to the tenets of congressional Reconstruction. The trustees' faculty was fired; William Stokes Wyman, himself a professor and originally chosen for president by the trustees, refused the position, and the Reverend Arad S. Lakin of Ohio was named as the president. When Lakin and state school superintendent Noah B. Cloud came to Tuscaloosa in September 1868 to take control, the resolute Wyman refused to hand over the keys. Ryland Randolph, the intemperate and forever unreconstructed editor of the Tuscaloosa *Independent Monitor,* laid down a barrage of cartoons and editorials on Lakin and the Radical Republicans, and the local Ku Klux Klan mounted a campaign of intimidation. Lakin resigned, and Randolph continued the attack on his successor, R. D. Harper of Ohio, who also resigned. When the regents, in a state of extreme pique, voted to move the university from Tuscaloosa, Randolph threatened to follow it with his newspaper wherever it went. Not until 1869–70 did the university manage to recruit a class, and it had an exceedingly favorable student-teacher ratio: there were six students and five professors.

Matters improved slightly in 1870 with the appointment of William Russell Smith as president (he was a native Southerner and a former Confederate officer), but when he resigned in 1871 the enrollment stood at ten students—and four of those were sons of faculty members. This, as it turned out, was the low point before the process of rebuilding accelerated. Members of the alumni met with the regents and both groups determined to save the university from its embarrassing situation. The highly respected Matthew Fontaine Maury, the "Father of Oceanography," was named president, and though he served for barely half a year, he recalled the standards of academic integrity, the legitimizing virtue of any institution.

333

Under its next presidents (long tenure was still hard to find) the university grew and expanded its horizons. Henderson Middleton Smith founded a law school in 1872, and by 1878 the university had an enrollment of 179. Clashes of authority occurred between the board of trustees (the Bourbons dropped the board of regents) and the presidents; women were finally admitted as regular students; and in 1900 there was a notable student rebellion against the strictness of military discipline—and the students won. Through all these years, and supplying the continuity of purpose often lacking in a rapid succession of presidents, was the enduring figure of Professor William Stokes Wyman, the "Keeper of the Keys." He had graduated from the university in 1851, then served as professor of Latin and Greek and as historian and librarian for more than fifty years. He was acting president four times, the adviser to eight presidents, and finally the president in 1901 on the promise that he could continue teaching. He served for one year and happily returned to the classroom.

No one could overlook the strength and leadership of John William Abercrombie, who succeeded Wyman in 1902. In 1909 he introduced the plan of schools and colleges still followed today; he founded the Schools of Education and Engineering, and he reorganized and named the College of Arts and Sciences. He coupled these actions with the "Greater University" building program, and by 1911 he had built a modern university. Abercrombie was a man of firmly held standards. He clashed with his successful football coach, J. W. H. Pollard, who enrolled players under fictitious names and who handed out "scholarships" that were in fact pay provided by the alumni. When Pollard (who had strong alumni support) threatened to resign, Abercrombie, with faculty approval, stood up to the threat and accepted the resignation. It was during Abercrombie's tenure that the last football game for the next forty-one years was played between Alabama and Auburn. The teams. had met eleven times, and Auburn had won seven of the contests. In the twelfth year the teams battled to a 6–6 tie before a crowd of 5,000 spectators.

Abercrombie's successor was George Hutcheson Denny, who was to serve as president for almost twenty-five years, through both prosperity and depression. Denny was a strong hand on the helm. In 1912 the university had nine major buildings and an enrollment of 400 students. When Denny retired there were twenty-three major buildings, a football stadium, and almost 5,000 students. When the chimes in Denny Tower ring out they surely toll for the years of hard work, the sacrifices, and the determination that resurrected a university from the ashes and rebuilt it as a major institution.

What had been and what was to be in the growth of Alabama education were only partially perceived as Governor Johnston and his contemporaries defined and refined their own choice of pertinent issues. Before Johnston finished his second term (after an easy victory over the Populist candidate, state senator George B. Deans of Shelby County), he was deeply embroiled in the issue of a new constitution. At one time or another he stood on both sides of the question. The constitution of 1875 was a perfect product of its times. It locked Alabama into a straitjacket of endless reaction to Reconstruction. Local governments operated under tax ceilings that stifled any response to growth, and the prohibition on the state in sponsoring internal improvements—while saving it from railroad schemes—prevented it from building a decent road system. The most workable part of the constitution was its unchanging continuity. In twenty-six years only five amendments had been proposed, and only one had been accepted.

As Alabama moved toward a new century there was a strong case for writing a new constitution. The 1875 frame of government was clearly inadequate to meet the state's future needs. Supporters of efficient city and county government were drawn toward a new constitution. Those who believed in the need for educational reform demanded a constitutional convention. Citizens desirous of democratic reforms, including the direct primary for nomination, became partisans of constitutional change.

To such laudable goals and constructive motives was added another and often stronger incentive for change. The most charitable explanation—and one used by contemporary advocates—was that because manipulation of the black vote had utterly corrupted the election process, political morality demanded black disfranchisement. Accepted by many whites, the assertion enunciated the curious thought that white dishonesty and fraud and corruption could only be stopped by denying the black man one of his constitutional rights. That was the shortest step away from blaming the black man for white chicanery.[9]

The conservative Democrats' intent back in 1892 to pass election laws that placed government "in the hands of the intelligent and the virtuous" (the chairman of the platform committee who used that phrase was Joseph F. Johnston) had not been forgotten by either side of the argument. Whether Populists, Jeffersonians, or tenacious Democrats, small and usually poor white farmers were deeply suspicious of the aims of constitutional reform. They would shed few tears over black disfranchisement, but their own right to vote was also swinging in the balance. That sentiment, strong among citizens in north Alabama's rural areas, was reinforced by the prospect that an increase in tax and debt ceilings would add to their unmanageable burden. Urban leaders could wax eloquent on the need for a broader tax base to enlarge social services, but they were voices from another world to the little farmer worried about feeding his family and his mule.

335

For the rulers of the Black Belt, constitutional revision was a thing of pluses and minuses. Black disfranchisement would remove the threat of a black–poor white coalition that might have allowed a majority of Alabamians to control their own government. That was a goal worth fighting for after the fears and alarms of the Populist years. But if the black man could not vote, what would happen to the political power of the Black Belt? How could it save the party (and that meant its own interests) if there were no votes to control? Would its voice fall to a whisper in party councils, and would it lose representation in the legislature? In the face of such uncertainties there was division and disagreement on the correct course to follow.

In 1896 the Democrats took no formal stand on calling a constitutional convention, but Governor Johnston's first message to the legislature proclaimed approval. The "good" reasons, said Johnston, were so important that they should have precedence over the "fear of improper restriction on the right of suffrage."[10] The statement was in keeping with the view of the Alabama Education Association and the Alabama Commercial and Industrial Association.

In response to the governor's request, a bill to call a constitutional convention was introduced in the house—and killed in the senate. There was Black Belt support and north Alabama opposition. The Black Belt now looked favorably on the idea of black and poor white disfranchisement, while in the north the former was acceptable and the latter was not. In 1898 a strong effort to make the "condition of the right of suffrage" a major plank in the Democratic agenda was excluded by the platform committee. The party was of two minds, and Governor Johnston, the advocate of revision in 1896, now expressed his opposition. On second thought it seemed clear to the governor that the poor white voters who underwrote his political career might be doubly lost: he would alienate them if he supported revision, and he would lose them forever if they were disfranchised.

Johnston did not speak for the legislature. A majority accepted the idea of a convention with conditions: no disfranchisement of war veterans, and no power to move the capital to another city. In deference to the Black Belt, apportionment of representation would be based on total population, and there would be no change in the ceilings on taxation. The vote was close in both senate and house (18–11 and 52–41), but the measure prevailed after an amendment required a statewide vote on calling the convention. Opposition came from across the Alabama political spectrum. Populists attacked the whole idea of suffrage restrictions as violative of the U.S. Constitution. Reformers for good government and ethical conservatives were offended by the absence of any provision for popular ratification.

In March 1899, three months before the convention referendum in July, the Democrats met in party assembly. The meeting opened with the temporary chairman declaring that the issue was whether Alabama would remain under Anglo-Saxon control or become a hybrid state. The task at hand was "to eliminate the negro from the ballot box." Alabama would be playing its part in the great Darwinian cleansing known as "the rejection of the unfit."[11] But with Black Belt support and north Alabama opposition, all the Democratic conclave did was pledge the party to a convention with the proviso that Democrats would support only party nominees for delegate positions.

At that point Governor Johnston entered the fray. With many anti-Johnston men nominated as delegates, the governor speculated on the increasing likelihood of poor white disfranchisement. It was clear that if he opposed a convention he was widening the breach in the party. Yet Johnston believed that a majority of the legislature would support him. He called a special session to repeal the convention law, and he recommended constitutional change through amendment, including suffrage limitations and a primary election law. Although the legislature repealed the convention law, it was in no mood for substantive action. The members adjourned without suggesting amendments and without providing for a direct primary. The issue appeared to be back where it started. In reality it was only one step away from success.

Before the special session declared an intermission in the drama of constitutional change, larger events captured the attention of Alabamians. State newspapers detailed the steps by which the vacillating administration of President William McKinley finally responded with military action to the cause of Cuban independence. Alabamians, along with their fellow Americans, had digested a heavy diet of presumed Spanish evil, atrocities, and perfidy. For some of the young men raised on legends of lost causes and heroes and the glory of battle, a war with Spain was neither unwelcome nor undesired.

Once the nation was converted from diplomacy to battle, swift action followed. The Spanish-American conflict was the shortest war ever fought unilaterally by the United States. From its declaration on April 25, 1898 (retroactive to April 21), to the signing of the treaty of peace on December 10, the war lasted 229 days and the fighting much less than that. It was a war of minimal national effort, and a majority of the troops raised to fight it never left the United States.

Such was the fate of the First, Second, and Third regiments, Alabama Volunteers. They saw no combat but illustrated the age-old problems of soldiers and wars. President McKinley initially called on Governor Johnston to furnish two regiments and a battalion. The War Department suggested units of volunteers from the Alabama National Guard. The conflict was the last American war fought under the confusing hand of states' rights, the last before a president could simply call state troops into federal service. McKinley's request fell within Alabama's capabilities: it had three white regiments and one black battalion (the Capital City Guards of Montgomery and the Gilmer Rifles of Mobile).

Attempting to muster his white regiments, Johnston became aware of two controlling factors. The state troops enjoyed being lionized—dances, banquets, outings, parades—but such festivities did not automatically translate into a desire for combat or a commitment to bring the blessing of freedom to the Cubans. Moreover, not all the state troops who qualified as patriotic and adventurous met the War Department's fitness standards. They failed physical examinations (being at least 5 feet 4 inches tall, having no deformities or diseases, and weighing between 120 and 190 pounds) at the appalling rate of 50 percent. Even with the mixture of new volunteers, the rejection rate was 30 percent.

The consequence was a long period of recruitment to bring units up to strength and therefore a delay in readiness. A short war would mean no Alabama service abroad. Governor Johnston had a manpower shortage, one that affected the issue of raising black troops for service. The third regiment of Alabama state troops (with additional recruits) became the First Regiment, Alabama Volunteer Infantry, while the core of the first and second regiments formed the Second Regiment, Alabama Volunteer Infantry. It took almost a month to muster the units into federal service at Camp Clarke near Mobile. Next the troops received a lesson in War Department policies and in the state of American military preparedness. Units received no federal subsistence or arms or uniforms until they were mustered. The men had not been instructed to bring civilian clothes to Camp Clarke, and some were soon reduced to strolling around the camp wrapped in blankets. Beans, bread, and beef were the initial menu. The men lived in tents, but the first easy-going schedule of a two-hour drill a day was soon increased to a more determined four-hour period.

At Mobile the men were soon reminded that death arrives in many guises. Four men died at the hospital, some perhaps of "fever," and Sergeant Hugh Collins died from a pistol bullet following a fracas with a black Mobile citizen "after a quarrel over a soda."[12] Matters improved with the arrival of uniforms, an increase in rations, and a move to Spring Hill, where a regiment of regulars had an excellent band.

On June 24 the Alabama troops, now a part of Major General Fitzhugh Lee's Seventh Army Corps with troops from Texas and Louisiana rounding out the First Division, moved from Mobile to Miami and the promise of action. The fifty-four-hour train trip was relieved by crowds of people along the way cheering and offering food and by a parade through the streets of Waycross, Georgia.

Events in a fleeting war were already outrunning any hopes of foreign service. The American expeditionary force for the Cuban invasion sailed from Tampa ten days before the Alabamians left Mobile. The battles of El Caney and San Juan Hill took place on July 1, and Admiral Cervera's fleet was destroyed on July 3. By July 25, Puerto Rico was occupied. With the war slipping away into a victory that denied them admittance, the troops suffered a loss of discipline and morale.

Miami was tropical but not exotic. The combination of heat, mosquitoes, and polluted water was matched by a lack of adequate medical attention. The shortage of liquor was much lamented. Once the latter problem was improved, wild adventures were had in the streets of Miami. Even so, Miamians declared that the Alabama troops were the best in the camp (some Louisiana and Texas troops refused to drill). Dissension occurred in the First Alabama: the officers wanted to go to Cuba for garrison duty, but the troops wanted to go home. At least health matters improved (along with the liquor supply) when the troops were moved north to Jacksonville.

Even as Alabama officers told the press that their men did not want to be discharged, almost complete companies wrote Governor Johnston asking to be mustered out. The enlisted men prevailed. In September the First Alabama came back to Birmingham, and the Second returned to Montgomery. There the men were given thirty-day furloughs and were mustered out. The great adventure—otherwise known as a trip to Florida—was over.

Although the Alabama troops played a subordinate role, the state furnished two of the war's most highly publicized individuals: "Fighting Joe" Wheeler and Richmond Pearson Hobson. Wheeler, a lieutenant general in the Confederate army at age twenty-eight and then a long-term congressman (he served as chairman of the House Ways and Means Committee), was commissioned major general of volunteers. It was a shrewd move by McKinley, as Wheeler became a potent symbol of national reunification. He was still an excellent officer in 1898.

Hobson, born in Greensboro, was a regular naval officer. He commanded a group of seven volunteers who attempted to sink the collier *Merrimac* in the channel of Santiago harbor. The objective was to bottle up Admiral Cervera and his Spanish squadron. The attempt went badly when heavy Spanish fire damaged the steering gear and several of Hobson's charges failed to explode. The place where the ship sank was improperly aligned to block the harbor's entrance. Nevertheless, Hobson emerged from brief Spanish imprisonment as a national hero. He later served as an Alabama congressman, gaining fame as a leader in the prohibition movement. Hobson's services in the war were tardily but nostalgically remembered in 1933 with the Congressional Medal of Honor.

If Alabama's white troops suffered frustration, and if Alabama's heroes performed exemplary acts, the state's black soldiers had their own unique experiences. They never left the state, although relentless racial confrontations gave them their share of combat. The egregious saga of what became the Third Regiment, Alabama Volunteer Infantry, deserves more than the hurried résumé that follows.

At the outset, Montgomery's Capital City Guards and Mobile's Gilmer Rifles offered their services. The War Department, despite the excellent record of black troops in the West, remained a bastion of racial prejudice, and black militia units were not accepted in the first call for volunteers. The issue was less a matter of whether blacks should serve than whether they could serve under black officers. Alabama's two companies had their own officers—Major Reuben R. Mims commanded the minuscule battalion (181 officers and men), while the Montgomery companies were led by Captain A. C. Caffey and Captain Charles T. Holbert.

Prejudice soon encountered reality. Johnston had trouble filling his regiments with whites and still lacked a battalion to answer Alabama's quota. The governor was also seeking reelection, and additional patronage was always helpful. Raising a black unit would answer their leaders' request for active service, and black votes—if not won by alienating whites—were quite acceptable. But there was a problem: blacks wanted at least their own company officers, while Johnston did not want to push white sensibilities that far.

The governor found a regular white officer—Captain Robert Lee Bullard, a West Pointer who grew up in Russell County—to command his black battalion as a major of volunteers. The governor and Bullard agreed on a policy of all-white officers (it made Alabama unique among the states with black units), but there was an immediate backlash. Mobile's Gilmer Rifles, with some white support, refused to accept a white officer, and there was dissension in the Montgomery company for the same reason. Black recruiting efforts went much slower than expected, and Governor Johnston lost face by attempting to blame his own policy on the War Department.

Even so, Bullard and his new volunteer officers began building a battalion in the muddy camp at Mobile. After June 26, when Johnston expanded the battalion to become the Third Alabama, the new Colonel Bullard intensified his efforts. By August 6 the unit was finally mustered with 1,200 men. The troops and their officers trained hard; discipline was firm but fair. Bullard discovered that his troops did not respond well to formal punishment or to appeals to honor. Promotions, praise, and rewards were the motivators. The colonel had stumbled on an approach that knew no racial barriers.

Such were the regiment's glory days. The men were disciplined, morale was high, and except for harassment by white Mobile streetcar conductors (Bullard got one of them fired), there was little racial trouble. Governor Johnston was pleased. The Mobile *Register,* showing both praise and prejudice, expressed its "general astonishment" at the level of discipline.[13] Yet in August the War Department announced that the Third Alabama would be mustered out. Bullard, knowing that most of his men enlisted after hope of combat had passed, assembled his regiment. How many men wanted to stay with the Third? With cheers and waving arms the men voted six to one to stay. Next Bullard and a delegation of his officers went to Washington to plead for garrison duty. The War Department, with white volunteers demanding to go home, agreed to keep the Third in service. Spirits soared, and the troops prepared to sail to Cuba. But with a change in orders they headed north to Camp Shipp at Anniston, Alabama—and into serious trouble.

White volunteer regiments from Arkansas, Kentucky, and Tennessee were stationed at Camp Shipp. Disgruntled and poorly disciplined, they objected to black troops in the camp. When Bullard allowed his troops to visit Anniston they were assaulted by a large crowd of soldiers and civilians. The beleaguered Third Regiment "was formed in column of fours" and marched to camp.[14] That was the beginning. Soldiers of the Third were beaten. Anniston hackmen drove through the Third's designated area streets at high speeds, until a sentry bayoneted a horse and stopped that form of harassment. Bullard had to send officers with every detail that went into Anniston, and by November the Third's sentries were being fired on.

The white press labeled what followed as the "battle of Anniston." On Thanksgiving night Corporal James Caperton, a regimental clerk, and two other soldiers were returning from church services. The men were ambushed and shot in the back. Caperton was killed, and the two others were wounded. Black troops fired back, seriously wounding one white soldier and hitting a few others. Alabama newspapers described the incident as a black "mutiny, " and Senator John Tyler Morgan, no friend of Governor Johnston, denounced the policy of "putting guns in the hands of negroes as soldiers and making them the peers of white men."[15]

In spring 1899, some men of the Third hoped to serve in the Philippine insurrection and keep the regiment alive. But on March 20, the regiment was quietly mustered out, in contrast to newspaper predictions of wild disorder. Some blacks hoped that their patriotic offering would foster white goodwill. They wanted to believe Governor Johnston's thought that the Third Regiment's sacrifices would "receive the grateful recognition of all the people of Alabama."[16] Such expectations were not realized. After the war the Gilmer Rifles were never revived. The Capital City Guards survived for a short time on the sufferance of white interests. As Adjutant General William W. Brandon ("Plain Bill" was a future Alabama governor) explained, it was "not a part of the National Guard."[17] In August 1905, as the unit paraded up Dexter Avenue in its home city, the band struck up "The Battle Hymn of the Republic." The stirring song was an unfortunate musical selection, and there was immediate criticism by whites. On November 8, 1905, the Capital City Guards, an "ineffective organization," were mustered out "for the good of the service."[18]

TWENTY-ONE

The Constitution of 1901

HISTORIANS have often noted the rising tide of racial prejudice that flooded the white Southern mind at the turn of the century. Slavery had at least fostered familiarity, while segregation bred suspicion through separation. The tentative promises of racial cooperation that emerged in the Populist Era were obliterated. In Alabama the reaction inaugurated a rigidly segregated society, legalized inequality, and, incongruously, overthrew old constitutional rights by means of a new constitution. The last vestiges of Reconstruction hopes were crushed by the Southern states whose actions were upheld and endorsed by compliant chief executives, sympathetic Congresses, and a Supreme Court whose views on race were one-dimensional. Faced with the crossroads of decision and direction, the political and economic leadership of the South and Alabama chose the one-way street that led through decades of reaction, injustice, recurring violence, and sectional stagnation.

Long before the brief interlude of 1898 and foreign distractions, agitation for a new constitution had flickered, blazed up, and then died away again as fears and doubts withheld the necessary fuel for action. The demand for black disfranchisement had been balanced by poor white fears that they too would lose the vote. Alabamians who saw the need for greater governmental services and a broader tax base were stymied by the interests that were served by rigid tax ceilings or that approved a government that governed least. Through the terms of Governor Johnston the issue of constitutional change rose and fell. No one had yet managed to build the promises and compromises that would allow some action. It was only a matter of time.

In opposing a constitutional convention, Johnston had won his point when he persuaded the legislature to cancel the process. Yet the success or failure of the issue centered directly on Johnston's own fortunes. After serving two terms as governor, Johnston attempted to prolong his power. He focused on displacing John Tyler Morgan, who, as a U.S. senator, had won national attention by championing a canal across Nicaragua. Johnston's success with the legislature seemed to indicate his strength. If his wing of the party was triumphant, it would at least mean a further postponement of constitutional revision.

Thus the major themes and factions of Alabama life were crammed into the unlikely vehicle of a senatorial race. Johnston was opposed to a constitutional convention, while Senator Morgan was a strong supporter. As Johnston played the champion of north Alabama and the small farmers, Morgan saw the drive as a move to displace him and as an effort to destroy Black Belt control of the party. Johnston opposed a national policy of imperialism while Morgan was its stentorian champion, but the campaign's emphasis turned sharply on state issues and the fundamental question of which direction the state would go on black disfranchisement.

Out on the hustings it was Morgan who had the heavier guns and who laid down the most devastating barrage. His attack centered on the emerging story of Johnston's involvement with the effort by H. C. Reynolds, president of the Girls' Industrial School, to sell state coal lands to Henry F. DeBardeleben. Johnston had attempted to clear his skirts of the embarrassment by firing Reynolds. More difficult to hide was Johnston's role in persuading the board of trustees of the University of Alabama to sell 4,400 acres of coal lands to the Sloss-Sheffield Steel and Iron Company. Johnston had helped to organize the company, and its vice-president was an associate of Johnston in the Alabama National Bank. Johnston's defense that holding the lands kept the acreage off the tax lists was a thin and inadequate excuse.

The governor's efforts to turn the election on his previous appeals as the poor man's champion against the "interests" conflicted with his own wealth and charter standing among those very interests. Here was exactly the flaw in forging an alliance of a few Birmingham businessmen with the numerous poor of north Alabama. It was either an alliance of subterfuge in which the rich misled the poor or it necessitated a transcendent common enemy to hold north Alabamians in an uneasy embrace. Only the Black Belt could play the role of designated villain and only then if its leaders lapsed into political ineptness and self-destruction.

With Morgan hammering away at Johnston's big business connections, and with the Black Belt leaders assuring north Alabamians that black disfranchisement would not affect white voting privileges, the April primary was a Morgan triumph and a Johnston debacle. Johnston carried only five counties, and four of them were die-hard Populist enclaves. The Johnston wing of the party lost again when the proconvention William J. Samford of Lee County won the party's nomination for governor (he defeated Jesse Stallings and three other candidates). In the general election Samford swamped the token opposition of the

344

Populists and Republicans. The doors of opportunity now swung open, and the obstacles to constitutional change were removed. As Frank S. White of Birmingham cynically prophesied, "We have disfranchised the African in the past by doubtful methods; but in the future we will disfranchise . . . [him] by law."[1]

The Alabama legislature now swung into action. In late November 1900, the house (followed shortly by the senate) approved a bill for a popular vote to call a constitutional convention. The only objection to what everyone knew would be black disfranchisement came from the beleaguered little group of Populists and Republicans. The vote in the house was 65–17; in the senate it was 22–8. It was time to turn back the clock.

The new law was similar to the one repealed in 1899. The promises and restrictions on convention action were still there, and a pledge was made to submit the new constitution to the people for ratification. On April 23, 1901, the voters would elect 155 delegates to the convention. Delegate apportionment followed the formula for the state legislature and thus guaranteed control by the Black Belt and south Alabama. If the voters turned down the convention plan, 155 useless delegates would be abroad in the state.

The April election was a spotty replay of traditional Alabama divergence. The cotton counties in the Tennessee Valley voted in favor; the hill counties (with some exceptions) voted against; the Wiregrass returned an opposing vote. Mighty Jefferson County (and Birmingham), in spite of Johnston's influence, went in favor by the narrow margin of 20 votes. Statewide the vote was 70,305 in favor and 45,505 votes against a constitutional convention. And what had the Black Belt done? It delivered a huge and overwhelming vote for a convention. It seemed as if blacks had voted for their own disfranchisement. Surviving Populists, transported back to the governor's races of 1892 and 1894, suffered from déjà vu. Lowndes County, for example, had 5,500 registered black voters to 1,000 whites. It went for the convention by a vote of 3,226–338. Democratic officials had promised such a vote. As J. Thomas (Tom) Heflin of Randolph County put it, "we have a very patriotic set of managers and probably all the Negroes will vote for the constitutional convention."[2]

The 155 delegates who assembled in Montgomery on May 21, 1901, have been dissected and analyzed by historians in terms of motive and interest, of alignment and ideology. The scholars' basic interpretation has been that of a convention dominated by the Black Belt–industrial alliance. Without arguing that all Black Belt planters or all industrialists thought alike, the interpretation is accurate. Not unexpectedly, different issues produced different coalitions and exposed different factions.

Less evident is one historian's conclusion that the convention "was not simply an occasion for the continuation of the bipolar conflicts of the 1890's . . . [but] a crucial midpoint in . . . [Alabama's] transition from the politics of revolution to the politics of pluralistic interest groups."[3] That view mistakes a commonplace for uniqueness. The secessionist years of the 1850s were filled with pluralistic interest groups, as were the years of Reconstruction. The Jeffersonian Democrats and the Populists teemed with diverse factions. Although the convention illuminated the interest groups of 1901, it also closed an era; it marked the end of a long fight. Did the delegates of 1901 march off to a new life of "pluralistic interest groups" or did they set the old themes and the old values in enduring concrete?

Dominating the committee chairmanships, the Black Belt–business alliance went to work. The major thrust of the convention—to disfranchise the black man—centered debate primarily within the committee on suffrage and elections and then on its recommendations. The committee's job—and one not approved of by all its members—was to find some formula for handling the impossible. In one direction the Fifteenth Amendment seemed an unscalable wall on the road to disfranchisement. Neither the national government nor the individual states could deny a citizen's right to vote because of "race, color, or previous condition of servitude." Beyond that challenge lay more. The state Democratic party had promised not to disfranchise white voters. Yet one of the favored grounds for disfranchisement was illiteracy. That basis of exclusion would have removed a still inadequate 59.5 percent of the black vote while also taking at least 14 percent of the supposedly untouchable white vote. Would the party break its pledge?

Promises aside, the Black Belt and business leaders had long intended to take away the vote from the poor whites and keep it in the hands of "the intelligent and the virtuous." The possibility of another Populist-black alliance had to be attacked at both ends: blacks and poor whites had to be rendered harmless. While black disfranchisement could be openly discussed and loudly championed, white disfranchisement operated on a quieter agenda. A great many of those same whites had opposed the convention, and even more might oppose ratification if they were unduly aroused.

For a month the suffrage committee communed with precedent and practice in the neighboring states and considered a diversity of plans. While it was so occupied, the convention, by a vote of 87–22, jettisoned the radical thought of allowing women to vote. The future U.S. senator Tom Heflin noted that women's suffrage was the work of "a few cranks strolling over the state."[4] An impatient Alabama press, anxious for news, might have gleaned salient clues from convention president John B.

Knox's opening address to the delegates. The pledge for no white disfranchisement, said Knox, did not extend "beyond the right of the voters now living."[5]

On June 30 the suffrage committee entered majority and minority reports. The documents were studies in disparate views. The majority report divided a complex system of suffrage requirements into a temporary and a permanent arrangement. Until January 1, 1903, a citizen who met age, residence, and poll tax requirements could register to vote for life provided he had been in the army or navy in previous wars. It was, in modern terminology, an extreme example of veteran preference. The provision must have brought some wry smiles to the faces of Alabama's black Third Volunteer Regiment. Failing military service directly, the descendants of soldiers or sailors (including those serving in the American Revolution) could also register. If even this stipulation was insufficient, the vote was also given to "all those of good character who understand the duties of citizenship in a republican form of government."[6]

The permanent plan to establish voting requirements turned from military service and ancestors to other matters. A prospective voter had to reside in the state for two years, his county for one year, and his ward for three months. On or before February 1 in an election year, he had to pay a poll tax of $1.50, retroactive to 1901 or to the year when voting age was reached. Either the voter or his wife had to own real or personal property worth $300 or more or forty acres of land on which the taxes had been paid. The potential voter had to be able to read and write any article in the constitution—in English—and that meant to the satisfaction of the registrars. He must have been engaged in a lawful business for the previous year and could never have been convicted of crimes ranging from treason and murder to vagrancy and buying votes. While the poor white might initially win a vote under the ancestry clauses, it would not be difficult to disfranchise him after 1903. The black man had almost no chance at all.

The minority report—an upstream dissent against the current of racial antagonism—was signed by four men. Former governor William C. Oates, the bane of reformers in 1894, presented the report. Stanley H. Dent of Eufaula, a paragon of conservative but strongly held ethical principles, placed his name on it, as did George P. Harrison, a fellow Gold Democrat. Frank S. White, Senator Morgan's campaign manager in 1900 and an ally of Braxton Bragg Comer in the fight for railroad regulation, rounded out the group.

The opponents favored a literate electorate and strict requirements to vote. Yet they strongly objected to the duplicity inherent in the effort to disfranchise the black man. They charged that despite the Fifteenth

Amendment the majority report had deliberately erected a system that would operate unequally on whites and blacks. Besides setting up a "permanent, hereditary, governing class," it would be impractical to administer (it might have caused an early boom in genealogical studies) and was simply unnecessary: "The ballot can be secured to the honest and dependable without resorting to this subterfuge."[7] If Oates wanted to disfranchise whites and blacks, at least he wanted to do it openly. Oates and his supporters were paternalistic and full of the white man's burden to help the inferior. Still, in 1901, these few voices pleading for requirements that bore equally on whites and blacks were in sharp contrast to men such as Tom Heflin who raged about the coming race war.

In the larger arena of convention debate and of public notice, many spoke and wrote against the majority plan, and particularly against the "grandfather clause." Yet it had strong supporters, not least among some hill country whites who shortsightedly saw it as a way to protect their franchise. But it was not a time for broad views, for tolerance, or for statesmanship. The convention rejected the minority report 109–23 and accepted the majority plan 104–14. Eight Democrats and a combination of six Republicans and Populists were the final opposition.

The suffrage issue occupied much of the convention's time and almost monopolized the public debate. Even so, a host of economic and political questions remained, and they affected every Alabamian. While not equaling the fundamental matter of who could vote, they touched the whole structure of state government and the bedrock issues of taxes, business regulation, and education.

The chances for effective corporation control—and most specifically the strengthening of the railroad commission's inadequate powers—seemed to fluctuate between slim and none. Railroad attorneys were present in impressive numbers, and the convention's president and the chairmen of the rules and the corporations committees were in railroad employ. But strident advocates of regulation were also present. Already the best-known apostle was businessman Braxton Bragg Comer. As will be seen, Comer rode the railroad issue down the tracks to notoriety, to political power, and into the governor's office. A minor war of words ensued between Comer's Birmingham Freight Bureau and the railroads. The Comer forces argued the need for a railroad commission on the Georgia model. They cited the almost $2 million more collected by Alabama railroads on the same tonnage as shipped in Georgia. The railroad's reply had much to do with money and profits and little connection with facts or logic. The railroad commission, the carriers argued, was doing an effective job and therefore had adequate powers.

The results of the railroad fight were mixed. The issuance of free

Left: Braxton Bragg Comer, Birmingham textile manufacturer, became known as a Progressive politician by virtue of his efforts to regulate the railroads as president of the Alabama Railroad Commission and to improve education as governor from 1907 to 1911. *Right:* Joseph F. Johnston, native of North Carolina, was a Birmingham industrialist who was elected governor in 1896 and became United States Senator in 1907 following the death of Edmund W. Pettus. (Photos Courtesy of the Alabama Department of Archives and History)

passes, always a potent means of railroad influence on state officials, was the object of compromise. Neither legislators nor judges could legally accept free passes, but all other state, county, and municipal officials were free to be bought by the railroads. The fight for an effective railroad commission failed, but at least the legislature's basic right to regulate the lines was written into the constitution.

As went the railroads so went most other issues of business regulation. Usury won its usual victory with the refusal to limit interest charges to 8 percent. No changes were made in the vicious but profitable convict leasing system (by the narrowest vote the convention even refused to stop working misdemeanants in the mines). Nothing was done to ameliorate the proved evils of child labor, although the fight on that issue was a necessary step in education and agitation.

Advocates of intellectual progress marshaled the argument that enlightenment produced perspective and proportion, and together the two set the priorities for progress toward an equitable society. Without a commitment to education a poor and less than progressive state would be trapped in a self-perpetuating cycle of ignorance and social stagnation. In short, states that needed public education the most were inclined to grant it least. And so it was with Alabama.

It might have been the occasion for statewide mortification that its earlier constitution stood alone among the states at the end of the century in denying local school taxation. Here again the disparate demographics and attitudes in Alabama accentuated the problem. "White" counties realized the need to increase existing state appropriations for education, while Black Belt counties found the current appropriation more than adequate to support their white schools. While educational funds were split heavily in favor of whites in north Alabama, under the prevailing view that education "ruined a good field hand" the Black Belt hardly funded even a token school system for blacks.

The constitution of 1875 placed a tax limit of 7.5 mills on evaluated property, and advocates of school appropriations above the old $100,000 level and those seeking funds for other state services hoped to raise the tax ceiling. But the tax committee was dominated by the same men who fought against an effective railroad commission and for the convict lease system. Their enthusiasm for higher taxes was decidedly lacking. The tax committee proposed a new tax limit of 6.5 mills. Its chairman (with a blend of hypocrisy and honesty) defended the reduction as a reward to the "poor farmer" and to the "welfare and industrial development" of Alabama.[8]

The convention accepted the 6.5 mill ceiling, and this action caused a flurry of basic accounting. If education received 3 mills, as the education committee proposed, if pensions for Confederate veterans took 1 mill (and that was untouchable), only 2.5 mills were left for all other state purposes, including a refunding of the state debt. The education committee (fourteen of the nineteen members were from the Black Belt) endorsed 3 mills for education and added an optional 1 mill local county tax for schools. If used, that option returned the tax ceiling to its old level of 7.5 mills. After rejecting the extreme antiblack proposal to divide school funds on the basis of taxes paid, and after giving state debts priority over everything, the convention adopted the education clauses. Some fractional victories were won, although it seems clear that the minuscule generosity to education was a political ploy by Black Belt leaders to win north Alabama ratification.

The state remained under the prohibition on internal improvements. Cities and counties could build streets and courthouses and bridges, but they were locked into almost the same repressive 1875 tax ceilings. If they attempted to borrow the funds denied them by taxation, they now ran into borrowing limits that stopped them. The problem of local legislation by the state legislature was marginally improved, and for better or worse the executive gained power at the expense of the legislature. Some provisions were the immediate consequences of recent events. No governor would be eligible to serve as a U.S. senator during or for one year after he left office—and that was a retroactive attack on Johnston and his effort to unseat Senator Morgan.

The office of lieutenant governor was reestablished (the Radical Republicans had provided for it in 1868) as a solution to the pending problem of succession. William J. Samford was gravely ill prior to his inauguration, but lacking a new legislature, no president of the senate was available to succeed him. Samford solved the immediate problem by being inaugurated; he died with the convention in session and ready to remedy the problem. William D. Jelks, the new president of the senate, became governor when Samford died on June 11, 1901.

Coverage of a complex constitution by reduction and résumé leaves much unsaid and more unanswered. But the sharp contours of who controlled the convention and what they did with their power were obvious. Black Belt delegates teamed with industrial allies to make their world safe for themselves. Black men, with token exceptions, would lose the right to vote. The poor whites, as the future quickly proved, progressively lost the right to vote as well. The rich, barring their own failure, would stay rich, and the vast majority of poor Alabamians would stay poor and remain a limitation on the social progress the state could ever achieve. In the crushing response to the hopes of social progress, in the deliberate expansion of white supremacy, what had the black man done?

The vote that he still possessed had been perverted into a vote to hold a constitutional convention in which he was denied representation. Before even that vote was finally taken away it was used one last time to ratify his disfranchisement. He knew what was happening to him. The authorities on prejudice and oppression are always those who suffer from it. Whether there were better or worse ways to protest the march of events has been debated ever since, but the black man did not surrender in silence and resignation. Four petitions were submitted to the convention that spoke for the blacks, and the most prestigious was the one signed by Booker T. Washington, William H. Councill, and thirteen other black leaders.

The emphasis of Washington and Councill on economic advancement could be viewed as renunciation of black political participation. But it is difficult to follow some historians who see their position as having "an important bearing upon the movement for disfranchisement."[9] Blacks were not disfranchised in Alabama because they promised to work hard or "know their place" and not cause trouble. They were disfranchised because the white majority took the vote away from them. That decision would have only been more firmly and violently enforced if the blacks had sharply protested. The first decade of the twentieth century was not the sixth decade, and reading racial strategies backward leads to distortion and historical injustice.

The Washington petition was indeed a long ode to humility and supplication. It asked for "some humble share" in electing government officials and made a major point against the assignment of educational funds on a basis of taxes paid. The petition closed with a thought that deserved closer attention than the convention gave it. If hope and aspiration were removed, if effort and intelligence were denied reward, then the black citizen might become "the ignorant, shiftless, criminal negro" of white stereotypes.[10] White progress would be endlessly retarded by black retrogression. The other black petitions touched on the same and broader themes. Several stressed the economic utility of black labor, and a few blacks sought to implement the threat of withdrawing their labor by forming the Afro-American Exodus Union to finance a return to Africa. One petition appealed to employers on the grounds that black labor promised (although the pledge lacked historical accuracy) not to "trouble your sleep with dynamite nor your waking hours with strikes."[11]

The black protests were softly worded and cogently argued, but their presentation made no difference. When the only words in black defense came from the paternalists in the convention—the Joneses, the Oateses, and the Dents—there was not the slightest hope of an equitable outcome. It is always easy to shed others' blood in the past, and bloodshed would have been the result had blacks followed the implied advice of some historians a half century later.

One more step was required to complete the ritual of constitution making. Governor William D. Jelks set November 11, 1901, as election day for a vote on ratification. For two months the Alabama air resounded with the rhetoric of politicians and the fulminations of the editors. Although it was obvious that the constitution was the work of Democrats, the party pushed ratification as an "impartial issue." The approach recognized that not all Democrats were in agreement on the suffrage provisions. The State Democratic Executive Committee established a campaign committee, headed by Representative Oscar W. Underwood of Jefferson County, to support the cause of ratification. Underwood's committee rallied the voters under the slogan "White Supremacy! Honest Elections! and the New Constitution! One and Inseparable!"[12] While the Republicans opposed ratification (the Lily Whites favored black disfranchisement) and the vestigial Populists would vote against it, the real fight occurred among the Democrats. A one-party state was becoming more and more a reality.

Former governor Joseph Johnston played a major role in opposition, and he was joined by future governor Bibb Graves and a group of north Alabama leaders. There was no spokesman here against black disfranchisement. Their constant emphasis concerned the issue of depriving the poor white of his vote and themselves of public office. Of all the ironies in a sea of the ironic, nothing surpassed the action of the black convention in Birmingham that appealed to poor whites who were "being used as instruments to effect their own political destruction."[13] In the election it was the black voter, or nonvoter, who would be used for the purposes of self-destruction. There was no chance that an alliance of the threatened would emerge. Far too many whites approved black disfranchisement, and, lacking an honest count, it simply did not matter how blacks actually voted.

The ratificationists, including the old Populist leader Reuben F. Kolb, blanketed the state with speakers, and their relentless plea was the cause of white supremacy. Political discourse presented a baleful picture of white supremacy hanging in the balance and unspeakable evils about to engulf the state should the constitution fail to be ratified. Just before the election, Senator John Tyler Morgan broke his enigmatic silence and laconically announced, "I hope the people will ratify the constitution."[14] It was not at all clear that it was the "people" who ratified it.

The contest was a repetitive story in Alabama's history of "stolen" elections, fabricated returns, and a perjured black vote. It was enough to tire the most stouthearted and to numb the sensibilities of the strongest champions of political morality. Black spokesmen meeting in Birmingham in September adopted the strategy and spread the word for blacks not to vote in the ratifying election. They hoped—in the face of a hostile record—to prevent their votes from being counted in favor of ratification. Their action did not guarantee that no blacks voted in the election, and it does not allow the conclusion that blacks were not forced to vote. The question of what happened in the election does not turn on this issue.

The statewide vote on ratification was 108,613 in favor to 81,734 opposed—a total vote that rivaled the great fights of the agrarian revolt. The constitution was adopted. How had this ratification passed? The vote in twelve Black Belt counties was 36,224 in favor to 5,471 against, while the vote in the remaining fifty-four counties was 76,263 against and 72,389 in favor. The winning majority came from the Black Belt, and over one-half of that majority came—it had to come—from black votes. There were ten counties—Black Belt or on its fringe—where more votes were cast for ratification than there were legal voters (males over age twenty-one). Even historians who note they cannot "prove" the black vote was fictitious admit that "in some counties almost every eligible Negro was 'voted' although thousands never appeared at the polls."[15]

There was a close correlation between the vote on ratification and the Populist elections of the 1890s. Counties that had gone strongly for Kolb in the old days now went heavily against the constitution, and vice versa. In this sense it was the ratifying election of 1901 that marked the end of the Populist Era. What the election meant for Alabama was plain. It is one thing to argue that majorities went down reactionary roads because the voters wanted it that way. It is another matter to confront the fact that the majority read its interests with some exactitude, but that an entrenched minority kept itself in power through extralegal and therefore criminal means. Those who saw ratification as retrogression believed that many convicts mining coal in expiation of their transgressions had harmed their fellow man far less than the architects of the constitution of 1901.

TWENTY-TWO

The Chimerical Impulse
of Progressivism

THE Alabama constitution of 1901, like so many state efforts, was a long compendium of what should have been legislation. Instead of providing a document of fundamental powers and general processes, the Alabama framers crafted a constitution of minute specifications designed to freeze change in desired channels. There were worlds of ideological difference between a constitution that would broadly say, "the Alabama legislature shall have the power to levy such taxes as it deems appropriate" and the actual document crafted in Alabama that spelled out the maximum millage rate on property. The first placed the power of decision in the legislature—with at least the possibility that it represented the majority; the second expressly took power away from the legislature and, therefore, from the people.

Despite the issuance of paeans to abstract democracy, that same democracy has often been denied at the state level. Elections in Alabama could not be dismissed as making no difference. But the fact remains that a voter's choice of candidates always operated within much narrower parameters of change than theory might have indicated. Yet inevitably the people of Alabama would be affected by what happened in 1902 when Governor William D. Jelks (who had long since established his conservative credentials as editor of the Eufaula *Times*) sought election, and when a new legislature—uniquely limited to a session of fifty days once every four years—made laws under the new constitution.

While the antiratificationists had no hope of prolonging the fight over the constitution, their coalition was an alignment worth keeping. Whether its course was necessarily the same as Johnston's was not long in doubt. On November 6, 1901, the opponents of ratification met in Birmingham, and Johnston was prominently in attendance. The group's demand that the State Democratic Executive Committee conduct a primary election (a white primary) was an endorsement of a Johnston issue. The former governor had been advocating primaries, and his heavily subsidized and partly owned Birmingham *Alabamian* was a loud voice of agitation. It may be that the campaign for a primary went too well. With support growing all over the state, even Governor Jelks praised the idea in June 1902. Johnston had decided a month earlier to oppose Jelks, but it was hard to make the primary an issue when there was no opposition. In July the executive committee met and called for a primary on August 25, 1902. It would be limited to Democrats on party rolls at the time—thus excluding Populists and Republicans—but a saving clause conveniently allowed Gold Democrats to participate.

The primary campaign indicated as much about coming attractions as it did current performers. This situation resulted from the campaign launched by the Comer camp in Birmingham. Comer's partisans tried to get commitments from primary candidates that they would support an elective railroad commission. The railroads counterattacked, and although Johnston came out for an elective commission, Comer did not reciprocate and endorse him. Many of Johnston's reform friends were barred from voting in the primary. Yet contrary to the usual interpretation, it is not clear that his opposition to the constitution determined the outcome. Johnston's political position in 1902 was confused and confusing. If there was a possible north Alabama coalition to assemble, Joseph F. Johnston was no longer a staunch rallying point. On August 25 Jelks won the party nomination with a vote of 63,490 to 25,746. Johnston carried only four counties, and the election demonstrated that a majority of the legislative candidates were pledged to support an elective railroad commission.

The general election was still to come, but it was of little matter in 1902 and a pure formality in the decades that followed. In 1902 Jelks swamped J. W. A. Smith, his Republican opponent, by a vote of 67,649 to 24,190. Even so, Jelks lost the old Republican-Populist strongholds of Winston, Chilton, Marshall, and St. Clair counties.

Governor Jelks's address to the legislature was not the call of positive leadership and a new era. Neither had been expected or promised. Jelks wanted a new municipal incorporation law, improved laws governing primary elections, and reductions in funds for schools for the blind and deaf. It is often reported that the governor wanted to end the leasing of county convicts. Actually, his suggestion came closer to providing working conditions where the convicts would be subject to better supervision.

The governor's prescription for legislative action was important for what he did not mention. The two profound reform issues of the day were the questions of making the railroad commission elective—as the first step in reducing rates—and the need for further regulation of child labor. Even for reformers these were divisive issues, as witness the stance of Braxton Bragg Comer. The leading advocate of railroad commission reform, and a major textile manufacturer, was no friend to the cause of protecting children from industrial exploitation.

Both issues received the ministrations of the legislature. There were rewards for the educational and agitational efforts of Edgar Gardner Murphy and Irene Asby McFayden for child-labor legislation. The legislature passed a law making twelve years the minimum age for factory labor and forbidding night work for youths under thirteen. Compromises weakened the law, and it did not provide for factory inspection.

With railroad attorneys presiding over the house and senate it was an inauspicious time for an elective commission. Still, the Comer strategy of concentrating on legislators was rewarded. House and senate agreed to an elective three-man commission with four-year terms to begin in November 1904. The burden of proof in rate justification was put on the railroads. Before signing the bill, Governor Jelks appointed two staunch friends of the railroads to the commission, and the law was later amended to make the two associate commissioners elective in 1906 instead of 1904. That still left the position as head of the commission elective in 1904. Few believed that Comer wanted to be an associate commissioner of anything.

If such matters seemed to fall on the more progressive side of the line, the conservatives were not major losers. While most Alabamians assumed that the legislature would meet once and not be heard from again for four years, the conservatives decided that a recess was in order until September 1. The senate named a committee to decide on legislation for the September term and stacked it heavily with reliable members of the Black Belt–heavy industry coalition. When the legislature reassembled, Governor Jelks contributed the ideas of selling the prison mill and farms and implementing the already specific suffrage requirements of the constitution. The latter matter was duly provided for in the Bankhead Act.

The view that the senate legislative committee's report was surprisingly progressive is better rendered as being less conservative than it might have been. There were special school taxes and adjustments to the primary election laws and to municipal incorporation, but there was nothing to threaten the essential status quo. Governor Jelks had not been a voice for change, but by 1907 he endorsed most reforms currently popular in Alabama except railroad control. The change said something about Jelks, but it said much more about Alabama reforms.

At the state level events now marched in a straight line toward the future. Failing in 1903 to convince the railroad commission to lower rates, Comer offered himself for president of the commission in 1904. The incumbent president, John V. Smith, easily gained railroad support in the race, and nostalgia was served by the attempt of Reuben F. Kolb to win election to state office. Conservatives opposed Comer, it has been argued, because they failed to realize that black disfranchisement made the need for white unity unnecessary. That the architects of disfranchisement did not know its effects and consequences strains credulity. Splits in white unity were still dangerous. Conservatives opposed Comer, not because they viewed him as a radical reformer, but because the changes he championed either did not benefit them or directly harmed their allies.

The Comer forces were well deployed for battle, and both sides spent large amounts of money to fuel their organizations and convert the voters. Comer polled 59 percent of the vote to Smith's 32 percent, and a major political career was off and running. The Montgomery *Journal* spoke of Comer as a "new force and a new power" in state politics and saw the dawning of a new era and "a new order of things" in Alabama.[1] Comer's personal success was clear enough, but it was questionable that lowering railroad rates was the key to rearrange Alabama society and inaugurate "a new order of things."

Comer, very much like Theodore Roosevelt when the latter was president of the New York City police commission, found himself a prisoner of his position. He was outmaneuvered and frustrated by his oppositional colleagues. To Comer, as to Roosevelt, it was clear that success depended on gaining greater power. By midsummer 1905 Comer had made up his mind to run for governor in 1906, and he traveled about the state taking the pulse of the people. Comer's political position was not clear. In 1905 he privately wrote, but he did not publicly say, that there had been "too much class law in Alabama and too much class rule."[2] The real question was what class did Comer himself represent and how broadly would he embrace reforms other than railroad regulation?

A month before Comer announced his candidacy, Lieutenant Governor Russell M. Cunningham, a medical doctor turned politician, publicized his own race for governor. Cunningham was well liked and had conservative support although his platform was as progressive as Comer's. It was not clear that the Birmingham businessmen who were the hard core of the Comer Rate Reform Club and the neo-Populist Farmers', Merchants', and Laborers' Association were any more liberal than Cunningham and his supporters. It was clear that different interests were struggling for recognition. They wrapped themselves in rhetoric and sought identification with the images that would attract the necessary votes. As one historian has explained, organized interest groups saw Comer's "narrow program" as "a vehicle for change." The "extraneous interests" were welcomed, and each brought "his own pet reform along with him."[3]

The campaign was enlivened with joint debates between Comer and Cunningham, attacks on Comer by the Montgomery *Advertiser* for his stand on child-labor legislation, and recrimination by the Comer forces. Comer was confident of victory, and when the votes were counted he had 61 percent of them—almost his same percentage as in 1904 when slightly more voters went to the polls. Comer would control the state convention, the State Democratic Executive Committee, and the legislature.

When the Democrats held their state convention they constructed a platform that betokened the "new era." Here was railroad regulation, a child-labor law, and the demand for compulsory education and better schools. Also in the platform was that harbinger of coming concerns— the call for a local option law on the sale of alcoholic beverages. In fact, the Comer wing was not alone in grading a reform road to the future. The Republicans produced a platform that matched the Democrats plank for plank and then went further to demand better roads and an end to the lynching of blacks. Alabama even had a Socialist party candidate for governor in the person of J. N. Abbott. His platform added the ideas of the eight-hour day, the abolition of the poll tax, and the initiative, referendum, and recall. The general election had now become a redundant sideshow, and on November 6 Comer was duly elected governor with 61,223 votes. His Republican opponent, Asa E. Stratton, polled 9,976, and Abbott, the incongruous Socialist, miraculously found 417 supporters around the state.

As the governor's race had waxed, the contest for the U.S. Senate had not waned. It seemed certain that neither of Alabama's senators—John Tyler Morgan and Edmund W. Pettus—could possibly live through another term, but each was duly nominated in the primary. To handle their expected demise a "pallbearers" slate of alternates was provided. When Spanish-American War hero Richmond Pearson Hobson ousted John H. Bankhead, Sr., from his representative's seat, Bankhead (who began his major career with a highly questionable reign as warden of the penitentiary) entered the lists for alternate senator, as did Joseph F. Johnston and five other hopeful statesmen. Bankhead and Johnston took a plurality of the votes. Neither man had long to wait. Morgan died on June 11, 1907, and the legislature elected Bankhead to replace him. Senator Edmund W. Pettus quickly followed on July 27, 1907, and Joseph F. Johnston finally became a U.S. senator.

As expected, the first item on the Comer agenda was railroad legislation. As matters turned out it was not a simple case where Comer asked and the legislature answered. The issue of the railroads ran all the way through the Comer administration, and he left office without some final answers. The issues were complicated, and the maneuvering was complex.

Comer asked his legislature for twenty different railroad laws. He wanted not only to strengthen the commission's power but also to regulate such matters as free passes, lobbying, and rebates. An enthusiastic legislature gave the governor almost everything he asked for—with the exception of a law forbidding freight trains to run on Sunday. Three laws dealt directly with regulation: the first was an interim measure that froze rates at their existing levels, while the second and third reduced both freight and passenger rates. Among the acts was an ingenious ploy permitting revocation of any corporation's business license if it began a suit in a state court and then took the proceeding to federal court. The assumption was that a railroad would think long and hard before appealing a rate case to a federal court in the hopes of getting an injunction.

The state had acted, and the railroads promptly reacted. On March 25, 1907, several lines asked the judge of the middle district of the United States District Court of Alabama to issue an injunction to stop the state's enforcement of its new laws. The sitting judge was the pristine conservative, former governor, implacable foe of the Populists, and longtime attorney for the Louisville and Nashville Railroad, Thomas G. Jones. The railroads based their case on the Supreme Court's decision in *Smyth v. Ames* (1898). Rates had to yield a "fair return" on a "fair value" of the railroad property. If a "fair return" was not received, the offending rate had deprived the railroad of property without due process of law. Although the Supreme Court's formula was in error, it did not follow, as often implied, that had the state attorneys pointed out this error, Jones would have denied the injunction. Judge Jones was pleased to continue the temporary injunction while the state lawyers communed on a rebuttal to the railroads.

When the legislature resumed its session in July it found an angry Governor Comer desperately looking over his narrow list of alternatives. An opportunity occurred when the Southern Railway Company moved a case from an Alabama circuit court to a federal court. Judge Jones had ruled unconstitutional the state's prohibition of such actions by railroads, but he had not enjoined the enforcement of the statute applying to general corporations. Acting under the latter law, Attorney General Frank Julian on August 1, 1907, revoked the Southern's license to do business in Alabama. After a week of uncertainty and tension, the Southern agreed to implement the statutory rates and ask Judge Jones to amend his injunction. An unhappy Jones did as he was asked after voicing his displeasure with the compromising railroad. The judge excoriated Governor Comer for his "lawless use of state power"[4] A majority of Alabama railroads now joined the Southern in compromise.

Among the recalcitrant railroads was the Louisville and Nashville under the redoubtable Milton H. Smith. A good friend of Henry F. DeBardeleben, Smith had come to Alabama from Kentucky, invested heavily, and grown rich following the maxim that what was good for

Birmingham and the mineral belt was good for the Louisville and Nashville. Smith now assumed the offensive. In speeches, letters, and the editorials of anti-Comer newspapers, Smith worked the issue that Comer's attacks on the railroads were scaring off capital investment. A more imaginative man than Smith might also have wondered how Comer would have reacted to the passage of twenty bills regulating the textile industry and setting maximum prices on cotton cloth. Not only did a face-to-face meeting between Smith and Comer fail to help, it made matters even worse.

Smith gained ammunition as the panic of 1907 brought financial troubles and threatened hard times, but Comer was undeterred. He called the legislature into special session with the assignment of providing "injunction-proof" laws against the railroads. By enacting new laws with different rates to bypass existing injunctions, and by allowing citizens to sue if they were denied the statutory rates, Comer threw down the gauntlet to Judge Jones. While it was unprecedented to enjoin every citizen of a state, Jones promptly did exactly that. Comer then appealed the question of the injunction to the federal court of appeals in New Orleans. This time he won. Jones's "improvidently issued" injunctions were overturned. Now the railroads put the statutory rates into effect, while the questions of rate changes themselves made their glacial way through the courts.

In 1912, after Comer had left the governor's mansion, Judge Jones issued permanent injunctions against the rate laws. But the state—with a new Supreme Court decision in the "Minnesota rate cases" to back it up—had its passenger rates upheld by the court of appeals. In 1914 Governor Emmet O'Neal, no friend of Comer, made an agreement with the railroads. The railroads accepted the passenger rates but were free to challenge future freight rates in the courts. Some scholars believe that Alabama won the Great Comer Rate War. If so, it was a strange victory.

The amorphous Progressive movement has bedeviled historians—they have difficulty even deciding when it began. Progressivism included the most opposite and contradictory people and policies. Its coherence is not helped by the interpretation that both Theodore Roosevelt's "New Nationalism" and Woodrow Wilson's "New Freedom" were "Progressive" programs. It was a time when a great many people endlessly talked reform but provided little of it. It always seemed to be composed far more of image and intent than of reality and drive and purpose. Some progressives were satisfied with a cleansing of the governmental process, but others, such as Robert M. LaFollette of Wisconsin, made substantive efforts to protect the public and the environment against the profit-seeking corporations. There were single-minded advocates of this reform or that, and there were the centralizing nationalists who saw an orderly, efficient, disciplined society. At the time and in retrospect it has been possible to affix the progressive label to all but the most cynical reactionaries, and historians have bestowed the sobriquet liberally. In the case of Alabama, Edgar Gardner Murphy—rector of St. John's Episcopal Church in Montgomery, social critic, author, and champion of child-labor laws—had little in common with Governor Braxton Bragg Comer, a wealthy textile manufacturer who wanted lower freight rates.

Railroad regulation was a dubious reform in Alabama—as well as nationally—not because it was not needed, but because it cast a shadow far larger than its substance. Between railroad regulation on the one hand and prohibition on the other, reform's time and energies were channeled into narrow streams and limited accomplishments.

Governor Comer, like his predecessors, faced the problem of procuring the revenue necessary to fund his projects. In his messages Comer preached frugality, but in fact the state spent more in every year of his term than it received. The surplus accumulated by Governor Jelks helped for a brief time, but Comer, who was opposed to borrowing, had to borrow. Once again efforts were made to increase the tax assessments on property. The legislature created a state tax commission, and it was an improvement. Yet opposition in the counties was a constant problem. By 1912 assessed property valuation for taxes stood at one-fourth estimated property value. Nor was revenue enhanced as the rising drive for prohibition closed the saloons and reduced the revenue from license fees.

In the search for revenue the convict lease system took on increased importance. In the four years of 1907–10 it produced a profit of $1,366,261—no inducement at all to end it. One historian reported that "in several ways the convicts' plight was worse under Comer than during the 1890's."[5] Another, more optimistic, wrote that "the legislature edged closer to the ultimate abolition of the lease system."[6] What the Comer legislature did—while a much needed reform—had nothing to do with abolishing the system. It simply provided that county convicts would come under state supervision. In like manner the appointment of a state inspector of jails promised at least a degree of publicity for the wretched county places of detention. But reading the inspector's report in 1911 gave no evidence of any improvement.

No issue shows Comer as the reluctant reformer so clearly as the continuing fight for effective child-labor legislation. Comer was committed to support his party's pledge for action, but neither his rhetoric nor his accomplishment was impressive. The 1903 act failed to provide factory inspection (Comer believed that textile owners could enforce the act themselves). The first session of the legislature deadlocked on the issues, and the second gave the task of inspecting the cotton mills to the inspector of jails and almshouses. The inspector's report indicated that the act of 1903 had been widely abused and disproved statistically the idea of self-enforcement.

Comer was forced to ask the legislature for further action while still warning against "an extreme provision of the law."[7] The result was the act of 1907. Factory inspection was still lumped with jails and alms-houses, the school attendance requirement was lowered, and weekly hours of work for minors were raised. Even with these changes Comer delayed the act's implementation and in 1909 tried to reopen the question. He claimed that there were constitutional questions about its passage. Governor Comer was less than pleased with reforms for labor. The child-labor agitation directly involved his interests, and the issue was used against him in his campaigns. Even symbolically it was a tainted issue to Comer: the hated Thomas G. Jones was a member of the Alabama Child Labor Committee. As it turned out, Comer's dealings with organized labor easily bested Jones's record of 1894.

It was a bright spot in the Comer years that the governor proved to be a champion of education. It was not an area where four hard years of work could wipe out the appalling past. The legislature greatly increased school funding, and an act located a high school in each county with state requirements for its building and operation. More funds were given to higher education, which was as threadbare as the public schools. These were much needed moves, and they owed a great deal to Comer's emphasis on education. Problems were inevitable. By 1911 one-half of the counties still did not have high schools.

The drive for compulsory public education ran afoul of the un-willingness to educate blacks—and again to Comer's credit he attacked the idea that black education was wasted effort. But no compulsory education law was passed until 1915, and it was plainly meant for whites only. In precise understatement one historian concluded, "a wide gap existed between white and Negro schools, both as to quality and quantity of education."[8] Many areas saw improvement, but on a national basis Alabama continued to fare poorly. It enrolled only 62.2 percent of its potential schoolchildren in 1910 (the national average was 71.2 percent), and it ranked forty-sixth among the states in that basic category. Most discouraging was that in 1900 the enrollment percentage had stood at 61.7 percent. A long road stretched ahead.

There were echoes in Alabama of the broader concerns of national progressivism, and one of these thrusts deserves some special mention. The problems and the response to public health predated the Progressive Era and led into a fundamental area of social development. The difficulties of life and society are not entirely of human manufacture. The Bourbons did not cause hookworm or pellagra. Racial prejudice did not produce the scourge of tuberculosis, nor did stolen elections lie at the

Left: Dr. Jerome Cochran was a pioneer leader in the state's public health program and a major figure in the Alabama Medical Association. (Courtesy of the Alabama Department of Archives and History) *Right:* Dr. Peter Bryce, a physician who became superintendent of the Alabama Insane Hospital when it opened in Tuscaloosa on April 5, 1861, had wide experience in Europe and the United States. In the last half of the nineteenth century, his concepts of occupational therapy earned him and the institution wide renown—all accomplished on a limited budget. Dr. Bryce's efforts resulted in physical expansion, including facilities for blacks. After his death in 1892, the hospital was named in his honor. (From Owen, *History of Alabama,* III: 273)

heart of the appalling levels of infant mortality or the abbreviated life span of the average Alabamian. In the beginning even the woeful straits of education were not to blame because causes and cures were unknown, undiscovered, and therefore unteachable.

The public health movement in Alabama began almost exactly in step with those giant advances in bacteriology that revolutionized the study and practice of medicine. In 1875 Dr. Jerome Cochran of Mobile—a man long overdue for statues and memorials—finally prevailed upon the legislature to create a state board of health under the supervision of the Alabama Medical Association. On his way to that accomplishment, Dr. Cochran reorganized the medical association in 1873 in order to make it an effective instrument for change. Dr. Cochran's plans were short on democracy but extremely long on action. He held the position of state public health officer until his death in 1896. In his investigations of convict leasing he was a loud and authoritative voice of exposé and reform, and he applied the new tools of modern medicine for the education of his fellow doctors, who were still worrying about miasmas and poultices.

The drive to improve public health was a daunting struggle with the promise of immense rewards. The first Alabama law requiring registration of births and deaths—the basic information of public health—was passed in 1881. It was poorly observed. The following year the legislature turned down recommendations for compulsory smallpox vaccinations, but by 1891 it allowed a quarantine against the spread of yellow fever.

Perhaps the most dramatic and surely one of the most far-reaching discoveries in public health came in 1902 with the identification of the American species of hookworm. This work by Dr. Charles Wardell Stiles, a United States public health officer, did not initially receive a Southern welcome. The more the Northern press talked about the discovery of "the germ of southern laziness" the less likely Southerners were to accept the accuracy of the information. When Alabama was surveyed for infestation—after John D. Rockefeller's donation of $1 million to eradicate hookworm in the South—the results were startling. Hookworm cases were found in every county in Alabama, and in some southern counties infection rates were over 62 percent. Something of the same quantum improvement in health care came as a result of the Julius Rosenwald Foundation's funding of the National Negro Public Health movement. Both races benefited from the discovery that pellagra was due to a dietary deficiency. Southerners were steeped in a poverty that affected their diet, but this discovery was a happier conclusion than the thought that an abnormally large number of people had a genetic propensity for insanity.

The Alabama public health movement was a success that would have delighted Dr. Cochran. It was the product of organization, leadership, and education—and a willingness to accept monetary help and expertise from outside the state. It suggested, more in retrospect than at the time, that there was no limit to progress and a better life when the sectional door was thrown open and the best of the world was invited in.

Public health was the child of the Alabama Medical Association, which was composed of the medical practitioners of the state. How did Alabama produce its doctors and what was the emphasis placed on medical education? In the earliest days Alabama's "medical students" (borrowing the methods of the lawyers) often learned their art by studying with an established doctor. As long as being a medical doctor consisted of claiming to be one, this method of education depended heavily on the merit of the teacher. Attempts had been made at more organized medical instruction, but a major step came in 1859 when the noted South Carolina surgeon Dr. Josiah C. Nott founded the Medical

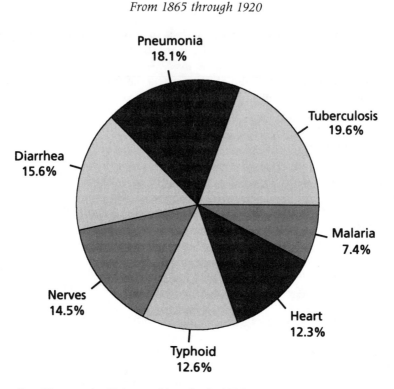

Leading Diseases in Alabama: Mortality in 1900

College of Alabama in Mobile. The next year the legislature made the college a department of the University of Alabama with its own board of trustees and appropriated $50,000 for its classrooms and laboratories. After the hiatus of war the school was reopened in 1868 with twenty-two students. By 1893 the school offered a three-year course of instruction, and in 1899 the program was expanded to four years. This growth spoke of progress and the pursuit of high standards, but in fact these virtues were either relative or illusory. The school had low entrance requirements (the equivalent of three years of high school), poor laboratory equipment, and far too many part-time teachers. Once again the problem was less a matter of leadership than a question of money. In 1907 the legislature styled the school the Medical Department of the University of Alabama and gave it a grant of $45,000. In 1911 an annual appropriation of $25,000 was made—but until 1914 only half of that was actually paid. Where earlier it was impossible to maintain a first-class medical school on student tuition, it was now impossible to support a reputable institution on a state appropriation of $10,000 a year.

What had been a difficult job of persuading the legislature to deal with the educational effects of the explosion of medical knowledge and techniques soon became a question of municipal rivalry. In 1894 nine Jefferson County doctors (including Russell M. Cunningham, the doctor-turned-politician) established the Birmingham Medical College. When the American Medical Association's Council on Medical Education—in a misguided act of positive thinking—classified Mobile as a Class A institution, it bestowed a Class B rating on the Birmingham Medical College. In response, the backers of the Birmingham school asked the legislature for one-half of the appropriation going to Mobile— and the tale and travail of two cities began. Simply put, Birmingham wanted the medical school as both symbol and instrument of its growth. Mobilians fought back with all the claims of outraged civic virtue, including the thought that the Panama Canal would make Mobile "the leading port of the Gulf and possibly of the United States."[9]

In larger purview, as the historian of the medical school controversy observes, the supporters of the two cities had some beliefs in common. Both feared that Alabama medical students would leave the state for training. They were "well aware of the state's inferior standards of medical education in comparison with the rest of the country," and they "recognized the necessity of establishing one first-class medical college."[10] These salient and shared truths did little to settle the argument. The war continued until 1920 when the legislature stopped its appropriation to Mobile. A medical college on the edge of the "red light district" had always allowed Mobile's critics to confuse medicine with morality.

It was doubtful that no medical college was better than an inferior one, but time healed and cured even this wound. After 1920 the University of Alabama offered a solid premedical course of study, and in 1944 Birmingham was finally selected as the site of the University of Alabama's medical school. The Magic City had successfully cast its spell.

While public health was progressivism in action, Governor Comer could take little credit for the movement. His substantive ties to reform centered on his attack on the railroads, and in his policies and actions toward labor he failed the simplest test of progressivism. The attempts by Alabama labor to organize and bargain collectively—first seen in the area of coal mining—had been a succession of minor ups and major downs. In 1890 the miners affiliated with the United Mine Workers of America. They went on strike for a pay increase and were completely defeated. When the strike began, the companies immediately evicted workers from company houses. A host of armed guards protected a force of black miners hired to break the strike. Miners were fired for union activity, and the United Mine Workers of America simply vanished from Alabama. In 1893, as already noted, even harder times came with

Alabama coal miners engaged in a dangerous occupation made more difficult by low pay and public and official hostility to union organization and strikes for better working conditions. (Courtesy of the Alabama Department of Archives and History)

economic depression. When the coal companies cut miner wages by 10 percent, the United Mine Workers of Alabama was born. Once again the coal companies, with major help from Governor Jones and the state troops, brought in strikebreakers, and after four months of violence-prone struggle the union collapsed.

Once again a slow rebuilding was in order, this time under the aegis of the national union. In 1902 the UMW claimed to have organized 65 percent of Alabama's miners, with blacks making up about half of the membership. The companies struck back with the open shop, and in 1904 the UMW went on strike. The walkout lacked the sharp focus of earlier strikes, and the standoff dragged on for two years. In 1908, with contracts expiring and the companies threatening a 10 percent reduction in wages, the UMW called a strike once again. The operators countered by importing laborers; the striking miners attempted to keep them out either by persuasion or violence. Hundreds of deputized company guards harassed and did battle with the strikers. When Governor Comer, like Governor Jones in 1894, ordered state troops into the coalfields, the miners welcomed what they thought was an impartial force that might neutralize the company guards. Considerable fraternization occurred between the strikers and the soldiers—to the disgust of the operators and Governor Comer. Forced to live in the same conditions as the miners (the operators paid expenses), the troops received an on-the-spot education in company beneficence.

The strike proceeded along predictable lines. Once it was called the operators refused any further negotiations and devoted their energies to increasing production and breaking the strike. The convict lease system once again proved its value in providing a strike-proof labor force. If the operators could bring in enough new labor they would win. If the strikers could not stop the importation of "scabs" they would lose. Violence escalated, and greater violence brought greater repression by the guards, the sheriff's deputies, and the troops. Had such activity remained the basic formula, the strikers would have inevitably lost. But they lost the strike in a remarkably short time because another ingredient was added, and it was the catalyst that could always convert even minor affairs into inflammatory issues.

The United Mine Workers of America (like the UMW of Alabama before it) was an integrated union. Whites and blacks met together, either sitting on different sides of the room or with their own group. Blacks were routinely elected to union posts, and the miners realized that without such unity and cooperation union activity would be virtually impossible. By the middle of August, Governor Comer had decided to end the strike, although he more tactfully phrased it as protecting the right of nonunion miners to work. Comer and the operators turned to the long-standing Southern fear of "outside influences"—aliens had come into the state to disrupt the peaceful working conditions of the coal miners. In this case the alien influences were brought in by the UMW officials who came to Alabama to direct the strike.

On August 28 Comer met with the union leaders and laid down his terms. Either the strike would end quickly or he would summon the legislature into special session to amend the vagrancy laws. Next, he would arrest every striking coal miner. The legislators, said Comer, were "outraged at the attempts to establish social equality between white and black miners."[11] The UMW denied the charge, but a rising tide of racial attack came from the operators and the newspapers. Frank Evans of the Birmingham *Age-Herald* first spied danger in having idle black workers. "Idleness," he declared, "always begets crime."[12] Then he discovered a greater "racial danger." After attending a biracial meeting of striking miners at Dora, Evans penned his own distillation of Southern images and values. "It is a lamentable condition," he wrote, "that incites and permits ignorant Negro leaders to address assemblies of white women and children as social equals advising as to moral and social questions and alluding to those delicate matters of social status which can only be discussed properly with fair women in the private home and by husband and father."[13]

It was doubtful that any people in Alabama were greater realists on the "moral and social" questions of the day than the wives of coal miners. What shocked Evans surely did not shock them. It did repel one Dolly Dalrymple, the purported author of "What the Women Think About It" in the *Age-Herald*. She was appalled that anyone would "set about to upset the primary social laws of our beloved South." Dalrymple took a firm stand on the principle that "social equality cannot be tolerated or even countenanced," and she made no effort to conceal her disdain for the camps that the miners had set up in the woods for their families.[14]

It was exactly on the point of the camps that Governor Comer took his most dramatic and revealing action. The camps had been established on rented land (an expedient used in earlier strikes) as the only alternative to company eviction. On August 26 Comer ordered the troops to cut down all the tents. The militia was not to "allow the establishment of more tented camps by the coal miners."[15] Comer claimed that he was motivated by public health conditions. Had that been his real concern he might much earlier have closed half the company towns in the state. When J. R. Kennamer, head of UMW District 20, tried to persuade Comer to reconsider his order, the governor refused. He stated bluntly: "You know what it means to have eight or nine thousand niggers idle in the state of Alabama, and I am not going to stand for it."[16]

Faced with these pressures and with racial sentiment rising in the Birmingham area, the UMW called off the strike. Only a remnant of the union existed during the next years. The operators, now running a labor force of about 70 percent blacks, were coming closer to Henry F. DeBardeleben's old boast of making the mining section "a Negro Eden."

Where Comer had been the author, starring actor, director, and producer of the Great Railroad Drama, he played little more than a supporting part in the long-running epic of prohibition. Following the adoption of the constitution of 1901, the dry forces were convinced that the disfranchisement of blacks improved their chances for success. Some believed that it made a fair count on prohibition possible, while others assumed that the black vote would have supported the whiskey forces. Prohibitionists exploited the prevailing racial attitudes with talk (as the historian of the movement explained) of safeguarding "the white man and white woman from the violence of the liquor-crazed black."[17]

The prohibition movement took form before the Civil War. It evolved in an age that produced a plethora of reform movements, running from women's rights to utopian socialism and on to the antislavery crusade. The national Sons of Temperance were strongly organized in Alabama, but its flirtation with the Know-Nothings, and a penchant to mix politics with its antialcohol message, hurt the order's primary mission. The Civil War itself did more to alter drinking habits than decades of agitation. Shortages produced the question of how much grain should be eaten and how much should be drunk. Wartime measures on the side of eating demonstrated that government control over alcoholic beverages was possible.

The immediate postwar laws that touched on alcoholic beverages regulated on two different levels. Saloons were licensed with bans on selling liquor to minors, the intemperate, and to those of "unsound mind." The legislation was based on the hope of preventing the misuse of alcohol. But the legislature also passed laws prohibiting sales on a microgeographical basis. Sales might be denied within some specified distance of schools, churches, coal mines, factories, or even whole towns. By 1874 legislation allowed local option elections on the petition of a single freeholder for the exclusion of sales from any area he might designate. In its always curious habit of "courtesy" (local) laws, the legislature permitted local option elections in twenty-two counties.

Although the prewar Sons of Temperance returned to give battle in 1869, it was soon replaced by the Independent Order of Good Templars. By 1875 that organization ran afoul of the race issue when its grand lodge decreed integrated lodges. White Southerners were equally constrained from drinking with blacks or meeting with them to stop drinking. There had to be segregated attacks on the liquor traffic. So the Templars of Temperance were organized with an all-white membership. At that point in the temperance movement, no organizational ties with the churches existed. Still, within their own groups the Baptists, Methodists, and Presbyterians preached either temperance or abstinence to their members.

By 1880 the movement was changing. Where early efforts were focused on individual renunciation—a free will approach as people made the decision to drink or not to drink—the emphasis moved toward influencing public opinion as a basis for political action. What individuals would not do for themselves they would be made to do by force of law. With the change in direction new organizations entered the field. The Women's Christian Temperance Union (WCTU), founded in Ohio in 1873, had a Tuscaloosa chapter in 1881. The WCTU was soon active across the state in a militant campaign of education. It provided one of the few direct channels for women's involvement in public affairs. Under unremitting pressure from the WCTU, the legislature in 1891 ordered the public school teachers to instruct their students on the evil effects of alcohol on the human body.

Whatever the social consequences of alcohol, it was not certain that its

371

consumption constituted one of the major problems confronting the state. In a poverty-stricken land, in a society based on inequality, with a less than responsive government, prohibition took up a disproportionate amount of money, time, energy, and moral outrage. The churches—and some responded to the social gospel—spent an inordinate amount of effort over the issues raised by the WCTU's "Committee on Unfermented Wine." The use of grape juice in the observance of the Lord's Supper was not a major social reform.

Perhaps the prohibition issue came to dominate Alabama life and politics because it was one of the few changes that was socially arguable. In a tightly closed society marked by a narrow range of acceptable aberrations, protest was a rare commodity. Prohibition conformed to the Alabama situation, and by promising the state a population of sober and industrious blacks, it reinforced existing patterns. In a freer atmosphere protest on one issue brings protest on a host of real or imagined wrongs. That was what happened to the prohibition movement in other parts of the country. But in Alabama the Prohibition party that fused with the Republicans in 1886 was soon criticizing its national leaders for broadening their demands to include such reforms as women's suffrage.

The attempt to politicize prohibition ran into a host of problems. The licensing of saloons created an economic interest for government exactly in the fashion of the convict lease system, and in neither case did the legislators want to imperil revenue. In 1886 Alabama's Democratic party convention was asked to endorse the principle of local option. The convention refused on the grounds that it would be impractical in the Black Belt because of "the large Negro vote which would always favor whiskey."[18] For political leaders majority decisions—and particularly black majority decisions—were best avoided. Prohibitionists came close to the same thought. It was not the process of democratic decision making that they wanted or respected; it was the much narrower right of the people to vote no on alcohol.

During the 1880s and 1890s the legislature extended the list of counties that could exercise local option, but the results, with two counties outlawing the sale of liquor and six approving it, confirmed the undependable nature of the people's voice. An alternative was soon discovered. State senator Frank S. Moody of Tuscaloosa became converted to the South Carolina dispensary system. In 1898 the legislature approved a trial run for the towns of Clayton (Barbour County) and Columbia and Dothan (Henry County). The law gave the municipalities a monopoly on the sale of liquor under the direction of town dispensary commissioners. While government sales operated to force saloons out of business, the system had more to do with government revenue than with prohibition. The range was broadened in 1899, and any incorporated town where liquor was not prohibited could vote on having a dispensary system.

Dozens of local fights occurred as town voters argued the merits and drawbacks of establishing dispensaries. Some charged that it put the government in the role of purveying impure liquor. One editor reported the results of an analysis made on liquor sold in his county. It contained, he said, "alcohol, arsenic, alum, aloes, bitter almonds, blood, chalk, cherry laurel, coculus, idicus, copperas, gypsum, henbane, isinglass, lime, lead, logwood, nux vomica, opium, oil of juniper, oil of turpentine, tobacco, sugar of lead, resin, etc."[19] Clearly the mixed drink had come to Alabama.

The dispensary system never satisfied those who wanted prohibition, and temperance was less and less a goal or an ambition. A major step for prohibition came when the Anti-Saloon League of America entered Alabama in 1904. It was organized with W. B. Crumpton as its president and the Reverend Brooks Lawrence of Ohio as superintendent. The movement's disparate factions began to fuse. Prohibition forces allied with the churches, and in 1906 the Democratic party included a state-wide local option plank in its platform.

Comer had never advocated prohibition, nor was he a partisan of the local option alternative. But with his election he accepted the idea and proclaimed that "the essential feature of our great democracy [is] that the great majority will rule."[20] A sharp split existed between rural areas that tended to be dry and the cities that were strongly wet. Cities demanded a separate vote for themselves, but the Lovelady Local Option Law of 1907 made the county the unit of decision. In only four months of 1907, twenty-four more counties joined the previously dry twenty-one. Even wet Birmingham was dried up by the spongelike vote of Jefferson County.

On the road to a dry utopia, the prohibition forces were not inclined to glory in partial victories. When Comer called his special legislative session to deal with the railroads in 1907, he resisted efforts to list statewide prohibition among the authorized subjects. By the rules this omission meant that any vote for prohibition had to attain a two-thirds vote in each house. When the requirement proved to be no obstacle, Comer rapidly trimmed his sails to "get right" on prohibition. The house passed the Carmichael Statutory Prohibition Law by a vote of 66–25, and the senate surpassed that with a vote of 32–2.

The passage of prohibition for Alabama was regarded (at least by prohibitionist groups) as a momentous historical event, one future generations would point to with awe and pride. Governor Comer's signing of the bill was staged with more than the usual perfunctory signature. With the state prohibition leaders in attendance, Mrs. J. B. Mell produced a pen given to her on her wedding day twenty years earlier—but never used—and handed it to Governor Comer. The governor affixed his name and dutifully wiped the pen on a "fresh linen handkerchief," the property of Mrs. J. B. Chatfield of the WCTU. Mrs. Mell completed the ritual by furnishing a "piece of blotting paper" to dry up the governor's signature.[21] The sinners had one last year to celebrate, but after December 31, 1908, it would be illegal to manufacture or sell intoxicating beverages in Alabama.

The prohibition movement had a propensity to march on from climax to anticlimax. Next came agitation over the antishipping bill in Congress that was designed to stop the transfer of alcohol into dry counties and states. Problems quickly surfaced on the enforcement of prohibition. Supporters were convinced that the law would be more enforceable if elevated to the rank and status of an amendment to the state constitution. Comer had seen the necessity of riding the prohibition wind, but his support for a constitutional amendment generated a tempest that almost blew him out of power. Comer wanted the issue disposed of so that it would not be a "disturbing factor" in state politics, but the act of passing an amendment ran into serious trouble.

The first step came easily as each legislative chamber passed an amendment by solid votes. But in the ensuing campaign for ratification, Comer's leadership was put directly on the line. The Safe and Sane Business Men's League opposed ratification. A state committee was established to mount an offensive, and a phalanx of former governors and conservative leaders—hearing the threatening knock of statism at the door—rallied to defeat the amendment. Emmet O'Neal of Lauderdale County, drawn by the lure of power and the governorship, led the fight. O'Neal used the stick of prohibition to smash away at all of Comer's programs while trumpeting his beguiling but meaningless theme that "the sanctity of the home must be kept inviolate."[22]

On November 29, 1909, when the votes were counted, both sides were surprised. There were 72,272 Alabamians who voted against and only 49,093 who voted for prohibition. It was a stunning and unexpected defeat. Governor Comer discovered that once questions are made into moral imperatives, there is zero tolerance for compromise, and "safe positions" are destroyed as rapidly as politicians find them.

As the Comer years came to a close, many questions were left about the scope and influence of Alabama progressivism. How far down the tracks could the Comer Express have run before exhausting its small load of railroad regulation fuel? Could Comer have taken on new supplies of causes and issues and traveled further against an opposition busy throwing the switches and burning the trestles to stop him? Comer as a conservative businessman attacking railroad rates was one thing.

Comer uneasily enlarging a narrow vision to add other reforms— including the fearful ones supported by "outsiders"—meant the end of his power. Comer's supposed fight for a more equitable society—and his pose as a "real" progressive—finally rang hollow. Progressivism in Alabama was a chimerical impulse, at best one of limited dimension and precarious balance. Without reform consensus or meaningful self-criticism, the Alabama of 1907 and 1909 lacked the leadership to reeducate a generation. Even tiny steps toward the progressive side of things doomed Comer to repudiation and failure.

In Alabama there was a connection and a continuity between populism and progressivism even as there was a difference in their orientation and their emphasis. At least in the hill counties, Populist leaders became Progressive leaders. They acted out their new roles as Republican reformers. Comer's progressivism was urban, middle class, and business oriented—the Populist program of helping poor farmers and laboring men was not in the Progressive plan of action. In this sense the north Alabama reformers—strong supporters of Theodore Roosevelt and the Progressive party in 1912—were far removed from and infinitely more advanced than the circumscribed vision of Democratic Comer Progressives.

The Populist crusade had preached political democracy and, for its time, was remarkably enlightened on matters of race. The Progressive agenda was compromised and inherently flawed because it was restricted to whites. Because it was divided into separate programs and goals that were often at odds, progressivism was difficult to implement. As a whole, progressivism was weaker than its parts. Just as the antislavery crusade had absorbed its attendant reforms before the Civil War, so too did prohibition consume its partners for change after 1900.

TWENTY-THREE

Women in Alabama
from 1865 to 1920

THE culture of those Americans who came to settle in Alabama was premised on the legal and social sanctions of a male-dominated society. Yet there was a world of activity and action in which women, under a host of cultural disabilities, influenced the nature of life and the direction of the state's affairs. The female journey was not a straight line of progression that started with complete legal inferiority and culminated in the ratification of the Nineteenth Amendment in 1920. It was a thing of twists and turns, of advances and retrogression that started long before and continued long after women acquired the right to vote. In Alabama, as in the rest of the South, family was the central unit of society, and Southern women were central to the family.

Before 1861 males were de facto and de jure heads of households, but the Civil War was a strong influence on Alabama's patriarchal society. The abolition of slavery, military defeat, and economic impoverishment lessened the power of men and especially the influence of the planters. Such events compelled white women, most clearly seen in the case of widows, to assume the role of family provider and head of the household. Battlefield casualties and migration out of the South by men left Alabama in 1870 with 255,023 white males and 266,361 white females (the total white population was down 4,887 from 1860).

On plantations slave women had often headed households, and with freedom, women-dominated families were evident. In 1870 Alabama had 233,677 black males and 241,833 black females. In contrast to the white population, the total number of blacks increased from 1860 to 1870 by 37,740 people. Thus by 1870 the state had almost a million people (996,992), and while this was an increase from 1860 (964,201), Alabama's white population had declined, its black population had increased, and there were more women than men in both races.

Despite the growing inroads of urbanization and industrialization, most of Alabama's men and women were dependent upon agriculture until well into the twentieth century. In 1900, 58.5 percent of Alabamians over the age of ten were engaged in a gainful occupation, and of those, 68.7 percent of the men and 64.5 percent of the women relied on farming for their livelihoods. At 13.4 percent, domestic and personal service was a distant second as a means of income, and even that statistic was the product of the large number of women so employed (27.4 percent). In 1920 the state's rural population was 78.3 percent, while its urban citizens (living in cities of 2,500 or more) made up 21.7 percent of the total population.

For black and white tenant farmer families, the desire to have males work in the fields and wives in the home was sought but rarely achieved. Women of both races whose husbands were sharecroppers frequently had to manage their households *and* work in the fields. Class more than race determined their condition. Within this social framework Alabama women continued to marry young and carry the demanding responsibilities of raising large numbers of children. This was a carry-over, a continuation, of conditions of the pre–Civil War era with its limited knowledge of birth control. In addition, high mortality rates required large numbers of children to ensure that some would reach maturity and sustain an adequate labor force. What was true of sharecroppers' wives was also true, if slightly less so, of small independent farm families.

Women who first made their voices heard and their influence felt in the public arena were middle or upper class whites who lived in towns and cities (the dominating role of women in literary endeavors is treated in chapter 24). Yet rural white women were also a factor in the early agrarian reform movements. As previously noted, they held offices in the Patrons of Husbandry (Grange) and participated in the activities of the Agricultural Wheel and the Farmers' Alliance. If women could not vote for the Populist cause, they could work for it, and in 1892 Nora Gaither edited a reform newspaper, the *Progressive People* at Walnut Grove in Etowah County. There were only a few black Granges, but in those that existed and in many of the black Farmers' Alliances it is probable that women were active participants.

White women in Alabama were particularly affected by the rise of the textile industry that accelerated in the South after 1880. Young white farm girls became the first recruits for the cotton mills, and they were followed by farm families headed by women. By the turn of the century, continued rural economic depression drove male heads of families to the mills where they displaced or joined women workers. In 1900, 3,152 men and 2,743 women were working in Alabama mills. By 1920 the numbers were 7,127 and 6,241.

Blacks who moved to Alabama's towns and cities in the decades after the Civil War did not become part of the textile mill labor force. At best they held temporary jobs. The reason was simple: textile mill owners and prevailing public attitudes enforced a policy of discrimination that continued as long as there was an abundant supply of cheap white labor. It was argued that blacks lacked the mechanical skills required by the mills and that working in close proximity with whites could lead to violence.

Urban black women in the state worked in low-paying domestic jobs for white families. Black women cooked, cleaned, and helped raise the children of whites. Washing and ironing the clothes for white women became an important cottage industry for black females in most Alabama towns. In 1870 the vast majority of Alabama's 18,506 female domestic servants and 1,924 laundresses were black. Little had changed in 1900 when black women constituted nearly all of the 22,921 female "servants and waiters" and 17,427 laundresses in the state. These labors freed white women from domestic responsibilities and enabled the more affluent to work with volunteer associations and participate in women's clubs. Through 1920, when 81 percent of the state's 70,812 wage earners employed in domestic and personal service were women, and on into the next decades, there was little working class commonalty between urban and small town black and white women.

During and after Reconstruction the lives of Alabama's women were profoundly affected by public education that included both races for the first time. Education for whites was superior in every way, but literacy itself transcended many inequities. Publicly funded education meant that mothers no longer provided that unpaid function, and it meant that some women would now, as professionals, specialize in teaching as a wage-earning occupation. Black and white women were able to command jobs that carried community prestige and brought some economic freedom. A teaching career had its own limitations and injustices (white women were consistently paid less than white men, and black women less than black men), but intellectual ability transformed into professional training and then into employment was still a major achievement. The rise of the coeducational normal schools and the state women's college permitted women to form a larger circle of relationships and enlarge their horizons far beyond the constricted circles of family and church.

While women profited immensely in the classroom as students and as teachers, they also benefited from participating in professional educational organizations. In the post-Reconstruction years the state's white women teachers became active (although not, with a few exceptions, as policymakers) in the Alabama Education Association. From the beginning of the Alabama State Teachers Association in 1882 black women teachers took part in its deliberations.

The most important initial springboard to influence and public visibility for women came through the church. After 1865 Southern women helped rebuild their churches and formed female missionary societies. The Methodist Board of Home Missions was organized in 1881, and the Baptist Woman's Mission Union followed in 1888. Presbyterian women established auxiliary groups and promoted missionary work. The Methodist Women's Board was a wealthy and far-flung organization with multiple enterprises. Black churchwomen, who won positions of leadership somewhat earlier than white women, organized diverse associations and gave genuine meaning to the expression "pillars of the church." Through church groups women acquired organizational skills and became effective and confident leaders. Religious activities established the validity of ventures into the public arena—education, suffrage, aid to the poor, prohibition, improved working conditions for women, and regulation of child labor. Women would argue that none of these social missions violated the traditional "domestic sphere" of home and family that society (for which it is possible to read "men") conceded to be their legitimate domain.

In the last half of the nineteenth century and beyond, middle and upper class women became more engaged in reform work as the development of labor-saving devices gave them more time. Under the special leadership of Susan B. Anthony, the National Women Suffrage Association was formed in New York in 1869, and later that year the American Woman Suffrage Association was organized in Cleveland, Ohio. The groups differed as to how suffrage could be achieved, but both groups championed voting rights as a liberal, moderate, and rational reform. The new suffragists tended to be financially secure professionals rather than housewives. Because many men in the 1880s denied that suffrage was a natural right (blacks, women, and immigrants were favorite groups for exclusion), women often emphasized that their vote would improve government and local communities. Suffrage became not only a reform but a means of reform.

The rival suffrage organizations merged in 1890 as the National American Woman Suffrage Association; in that same year the movement came to the South. In Alabama white women took the lead, but black women, acting separately, were also involved. In the antebellum era abolition had served as a catalyst for the women's rights movement. Now some advocates of women's suffrage contended that it would help preserve white supremacy, and they pointed out the irony of uneducated black males who could vote while educated white women could not. It was not assumed by whites that black women would vote in large numbers. In fact, Alabama's black women, with great unanimity, championed suffrage for women. Theirs was the indisputable logic that if obtaining the vote would benefit white women, black women, virtually ignored in society, would profit even more.

Alabama white women and their counterparts throughout the South were both the victims and the practitioners of the image of the Southern belle and lady. According to this social illusion the rough and tumble world of politics was reserved for males, not for sensitive, domestically oriented, highly moral, and modest Southern ladies. Not until the Southern women had worked in church organizations, teachers' associations, and temperance groups did they see any hope of descending from the pedestal created by male fantasy and female acquiescence. Women had first to emancipate themselves.

Central to the role of women, lying at the heart of the public inequality that proclaimed their inferiority, was the question of the right to vote. Alabama's women initially attempted to win the vote by amending the state constitution; failing to accomplish that mission, they later championed a national suffrage amendment as the most permanent guarantee of political freedom.

As early as 1867 Pierce Burton, a Massachusetts native and Republican leader residing in Alabama, wrote a newspaper article that proposed permitting Alabama women to vote. Burton qualified his thought by suggesting that both literacy and property qualifications might be in order. For most this was probably dismissed as the ravings of a carpetbagger. There was no support for the idea and Burton never mentioned it again. The first meaningful involvement of women came with Alabama's first suffrage club, a small group founded in Decatur in 1892. That same year five suffrage clubs formed a state organization and elected Ellen Hildreth of Decatur as president. The group's main activity was mailing out literature. Interest was revived in 1897 by Alberta C. Taylor of Huntsville who had visited Colorado and observed the effect of women voting. Taylor reorganized the Huntsville association, and a state group was headed by the elderly and respected Virginia Tunstall Clay-Clopton. Again the organization limited its activities to mailings and press releases.

A stirring occurred in 1901 when Frances Griffin, a native of Wetumpka and graduate of Judson Female Institute, became president of the state suffrage group. Griffin, also active in prohibition work, raised the issue of women suffrage at the 1901 state constitutional convention. She addressed the delegates, and B. H. Craig of Selma introduced a resolution to give all white females over the age of twenty-one the right to vote. Nothing came of the resolution or from the effort to permit all unmarried taxpaying women to vote on municipal tax issues. The mystique of the Southern belle was too strong, the urge to dominate too encompassing, and satisfaction with the status quo too widely spread. Contrary to the national trend, the Alabama state women's suffrage organization and its local groups ceased to function actively after 1901.

Revival came in 1910 with the work of Mary Partridge of Selma. A strong prohibitionist, Partridge organized a new suffrage association with the argument that arming women with the vote would hasten the day of abolishing the liquor traffic. Organization of the Selma Suffrage Association was followed in 1911 with the founding of the Equal Suffrage League of Birmingham. Leaders included Pattie Ruffner Jacobs, a native of Virginia, social leader, and wife of a prominent businessman, and Nellie Kimball Murdoch, a leader in the child-labor reform movement. Bossie O'Brien Hundley (wife of Oscar R. Hundley) reorganized the Huntsville association, and a state group, the Alabama Equal Suffrage Association (AESA), was established in Birmingham in 1912. At the first state convention in 1913, Jacobs was elected president (she later became Alabama's first Democratic national committeewoman). The AESA adopted the motto, "We mean to make Alabama lead the South for Woman's Suffrage."

As its parent body—the National American Woman Suffrage Association (NAWSA)—grew in strength and influence, so too did the AESA expand its domain. It continued to form new local associations and by 1915 was powerful enough to force political action. An intensive campaign ensued to amend the state constitution and enfranchise women. Jacobs, Hundley, and Lillian Roden Bowron of Birmingham stumped the state. Funds were raised from bazaars, teas, and dances, and suffragists maintained booths at local and state fairs. A resolution to add a suffrage amendment to the constitution was introduced in the house in 1915 by Representative J. H. Green of Dallas County. H. H. Holmes of Baldwin County introduced a similar bill in the senate. At a joint session of legislative committees the suffrage lobby was given a hearing, and Jacobs and Julia S. Tutwiler, the state's best-known woman reformer, spoke. Advocating change and the status quo at the same time, they pointed out that the amendment would not enfranchise black women— they would continue to be barred from the ballot box by the existing election laws that applied to black men.

There was strong opposition to a suffrage amendment, and it came from prominent people. Individual males lent their support, but not one single influential male organization rose up in advocacy. The Alabama Federation of Women's Clubs, oriented toward family and home, stood on the sidelines. Nor were women teachers among the leaders. Their neutrality may have been the product of real or imagined economic fears. Women in Alabama's leading religious denominations, the Evangelical Baptists and Methodists, were less active in the suffrage campaign than women in the more affluent Episcopal and Presbyterian churches.

On the day of the house vote on the suffrage measure, the suffragists were out in force and filled the balcony. A huge suffrage banner was prominently displayed, and yellow and black, the movement's colors, were seen in the bunting that decorated the chambers. Many legislators wore yellow flowers in their lapels. Unfortunately the decorations failed to match the political sentiments of the representatives. The sponsor of the measure, J. H. Green, reversed his stand, and further damage came from an anonymous pamphlet that argued that most Alabama women did not want to vote. After various delays, the amendment received a majority vote (52–43) but not the required three-fifths majority. The senate concurred in the judgment and also defeated the measure. Because the legislature did not meet again until 1919, this was the only attempt to amend the constitution. Suffrage for Alabama women would not come at the state level. Alabama would not give its own women the right to vote.

On the national level the NAWSA adopted a more militant stance and took more direct control of state activities. More suffrage clubs were organized in Alabama, and the women's leagues in Auburn and Opelika in 1916 held the South's first public demonstration for suffrage. The First World War not only saw NAWSA and its local groups deeply involved in food production, conservation, and Red Cross work, but these activities dramatized the injustice of excluding women from government participation. It was argued—with more innocence than fact—that women were advocates of peace and if given the vote they could help prevent wars.

A constitutional amendment was introduced in Congress, and in January 1918 President Woodrow Wilson (who had earlier favored leaving the matter to the states) declared his support. Both houses of Congress passed the amendment, but Alabama's delegation, with the exception of Representative William B. Oliver of Tuscaloosa, voted against the Nineteenth Amendment. In 1918 the AESA had endorsed a national amendment, and in summer 1919 a telegram from President Wilson to Governor Thomas E. Kilby pressed for ratification. Kilby favored the amendment, but there was powerful opposition. The fight was on.

U.S. Senators Oscar W. Underwood and John H. Bankhead viewed the amendment as a threat to states' rights. They argued that it would give the federal government control over voting rights and might lead to the enfranchisement of blacks. In Montgomery the Alabama Association Opposed to Woman Suffrage, organized in 1916, was active. So was the Southern Women's Anti-ratification League—with Marie Bankhead Owen, who would succeed her husband as director of the Alabama Department of Archives and History in 1920, as head of its legislative committee. There was an endless repetition of the old arguments about politics being unsuited for women, and Representative Tom Heflin believed that giving women the vote was a threat to family life.

The amendment, with its advocates and opponents, attracted wide attention. The suffragists, disappointed in 1915, were disappointed again. In separate action both houses voted against the amendment and then proceeded to reject it by joint resolution. The Black Belt voted heavily against ratification. That section's leaders were no more willing to accept democracy for white women than they were to extend it to blacks.

Alabama might refuse to ratify the Nineteenth Amendment, but its action was little more than a salute to conservatism. In late summer 1920 Tennessee became the thirty-sixth state to ratify and the amendment was added to the Constitution. Governor Kilby called a special session of the legislature to ratify the already ratified. That action was duly accomplished, the amendment was officially proclaimed in August, and Alabama's white women could vote. An immediate effect was that polling places—long notorious for card playing, drinking, and raucous behavior—were forced to become more sanitary and decorous. Men still dominated society, but women had taken a major step toward equality.

The National American 'Woman Suffrage Association was succeeded by the League of Women Voters, and in Alabama the AESA ended its work and the Alabama League of Women Voters was organized. The organization's potential was demonstrated when male political candidates appeared at its first state convention. Lillian Roden Bowron headed the new organization, and Dixie Bibb Graves (reformer, wife of future governor Bibb Graves, first Alabama woman to sit in the U.S. Senate) was her chief lieutenant.

The long drive for political equality was surely the most dramatic aspect of the slow emancipation of women, but it was only one design on the wide fabric of change. After the Civil War, upper and middle class white women in Alabama's towns and cities began to form literary clubs. While women had long dominated the Alabama world of arts and letters (see chapter 24), these literary organizations were influential in the development of the late-nineteenth-century women's movement. At first the clubs were nonpolitical and only mildly if at all concerned with local or statewide economic or societal problems. Their primary purpose was intellectual and social. At the urging of Mary LaFayette Robbins of Selma, several literary clubs sent delegates to Birmingham in 1895 and formed the Alabama Federation of Women's Clubs. It was the nation's fourth such organization.

The AFWC's constitution proclaimed the group's purpose: to "bring together for mutual help, for intellectual improvement and for social union the different women's literary clubs of the State." The organization would be nonsectarian and nonpolitical. As Mary Robbins put it, "we are not reformers in any sense of the word . . . , but if hereafter we should desire to pursue an object apart from the one already stated no one can prevent us."[1] In fact, the AFWC pursued several objects. By 1915 its 153 clubs representing 4,250 women were a strong force in the state's educational, civic, and social life.

In 1897 the AFWC was busy promoting new libraries, increasing library holdings, and forming "traveling" libraries (the forerunners of bookmobiles). A year later it was urging the establishment of a reformatory for white boys, the elimination of illiteracy, and a new state constitution to provide educational reform. It supported the Alabama Education Association, the state's primary lobbying group for teachers and the cause of education. The AFWC moved surely from the needs of its clubs to the needs of Alabama's women and children. It championed the Girls' Industrial School at Montevallo and set up a number of scholarships for girls attending the school. Mrs. R. D. Johnston was the prime mover in the establishment of the East Lake Reformatory School for Boys, and though it was a state school, the AFWC for years helped to fund it. In the early 1900s the organization was active in its support for the Alabama Child Labor Committee. In 1907 it demanded a system of juvenile courts, and eventually (1919) the legislature acquiesced.

The AFWC was a vigorous champion of specific goals and its leaders were constantly going to legislative sessions in Montgomery to lobby the lawmakers personally. In spite of good intentions and a well-earned reputation as Alabama's most effective organization for change, the AFWC had its difficulties and its less happy moments. In 1903 the organization received major credit for the passage of the child-labor law, although Edgar Gardner Murphy and members of the Alabama Child Labor Committee believed that Lillian Milner Orr, president of the AFWC, agreed to a weaker measure because she and her family were stockholders in Avondale textile mills. Certainly there were limitations on the liberalism of the AFWC. Four times between 1899 and 1907 the Alabama organization refused to join the General Federation of Women's Clubs; by 1904 it was the only state organization without national affiliation. The reason, as attested by the group's makeup of affluent white women, was racial. The Alabama federation cited the existence of integrated clubs in Massachusetts and Chicago and protested that admitting blacks to membership was a declaration of social equality. Not only would they not admit black women to membership but no one else should either. The general federation continued to issue invitations (including a denial that a black woman had been seated at a national convention), and in 1907 the state group finally went national.

With all of its efforts, the AFWC was the direct agent in the emancipation of a great many Alabama women. Attending a state convention for the first time, and seeing women in the throes of a very verbal democratic process, one delegate said, "I didn't know before that women could speak out in a convention like men."[2] That was priceless information.

There was irony aplenty in the fact that Alabama black women also became active in the women's club movement. As early as 1886 a group assembled in Selma and formed a colored state union with Mrs. C. C. Booth as president. This organization ceased to exist by 1890, but city women's clubs were being organized—Montgomery in 1890 and Tuskegee in 1895. The different clubs united to create the Colored Women's Clubs in 1898 and affiliated with the newly organized National Association of Colored Women. By 1904 the state had twenty-six black women's clubs. Their motto was "Lifting As We Climb."

The Tuskegee Woman's Club, led by Margaret Murray Washington, wife of Tuskegee Institute's famous president, established a settlement house where mothers and children could take cooking and sewing classes. The group created a reform school for black boys and a home for delinquent black girls, both at Mount Meigs in Montgomery County. Margaret Washington helped found the National Association of Colored Women in 1896, later serving as its president as well as president of the Alabama State Federation of Colored Women's Clubs. Leaders of the local and state organizations, like their white counterparts, were largely middle class. Unlike white women, the rank and file members were often working women and farmers' wives—and poor. Like the white clubs they stressed education and self- and community improvement. They placed additional emphasis on racial pride, race advancement, and defense of the black community and home. Lacking the resources or the support of the AFWC, the black women of Alabama learned the benefits and personal rewards of cooperative effort.

Not all post–Civil War women's organizations in Alabama had reform as their basic aim. Still, early on they stressed feminist activity that had beneficial results for women not anticipated in their original purposes. On March 2, 1896, at the request of the Camden camp of the United Confederate Veterans (UCV), Sallie Jones organized a United Daughters of the Confederacy chapter. Previous groups such as the Soldiers Aid Society and the Ladies Memorial Association offered ample precedent. The UDC became an auxiliary to the UCV.

In Camden, seat of government for the Black Belt's Wilcox County, it seemed appropriate for women who had shared the burden of war to honor a common heritage, and Jones quickly got the necessary seven chapters to meet and form a state division. The first state convention was held at Montgomery on April 18, 1897, and Jones was elected president. The division soon launched a drive to purchase and refurbish Jefferson

Davis's home in the capital, the first White House of the Confederacy. The home was bought and moved to public grounds near the capitol. Under the aegis of the White House Association, chartered in 1901, renovation continued, and under the leadership of Mrs. Jesse Drew Beale, the association combined lavender and lace diplomacy with steel-hard determination, and the home was dedicated in 1921.

The UDC was nonpolitical, but it seems unthinkable that individual members or chapters endorsed or voted for Republican candidates at any level. Most Alabama towns had chapters (Montgomery had four), and during World War I the members engaged in the supportive home-front activities that engaged most women's organizations. With membership based on kinship to someone who had served the Confederacy, the UDC was limited in numbers and limited in goals. Original members were not replaced in equal numbers by later generations. Yet the UDC survived and the organizational skills honed at chapter meetings could be (and were) transferred to other women's groups that had no relation to the Lost Cause. Generations of scholars are in debt to the UDC for its preservation of Civil War records.

In militant fervor alone, the Women's Christian Temperance Union was the opposite of the UDC. The WCTU was founded in Hillsboro, Ohio, in 1873, and Alabama's first union was organized at Tuscaloosa in 1881. The organization soon caught and held the imagination of many Alabama women. Mrs. Thomas La Crade became the president of the Tuscaloosa union, and a second unit was founded at Gadsden in 1884, with local ministers lending their strong support. A state union was incorporated in 1887. Members pledged total abstinence, paid their dues, worked to form new unions, and supported measures to abolish the liquor traffic. By 1908 Alabama had forty-three unions with 945 members—some of them men who paid their dues and became honorary members. The WCTU set up ten departments of work, but they were so wide ranging in their initial missions (including "work among the colored people") that the primary goal was weakened. Even so, other departments were added as time passed (juvenile, prison reform, work among railroad employees, work among lumbermen, to mention a few).

The political aspects of the prohibition struggle have been recounted earlier, and it is well to remember the dedicated work of the WCTU in getting a law enacted in 1891 that required teachers to give temperance instruction. In 1909 the legislature went further and required public schools to stage an annual temperance day. The WCTU was practical enough to endorse state control of liquor sales (the dispensary system), but prohibition became the ultimate goal. The effort here was the presentation of statistics demonstrating alcohol's debilitating effect on health and family unity along with strong emotional propaganda. The redoubtable Julia S. Tutwiler, longtime head of the WCTU's prison and jail department, contributed a prohibition rally song:

> *Where's the man who fears opinion?*
> *He is not the friend for me.*
> *Let him cringe to rum's dominion,*
> *Sister, you and I are free.*
> *So, let the cowards vote as they will,*
> *I'm for prohibition still.*
> *Prohibition, Prohibition,*
> *I'm for prohibition still.*

It was, of course, the stills that were producing a great deal of the whiskey in Alabama.

The WCTU was a prominent example of the power of women. Whether their cause was just or wise or misdirected does not tarnish the dedication and the effort that they gave to their movement. Societies do not vote on the proper issues for moral fervor, change comes in complex packages, and yesterday's reforms become today's issues for alteration.

Some women in Alabama made contributions to the state that singled them out for distinction. Julia S. Tutwiler was such a person. She was born August 5, 1841, in Tuscaloosa. Her father, Dr. Henry Tutwiler—the first man to take a master's degree at the University of Virginia and the first professor of ancient languages at the University of Alabama—gained his greatest fame as founder in 1847 of Greene Springs School for Boys at Havana in Greene (present-day Hale) County. His was the finest secondary school in the state, emphasizing the classics and mathematics and pioneering in science. Julia Tutwiler grew up under his tutelage. First she was sent to a private school in Philadelphia run by a French family. After a year at newly opened Vassar College in New York, she taught at the Greene Springs school and then pursued further study in Virginia. Then came teaching and study in Germany, teaching at Tuscaloosa Female Academy, and a year in Paris investigating the educational system. This splendid preparation for service, this collection of "outside influences," was the foundation for what she did. She brought the outside world to Alabama.

In 1881 she became coprincipal of the Livingston Female Academy, a private school chartered in 1835. In 1883 she persuaded the legislature to subsidize the Alabama Normal College for Girls as a department of the Livingston Female Academy. By 1891 Julia Tutwiler was its president and the name was changed to Alabama Normal School.

It was Julia Tutwiler who persuaded the trustees of the University of Alabama to admit women students—and it was one of her students, Rose Lawthorn, who became the first woman graduate of the university

Left: Julia Strudwick Tutwiler, daughter of the educator Henry Tutwiler, was an author and champion of industrial education for women, coeducation, prison reform, prohibition, and women's rights. (Courtesy of the Collections of the Birmingham Public Library) *Right:* Born at Tuscumbia, Helen Keller lost her sight and hearing at the age of eighteen months, but she courageously overcame those disabilities to become known internationally as an author, lecturer, and inspiration to others, especially to other handicapped people. (Courtesy of the Alabama Department of Archives and History)

in 1900. In 1902 Lila McMahon, a Livingston graduate, and one other woman became the first women to earn master's degrees from the university. Based on what she had observed in France, Tutwiler became a champion of vocational schools for women. Her tireless pressure on the legislature resulted in the establishment of an industrial school for women at Montevallo (today the University of Montevallo).

Her work for prison reform and an end to the convict lease system was particularly notable. At her urging, in 1887 night schools were opened for convicts—the first such important program in the South. The "Angel of the Prisons" failed in her efforts to have the state establish an institution separating youths from adults, but she was a strong supporter of the Alabama Federation of Women's Clubs in setting up the boys' reformatory at East Lake.

While Julia Tutwiler was a proud Alabamian (her "Alabama" became the state song), she was no pleader for the Lost Cause and no professional Southerner. Some of her songs reflected her patriotic spirit: "The Star Spangled Banner of Peace" and "Southern Yankee Doodle" are cases in point. Julia Tutwiler had an impressive presence. She was a woman of action and ideas. She took the best of what she found around the world and she devoted her life to making Alabama the best that it could be. One person, noting her distinctiveness, observed that for decades the "busy, white-haired woman with the face of a saint, clad in a faded black shirt, coat of obsolete fashion, and bonnet slipped sideways and backwards," was ubiquitous in the cause of reform and change.[3] She died March 24, 1916, and Alabama was much the poorer with her passing. It is difficult to believe that there could ever be too many Julia Tutwilers.

The individual who triumphs over great odds, who achieves where lesser people might stumble and turn away, earns the respect (and sometimes the love) of society. It was for those values that another native Alabamian, Helen Keller, born in Tuscumbia on June 27, 1880, acquired an international reputation. For the first eighteen months of her life she was a healthy little girl. Then she was stricken with a fever that destroyed her sight and her hearing and effectively cut her off from the world. When Keller was five years old her father sent her to the Perkins Institution for the Blind in Boston, and when she was seven years old Anne Mausfield Sullivan came to teach her in Alabama. Helen learned the alphabet by having letters spelled out on her hand, she connected words with objects, and she learned rapidly.

At ten years of age another remarkable teacher, Sarah Fuller, taught Helen to speak. "I shall never forget," Keller wrote later, the feeling "when I uttered my first connected sentence, 'it is warm.' It is true, they were broken and stammering syllables; but they were human speech. My soul came out of bondage and was reaching through those broken symbols of speech to all knowledge and all faith."[4]

Helen Keller graduated from Radcliffe College with honors in 1904 and devoted her life to working with those who were impaired in sight or hearing. She was a prolific writer (her first book, *The Story of My Life*, appeared in 1903) and an excellent speaker. When she died on June 1, 1968, she left a life of personal accomplishment equally matched by the inspiration and example she gave to so many others.

How far had Alabama women come from 1865 to 1900 and how far during the first two decades of the twentieth century? Few women would have answered the question by replying "far enough." As in other states the law bore unequally upon them. A state law of 1887 (reenacted in 1895) permitted a married woman to sell her land without her husband's consent—but only if he was *non compos mentis*, had abandoned her, was a nonresident of Alabama, or was serving time in prison for at least two years. It was a sign of progress that legislation in 1887 permitted the governor to appoint a woman as a notary public, but he still could not give her the power of a justice of the peace. Not until 1903 could married women and minors control the deposits they made in banks, and not until 1915 was there a statute protecting married women and children from desertion and nonsupport.

In the professions the dominance of men was overwhelmingly one-sided. In 1900 there were 2,212 male and 18 female ministers; 1,593 male and 3 female lawyers; 2,097 male and 16 female doctors; 1,593 male and 1 female dentists (the woman may have been C. C. Collins of Athens). Not until 1917 did Alice Walkins of Montgomery become the state's first licensed black dentist. In 1900 teaching was the only profession where women outnumbered men.

In 1900 only 2 women could be found among the state's 582 bank officials and cashiers. There were 50 male architects but no women, nor was a woman included among the 28 veterinarians. Within the ranks of 224 journalists there were 212 men. Although women had begun working in stores and businesses, Alabama had 5,461 salesmen and 781 saleswomen. While women far outnumbered men as boarding- and lodging house keepers, the reverse was true for hotel keepers.

The invention of the typewriter in the 1870s helped women get clerical positions as men moved up from clerks to managerial positions. After the invention of the telephone in 1876, the instrument became central to the nation's expanding communication system. In Alabama, as elsewhere, women proved adept operators, and they did not have to compete for employment in a traditional male-dominated vocation. With an expanded job market, women at the turn of the century generally held the lowest-paying and the most menial jobs. As domestic servants and waiters they outnumbered men 22,921 to 5,343. The disparity was even greater among those who laundered clothes: 17,427 women, 240 men. At the higher creative level, where there were few men or women—authors, musicians, scientists—women held their own. The same was true for librarians.

Theoretically, the effects of progressivism and its programs should have closed the gap of inequality between 1900 and 1920. Changes in attitude surely occurred among many women and some men, but no surge of statistics marked the dim path of Alabama progressivism. While the admission of women to the professions had advanced, the inroads, except for teachers, were hardly dramatic: doctors, 2,244 to 22; dentists, 583 to 23; veterinarians, 52 to 0; ministers, 2,735 to 21. In 1907 Louelle Lamar Allen became the first woman to graduate from the University of Alabama law school, and Maude McLure Kelly, who graduated in 1908, became the first woman admitted to the Alabama bar. It would be another forty years before Mahala Ashley Dickerson became the first black woman recognized to practice law in Alabama.

In 1920 the state's 26 female bankers had little influence among their

828 male counterparts. In twenty years only 1 woman had been added to the state's 88 architects, and 44 women editors and reporters were outnumbered by 231 men. Predictably, women had taken a wide lead among stenographers and typists (3,469 to 403) and telephone operators (1,288 to 152). They maintained a crushing majority as seamstresses and in laundry and domestic service, held their own as librarians and religious and welfare workers, and outnumbered men as osteopaths, authors, artists, sculptors, and art teachers.

In the realm of economic opportunities for women there were a few major exceptions to the norm. On the death of her husband in 1895, Rosa Zinszer took over his business and built it into Birmingham's largest installment credit furniture company. "Peter Zinszer's Mammoth Furniture House" prospered for decades due to her hard work and creative advertising. Two women, Winifred Collins, a white social worker with settlement house experience in Chicago, and Sue Berta Coleman, a black native Alabamian and graduate of Fisk University, were pioneer social workers in "welfare capitalism." The program was begun around 1910 by George Gordon Crawford, president of the Tennessee Coal, Iron and Railroad Company in Birmingham. Collins directed the hiring and training of employees and Coleman taught and trained rural workers in the unfamiliar ways of urban living. Their personal success may have transcended the achievements of the program.

Overall, progressivism in Alabama was far more a failure than a success. As a result of their labors, women gave progressivism its largest achievement and they surely contributed more to the movement than they gained from it. Their efforts after 1900 were opposed by many antidemocratic political leaders who feared the effect of women's votes and who were singularly unaffected by Progressive rhetoric. As individuals and as groups, women gave light to the shadows that darkened Alabama's highly selective encounter with Progressive reform.

In 1920 there was cause for hope. Women could vote, their suffrage campaign had succeeded, some few had entered the professions, and they had made a difference in the success of reform campaigns. There was reason for confidence. They had moved from no voice to a few voices crying in the wilderness and then to a chorus of voices heard and sometimes heeded. From church groups to literary clubs, from temperance movements to family-oriented reform, from teachers' associations to public crusades for change, Alabama's middle and upper class women, and to a lesser extent black women, had made a move. It was an enviable journey.

TWENTY-FOUR

Domestic Issues, the Creative State, and the Great War

EMMET O'Neal could have been one of Alabama's most brilliant and productive governors. He had great ability and far more vision than his reactionary campaign in 1910 for the governorship suggested. But O'Neal was the victim, not the master, of Alabama politics. He played the game in order to be elected, and he became a prisoner of his choice. The game was a vicious circle of images and self-proving expectations. The voters were lectured on the virtues and glories of doing nothing and the evils of doing anything. This was their constant education, the image of what they were, the vision of solid Alabamians—the enduring Southerners—who saw their values in the time-honored verities, who feared and thus opposed the new and the alien and the different. It was the ultimate appeal to inertia, the apotheosis of the known and the tried and the true. And the more the image was presented as an honorable estate the more the voters became what they were told they ought to be.

Governor O'Neal had a difficult and less than rewarding four years. His recommendations to the legislature read far more of progressive reform than the best of Braxton Bragg Comer, but O'Neal learned the difficulties of campaigning as a conservative and governing as a reformer. O'Neal got a state highway commission, but selfish interests, as he styled them, defeated his attempt at more equitable tax laws. The governor spent far more of his time defending and explaining frauds and embezzlements than he did on constructive government programs. There were major reasons for his concern, as the often seamy side of state government moved into one of its periodic public displays.

O'Neal's major scandal centered in the Convict Department, an agency that bred corruption with the certitude of the seasons. The scenario was always the same. Large amounts of money came to state officials who operated with the unaccounted authority of a provincial satrap. Without bond or supervision, appointed by a political process that stressed who knew whom and with slight reference to ability or responsibility, Alabama government had for years been an unguarded treasure waiting for thieves to steal the people's money and haul it away.

The chief thief was the head of the Convict Department, James G. Oakley, aided and abetted by his clerk Theodore Lacy. In the face of less than anticipated revenues from convict leasing, Governor O'Neal decided to examine Oakley's records before reappointing him in 1913. The state examiners soon concluded that as much as $150,000 was missing, and the score was raised when Lacy then disappeared with an additional $90,000. The evidence suggests that Oakley, with the finger of blame already pointing to him, ordered Lacy to steal the second installment, for which he paid him only $1,500. Lacy turned himself in and in two trials was sentenced to sixteen years in prison; he served ten of them. Oakley, on the other hand, was also tried twice, and the juries, in flagrant disregard of the facts (and the judge's declaration), found him innocent and free to enjoy his stolen $240,000.

Governor O'Neal then spent time and energy in a major investigation of the Convict Department. Even before the Oakley-Lacy exposé, a tragedy of major proportions rocked the state's penal system. On April 8, 1911, an explosion at the ironically named Banner Mine (near Birmingham) killed 129 miners. Most of them were prisoners serving time under the convict lease system. They were in the employ of the Pratt Consolidated Coal Company. Sensational newspaper stories followed, and in the aftermath there were reports, investigations, and demands for improved methods in mining coal and for abolishing the brutal "renting" of human beings for corporate profit.

With the stain of fraud and malpractice added to the sensational explosion in the Banner Mine, the legislature passed a new mine safety law. But once again vested interests—and none was greater than the state itself—rallied to prevent an end to convict leasing. To his credit, Governor O'Neal pushed hard and without compromise for the mine safety law. To his discredit, O'Neal was content to accept half a loaf and label it a feast of reform. The convict lease law remained on the books.

As discussed in the treatment of higher education, it was Governor O'Neal who presided over the plan to distribute the federal funds of the Smith-Lever Act. O'Neal's own committee (composed entirely of whites) recommended that 30 percent of the money be divided between Tuskegee Institute and the Agricultural and Mechanical College for blacks at Huntsville. But the governor proceeded with his own decision to let Auburn handle all of the funds. O'Neal knew about black needs and black expectations but he did not heed them.

On the eve of the First World War, when the major nations of the world were about to begin an irrational orgy of bloodletting, Alabamians were still secure with the tempo of their own concerns. Braxton Bragg Comer wanted to be governor once again, O'Neal still smarted from the charges and innuendos concerning his administration, and the forces of prohibition were prepared to save Alabamians all over again. As it had before, prohibition muddied the waters of ideological cleavage. It tended to subordinate other issues, and it dressed many candidates in costumes alien to their roles. It did not follow that the politician—or the voter—who wanted to save his fellows from drunkenness also wanted a strong child labor law, or the end to convict leasing, or a stronger educational system.

Four candidates announced for the governor's office in 1914. Comer and Lieutenant Governor Walter D. "Bone-dry" Seed both advocated prohibition, while Charles Henderson, the president of the railroad commission, and the perennial Reuben F. Kolb spoke the language of local option. This alignment split the vote on both sides of the prohibition issue, although with Kolb expected to draw only a sympathy vote away from Henderson, the prohibitionists were probably hurt the most. Comer still equated reform with railroad regulation. He attacked both O'Neal and Henderson for surrendering to the railroad interests, and he suggested that under Henderson the scandals and the fraud would continue. Comer's obvious enjoyment and appreciation of himself led his opponents to trumpet the evils of "Comerism" and warn the voters not to subject the state to his adventures.

The State Democratic Executive Committee decreed that if a candidate did not win a majority of the votes, the two top candidates would participate in a second run-off primary. Kolb and Seed were eliminated in the first primary, and Comer and Henderson tried the matter a second time. O'Neal campaigned vigorously for Henderson—or more accurately, he attacked Comer in a blistering contest. By a majority of 10,327 votes, Henderson was elected, and Comer saw his dreams evaporate. The prohibitionists lost the governor's race but won a large majority in the legislature and elected Thomas E. Kilby, a manufacturer and banker who had served as mayor of Anniston, as lieutenant governor. Relatively unknown, Kilby would soon emerge as a powerful and effective leader.

Henderson found his first year in office vastly different from the pleasant routine he had enjoyed as a civic leader, businessman, and banker in his hometown of Troy. It was a disturbing fifty-two weeks. The state was suffering from one of its worst deficits in history; the war initially disrupted the cotton market; and Henderson, with little experience, had to battle with a prohibitionist house and senate. The legislature passed statewide prohibition over Henderson's veto. Alabama thus remained a part of the movement that culminated in national prohibition with the Volstead Act and the Eighteenth Amendment in 1919. A new primary election law specified how whites would conduct their political affairs. Educational change came with the passage of a constitutional amendment that allowed counties to levy a special school tax up to three mills. While helpful, the additional revenue only prevented Alabama from falling even further behind in per capita spending on education.

To pause in the progress of public affairs for a brief look at art and the written word—at the Alabamians who tried their hand at poetry and prose and painting—may seem an exit from the hard and exact indicators of reality and an entry to the confusing realms of creativity. But while art is an individual expression, artists are children of their time—a part of the great collective—and they speak its language and reflect its many values. Much can be learned about Alabama and Alabamians by looking at the artists and the authors. Truth is often revealed through the pages of fiction, while fiction can be written in the hardheaded pursuit of truth. Literature deals with life as readers think or hope it was, as it sometimes is, and as they want it to be. In its own time a work may be popular when it touches readers with its current relevance, when it affects a wide audience by turning individual experience into shared communion, or when it leads to social revelation. The work may become great literature when it transcends those same contemporary appeals and deals with themes at the very core of human experience.

In the ceaseless judgment of the written word, Alabama authors between 1865 and 1920 have not fared well in the appraisement of talent and success. H. L. Mencken, the professional exploder of the balloons of pretense (and himself a study in pretentiousness), condemned the entire South as a cultural wasteland. Modern scholars have noted that Alabama's literature did not match that of Mississippi, Tennessee, or the southeastern seaboard states. It was true that many Alabama authors and artists left the state (although some came in from other areas) and equally certain that there were few literary societies and only short-lived literary magazines. But it does not follow, as the blanket judgments may suggest, that there were no Alabamians whose works were read on the national stage, no Alabama paintings to bemuse and delight, and nothing substantial in the "literature of scholarship." A survey of the authors will more than make the point.

The classification of literature by time and place, by emphasis and theme and style, can offer immediate entrée to the major steps of development. In what rationally might have been an unswerving sequence of progression, and what was in fact a subtle series of overlapping steps, Southern literature opened in 1865 with apologia for slavery and the Civil War, moved on to romanticism and the creation of a South that never was, turned back to local color, dialect, and the humorous, and finally began to practice the cleansing regimen of realism.

Participants in and observers of great events are naturally moved to share their stories with a wider audience. Every war is followed by a surviving generation intent on recording its exploits, detailing its suffering, and defending its decisions. Alabamians were not left out of the national avalanche of books about the Civil War. Raphael Semmes, the captain of the Confederate raider *Alabama,* published his *Memoirs of Service Afloat, during the War Between the States* in 1869. In 1874 Robinson Hundley touched a different aspect with his *Prison Echoes of the Great Rebellion,* and Richard Hooker Wilmer, the Episcopal bishop of Alabama, defended Southern actions in *The Recent Past from a Southern Standpoint,* published in 1887. At about the same time, Parthenia Antoinette Vardaman Hague recounted the trials and tribulations of the home front with her *A Blockaded Family: Life In Southern Alabama during the Civil War.* In 1895 Kate Cumming published *Gleanings from the Southland,* a revision of her earlier work on nursing during the war. Henry W. Hilliard, the paragon of prewar Whig politics (and a professor of English at the University of Alabama), stilled his oratory long enough to publish his memoirs, *Politics and Pen Pictures,* in 1892. Even the turn of the century did not stop the reminiscences. In 1904 Virginia Tunstall Clay-Clopton, wife of the eminent Clement Claiborne Clay, wrote (with the aid of Ada Sterling) *A Belle of the Fifties: Memoirs of Mrs. Clay of Alabama, Covering Social and Political Life In Washington and the South, 1853–1866.*

Alabama novelists also had their say in the realm of explanation, defense, and heavy nostalgia. Perhaps the best example was Sutton S. Scott. He was born in Huntsville in 1829, practiced law and entered politics, and served during the war as Confederate commissioner of Indian affairs. He settled in Russell County and in 1880 published *Southbooke,* a compendium of novelette, poetry, and prose pieces. Scott glorified and idealized Southern manhood and the Old South, and he repeated the theme—in a much better book—with the *Mobilians,* published in 1898. Scott had a sincere lack of objectivity, but his portraits of Alabamians were useful, and he established a benchmark for the quintessential position of Unreconstructed Southern Writer. A better-defined novelist was William Falconer, who combined romance and sentimentality (with occasional redeeming flashes of realism). His *Bloom and Brier; or, As I Saw It Long Ago* came out in 1870 and its nostalgia was well mixed with bitterness.

Depending on the author, the popular form of the historical romance ran the gamut from almost terminal sentimentality and pathos to effective use of realism and good touches of the local scene. Alabama furnished authors for all seasons. Ella ("Beryl Carr") Byrd's *Marston Hall* (1880) hewed tightly to the guidelines of romantic escape literature, as did George Roberts Carter's *Dora's Device* (1885). The first two novels of Elizabeth Whitefield Croom Bellamy—a Floridian by birth, a Mobilian by choice—were unremarkable romances, but her last two novels were illuminated by realistic touches and interesting local color. Louisa A. Jemison, who sometimes wrote under the name "Ellery Sinclair," gained local fame as a philanthropist and wider fame as a writer. *Christie's Choice* and her other five books combined local color with sentimentalized and melodramatic plots.

It is a marginal claim to see Mary Johnston as an Alabama novelist—she was born in Virginia and placed her novels there—although her stay in Birmingham and her success have advanced the claim. There are fewer constraints in the case of Augusta Evans Wilson. A Georgian by birth and a Texan through brief residency, she settled in Mobile in 1849 and remained an Alabamian until her death. Her first two books were written before the Civil War, and her wartime novel *Macaria; or, Altars of Sacrifice* was such effective Confederate propaganda that a Union general—setting new standards for critics—confiscated copies and burned them. Wilson went on to publish six more novels. Her best-known work was *St. Elmo* (1866), a best seller of its time and the basis for two silent movies. One might decry Wilson's heavy hand with pathos and moral admonitions (one critic declared that the tortured erudition of *St. Elmo's* heroine was the result of having swallowed an unabridged dictionary as a child), but her books were financial successes. It is worthy of note that Wilson opposed feminism, evolution, populism, and—that child of idle hours—bridge.

If Wilson spoke with strict moralisms, Mary Elizabeth McNeill Fenollosa surely represented the image of the ultimate exotic romanticist. She married Ernest Fenollosa, and the couple lived in Japan, where Ernest pursued his study of Japanese art and his wife became a prolific poet and novelist. Her first novels were splendid successes, and she remains the only person to write a novel with an Alabama setting while living in Japan and another about Japan while residing in Mobile. She remains an enigmatic figure—not least for the fact that while she lived until 1954 she did not write again after 1919.

Where Mary Fenollosa looked outward to a larger world, other Alabama authors discovered the richness of the local scene. Louise Clarke Pyrnelle, raised on her father's plantation in the Black Belt, learned the folktales and the dialect of the south Alabama black. In *Diddie, Dumps, and Tot* (1882) she told the story of the plantation and recreated its hierarchy of slave labor. This work, along with *Li'l Tweety*, published ten years after Pyrnelle's death in 1907, were children's books that contained useful social history and authentic black speech patterns. Their reprinting attested to their popularity.

What Pyrnelle did for the Black Belt, Idora McClellan Plower Moore did for the hill country. By the 1880s her sketches of blacks and poor whites were being published in the Atlanta *Sunny South* and *Harper's*

Weekly, and Joel Chandler Harris persuaded the Atlanta *Constitution* to publish her pieces. For fifteen years her stories appeared with Harris's "Uncle Remus" tales and Charles H. Smith's "Bill Arp" accounts of Georgia crackers. Writing under the pseudonym of "Betsy Hamilton," Moore used the dialects of her subjects to good effect and she was equally successful as a national lecturer. *Betsy Hamilton: Southern Character Sketches* was published in 1921.

Plowing the same field of local color was Francis Bartow Lloyd, the author of the "Rufus Sanders" stories. Lloyd was solidly in the tradition of the antebellum writers Johnson Jones Hooper and Joseph Glover Baldwin. Lloyd was born at Mount Willing, deep in the Black Belt's Lowndes County, and, forsaking the practice of law, opted for a career in journalism. As the city editor of the Montgomery *Advertiser,* he began his Rufus Sanders sketches. The column grew in popularity, and syndication brought in enough money to retire from journalism and enter politics. Rufus Sanders displayed the durable character of the frontier con man and practical joker, and Lloyd had a fine talent for depicting politicians and horse traders with humor and telling aphorisms. It is a timeless observation on the human condition "that every man that gits there ahead of the regular crowd has got to know sometin about cuttin across lots." Lloyd's stories promoted the Democratic party, and though his characters were of common clay, he was a strong opponent of the Populists. Both a solid literary career and a burgeoning political role came to an end when Lloyd was murdered on a rural road in Butler County. In 1898 his wife published a collection of his Rufus Sanders stories as *Sketches of Country Life: Humor, Wisdom, and Pathos from the "Sage of Rocky Creek."*

While most authors limited themselves to one mode of expression, Thomas Cooper DeLeon defied categories to become Alabama's first professional man of letters. His Civil War reminiscences (he was secretary to President Jefferson Davis) were published as *Four Years In Rebel Capitals.* He edited newspapers in New York and Mobile, published a collection of Confederate poems and songs, managed a printing company, organized the Mobile Mardi Gras, and qualified as editor, publisher, poet, pamphleteer, playwright, essayist, translator, novelist, and biographer. His last book, *Belles, Beaux and Brains of the '60s* (1909), was one of his best offerings.

If novelists were relatively scarce on the Alabama scene, poets of serious import were only a few steps removed from invisibility. There were certainly those who tried. Ina Marie Porter was a solid journalist who contributed poems to various publications. There were Samuel Lowrie Roberts and Warfield Creath Richardson—and Richardson's daughter, Belle Richardson Harrison, who gained recognition for her verses in black dialect. Kate Slaughter McKinney of Montgomery published two volumes of poetry, and Ellen Henry Ruffin of Mobile provided *Drifting Leaves* in 1884. Marie Howard Weeden of Huntsville accompanied her paintings with her poems, but it was the former that made her reputation.

Alabama's best-known and most prolific poet was Samuel Minturn Peck, who published his first poem while still in medical school. That might have been an odd education for a poet, and in fact Peck never practiced medicine but devoted his life to literature. His first volume of verse, *Cap and Bells,* appeared in 1886. It proved his talent for light verse (some of his best poems recall his boyhood in Alabama) but characterized him as less than a serious poet. More volumes followed, there was strong reader response, and Peck became a widely known figure. He retained his popularity over a long span of years, and he was selected as Alabama's first poet laureate in 1931.

The Alabama contribution to music allows the tenuous thought that William C. Handy, the "Father of the Blues," was born in Florence, but he lived his productive years in Mississippi and then in Memphis, Tennessee. Matters were better in the field of painting. Howard Weeden, as she was called, established an international reputation with her sensitive and accurate portraits of former slaves. By the mid-1890s her work was being exhibited in Europe, and in 1898 her *Shadows on the Wall,* a collection of drawings and accompanying verse, gave her a solid reputation. Weeden made her way in the world of art without leaving Alabama to enter a larger sphere of study and influence.

Other Alabama painters pursued their work in the mainstream of artistic life. Roderick McKenzie was born in London but came as a child to Mobile in 1872. He trained in art at Mobile's Barton Academy, studied in Boston, and spent the next twenty-five years abroad. For some of this time he lived in Paris but more was spent in India, where he painted the Bengal tiger for local potentates and the sahibs of the raj. McKenzie returned to Alabama and some of his finest work included a historical mural in the state capitol. Hannah Elliot of Birmingham studied art in Paris and won international fame for her miniature portraits; Anne Goldthwaite of Montgomery trained in New York and Paris, exhibited widely, and was particularly renowned for her paintings of Alabama Black Belt landscapes; and Clara Weaver Parrish was a superb painter who in later years promoted Southern art and artists. Kelly Fitzpatrick of Wetumpka, the grandson of Governor Benjamin Fitzpatrick, studied art in Paris and came home to start the Dixie Art Colony at Wetumpka and to help found the Alabama Art League and the Montgomery Museum of Fine Arts. While Alabama artists were studying abroad, Italian-born Giuseppe Moretti was contributing his giant statue of Vulcan to the

World's Fair (for years afterward Vulcan watched the Alabama State Fair until he was given a more heroic vista on top of Red Mountain). Moretti moved to Sylacauga and executed many works in Alabama marble.

There may have been a relative paucity of creativity in these years, and, if so, how can it be explained? Art and literature flourish—as does education itself—where it is viewed as a matter of importance and value. Where it is not supported by public approbation and finances, it is left to scattered individuals and their own resources to supply the drive and seek an audience outside their native milieu. There is no way to know how much talent, how much world-class ability, never had the chance to rise above the fleeting dream and the dimly seen aspiration. In Alabama one race had little opportunity and less encouragement; the other race had almost no chance at all.

When historians write about historians it is often with unstated ambivalence and unresolved doubts and confusions. Historians seem perpetually stranded between a literary re-creation of the past and recurring delusions of scientific rigor and reasoning. Yet it was exactly in these years that Alabama historians began their passage from history as informative and entertaining story (and sometimes as dry compendium) to the "scientific history" that had its day in the sun. Even in their literary phases historians used the past to comment on the present, although it is always preferable and often enjoyable to be propagandized by good writers and the deft phrase.

The first phase of Alabama historical writing was exactly in the tradition of the man of public affairs as historian. William Garrett's *Reminiscences of Public Men In Alabama for Thirty Years* (1872) and Willis Brewer's *Alabama: Her History, Resources, War Record, and Public Men* (1872) were natural extensions (but lacking the synthesis) of Albert James Pickett's path-breaking *History of Alabama* (1851). In 1876 Joseph Hodgson, editor of the Montgomery *Mail*, published his *The Cradle of the Confederacy; or the Times of Troup, Quitman, and Yancey,* and in 1899 John Allan Wyeth (a native of Marshall County and distinguished New York surgeon) contributed his *The Life of General Nathan Bedford Forrest.* John Witherspoon DuBose—planter, journalist, and sometime state employee—was a dedicated historian. In 1892 he published *The Life and Times of William Lowndes Yancey,* and in 1912 he produced *General Joseph Wheeler and the Army of Tennessee.* His titles suggest his interest, and DuBose was a narrow and uncritical partisan of Southern affairs. Some of his newspaper pieces on Reconstruction have been published, but his handwritten 2,000-page manuscript on Alabama from 1865 to 1901 rests appropriately in acid-proof boxes in the Alabama Department of Archives and History.

Some Alabamians wrote political accounts and exposés on matters other than the Civil War. The Populist politicians Joseph C. Manning, Milford W. Howard, and William H. Skaggs produced telling attacks on the Bourbon Democrats. Manning wrote *Politics of Alabama* (1893), *The Rise and Reign of the Bourbon Oligarchy* (1916), and *The Fadeout of Populism: Pot and Kettle In Combat* (1928). Howard was a full-bore muckraker. His *If Christ Came to Congress* (1894) strongly suggested that the visit would have been without an invitation and that Christ's scourge would have been put to good use. Skaggs published *The Southern Oligarchy: An Appeal In Behalf of the Silent Masses of Our Country Against the Despotic Rule of the Few* in 1924. Skaggs was a man of enormous political talent, and while he lacked a national reputation, his book was both better written than those of Upton Sinclair and better reasoned than those of Ida Tarbell.

These were, of course, avowedly partisan works (though perhaps no more so than those of DuBose), but historians, amateur and professional, began to approach matters with the appearance and paraphernalia of telling it "as it actually was." The lawyer Peter J. Hamilton published his fine *Colonial Mobile* in 1897, a well-written work based on intensive research. In 1910 Ethel Armes, a newspaper reporter, wrote her *Story of Coal and Iron In Alabama*. The work romantically portrayed the coal and iron entrepreneurs as a beneficent force in Alabama life, but the lack of critical analysis was balanced by the depth of her interviews. The book has been reprinted and remains a major source in Alabama history.

Two men, each in his own way, led the march toward the professionalization of Alabama history. The first was George Petrie of Montgomery who professionalized himself. In 1892 he was the first Alabamian to earn the Ph.D. degree. For fifty years Petrie served as professor of history at Alabama Polytechnic Institute, where he was mentioned as the first coach of the Auburn football team. Petrie was the promoter of professional research in Alabama history. Walter L. Fleming of Brundidge was a Petrie student who went on to establish a national reputation as a student of the Civil War and Reconstruction. Both Frank L. Owsley and Albert Burton Moore—major Alabama historians—were trained by Petrie, although their most important work came after 1920.

The other formative force was Thomas McAdory Owen, who contributed significantly to the writing and preservation of Alabama history. What Owen may have lacked in formal training he made up for in drive and organizing ability. He was the moving spirit in the Alabama Historical Society and led the Alabama History Commission in its call for the establishment of a state archives. He became the first director of the first archival agency to be established by a state. Owen published his "Bibliography of Alabama" in 1897 (he did another on Mississippi); his four-volume *History of Alabama and Dictionary of Alabama Biography* was published posthumously in 1921.

The writers and historians of Alabama were, with few exceptions, white men and women. One of the exceptions deserves consideration. John William Beverly was born a slave near Greensboro in 1858. His parents became landowners, and Beverly attended William Burns Paterson's Tullibody Academy in Greensboro. He followed Paterson to the normal school for blacks at Marion and became the first black faculty member in 1886. After graduate work at Brown University he came back to the normal school at Montgomery. Beverly taught history and was the author of five books including, in 1901, *History of Alabama for Use in Schools and for General Reading.* His balance is best attested by the fact that the book won state approval as a supplemental textbook for the public schools, white and black.[1]

While novelists invented other lives, while poets sought the spirit and the essence, while artists froze some moment, real or imagined, on their canvas, while historians poked about and examined the debris of the past, a very hard and present reality was descending on the state and nation. War loomed on the horizon, a war that produced the logical, if incongruous, picture of Roderick McKenzie (of tiger-painting fame) hard at work applying camouflage paint to the vessels in the shipyards of Mobile. Life itself is always the greatest novel.

As the war abroad continued to a bloody stalemate, as American interests were affected by the policies of both sides, Alabamians were drawn to an increasing concentration on matters far larger than themselves. If the Wilson administration decided on war, Alabama's influence in Congress promised to be a source of pride and power. Oscar W. Underwood, the Democrats' authority on tariff matters, majority leader of the House, and after 1914 a U.S. senator, was a major figure in the party. Henry D. Clayton was a trusted adviser to the president on antitrust matters and was the influential chairman of the House Judiciary Committee. Stanley H. Dent, Jr. (the son of Barbour County's conservative stalwart in the constitutional convention of 1901), was the chairman of the important House Military Affairs Committee. Overall, the president's progressive domestic program had the support of Alabama's congressional delegation.

President Wilson asked Congress for a declaration of war on April 2, and it was voted on April 6. It seemed certain to patriotic Alabamians that Dent would play a leading role in passing the new war leader's mobilization plans. Their shock was profound when it became apparent that Dent (along with a majority of his committee members) opposed the administration's call for conscription (selective service) and favored a plan to allow volunteering before resorting to a draft.

Americans were newcomers to the realities of total war and the overwhelming powers that it brings to government. Dent's allies deserted him, and President Wilson had his way. But when the war was over and the Wilson administration proposed a highly centralized military establishment, Dent not only blocked action on the legislation but helped lead a revolt against Wilson by the House Democratic caucus.

The First World War was the first modern conflict to attempt the total mobilization of society. Efforts were made to organize every segment and every activity of civilians in support of collective policy. Governments proclaimed their power and persuasion in hundreds of areas where they had never ventured in time of peace. Every aspect of life felt the organizing hand of government. Giving and sacrifice and obligation were preached as new national gospel. Alabamians—whatever their states' rights heritage—rallied to the collectivizing program with the same fervor of nationalism that marked Americans from every section of the nation.

The first job was to raise an army, and the effort was not a replay of the Spanish-American War. Huge numbers of troops would be raised—and that meant housed, fed, equipped, and trained. The United States participated in the war for only twenty months, but in that time it raised more than four million men and sent more than two million overseas to France. In spite of frenzied efforts to produce the implements of war, the nation after two years was still heavily dependent on its allies. In all of this activity, the Alabama experience—with some notable idiosyncrasies—was the national story in microcosm.

The 74,000 Alabamians inducted into the army through selective service lost their state identity and were tossed and turned in the giant melting pot of military service. In contrast, many Alabama National Guard troops maintained a state coherence even as they lost their old guard designations. The Fourth Infantry of the guard became the 167th United States Infantry, and it in turn became a part of the Forty-second "Rainbow" Division.

The Alabama guard had been called to duty in 1916 for service on the Mexican border while General John Pershing's regulars had futilely searched for Pancho Villa. They had come home to be greeted by the war with Germany and started further recruitment in their camp at Vandiver Park, three miles north of Montgomery. Renamed Camp Sheridan, and greatly enlarged, the base became the later home of the Thirty-seventh Division from Ohio before it went to France. It was the temporary home as well of young Lieutenant F. Scott Fitzgerald, not yet a novelist but

Company inspection at Camp Sheridan. Located near Montgomery, the base housed many World War I soldiers, including Lt. F. Scott Fitzgerald. (Courtesy of the Alabama Department of Archives and History)

who, with the stuff of novels, drew his pistol and forced a conscientious objector to drill at gunpoint. In his spare time Fitzgerald met young Zelda Sayre (daughter of a prominent Montgomery family—her father was the author of the restrictive Sayre election law of 1893). He courted her extravagantly; despite certain misgivings on her part, she finally married him on April 20, 1920.

The Fourth Alabama, in the throes of becoming the 167th Infantry, was sent to Camp Mills in New Jersey to join its fellow regiments of the Forty-second Division. One of the regiments was the famous—or notorious—Sixty-ninth New York. The melting pot failed to function, or perhaps it functioned too well, in what became a clash of pride and culture. Classic mass fights occurred between the regiments. By November 1917, the Forty-second's headquarters units were in France. The division followed and participated in the grand roll of American campaigns: Chateau-Thierry, St. Mihiel, and the Argonne. The Forty-second Division took its losses—2,810 deaths and 11,873 wounded (Alabama's total losses were 2,401 killed in action, 3,861 died from wounds or disease)—and it gained some heroes. The 167th had two winners of the Congressional Medal of Honor (one was a native Alabamian, Corporal Sidney E. Manning of Flomaton, Escambia County). A host of other decorations and medals attested to the bravery of Alabamians under fire. This was indeed a different story from 1898—and a vastly different war.

While soldiers trained, suffered, and sometimes died, Alabama civilians went through the months of wartime with some privation, great

404

relative prosperity, and the boom of war building and expansion. Operating under its parent body in Washington, the Alabama Council of National Defense attempted to coordinate the activities of eleven subordinate groups in the broadest organization of national life yet attempted. There were men's and women's groups and further division along the lines of occupation and activity. The aim of it all was "to involve the entire population in the domestic war effort."[2] That goal ran into difficulties in the South and in Alabama.

Both men's and women's national sections put an uneven but unceasing pressure on the Southern state councils to organize black men and women for the war effort. The idea of black involvement, the recognition of a participatory role, was a logical application of the constant preaching of democracy. But while the advance of democracy might be a major war aim, Southern racial attitudes and practices were as firmly opposed to the concept as they had always been. Black women's committees were established in Birmingham, Bessemer, and Selma; in Mobile black women set up their own "War Service Club" while waiting for official organizers to discover them. These groups—like their white counterparts—sewed, prepared soldiers' "comfort kits," canned food, and sold savings stamps. It was exactly the sort of service that was being urged on everyone, but it gave some white Southerners an uneasy sense of change. There was a potential for reform in the collectivizing pressure of war, but it would have taken much longer and required much greater force to have left its imprint on the state.

Not until the Second World War were Americans again subjected to such unremitting appeals to patriotism—the euphemism for the thoroughly pragmatic weapon of propaganda—as they were in 1917–18. They were exhorted by speakers, inflamed by poets, and carried through miles of verbiage by the writers of prose. There were endless reminders to buy war bonds, to observe the meatless days, to economize on fuel and fats. The kaiser's spies were apparently lurking everywhere from Scottsboro to Bay Minette, and Alabamians were admonished to maintain a wary silence. In massive overkill Americans were bombarded with reminders of why they were fighting. In this process of mass communication the poster reached its highest point of development and left a puzzling and bemusing legacy for later readers. "Uncle Sam Wants Fruit Pits" made more sense than first appeared. "Tear Off Your Clothing and Sell It" seemed an overly rash reaction to the principle of doing one's part, while "Hold Up Your End" was ripe with imagery. In later times "Our Boys Need Sox" might be taken as a typographical error, but at the time it was testimony to the sock mania that swept the nation.

In the midst of war work, Alabamians were not spared the domestic appearance of the international flu epidemic. The virulent strain of influenza that killed millions around the world added its ravages to the suffering of war. In October 1918 it struck with full effect in Alabama. Camp Sheridan had five hundred cases, with three deaths reported on October 8 and twelve more on the following day. Every Alabama county played host to the virus, and across the state schools, soda fountains, and movie theaters were closed. No immunization and no effective medicine existed. The Montgomery *Advertiser* gave its readers advice on treatment that stressed keeping everything open—doors, windows, and bowels. Hot soup was deemed helpful, but patent medicines were to be avoided. On the other hand, one enterprising merchant claimed that the flu could be avoided entirely by spraying oneself all over with a DeVilbiss Nose and Throat Atomizer (only one dollar) filled with Dobell Solution (fifty cents a bottle).

Alabama's iron and steel industry felt the flush times of wartime demand and greatly expanded production, and the hostilities promised to change the very face, fortunes, and future of the Tennessee Valley. The region had long resented the greater wealth (and power) of south Alabama, and the war revived old dreams of prosperity. Not only did it seem possible to open the Tennessee River to full-length navigation, but there was the newer ambition of making it a center for electrical generation.

With the National Defense Act of 1916, the government began a search for a suitable site for a nitrate plant that could make the United States an independent producer of explosives. The search proceeded through a labyrinth of committee investigation followed by the thicket of quarreling local interests. Not until September 1917, five months after the United States entered the war, did President Wilson announce that a nitrate plant would be built at Muscle Shoals, Alabama. A month later a second and larger plant was announced. The news ignited not only a frenzied construction program but an equally heated boom of land prices. The flame of boosterism burned brightly, and future prosperity was painted in hopefully permanent colors. Thousands of workers poured into the area, and new camps and villages grew up to house the newcomers. Farfetched dreams seemed realizable when it was announced in February 1918 that the government would build a major dam and hydroelectric works next to the largest nitrate plant.

All of these plans seemed to be a bonanza for labor—unskilled workers were being paid thirty cents an hour—but labor turnover, pushed by the frenetic pace and bad housing, was extremely high (60,000 hired to fill 20,000 jobs). One-third of the work force was black, and while they filled the unskilled positions, the work was at least an alternative to the cotton field and the coal mine.

By the time the war was over the first nitrate plant had produced one experimental run. The second plant started production two weeks after

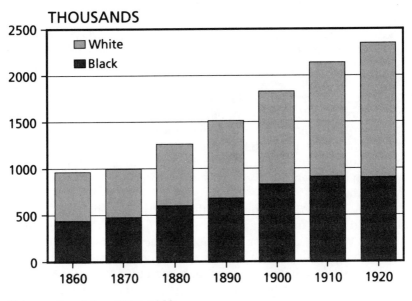

THOUSANDS

Alabama Population, 1860–1920

the armistice, and the dam was either half-completed or half-unfinished, depending on one's point of view. As it did with all its wartime industrial activities, the government stopped its projects, canceled production, and laid off workers with a dislocating suddenness. What would become of Muscle Shoals was a question of policies and politics that would work their way through the 1920s. Not until the 1930s did the New Deal and the Tennessee Valley Authority begin to fulfill the promise of north Alabama.

For a war now receding into secondhand memory it is easy to forget its central importance to its own time and the overpowering emotion that seized people when they learned that it had finally ended. News that an armistice had gone into effect on November 11, 1918, set off wild demonstrations across Alabama. In Montgomery few bothered to see "The Girl of the Golden West" playing at the Plaza, or to go to the Strand for a movie with even more popular appeal, "Johanna Enlists," starring Mary Pickford. Instead, it was a time to throng the streets as sirens wailed, steam whistles roared, bells rang, and rifles and pistols were fired in the air. Firecrackers popped constantly and hundreds of garbage can lids were banged and rattled as 6,500 schoolchildren swarmed across the town. Governor Henderson—perhaps unheard—spoke at the capitol.

If possible, wilder scenes occurred in Birmingham. A casket containing an effigy of the kaiser was lowered from the roof of a downtown building twenty-seven stories to the ground. People inside, pistols cocked and at the ready, shot at the casket as it passed their windows. A giant parade (there were 200,000 celebrating citizens) was held with banners carried high to pronounce that the kaiser was "Hell-Bound." A division of black civilians marched in the parade, accompanied by black Liberty Loan workers with a banner whose inscription reminded that "A Negro First Died for American Independence." In Selma the celebration lasted for nine hours, and in Huntsville the noise could be heard twenty miles away. Matters became so excited in the latter city that two cars collided on East Holmes Street, a frightened team of horses ran away on Meridian Street, and Henry Haines was accidentally shot in the foot by Archie Hawkins.

The Huntsville *Times* announced that "not since the birth of Christ has the world passed through a more important day than this November 11, 1918."[3] Without even that qualification the Birmingham *Age-Herald* stated on November 12 that "yesterday was the greatest day in history. It marked the beginning of a new era for humanity."[4] Neither the assumed prizes of peace nor the idealistic expectations of the future lingered long in Alabama or the nation. Having aimed too high with a crusade to save humanity, Americans quickly fell back too far. The 1920s would be the stuff of tarnished illusions, failed ambitions, and defeated dreams. The return of reality brought the same old struggle against poverty, the same fight against exploitation, and the same blinding prejudice and fear.

In Alabama the year 1919 surely differed in a thousand ways from that other postwar year, 1866. Only fifty-three years separated the two dates, and they had been crowded and sometimes tumultous times. There had been progress and cries for more progress. There had been material growth and the rise of industrial life. There had been happy times in the worst of circumstances and personal misery in the midst of prosperity. That was the matrix of life in anyplace and at anytime. But would there be a better life for everyone? Perhaps the next fifty years would make a difference.

PART THREE

From the 1920s to the 1990s

by
Wayne Flynt

Tradition amid change. Automobiles are parked in front of an antebellum mansion in Montgomery in the 1930s. (Courtesy of the Alabama Department of Archives and History)

TWENTY-FIVE

The Politics of Reform
and Stability
during the 1920s

HISTORY often plays tricks on people. Those living in Alabama in 1920 believed they witnessed the dawning of a new era. In fact they lived in the twilight of an old one. The war to end wars had filled their heads with naive faith in the possibilities of American democracy to emancipate totalitarian and backward societies. In fact the war had accelerated forces of bigotry, nativism, and exclusion seldom seen before in Alabama. Evangelical Protestants had just won their greatest victory by prohibiting the manufacture and sale of alcoholic beverages. Their moral crusade would soon flounder in the shoals of cultural change and bootlegging. Women bobbed their hair, smoked, let their necklines plunge, went to work, danced the Charleston, attended racy movies, and necked in automobiles. Controlling the changing patterns of behavior of their sons and daughters would prove far more difficult for Evangelicals than restricting alcohol consumption or immigration.

Women emerged in 1920 with the vote and with powerful political organizations. But their bright dreams ended in squabbling and partisanship. They experienced the frequent fate of all successful causes won by one generation: the apathy of the following generation.

Economic prosperity and agricultural diversification seemed the result of a kind providence. Instead, the worst economic cataclysm in Alabama's history awaited them less than a decade away. Their agriculture remained mired in the world of their grandfathers—a world of share-cropping, one-mule farms, slavish reliance on cotton, and ruinous economic cycles. Urbanization and mechanization focused attention on cultural modernization, on automobiles, urban gridlock, construction of skyscrapers, and on a daring generation of young men and women who were as bold when starting new businesses as when flying the state's first airplanes.

But most Alabamians remained rural, treasuring folkways that featured "conjure women," midwives, sacred harp singings, fiddle festivals, quilting, and basket making. Their traditions, like their fashions, belonged more to the nineteenth century than to the twentieth. So Alabama presented contrasting images during the decade of the 1920s. The historical lens seemed to have produced a double exposure. The foreground revealed a picture of rapid change and urban prosperity. The background revealed persistent agrarian values amid agricultural poverty.

Later decades would cause some Alabamians to wonder if political leadership, efficient administration, progressive change, and a clear vision of the future had ever been a part of the state's tradition. Before 1865 the answer would have been a qualified "yes," but after 1865 it would have been "no." The decade of the 1920s, strangely enough, was more positive than negative. The state enjoyed what was to prove the most progressive, efficient political leadership of any decade in the century. That fact is even more remarkable in light of the unlikely coalition of working class whites, Evangelical Protestants, women reformers, and Ku Klux Klansmen that installed it in power. Parts of this progressive coalition produced a witch's brew of mischief that embarrassed the state and brought down upon it ridicule and censure.

The same patterns that had dominated Alabama politics since Reconstruction prevailed during the 1920s. The Democratic party had no serious opposition to discipline its ranks. Not once between 1876 and 1960 was a Republican presidential candidate to carry Alabama. Nor was the state to elect a Republican governor until 1986. In many sections of the state during the first decades of the twentieth century, a Republican was a rare curiosity and considered a community eccentric. Hence Democrats divided along both philosophical and personal lines. Political scientist V. O. Key, Jr., characterized the state's political system as one dominated by localism. Parochial issues and local elites—consisting of sheriffs, probate judges, prominent businessmen, and planters—controlled county politics. A candidate for office campaigned not so much among the general population as for the endorsement of these elites. Another principle that Key found dominant in state politics was a "friends and neighbors" phenomenon. Candidates for statewide office tended to run strongest in their home county and in adjacent counties where they were known personally. Because Alabama was a large state with sixty-seven counties, it was usually necessary in the pretelevision age for candidates to run twice, the first time to establish name recognition and the second time to win. A persistent gubernatorial pattern developed in the middle decades of the twentieth century: a candidate ran, came in second to the eventual winner, then won the ensuing contest. The fact that a governor could not succeed himself denied the advantages of incumbency and encouraged this pattern.

Another age-old pattern consisted of sectionalism between north and south Alabama. Planters in the Black Belt often allied politically to four or five counties in southwestern Alabama and to industrialists and businessmen in Birmingham. Governor Bibb Graves is credited with calling Birmingham entrepreneurs "Big Mules." He said they reminded him of a farmer who had harnessed a small mule to a wagon heavily loaded with corn. Behind the wagon he had hitched a big mule who amused itself by leisurely munching corn out of the wagon, while the small mule strained every muscle to pull the entire load. The imagery was memorable, and the Big Mules were latter-day urban Bourbons. Businessmen and planters saddled small farmers and those least able to pay with an inequitable tax burden while they conspired to pass legislation for their own benefit. The masses might occasionally become outraged enough to elect a reform governor, but as long as the conservative coalition controlled the legislature, no particularly pernicious class legislation could pass. The 1901 constitution required that the Alabama legislature reapportion its membership following each census. In fact the legislature refused to reapportion itself until the U.S. Supreme Court compelled it to do so in the 1960s. On the surface the interests of industrial Birmingham, which had only one senator despite containing a fifth of the state's population, seemed inimical to those of Black Belt planters. In the Black Belt the population steadily declined throughout the century. But appearances were deceiving. Because Birmingham's Big Mules opposed higher taxes, labor unions, and political change as much as Black Belt planters did, they were determined to allow Birmingham's volatile, polyglot population to go underrepresented rather than risk a reapportioned legislature that might be unsympathetic to their interests.

Conversely, north Alabama's plain folk, consisting mainly of white subsistence farmers and industrial workers, had little in common with Big Mules and Black Belt planters. Oftentimes they made common cause with small farmers in the mainly white southeast Alabama Wiregrass region.

At the state level, the 1901 constitution and political practice invested considerable power in the governor. Historically the chief executive controlled the house of representatives by selecting its speaker. The speaker in turn loaded key committee chairmanships with the governor's allies. Until 1975 senators also allowed the chief executive to organize the upper house. Using patronage and pork barrel budget expenditures, the governor could reward friends and punish enemies.

This political system did not encourage visionary thinking in a time when the problems confronting a new generation seemed daunting. Wartime governor Charles Henderson requested the Russell Sage Foundation of New York to conduct a study of conditions in the state. The report, submitted in December 1918, detailed a grim landscape of neglect and inequity.

In education Alabama spent only 54 percent of the national per pupil average. The average annual salary of teachers was only 79 percent of the national figure. State expenditures on higher education per inhabitant were less than any state other than Arkansas. Only 50 percent of black elementary-age children attended school, and they attended terms that averaged less than five months. The entire state contained only three four-year public high schools for blacks.

Despite the herculean volunteer efforts undertaken by the state's illiteracy commission to educate adults, Alabama's rate of illiteracy for people age ten or above was 16.1 percent in 1920. Even native-born whites had a rate of 6.4 percent; black illiteracy in that age group soared to 31.3 percent. As late as 1927 Alabama's literacy ranking was forty-fifth among forty-eight states. Its white illiteracy rate was the seventh highest of any state.

The second problem spotlighted in the Sage Foundation report was Alabama's penal system. The decades-old problem involved the unwillingness of citizens to pay taxes in order to provide prisons. Instead, the state continued to realize a profit from the rental of convicts to coal mines and other industries. Should the system be reduced or terminated, such action would require costly construction of additional facilities.

Child labor had declined from the frightful levels of early century. Yet in 1920 Alabama agriculture and industry still employed more than 130,000 children ages ten to seventeen, divided almost equally between whites and blacks.

State law required children to attend school until age fourteen and prohibited a child from working while school was in session. But desperately poor parents and employers seeking cheap labor ignored the ordinance. The first state child welfare survey in 1920 found more than 1,200 children below the age of sixteen working in cotton mills. In one small Covington County community an inspector found fourteen children living with their mother who operated a house of prostitution. One daughter, age thirteen, was pregnant. Several daughters had contracted venereal diseases. In another community near Montgomery, the inspector discovered a white sixteen-year-old girl operating a brothel. In one cotton mill town she found eighteen illegitimate children, four crippled children receiving no medical attention, and twenty-eight families deserted by the male head of family.

Such conditions were typical of care for the poor and powerless. Although Alabama contained high-quality institutions for the insane, the state virtually ignored 3,000 feeble-minded citizens, 1,000 neglected children, and a similar number of epileptics. State appropriations for public health were woefully inadequate. In 1918 Alabama ranked eleventh among twelve Southern states in appropriations for its state Board of Health; the state's total expenditures amounted to only one-fourth the Southern average. That same year the legislature appropriated $26,200 to fund public health programs. But all except $6,500 of this sum went to pay administrative salaries and expenses. That same legislature appropriated $28,000 to prevent hog cholera and $25,000 for eradicating cattle ticks. In all, legislators that year authorized $83,000 for treating sick animals compared to $26,200 for treating sick people.

At the root of these social problems stood an inadequate and inequitable tax system. The state was fully able to pay for public services, the Sage Foundation argued. The state debt was low, and taxation was not excessive. The state revenue code provided for assessment of all taxable property at 60 percent of fair cash value. But statewide assessments fell well below this level. The U.S. Census Bureau estimated average assessments at only 25 percent of true value. The Sage Foundation report recommended that the legislature enforce the 60 percent figure in order to generate sufficient funds to operate state government at a decent level. This reform alone would enable the state to pay its bonded indebtedness, increase the salaries of underpaid state employees, improve education at all levels for both races, construct adequate prisons and hospitals, and adequately provide for public health. Not only was Alabama's tax structure inadequate, it also levied the heaviest burden on those least able to pay. Critics of reform would reply that citizens opposed additional taxes, and legislators who voted for them would be committing political suicide. Not so, the report contended. Alabamians, including progressive businessmen, cared about health, education, and the feeble-minded. The author of the report, Hastings H. Hart, concluded: "Surely the people of the splendid state of Alabama intend that their social progress in education, philanthropy and public education shall keep pace with their progress in wealth, industry, agriculture, commerce and home-building, and shall not be inferior to other southern states."[1]

Whether because of Hart's challenge, embarrassment at the woeful performance of state government, or heightened social consciousness, Alabama citizens responded by electing two of the most reform-minded governors of the century. Within a decade after the publication of this report, governors Thomas E. Kilby and Bibb Graves had addressed virtually every item contained within it plus many additional problems.

Never in Alabama history did a governor profit so greatly from an academic endeavor as did Thomas Kilby from the Sage Foundation study. In many ways the agenda of the times suited Kilby perfectly. He had come to Anniston from Georgia in 1887 as an agent of the Georgia and Pacific Railroad. Following business successes in iron, steel, and banking, he entered politics; he served as Anniston's mayor, as state senator from Calhoun County, and as lieutenant governor. Renowned for his efficient and honest administration and his pious religious concern for the less fortunate, he entered the 1918 governor's race as a distinct favorite. Tapping his personal fortune, he paid all his own expenses and returned contributions to those who sent donations anyway. As a consequence he owed no favors to special interests. Two-thirds of the state's newspapers endorsed him and a platform that promised to reform the state's business practices, improve education, revise tax laws to eliminate exemptions that penalized out-of-state corporations, enforce prohibition, abolish the convict lease system, put prisoners to work improving state roads, and enact workmen's compensation legislation. Kilby defeated the more conservative candidate, William W. Brandon, by a vote of 47,500 to 38,300. He carried northern and eastern counties but lost the Black Belt and southwestern Alabama.

Hardly had Governor Kilby taken his oath of office in January 1919 than two national issues forced immediate action. Congress had recently enacted both the Eighteenth (prohibition) and Nineteenth (women's suffrage) amendments and sent them to the states for ratification. Kilby strongly endorsed ratification of the first and proposed a strong enforcement agency; but he maintained cautious neutrality on the second. After the Alabama legislature rejected the women's suffrage amendment, he expressed regret at its decision. When Tennessee ratified it months later and provided the necessary margin for enactment, Kilby immediately summoned the legislature, at the request of suffragists, and submitted a legislative package allowing Alabama women to vote in the 1920 elections. In private correspondence with officials of the Alabama League of Women Voters, he expressed enthusiastic support quite at variance with his official neutrality of previous months.

With these urgent matters resolved, he turned attention to enacting his platform. At the heart of his agenda was creation of a new budget commission. As with so many other "businessmen progressive" governors of the 1920s, he determined to put government on a businesslike basis. At one level of fiscal policy this plan meant implementing the Sage Foundation recommendation of tax reform. Defying political wisdom, Kilby proposed tax equalization, enactment of a graduated state income tax, and a severance tax on coal and iron ore mined in the state. The legislature passed his tax program, but the state supreme court struck down his income tax proposal. This action forced Kilby and the legislature to increase property tax assessments toward the constitutionally mandated level of 60 percent, but public opposition coalesced in the form of the Taxpayers' League, which petitioned for lower taxes. Kilby stood his ground, arguing that Alabama's taxes were already low compared to other states and that cuts would disrupt all state institutions and services. Despite the growing taxpayer revolt, Kilby prevented a rollback.

With a funding basis secured by new taxes and booming state industry, Kilby could now address the manifold social, educational, and health problems confronting citizens.

Although he had campaigned for abolishing the convict lease system, he grew cautious on this issue after his inauguration. Practical issues largely dictated the pace of change. By withdrawing convicts from coal mines, the state would absorb a double financial blow. It would lose revenue paid the state in order to lease the convicts, and it would have to provide prisons in which to house them. He began the largest prison construction program in state history, including one of the most modern prisons in the South near Montgomery that would eventually bear his name. But he delayed abolition of convict leasing, persuading the legislature to push back the effective date until 1924. He also obtained funds for a new state training school for girls, which was completed in 1921.

Care for the insane and feeble-minded expanded enormously during Kilby's term, but he was specifically interested in mentally handicapped children who could not care for themselves. Kilby requested $200,000 for the establishment of the Alabama Home for Feeble-Minded plus $5,000 a month to operate the facility. The legislature complied, and the home opened in Tuscaloosa in 1922. Kilby was the first governor to differentiate between the insane and those who were only mentally handicapped.

The governor's interest in children extended beyond those with mental problems to the entire issue of child welfare. Kilby persuaded the legislature to establish the state Child Welfare Department in 1919, two years before the first federal grants for maternal and child health care and nearly two decades before the Social Security Act. Alabama, which historically lagged in so many areas of human concern, actually pioneered publicly financed child welfare. Under the direction of Lorraine Bedsole Tunstall-Bush and child-labor inspector Augusta Martin, the agency transformed conditions for Alabama's children. They not only enforced the state's child-labor laws but also surveyed children to find out why they dropped out of school and went to work (79 percent did so to assist widowed or deserted mothers). In addition they inspected cotton mills and coal mines that employed children.

Education received similar attention. Kilby established a five-member agency headed by the U.S. commissioner of education, Dr. P. P. Claxton. The commission called for increased financing and reorganization. The 1919 legislature promptly adopted a new school code placing all non-college education under a newly established state Board of Education. The state's illiteracy program, previously a volunteer effort since its inception in 1915, now became a state-funded program under the Division of Exceptional Education within the new state department. During

Kilby's four-year term, appropriations for schools nearly doubled those from the previous administration.

The governor was also faithful to other platform promises. Funding for public health increased by 50 percent. He presented a workmen's compensation bill to the legislature in 1919, backed by both business and labor, that won speedy enactment in July of that year. The same legislature passed a bond issue of $25 million for road construction. After the state supreme court struck down the law, a special session of the legislature passed it again in 1921, and voters ratified the issue by a margin of five to one.

Kilby's efforts to construct state-owned docks at the port of Mobile ran into tougher opposition. The federal government had urged each coastal state to develop a major dock facility, and Mobile officials and businessmen pushed hard for the project. But voters narrowly defeated such legislation in 1920. Kilby renewed a spirited public campaign in 1922, drawing upon the backing of the powerful president of the Tennessee Coal and Iron and Railroad Company (TCI), George G. Crawford, who realized the potential of Mobile for the export of coal, iron, and steel. This time better-informed voters approved an amendment creating the state docks and a three-man State Docks Commission by a vote of five to one. The $10 million docks opened in 1927 and were among the most modern in the nation.

By 1922 the legislature had passed every major bill proposed by Kilby, an unprecedented cooperation that won praise even from cynical editors who had opposed him in 1918. Kilby left the state treasury in its best condition since before the Civil War. And an official of the Russell Sage Foundation commented at the end of his term that Alabama had advanced "from the rear ranks to the front rank of states of the union in her social progress."[2] He had moved the state from a posture of crisis management to long-range planning.

Amid his many successes Kilby's reputation was marred by two failures. Despite his good intentions, the convict lease system remained largely intact at the end of his term. And those who lived at the bottom of Alabama's industrial ladder did not share the prosperity trickling down from above. In fact industrial workers waged open warfare against what they viewed as a wicked and unjust industrial system.

Economic conditions between 1917 and 1919 crippled industrial workers. Spiraling increases in the cost of living coupled with modest wage increases threatened their standard of living and encouraged the growth of labor unions. In Birmingham iron- and steelworkers struck in September 1919. The Birmingham *Age-Herald* expressed a typical establishment reaction by arguing that the strike was "fomented from the outside by radical leaders" and warned that Alabama was "not ready for a proletariat dictatorship."[3] The strike was poorly coordinated and fizzled after only two weeks. One legislator responded with an antistrike bill fining strikers $1,000 and sending them to jail. His bill passed the legislature by a large margin, but Kilby vetoed it.

The United Mine Workers took advantage of troubled economic conditions to organize a quarter of all Alabama coal miners by 1917. Coal operators resisted the organizing drive, precipitating two strikes by miners, the first in 1919 and the second a year later. The 1919 strike involved about equal numbers of blacks and whites, a total of some 15,000 of the state's 26,000 miners. Kilby refused the request of Jefferson County's sheriff for machine guns and accused coal operators of profiteering. But he also dispatched six companies of the National Guard to protect company property and maintain order. By November operators obtained a federal injunction against strike leaders and broke the strike, and Kilby removed the troops. But the lull was brief. Operators refused to reinstate strike leaders, provoking a second strike in 1920–21. These strikes continued the troubling racial division that had characterized economic conflicts in 1908 and even earlier.

Coal companies refused to institute wage increases and other provisions recommended by the U.S. Bituminous Coal Commission. The Alabama Coal Operators' Association, which represented organized business, denied that it had entered into any agreements with the federal commission and was therefore not bound by its recommendations. Some 11,000 Alabama miners refused to dig coal. Unlike the 1919 strike, the walkout was purely local and tried Kilby's patience. He condemned the strike and sent seven companies of National Guardsmen back to north Alabama. The guard stayed nearly half a year, broke up union meetings, harassed organizers, and generally sided with management. Such favoritism was not surprising because mining companies paid part of the guard's salaries and expenses. One officer resigned, protesting that his commander instructed him to "have your men beat hell out of the agitators . . . every time you catch them out" and promised to pay his fine if he got in trouble.[4]

The 1920 strike introduced a troubling racial dimension to Alabama's economic conflicts, which helped to explain Kilby's hostility as well as lack of public support for organized labor. More than three-fourths of the strikers were blacks. Operators shrewdly aimed their public attacks at the UMW because it included in its membership pledge a promise not to discriminate against a fellow miner because of "creed, color, or nationality." This pledge, the owners claimed, caused the union to practice social equality between the races. Although UMW locals elected some black officers, most white Alabama miners harbored the same racial prejudices as fellow citizens, and many white miners refused to strike.

Exacerbating racial divisions was the fact that most strikebreakers hired to replace the striking miners were black. By the end of the strike a mine force that had been nearly equally white and black in 1919 was three-fourths black.

As the beautiful fall of 1920 gave way to the harsh winter of 1921, striking miners became desperate. Companies evicted them from company houses and built fences around coal camps. Working miners and their families could not leave some camps without written passes. Some 11,000 strikers—and 8,000 wives and more than 21,000 children—crowded into tent cities. The national UMW and sympathetic Alabamians donated $70,000 and surplus army tents. Violence became common. In September striking miners and deputy sheriffs fought a pitched battle near Patton in Walker County. A general manager of the Corona Coal Company and a deputy sheriff were killed, and three deputies were seriously wounded when they attacked houses and a union hall where miners had taken refuge. Company thugs brutally beat the publisher of a prolabor newspaper, and retaliating strikers fired on trains carrying strikebreakers and dynamited company houses.

Gradually company policy strangled the strike. Strikebreakers restored near-normal coal production. Armed guards prevented farmers from carrying provisions to strikers and closed company commissaries to them. National UMW relief funds dried up and strikers' families froze in the cold January weather. The strike finally ended in failure in February 1921. TCI and other companies published the names of UMW miners so they could be blacklisted and denied employment. Many union families, especially blacks, left north Alabama for the Kentucky and West Virginia coalfields, where they incidentally spread their folk music, especially "blues" songs born from generations of such defeats. Miners deserted the UMW en masse, and membership dropped from 25 percent of Alabama miners in 1917 to 1 percent in 1929. In 1920 nearly 25,000 black miners belonged to the UMW nationally, and most of them lived in West Virginia and Alabama. By 1927 the union retained only 5,000 black miners.

Other union drives fared no better than those of mine workers. Efforts by the state unit of the American Federation of Labor to organize Jefferson County schoolteachers failed and raised furious public outcries. A three-month strike by railroad employees in 1922 idled some 7,000 Birmingham railroad workers and resulted in violence when the lines hired strikebreakers. Governor Kilby summoned the National Guard to Birmingham for the third time in four years. One man was killed and others were injured before the guard restored order. Again the union lost, and fewer than a third of the strikers were able to reclaim their jobs. In fact the intensive efforts to organize Birmingham district

420

industrial workers between 1920 and 1930 failed entirely. On the eve of the Great Depression industrial unionism in north Alabama was weaker than when the decade began, and many of the area's best labor leaders were blacklisted and working in other states. Although Governor Kilby had sympathized with efforts to obtain workmen's compensation and fair treatment, his business background made him unsympathetic to strikes and collective bargaining.

William W. ("Plain Bill") Brandon, who had run second to Kilby in 1918, won the governorship in 1922. Continuing prosperity fueled tax revenues and allowed additional spending on roads, public health, and education. But Governor Kilby's long-range initiatives, just coming on line, were so well planned that Brandon's administration was little more than that of a caretaker. No significant legislation emanated from his term, and that fact fit his status quo philosophy of government quite well. No innovator, he in fact rolled back at least one reform of the Kilby era.

Under terms of legislation passed during the Kilby administration, the state withdrew convicts from the lumber and naval stores industries because of abuses to prisoners but left them in coal mines. Governor Brandon argued that the state had no way of housing the convicts adequately, and he recommended extending the lease system until January 1927. His only change was to lease the mines instead of the convicts. Operating in this fashion, Brandon placed convicts in the Belle Ellen, Flat Top, Banner, and Aldrich mines.

This slightly altered procedure did not improve treatment of prisoners. State guards dispensed the same brutality as had private company guards. In reaction, five hundred convicts at Banner Mine rebelled over abusive treatment in September 1923 and briefly held mine officials hostage. A furious Governor Brandon announced reestablishment of the policy of whipping prisoners and defended the entire convict lease system, which generated $3.3 million in revenue for the state during his four-year term. Following Brandon's announcement (the restored lash was a deadly instrument), the rebellion ended and the leaders were captured and whipped, one so badly that he required hospitalization. Brandon refused to allow an investigation of conditions at the mines and blocked an inquiry by a Jefferson County grand jury.

This time reform would not die easily. Unlike the late nineteenth century when nearly all convicts were black, by the 1920s a growing percentage of abused convicts were white. Former governor Kilby called Brandon's reinstitution of legalized beatings "barbarism that no civilized government should sanction and no enlightened people should tolerate."[5] He also regretted that he had not entirely abolished convict leasing during his administration. Ministers, led by pastors of St. John's

Episcopal Church in Mobile and First Baptist in Montgomery, condemned convict leasing. Progressive journalists joined the chorus of criticism, as did suffragist Pattie Ruffner Jacobs of Birmingham (a vice-president of the national League of Women Voters), who led the state LWV to lobby for abolition of the system. The legislature remained impervious to such moral outrage, deploring continued attacks by "certain newspapers, public agitators and ill-advised and misled citizens."[6] Brandon also remained oblivious to such protests and even advocated extending convict leasing.

Perhaps the material interests of the state would have prevailed over its moral sentiments had it not been for a major scandal in 1924. James Knox was a West Virginia native who had been convicted of forging a thirty-dollar check in Mobile and was sent to Kilby Prison. Shortly thereafter he was transferred to Flat Top Prison Mine, where he died a few days later. Prison officials filed an official report listing cause of death as suicide. But Knox's family contacted Alabama's attorney general, Harwell G. Davis, who launched an investigation. He discovered that Knox had been beaten with a heavy steel wire and then dipped into a laundry vat full of hot water, where he had a heart attack and died. The national press picked up Davis's report of the affair. The Washington *Post* editorialized that the honor of the state was at stake, and the New York *World* sent a reporter to Alabama to write a story on the death of Knox and the last state in the Union to retain the convict lease system. Attorney General Davis turned his report over to a Jefferson County grand jury, which indicted warden Charles R. Davis and four of his associates. Although a jury acquitted them, one of the defendants encountered the attorney general, whom they blamed for their trouble, on the streets of Birmingham and beat him. This attack on Harwell Davis, a respected Black Belt attorney and active Baptist layman, shocked the state more than had the national media denunciation. It was within this context that Bibb Graves made total abolition of convict leasing a major plank in his 1926 gubernatorial campaign despite its defense by business interests, Governor Brandon, and the legislature.

Graves was a native of Hope Hull in Montgomery County. After taking a degree in civil engineering from the University of Texas, he completed law school at Yale. He served two terms as a legislator from his home county and in 1916 won election as chairman of the State Democratic Executive Committee. Following the pattern of so many before him, he lost his first race for governor, placing second to Brandon in 1922. In 1926 he launched his campaign with pledges to abolish convict leasing, establish a minimum seven-month school term statewide, increase funding for education, improve social services and highways, and enforce prohibition. The coalition backing him included Evangelical Protestants attracted to his prohibition views, the Ku Klux Klan to which he belonged, organized labor, veterans of World War I, and educators. Black Belt planters, Big Mule interests, and Governor Brandon backed Lieutenant Governor Charles S. McDowell, Jr., of Eufaula, and Graves actually entered the race a dark horse with almost no support from big city daily newspapers. But his shrewdly constructed coalition and his speaking skills won him large majorities in rural north Alabama, among Klansmen and laborers in towns and cities, and among veterans and teachers statewide. He ran well in every area of the state except the Black Belt.

Graves had barely taken his oath of office when in February 1927 he removed state convicts from the mines. He proposed a bill officially ending the system in Alabama, and both houses agreed to a compromise date of June 30, 1928. The Knox affair was still on everyone's minds, and public outrage made this decision popular. Graves transferred convicts to state road construction and put them to work at the two prison cotton mills or at making auto tags and road signs. But before he left office an avalanche of prisoners entered the penal system for making illicit alcohol. As a consequence the five state prisons overflowed. Kilby Prison, the new facility near Montgomery, was designed to house 900 but contained 1,400 in 1931.

The state's urban industrial prosperity continued during the first part of the Graves administration. New industries located in the state and the tax reform package produced additional revenue for state services. Graves also persuaded the legislature to pass higher taxes on tobacco products and corporations, the proceeds of which funded educational improvements.

Despite better support during the Kilby years, education in the state still experienced real problems: illiteracy rates were high, teacher salaries low, expenditures per child inadequate, and poorer counties could not supplement state funding the way richer counties could. Graves addressed these problems at a special session of the legislature in December 1926. His educational reform package passed in January 1927. It called for $600,000 in emergency funds for schools. It also proposed a four-year appropriation of $25 million, the largest by far in state history (total educational expenditures during the Brandon administration had amounted to only $9.9 million). Graves persuaded the Alabama Education Association and the presidents of the University of Alabama, Auburn University, and Alabama College to coordinate their programs and eliminate wasteful duplication. With this agreement in hand, the legislature passed his budget in August. In 1929 he upgraded the four normal colleges at Florence, Troy, Jacksonville, and Livingston to the status of state teachers' colleges and empowered each to grant the bachelor of science degree. Like Kilby, he pushed through a complete revision of the state education code. He added the Division of Negro Education in 1927 with a black agent partially supported by the state and partially by the philanthropic Rosenwald Fund. Another black agent in the new department received his entire salary from the state. Graves continued consolidating one-room rural schools into larger and more efficient units. Teacher salaries also increased during his term, from an average of $689 a year in 1926–27 to $761 in 1929–1930.

In his inaugural address Graves emphasized the importance of all the state's human resources, not just education. Under his stimulation the legislature authorized construction of a new 225-bed hospital for blacks at Mount Vernon, a 200-bed unit at Bryce Hospital in Tuscaloosa, a new water sprinkler system to prevent fires at Bryce, and considerable improvements at what was then called the Blind Institute at Talladega. The state also doubled appropriations to the Child Welfare Department. He expanded the Health Department's operations into fifty-four of Alabama's sixty-seven counties, reaching nearly 90 percent of the state's population. The Brandon administration had spent $820,000 on public health; the Graves administration spent $2.25 million. Graves also implemented $30 million bond issues for road and toll bridge construction.

Unfortunately, the collapse of the economy beginning in 1929 dried up revenues at precisely the time that Alabama was rapidly expanding social and health services, education, roads, and the number of state employees. Defenders of the status quo opposed Graves's administration throughout his term, and newspaper editors began referring to his "orgies of extravagance and waste." The editor of the Montgomery *Advertiser*, no friend of the governor, reluctantly concluded that "Bibb Graves makes a good governor, but an expensive one."[7] The governor also failed in his attempts to reapportion the state legislature and to obtain biennial legislative sessions.

Despite such defeats, the state made remarkable strides in every category of public life. Although the last state to do so, Alabama had finally abolished the convict lease system after four decades of agitation. The Child Welfare Department, begun in 1919 with a budget of $12,400, received $450,000 during the Graves years. By 1927 all but one county conducted some child welfare services, and fifty-three counties employed a social worker to deliver these services. Child employment had plunged. A report by the Brookings Institution at the end of Graves's term praised the state's public health program and reported that Alabama spent a quarter more per capita on public health than the national average. But perhaps education had made the greatest strides. Once the illiteracy program became a state responsibility in 1919, significant improvement began. In 1920 rates of white illiteracy stood at 16 and 15 percent in Geneva and Coffee counties and as high as 15 and 14 percent in Cherokee and Cleburne counties. For the state, 57,200 white adults could not read in any language, accounting for a little more than 8 percent of the white voting-age population. But for blacks, illiteracy statewide in 1920 was nearly 39 percent.

Opportunity Schools offered instruction to adults age twenty-one or older or to teenagers between ages sixteen and twenty who had completed less than four grades. Officials located the schools where a minimum of fifteen people promised to enroll. In farming areas the schools met twenty hours a week in four-hour sessions for six weeks during the winter. In large cities the school term extended from October to April with three two-hour meetings a week. The University of Alabama in 1926 conducted a conference to instruct teachers of illiterates. Home demonstration agents from Auburn University wrote simple instruction booklets explaining how to install a water system or bake bread. Other supplemental "texts" included Sunday school literature, newspapers, and public signs. Teachers reported individual triumphs from around the state. In Tuscaloosa fifteen people enrolled the first night, but they could do little because only one brought a lantern and a miner's carbide lamp. The next night one student brought lanterns and others supplied oil. By the end of the first week twenty-six students had enrolled and by the end of the second, forty-two. "Tonight we had our regular classes with lectures on geography and health," the two teachers reported, and "we had a very hot discussion in geography about the world's being flat." Two other teachers reported: "Work seems to be the only objection the people have for not attending school. My, but these people are slaves to work" (sixty-five- to seventy-hour work weeks were common). An illiterate woman from Cleburne County spent two years in an Opportunity School, became a school trustee, and wrote her gratitude in careful if incorrect English in December 1926. She rejoiced that she could read the letters her children sent her and books impossible to understand before: "if this school had not come about I would not learn to read those Books. Sometime I cry when I think how long I stayed in this old world and could not read or write."[8] Birmingham's Opportunity Schools enrolled more than 1,000 students in 1926. Cleburne County enrolled 321, Cullman County 294, Jackson County 216, and Covington County 198.

Traditional schools improved as well. Given conditions in 1918, schools could hardly go anyplace but up. Alabama's educational system ranked fourth from last in one national survey, ahead of only Arkansas, Mississippi, and South Carolina. Nearly two out of three white students attending rural schools studied in one- or two-teacher schools. Seven of ten rural teachers held the two lowest grades of certification, compared

Old one-room schoolhouse, Gum Springs District, Clay County, built about 1892 (Courtesy of the Alabama Department of Archives and History)

to only three in ten of the state's urban teachers. Only one white student in eleven attending rural schools was in high school compared to one in six in towns. The state provided a disproportionate share of funding, 53 percent compared to 47 percent local. The average school term for white rural schools in 1919–20 was 123 days; for white urban schools it was 174 days. The average for black urban schools was 170 days; in rural Alabama it was only 87 days. Over the preceding five years the average length of school terms in urban areas had actually declined. One in eight teachers possessed inadequate credentials, but "a poorly prepared teacher was deemed better than no teacher."[9]

So bad were conditions in fall 1919 that more than five hundred white schools and a similar number of black ones were unable to open because no teachers were available. The reason for the shortage was simple: teachers could hardly survive on the salaries. For the 1919–20 school year, white male teachers in rural schools earned $630 and white females $430. Black male and female colleagues earned $206 and $167. White male urban teachers earned $1,481, white females $762. In the state capital of Montgomery that year 1,000 children attended school part-time because of inadequate facilities and teacher shortages. Between 1904 and 1920 the city had erected only one small elementary school. Sidney Lanier High School, with a capacity of 700, enrolled 1,012 students.

The First World War and the Kilby administration changed these wretched conditions, though the transformation took time. War generated tremendous public concern about educational inadequacies and led to legislation establishing the county unit of school administration with a county superintendent and a new three-mill district tax. By January 1920 voters in every county except Lowndes had ratified the new three-mill local tax. Thanks to Kilby's reforms, white high school enrollment exploded from 27,700 in 1918–19 to 45,500 in 1921–22. The school dropout rate also declined.

The Bibb Graves administration brought further improvements. When Graves took office, forty-four counties had school terms shorter than seven months. His "unified program" to upgrade education increased the school term to at least that length in every county. By 1929 Alabama had nearly 600 consolidated white schools, a reform made possible both by increased funding during the Kilby and Graves administrations and by improvements in state and county roads.

Even with all these improvements the state's public schools entered the depression with serious inadequacies. A 1925 survey revealed that Alabama spent only 33 percent of the national average on its schools. In 1928–29 only a little more than half the state's teachers possessed standard credentials. That same year urban elementary teachers earned 46 percent more than their rural counterparts, and urban high school teachers earned 23 percent more. In towns, 28 percent of elementary teachers had completed four or more years of college; in rural areas only 7 percent had done so.

As bad as discrepancies were between rural and urban schools, differences by gender and race were as bad or worse. In 1922 white male teachers averaged salaries of $666 a year, white females $628. But that same year black male teachers earned an average $248, black female teachers $299. In 1924 blacks composed approximately 40 percent of Alabama's population, but the state spent $1.4 million on their schools compared to $13.1 million on white schools. Throughout the decade Opportunity Schools for blacks had to raise much of their funding from the local black community or from Northern philanthropic foundations.

But even education for blacks improved. Labor shortages due to the war and an exodus of blacks to the North provided leverage to black leaders to demand better schools. The Birmingham school board built several new schools for blacks despite protests from labor unions and that city's powerful Ku Klux Klan. In 1923, 70 percent of the city's black students studied in older, inadequate wooden buildings; by 1931 only 33 percent remained in such structures. In 1916 only a quarter of black

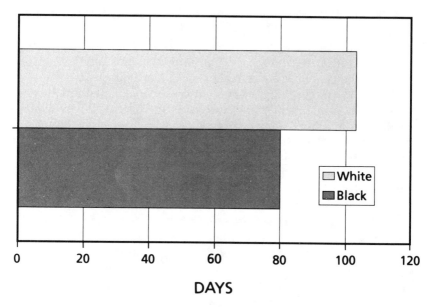

DAYS

Length of Average School Term, 1922

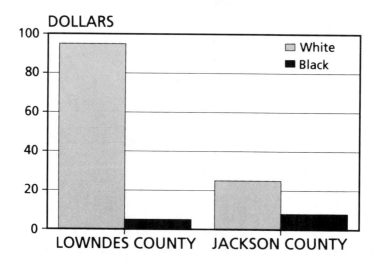

Average Per Child School Expenditure in a Black Belt County and a Hill County in 1930

students attended city schools; by 1931 two-thirds did so. Black teacher salaries doubled along with white salaries, but at least they did not lose ground compared to their white colleagues. And in some areas black education closed the gap a bit during the decade. Per capita expenditures for black students actually increased relative to whites. Even black educators considered the 1920s a period of substantial educational progress in Birmingham. Unfortunately, improvement came much slower for blacks in rural Alabama, and in 1928 the state still had nearly 62,000 illiterate black children.

One reform that made possible the consolidation of rural schools was the good roads movement. The number of motor vehicles registered in Alabama increased steadily from 3,385 in 1912 to 74,637 in 1920 and to 277,146 in 1930 before declining to 206,361 in the deep depression year of 1933. Early lobbying by the Alabama Good Roads Association resulted in the creation of the state Highway Department in 1911. Its function was to build and maintain roads, prepare highway maps, and promote, maintain, and publicize motorized transportation. Unfortunately, many counties were no more willing to promote county roads than they were county schools, so rural roads rapidly deteriorated. In 1916 Alabama's senator John H. Bankhead, Sr., had sponsored a federal highway law appropriating $200 million to match state highway funds. The $25 million highway bond issue passed during Kilby's administration in 1921 (the motto for the ratification campaign was "Get Alabama Out of the Mud") provided Alabama's match necessary to obtain federal funds, as did a comparable bond issue passed in 1927. The legislature financed both bond issues with license and gasoline taxes. As a consequence Alabama obtained some $50 million in federal highway funds between 1916 and 1934. When the building program began, the state contained 55,000 miles of rural roads, only 5,000 of which were hard-surfaced. By 1930 some 20,000 of 68,000 miles of rural roads were surfaced. State expenditures for roads amounted to only $1 million in 1921 but peaked at $20 million in 1928 before sharply declining during the depression.

Although gubernatorial politics dominated the course of state affairs, other races and patterns reflected fundamental changes in political ideology and opinion. No political decision occurred without some reference to race. Even though politicians had erected an elaborate structure of disfranchisement that kept all but a handful of blacks from voting, the racial issue would not disappear from political discourse. An incident in Tuskegee demonstrates the pervasiveness of racial politics.

In 1921 Tuskegee mayor William Varner noticed an announcement about plans to construct a new hospital for black veterans. He contacted Tuskegee Institute president Robert R. Moton to suggest that he use his contacts in Washington to acquire the hospital for Tuskegee. Moton agreed and successfully recruited a complex of twenty-seven buildings by 1923. No sooner had the hospital opened than Varner and Moton engaged in a power struggle over staffing. Tuskegee whites demanded an all-white staff, while Moton firmly insisted it be all black. Using his contacts with President Warren G. Harding, Moton won the skirmish. The presence of so many highly trained black physicians, clinicians, administrators, and other professionals frightened local whites. In fact, the prospect of aggressive, competent blacks unwilling to accept traditional racial patterns was a specter capable of terrifying Alabama whites for decades to come. The Tuskegee affair in the early 1920s was merely the first shot in a long battle.

Nor would white Alabamians passively accept any others whom they considered to be "uppity" people or provocateurs. Even folks minding their own business who were in some way strange or alien to Alabama culture provoked reaction during the 1920s. It had not always been so. Racial relations were usually stable when blacks "recognized their place," and whites paternalistically protected them from the violent excesses of white rabble-rousers. People with different religions and cultures often lived peaceably with their neighbors. Montgomery and Birmingham elected Catholic mayors early in the century, and Mobile's Catholic population often dominated that city's political and social life. But the war had released strange currents, which now raged out of control in Alabama.

Of the many nativist organizations that flourished in the state early in the century, the most important was the Ku Klux Klan. Reborn from its half-century slumber in 1915, the Klan of the 1920s differed markedly from the Klans of the 1860s and 1960s. When the First World War ended, the tidal wave of immigration from southern and eastern Europe renewed. Before Congress had time to fashion restrictive legislation, native-born Americans became alarmed at the influx of Catholic and Jewish immigrants. Nearly two thousand Italians had already settled at Fairfield and Ensley to work for TCI. Now in their wake came more Italians along with Greeks, Slovaks, Russians, Czechs, Poles, and a dozen other nationalities. Speaking strange languages and practicing what Americans of British ancestry considered bizarre, superstitious religions, the "aliens" seemed to threaten traditional values. Unaccustomed to a prohibitionist ethos, they made, sold, and consumed alcoholic beverages in violation of prohibition laws. In this way immigrants threatened the central moral reform of the Progressive Era. Furthermore they corrupted politics by joining urban political machines that provided social services in return for their votes.

Immigrants threatened to erode the status of blue-collar workers by taking jobs for lower wages as well as working as strikebreakers. Politically active women disliked patriarchal immigrant cultures and their support of corrupt urban political machines that winked at prostitution and illegal liquor traffic. Labor unionists resented the threat they represented to jobs and the way they undermined wage scales. Evangelical Protestants resented their papist views and the Catholic heritage of religious persecution. Nativist Americans opposed their strange languages and customs. Taken all together the resentments represented a potent political force waiting for an organizer. William Joseph Simmons and Dr. Hiram Wesley Evans were the right men, at the right place, at the right time.

William J. Simmons, who presided as spiritual midwife to the Klan in 1915, was born at Munford, Alabama, in 1880. Following an unsuccessful career in the Methodist ministry, Simmons turned to organizing fraternal clubs. From its birthplace at Stone Mountain, Georgia, the Klan expanded first into Alabama, then into other Southern states, and finally to other regions. The first Alabama Klan both in chronology and in importance was Birmingham's Robert E. Lee Klan, organized in 1916, followed by the Klans in Bessemer and Montgomery.

The Klan grew slowly until 1921 when Imperial Wizard Simmons launched a membership drive in Birmingham with huge rallies. A spectacular at Edgewood Park in Homewood during 1923 featured swimming, fireworks, barbecue, stunt flying, and a concert by the Chattanooga Klan band. The Klan initiated 1,500 new members that night while an estimated 25,000 curious onlookers observed the ceremony. The new Imperial Wizard, Dr. Hiram Wesley Evans, a native of Ashland in Clay County, presided. A Vanderbilt graduate and Dallas, Texas, dentist, he did not fit the stereotype that many had of the Klan—racist "poor white trash"—nor did one of the initiates that night at Edgewood Park: young lawyer, Baptist Sunday school teacher, and future Supreme Court justice Hugo L. Black. In fact, one brief list of known Birmingham Klansmen included carpenters, plumbers, merchants, a police sergeant, and a former schoolteacher. By 1924 the alluring mixture of racism, nativism, moralism, fraternalism, and ritualism had attracted 10,000 members to the Robert E. Lee Klan, including many of Birmingham's leading businessmen and politicians. A women's auxiliary, called Kamelias, flourished as well. All the Birmingham Klans together enrolled an estimated 18,000 of the city's 32,000 registered voters by 1924, including the sheriff, at least two city judges, and probably a majority of the city's Protestant ministers. It elected its entire slate to the city commission in 1925. The following year it played a major role in the election of Bibb Graves (who belonged to the Montgomery Klan) as governor and Hugo Black to the U.S. Senate. Statewide Klan membership reached an esti-

A 1920s Ku Klux Klan parade in Montgomery, where future Governor Bibb Graves was a prominent member (Courtesy of the Alabama Department of Archives and History)

mated 95,000 members, and it even produced its own multicolored journal, the *TWK Monthly.*

Beginning in 1921 individual Klansmen, often without the knowledge or support of fellow Klansmen, began enforcing their own moral standards with whip and club. They lashed a Greek artist in Clay County for marrying an American woman. They flogged a white couple for "friendly relations with Negroes" and alleged miscegenation. In 1925 the Klan launched a campaign to stop prostitution in Birmingham. Its members raided brothels and roadhouses and even a prominent Chinese restaurant, Joy Young's, which they accused of serving liquor. Carousing in automobiles also offended their sensibilities, and Klansmen began patrolling roads and routing parking couples. In Troy, Klansmen reported to their parents the names of teenagers they caught parking. On Red Mountain overlooking the sparkling lights of Birmingham, robed Klansmen flashed lights on occupants of parked cars and ordered them to move along. They kidnapped a white divorcée, stripped her to the waist, tied her to a tree, and whipped her savagely. Such tactics by the Klan offended decent people. Some clergymen, bar associations, chambers of commerce, and editors began to denounce Klan depredations.

Chief among the Klan's newspaper critics was the Hall family. One of the most successful journalist families in the nation, family members began, operated, or edited the Dothan *Eagle,* the Dothan *Journal,* the Alexander City *Outlook,* the Anniston *Star,* and the Montgomery *Advertiser.* Defenders of both the fiscal and the political status quo, they

432

particularly disliked political demagoguery, religious bigotry, and populistic causes. Julian Hall refused to join the Klan when the Houston County superintendent of education tried to recruit him and became a vigorous foe of all things Klan. He used his Dothan *Eagle* to denounce the Bibb Graves administration as a "wild debauchery of spending by a be-Kluxed Governor and a be-Kluxed legislature." On another occasion he referred to the administration as a "callous gang of third-rate lawyers and backwoods politicians."[10]

Grover C. Hall, Sr., another member of the dynastic family, became editor of the influential Montgomery *Advertiser* in 1926 and began writing editorials against the Klan almost immediately. A series of editorials attacking floggings and racial and religious intolerance, written in 1927, won Hall the Pulitzer Prize in journalism.

Other forces also undermined Alabama's Klan. Organized labor grew wary of the secret empire. In 1928 Mabel Jones West, president of the Alabama Woman's League for White Supremacy, resigned from the Klan, blasted its violence, and denounced its attempt to control state politics. Emboldened city officials began to prosecute flogging cases; scandals involving national Klan officials shook their credibility among rank-and-file members; and the leadership of Alabama Klan officials in bolting the Democratic party and supporting a Republican for president in 1928 further discredited the organization. Membership and influence peaked in the 1926 state elections, a bit later than in other Southern states, then dropped sharply to an estimated 10,400 members by the end of 1927 and to only 5,500 a year later. Although the Klan provided a vehicle for the political ambition and racism of many white Alabamians, it also allowed plain white voters to achieve a substantial amount of political power.

The Klan constituted only one of several new elements in Alabama politics. Women voters formed another. Alabamians have not been very hospitable to women's issues, but individual Alabama women have been remarkably prominent in various women's movements. Alva Belmont, a native of Mobile, was the major source of financial support for all three major American women's suffrage organizations that competed for leadership between 1900 and 1920. Pattie Ruffner Jacobs of Birmingham was one of the most respected orators and strategists within the largest of the three, the National American Woman Suffrage Association. In the early 1920s she became vice-president and chief congressional strategist of the national League of Women Voters. Although Alabama males refused to extend women the right to vote, an estimated 123,000 white women and 100 black women registered to vote for the November 1920 presidential election.

After women achieved suffrage, the most important women's political organization was the Alabama League of Women Voters, begun in April 1920. Members elected prominent and wealthy Birmingham suffragist Lillian Roden Bowron president and Dixie Bibb Graves vice-president. Pattie Jacobs held no office in the Alabama league but remained its most influential member. The organization championed liberal causes such as the League of Nations, raising the female age of consent to marry from fourteen to eighteen, increasing teacher salaries, abolishing the death penalty, establishing the eight-hour workday and the forty-hour work-week for women, and providing vocational and physical education to all female students. The league also conducted citizenship schools to educate women about public issues, voter registration and voting procedures, and American history and government. It worked closely with the Kilby administration, particularly aiding the work of Lorraine B. Tunstall-Bush, a league member and head of the Child Welfare Department. Kilby welcomed their efforts on behalf of reform and made Alabama one of the first states to accept federal money to implement the Sheppard-Towner Act for Maternal and Infant Care. By 1923 Alabama supported from federal funds thirty-three nurses to care for mothers and infants. Many women played roles in the Kilby administration, including Tunstall-Bush and Augusta Martin in the Child Welfare Department and Sarah E. Luther, who headed the Division of Exceptional Education under the state Board of Education.

In 1922 another prominent politician tipped his hat to the women. Bibb Graves in his first race for governor spoke to a Mobile County LWV meeting. Although he lost that race, he maintained a strong connection to the league through his wife and won considerable support from members in 1926.

The league rapidly increased its membership in the 1920s. Its strongest chapter, in Jefferson County, peaked at two thousand members in 1924; the Montgomery league reached half that total, and smaller but active leagues functioned in Anniston, Sheffield, Grand Bay, Auburn, Tuscaloosa, and Bessemer, as well as in Dallas, Baldwin, and Sumter counties. Collegiate chapters began at Huntingdon and Alabama colleges and at the University of Alabama. In 1924 Pattie Jacobs resigned her national office at the urging of Eleanor Roosevelt to serve on the national Democratic Platform Committee, which she used as a forum for the LWV legislative agenda. In Alabama Jacobs personally inspected convict mining camps, publicized in newspaper articles the wretched conditions she found there, and supported legislative attempts to abolish the system. Although she and the league failed with Governor Brandon, they had better success with Bibb Graves. In 1927 they opened a state office in Montgomery to serve as a base for lobbying. When Graves signed the bill finally abolishing convict leasing in Alabama, he presented the pen he used to the Alabama League of Women Voters.

Women won other political victories as well, some philosophical, others personal. Due partly to efforts by the bipartisan state LWV, Alabama's vote in the 1924 presidential election increased to more than 54 percent from only 30 percent in 1920. Two years later the Mobile LWV urged Governor Brandon to commute the death sentence of a black man who had murdered a Wetumpka judge. Grover Hall, Sr., of the Montgomery *Advertiser* endorsed the request, and Brandon responded by commuting the sentence to life in prison. In 1921 the Birmingham league invited the public safety commissioner, who was seeking reelection, to speak. After his address the women began to grill him about what he was doing to control prostitution and the Ku Klux Klan in the city. They fired question after question in what one reporter called the most intense grilling he had ever witnessed. Although all three female candidates lost their bids for city offices in 1921, the league defeated every incumbent and elected its entire slate of endorsed males to the city commission. One newspaper critical of the league announced the results of city elections by stating simply: "the women did it."[11] The following year, 1922, a number of league women ran statewide. Only one triumphed, but what a sweet victory that was. Hattie Hooker Wilkins of Selma, a forty-seven-year-old suffragist and civic and church leader, beat the incumbent male to win a seat in the state house. The man she defeated was initially the leading legislative advocate of women's suffrage in the 1915 legislature. Then he betrayed the women by reversing himself only days before the final vote. As a member of the house, Wilkins promoted legislation on behalf of health, education, and children's issues.

League membership and influence peaked the same year as the Klan's in 1926 and began a steady decline until the organization was completely moribund by the 1930s. Like the Klan, the league lost much of its influence because of the 1928 presidential election. It was as fiercely partisan on behalf of Democrat Alfred E. Smith as the Klan was for Herbert Hoover. This partisanship hurt the league because it included many wealthy Republican women as well as independent Democrats who could not abide a Roman Catholic presidential candidate.

The first statewide politician to experience the brunt of the new politics was Alabama's U.S. senator Oscar W. Underwood. One of the most influential members of the Democratic party, Underwood was a presidential candidate in 1912. He was a states' righter who opposed federal women's suffrage, child labor, and prohibition enactments as well as most legislation advocated by organized labor. Entrenched in his political base at Birmingham, he had won several terms in Congress with the backing of the city's Big Mules as well as Black Belt planters, antiprohibitionists, and small businessmen. When he announced for reelection to the Senate on the last day of 1919, his reelection seemed a sure bet. But in February 1920 the American Federation of Labor announced that Underwood was one of six U.S. senators with the worst labor records. Unions targeted them for defeat. Birmingham-area industrial workers, most of them experiencing financial problems because of inflation and some already on strike, organized against Underwood. Jefferson County unionists estimated their registration drive had quadrupled the union vote between 1919 and 1920. Mobile-area labor unions launched a poll tax drive that added 1,400 laboring people to the city's voting lists.

Unionists found an unlikely champion in Lycurgus Breckenridge Musgrove. Despite the liability of a name that sounded like a Roman proconsul and despite a fortune earned in banking and coal mining, L. B. Musgrove proved to be a formidable candidate. He possessed a solid reputation as a Methodist layman and was a past national chairman of the Anti-Saloon League. He had supported a progressive candidate against Underwood in 1914 and favored such liberal causes as federal aid to education, women's suffrage, the right of labor to join unions, and farm extension programs. In 1920 he won support from farmers' organizations, unions, women suffragists, prohibitionists, and even the Klan, which called Underwood a friend of Catholicism.

Musgrove made a powerful impression as a campaigner, which was not Underwood's best skill. A bachelor and storyteller renowned for his humor, Musgrove was famous also for his possum dinners. He liked to recount one particularly memorable dinner he gave at the Hotel Malborough in New York City where he always stayed when in the city on business. He invited a number of business acquaintances for dinner, then sent ten possums and a cook from his native Jasper to New York to prepare the meal properly for his wealthy (and perhaps anxiety-ridden) guests.

At first Underwood tended his Senate duties in Washington and ignored Musgrove. But his strategists began to warn him about the incipient rebellion back home. One aide tried to explain the bizarre coalition aligned against him: "the prohibitionists, the Unionists, the Suffragettes, the Bolshevists and where they could be prevailed upon, the pulpit."[12]

Underwood heeded their pleas, returning to the state and launching a furious campaign against what he described as labor upheaval and radical anarchy. He warned farm leaders and businessmen of an imminent labor union takeover of the state, a theme that usually played well in Alabama politics. In 1920 the violent north Alabama coal strike gave the charge larger credibility than it otherwise would have had. Urban newspapers endorsed him, and he narrowly escaped an upset, beating Musgrove by a vote of 69,000 to 61,000 but losing his home county of

Jefferson for the only time in his career. He also lost most of north Alabama. Although the union effort failed to unseat Underwood, it elected two members of the Birmingham Board of Education and re-elected prounion congressman George Huddleston, Sr.

Musgrove and Underwood fought another round in their decade-long conflict in 1924. Underwood made a second run at the presidency that year. Representing the Southern wing of the Democratic party, he launched a risky speaking tour in 1923, attacking the Ku Klux Klan in speeches across the nation. The national press praised his courageous stand, but the Klan denounced him as the "Jew, jug, and Jesuit" candidate (Klansmen preferred their alliteration with the letter *K*, but *J* would also do). Unfortunately the attacks on the Klan that made the Alabamian respectable in the North hurt him badly in Southern presidential primaries. The Klan turned out its members to vote against him, and in Alabama Musgrove entered the Democratic primary against him. The Great Commoner William Jennings Bryan campaigned for Musgrove, calling Underwood a wet and a Wall Street reactionary; but this time Underwood mobilized his business and planter backing for an easy victory with 65,000 votes to Musgrove's 37,000. Underwood lost every other Southern state due partly to solid Klan opposition and limped into the Democratic National Convention one of sixteen candidates who deadlocked the proceedings for 103 ballots, the longest nominating ballot in history. He tried to persuade the convention to denounce the Klan openly by name, but he lost even that battle. Dispirited and disappointed, Underwood decided not to risk Klan wrath again and retired in 1926, setting the stage for another showdown between the old patrician forces and the new politics.

Underwood's retirement opened the way for every Democratic heavyweight in the state. Because no candidate would enjoy the advantage of incumbency, former governor Thomas Kilby, Musgrove, John H. Bankhead, Jr. (son of a former U.S. senator), and young Birmingham lawyer and Klan member Hugo L. Black entered the race, along with others. The Klan, most prohibitionists and suffragists, and most of organized labor endorsed Graves for governor and Black for senator. Both won. Jubilant Klansmen celebrated, but their 1926 victories proved to be the high watermark of the "invisible empire" in Alabama. Paradoxically, the Klan had provided the mechanism by which plain whites had installed their champions in both the governorship and the U.S. Senate at the same time, an unprecedented development in post-Reconstruction Alabama politics.

Given the volatile and changing politics of the 1920s, it is appropriate that the decade should have ended with the most divisive campaign in years. The 1928 Democratic convention nominated Governor Alfred E.

Smith of New York for president. No candidate other than a resurrected Thaddeus Stevens could have worse offended Alabama Democrats. Smith was a Roman Catholic and a son of immigrants, and he opposed prohibition, was tied to New York City's Tammany Hall political machine, and understood next to nothing about rural farm people. Even before Smith's selection in summer 1928, Alabama Democrats made it clear that he was unacceptable.

Smith's nomination split Alabama's Democrats and was the harbinger of a shift toward the Republican party. Before 1928 the GOP in Alabama primarily consisted of two groups: blacks who attributed their emancipation to the party, and hill country whites who had opposed secession and Black Belt Democratic rule of the state. But in 1928 many suburbanites, Evangelical Protestants, and Klansmen began moving into the GOP. The Great Depression and Franklin D. Roosevelt's popularity obscured this weakening of Democratic party ties in Alabama, but the return of normality in the 1940s would demonstrate that many 1928 bolters never again felt comfortable in the Democratic house of their fathers.

Hardly had the embittered Democratic electors returned from their convention in Houston than unhappy party members held a mass meeting on August 13, 1928, in Birmingham. Among the hundreds of rebellious Democrats who attended were large delegations from the Women's Christian Temperance Union, the Anti-Saloon League, and the Ku Klux Klan, a coalition now familiar in the new politics of the 1920s. Judge Horace Wilkinson of Birmingham, a Klansman and close associate of Governor Bibb Graves, offered a resolution to create an Alabama Conference of Anti-Smith Democrats. The meeting elected Judge Hugh A. Locke of Birmingham, a prominent Methodist layman and member of the State Democratic Executive Committee, as chairman and director of Republican Herbert Hoover's campaign in Alabama. The Reverend Bob Jones, an independent Baptist evangelist, inflamed the gathering by warning of the immigrant menace to traditional American values. Dr. A. J. Barton, head of the Southern Baptist Social Service Committee, praised the prohibition views of Herbert Hoover and denounced the "wet" Al Smith. Those who attended the meeting included a number of prominent Methodist and Baptist pastors as well as a number of state appointees of the Graves administration, a veteran coalition that began in the anti-Underwood campaign of 1920 and held together throughout the decade. The one new element to this now-familiar alignment was its alliance with Republicans. Horace Wilkinson negotiated a bizarre agreement with state Republican leaders to name anti-Smith Democrats as Hoover electors. In the ensuing campaign Republicans played a minor role compared to Democrats in rebellion against their own party's nominee.

438

Although Evangelicals, prohibitionists, and Klansmen took leading roles in the party bolt, businessmen such as the respected textile baron Donald Comer also bolted the party and endorsed Hoover. Longtime Underwood antagonist L. B. Musgrove also voted Republican in 1928 for the first time in his life. Even the state's two leading Democrats, Governor Bibb Graves and Senator Hugo Black, sat out the campaign fearful of the reaction of their own followers, many of whom were active in the anti-Smith movement.

Chief among the anti-Smith orators was U.S. senator Tom Heflin, perhaps the nearest thing Alabama had to a genuine Southern demagogue. A native of Randolph County, Heflin had manipulated his bombastic oratory, mimicry, and rustic wit into a lengthy if undistinguished political career as state legislator, congressman, and U.S. senator. Aside from a 1913 resolution he introduced that created Mother's Day, he had nothing of consequence to show for nearly three decades on Capitol Hill. Neither colleagues nor Alabama journalists tendered him much respect. One diminutive opponent said of Heflin's pompous, largely irrelevant, and long-winded speeches, "If you stick a pitchfork in Tom Heflin and let the wind out, a pair of my breeches would swallow him." In 1923 the Birmingham *News* concluded that Heflin, "who might have been the nation's one really genuine Picturesque Statesman in the drab and drear Coolidgian epoch is burning with an inner and . . . unhealthy fire."[13] Heflin merely turned such home-state attacks to his advantage, denouncing "subsidized" big city daily papers as enemies of the people.

The object of the journalistic scorn was Heflin's long flirtation with the Ku Klux Klan. Although he denied having ever been a dues-paying Klansman, he sided with the "invisible empire" on virtually every public issue, launched highly publicized attacks on the Catholic lay organization Knights of Columbus, warned of a Catholic conspiracy against Democratic institutions, and earned generous speaking fees for addressing Klans nationwide. Beginning in 1920 he subscribed to "one hundred percent Americanism" and warned fellow senators about Catholic domination of U.S. policy toward Mexico. So wild were his rantings that one fellow senator dismissed his charges as "the flimsiest bubble that ever found lodgement in an empty head." When Heflin reported mysterious threats on his life that he attributed to the Catholic hierarchy, another Senate colleague satirically pleaded for "immediate and effective steps . . . to protect this Senator. The army should assign troops to surround the Capitol. The navy should send a large part of the fleet into the Potomac. The Marines should be called . . . to protect his precious life." The New York *Sun* editorialized: "The feeling of most Americans toward Heflin is one of undescribable loathing."[14] In 1928 Heflin had an issue perfectly designed for his talents, and he roasted Al Smith in speeches from the Tennessee River to the Gulf of Mexico.

In this undertaking he had plenty of help. Methodist and Baptist ministers, allegedly spiritual and otherworldly, were about as passive as a spring tornado. Methodists were the most politically active, urging their members to "vote as you pray" or "vote as Jesus our Captain would have us vote." Methodist evangelist Bob Shuler predicted that Smith's election would make the Democratic party the "party of Rome and rum for the next hundred years." The Methodist state journal, the *Alabama Christian Advocate,* combined alcohol abuse, racism, and Al Smith in a warning against placing "this passion inflamer in the hands of this child race not far removed from their savage haunts in the jungles of Africa." Baptist evangelist Bob Jones warned that if Smith won, "marriage . . . will be legal only if performed by a priest." The *Alabama Baptist* printed an essay describing the historic 1928 Democratic convention at Houston as a transition from "honest and upright rural and village and town folk," whom Thomas Jefferson trusted with the reigns of government, to "boss-ridden city masses—largely foreign and thirsty," whom Jefferson distrusted. The editor denied that the Baptist journal was nonpartisan but vowed that he would have avoided politics "if there were not a moral and religious issue involved."[15] Dozens of Baptist associations, ministers, and the state convention vowed to support for president only men who endorsed prohibition. One anti-Smith speaker in Anniston even contended that every assassin of a U.S. president had been Catholic or inspired by Catholics.

To counter the avalanche of defections, loyalist Democrats could offer their own politicians, most editorial pages of major dailies, and their own brand of racism. The Smith forces were led by Congressmen William B. Oliver, John McDuffie, Lister Hill, George Huddleston, Sr., Henry B. Steagall, and John H. Bankhead, Jr. The pro-Smith forces emphasized historic loyalty to the Democratic party while trying to tie Republicanism to the Civil War, Reconstruction, and blacks. Archie H. Carmichael of Tuscumbia urged: "So long as there is a Confederate soldier with a dangling empty sleeve in his coat, we can never vote the Republican ticket." Thomas D. Samford of Opelika, son of a former governor, reminded listeners that the Democratic party was "the white man's party and we are white men." Hugh Mallory of Selma proclaimed that "God meant Alabama to be a white man's state and the Democratic party has been His instrument in keeping it a white man's state."[16] State Democratic officials charged that Hoover had forced white girls to "sit alongside buck Negroes" in the Commerce Department, which he headed—"a shocking outrage on these fine American girls." Others accused Hoover of advocating interracial marriage. Congressman McDuffie denounced Tom Heflin as the "most consummate demagogue Alabama has ever sent to the U.S. Senate."[17]

McDuffie was not alone in his attacks on Heflin and other anti-Smith leaders. Grover Hall, Sr., of the Montgomery *Advertiser* denounced Heflin as a "callous and wretched demagogue," and Montgomery mayor William A. Gunter, Jr., refused to allow Heflin to speak in a city building, vowing that "as long as I am Mayor I will not permit the use of city property to persons who preach religious hatred."[18] Various Hall-family newspapers denounced Protestant ministers for violating separation of church and state by using their pulpits for partisan political causes. They also condemned Ku Klux Klan involvement in the bolt from the Democratic party. It was the lunacy of the 1928 campaign that inspired journalism professor Clarence Cason to write that newspaper articles about Southern elections should be printed on the sports pages.

When all the shouting and denunciations ended, an unprecedented 250,000 of Alabama's 300,000 registered voters cast ballots. Al Smith held Alabama but only barely, 127,000 to 120,725. He won Mobile and Montgomery counties, the Black Belt, and farm areas in northwestern Alabama. Hoover carried Jefferson County, northeastern Alabama, and most central Alabama counties above the Black Belt. Of the twenty-seven counties Hoover won, only five had more than 30 percent Negro population. Eleven Black Belt counties saved the Democrats, furnishing Smith a margin of 10,200 votes, more than his victory margin statewide. Obviously, in these counties the realities of race mattered more than the whims of evangelical religion and prohibitionist morality.

Victorious Democrats turned their attention to those who had led the anti-Smith movement. Party leadership divided over whether or not to expel the 1928 bolters, but party loyalists on the State Democratic Executive Committee prevailed by a vote of 27–21 and refused to allow any Democrat who had voted Republican or openly opposed Smith to run as a Democrat. Paradoxically, E. C. Boswell, who himself would lead the 1948 Dixiecrat bolt against Democratic nominee Harry Truman, played a major role in expelling Tom Heflin and Judge Hugh Locke from the party. Senator Hugo Black, north Alabama Democrats, and organized labor unsuccessfully opposed this purge.

Heflin, who had to stand for reelection in 1930, and Locke, who had decided to run for governor, organized a rump party, which they called Jeffersonian Democrats, to furnish a base for their independent campaigns against Democratic nominees John H. Bankhead, Jr., and Benjamin M. Miller. The Ku Klux Klan, many Protestant ministers, and prohibitionists supported Heflin, as did the state Republican party; but of Alabama's 151 newspapers, only 19 small weeklies endorsed Heflin. Bankhead went straight for the jugular in his campaign. He denounced Heflin's career, its sole accomplishment being a Mother's Day bill that was easier to pass "than one endorsing the Ten Commandments."

Mincing no words, he branded Heflin "a character assassin, a creature more detestable than a man-killer. The only extenuating circumstance is the unfortunate state of his mind. It is impossible to doubt that he is a crazy man."[19] Once again public interest in the campaign was overwhelming. Of 357,000 qualified voters, 252,000 cast ballots, with Bankhead winning 151,000 to Heflin's 101,000. Hugh Locke lost to Democrat Benjamin Miller by a similar margin of 59,000 votes. County returns mirrored the 1928 results, with Heflin and Locke running strongest in Klan areas and the prohibitionist strongholds of north Alabama, while Bankhead and Miller rolled up huge margins in the Black Belt and southwestern Alabama. Although Heflin would run again for Congress in 1934 and 1938 and oppose Lister Hill for a U.S. Senate seat in 1937, he would never again hold office in Alabama. Like Hugo Black and Bibb Graves, he had hitched his wagon to the powerful forces of political change sweeping across Alabama in the 1920s. But Graves and Black perceived far more clearly than Heflin the complex socioeconomic interests arrayed against the state's traditional conservative leadership. They joined the Klan because they understood the frustrations it vented and the coalition of moralists and working class people to which it belonged. But they used it, then discarded the Klan (and its nativism and bigotry) when it no longer served their purposes. Heflin was far slower in perceiving the passage of moralistic politics and became the chief casualty of a new political era in which the Great Depression redefined all conventional political wisdom.

TWENTY-SIX

Change and Stability
during the Roaring Twenties

WHAT fueled the swollen budgets of the Kilby and Graves administrations was a booming state economy. To be sure, Alabama's fiscal health during the 1920s was uneven. Agriculture languished throughout the decade; even portions of industry turned sour after 1926. But generally business and industry surged ahead until 1929. Before the First World War Alabama's economy was isolated and characterized by high population growth, fluctuating cotton demand, isolated regional markets, backward technology, and scarcity of skilled managers and technicians. Low agricultural wages meant industrialists could recruit adequate labor with low wages. But during and just after the war national economic patterns became more pronounced.

During the First World War Alabama established agencies to publicize state resources and recruit prospective industries. Working with local chambers of commerce during a period of rapid economic growth, these efforts resulted in substantial improvement in Alabama's economy between 1910 and 1929, but an even more precipitous decline followed.

By 1925 Alabama ranked fourth in the South behind North Carolina, Georgia, and South Carolina in number of manufacturing jobs. That rank was misleading, however, because the other three states contained little industry other than textile mills, whereas Alabama was by far the most diversified Southern industrial state, listing thirty different manufacturing categories. Of its 66,800 industrial wage earners, 23,400 labored in textile mills, 19,300 in steel and iron mills, 4,900 in smelting, refining, and blast furnaces, 8,500 in railroad and car shops, and 10,700 in a variety of other industries. The value of coal, textiles, electricity, pig iron, and steel accounted for half the aggregate value of all of Alabama's industrial production between 1914 and 1930.

Many of these industries, especially timber and textiles, traced their origins to antebellum roots and were closely tied to agriculture. Forest products accounted for nearly half of Alabama's 2,848 manufacturing establishments in 1929 but most were small planing, saw-, or turpentine mills employing 10 to 30 workers. The industry also fluctuated season-

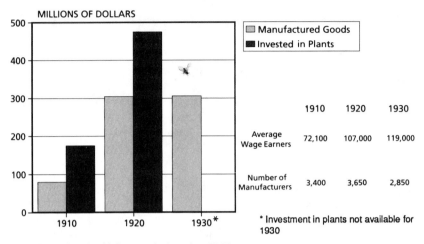

MILLIONS OF DOLLARS

| | Manufactured Goods |
| | Invested in Plants |

	1910	1920	1930
Average Wage Earners	72,100	107,000	119,000
Number of Manufacturers	3,400	3,650	2,850

* Investment in plants not available for 1930

Manufacturing in Alabama during the 1920s

ally and experienced a high rate of labor turnover. Employment began and ended the decade at 30,000 but slumped in the early 1920s and dipped to only 15,000 in 1931.

Despite the fragmented pattern of the industry, the little town of Chapman in Butler County was the site of a baronial lumber empire begun by W. T. Smith. Early in the century James G. McGowin moved from Mobile and became secretary and treasurer of W. T. Smith Lumber Company and in 1925 was elected president. He provided his three sons fine educations at the state university and then at Oxford University (Earl McGowin won a Rhodes Scholarship to Oxford). Then he brought them back to manage various branches of the company. They devised a sustained-yield strategy that consisted of reforestation and conservation rather than wasteful clear-cutting. By the time of McGowin's death in 1934 he owned 140,000 acres of timberland. He also ran the town of Chapman as a personal fiefdom. His firm but paternalistic rule provided houses, churches, and schools for his employees. The family always furnished the mayor, a pattern made easier by the fact that only fifteen or twenty people registered to vote (including no blacks). Even in oral histories family members referred to the W. T. Smith Lumber Company as a "benevolent dictatorship."

From the standpoint of workers, forest products was one of the hardest, most demeaning sources of employment in Alabama. Within the racially mixed work force violence between blacks and whites often occurred. Wages were among the lowest in any industry and peonage was not unheard of. Convicts worked some of the turpentine camps and sawmills until the mid-1920s, and despite state laws forbidding it, nearly 1,800 boys between the ages of ten and thirteen worked in the dangerous occupation in 1920.

The textile industry ranked highest of all Alabama industries in total value of products from 1914 to 1930 and second to iron and steel in largest manufacturing units. In 1929 the state's eighty-three cotton mills consumed nearly a tenth of all cotton used in the nation. The industry reached its apex that year, the only Alabama industry to peak that late. During the 1920s textile employment increased 60 percent and by 1931 provided jobs for one-third of all Alabama's manufacturing workers. Unlike the forest products industry, the labor force was largely white and female. Although average full-time cotton mill wages for males in Alabama were the lowest of any state in 1920 (about $700 annually), the wages were princely compared to the $410 a typical farm laborer earned.

The largest textile owner in the state was former governor Braxton Bragg Comer, who had established Avondale Mills in 1897. He and his son and successor, Donald, who became president of Avondale in 1927, constantly expanded the mills, opening branches in Bevelle, Eufaula, Pell City, Sylacauga, Sycamore, and elsewhere. The Comers, like the McGowins, were an old Alabama family with political power and paternalistic instincts. Active Methodist laymen, they endowed scholarships and churches and treated cooperative workers kindly. They vowed that they located their plants in towns only because business and civic leaders begged them to provide jobs for the multitude of illiterate or poorly educated whites living nearby on tenant farms. But Donald Comer also backed reactionary political forces in the state and opposed a 1923 federal bill to restrict child labor.

Although the Comer family dominated the industry, the town of Huntsville was the single largest textile center, followed closely by the Chattahoochee Valley. Huntsville was a one-industry town but also the second largest textile town in the South. The five mills belonging to LaFayette Lanier's West Point Manufacturing Company in Lanett, Shawmut, Langdale, Fairfax, and River View (all in Chambers County on the Chattahoochee River) constituted one of the six largest textile manufacturing centers in the United States by the 1930s. Like the Comers, the Lanier family tried to win the loyalty of workers with elaborate recreational, educational, and social programs.

Although coal and iron ore mining did not have agricultural roots, mining had a long history in the state. Mining employment stood at 35,700 in 1920, peaked in 1926, then declined to 31,400 in 1930. High production and transportation costs of Alabama coal due to small, steep coal veins, dirty bituminous coal, and high railroad rates put the Birmingham district's product at a cost disadvantage compared to Pennsylvania's anthracite. Coal mining was a dangerous, low-paying job. Between 1918 and 1928 the average coal production per fatality in Alabama was 186,000 tons; nationwide the rate was 259,000 tons per fatality. In November 1920 an explosion at the Parish Mine killed 12; in 1922 three blasts, the largest at Dolomite in November, left 106 dead; in December 1925 an explosion at Overton Mine No. 2 took 53 lives. In compensation for this danger Alabama coal miners earned a median wage of $800 in 1921 compared to $1,425 nationwide. As a consequence of high risks and low wages, labor turnover was high (180 percent a year at Montevallo Mining Company in Shelby County, 120 percent at Alabama Fuel and Iron Company, 80 percent for seventeen companies in 1921).

Like the textile industry, mining relied on poor rural people to fill its ranks. Unlike textiles, mining employed no women and divided its labor force in 1920 almost equally between whites and blacks. It also contained nearly 4 percent foreign miners, most of them from Italy and eastern Europe. One such miner was orphan John Gioiello, who immigrated to Alabama from Torino, Italy, in 1921. He began mining coal for TCI in 1922 at age twenty-three and mined for twenty-nine years. At first he spoke no English and had great difficulty understanding instructions. The small community of Brookside became an ethnic enclave especially for eastern European immigrants. A Russian Orthodox church and cemetery still bear tribute to the struggle of Czech, Russian, and other Slavic miners trying to build a new life in Alabama. Most miners (66 percent in 1922–23) lived in company-owned houses. Few of them had running water, less than half had electricity or gas, and none had bathtubs, showers, or flush toilets. The labor-management tensions of the coal mine camp with its payment in scrip rather than cash, its expensive company commissary, and its closely guarded isolation produced bitter strikes like the 1920 conflict and would soon produce the state's bloodiest union campaign.

Iron and steel employment peaked at 25,000 in 1925 and dropped to 23,000 by 1929. By the latter year Alabama produced 9.1 percent of the nation's iron ore, and the Birmingham district experienced the largest growth in pig iron of any state between 1913 and 1930. Anniston's ten plants produced more cast iron pipe and fittings than any place in the world, and the city shipped pipe to every part of the globe. In 1926 Alabama produced 87 percent of the South's pig iron, and Birmingham steadily increased its share of the nation's steel production: 2.4 percent in 1919, 3.3 percent in 1929. The increase was even more remarkable considering that a consumer of Birmingham steel in 1920 still had to pay the price of steel at Pittsburgh plus a five-dollar per ton differential levied by TCI's parent company, U.S. Steel. The "Pittsburgh differential" theoretically was based on higher production costs for Birmingham steel, although the Federal Trade Commission estimated that the actual cost of producing Birmingham steel was lower than elsewhere.

Fueling all this industrial growth was the new Alabama Power Company. Under the direction of Thomas W. Martin, who became president in 1920, the utility expanded its system of hydroelectric dams and its considerable influence in the Alabama legislature.

Although industrial progress occurred within pockets across the state, most of it was confined to urban areas. In 1920 Alabama contained 2.35 million people, a figure that increased by almost 13 percent to 2.65 million in 1930. Although most Alabamians lived in rural areas in both censuses, the urban population climbed from 21.7 percent in 1920 to 28.1 percent in 1930. Unquestionably Birmingham was the state's primary city. Despite its late start, the city boomed between 1910 and 1930, thanks largely to the 1910 annexation of suburbs. Its population of 179,000 in 1920 raced to 260,000 in 1930, figures that compared favorably to Atlanta's 201,000 (1920) and 270,000 (1930). During the decade the city constructed the South's largest and tallest skyscrapers. When Birmingham celebrated its fiftieth birthday in October 1921, it could attract President Warren G. Harding to deliver the primary address.

An elite of small businessmen, industrialists, professionals, and civic boosters organized into various social, economic, and civic clubs and dominated the city's life. One list of 296 designated leaders in 1920 contained 200 businessmen who belonged to the chamber of commerce, Business Men's League, Merchants and Manufacturers Association, and the Civitan Club (an organization founded in Birmingham in 1917). By 1924 the city boasted 788 manufacturing plants employing an estimated 106,000 workers. Although labor was poorly organized during the 1920s, unions actually supported two newspapers, the *Southern Labor Review*, published by A. H. Cather, a businessman with iconoclastic Christian Socialist views, and the more traditional *Labor Advocate*. Although only 2.3 percent of the population was immigrant in 1930, 38.2 percent was black, down 1 percent from 1920. The black racial component was the highest of any major American city. In 1923 officials segregated streetcar riders by race; residentially, blacks clustered into a section of the city known as Tuxedo Junction.

Within their poorly understood subculture and beyond the view of most whites, black leaders forged a distinctive world. Carrie A. Tuggle, born a slave, moved to Birmingham in 1884 with her railroad worker

Carrie Tuggle, born a slave, became a leader in the black community in Birmingham and established Tuggle Institute as a school for black children. (Courtesy of the Birmingham Public Library Archives)

husband. The Carrie Tuggle that most Birmingham whites knew was a kindly maid and washerwoman. But within the tightly constricted black community, Tuggle became a member of many black women's fraternal organizations, a leader in the Methodist Episcopal Church, Zion, and a leading prohibitionist. She established a black newspaper, the Birmingham *Truth*, and wrote editorials denouncing lynching, the convict lease system, and racial discrimination. She began Tuggle Institute, a school for black children that was supported by prominent Protestant and Jewish leaders and business people. When the school burned in 1919 local citizens of both races donated $25,000 to rebuild it. By 1924 the institute bearing her name boasted two double-story buildings, a one-story structure, three cottages, and an infirmary. Among its distinguished alumni from this era was an ambitious, shrewd newcomer from the Black Belt, A. G. Gaston, who would in time become a millionaire businessman and one of the city's most influential citizens. When Tuggle died in 1924, the Birmingham *News* eulogized her as the "female Booker T. Washington."

Businessmen and blacks certainly had no monopoly on power. Nativists, white laborers, and prohibitionists constantly challenged city leadership. By 1920 anti-Catholicism was rampant, and the Ku Klux Klan exercised tremendous influence. By the time James M. (Jimmy) Jones, Jr., a Klan-endorsed trucking company executive, won the presidency of the city commission in 1925, the "invisible empire" controlled city politics.

The worst of many acts of violence occurred in 1920. The Reverend E. R. Stephenson was an itinerant Methodist preacher who specialized in corralling eager young couples headed out of the courthouse with marriage certificates and performing the ceremony on the spot. Already inflamed by the nativist sentiment of the times, Stephenson was additionally outraged when Father James E. Coyle, pastor of St. Paul's Catholic Church, performed the wedding ceremony for his only daughter, Ruth, and a Puerto Rican Catholic, Pedro Gussman.

Unable to get his hands on his new son-in-law, Stephenson took out his rage on Father Coyle, shooting the priest to death while he sat on the front porch of the Catholic parsonage. Stephenson hired attorney Hugo Black to defend him, and Black mounted a defense based on a plea of insanity induced by allegations that Puerto Ricans were mulattoes (Ruth had thus married a black) and that the priest had seduced his daughter away from her Methodist upbringing. The jury, composed primarily of Klan members, found this to be a perfectly reasonable defense and acquitted Stephenson of second-degree murder. For the first but not the last time, the national press roasted the young city. Journalist Charles Sweeney wrote two particularly devastating essays in the *Nation* magazine (in August 1921 and November 1924) accusing Birmingham of being "the American hotbed of anti-Catholic fanaticism," where the "murder of a priest had been added to the achievements of bigotry."

Moral crusades against Catholics merged easily into a broader effort against drinking, dancing, movies, and prostitution. City voters defeated proposals to allow public dancing at East Lake Park or movies after church hours on Sunday. In 1921 and again in 1923 women's organizations and churches tried to pressure city officials to end open prostitution in the city. They cited one police report estimating that five hundred boardinghouses and four downtown hotels drew their primary income from prostitution. One of the leading "madams," the illiterate Fannie J. Barefield, operated the "White House" at 2221 Avenue A that featured fifteen paintings of nudes by an Italian painter who lived there for a year. Barefield included many prominent businessmen among her clients, counted the police chief among her friends, and included Hugo Black among many lawyers who handled her legal business.

Although women's organizations proved less politically powerful than the city's brothels, they influenced all aspects of city life and played a prominent role in reform efforts. Organized into the Birmingham League of Women Voters, the Business and Professional Women's Clubs, the Federation of Women's Clubs, the Alabama Woman's Committee on Interracial Cooperation, and numerous literary clubs (notably the Cadmean and Highland book clubs), they pioneered new roles for women.

One problem they could not solve was traffic. Between 1920 and 1930

The automobile changed the urban landscape of Alabama during the 1920s, creating traffic jams and new problems. (Courtesy of the Eric Overbey/Mobile Public Library Collection, University of South Alabama Photographic Archives)

the number of registered motor vehicles increased from 16,000 to 70,000. By 1930 the city contained a quarter of the motorized vehicles in Alabama. Traffic congestion became so bad that the chamber of commerce called the auto "the greatest menace in the country," and moralists proposed outlawing cars in order "to save the womanhood of the country" from these "assignation houses on wheels."[1] Streetcars, private automobiles, taxis, and jitneys (large touring cars converted to carrying five to seven passengers that were more flexible and rapid than streetcars and cheaper than taxis) competed for space on city streets. Gridlock became so bad in the early 1920s that officials created one-way streets, imposed speed limits, limited parking to one side of the streets, modernized traffic lights, created a motorcycle squad within the police department, and tried to ban jitneys from downtown. The debate between streetcar companies and jitney owners was the first spat over methods of urban transportation and resulted in an initial victory for the streetcars, which transported 64 percent of all passengers in and out of the city by 1926. Despite the effort of city officials to persuade citizens to use streetcars and the institution of fare reductions on the vehicles, more and more citizens turned 1920s prosperity into purchase of private autos. Cars became the ultimate urban status symbol, and once purchased few owners chose to use the streetcar, a fact that destroyed the streetcar's potential to provide a cheap, effective, nonpolluting urban traffic system. Future generations would pay in many ways for the protracted love affair with the automobile.

Befitting its reputation for adventure and experimentation, Birmingham's population was less tradition-bound than those of Mobile and Montgomery. Not only did successful newcomers find it easier to join prestigious business and women's clubs, but they found an atmosphere congenial to taking chances. Electronics whiz Donald Croom Beatty and a small group of adventurous young aviators established a flying group. A member of the group, Johnny Meissner, used connections in Washington to obtain federal funding in 1922 and formed the nation's first Air National Guard unit (the 106th Observation Squadron). Glenn E. Messer began an aviation charter service out of the city and even made plans to manufacture planes there.

Other industries were more conventional but still pioneered new products and strategies. Solon Jacobs, husband of suffragist Pattie Jacobs, and Henry L. Badham began Birmingham Slag Company to utilize industrial wastes as a base for highway construction. Later Charles Ireland bought the company and expanded operations during the 1920s to Montgomery and Atlanta. The good roads movement in the South produced a huge market, and from these modest beginnings grew Vulcan Materials, by the 1980s the largest aggregate company in the world. In 1927 an insurance company originally named Heralds of Liberty moved to Birmingham. A number of mergers and name changes later, Liberty National Insurance Company emerged as one of the best-managed and largest units in the industry.

Two entrepreneurs deserve special attention for their unique approach to labor-management relations. Although the prevailing management attitude in Birmingham was rooted either in paternalism or in the notion that workers had no rights, at least two entrepreneurs perceived industrial organization in different ways. George G. Crawford came to run TCI after its purchase by U.S. Steel in 1907 and created the most elaborate company welfare system in the South. The professional physicians, dentists, and social workers hired by TCI improved conditions, reduced workdays lost to illness, and reduced labor turnover from 400 percent a year in 1908 to just over 5 percent in 1930. A key person in the program was Winifred Collins, an experienced social worker from Chicago, whom Crawford hired to head his new Department of Social Service. It was Collins who recruited a staff of professionally trained women to staff social service positions in TCI villages. But beyond his revolutionary changes in company policy, Crawford became the chief advocate of a state docks complex in Mobile that by the late 1920s made the port city the cheapest coaling seaport in the world and TCI the largest shipper through the port. Crawford also inspired creation of the city's first industrial board to recruit industry, and he helped persuade Goodyear to locate a tire plant in Gadsden in 1929.

The other entrepreneur was even less conventional. Georgian John J. Eagan had organized American Cast Iron Pipe Company in 1905. An active and philanthropic Presbyterian who had already funded Appalachian schools, championed the rights of labor, and helped organize the Southern interracial movement, Eagan in 1920 became interested in English patterns of labor-management relations. In June 1921 he announced his "Golden Rule Plan." He established a five-member board of management, with himself as president, and a twelve-man board of operatives selected by workers. Blacks voted for the operatives but could not serve on the board. Together the two boards established policies. He invested all dividends to provide continued employment and wages during hard times. He also established profit sharing for workers, an unemployment fund, life insurance policies for all employees, pensions, medical care, athletic teams, housing, gardens, and a savings bank. In 1923 he changed his will to leave all common stock to the two boards in order to demonstrate his faith that labor and management could profitably and effectively supervise a company. When he died in 1924 a delegation of black and white laborers traveled to Atlanta for his funeral, and despite warnings from friends that his utopian scheme would fail, ACIPCO ultimately became the world's largest pipe shop under a single roof, and in 1990 it was still run as a trust for its employees.

Other Alabama cities grew also, though none to the importance of the Magic City. Mobile began the decade with a population of 61,000 and ended it with 68,000; Montgomery grew from 43,000 to 66,000; Anniston from 18,000 to 22,000; Huntsville from 8,000 to 12,000. Construction of state docks in Mobile fueled growth of the port city. Montgomery acquired textile mills and experienced growth as a livestock marketing and agricultural center. But most important, the U.S. Air Service bought land in January 1920 for an Aviation Repair Depot, which began Maxwell Air Force Base, the city's most important economic resource. The number of Montgomery wage earners nearly doubled during the decade, and more than 4,000 women earned salaries in 1929, 21 percent of them in professional jobs, 28 percent in factories and mills, 20 percent in retail stores, and others in a variety of domestic occupations.

Picking cotton in the late summer and early fall was hard work, as shown in this photograph of workers in DeKalb County in the 1930s. (Courtesy of the Auburn University Archives)

Even city fathers in Selma, the state's fifth largest city, got in on the boosterism. They erected a sign proclaiming Selma the "fastest-growing city in Alabama—50,000 people by 1930." The city fell a bit short: in 1930, 16,000 people lived there. Despite efforts by some promoters to attract industry, many white residents of both Selma and Montgomery were too deeply wedded to traditional Black Belt values and too frightened of change to seek factories actively. When the wind blew their sign down, city officials did not bother to replace it. In many ways the incident was representative of the extravagant dreams and disappointing realities of urbanizing Alabama.

Extravagant dreams never were a problem for the 78 percent of Alabamians who lived on farms in 1920. The prosperity of the decade passed them by. Although the number of farms increased slightly during the decade, their value declined by nearly 8 percent. In 1920 tenants operated 58 percent of all Alabama farms; by 1930 the number of tenant farms had risen to 65 percent, a rate surpassed only in four other Southern states. White sharecroppers outnumbered blacks 37,600 to 27,500, and the races split almost evenly among other forms of tenants. Other factors contributing to the decline included the effect of the boll weevil (Alabama harvested 719,000 bales of cotton in 1919, only 580,000 bales in 1921), loss of international markets, bad weather, and soil erosion.

One reason for the majority of white tenants was the exodus of blacks from rural Alabama. Many left for Birmingham or Mobile first, then once they had acquired industrial skills, they departed for better opportunities in the North. Hardening patterns of urban segregation, racial violence, the growth of the Klan, the failed coal strike of 1920—all contributed to the exodus of young, skilled and semiskilled labor north to Kentucky, West Virginia, Ohio, and Michigan. Some Northern industries even sent recruiters to Alabama looking for ambitious blacks. One student of black migration estimated that half a million blacks left the South between 1921 and 1925. Birmingham lost an estimated 38,000 blacks in 1922–23 alone, but within three months their vacant jobs had been filled by new migrants from the countryside. Migrants often recruited friends and relatives, as did one laborer in the North who wrote friends back in Alabama that "people are coming here every day and are finding employment. Nothing here but money and it is not hard to get."[2] In 1923 the Alabama Cooperative Extension Service and Tuskegee Institute dispatched Thomas Monroe Campbell, the state's first black extension agent, to the North to report on conditions of Alabama's migrants. He reported that many former tenant farmers said they left because of unfair treatment by their landlords.

By the mid-1920s Thomas Monroe Campbell directed a considerable staff of black men and women who tried to stabilize farm life. Alabama had a more highly developed system of black extension work than most Southern states, thanks to Campbell and Tuskegee Institute. In 1923, 30,000 black and white farmers donated money to buy a Ford truck, which Campbell called the "Booker T. Washington Movable School on Wheels." From the back of the truck black agents conducted demonstrations on agriculture, health, and domestic skills. In 1920 Tuskegee hosted the first annual conference of white and black extension workers, and later in the decade the Alabama Farm Bureau allowed black farmers to join. But Campbell never felt adequately supported by white extension officials at Auburn University and grew concerned over the number of whites sent by the state and federal governments to teach agriculture classes at Tuskegee Institute.

Luther N. Duncan, who became the first director of the Alabama Cooperative Extension Service in 1920 after it split away from the research station, made it a semi-independent and highly political agency. When funding problems arose in 1922, he tried to move the agency to Montgomery, the site of the State Department of Agriculture, the Alabama Farm Bureau Federation headquarters, and the legislature, but Auburn's trustees rejected the idea after much debate. Duncan also took the lead in organizing Alabama's Farm Bureau from the founding of the national organization in 1919. By the end of 1922 the bureau had organized in thirty-six counties and by 1930 in all sixty-seven counties.

By mid-1926 the federation contained 26,000 members. The bureau helped farmers organize and better market their cotton crop.

Under the leadership of Edward A. O'Neal III, from Florence, the bureau departed from its pledge to be a "non-partisan, non-political business organization." O'Neal came from a well-educated family of farmers, lawyers, and politicians, including two former governors. In 1925 he became vice-president of the American Farm Bureau and later became president. He served in that office for eight terms and became one of the most influential Americans in charting federal agricultural policy. But his highly political leadership of Alabama farmers alienated many small producers, and a number of county bureaus withdrew from the state organization, accusing it of becoming a political machine. O'Neal and Duncan worked closely together, making it hard to decide where the extension service ended and the farm bureau began. Extension agents paid by Auburn from state and federal funds became heavily involved in political campaigns, usually on behalf of Black Belt or Big Mule candidates. Although the bureau lobbied successfully for many needed reforms during the 1920s (a code requiring accurate labeling of fertilizers and feeds, increases in the severance taxes on coal, iron, and water power to better fund education, the creation of a milk control board), the net effect of the bureau was to strengthen entrenched political forces in the state and create perhaps the single most powerful lobby in Alabama for the next half century.

The work of Auburn's extension service is not so clear. Generally agents favored large productive farmers and became involved with bureau politics. But many agents began to help poor farmers as well, creating farmers' markets and crafts programs to help small farmers earn extra income. Many female home demonstration agents staked out new roles for women. Only single women could hold the jobs, and some of them meddled with traditional gender roles. Gladys Tappan, an assistant demonstration agent in Auburn, urged the election of women farmers to membership on the county farm bureau's board of directors. By 1924 she had already won this reform in Perry and Dallas counties. Auburn also began a fisheries program in 1929. The ponds constructed were designed to provide farmers an alternative source of income in the form of catfish production. Designed entirely for domestic development at first, the program would later become international in scope and the largest aquaculture program in the world. Farmers showed little interest in 1929, but by the 1980s catfish production would become a major agricultural business.

Such reforms came far too late to help the bottom rung of Alabama's farmers. They lived out their lives in a downward cascade of troubles. Rootless and powerless, they moved every few years in search of better land and fairer treatment. One tenant in Lamar County moved from Mississippi to the Bankhead farm in November 1927. In November 1928 he moved to the Yerby place. A year later to the month he moved to the Alabama Mills Company in Fayette. In February 1930 he relocated his family to the Strother farm and in December of the same year to Seth Lawrence's farm. The next decade was no different except he could then supplement his rabbit hunting, which supplied wintertime meat, with a cash income from his son, who worked at a Civilian Conservation Corps job. For his family the Great Depression began early.

But even he was luckier than sharecropper Jim Washington. In January 1920 E. A. Stoudenmire, a prominent Prattville farmer, traveled to a large farm he owned to collect the year's debt owed by Washington. Fallen on hard times, the sharecropper refused to allow the owner to take any of his crops and threatened him with a shotgun. Stoudenmire left but returned shortly with the sheriff and an arrest warrant. Washington reached for his shotgun, but the sheriff took it off the porch. Washington reached for a knife in his pocket, and Stoudenmire shot him dead. The Montgomery *Advertiser* reported that though the sheriff charged Stoudenmire with manslaughter, he was a man with many friends and had a reputation of getting along well with his tenants.

It takes little effort to understand the frustrating world of Jim Washington. By 1929 Alabama's per capita income had dropped to forty-fourth among the forty-eight states. More than half the state's income was concentrated in the six urban counties of Calhoun, Etowah, Jefferson, Mobile, Montgomery, and Tuscaloosa that contained less than a third of the state's population. In Cleburne County in 1928 farm income dropped 37 percent from the previous year and in Cherokee County by 35 percent. Within this rural world the "Roaring 1920s" sounded more like a desperate whimper.

Just as national trends eroded Alabama's economic isolation, standardized American patterns eroded the state's cultural isolation. Movies vividly portrayed how people in California and New York dressed, smoked, danced, spent leisure time, and even made love. The Ziegfeld Follies played to packed houses in Montgomery. Birmingham's Empire Theater showed *Matinee Ladies* in May 1927 starring May McAvoy and Hedda Hopper. A newspaper advertisement attracted the audience to a "lively story of a Broadway cigarette girl and a 'gigolo'; of thrill-seeking wives who spend their afternoons in cabarets with younger men. Carefree comedy and exciting drama!" When the movie *Two Weeks* came to Birmingham in 1920, the newspaper ad inquired: "If you saw a pretty young thing bathing in the moonlight would you shut your eyes? Now would you?" For more conservative patrons the movies also offered biblical epics such as *Ben-Hur,* and for adventure buffs there were Tarzan movies.

More traditional entertainment centered in sports. Alabama's obsession with sports has many explanations. The South remained a raw, agricultural frontier longer than other sections, and frontier people tend to denigrate high forms of culture (college education, classical music, opera, the fine arts) in favor of folk art. They also are closer to nature (best illustrated by their love of hunting and fishing) and are more physical (hard physical labor was central to an agricultural system little influenced by modern technology). Furthermore, their society offered poor people few avenues of economic mobility. Denied decent education by woefully underfunded schools and by a culture that ridiculed "eggheads" and "teacher's pets," poor kids found an outlet in sports. And broader Alabama culture affirmed sports as having great value, especially for males. The pattern notably prevailed among black males. Shut off from adequate schools, union apprenticeships, or traditional subservient jobs, and barred from most professions by multiple layers of prejudice, blacks survived as best they could, women by sewing and washing and men by physical prowess.

In a strange but different way, the United States also denied Alabama's white football players the respect they believed they deserved. Although Southern college teams began playing football in the 1870s, they had little success in intersectional games. In fact Virginia lost the first such game to Princeton by a score of 116 to 0. Gradually Southern universities hired outstanding Northern coaches such as John W. Heisman (Auburn, 1895–99) and Pop Warner (Georgia, 1895–97), and Southern teams improved. Southern schools organized their first conference, the Southern Intercollegiate Conference, which enrolled forty-six different teams during its lifetime between 1894 and 1922. Alabama schools did well within the region, winning the conference championship many times (Auburn in 1908, 1913, 1919, and the University of Alabama in 1924, 1925, 1926, and 1930).

In 1925 conference champion Alabama had combined the forward pass, developed earlier at Notre Dame, with a crunching defense that allowed only one team to score during the regular season. On December 6, the Pacific Coast Conference invited Alabama to play in the Rose Bowl. Unfortunately, rumors circulated that Alabama was a distant fourth choice, selected only because more respected Eastern teams such as Colgate, Dartmouth, and Princeton had declined owing to interference with academic programs. Initially the University of Washington, a perennial West Coast power, also declined to be the host team. When Rose Bowl officials first contacted Alabama coach Wallace Wade, he allegedly told them that he was not interested in a bowl game that was being peddled from team to team. But officials in California denied the allegations and invited Alabama to become the first Southern team ever to play in the Rose Bowl.

December football ratings had listed Michigan first, even though the team had lost one game, Dartmouth second, Washington third, and Alabama and Tulane tied for fourth. The entire affair smacked of condescension, and Zipp Newman, sportswriter for the Birmingham *News,* editorialized that this game was a great opportunity for Alabama and the South. Adding to the hype for the game were comments made by a professor at Princeton, which allegedly had turned down the invitation that Alabama accepted. The Birmingham *News* quoted Dr. Stewart Paton, a psychiatrist and author, as saying that football was a physical and mental menace to the health of players. Practices and tense games imposed "unbearable emotional strain," the doctor believed, and a "national football hysteria" was "causing players to be slaughtered to make a Roman holiday."[3]

Alabama's team and fans could hardly wait for the tension and slaughter. They departed by train for California on December 19, two full weeks before the game. Once they arrived in California the Civil War seemed not to have ended at all. A writer for a Seattle newspaper described the encounter as a test of the supremacy of Southern and Western football. Washington had the highest-scoring team in the country and entered the game a two-to-one betting choice and a two-touchdown favorite. Their players also outweighed Alabama's competitors by an average of ten pounds.

Back in Alabama questions from the Eastern press about the worthiness of a Southern team in the Rose Bowl infuriated residents. One enraged Alabamian bet $3,750 he could ill-afford to lose on an Alabama upset. Governor William W. Brandon sent the team a telegram urging their greatest effort, and even Dr. Spright Dowell, president of fierce state rival Auburn, wished Alabama success in a telegram that read, "We are with you in spirit; we have absolute faith in your skill and performance."[4]

Writer Damon Runyon covered the game and reported rumors that Washington players took the Southern team so lightly that they barely practiced. Washington had the better team, he believed, but he warned that "these Southern lads have a tremendous desire to take a victory back to the home folks" and that they played with greater spirit than most teams: "You see, Alabama realizes the importance and value of this game as a medium for attracting attention to itself, and to Southern football in general. It knows that the gridiron interest of the country centers on Pasadena New Year's Day, and that a victory over Washington will put Alabama up among the pictures so to speak."[5] Whereas Runyon criticized Washington for taking the game too lightly, he wrote that perhaps Coach Wade took it too seriously, practicing his team mercilessly and in seclusion.

When the long-awaited game day arrived, transplanted Southerners from as far north as Portland, Oregon, and as far south as San Diego swelled the crowd of 50,000 in order to "uphold traditions of the Old South," as the Birmingham *News* put it. Washington led 12–0 at the half, but Alabama stormed back to take a 20–19 victory. It was only the third time in Rose Bowl history that the Eastern team had won, and Alabama's victory shocked sports enthusiasts from coast to coast.

Sectional pride dominated newspaper coverage of the game. Birmingham sportswriter Zipp Newman could not resist a pun when he wrote that "the whole Pacific coast cringed while the Middle West and East trembled from the shock of a tidal wave" as the "Southland swept into its own . . . in the South's greatest intersectional football victory." The Birmingham *News* editorialized rhapsodically that prose could not do justice to Alabama's "miracle at the Rose Bowl." Such events needed "a ten-league canvas with brushes of comet's hair." It was a victory of "Southerners over the Westerners" that challenged the "imagination of a great epic poet." Washington's team was great but ran up "against men toughened by Southern suns into something akin to elastic steel," men who possessed "an unconquerable, undying fighting spirit, worthy of the highest traditions of the state, the South, the nation." Luny Smith, an Alabama player, admitted that "we felt an enormous responsibility to our state and to the Southern Conference." Alabama's president George Denny called January 1 a historic day when his team had won a "great victory for Alabama and the South." And Dr. S. V. Sanford, president of the Southern Conference, proclaimed that "the South should be proud of Alabama. It upheld the traditions and fighting spirit of the Old South."[6]

Wallace Wade would win national championships in 1925, 1926, and 1930; Frank Thomas, who succeeded him, would accomplish the feat in 1934; and Paul ("Bear") Bryant would do so repeatedly in the 1960s and 1970s. But no game ever again mattered so much as the 1926 Rose Bowl. Reading reports of the victory in Southern papers makes one uncertain of whether the articles are about reaction to a 1926 football game or to the first accounts of Confederate victories at Chancellorsville. Nearly half a century passed without dimming the memory for Zipp Newman, who wrote with hyperbole in the mid-1960s amid another triumphal Alabama dynasty: "No victory in football ever changed the destiny of one section of the country like Alabama's furious seven-minute comeback against . . . Washington."[7]

For those less athletically gifted, music provided an alternative route to fame. Former slave W. C. Handy of Florence had given birth to the "down home blues" earlier, but many less-famous black musicians joined the exodus to the North and to greatness. James Reese Europe was born in Mobile in 1881 but migrated to Washington, D.C. Later in New York City he organized a band and the Clef Club, which served as a union and musical contractor. He organized the Negro Symphony Orchestra (which played Carnegie Hall), the National Negro Orchestra, and Europe's Society Orchestra. All emphasized black rhythms, and his music was among the first to be called "jazz." During the First World War he organized the 369th Infantry Band for a black army regiment. It won fame in Europe as the best regimental band and was invited to play for French troops and civilians in Paris.

In Birmingham, Fess Whatley began teaching music at the Negro Industrial High School (later Parker High) in 1919. He organized a band called the Jazz Demons, which played dances in hotels and clubs and introduced the new musical sound to white Birmingham. Seven of his musicians later played in the famous Erskine Hawkins Band. Hawkins was a city native and graduate of Tuggle Institute who took his college jazz band, the Alabama State Collegians, to New York in the 1920s. His greatest composition, "Tuxedo Junction," celebrated in jazz idiom a trolley stop in Ensley. Jazz enthusiasts cheered the Hawkins band at the Savoy Ballroom in New York City, but it was not until Glenn Miller made "Tuxedo Junction" a smashing success that most white Americans heard the song.

Charles Melvin ("Cootie") Williams, born in Mobile in 1908, achieved less recognition. But as a member of Duke Ellington's band beginning in 1929 and later in the Benny Goodman Band, he became a renowned trumpet soloist.

Of all native Alabama musicians from the jazz era, Nathaniel Adams Cole achieved the greatest fame. Born in Montgomery in 1919, Nat "King" Cole left the South when his family joined the exodus to Chicago during the 1920s. The Windy City's environment afforded the proper challenge for his musical talents. He formed a band while in high school, and as pianist for the King Cole Trio he introduced a light, seamless style that formed an important transition from swing jazz to modern jazz. Although his band played mainly in the "race market" (on black stations) during the 1930s and 1940s, Cole broke into the white American audience in 1948, one of the first black male singers to cross over completely into the white market.

The decade also witnessed Alabama's coming of age in literature. In Birmingham a group of journalists for the Birmingham *News* and the newly established Scripps-Howard newspaper, the Birmingham *Post* (founded in 1921), began meeting on Wednesday evenings at the home of Octavus Roy Cohen to discuss their fiction. Cohen wrote fiction that was published in a number of magazines; he became a Hollywood scriptwriter, novelist, and dramatist. Others in the literary group that

Left: Zelda Sayre Fitzgerald, Montgomery native, became a 1920s symbol of "flaming youth" through the novels of her husband, F. Scott Fitzgerald. (Courtesy of Frances Fitzgerald Smith). *Right:* Tallulah Bankhead was a flamboyant actress at an early age. (Courtesy of the Alabama Department of Archives and History)

called themselves "the Loafers" included Edgar Valentine Smith, who won the first of his three O. Henry Prizes for the best American short story of 1923, and James Saxon Childers, who took a Rhodes Scholarship to England before settling down to writing novels and travel books and teaching literature at Birmingham-Southern College. Marie Bankhead Owen, better known as Alabama's state archivist following her husband's death in 1920, wrote eight volumes on Alabama history, three novels, and several plays. T. S. Stribling began writing about the plain white folk of the Tennessee Valley, beginning a career that would reward him with a Pulitzer Prize in 1933 for *The Store.* Zelda Sayre Fitzgerald and Sara Haardt Mencken nearly lost their own identities to their eminent literary husbands, but both produced important short stories during the decade. Most notable of all Alabama writers was William March of Mobile, author of *The Bad Seed,* which was made into a successful motion picture. He gave nearly all his stories an Alabama Gulf Coast setting except *Company K,* an epic First World War novel

461

considered by some critics as one of the finest antiwar novels in American literature.

In the field of drama Tallulah Bankhead became one of the most celebrated actresses of her generation both in England and in the United States. Coincidentally she lived in Montgomery with her aunt, Marie Bankhead Owen, at the same time and in the same neighborhood as Zelda Sayre and Sara Haardt. Ironically, all left one of Alabama's most conventional and conservative cities to become three of the country's most iconoclastic and liberated women. Haardt became a radical feminist by the standards of her time and debunked Alabama's romantic pretensions in her short stories. Zelda became F. Scott Fitzgerald's model for his fictional flappers, women who defied tradition and snubbed their noses at conventional values. Tallulah became one of the wildest extroverts of the twentieth century as well as a serious and celebrated actress. One Birmingham reporter recalled obtaining permission to interview Bankhead at her family home in Jasper. She pondered whether she was underdressed in her typical reporter's garb to interview such a distinguished person. When she rang the bell of the Bankhead home at the appointed hour, an elderly black male servant admitted her and ushered her to the garden where she encountered Tallulah, stark naked, draped onto a lounge chair. The servant served drinks while the reporter interviewed her nude celebrity. Bankhead left New York for London in 1923 a virtual unknown, but she returned to the United States in 1931 after seventeen plays as an international celebrity.

By no means were these three Montgomery women typical of Alabama's values. In fact, conventional religion provided a powerful anchor among the swirling cultural currents of the 1920s. Of Montgomery's 66,000 people, 55,000 (or 83 percent) enrolled in the city's ninety-three churches, and 61 percent of the members were women. Between 1916 and 1926 church membership in Birmingham increased from 77,000 to 125,000.

Denominations of many varieties thrived, led by Baptist and Methodist churches of both races. The state's 2,415 Negro Baptist churches (230 urban and 2,185 rural) had 365,000 members in 1926. That same year white Southern Baptists boasted 2,083 churches (109 urban and 1,974 rural) with 272,000 members. White Methodists counted 197,000 members of 1,422 churches and black Methodists some 126,000 members in 944 churches. Catholics actually lost 14,000 members between 1906 and 1926 (50,000 members compared to 36,000). Many Italian immigrants left Birmingham as the Klan and other nativist groups began to persecute them, and others converted to Protestant churches out of conviction or expediency. Churches of Christ (30,000 members) and Presbyterians (24,000 members) trailed well behind the others. Al-

Tent revival at Fairmont Baptist Church, Red Level (Covington County), ca. 1925 (Courtesy of the Samford University Archives)

though Pentecostal congregations were not numerous (the Church of God counted only 2,200 members in 57 churches in 1926), much of the old-time evangelical fervor had passed to Holiness and Church of God groups that grew rapidly in mill towns and depressed rural areas. As "hard time churches," they provided emotional outlets important to poor people.

Even within main-line denominations enormous variety existed, especially between part-time rural churches with poorly educated bivocational ministers and large, sophisticated urban churches with seminary-trained clergy. L. L. Gwaltney, Baptist pastor and editor of the influential *Alabama Baptist* from 1919 to 1950, deplored the fundamentalist witch-hunts of the 1920s. If Fundamentalism referred to belief in divine inspiration of scripture, the Virgin Birth of Christ, his vicarious atonement, bodily resurrection, and second coming, Gwaltney claimed to know no Baptist preachers who were not Fundamentalists. But he deplored the time and energy wasted by Baptists arguing religion. He denounced both Modernists who held a shallow, humanistic faith and Fundamentalists who tried to force their creeds on others. He was a

463

theistic evolutionist who wrote privately that every farmer who bred his stock knew evolution to be a reality. The 1925 Scopes "monkey" trial in Dayton, Tennessee, he wrote, was unworthy of both science and religion. The Bible no more taught science, he argued, than science books taught religion.

Although Gwaltney supported Herbert Hoover in 1928 because of Al Smith's Catholicism and opposition to prohibition, he also criticized the convict lease system, capital punishment, and lynching of blacks (which he called a "lapse into barbarism and savagery"). Although a Social Darwinist who believed in Anglo-Saxon racial superiority, he held that such notions required whites to assist weaker races. Gwaltney enjoyed telling a story of a white juror who told him: "He was a Negro and we gave him Hell." Gwaltney replied, "Since he was a Negro why did you not give him justice?" During the 1930s Gwaltney applauded the U.S. Supreme Court for overturning the convictions of nine black boys accused of raping two white girls on a train near Scottsboro, and he suggested that socialism might be a more just economic system than capitalism.

If Gwaltney was the symbol of reasoned religion, evangelist Samuel Porter Jones epitomized old-time fire-eating religion. A former drunk turned Methodist minister, he was a native of Chambers County, Alabama. Although dead by the 1920s, his memory lived on among rural Alabamians who had revered him. More learned auditors referred to Jones as the "Savonarola of the hillbillies." His earthy language might offend effete urbanites, but rural people delighted in his denunciations of women's attire. He brought roars of laughter describing a dinner he attended where plunging necklines revealed so much feminine nakedness that he dared not look under the table. Nor did he value education, preferring to be in heaven studying his ABCs, "than sitting in hell reading Greek." Many persons imagined themselves to be religious, he warned, when all they had was a liver ailment.

Such rural folkways lend themselves to negative stereotyping. But in fact such values helped entertain and stabilize Alabama's rural society and provided a sense of community and belonging that was rapidly disappearing in cities. So the 1920s revealed a society not unlike Alabama's politics and economy, with new ways and change everywhere apparent but with subterranean elements of persistence and tradition.

TWENTY-SEVEN

Hard Times, 1930–1940

HARD Times. The Great Depression. The Cataclysm. The decade of the 1930s went by lots of names, but all stood for trouble. In fact, Alabamians born during the first third of the twentieth century would live through the most severe depression and the bloodiest war in the history of the world. They were a tough generation and lived in trying times. The world would never quite be the same again. Neither would Alabama.

Although most people think of the Great Depression as a sudden event triggered by the stock market crash of November 1929, it actually was a gradual collapse. As already noted, agriculture entered a depression during the early 1920s and did not fully recover for two decades. Most industries peaked in 1926 or 1927, then began to decline, usually hitting bottom sometime in 1933. Even after hard times began, some industries and cities suffered more than others. Forest products sustained perhaps the worse decline; textile production held up fairly well. Some experts considered Birmingham the worst-hit city in the United States; Montgomery experienced difficulty, but to a lesser extent.

Between 1930 and 1940 employment rates declined for both races in Alabama. For whites the decline amounted to 5.6 percent, but for blacks employment fell by 13.6 percent. Only three Southern states registered an absolute drop in white employment during the decade; Alabama had the dubious distinction of leading the way. Nonfarm employment declined by 15 percent between 1930 and 1940—also a rate higher than any other Southern state. Because nonfarm jobs fell faster than farm employment, Alabama momentarily reversed its historic trek from country to city. During the twelve months from April 1, 1929, to March 31, 1930, 17,580 people returned to the farm and only 7,836 left. The state began the decade 28 percent urban and ended it only slightly higher at 30 percent urban. Whereas Alabama's urban population had increased a little more than 37 percent between 1910 and 1920 and about 46 percent from 1920 to 1930, it increased only 15 percent between 1930 and 1940. By 1940 Alabama had a population of

2,833,000; of these people, 1,977,000 lived on the land and 856,000 in towns and cities.

Even under the best of circumstances the Great Depression ravaged people's lives. But Alabama's population was weakened already from debilitating problems of sickness and illiteracy. The state Board of Health operated in only fifty-two of Alabama's sixty-seven counties and maintained clinics to serve indigents in only fourteen. Within Alabama nearly 200,000 of the state's farmers and industrial workers were illiterate. Native white illiteracy stood at 5 percent (61,000) despite years of efforts by the illiteracy commission and education department. Agriculture languished. In 1930 Alabama contained 207,000 cotton farms, 30 percent operated by owners and 70 percent by tenants. Among all Alabama farmers 65 percent were landless tenants in 1935. The 600,000 who earned a living in industry worked mainly in low-wage, low-skill, or unskilled jobs.

Paradoxically many of Alabama's poor people hardly knew that a depression had swept across the land. As one wit phrased it, the depression came at a bad time when conditions were awful. Or as blues musician Lonnie Johnson contrasted conditions before and after 1929: "Hard times don't worry me, I was broke when it first started out." Senator John H. Bankhead, Jr., noticed the same phenomenon. During 1935 virtually all industries in Walker County operated at near full capacity; yet county relief rolls contained 2,181 persons, and rural rehabilitation provided for 400 tenant farmers. Bankhead wondered how these figures could be correct and finally concluded that many Walker Countians must not have had jobs even before the depression. Noting sharp declines in both rural and urban conditions in Alabama, one federal investigator concluded: "In all probability these conditions are the accumulation of many years of dwindling income."[1]

For such people poverty was a matter of degree. The old lived in greater dread of ending their lives in a poorhouse. As one elderly Birmingham man wrote national relief administrator Harry L. Hopkins, "Many old people had almost rather die than to go to the poorhouse."[2]

Industrial workers suffered more because they could not grow their own food; and they lost cash income even if their wages had been woefully inadequate before. Mary Dolliver, one of the social workers hired by George Crawford to assist TCI employees, tried to maintain the morale of miners at Docena where employment had declined from 1,000 to 78 by 1933. But privately she wrote her brother:

All I am doing now is taking care of clothing relief cases and flour lines, and all the people I deal with have been without work for months, and they are getting to the point where they are without hope. Like the fool that I am, I'd spend all my earthly goods on them, but it's just a drop in the bucket. . . . Tuesday is always a bad day, with a line of discouraging length to listen to one by one—a tale of woe, insufficient clothing and food, sickness. Pellagra is increasing and I wonder what the end will be. . . . If this thing continues, I will have forgotten how to play.[3]

Those who noticed the most change were middle and upper class folk whose world seemed to come apart. Toccoa Cozart lived in Montgomery where she was a woman of standing in the community. She held a history degree from Auburn and had studied under the legendary George Petrie. She had worked for many years for Thomas McAdory Owen at the state archives. Cozart described herself in a letter to Eleanor Roosevelt as "very proud and independent" and a friend of Congressman Lister Hill and his family. She had resigned her job when Owen died because of advancing age and ill health. But the depression had forced her back into the job market despite her seventy-eight years. Owen's widow and successor, Marie Bankhead Owen, used funds from the Reconstruction Finance Corporation to pay Cozart $3.60 for two days' work each week. Then in the fall of 1933, RFC administrators decided she was too old and removed her from her job of arranging, indexing, copying, and filing state documents. She refused to take a "dole" for doing nothing, and finally her boss sent work for her to do at home in order to justify her tiny salary. She wrote Eleanor Roosevelt because she was furious at the relief agency for hiring young debutantes and society women while elderly historians lost their jobs.

Dr. H. W. Stephenson practiced medicine in Walker County in 1935. He was the only doctor left in a coal mining region that had recently supported seven. Unemployed coal miners could barely afford groceries, much less doctor's bills. For a year he had tended their medical needs but now "they cannot pay," and he could no "longer work for nothing." He believed that "the doctor is the forgotten man during these trying days."[4]

Belle Ogle of Birmingham was much angrier than Cozart or Stephenson. A single woman had no chance to obtain work, she wrote Harry Hopkins in a letter both bellicose and poignant. For ten years she had worked hard; she bought a home; she paid her taxes. Then she had lost her job and walked the streets looking for work. Unsuccessful and in danger of losing her house because of lapsed mortgage payments, she had reached the point where "I will steal for what I have to have, I will join any Communist or any other party and just as soon shoot to kill and get killed as to breathe—All I am waiting for is to find the ones to join up with."[5]

Lorena Hickok came from Washington to report on the response to federal programs in Alabama. She interviewed fifteen unemployed white-collar Alabamians in Montgomery and Birmingham during 1934. They included a certified public accountant, insurance salesman, pharmacist, two engineers, an architect, musician, masseur, pawnshop clerk, and the owner of a lumberyard. All wanted work "to save their self-respect," she reported, but "generally I'd say they were dumb with misery." One explained that taking relief payments to feed his wife and baby was not so bad for a few weeks, but "when it runs into months— you get damned discouraged." The federal analyst explained that relief did not meet middle class expectations because such people tried to cling to "some semblance at least of their normal standards of living." Relief agents provided such people clothes, but the raiment consisted of overalls, not business suits. One relief official explained callously, Hickok wrote, that "we can't keep those white collars laundered." Unemployed professionals tried especially hard to keep houses or apartments in nice neighborhoods. Another person explained: "I do everything I can to pick up a little money to pay that rent. I've washed windows. I've even gone out and competed with Niggers to get jobs mowing lawns. But some weeks I don't make it."[6] One mother had cut her children's meals to two a day.

Such conditions changed Alabama's middle class in profound ways. Even a man long allied to the state's establishment knew that the old order had been swept away. Montgomery *Advertiser* editor Grover Hall, Sr., wrote the fellow editor of an Atlanta paper:

> However much we may love the days of Harding and Coolidge, they are gone forever— they will not be recaptured, no matter how much the newspapers of the land may rant and strain. Personally I fared much better under Pickle Coolidge than I have under any subsequent President—but I saw his world and mine die. Under Roosevelt I saw a new world born, even though much that Roosevelt has done annoys me and will not receive my approval. . . . But a new day, a new world, a new leadership, a new responsibility are here and you and I would be foolish to ignore the fact.[7]

The poor and businessmen alike had to cope in that new world as best they could. Many of the poor believed that somewhere else offered better prospects. They became the rootless people of the Great Depression, the despised "transients."

During four months in 1933 four detectives working for the Louisville and Nashville Railroad expelled more than 27,200 transients from trains and reported they could have expelled twice that number with more detectives. Two detectives riding a train from Birmingham to Montgomery on the night of July 1, 1933, removed 730 "hoboes" and 350 trespassers on railroad right-of-way. But identification of these riders as hoboes distorts their condition. Between 25 and 30 percent were teenage boys without work; another 10 to 15 percent were teenage girls.

Birmingham-area transient camp, 1930s (Photo by Arthur Rothstein, Farm Security Administration, Library of Congress)

Others consisted of entire families on the move. The mood was often angry. Railroad detectives reported that one group of transients believed that newspaper reports of improved economic conditions were "'huey' so the working people would not start a revolution. Many expressed the hope that we would have a real revolution this winter and were expecting to take part in it."[8]

The government established the Alabama Transient Bureau to assist such people. In some towns the bureau cared for transients in private boardinghouses; at other places it created transient camps with tents and soup kitchens. By December 1934, four Alabama transient camps cared for more than 8,000 people, including 424 family groups. When asked in one survey why they went on the road, they responded with answers ranging from "chronic hobo" (446), to "run away" (43), to "adventure" (150). By far the largest number responded that they were "unemployed" (2,245) or "looking for work" (1,911).[9]

A fifty-year-old transient traveled an estimated 38,000 miles from Georgia to Texas to Michigan between 1930 and 1933. All his odd jobs produced less than $1,000. Settled in Mobile, he was startled one night by a frantic knock. When he opened the door, a nearly hysterical black woman stood before him in the dark. She offered to do any kind of work in order to obtain milk for her baby. In her hand she held a paper sack with scraps of food given her by neighbors. He gave her some change, then took out pen and paper and wrote Secretary of Labor Frances Perkins demanding help for the poor.

Business calamities paralleled personal ones. Huntsville's textile industry collapsed like a deck of cards. Dallas Mill, which had reported a profit of nearly $800,000 in 1920, earned only $6,559 in 1929 and in 1930 lost $279,039. Auctioneers sold Lowe Mill at a bankruptcy auction in 1932.

Change also swept over TCI, the state's largest corporation. After the death of Judge Elbert Gary, who had been U.S. Steel's chief executive, the new management of the parent company was less favorable to welfare capitalism. George Crawford resigned as president of TCI in 1930 to become president of Jones and Laughlin Steel Corporation in Pittsburgh. The new president of TCI took advantage of New Deal welfare programs to phase out the expensive company efforts. The head of Crawford's Welfare Department wrote him sadly in 1932 that the new management considered the work of her division to be "needless expense." U.S. Steel also looked less favorably upon its Birmingham facility and extended less autonomy to presidents of its subsidiaries. As a result the TCI operation experienced considerable upheaval.

Three presidents led the corporation during the decade, and their policies changed from Crawford's cooperative management strategy to one of confrontation. They organized a company union to try to prevent unionism. Company officials also probably conspired with Birmingham police to intimidate union organizers and local radicals, sometimes using thugs and physical violence as tactics. Despite its antiunionism, TCI was forced by U.S. Steel to sign an agreement with the United Mine Workers in 1934, with the Steel Workers Organizing Committee in 1937, and the Mine, Mill, and Smelter Workers Union in 1941. But by the latter date production had soared due to wartime demands. By fall 1939 the company operated at 100 percent capacity, but company welfare expenditures during that recovery year amounted to only 14 percent of TCI's 1928 expenditures.

Other Alabama companies fared little better. Birmingham Slag, which depended heavily on road construction for its market, discovered that highway projects were expendable luxuries during hard times. In 1932 the company suffered the only operating loss in its history. Southern Natural Gas Corporation began constructing its first national gas pipeline from northeastern Louisiana to Birmingham. The company began gas deliveries on the last day of 1929 and extended service to Atlanta the following year. But the stock market crash and depression forced the company into receivership.

Alabama Power Company continued construction of its planned series of six hydroelectric dams, but it lost its longtime goal of gaining control of the government's Wilson Dam at Muscle Shoals on the Tennessee River. President Franklin D. Roosevelt incorporated the dam into the new Tennessee Valley Authority system begun in 1933. Arguing that TVA constituted a government entity in competition with free enterprise, attorneys for Alabama Power kept the issue in litigation for half the decade. They finally agreed to divide the state into TVA territory in the northern third of the state and Alabama Power territory in the central and southern two-thirds. Growing state and federal regulation and encroachment led Alabama Power president Thomas W. Martin to help organize the Alabama Chamber of Commerce in June 1937 with headquarters in the state capital. This step strengthened business interests in the legislature and further polarized the state politically, contributing to the rise of bifactionalism between ideological elements within the Democratic party. Meanwhile many residents of the Tennessee Valley received electricity for the first time.

Although state government regulated business abuses through the Public Service Commission, labor, insurance, and banking departments, and factory and mine inspectors, it also encouraged new business by creating the Alabama State Planning Commission in 1935. In time the agency adopted a number of industry-recruiting techniques from Mississippi. A community could sell municipal bonds to construct factories for companies willing to hire a stipulated number of employees or pay a certain payroll. The bonds were exempt from federal taxes. The community often charged the company a nominal rent of a few dollars a year that it could charge as a tax write-off. The industry paid no state taxes because, technically, the building remained public property and thus tax-exempt. State officials rationalized this subsidy for industry by reasoning that the companies created jobs, the state's most critical need during the 1930s. Later raised to a high art form by the Cater and Wallace acts, the strategy attracted many low-wage, labor-intensive factories but at great expense to the state's long-term welfare.

Alabama industrial leaders certainly left no doubt how they felt about political progressivism, whether it emanated from Montgomery or

471

Washington. Thomas Martin led Alabama Power Company into court challenging TVA, but most opposition took the form of bitter denunciations of the New Deal. Scott Roberts, president of the Alabama Cotton Manufacturers Association, blasted New Deal officials for allowing relief benefits to be given to striking textile workers. Associated Industries of Alabama, another powerful political action group, condemned federal relief director Harry Hopkins for feeding striking coal miners. The state's lumber company officials complained that Alabama relief agencies also cared for striking lumber workers.

The New Deal tried to blunt the charges by appointing businessmen to the state board that administered relief in Alabama. Board members included Algernon Blair, Montgomery real estate developer; Donald Comer, Birmingham's textile tycoon; Milton H. Fies, vice-president of the militantly antiunion DeBardeleben Coal Company; and Grover Hall, Sr., Montgomery newspaper editor and longtime ally of planters and Big Mules. But such appointments satisfied neither camp. Workers blasted the relief board because it contained so many businessmen hostile to unionism. Businessmen criticized the board for allowing striking workers to receive relief payments. In time some industrialists painfully acquiesced to the new order of economics, but others held out to the bitter end. Perhaps Huntsville *Times* editor Reese T. Amis best summarized the changing times. Discussing the Social Security Act of 1935 (which provided pensions to the elderly), he surmised that had the proposal been introduced in 1933, businessmen would have called it "dangerous experimentation" or an "un-American form of coddling." But by 1935 businessmen were ignored and most critics thought the bill did not go far enough: "We have had a revolution in this country, after all, and it has taken place in our minds. Our point of view has shifted. We don't look at things with the same eyes that we used to half a dozen years ago. Yesterday's dangerous radicalism is the height of today's conservatism."[10]

One group of Alabamians who were only too aware of the changed conditions were clergymen. In 1935 Roosevelt, gearing up for his 1936 reelection campaign, addressed a letter to 10,000 clergymen, asking them to describe conditions in their communities and to send their opinion of the Social Security bill. Of the Alabama clergymen who received the letter, 327 replied; of those who answered, nearly 79 percent favored FDR and the New Deal—quite a contrast to the reaction of Alabama businessmen. The favorable rating was slightly less than in the nation as a whole, but conditions in Alabama were so desperate in 1935 that many ministers criticized Roosevelt for doing too little.

Little did Roosevelt understand when he sent his letter that many of the clergymen-recipients were themselves bivocational farmers, miners, or mill workers who were as down on their luck as were their impoverished neighbors. As a consequence the responses they sent constituted a personal cry of anguish as well as a social critique of the times.

Most of the ministers served rural congregations. Their cosmology spanned the theological gulf from a Dothan-area tenant farmer–minister who believed the depression would bring the end of the world to another minister who believed FDR's election "must have been God's plan to save our country from ruin." One poetic Methodist minister in Wilsonville, a loyal Democrat who had not voted in three years because he could not pay his poll tax, described his community. Small farmers were losing their farms through foreclosure and farm laborers could not earn enough in a day to buy a bucket of hog lard: "11 cent cotton and 40 cent meat, how in the world can a poor man eat?" A minister near Hartford concluded that the New Deal's Agricultural Adjustment Act had not helped tenant farmers and that the 80 percent of farmers in his neighborhood who were tenants had been "reduced to practical serfdom." A Methodist minister at Courtland had preached throughout Marion, Franklin, and Lawrence counties to people who wore clothes made from feed and fertilizer sacks. Many people refused to attend religious services at all because "they are embarrassed by their poverty and lack of better apparel."[11]

Pastors of industrial workers sent the same kind of letters. The bivocational Baptist pastor of a textile mill church in Florence worked in the knitting mill along with his wife. They made all their own clothes and could not send their children to college because they had no money. A Baptist coal miner–preacher in Walker County lost his job in the mine and was working on the public roads. He lived in an abandoned coal camp with thirty-seven families, thirty white and seven black. The sixty children within these families suffered from malnutrition and lack of health care. He belonged to the United Mine Workers local because "union means onesty [*sic*] friendship love and truth—everything else beside these is ununion ungodly inhuman and unconstitutional."[12] Another minister from the mining/textile town of Cordova reported hundreds of children kept out of school because their families had neither clothes nor food.

Some Alabama ministers expressed misgivings about the fundamental assumptions of the nation's economic system. A clergyman from Union Springs deplored the condition of tenant farmers and warned that the nation had to abandon capitalism. The pastor of Parker Memorial Baptist Church in Anniston voted for Socialist Norman Thomas for president and tried to create a cooperative farm.

Even ministers who refused to abandon capitalism expressed class grievances against big business, which they blamed for the depression.

A minister from near Haleyville complained that the little one-horse farmer had lost out to "the Big fellow and the Landlord" who were "in the saddle in a big way." An evangelist based in the steel community of Fairfield believed the depression would have been over had big business cooperated with the New Deal. He urged a fifteen-year moratorium on new machines that displaced steelworkers and federal legislation limiting business profits to 20 percent. A minister in Alden warned the president that "operators of big business is against you and they are going to come against you hard." A minister at Thorsby believed that big business had "no regard for anything but Big Business." Therefore Roosevelt should tell businessmen that he favored the conduct of the nation's economy for "supplying the needs of the people" rather than merely for the sake of profits. Another minister wrote that "State Agricultural Institutions" used federal programs to strengthen "their grip on the tiller of the soil."[13]

Of course some ministers continued to believe in a more traditional Alabama culture out of loyalty either to the Protestant work ethic, class, or race. A Baptist cotton farmer–minister near Haleyville believed the New Deal had taken away freedoms and reduced the work ethic. He could not hire people on relief to work at picking cotton. Roosevelt was not a president; he was a "dictator." Three-fifths of the members of St. John's Episcopal Church in Birmingham worked in management for TCI. The pastor condemned "selfish" union leaders and protested Roosevelt's policy of "forcing unionization" on the steel industry. A Baptist pastor in Mobile, who believed in white supremacy and the forced expulsion of all blacks back to Africa, warned Roosevelt that "[you] put more stress on your African jungle friends than you do on your white friends." New Deal officials in Mobile, he charged, had made their agencies incubators for communism and interracial marriage.[14]

The conditions of rural poverty described by so many ministers bred despair. In 1931 a physician employed by the Public Health Service visited Macon County in the Black Belt. There he found four women living on nothing but corn bread and sweet potatoes while trying to breast-feed their babies. He found an elderly man who had died after eating raw potatoes he found in a field. The visit to Alabama left him shaken. He had seen crop failures and hunger in the Philippines and China, he wrote, but "this is the first time I realized what is going on in the South."[15]

Lack of stability characterized rural life. Of nearly 160,000 farm families questioned in 1940, 29 percent had lived on their land for less than a year and 50 percent for fewer than three years. Sociological reports by Harold Hoffsommer, a specialist in rural sociology at Auburn University, Paul W. Terry and Verner M. Sims at the University of Alabama, and

Charles S. Johnson, a black sociologist who studied Macon County intensely, revealed devastating and long-lived patterns of poverty. Hoffsommer found that one-third of the adult tenants he interviewed were essentially illiterate, and another third were insufficiently literate to follow simple instructions. The average white sharecropper family moved every 2.6 years while comparable black families moved every 5.1 years. Terry and Sims found that 20 percent of the sharecroppers they studied owned no cows, 35 percent no chickens, and 45 percent no hogs. They attended different, often Pentecostal churches, seldom intermarried with landowners, and rarely voted because they could not pay the poll tax. Their children seldom made it through high school, and when they did they infrequently held positions of leadership.

As statistically compelling as these studies were, it was a different work that bequeathed an everlasting account of Alabama's rural poor. During the middle years of the Great Depression New York photographer Walker Evans and author-critic James Agee came to live briefly with three white sharecropper families. Their efforts resulted in a magisterial but tormented book published in 1941 entitled *Let Us Now Praise Famous Men*. One of the innovative literary feats of the era, the book began with a series of stark, if highly stylized, black and white photographs by Evans. Agee fully intended that the photos and the brilliant, labored text would complement each other. By the time the volume appeared in 1941, interest in the South's poor had waned. But another era resurrected the nearly forgotten book, and by the late 1960s it had become a classic. Television crews from the British Broadcasting Corporation trekked to the country south of Tuscaloosa to interview the families' descendants, and in 1989 two California journalists won a Pulitzer Prize for a history of the families' survivors. Unfortunately during the 1930s sharecroppers were Alabama's forgotten people, not the subject of curiosity.

Agee described lives of desperately poor people who somehow managed to retain family stability and even a fierce kind of pride. J. H. Flynt recalled growing up in the 1930s on a 180-acre sharecropper farm near Ohatchee in Calhoun County. Deprivation affected the way the family dressed, the food they ate, and even the way they celebrated holidays. He tells a story, apocryphal but plausible, about comparative poverty. One sharecropper's son grew weary of the collard green sandwiches that his mother sent to school for his lunch. So he secretly switched lard pails with another child and retreated to a stand of trees to enjoy a little variety and better fare, only to discover that the pilfered lunch contained six hickory nuts and a rock. The family faced one particularly bleak Christmas with resolve to make the best of hard times. They cut a cedar tree from the woodlot and decorated it with strings of popcorn and cotton balls on stringers. Fresh fruit, a rarity in their winter diet, and peppermint candy came from barter of eggs and chickens. Christmas dinner consisted of the turkeys they raised and rabbits that the five boys ran down in a sage field. Their parents gave them homemade toys: jumping jacks, wagon wheel metal hoops to roll, old tire swings, carved animals, and one special store-bought treasure—a tin monkey on a string. Tighten the string and the monkey climbed higher; release the string and the monkey descended.

Rural folkways prevailed in their family. Annie Flynt, their mother, birthed and raised the children, worked in the fields, made all their white-oak cotton baskets, carved goblets and plates from wood, made dresses from feed and fertilizer sacks and quilts from scraps left over from her sewing. She bartered thread and needles from the "rolling store," a truck with sundries that periodically visited their isolated farmstead. Their father arose early, ate a big breakfast of biscuits and "saucered coffee" (poured into a saucer to cool and loudly sucked into the mouth), then departed to harness his mule. He was in the fields ready to plow by first light. Older boys worked with him plowing, chopping, hoeing, or carrying 200-pound guano sacks to fertilize crops. Children grew up fast, assuming the full responsibilities of adults by their early teens. But they also developed close ties with neighbors, helping each other in times of trouble and socializing at church and school. They could plow all day and still dance till 2:00 on a Sunday morning.

The urban poor had no literary genius such as James Agee to describe their plight. During most of the decade at least 35 percent of Alabama's relief load was located in three urban counties: Mobile, Montgomery, and Jefferson. Of 56,000 families on relief statewide in December 1934, 28,000 lived in Birmingham alone. In June 1932 the steel city contained 100,000 wage and salaried people; of these, 25,000 were jobless and 60,000 worked only part-time. The Red Cross estimated that 6,000 to 8,000 people lacked adequate food, fuel, and housing. The county poorhouse at Ketona, designed to hold 220, contained 500. Three years later, in January 1935, Jefferson County listed 100,000 people on its relief rolls, causing President Roosevelt to describe Birmingham as the "worst hit town in the country." The city's normal employment of 45,000 workers in its durable goods industries dropped to 25,000.

Between 1930 and 1940 the population of Birmingham remained almost the same (260,000 in 1930, 268,000 in 1940), as did that of its longtime rival Atlanta (270,000 in 1930, 302,000 in 1940). To care for its citizens the city relied initially on charity: churches, the Community Chest, the League of Women Voters, the chamber of commerce. One reason for the private approach was that of sixty-eight American cities containing more than 120,000 people in 1933, Birmingham ranked next to last in per capita expenditures on vital city services. The massive economic collapse simply overwhelmed the charitable resources of the city. Hattie Freeman, a white unemployed widow caring for a number of small children, wrote President Roosevelt in June 1934 that her black landlord threatened to evict her and confiscate her household furnishings to pay back rent: "Please for God's sakes," she wrote, "send some one to help me in this distress."[16] The president sent a program rather than a person, and the Federal Emergency Relief Administration literally saved the city's desperate population. But even federal relief payments were below the average provided in other Southern cities (they averaged nine dollars per month in Birmingham compared to twenty-one dollars a month in Louisville, Kentucky).

Mobile shared Birmingham's fate, though not to the same extent. By 1935, 10.3 percent of the port city's native-born white families were on relief; 21.7 percent of the white wage earners took home less than $500.00 a year; and 51.7 percent earned less than $1,000.00 a year. The relief payment of Emmett Gale, a father of three, was $2.15 per week. He had to find a way to pay nine cents for cooking oil, $2.06 for groceries, and $2.50 for room rent. Gale begged for a pair of overalls for himself and a pair of shoes for his nearly blind and cancer-stricken wife, but he had to wait until funds could be found to help. After hearing countless desperate stories, the publisher of the Mobile *Post* reported that there were "sparks of revolution in the air that may burst into flame at any moment."[17]

The capital city of Montgomery suffered less than other Alabama cities due to the presence of so many state employees and of Maxwell Field. But by no means was its population immune to the tidal wave of trouble sweeping across the state. Middle class families hit by the depression simplified their lives. In 1930 the city had 11,607 telephones; by January 1933 only 9,899 families still had them. J. H. McCormick renamed his store on Commerce Street "the Poor Man's Store" and accepted city scrip or warrants in lieu of cash. A man's suit sold for $7.14 in November 1934, a five-pound bag of sugar for twenty-seven cents, hams for twelve and one-half cents per pound.

The Montgomery Board of Education decreed in January 1933 that schools could not remain open. The board tried to persuade teachers to take a pay cut and recorded the names of all teachers who rejected the proposal. The attempted intimidation did not work; hard-pressed teachers rejected the proposal by a vote of 276 to 6. Some four hundred parents, PTA and AEA members, and interested citizens demanded that the board of education resign instead, but Mayor William A. Gunter, Jr., finally worked out a compromise to keep the city's 10,000 children in school. Teachers received two-thirds of their salaries, part in cash and part in warranties (promises to pay cash to redeem the warrants at some future time). The Poor Man's Store and other local businesses accepted the warrants in exchange for merchandise in order to keep the school system operating. But the Montgomery *Advertiser* editorialized, "It is deplorable to see Montgomery County's widely celebrated school system collapse, but that is what we have at last seen."[18]

Not even the famous Bankhead family could escape financial trouble. Despite the fact that her brothers were powers in Congress and she was Alabama's state archivist, Marie Bankhead Owen experienced financial setbacks. In May 1931 Owen wrote her niece Tallulah of her great distress both personally and in her career. Her state salary did not cover expenses, and she faced the loss of her property. Her son Thomas made so little working for a Huntsville newspaper that his wife and two children had to live in Montgomery with Owen. She also was frustrated by the state's unwillingness to build a structure to house the crowded state archives then jumbled in the south wing of the capitol. She asked Tallulah if she could come to Hollywood and take a job as secretary for her famous niece. She reassured the flamboyant Tallulah that she would not interfere with her extroverted life-style. Given her niece's legendary reputation for debauchery, Owen wrote in cautious understatement:

Of course, I realize that you are not the child that I used to chaperon but that you are a woman of wide experience and arrived at years of discretion. You have made your own reputation and it would be very unfitting of me to attempt to impose any old fashioned ideals upon you. The fact of the business is I am not as old fashioned a person in my own ideals as most of my generation.[19]

Perhaps not, but Aunt Marie was conventional enough to have opposed women's suffrage in 1919, and Tallulah tactfully declined her aunt's offer. She was much too Victorian for Tallulah Bankhead.

But that was not the end of the matter. Owen borrowed five hundred dollars from Tallulah in 1931 to pay property taxes and asked for the same amount in 1932. This time Tallulah was without funds herself and could offer no help. Alabama's archivist improved her personal finances by the late 1930s and even managed to acquire a spectacular building for the state archives. By then her brother John was an influential U.S. senator and her brother William was Speaker of the House. The economy had improved and she persuaded Governor Bibb Graves to go with her to present her case for an archives building to Harry Hopkins.

Unfortunately Hopkins made no connection between Marie Bankhead Owen's middle name and her famous brothers who wielded such great power in Congress. After impatiently listening to Owen's presentation, he peremptorily dismissed her request. When she was out of hearing he explained curtly to Governor Graves that the government did not have the money to construct a building for every little old lady who wanted an archives. Graves explained that Owen was not just any little old lady but the sister of John and William Bankhead. According to legend the information struck Hopkins speechless. Recovering, he excused himself from the room for a few moments. When Hopkins returned he walked over to Owen in the most felicitous fashion and inquired where in Montgomery she planned to build her new archives.

Dr. Harris P. Dawson practiced pediatrics in the Alabama capital. During the 1930s he charged a dollar for an office visit, three dollars for a home call during the day, and five dollars at night. Patients lacking cash paid him with hams, chickens, eggs, fresh fruits, and vegetables. He also supervised a charity pediatric clinic created by Mayor Gunter in the basement of the city hall. Dawson volunteered his time, and the city donated the medicine. His great cause during the depression was breast-feeding. The city's milk supply was so unsanitary that Dr. Dawson believed breast-feeding infants would save lives. In his diary the physician recorded one notable convert. He persuaded a woman who had already lost one infant to breast-feed her second. She had a third child soon after, and both children were robust, healthy babies. When the youngest child was three years old, it contracted pneumonia. The mother rushed the child to Dr. Dawson, and while he was examining it the child began to scream.

Without warning, his mother immediately opened her dress and dropped out one of her breast[s]. He nursed a few minutes and stopped crying. I was horrified and said "This child is three years old. Why have you not weaned him?" She laughingly answered "I nursed two babies and they did well and I was advised that if I nursed I would not be pregnant; so I have been allowing him to nurse at least once or twice a day since he was a year old." I was convinced that breast feeding had taken hold in that family and that she would be a missionary for it.[20]

As in Birmingham, Montgomery's charitable organizations did the best they could to help the poor. The First Baptist Church began a food pantry and a job referral service. The referral service never worked; many people registered for jobs but no one had jobs to register. To try to raise money for missions the church devised ingenious strategies. In 1933 it sponsored an old gold drive. Members contributed 850 pieces of old gold, including 129 rings, seventy-seven cuff links, one gold head from a cane, ten thimbles, and eight gold tooth fillings (presumably not extracted solely for the occasion).

At the other moral extreme of Montgomery life another institution survived as best it could. During the late 1930s the capital contained 274 bawdy houses scattered across the city, although most were concentrated along Pollard Street near the Alabama River. Most were located on the second floor of buildings with the bottom floor serving as a saloon. A Coca-Cola salesman who delivered Cokes to the saloons counted the brothels and preserved this bit of social history from the Great Depression. Shortly after he completed his calculations the Second World War began and Air Force officials at Maxwell Air Force Base insisted that the city clean up its red-light district. A sanitized, presumably more moral city resulted, though not one entirely welcomed by male citizens.

Perhaps the most poetic description of Montgomery during these dark years came from the pen of novelist F. Scott Fitzgerald. After removing his wife Zelda from a mental hospital in Switzerland, Fitzgerald brought her back to Montgomery for a brief period. When they returned to the city in September 1931 a giant Alabama Power Company sign located between the railroad station and the river wharves winked an optimistic greeting: "Montgomery: The Key to Your Opportunity." The welcome could hardly have been more inappropriate to the times. Old mansions Zelda had once loved were now overgrown and dilapidated, peopled by undertakers, fortune-tellers, and prostitutes. The couple rented a house on Felder Avenue in Cloverdale and tried to patch together a relationship far advanced toward disintegration.

Fitzgerald proclaimed that the city showed less effect of the depression than any town he had visited: "In Alabama, the streets were sleepy and remote and a calliope on parade gasped out the tunes of our youth. . . . Nothing had happened there since the Civil War."[21] The couple set up housekeeping with a white Persian cat called Chopin and a blood-hound named Trouble.

The dog's name was more appropriate to the times. George Pool, a black man whose family farmed on the edge of town, remembered transients of both races coming to his father's door and begging for food. B. Y. Farris, also black and born only two blocks from the capitol, recalled friends who borrowed money to buy Christmas toys, then spent all year paying the debts before borrowing again. And two poor women with four children wrote to President Roosevelt asking for house rent, food, and clothes:

I bleave you are to good to let poor little children go hungry and purnish them that way we wont even have a house to live in much less something to eat and wear and burn the Lord didnt put us here to go hungry and it is a sin before God the way some people is purnishing the poor people they ant no rest for such people the Lord says a rich man cant enter the Kingdom of heaven a bit more than a camel can go through the eye of a needle so you see they got a slim chance to get there when they go the burning they will wish they had turned the money loose and divided with the poor.[22]

Many of the poor were less resigned to waiting for heavenly judgment. They took matters into their own hands. Organized labor had collapsed in the 1920s, a casualty both of opposition from the business community and of apathy or fear among workers. When John L. Lewis began an organizing drive among Alabama miners in 1933, only 225 of them belonged to the UMW.

Between 1933 and 1938 the New Deal installed a legislative framework sympathetic to labor. Section 7(a) of the National Industry Recovery Act (June 1933) gave employees the right to organize and bargain collectively. The National Labor Relations Board (NLRB) enforced the legislation. Congress replaced 7(a) with the National Labor Relations Act (often called the Wagner Act after its sponsor) in July 1935. It prohibited a number of unfair practices used by employers against unions. The Walsh-Healy Act of 1936 established minimum labor standards for firms receiving government contracts, and the Fair Labor Standards Act of 1938 fixed minimum wage and maximum hours for companies engaged in interstate commerce.

Most of the workers affected by minimum wage laws lived in the South where industry paid the lowest wages (and Alabama had the largest number of industrial workers of any Southern state). Of 690,000 workers earning less than 30 cents an hour in the spring of 1939, 54 percent were Southerners. The 32½ cent minimum wage went into effect in October 1939 and raised the salaries of 44 percent of Southern textile workers compared to only 6 percent in the North. In the forest products industry half of all Southern laborers made exactly the minimum wage after the new law went into effect. The changes completed the transition of Alabama's economy from one of isolation to integration into national economic patterns. Furthermore, Congress, the NLRB, and federal courts became more persistent in prosecuting vigilantes who violated the civil liberties of union organizers. Finally the newly organized Congress of Industrial Organizations (CIO) focused its efforts on Southern industrial workers.

Despite such assistance the organizing battle gained ground grudgingly. Businessmen organized as effectively as labor and fought unionism at every step. They effectively branded CIO organizers as "Communists" and "integrationists," charges that would still echo in Alabama politics decades later.

The first skirmish in what became a protracted war occurred during a lengthy strike by coal miners in 1933–34. John L. Lewis sent two tenacious organizers, William Mitch and William Dalrymple, to Birmingham to resurrect District 20 of the UMW. Henry and Charles De-Bardeleben led company efforts to defeat the miners' union, and for two years sporadic violence by both sides crackled through the hills and hollows north of Birmingham. Strikebreakers and company guards clashed with 7,000 striking miners, and the governor once again sent in the National Guard. But this time the federal administration sided with

Birmingham barbershop window, February 1937 (Photo by Arthur Rothstein, Farm Security Administration, Library of Congress)

the miners, allowing them onto relief rolls and defending their legal right to join unions if they desired. As a consequence, by spring 1934 thirty-eight companies representing 90 percent of Alabama's miners had signed agreements with the UMW.

Textile workers ranked with miners and timber workers as the poorest paid industrial workers in Alabama. The state's average mill hand earned thirteen dollars a week in 1930 for a ten- to twelve-hour day. By comparison, truck drivers and stenographers made twenty to twenty-five dollars a week. The industry posed special problems for organizers. Unlike coal mining, which was concentrated in a few northern counties and involved similar kinds of work, textile mills were scattered in small units across the state and involved many different fabrics and proce-

Coal miners, Birmingham, 1930s (Courtesy of the Farm Security Administration, Library of Congress)

dures. The predominantly white and female labor force also differed fundamentally from the nearly all-male and mainly black mining force. Individual strikes broke out during the early 1930s but were put down by National Guard units sent by Governor Benjamin M. Miller.

A new phase of labor unrest began in July 1934 when Huntsville textile workers walked off their jobs. Despite the kidnapping of their leader by a former commander of the American Legion, threats of violence against them, and the opposition of the state Federation of Labor, 15,000 Alabama textile workers struck thirty mills, most of them in north Alabama. "Flying squads" of workers loaded aboard jalopies and trucks and drove from mill to mill, urging workers to walk off their jobs. Arriving at Lanett and Opelika, they were greeted by bales of cotton piled on the highway to block their passage and by guards carrying high-powered rifles and even manning machine gun emplacements. By the fall the work stoppage that began in Alabama spread nationwide into the largest strike in American history to that time. Although textile workers lost their strike, the industry continued to experience conflict for years. The worst episode during the 1930s occurred in Talladega, where a gunfight on a thoroughfare (appropriately called Battle Street) between strikers, law enforcement officials, and antiunion local businessmen resulted in two killed and sixteen wounded. As in the earlier case of federal assistance to striking coal miners, textile workers won support from the pro—New Deal Bibb Graves administration.

Although efforts by the United Rubber Workers to organize Gadsden's Goodyear Tire plant failed due to company-inspired violence, supported by local businessmen and law enforcement officials, even that company would succumb to litigation and union pressure in the early 1940s. So the 1930s produced a vigorous labor movement in Alabama supported by both federal and state New Deal officials. The strongly organized, biracial movement provided the core strength of Alabama's reform movement and furnished money and muscle for its candidates.

Allegations by businessmen of worker radicalism were wildly exaggerated. Most Alabama workers wanted a larger share of the pie, not replacement of the pie with some alternative dessert. Once given what they viewed as their fair share of the fruits of capitalism, white workers turned against their black brothers and sisters. Conservative unions denounced radical ones, and workers newly installed in the middle class quickly forgot the poor they left behind. Successful workers rationalized that they earned their way out of poverty whereas their less worthy companions slacked off or wasted their opportunities.

For a small fraction of Alabamians during hard times the charge of radicalism was correct. In 1930 the American Communist party established a Southern headquarters in Birmingham and began publishing the *Southern Worker.* The Communist-front International Labor Defense Fund also opened an office in the city. Communists sponsored a candidate for the U.S. Senate in 1930 and a slate that included a Birmingham congressional candidate and two presidential electors in 1932. Roosevelt easily defeated Herbert Hoover in Alabama by a vote of 208,000 to 35,000 (a drastic decline from the 120,725 votes Hoover had won against Al Smith in 1928). Radical candidates caused barely a ripple. The Socialist party polled 2,000 votes and the Communist party only 726.

During these years Communists operating from Birmingham organized a small Share Croppers Union in east-central Alabama that led to violent attempts by white officials and landowners to destroy it. They also rallied support for the nine "Scottsboro boys," blacks accused of raping two white Huntsville textile workers. Through the pages of the *Southern Worker,* Communists attacked lynching and exploitation of blacks, blamed unemployment on the foibles of capitalism, and denounced vigilantism aimed at Birmingham's small radical community. They even staged a fairly large demonstration at the construction site of Birmingham's 18th Street overpass in December 1930. Some 5,000 unemployed, two-thirds of them blacks, gathered at the construction site seeking jobs. The construction foreman made the mistake of passing through the crowd selecting a few of the unemployed for work while ignoring most of the others. The crowd became furious and began chasing the terrified foreman. He fled into the lobby of the Morris Hotel, followed by 4,000 unemployed workers. A black member of the Young Communist League addressed those who could crowd inside about the capitalistic roots of unemployment and how businessmen used racial prejudice to divide workers. Police arrived and broke up the demonstration, but the specter of radicals chasing a supervisor through the streets of Birmingham and occupying the lobby of a hotel sent shudders through many citizens.

Following the 1934 wave of strikes, both Birmingham and Bessemer enacted antisedition laws. The Birmingham police force also organized a "red squad" to raid homes of known leftists, harass labor organizers, and enforce the antisedition act. Police interpreted sedition to mean anyone who possessed a copy of the *Southern Worker* or even journals such as the *Nation* and *New Republic*. Vigilantes fired at one group of dissidents and kidnapped and flogged Joseph S. Gelders, the most prominent local radical. Gelders, the son of a prosperous Jewish restaurateur, attended Massachusetts Institute of Technology before earning a degree from the University of Alabama, where he stayed on to teach physics. Long troubled by the suffering of the poor, he became even more upset by violence and violations of civil liberties in his hometown during a 1934 strike. He was increasingly drawn into leftist causes and finally the Communist party. Opposition to Gelders increased when he organized weekly discussion groups for University of Alabama students.

The physical attack on him in 1935 enraged editors of state papers and led Governor Graves to order an investigation. Although local law enforcement officials dragged their feet and even covered up evidence, state investigators finally identified the likely perpetrators as members of the Alabama National Guard and TCI employees. A grand jury refused to indict them, but Birmingham's antiradical violence clearly occurred with the connivance or active participation of city officials and perhaps even TCI.

Radicalism would have made far more impact on Alabama had it not been for New Deal relief programs. Before Franklin Roosevelt's inauguration as president in March 1933, he visited Montgomery. The state's electorate had overwhelmingly voted for him, so the huge throng that greeted him at Union Station was no surprise. The Twenty-ninth Infantry Band from Fort Benning, Georgia, struck up his campaign theme song, the ironic "Happy Days Are Here Again," as he rode up Dexter Avenue to the capitol and was wheeled up a ramp to the rear door, then through the rotunda, and onto the speaker's stand facing Dexter Avenue. People crowded the street for three blocks down the hill. From the spot where Jefferson Davis had proclaimed a message of hope in 1861, where

Theodore Roosevelt had promised a Square Deal in 1908, another Roosevelt brought a message of renewal. He spoke of plans for developing the Tennessee Valley and restoring prosperity, and Alabamians listened and prayed that his optimism might be fulfilled.

In many ways it was. Within months after his inauguration Congress passed a measure establishing the Tennessee Valley Authority. The scheme would transform the valley through a series of hydroelectric dams. The network would provide navigation of the river, flood control, a vast recreational area, cheap electrical power to the state's northern third, and pave the way for eventual industrialization. Before the New Deal the valley, which drained parts of seven states, was the poorest area of the United States with a per capita income only one-third the national average. Only 0.2 percent of farms in the valley had electricity in 1930, only 3.0 percent had running water, and illiteracy rates stood at 6.8 percent compared to the national rate of 1.5. The decade-long construction program not only created thousands of jobs for the unemployed but also built dams whose generators electrified farms throughout the region, produced cheap fertilizers, and led to a flourishing trade in midwestern grains, which in turn stimulated the livestock and poultry industries. During the boom times of the 1940s, industry poured into the valley, attracted by its cheap labor and electricity.

All this change came at a price. Ancestral lands sank beneath the waters of TVA lakes. Ancient folkways gave way to modernity. Promises to hire black employees equal to the black proportion of the population translated into skilled, high-paying jobs for whites and menial, low-paying jobs for blacks. But the most significant manifestation of how Alabamians of both races living in the valley felt about TVA was political: the congressional district became the most pro–national Democratic party in the state.

New Deal agricultural programs had an even more ambivalent impact. The Commodity Credit Corporation advanced loans on crops. The Agricultural Adjustment Act encouraged farmers growing a specific crop to impose acreage restrictions and marketing agreements in return for guaranteed federal price supports. Unfortunately Edward A. O'Neal III, a north Alabama planter and president of the national Farm Bureau Federation, influenced the Department of Agriculture to administer the programs through a minority of Alabama farmers who actually owned land. As a consequence, landowners often received federal payments to reduce acreage. Then they removed the acreage of their tenants from production and forced them off the land. Next they used the money to buy tractors, consolidate farms into larger parcels, fertilize the remaining land heavily, and produce more crops on fewer acres. As a result the average size of farms increased, as did mechanization, and thousands of tenant farm families were forced out of agriculture altogether.

Later federal programs helped Alabama's rural poor more. A Division of Subsistence Homesteads funded the purchase of small farms (five to ten acres) near cities to combine subsistence farming and nonfarm employment. The Resettlement Administration, created in May 1935, undertook a broader task of selling larger plots of land to poor farmers, providing credit and supervision, and took over rural rehabilitation from the FERA. Senator John Bankhead, Jr., sponsored the Subsistence Homestead Program in 1933. Of the $25 million appropriated for the program, Bankhead obtained $6 million, or nearly one-fourth the total, for Jefferson and Walker counties. The money funded five subsistence communities at Palmerdale, Gardendale (Mount Olive), Trussville (called Cahaba Farms or "Slagheap Village"), Bessemer (called Greenwood), and Jasper (called Jasper Subsistence Farms or Bankhead Farms). Unemployed workers built the houses. Officials desired that each family combine part-time wage work with subsistence garden plots. Unfortunately the projects merely skimmed the top off Alabama's bottom class. Lengthy interviews, background investigations, letters of reference, employment records, and credit checks assured that most residents were formerly machinists, skilled artisans, professionals, or workers in service occupations.

Relief officials began two such projects for blacks at Prairie Farms in Macon County and Gee's Bend in Wilcox County, and black agricultural agent Thomas Campbell from Tuskegee helped organize the Black Belt Improvement League and the Tuskegee Self-Help Cooperative. The two agencies established a revolving fund to help other black tenants acquire land. Federal agencies loaned the cooperative $68,000 to begin canning, farming, livestock, and small farm implement manufacturing projects. Campbell also kept careful watch for Communists and radicals trying to organize black tenants. He calmed blacks who were furious over a shoot-out between black sharecroppers and county deputies at Camp Hill in July 1931 and reported "radical" activity to the white director of the Cooperative Extension Service at Auburn. He also used radio programs to reach black farmers with his reform ideas and won many awards for his efforts.

One of the most extensive resettlement efforts began in 1934 on Cumberland Mountain fourteen miles northwest of Scottsboro. White tenant farmers began to clear the land and build houses under careful government supervision. Internal friction among the fiercely independent Appalachian settlers, unrealistic expectations by government bureaucrats, jealousy, and mismanagement plagued the project. Although Skyline Farms became a superb laboratory of Appalachian folkways, it never succeeded economically, and the government sold the forty-acre farms in 1945.

The New Deal agency that touched the most lives in rural Alabama

Fiddler Mary McLean, Skyline Farms, 1937 (Photo by Ben Shahn, Farm Security Administration, Library of Congress)

was the Rural Rehabilitation Division of the Federal Emergency Relief Administration. It provided rented land, credit, work animals, and supplies for farmers, effectively assuming the role traditionally played by a landlord. Alabama was one of the first three states to initiate rural rehabilitation in early 1934, and its program soon became the largest in the nation. By December it enrolled families numbering 115,000 people. County extension agents and local rehabilitation committees administered the program. Clashes often occurred between county agents unaccustomed to working with poor farmers and relief officials who usually came from a more idealistic background in social work. Officials made heavy demands on clients, who were required to find a landowner willing to rent them land, to obtain permission for both the agreement and the land, and to plant food crops rather than cotton. They had to purchase supplies from the Rehabilitation Corporation because the government was "not giving anybody anything." The agency maintained a rigorous work ethic in its relief program, warning clients in its instruction booklet: "You will work for what you get and you will be expected to earn every cent. If you have an idea this is a 'set-up' and that you won't have much work to do, then don't come into the program because there is more work than anything else to it."[23]

Alabama's program was the first approved by FERA officials, and some of its procedures became models for other states. One federal investigator considered the state program simple, practical, and well administered.

The program's most memorable feature from the farmer's viewpoint was the provision of oxen or "steers" in place of mules for plow animals. A good mule cost between $100 and $150 in Alabama, whereas an ox cost only $15 to $30. Furthermore, feeding a mule for a month cost about the same as feeding a family.

Black Belt planters ridiculed both oxen and clients. One told a federal investigator that farmers would not be able to break steers to a plow. Furthermore, oxen would not work in heat. "Let it get to be noon," he warned, "and they jest lay right down—or wander off to the swamp draggin the Nigger with 'em." He added, "Hell, this ain't no New Deal if we all gotta go back plowin' steers." Planters demeaned the rural rehabilitation clients as well. One planter expressed amusement that the government should expend so much effort on "pore white trash and Niggers." More thoughtful planters estimated a rehabilitation success rate of 50 percent if the clients were carefully supervised ("You jest gotta stand right over 'em").[24] Relief officials were much more optimistic, blaming rural poverty on lack of opportunity. Despite its successes, rural rehabilitation at its best constituted only a stopgap effort.

Senator John Bankhead, Jr., proposed the most long-lasting effort to help the South's tenant farmers. A 1935 federal report, based on research in Georgia, Alabama, Mississippi, and Arkansas, concluded that the South's tenancy system had collapsed and could not be repaired. Agricultural policy should promote small landownership. The Agricultural Adjustment Act had failed in this objective, and Senator Bankhead introduced the Bankhead-Jones Farm Tenancy bill in February 1935. It proposed $1.05 billion in capital to provide land, equipment, and livestock for resale to tenants on liberal credit terms. The bill passed the Senate but died in the House for lack of presidential support. Two years later Roosevelt decided to support a scaled-down version of the bill, but the final Bankhead-Jones Act of 1937 appropriated only $10 million for direct farm purchase loans and gave preference to tenants who owned equipment and livestock or who could make small cash down payments. At its peak the Farm Security Administration, which administered the program, assisted only about one in every twenty-two land purchase applicants. In Region 5, which included Alabama, the FSA provided rural rehabilitation loans to some 35 or 40 percent of those who needed them. Many applicants experienced poor health (in Butler County 155 rehabilitation clients dropped by the FSA in 1937 had hookworm and four-fifths manifested other health problems). Relatively few blacks (22 percent of all loans) or sharecroppers (17 percent of all loans) received help. The program helped the most successful of Alabama's poor and largely ignored the rest.

Thad Holt, a native Alabamian, presided over the state's relief apparatus created by Governor Benjamin M. Miller in December 1932. Another native Alabamian, Aubrey Williams, who grew up poor in Birmingham, became field representative and later assistant administrator of the FERA. The Civil Works Administration began providing jobs in November 1933, just in time to save one Birmingham department store about to declare bankruptcy. The CWA expended $15 million before its demobilization in April 1934. At its peak it employed 129,000 Alabamians. The Works Progress Administration followed, also headed by Holt. It divided the state into six districts and pumped federal money into various construction projects. Federal relief director Harry Hopkins complained in 1935 that the state government had contributed nothing during the previous twenty-three months, during which the federal government had provided Alabama nearly $26 million in relief. He insisted that the state provide at least $3 million in assistance.

Although Alabama's relief program became a model for other Southern states, it experienced internal dissension and pleased neither clients nor critics. Thad Holt and Lorraine Tunstall-Bush, the state director of social services, did not get along well. Social workers and Auburn extension agents clashed frequently. Aubrey Williams advocated a biracial relief effort, which many white Alabamians opposed.

To many clients, relief payments were inadequate, delayed by bureaucracy, and unfairly administered. Even state relief officials admitted shortages of funds that interrupted relief and required cutting thousands of families from relief rolls. Tunstall-Bush wrote that even in good times Alabama relief was "far from adequate measured by any decent standards." But by summer 1933 the average relief payment in the state had declined to little more than eight dollars a month; even this figure was misleading because 20,000 families in Jefferson County averaged between seventeen and eighteen dollars monthly. Tunstall-Bush reported to Thad Holt that the health of relief clients was worsening: "Pellagra, tuberculosis prevail to undreamed of extents; nervous breakdowns attributed to mental strains resulting from inadequate relief are discernible on every hand."[25] Poor clients complained that middle class relief officials favored the white-collar unemployed and discriminated against union members. They denounced bureaucratic guidelines that cut off relief when clients moved to a new county. They alleged corruption. Relief officials sometimes discovered politically inspired relief appointments and occasionally gave extra construction work to skilled laborers, so that a minority of skilled clients received the majority of relief payments. Middle class clients complained that lazy blacks and poor whites received too much and performed no useful work. Furthermore they particularly objected to paying relief to striking workers who voluntarily left jobs where they could earn a living wage.

Prominent citizens who still had jobs divided welfare recipients into the deserving and undeserving poor. A Catholic priest wrote about chronic poor people willing to live on charity and middle class, industrious people who were anxious for work and embarrassed to accept relief. Businessman Herbert Stockham praised blacks who were satisfied with relief and criticized whites who always complained that the amount was too little. In his view the long-term solution to poverty was to curb federal efforts to force "closed shop unionism in industry" and try instead to locate the unemployed on farms. A prominent social worker attributed poverty to eugenics and lack of education. She claimed that children and women deserted by their husbands, together with the old and sick, constituted most of the poor. They had little education and few job skills, she added, and many of them also suffered from a deficiency in character. Labor leader Noel Beddow criticized the predominance on relief rolls of middle class college-educated workers, who hid their assets, and of blacks who, he argued, really did not desire to work anyway. As a result unemployed industrial laborers received too little to survive. Relief, he concluded, "is succeeding far better in making bolsheviks and radicals in the State of Alabama than any group or groups of Russian envoys could do."[26] Then as later, public welfare suited neither recipients nor those whose taxes paid for it.

In addition to these relief efforts, the federal government provided other forms of help. The National Youth Administration, which was headed by Birmingham native Aubrey Williams, provided jobs for college students that allowed them to stay in school. The Social Security Act of 1935 required the state to create the Alabama Department of Public Welfare to administer all public assistance programs. It replaced the older Child Welfare Department and assumed responsibility for the elderly, dependent children, the mentally and physically handicapped, and unemployed women.

The Civilian Conservation Corps enrolled nearly 67,000 youths during its nine-year lifetime (1933–42). Youngsters fifteen to twenty-four years old constituted 32 percent of the 1930 population, and the CCC enrolled about one-fourth of the eligible single men within this age group. It provided a military-like camp atmosphere that emphasized education, job skills, discipline, and organization. Relief officials selected the boys from local relief rolls. Although the agency conducted 150 types of work, it concentrated on forest protection, erosion control, irrigation, drainage, transportation, landscaping, and recreational construction. Nearby colleges provided courses in math, history, forestry, civics, grammar, spelling, radio, typing, and woodworking to supplement the more mundane skills learned in camps.

Although the legislature had begun the Alabama park system in 1923 as part of the new Alabama Forestry Commission, it was the CCC that constructed seventeen state parks with rustic cabins, hiking trails, dams, lakes, and picnic facilities. Taking advantage of Alabama's spectacular natural beauty, the CCC constructed spacious parks at Cheaha, Chewacla, De Soto Falls, and at many other sites. They also planted 4.5 million trees (they were the "tree army"), built forty-nine lookout towers and nearly 2,900 miles of truck trails, and reduced annual forest fires by more than two-thirds. As a by-product of this work, their families received a federal check for $25 a month, and the enrollees received medical care and nourishing food. The rigorous military-style discipline by regular army officers, the hard work, good medical care, and nutritious meals helped assure the nation a far better pool of fighting men for the Second World War than would have been possible without the CCC.

Thad Holt was unusual among Southern state relief directors in his willingness to appoint significant numbers of young black men to the CCC. Alabama led all Southern states in the number of black enrollees: of the eighty-three black CCC camps in the South, Alabama had eleven of them. Blacks and whites working on CCC roads received the same salary.

Many of the camps were located in wilderness areas where boredom became a problem. Innovative camp directors coped with the excess energy of the young men in imaginative ways. The supervisor of Florala's camp held rattlesnake contests with prizes for the largest snakes killed each day. He even utilized the meat resulting from this campaign to supplement the camp diet. Apparently recruits devoured snake meat as quickly as they did everything else in sight. Profiting from three hearty meals a day, many enrollees gained forty to fifty pounds during their first six months in camp. Cooks told one voracious recruit to slow down before he burst. He replied contemptuously, "pass the stew and get out of the way." Camp sports also played a major role in social life, with football and baseball attracting greatest interest. Some camp commanders became proficient at recruiting skilled athletes from poor families. One boy originally bound for a camp in Oregon wound up in Fort Payne because of his skills with bat and glove.

The heritage of the New Deal is hard to estimate. On the negative side its agricultural policies strengthened landowners, drove tenants off the land, and ignored the problems of the poorest farmers. TVA failed in its grandiose schemes of social planning and racial equality. Relief helped but often flowed through channels twisted by political and racial prejudices. But at least relief kept people clothed, housed, and eating. New Deal labor policies empowered workers to organize in order to protect themselves from capricious managers. Blacks received fairer treatment than at any time since Reconstruction. Social Security and creation of the state welfare department closed county poorhouses and provided a welfare system both more humane and more extensive than before. The TVA brought the miracle of electricity to rural north Alabama and laid the groundwork for an industrial boom in the 1940s. The exodus of tenant farmers and the imposition of a nationwide minimum wage and of maximum hours reduced the South's appeal to low-wage industry and further integrated its economy into national labor and capital markets. State government became somewhat less concerned about protecting white supremacy and social stability and more concerned about promoting business and industrial growth. On balance the New Deal accomplished more than its critics were willing to concede and less than its admirers claimed.

TWENTY-EIGHT

How New a Deal in Alabama?

G IVEN the dominating presence of President Roosevelt and New Deal liberalism, it was nearly inevitable that state politics would divide basically along the lines of FDR's supporters and opponents. The anti–New Dealers drew their strength from planters and industrialists. The New Deal appealed mainly to unionists and small farmers, especially in north Alabama. Familiar older divisions between hill counties/Wiregrass and Black Belt/southwestern counties added a new issue: ideological conflicts over the role of the federal government in providing assistance to needy citizens, whether in the form of agricultural subsidies, jobs for college students, or help to union organizers, farmers seeking electricity, or small businessmen seeking low-interest loans.

New Dealers ranged from unenthusiastic politicians, such as Congressman John McDuffie to progressives such as Aubrey Williams. McDuffie reluctantly supported the New Deal until Roosevelt appointed him to a judgeship in 1935. After that he criticized Hugo Black's appointment to the Supreme Court (Black was "wholly unqualified"), denounced the Farm Security Administration as a "socialistic schemer," and defined New Dealers as "a cross between Socialists and Communists."[1] In 1930, Congressman Henry B. Steagall of Ozark, descended from a Populist tradition, became chairman of the powerful House Banking and Currency Committee. He developed a warm personal relationship with FDR and loyally supported virtually all New Deal legislation. Steagall left a permanent mark on the nation's financial structure as coauthor of the Glass-Steagall Act of 1933, which reformed the banking system and created the Federal Deposit Insurance Corporation to guarantee bank deposits.

Congressman George Huddleston, Sr., of Birmingham represented labor and progressive elements in his district and also furnished consistent support for the New Deal. Ironically the same forces of labor, which kept him in office from 1914 until 1937, split with him and endorsed Luther Patrick in 1936. Influential Senator Hugo Black endorsed Patrick, who won by a vote of 20,000 to 14,000. Patrick's voting record was similar to Huddleston's in favor of New Deal measures.

Although conservative in his basic values, Senator John Bankhead, Jr., became a firm ally of FDR and a loyal New Dealer. On the issue of aid to tenant farmers, he actually pushed Roosevelt to the left. Bankhead's powerful positions on the Senate agriculture and banking committees gave him significant power from which to launch his Subsistence Homestead and Cotton Control acts. He split with Roosevelt in 1937 on the issue of packing the Supreme Court with liberals but otherwise supported the New Deal consistently, as did his younger brother William, who became Democratic majority leader and Speaker of the House in 1934. William Bankhead launched a campaign for the Democratic vice-presidential nomination in 1940 but could not win Roosevelt's endorsement. John Bankhead soured on Roosevelt following the family slight and helped block the appointment of fellow Alabamian Aubrey Williams as director of the Rural Electrification Administration.

When Roosevelt raised Senator Hugo Black to the Supreme Court in 1937, he created a justice who would leave a lasting judicial impression on interpretation of the First Amendment rights of privacy, free speech, and separation of church and state. Over a career that spanned parts of four decades, Clay County's Justice Black translated his Southern Baptist convictions of appropriate religious exercise in public schools, racial justice, and protection of free speech and privacy into American law. Despite initial public debate over the qualifications of a former Ku Klux Klansman for the high court, Black earned acclaim as one of the twentieth century's most influential jurists. Yet his decisions on racial integration, free speech, and school prayer did not win applause back home. Clay Countians erected no markers in his honor, and many Alabamians denounced him as a renegade and traitor to his people.

His appointment to the Supreme Court removed one of Roosevelt's most loyal supporters from the Senate and set the stage for a special election to fill Black's vacated seat. The major contenders were Tom Heflin, badly scarred from the 1928 and 1930 campaigns, and Congressman Lister Hill. Heflin suffered from poor health, heavy drinking, advancing age, and a reputation for demagoguery and congressional ineffectiveness. Hill on the other hand, descended from a distinguished Montgomery family, was an effective New Deal congressman with close ties to Roosevelt, and he had fashioned a superb campaign organization.

The fall 1937 campaign revealed deep rifts in Alabama politics. The state's industrialists, timber owners, planters, and business leaders reluctantly endorsed Heflin, more out of fear of New Dealers than for any personal liking of Heflin. Hill emphasized his support of the New Deal, Roosevelt, and especially TVA. Organized labor strongly supported Hill, as did north Alabama farmers. Paradoxically, Heflin ran strongest among poor whites, planters, and Big Mules, leaving Hill the great middle ground of Alabama politics, and Hill won easily.

Although congressional New Dealers attracted the most attention, other sympathizers exerted the greater impact on state politics. Numerous journalists endorsed the New Deal and defended it from detractors. John Temple Graves II came to Birmingham early in the decade and consistently supported the New Deal in essays that one national magazine described as the first successful syndicated newspaper column. A Princeton University graduate who also held a law degree from George Washington University, Graves originally supported FDR but gradually moved to the political right after the president's 1937 court-packing scheme. Neil Davis, editor and publisher of the *Lee County Bulletin;* Gould Beech, editorial writer for the Montgomery *Advertiser;* James H. (Jimmy) Faulkner, editor-publisher of the *Baldwin Times;* and Charles G. Dobbins, publisher of the Anniston *Times,* never wavered in their support of the New Deal. All except John Temple Graves participated in the Alabama Policy Committee, which charted a reformist course for state politics.

Others who played key roles in the committee were: Charles W. Edwards, Auburn University's registrar; Ralph B. Draughon, then an Auburn history professor but soon to be its president; and George Le Maistre, a Tuscaloosa attorney and University of Alabama law professor. The policy committee opposed discriminatory freight rates that penalized Alabama products, favored equal justice for blacks, and sought repeal of the cumulative poll tax (wherein voters had to pay for back years). A multitude of reformers allied to these policymakers, and together they left their mark on Alabama's political landscape for years: Birmingham-area CIO organizers/attorneys William Mitch and Noel Beddow; New Deal bureaucrat Aubrey Williams; radical poet and Subsistence Homestead administrator John Beecher; attorney Clifford Durr and his wife, Virginia Foster Durr, who used her family connection to Hugo Black (her brother-in-law) to lobby Congress for abolition of the poll tax; and Herman C. Nixon, a political scientist teaching at Vanderbilt but a native of Possum Trot in Calhoun County.

One of the most memorable events indicating the rising sentiment for change was the organization of the Southern Conference for Human Welfare in November 1938. It held its first meeting in Birmingham's historic municipal auditorium. Designed to unify Southerners behind a New Deal agenda, the assembly attracted a distinguished cast of Alabamians: Black, Bankhead, Hill, Williams, the Durrs, Nixon, Tuskegee Institute president F. D. Patterson, Bibb Graves, liberal young Baptist minister Charles R. Bell from Anniston, and many others. Nixon was both a chief organizer and secretary of the SCHW.

Despite the euphoria of shared idealism, an incident during the meeting was the harbinger of troubled times ahead for Alabama liberals.

496

While the audience listened to a speaker discuss farm tenancy, Birmingham police commissioner Eugene ("Bull") Connor informed conference leaders that he intended to enforce the city's segregation ordinance. They stopped the speaker and rearranged the audience with the central aisle dividing one thousand whites from two hundred blacks, who sat in a section prominently marked "colored." At subsequent sessions Eleanor Roosevelt symbolically protested Birmingham's racism by placing her chair in the center aisle separating the races. Despite the presence and support of so many prominent people, the interracial nature of the SCHW and attendance by Communists and other radicals compromised the organization in the eyes of most Alabamians. This handful of radicals seemed to confirm what many Alabama defenders of the status quo had long alleged: New Dealism had a "red" fringe to it.

Statehouse politics revealed similar New Deal/anti–New Deal divisions. In the 1930 gubernatorial campaign the major issue seemed to be outgoing governor Bibb Graves. He quietly endorsed his lieutenant governor, who also received the now-dubious backing of the Ku Klux Klan. But Benjamin M. Miller, a longtime attorney in the Wilcox County seat of Camden, combined the Black Belt and Birmingham's Big Mules into a winning coalition. He ripped into the extravagance of the Graves administration, criticized its tax increases, bloated bureaucracy, and wasteful spending, and accused it of Klan domination. If elected Miller pledged to restore economy to the state government and to fire state employees with Klan ties. In a speech at Luverne, Miller called Graves "the Ku Klux Klan Governor of Alabama" and blamed another opponent for "sucking the biggest teat at the Klan-ridden capitol"; he declared: "if you are satisfied with the rule of the Ku Klux Klan in your state government, don't vote for me. Vote for any of my opponents."[2] The Abbeville *Herald*, Alabama's Klan paper, and James Esdale, Birmingham attorney and Grand Dragon of the Alabama Klan, seemed to confirm the allegations by denouncing Miller as a "wet" pawn of the Big Mules who would repeal both prohibition and corporation taxes used to support education. The Montgomery *Advertiser* endorsed Miller, whom it dubbed "Old Economy" in honor of his personal frugality. So conservative was Miller, said acquaintances, that he used oil lamps on his south Alabama farm rather than install electricity. After winning the governorship, Miller reenforced that image by including only two cars in his inaugural parade.

Governor Miller discovered what many politicians before and after him learned the hard way: economic reality oftentimes plays havoc with campaign promises. Miller held office during the worst years of the Great Depression, from 1931 through 1934. The collapse of the state's economy made it impossible to pay state employees and forced the governor to advocate a two-cent tax on gas, creation of a state income tax, and a $20 million program to validate warrants given to state employees (and, it was hoped, to be redeemed later in cash). He won support for his package with the assistance of a Brookings Institution study of the organization of state government. The report's tax section reached conclusions similar to the 1918 Russell Sage Foundation report: Alabama assessed property at ridiculously low rates. State tax assessments on farmland were lower than any of eight adjacent states with the result that Alabama's landowning farmers paid less than 20 percent of the state's taxes. The governor, unwilling to challenge Black Belt planters and the powerful Farm Bureau, ignored the recommendation (not an uncommon fate for the tax reform proposals in Alabama history) and proposed gas and income taxes instead.

Although the state house of representatives passed Miller's tax package, the Black Belt–dominated senate rejected it as too extravagant. The governor finally got a version of it through the upper house only to run afoul of his erstwhile supporters. The Alabama Independent Merchants Association, the Economy League, and other business groups formed a Committee of 500 to oppose all tax increases but especially an income tax. Benjamin Russell of Alexander City and Carlisle Melvin of Selma led the coalition, which proposed to cut state expenditures rather than increase taxes. The chairman of the Shelby County Economy League denounced Miller for double-crossing "the very men that put [him] into office" and concluded that "hell is too good" for his protax supporters in the lower house. Miller fought back, arguing that his income tax would affect only 7,000 people in the entire state.[3] The effort did no good, and his income tax proposal went down to a crushing defeat at the hands of voters angered by the gas tax, 146,000 to 74,000.

Business interests that had successfully opposed his tax program now watched in surprise while the state government collapsed. Winston County teachers had gone nearly a year without pay except for worthless teacher warrants. Of 116 Alabama public school systems in May 1932, only 16 had paid their teachers in full for the school year. State education officials estimated that half the schools in Alabama would close for the school year at Christmas 1932. In March 1933 the Alabama Education Association met in Birmingham and refused to open schools unless the government adopted a plan to pay teacher salaries. Other state agencies experienced similar crises.

Without funds to operate state government, Miller summoned a special session of the legislature in January 1933. The house passed a tax package consisting of increased corporation taxes and a graduated income tax of 1 percent for incomes of $4,000 or more. The senate, sobered by the impending closing of public schools, passed the package

498

by a vote of 22–13. Miller launched a vigorous campaign on behalf of his tax proposals prior to the public referendum. The number of Alabamians who paid federal income taxes had declined from 15,000 in 1930 to 8,000 in 1932. He estimated that only 7,000 Alabamians earned enough to pay the new income tax. In a speech at Monroeville, Miller asked how many in the audience had paid a federal income tax for the previous year. Not a hand went up. Then he branded tax opponents as 7,000 selfish people unwilling to pay their fair share. He defended his tax package as a reasonable and just attempt to tax those best able to pay. The same business çoalition that had opposed him earlier—led by Benjamin Russell, Carlisle Melvin, Selma broker Sidney J. Smyer, Gerald R. E. Steiner of Montgomery, and the Independent Merchants Association—denounced the governor again for reneging on his 1930 pledge of no new taxes. But they failed. The impending closing of schools and the governor's assurances that the rich would carry the burden of the taxes led to a 37,000-vote margin in favor of the tax package.

Unfortunately, the taxes raised too little money to solve the state's funding problems, and in January 1934 two hundred schools closed while others remained open only because federal funds kept them operating. The refusal of local governments to levy taxes to educate Alabama children provoked the Hearst newspapers to inquire harshly: "Why should the people of the United States subsidize 67 county governments in the state of Alabama in order to save the public schools of that state from collapse?"[4]

Miller's administration was so totally dominated by financial crises that it had neither time nor energy to tackle other problems. As part of governmental reorganization, the governor abolished the state Law Enforcement Department, which enforced prohibition. Without enforcement machinery and scandalized by decade-long revelations of governmental corruption involving bootleggers, the agency came under fire from the state's urban newspapers. Despite allegations in 1930 that he was a "wet," Miller opposed repeal and vetoed a bill calling for a statewide referendum on the issue. But the legislature had the votes to override his veto and send the matter to a vote of the people. The indomitable Pattie Jacobs led repeal forces while Evangelicals tried to save the Eighteenth Amendment. One Methodist bishop disparaged the wet forces: "Every gambler, the rakes, the roves, the prostitutes, the brothel keepers are actively in support of the defeat of the Eighteenth Amendment."[5]

Either the bishop underestimated the breadth of the opposition or else Alabama contained an unsavory population, because repeal passed by a vote of 100,000 to 71,000. Although the margin was wide, it was still the third lowest ratio for repeal in the entire United States. After July 1933 Alabamians could once again imbibe beer and wine, although liquor sales did not begin until 1937. Prohibitionists rallied in 1935 to defeat statewide liquor sales. Miller also signed a bill into law restoring runoff elections in place of a first ballot plurality that combined first- and second-choice votes, a cumbersome system used during the 1920s.

Benjamin Miller began his term severely criticizing what he termed the extravagant Bibb Graves administration. But by the time he left office voters had grown nostalgic about the Graves years. Labor endorsed Graves for governor in 1934, as did most Alabama New Dealers. He won a hard-fought primary against Birmingham attorney Frank M. Dixon. Dixon resurrected the five-volume Brookings Institution report calling for complete overhaul of state government, but the issue was too esoteric for most voters. Furthermore, Dixon's attacks on Graves's Klan ties were by now irrelevant to voters obsessed with economic troubles and class grievances. Graves carried fifty-six counties on his way to a 157,000 to 135,000 runoff victory over Dixon.

As governor, Graves frequently sided with organized labor and created a new state Department of Labor in 1935 that administered wage and hour laws, conducted mediation of labor disputes, and regulated child labor. The governor appointed a member of the Bricklayers' Union (who also headed the state Federation of Labor) as director. He filled other positions with reform-minded women. Daisy Donovan became head of the Child Labor Division, and Molly Dowd (longtime suffragist, secretary of the Alabama League of Women Voters, textile union organizer, and founder of Alabama's branch of the National Women's Trade Union League) became one of the leading labor mediators in the new department. During the bloody Talladega textile strike of 1936 and again during a 1937 strike at Huntsville, Graves sided with workers. In fact Graves played as large a role in Montgomery as Roosevelt did in Washington to create a vigorous, politically assertive labor movement in Alabama.

Graves also addressed welfare problems and liquor sales. The governor signed a law creating the state Department of Public Welfare in 1935. The legislature, badly strapped for funds, hesitated to appropriate money to operate it until a coalition of civic clubs, chambers of commerce, and parent-teacher associations successfully lobbied for a $250,000 appropriation. He also proposed raising money to fund state services by giving a monopoly to state liquor stores. He vetoed a bill establishing a state liquor sales system because it contained no provision for a public vote, but legislators passed it over his veto. It created a state monopoly under a three-person Alcoholic Beverage Control Board appointed by the governor. The law allowed county wet-dry referenda, and twenty-four counties quickly voted wet, although statewide the result of county elections was a narrow margin for dry forces, 100,000 to 98,000.

In 1938 Frank Dixon continued the pattern of winning the governorship after finishing second in the preceding election. Dixon had strong credentials. Born in California and descended from a line of prominent North Carolina Baptist preachers, he attended Phillips-Exeter Academy, Columbia University, and the University of Virginia (for his law degree). He lost a leg as a U.S. Army pilot in France during the First World War. A foe of the Klan and a thoughtful advocate of governmental reorganization, Dixon drew support both from New Deal members of the Alabama Policy Committee and from some New Deal critics. His leading opponent was Chauncey M. Sparks, a Eufaula banker and attorney. Both attacked the Graves administration, although Sparks was the more vociferous critic. Organized labor endorsed Dixon while business backed Sparks. Dixon pioneered a new election technique in 1938 when he showed a sound movie extolling his merits in Alabama theaters. Dixon led Sparks 153,000 (49 percent) to 75,000, with the remaining votes scattered among a variety of minor candidates. Sparks conceded without a runoff.

As governor, Dixon quickly disillusioned New Dealers. His personality was cool and indifferent and his policies antilabor. As part of his governmental reorganization, he abolished the Department of Labor, transferring its duties to the new Department of Industrial Relations. The governor also hired a new staff for the department that was far less sympathetic to labor. Dixon created a merit system for state employees, a state personnel department, and a conservation department. A states' righter who would later play a key role in the 1948 Dixiecrat movement, he opposed congressional attempts to abolish the poll tax and prevent lynching. He also resurrected the gubernatorial practice of using the National Guard to break strikes. His two efforts at reform, state poll tax reform and legislative reapportionment, fell casualties to a status quo legislature. He had the good fortune to take office during the last year of the depression. Wartime spending allowed his frugal administration actually to bequeath his successor a large surplus in the treasury, something of a novelty in Alabama's political history.

Dixon's Birmingham base furnished more than its share of anti–New Dealers. Although the city elected George Huddleston, Sr., and Luther Patrick to Congress, both backed by labor unions and both loyal to Roosevelt, city government was a stronghold for established business interests. Jimmy Jones continued as president of the city commission until his death in 1940. During the 1930s he allied with industrialist Big Mules, slashed city services, and winked at violence directed at labor organizers and political radicals. The other two commissioners opposed him early in the decade, but in 1937 Jones's allies won control of the commission when Eugene ("Bull") Connor gained a seat. Connor was a salesman who had gained local fame as a radio announcer of Birmingham Baron baseball games. He and Jones generally opposed unions, federal housing, and any concessions to blacks. They seldom criticized the New Deal directly but privately sided with Birmingham's industrial leaders.

"Bull" Connor, who acquired his nickname for his ability to provide irrelevant chatter during boring intervals of baseball broadcasts on radio, became police commissioner on the three-person city commission. He reorganized the police force but also earned a reputation for autocracy and favoritism (he called his favorites in the all-white force "my nigguhs"). He used police raids to raise funds for his 1941 reelection campaign, transferred policemen who refused to support him to undesirable details, and transformed the force into a personal political machine. Big Mules, especially TCI officials, liked his union-busting tactics, and racists appreciated the sentiment, if not the syntax, when Connor informed the integrated 1938 SCHW meeting that "Negroes and whites would not segregate together."[6] Even some white unionists identified with his early union membership and impoverished background.

Jones and Connor had a close friend and philosophical ally in Jefferson County's state senator James A. Simpson. As a corporate attorney and foe of Bibb Graves, Simpson had endeared himself to the city's Big Mules. Elected to the state senate in 1934, he became a leader of the anti–New Deal forces in the upper house and a close ally of Governor Frank Dixon and later of Governor Chauncey Sparks. He wrote and steered to passage a bill prohibiting picketing by strikers and in 1939 wrote a bill prohibiting strikers from receiving unemployment benefits. He favored reapportionment and introduced legislation to establish a state merit system for city employees in order to weaken patronage politics.

Like the economy and politics, Alabama society demonstrated elements of both continuity and change during the decade. Historic patterns of racism turned violent when strained economic conditions forced whites to compete with blacks for what had once been called "nigger jobs." New Deal efforts to abolish the poll tax, raise minimum wages, shorten the workweek, and assist tenant farmers threatened long-established racial patterns.

The most spectacular racial incident began in March 1931 when a fight broke out between black and white men on a freight car rolling through Jackson County. Some of the white men thrown from the train notified the sheriff. He stopped the train in Scottsboro and removed nine black males. Two white women, taken from another car, alleged that the nine blacks had raped them. The defendants were tried, found guilty, and sentenced to death. The National Association for the Advancement of Colored People and the Communist-aligned International Labor Defense Fund came to the blacks' aid, and the Supreme Court overruled their conviction on the grounds that the state had not provided a defense attorney in a capital case.

Retried in Decatur, the black defendants were again convicted, despite the fact that one of the women had changed her testimony and denied her original charge. Again the Supreme Court overturned the convictions, this time because systematically the state of Alabama excluded blacks from jury duty. Retrials and appeals, complete with "Scottsboro boys" rallies in the United States and abroad, kept the case alive throughout the decade. Sympathetic whites formed an Alabama Scottsboro Fair Trial Committee, which included respected clergymen such as Dr. Henry M. Edmonds, pastor of Birmingham's Independent Presbyterian Church, politicians such as former governor Thomas Kilby, and educators such as Dr. Guy E. Snavely, president of Birmingham-Southern College, and Dr. George Denny, president of the University of Alabama.

But identification with accused black rapists could damage careers, as a Birmingham-Southern College professor discovered when he was fired for becoming too deeply involved on behalf of the nine blacks. A Jewish congregation in Montgomery dismissed its rabbi for the same reason. Over the years Alabama authorities dropped charges against the nine men.

However, three blacks accused of raping Vaudine Maddox, the daughter of an itinerant Tuscaloosa County sharecropper, were not so fortunate. In 1933, amid outcry that the Scottsboro boys had thus far escaped the noose, a half-dozen masked white men intercepted a sheriff's car carrying the blacks to Birmingham and lynched all three.

Less spectacular but more shocking was the Tuskegee syphilis experiment. Beginning in 1932 the U.S. Public Health Service—with the cooperation of the Veteran's Hospital staff at Tuskegee, the Alabama State Department of Health, the Macon County Health Department, Tuskegee Institute, and private physicians throughout the area—began a forty-year scientific study of the untreated evolution of a fatal disease. They deliberately withheld treatment from some 400 black men who suffered from syphilis. Most were uneducated sharecroppers and laborers convinced that "government doctors" were helping them. Told they had "bad blood," they were given aspirin and iron tonic. Thus did some of the most progressive officials of American medicine, deprived of funding for their research by the Great Depression, engage in one of the most scandalous experiments in the history of American science.

But not all was so bleak in race relations. Blacks gained unprecedented access to unionism through the CIO. Blacks constituted 41 percent of Birmingham's steelworkers, 56 percent of its ore miners, and 63 percent of its coal miners in the mid-1930s. CIO drives increased the black percentage of union membership to some 30 percent by 1940. In Sumter County white folklorist Ruby Pickens Tartt introduced renowned folklorist John A. Lomax from the Library of Congress to black folk musicians. Dock Reed—a farmer, basket maker, raconteur, and singer—thus moved from the obscurity of west Alabama to international fame. He gave Lomax and the Library of Congress some of its most famous recordings: "Tramping, Tramping," "Jesus Going to Make My Dying Bed," and "The Sun Will Never Go Down." Deeply religious and greatly beloved in the Livingston area, Reed refused to sing blues or secular songs, believing them worldly. But as a singer of spirituals the gentle Reed was considered by many folklorists to be without peer.

Black women were doubly dispossessed, suffering discrimination because of both race and gender. Nonetheless they wrote letters similar to those of whites demanding fair treatment from New Deal agencies. Their women's clubs formed an advisory council to help unemployed black women, especially in counties with a black population of more than 25 percent.

White women had many of the same problems. Widow Marie Bankhead Owen struggled with her finances and contemplated leaving the state. But she was an accomplished writer who had once turned down a salary of $10,000 a year to move to New York and write for the Hearst papers. Instead she turned her attention to Alabama history and literature, writing novels, thousands of pages of Alabama history, and in 1930 beginning the *Alabama Historical Quarterly.*

Irene Davis had a harder time. A widow from Greenville, she had a college degree and a record of good employment as a skilled stenographer before the depression. She lost her job and in 1934 her parents died, leaving her without home, job, or money. The destitute woman tried to provide for her three children through the rural rehabilitation program but officials denied her a loan, explaining that an inexperienced woman could not operate a farm successfully. She was desperate and persistent, and the official finally relented and loaned her one hundred dollars. She rented eight acres that contained a shack without windows, a leaky roof, and wide cracks in the walls. She borrowed a mule from a neighbor, and her fourteen-year-old son plowed. For each day she used the mule, she spent a day hoeing her neighbor's field. Despite drought, insects, and other problems, she harvested a crop, repaid her loan, and sold enough corn, cane, and vegetables to store sufficient food for winter. By the mid-1930s she was making plans somehow to send her children to college. The Birmingham *Post* selected her as "Alabama's Most Courageous Woman of 1934."

Because Eleanor Roosevelt sympathized with blacks and dispossessed people, many white Alabamians developed a keen dislike for her. Absurd rumors spread about Eleanor Roosevelt Clubs of black servants whom she inspired to rebel against their employers and whose motto was "a white woman in every kitchen." But the First Lady's files at Hyde Park, New York, contain many letters from Alabama women who obviously felt a special attachment to her. Mary Edna Carlisle of Leeds wrote because Eleanor Roosevelt seemed to have a "sympathetic understanding" of women's problems. Carlisle was a college graduate, unemployed, one of three candidates for the job as Leeds postmaster, and made the highest score on the civil service exam. But the job went to a male druggist, allegedly because of his political connections to the district's congressman. Carlisle complained:

> The work the government has given to women here has been cleaning the city park and things of that nature. I do not want to belong to that vast army of American people who are on charity. I only long for the opportunity to earn a livelihood for my family. . . . This letter is to "Eleanor Roosevelt the woman," and not to the President's wife.[7]

But it was a second letter that touched Eleanor Roosevelt deeply, although the author of it could not have known the similarities in their marriages. Eleanor Roosevelt, who knew nothing about birth control, had given birth to one child after another. Myrtle Rockett of Birmingham wrote Eleanor Roosevelt that she was a twenty-nine-year-old mother of four who had been married seven years. She also supported her mother, who was critically ill with tuberculosis, and her fourteen-year-old sister. Her husband owned his business, and the family had nice clothes, plenty to eat, and an educational fund for their children. But her husband refused to help support her mother and sister and refused to allow her to help them unless she took a job and earned the money herself. She had no time to work, having given birth to four children in seven years. She described her husband as "the old fashioned 'Lord and Master' type" who refused her spending money. She offered to do all the housework in their eight-room house if he would fire the maid and give her the five-dollar-a-week salary. But he rejected the proposal. She considered leaving her husband, but physical cruelty and adultery were the only legal grounds for divorce in Alabama. Divorce also violated her sense of moral obligation to her children and marriage. She asked Eleanor Roosevelt for advice and reference to some agency that could help her mother and sister.

Most such letters languished in files and then found their way into the Roosevelt presidential library. But not this one; something about it moved Eleanor Roosevelt in a special way. She wrote a female official of FERA who, in turn, contacted the director of women's relief efforts in Alabama, instructing them to assist Myrtle Rockett.

One person whom Eleanor Roosevelt sometimes entrusted with such special cases was Pattie Jacobs. She had been part of virtually every public debate in Alabama for two decades. Now Roosevelt brought her to Washington briefly to head the women's division of one of the federal relief agencies. When Jacobs's husband became ill, she returned to Birmingham to assume the job as Alabama representative on the TVA board.

It was generally not a good decade for Alabama women. The Alabama League of Women Voters collapsed like the economy. In 1936 Sybil Pool of Linden (in Marengo County) became the state's second female legislator, but she was the only woman elected during the 1930s. She won reelection in 1938 and 1942, beginning a thirty-four-year political career that would include terms as secretary of state, state treasurer, and membership on the Public Service Commission. But Pool's career was a spectacular exception to a general decline of female political activity in the state.

Literature often thrives during hard times, and Alabama authors produced some remarkable books during the 1930s. Most were iconoclastic, challenging traditional values just as the New Deal challenged traditional politics. In 1933 T. S. Stribling won a Pulitzer Prize for his novel *The Store*. Set in northwestern Alabama near his home of Florence, the story concerned a merchant who traded moral values for political office and material gain. James Saxon Childers's *A Novel About a White Man and a Black Man: In the Deep South,* published in 1936, explored an interracial friendship between two young men living in Birmingham and the inevitable tragedy that crossing the color line brought to both of them. Clarence Cason, author of a mildly critical essay on Alabama entitled *90° in the Shade,* published in 1935, grew so morose over its likely reception that he killed himself the week his work appeared. Lella Warren wrote more traditional novels, such as *Foundation Stone* and *Whetstone Walls*.

Movies and sports continued to provide escape from painful reality. The great theaters built during the 1920s in Birmingham, Montgomery, and Mobile filled with people even during the depression. It was as if the harder times became the more people retreated into fantasy. Sports continued to offer what they had in a previous decade: personal glory, racial pride, and economic opportunity. Virtually every community and company had a baseball team. Even Hosea Hudson, black Communist militant and organizer, took time off from the cosmic work of destroying capitalism to watch baseball games between Birmingham industrial league teams like ACIPCO, L&N, Sayreton Mine, Edgewater Mine, and Stockham Valves. Hudson loved baseball but found even in sports elements of class and racial conflict. He remembered a game between Stockham and Ensley. A white umpire called the game and infuriated the black ace pitcher for Stockham with one of his calls. Pitcher Jesse

Jeeters mumbled derogatory comments about the umpire, who charged the mound shouting, "By God, you better not dispute my word." Jeeters was sullen but knew "he better take it, better kind of stay cool."[8]

Joe Louis never worried about staying cool. Louis was born in May 1914 to a sharecropper family near Lafayette in east Alabama. After his father's health failed, his mother raised Joe and six siblings. The boy began picking cotton at age four; he did not learn to talk until six or read until nine. In 1924 his mother remarried, and the family became part of the great emigration of blacks from Alabama. They moved to Detroit in 1924, and it was from the Motor City that Louis launched a boxing career that made him Golden Gloves Champion and Heavyweight Champion of the World during the 1930s. He retained the heavyweight crown for ten years through twenty-five fights, more than all of his heavyweight predecessors combined. As prideful Alabamians (black and white) listened to his world championship bout with German Max Schmeling in 1938, they experienced mixed emotions. Black Alabamians felt a supreme triumph as Louis punched his Aryan opponent senseless in a matter of minutes. Some white Alabamians openly celebrated; others, more ambivalent, were quietly pleased at the triumph of a fellow Alabamian. A few preferred the triumph even of a Nazi over the "Brown Bomber" from Lafayette.

Two months before Schmeling's and Louis's first meeting, when Schmeling had knocked Louis out, 110,000 spectators stood in the rain in Berlin for the final event of the 1936 Olympics. The star of the event was Jesse Owens, who set a new world record for the 200-meter dash. He tied the world record in the 100 meters and won a third gold medal for the long jump. Not since 1900 had a track-and-field athlete won three golds in a single Olympics. He also shared a gold medal as part of the U.S. 400-meter relay team. Of the sixteen world records broken or tied in Berlin, Owens owned four. The unofficial point system gave the U.S. track-and-field team 203 points, and Owens accounted for 40 points by himself.

Owens was born in September 1913 in Oakville, eight miles south of Decatur. He was the youngest of ten children born to a sharecropper family. Despite their abject poverty, the Owens family provided James Cleveland ("Jesse") a happy childhood. His devoted Baptist mother made him memorize a Bible verse every day and exposed him to visions of a world not bounded by racial limitations. His timid, illiterate father bid him remember the circumscribed world of Oakville, Alabama. He once told his son: "J. C., it don't do a colored man no good to get himself too high. 'Cause it's a helluva drop back to the bottom."[9] His mother's expansive vision dominated his father's pragmatic one, and the family left Oakville for Cleveland, Ohio, and greater opportunities during the early 1920s. Like Louis, Owens would rise to fame far from his Alabama birthplace.

LeRoy ("Satchel") Paige began life in Mobile, though the date is uncertain. His mother put the event in 1903; Paige, perhaps for his own reasons, set it in 1906. The seventh of eleven children born to a gardener father and a washerwoman mother, LeRoy early found jobs selling bottles and carrying bags at Mobile's train station (carrying multiple bags, the boy looked like a tree of satchels, which provided his nickname). As a boy he threw so accurately that when his mother sent him to kill a chicken he allegedly would dispatch it with a rock. After a brush with the law and a term in the Negro Industrial High School at Mount Meigs, Paige began pitching for the Mobile Tigers, a black semipro baseball team. By 1926 he pitched for the Chattanooga Black Lookouts. Later he joined the Birmingham Black Barons, the Pittsburgh Crawfords, and other black teams.

His exploits were the stuff of legends. In 1933 he won thirty-one games for Pittsburgh, while losing only four. Through one stretch of the season he won twenty-one consecutive games and pitched sixty-two scoreless innings. So hard was his fast ball that humorists said it disappeared. Batters did not hit it and catchers could not find it in their mitts. Many baseball historians consider the 1932 Pittsburgh Crawfords one of the greatest teams in history and believe it could have beaten either major league champion. Cleveland manager Bill Veeck, who finally brought Paige to the major leagues in 1948, first saw him pitch in 1934 and called him the best pitcher he had ever seen. Joe DiMaggio, after batting against him in a minor league game in 1937, declared him the best pitcher he ever faced. Paige pitched teams to Negro World Series triumphs in 1942 and in 1946. After Jackie Robinson broke the color barrier in the big leagues, Bill Veeck brought Paige to Cleveland in July 1948, where 20,000 fans gave the legendary pitcher a ten-minute ovation. Even in the twilight of his career at age forty-two (or forty-five), he won 6 games, lost 1, recorded a phenomenal earned run average of 2.47, and helped pitch the Indians to a pennant. So impressive was he that baseball writers talked of naming him "Rookie of the Year." Remembering an estimated 2,500 games pitched for 250 teams and 2,000 victories, including 300 shutouts and 55 no-hit games, most of them in black leagues that kept no records and thus denied him the immortality he reckoned he deserved, Paige replied without bitterness: "Which year?" He pitched five more seasons in the big leagues, then returned to the minors where he continued pitching well into his fifties. Perhaps his most famous quotation, "Don't look back. Something might be gaining on you," was never intended to be as light-hearted as most bemused Americans believed. In 1971 the Baseball Hall of Fame finally got around to inducting Paige, but the now-famous athlete passed up a White House audience with President Ronald Reagan in 1981 to attend a reunion of players from the old black leagues. Shunned for so long by white America, perhaps it was Satchel Paige's moment to return the insult.

The popularity of baseball was by no means exclusive or confined to blacks. Virtually every town and community had a team and even CCC camps boasted a club. But whites took particular pride in college football. Coach Wallace Wade won a third national championship for the Alabama team in 1930. Frank Thomas, the first student of legendary Notre Dame coach Knute Rockne to come south, moved to the University of Alabama the next year. During the following fifteen years he won 115 games, lost 34, and tied 7. He produced four undefeated teams, won or shared Southeastern Conference championships in 1933, 1934, and 1937, and took 'Bama to the Rose Bowl in two of those years. Some football historians consider the 1934 Alabama team, which featured Dixie Howell, Don Hutson, and Paul ("Bear") Bryant, to be the finest football team the South ever produced. It provided the Capstone its fourth national championship and announced clearly that Alabama had become an American football dynasty. Even Alabama's 13–0 loss to California in the 1937 Rose Bowl did not reduce the pride Alabamians felt in the Crimson Tide. Times might be hard, but football championships eased the pain.

TWENTY-NINE

A State Forged by War, 1940–1954

THE New Deal did not end the Great Depression. The storm clouds that for so long had swirled over the United States seemed to gather over Europe and Asia by the end of the decade. As worldwide economies geared up for war, prosperity returned to Alabama. But the good times were born of heartbreak for many families who lost sons, husbands, and fathers in the maelstrom of war that swept across the earth.

Alabama had a long and honorable military tradition. Many elements contributed to this heritage: a long frontier experience that left males strongly devoted to hunting and other physical pursuits; a fierce national and regional pride ("American by Birth, Southerner by the Grace of God"); the popularity of volunteer military services such as the National Guard and the Reserve Officer Training Corps (ROTC). Not until the 1960s did Auburn University drop the requirement that all male students participate in ROTC. Auburn boasted that it had provided more line officers to the armed services than any university in the nation except the three service academies and Texas A&M. Auburn educated both General Holland M. Smith, the father of amphibious warfare, and General Franklin A. Hart, commandant of the Marine Corps. Alabama also gave the nation Admiral Thomas M. Moorer, who served as chairman of the Joint Chiefs of Staff during the early 1970s. Alabama's economy was closely tied to world markets. Foreign countries purchased half the state's cotton crop and much of its coal and timber. The state's white population was largely Celtic and Anglo-American, and its educated people had long been international in outlook.

All these factors inclined Alabamians toward an interventionist foreign policy. During congressional debates over U.S. preparedness, Alabama's delegation supported President Roosevelt's call for Lend-Lease to assist Britain and Russia and for a peacetime draft. After initial editorials in 1939 expressing support for neutrality and caution about U.S. involvement in the war, the state press became increasingly interventionist. Most papers ignored events in Asia until Japan's attack on Pearl Harbor; but then the Alexander City *Outlook* editorially expressed the sentiment of most Alabamians: "All right, little brown man, you asked for it."[1]

Gearing up the home front for war proved a gigantic boost to Alabama's depressed economy. The state was well positioned to take advantage of the war effort. Its mild weather afforded many more training days annually for airmen and soldiers than harsh Northern climes. Cheap TVA power, a large surplus labor force, and a strong industrial base made north Alabama an ideal location for war industry. No area of the state failed to profit economically from the war, but the northern third benefited most.

Huntsville's half-century dependency on the textile industry ended on July 3, 1941, when jubilant chamber of commerce officials announced that a new $40 million war chemical plant would locate in the city. Within months construction crews began building Huntsville and Redstone arsenals, which produced artillery shells and bombs. Together these facilities covered 40,000 acres, employed 11,000 at their peak, and pumped $70 million into the local economy. By May 1944 Huntsville contained 17,000 manufacturing employees, more than the entire city population in 1940. Although the city's nine textile mills before the depression declined to only three by wartime, the remaining mills expanded to 5,500 employees.

Birmingham, recently called the nation's most depressed city, now earned another nickname, the "great arsenal of the South." Factories began operating three eight-hour shifts around the clock. TCI, already operating at full capacity by fall 1939, enlarged its Wenonah ore plant, added a blast furnace and an electrolytic tin-plating mill at Fairfield, constructed a sheet-forging plant at Ensley, and opened a new coal mine at Short Creek. TCI's work force increased by 7,000 between 1938 and 1941 to a total of 30,000. Labor shortages by that year had become acute and plagued the steel industry throughout the war. Kirkman O'Neal founded O'Neal Steel, which manufactured steel fabrications for bombs and became one of the largest independent steel companies in the South. Bechtel-McCone Aircraft Modification Company opened a factory that equipped and modified half the B-29 bombers used during the war. Birmingham steel fabricator Robert I. Ingalls began a cargo ship–manufacturing facility at Pascagoula, Mississippi. DuPont Chemical built the largest smokeless powder and explosives plant in the South at Childersburg. That hamlet of 500 in 1940 had to absorb 14,000 construction workers who descended on Childersburg like a cloud of locusts. The government took 32,000 acres of land, uprooting 300 farm families in the process.

A few miles to the north, the Anniston Ordnance Depot and Fort McClellan hired thousands of construction workers. One farmer from just across the Georgia line had been earning three hundred dollars a year farming. He obtained work at Fort McClellan as a carpenter making seven dollars a day. Even though he had to leave home at 3:30 A.M. and returned about 7:30 P.M., he was able to pay his debts and actually save money.

Montgomery thrived on Gunter and Maxwell Air Force bases. In 1940 Major General H. H. ("Hap") Arnold established the Southeast Air Corps Training Center at Maxwell field to train all pilots, navigators, and bombardiers assigned to the Southeast. By spring 1943 more than 9,000 cadets underwent training continuously; more than 100,000 airmen received flight training at Maxwell during the war. Its B-24 and B-29 crews made nearly 350,000 practice landings without a crash by its B-29 contingents.

Gunter Air Force Base began in August 1940 on the site of an abandoned prison. The facility trained four classes a year and a total of 12,000 cadets during the war. Nearby, auxiliary fields to serve Gunter and Maxwell pilots opened at Shorter, Deatsville, Elmore, and Dannelly. Mobile perhaps profited from military growth more than any other Alabama city. In 1940 the Army Air Corps began construction of Brookley Field west of Mobile. The facility modified B-24s and served as a military depot. By 1943 Brookley employed 17,000 civilians. Mobile drained the second largest interior river system of any American city, so its harbor and port facilities strained to keep pace with growth in the interior of the state. Alabama Dry Dock and Shipbuilding Company (ADDSCO) launched a new 16,000-ton dry dock, constructed 20 liberty ships, 102 tankers, and repaired nearly 3,000 additional vessels during the war. Gulf Shipbuilding Corporation at Chickasaw produced 30 tankers, 7 destroyers, 29 minesweepers, and a landing ship dock. The Waterman Repair Division reoutfitted 50 ships. By 1943 the two largest firms, ADDSCO and Gulf Shipbuilding, employed 40,000 and were producing on average a ship each week.

When the war began Mobile employed only 17,000 in its entire work force, so the rapid industrial growth overwhelmed existing facilities. Mobile's population mushroomed from 79,000 to 125,000 between 1940 and March 1943. Most of the newcomers were poor farmers from southern Mississippi and Alabama. The Census Bureau estimated that 89,000 new people moved to Mobile County during those years, changing the area fundamentally. Physically the county had no way to house the newcomers, so tents, trailers, and "hommettes" (cheap, prefabricated boxlike structures) sprouted across the county. In the city boardinghouses rented the same room to three men on different shifts so that one slept on the bed while the other two worked. The city's genial aristocratic heritage of tolerance and festivity gave way to intolerance, religious bigotry, racial conflict, and exhausting labor.

512

Selma also received a facility in 1940. Craig Air Force Base—named for Selma native Lieutenant Bruce K. Craig, a test engineer killed in a bomber crash—provided advanced flight training to American and Royal Air Force cadets beginning in May 1941. At its height Craig employed a military staff of 2,000 plus 1,400 civilians. Because all cadets were single when they arrived, many courted Selma girls and were married soon after graduation.

Civilians responded enthusiastically to calls for volunteers to assist the war effort. Montgomery's Citizens' Service Corps enrolled 15,000 people in such projects as conducting war bond drives; planting victory gardens; canning; mailing gas ration coupons; collecting old magazines and paper; salvaging scrap metal, rags, and grease; and knitting sweaters, mufflers, and gloves. Some women in the corps were more patriotic than others. During summer 1943 the knitters fell behind their quota, complaining that the yarn was too hot and hard to handle. One unsympathetic mother of a serviceman chided that she had no patience with such excuses. She pointed out that the boys who would wear these winter woolens would not be consulted about the temperature before they went into combat.

Many Alabama women left their knitting for jobs in war industry. As manpower shortages began to increase in 1942, the government began to recruit women. One advertisement admonished every housewife to ask herself: "Can I be of greater service in my home or in a war plant?" Another proclaimed that "Every woman who takes a job hastens the day of victory for American arms and peace." Still another argued, "The more women at work, the sooner we'll win."[2] This patriotic campaign, combined with the poverty of the population, brought quick results. At Brookley Field's Mobile Air Service women constituted 49 percent of employees by 1944; at Bechtel-McCone in Birmingham, 40 percent; at the DuPont factory in Childersburg, 48 percent; at Redstone and Huntsville arsenals in Huntsville, 25 and 35 percent; in the Mobile shipyards, 10 percent. Shortages in other areas of the work force created unprecedented opportunities for Alabama women. In 1941 the state began appointing female physicians as county health officers. In 1943 the prison board employed its first woman as superintendent of Julia Tutwiler Prison for women. Women also became auto mechanics, pharmacists, school bus drivers, and legislative clerks.

The Alabama School of Trades in Gadsden admitted women, and they soon became a majority of the student body. So many women enrolled that the Birmingham *News* concluded that "the Alabama School of Trades is now a school of Maids."[3] This frilly description hardly fit the female welders who began to fill assembly lines at the state's aircraft plants and shipyards.

Women were not able to sustain the gains they made during the war.

By 1944 layoffs had already begun. Propaganda that had depicted war industry as women's obligation in 1942 began to emphasize their patriotic duty to step aside in order to make jobs for returning veterans. One advertisement congratulated women for "pinch-hitting for the boys who are fighting for freedom" but reminded them that the regular players were soon coming home and that would send the substitutes back to the bench. Many women were delighted to return to their homes, or to marry, have babies, and resume lives interrupted by war. Homemaking was an honorable and demanding profession requiring every ounce of energy and ingenuity they possessed. But other women—married or unmarried, enjoying good earnings and satisfying jobs—were not content to step aside. One survey of working women in Mobile revealed that 78 percent wanted to continue their jobs. Even during the war women earned less money than men for the same jobs and received fewer promotions. As the Birmingham *News* described the dominant male philosophy in May 1942: "Girls work better in factories if they have a man for a boss."

The war afforded new opportunities for blacks as well as for women. Blacks filled many of the new jobs created by war industry, though not always happily. The black population of Mobile spurted from 29,000 in 1940 to 46,000 in 1950. White resistance to this massive influx flared into racial riots in May 1943. White employees of ADDSCO went on a two-day rampage because the Fair Employment Practices Commission had forced the company to promote twelve black welders. Guards had to escort black employees to and from work. A year later at Brookley Field racial tensions erupted into a two-hour gun battle between Negro troops and white military police. The CIO helped arrange a settlement at the shipyards that established four "Jim Crow" ways (timber frameworks on which ships were constructed) manned altogether by blacks who advanced solely on the basis of seniority. Most of the workers on the other ways were white. Although racial tensions did not end, at least they abated.

The executive secretary of Mobile's chapter of the National Association for the Advancement of Colored People, John LeFlore, filed a voter registration suit that finally forced the state Democratic party to drop its restriction against black voters. Returning black veterans organized the Negro Voter's and Veteran's Association and, together with LeFlore, again successfully challenged state efforts to limit their franchise. But it was a program in Tuskegee that reflected the greatest wartime change in race relations.

Black aviation had an honorable tradition at Tuskegee Institute. John C. Robinson, a 1924 graduate, had flown his plane to the tenth anniversary celebration of his graduation. The next year he became

Black U.S. Army band from Alabama, Second World War. Although segregated, the Army offered new opportunities to black Alabamians. (Courtesy of the Alabama Department of Archives and History)

commander of the Ethiopian Air Force and flew combat missions against Italian invaders. When Ethiopia lost the war, he returned to a tumultuous homecoming reception and with Jesse Owens and Joe Louis became a hero to American blacks (paradoxically all three came from racially troubled Alabama or attended college in the state).

In 1939 the government established the Civilian Pilot Training Program at Tuskegee using two Auburn aeronautical engineering professors to teach courses. When a federal inspector administered the standard CPT exam, every black student passed, making Tuskegee Institute the first college in the South to have a 100 percent pass rate on the initial exam. One graduate who scored 97 percent on the test became one of seven southeastern students to compete for a prestigious national aviation scholarship. Advanced pilot training began the next year. By 1940 the Army Air Corps and NAACP locked into a fierce struggle over the army's refusal to accept black aviation cadets. When the Air Corps finally agreed to create an all-black unit at Tuskegee, the NAACP denounced the move as an attempt to prevent the integration of the Air Corps. But in this case Tuskegee officials sided with the Air Corps and began training the first black cadets, who formed the Ninety-ninth Pursuit Squadron. Although many black civil rights leaders referred to the squadron as "the Jim Crow air corps," Tuskegee made the best of its pioneering opportunity. By 1941 the government had constructed a new airfield using a black construction company for the first time in War Department history. Eleanor Roosevelt visited in March of that year and flew aloft in a trainer piloted by a black instructor. In January 1942 the War Department created a second black squadron, the 100th, and soon dispatched the Ninety-ninth to Italy, where its pilots distinguished themselves in combat. Pilots from the Ninety-ninth scored many kills against Italian and German aircraft, won a number of citations, and produced two future air force generals, Benjamin O. Davis, Jr., and Chappie James.

Tuskegee whites were not at all certain they approved these changes. Initially they welcomed the squadron. But businessmen objected to a black firm building the airfield, and Senator John Bankhead, Jr., lobbied Army General George C. Marshall to remove all black troops from the South because of increasing racial tensions. Some white officers at Tuskegee were frankly racist and maintained strict segregation of base facilities. Famous novelist Carson McCullers visited Tuskegee and inquired of the white base commander if it were not true that Negroes could fly better than whites "because they're closer to nature."[4]

Many other Alabamians distinguished themselves during the war. Jefferson County's Navy Captain John A. Williamson designed a special "Williamson's turn" for ships trying to rescue overboard sailors. Birmingham's General John C. Persons commanded the Thirty-first Infantry Division, and Brigadier General John E. Copeland commanded one of George Patton's Third Army divisions during the sweep through eastern France and into Germany. Lieutenant Colonel David L. Daniel, a former Birmingham-Southern College student, led paratroopers during the D-Day invasion of France.

Perhaps the most influential Alabama officer was General Holland M. Smith, who was born in Hatchechubbee (Russell County) and grew up in Seale. He attended Auburn University where he read history, especially every book he could locate in the Auburn library on Napoleon. He attended law school at the University of Alabama but did not enjoy his Montgomery law practice. He sought a commission in the Marine Corps in 1905 and spent the following forty-five years in the corps. He earned the nickname "Howlin' Mad" for protesting shabby treatment meted out to marines by army and navy brass. During a 1920s tour of duty at the Naval War College, he advocated a new use for naval vessels as supply and transport vehicles to land amphibious troops. Naval officers vigorously opposed his idea, but Smith began training marines for amphibious operations anyway. By the late 1930s he had trained one of the best-prepared amphibious assault forces in the world. Smith boasted with typical bravado: "I could have landed them in the mouth of Hell if the Joint Chiefs of Staff had picked the target." After leading the assault on Iwo Jima, he added: "and Iwo Jima was a fair substitute."[5] Smith became brigadier general in 1939, major general in 1941, commanding general of the Fleet Marine Force Pacific in 1944, and lieutenant general the same year. He helped plan the invasion of Okinawa and commanded U.S. forces in the invasion of Iwo Jima.

In all, some 250,000 Alabamians served in the armed services and approximately 6,000 gave their lives in the cause of freedom. Back home in Alabama the war sometimes raised fears but barely touched the state directly. Birmingham residents took considerable pride in reports that the steel city was the number two German target after Pittsburgh. Citizens hung heavy curtains over windows and regularly practiced blackouts. Women rolled their hair on old socks because metal curlers disappeared into the war effort. Gas and meat rationing changed transportation and nutrition.

In Montgomery a truck carrying a two-man Japanese submarine parked on Dexter Avenue, and long lines of curious citizens queued up for blocks waiting their turn to mount a catwalk and view this strange instrument of war. An estimated 25,000 people bought a one-dollar savings stamp to view the sub.

Farther to the south submarines of another nationality inspired considerably more fear. Some fourteen German U-boats operated in Gulf waters between May and September 1942. They destroyed fifty-eight Allied ships totaling approximately 300,000 tons. The shallow waters of the Gulf should have provided good hunting for defense forces, but the U.S. military was woefully unprepared for the 1942 campaign and sank only two U-boats. FBI agents in Mobile conducted antiespionage classes, but the city and other Gulf ports did not begin to dim their lights at night until June 1942. U-106 laid off Mobile Bay on the surface waiting for ships to enter open water. When they did, the sub found their silhouettes perfectly outlined against the bright lights of the city and sent several ships to a watery grave.

Perhaps a few German submariners from the two vessels sunk by U.S. forces got a view of Alabama a good deal closer than through a periscope. The state became a major location for prisoner of war camps. The government began constructing the first camp at Aliceville in fall 1942, and the first contingent of 1,000 POWs arrived in June 1943. Two years later the Aliceville camp contained nearly 3,500 prisoners. Many elite Nazi submariners were among the POWs. They kept German morale high and even plotted daring escapes in which several were killed by guards. Other camps at Opelika and Anniston housed 2,800 POWs each by June 1945. A smaller facility at Camp Rucker in Dale and Coffee counties contained 1,700. Some prisoners were assigned to twenty small auxiliary camps with tents where they harvested crops for farmers. The total number of German POWs assigned to Alabama camps numbered some 15,000.

Prisoners organized some of the camps thoroughly, forming athletic teams, newspapers, libraries, and study groups. At Fort McClellan a former circus employee built a small zoo, housing birds, snakes, alligators, turtles, squirrels, opossums, and raccoons, some of the animals exotic enough to mystify the Germans. Auburn University professors and POWs taught prisoners at Opelika Spanish, science, math, physics, and chemistry.

All these circumstances created by war accelerated changes already under way in the state. Total population increased from 2.83 million in 1940 to 3.06 million in 1950. The state's black population continued a historic decline, dropping 0.4 percent between 1940 and 1950 as many left for high-paying jobs in the North. In 1910 Alabama's population was just over 42 percent black; in 1950 it was only 33 percent black, and in 1960 only 30 percent. In 1900 nearly two-thirds of the state's working people engaged in farming; in 1954 more than 80 percent worked in nonfarm jobs and 15 percent in manufacturing.

Activity was increasingly centered in urban areas. Jefferson County contained more than half a million people by 1950, more than one of every six Alabama residents. Birmingham was the twenty-seventh largest city in the United States; only New Orleans and Atlanta were larger in the Southeast (Birmingham's population numbered 326,037 in 1950, Atlanta's 331,314). Since 1900 the population of the United States doubled, the population of Alabama had increased by two-thirds, and Birmingham's quadrupled. Atlanta grew by 311 percent during the half century, Birmingham by 298 percent, New Orleans by 123 percent, and Memphis by 214 percent. Jefferson County's population was 37 percent black, a figure exceeded only by Memphis among the fifty-seven largest metropolitan counties in America. Median income in Birmingham in 1950 exceeded that of both Memphis and New Orleans, thanks to high union wage scales, and lagged only slightly behind Atlanta's. In most categories Birmingham seemed poised in 1950 to overtake its longtime Georgia rival for Southern supremacy. In 1940 Mobile and Montgomery contained nearly identical populations of 78,000, but by 1950 war industry had pushed Mobile's population to 129,000 while Montgomery trailed behind at 107,000. Like the state as a whole, the black population of Montgomery County declined, from nearly 53 percent in 1930 to 50 percent in 1940. Anniston's total population increased to 31,100 by 1950 and Huntsville's to 16,400.

All sectors of the economy experienced dramatic change but no area more than farming. The ten years between 1935 and 1945 were a critical juncture in Southern agriculture. New Deal agricultural policies exercised a "push" effect on tenants and farm labor while war industry had a "pull" effect. The long-advocated changes of agricultural reformers finally occurred: deemphasis on cotton, a switch to alternative cash crops, mechanization, consolidation, increase in pasturage/livestock/poultry production, attention to soil conservation, and less dependence on cheap farm labor.

All of these patterns emerged in Alabama. The number of farms declined from 232,000 in 1940 to 212,000 in 1950. But the average size of these farms increased from 83 to 99 acres, and the total farm acreage increased from 19,143,000 in 1940 to 20,889,000 in 1950, the highest total that Alabama farmers would ever cultivate.

Mechanization transformed the way they tilled land and harvested crops. Manpower shortages during the war created higher labor costs and encouraged farmers to mechanize. High wartime profits and government subsidies provided the capital to do so. In 1930 Alabama farmers operated only 4,664 tractors. By 1940 that figure had risen to 7,638. But during the next five years the total more than doubled to 16,882 and by 1950 reached 45,751 (a 171 percent increase after 1945 alone). International Harvester perfected its mechanical cotton picker early in the 1940s, allowing a machine to pick 1,000 pounds of cotton an hour compared to a human limit of 15 to 20 pounds. Diversification finally reached Alabama also. In 1930 Alabama produced 9.0 percent of the nation's cotton compared to 6.7 percent in 1940 and 5.3 percent in 1950. In place of cotton, farmers turned to poultry, eggs, livestock, pulpwood, soybeans, and peanuts. By the late 1940s livestock provided a third of the state's agricultural income and poultry another 7 percent. In Montgomery County, long renowned for its rich cotton land, farmers received 57 percent of their income from livestock in 1944 and only 22 percent from cotton. By the mid-1950s Alabama farmers produced more pulpwood than any other Southern state, earning $50 million a year, and they had transferred 40 percent of their acreage to pastures.

Tenancy continued to decline from 55.3 percent of all farmers in 1935, to 49.6 in 1940, 32.2 in 1950, and 18.4 in 1959. By 1969 the state contained only 4,605 white tenants compared to 100,000 in 1935. New Deal programs coupled with wartime prosperity greatly improved the quality of rural life, bringing electricity, running water, indoor plumbing, and telephone service. Agricultural extension agents and experiment station scientists continued research on livestock and crop diseases, and state appropriations for such research more than tripled between 1940 and 1950. But even with all these changes the state derived only 9 percent of its income from agriculture in 1954.

Industry experienced comparable changes. The South lost its regional economic identity as its unskilled labor force was integrated into a national market and siphoned into Northern factories. Federal minimum-wage laws, unionization, and labor shortages forced wages up, thus encouraging new labor-saving technology. Five low-wage industries—textiles, tobacco, food, paper, and lumber—accounted for two-thirds of all Southern industrial jobs in 1939 but only one-third in 1976.

The end of the war dislocated some Alabama industry, especially in Mobile. By the end of 1945 the city's shipyards employed only 8,500, and Mobile's economy lost more than 40,000 jobs. An estimated 55,000 people left the area for better opportunities elsewhere.

Other fortunes began as these declined. Winton M. ("Red") Blount and his brother Houston left the University of Alabama for military service, intending to return to their father's sand and gravel business. When they returned, their father was dead and the family business was declining. So the brothers bought four surplus Caterpillar tractors and scrapers for $28,000 and began Blount Brothers Construction Company. They built fish ponds and state highways, developing a reputation for high-quality work. In 1952 they received a contract to build an air force wind tunnel that began their emphasis on high-technology engineering-construction projects (there followed an atomic reactor, the first U.S. intercontinental missile base, and complex 39A at Cape Canaveral from which all flights to the moon were launched).

John M. Harbert III took his Auburn engineering degree into military service and returned with a $6,000 stake he won at dice. He invested in building equipment, added his brother Bill and two young engineers (Edwin M. Dixon and Theodore F. Randolph) to his team, and began a construction business that would ultimately make him the richest man in Alabama.

These young entrepreneurs and many like them depended on different resources for success. The key to their profit margins was not so much cheap labor, a tractable labor force, or state inducements. Rather they depended on creative ideas, efficient management, and a well-trained labor force. In all these areas the South suffered serious deficiencies after the war. Research scientists were five times more numerous in the nation as a whole than in the South. Southerners received patents at a rate less than one-third the national average. Alabama contained no major research university during the era, and its educational system was inadequate. Birmingham in particular still suffered from the disinterest of absentee owners like U.S. Steel. The head of one corporation was so disdainful of the city that he had no local bank account, paying his bills with checks written on an Atlanta bank. But a new generation of homegrown entrepreneurs like the Blount and Harbert brothers would soon contribute heavily to the state's universities and cultural resources.

To compensate for the inadequate educational system and poorly trained labor force, state officials expanded their array of financial inducements and industry recruitment. The State Planning Commission, created in 1935, gave way to the State Planning Board in 1943, which in turn became the State Planning and Industrial Development boards. Some years later they were merged to form the Alabama Development Office. Yet other divisions followed (the Alabama Department of Economic and Community Affairs or ADECA), but all tended to be political and spent much of their time generating good press releases for the governor who happened to be in office at the time. In 1953 the legislature enacted an industrial revenue bond act as a way of financing manufacturing growth. In 1947 George C. Wallace, newly elected to the state house of representatives, sponsored the Regional Trade School Act to construct four new institutions at strategic points across the state. Unfortunately the presidents of such institutions were often political operatives and the curriculum out of date. Wallace also sponsored the 1951 Wallace Act, which, along with the 1949 Cater Act, allowed county industrial development boards to exempt new industries from local property taxes. As a consequence of a poorly educated work force and active recruitment, Alabama tended to attract a great deal of low-wage, low-technology industry.

After 1940 the South's per capita income grew at rates well above the national average. But Alabama's rank in the critical measure of per capita income stayed about where it had always been: in 1930, forty-fifth of forty-eight states; in 1940, forty-sixth; in 1950, forty-sixth. Among ten other states in the South, Alabama's per capita income ranked eighth in 1945, ninth in 1950, and eighth in 1955. Obviously its gamble on low-wage industry did not pay off, and many factories attracted by low wages and a favorable business climate in the 1940s and 1950s found even lower wages and more favorable taxes in Asia, the Caribbean, and Latin America during subsequent decades.

Alabama's economy still depended heavily on its traditional sectors. In 1950 Alabama's seventy-two textile mills employed 54,000 workers. The largest company continued to be Donald Comer's Avondale Mills Corporation, which operated ten mills scattered across northern and east-central Alabama, employed 7,000 in 1947, and consumed 20 percent of the state's cotton production. Benjamin Russell, another native-born textile innovator, brought his three sons into the business and diversified into military uniforms during the war and athletic wear afterward. Russell Mills doubled its floor space between 1945 and 1960, quadrupled its production, and became the largest manufacturer of athletic uniforms and seersucker in the nation.

Alabama's iron and steel industry readjusted from its peak war rates but continued to operate at a high level. Jefferson County led the South in the number of steel firms employing more than 100 workers (notably TCI, Republic Steel, Sloss-Sheffield Steel, Woodward Iron, Connors Steel, J. I. Case Company, O'Neal Steel, and ACIPCO). Birmingham mills employed 30,000 steelworkers in 1947 compared to Houston's 18,600. That year the manufacturing value of the industry in Alabama amounted to 20 percent of the state's total industrial output. By 1940 Mobile had become the largest shipper of steel products on the Gulf Coast, although it lost that standing to New Orleans by the late 1940s.

The forest products industry thrived on the state's heavy rainfall, humidity, and long growing season. But its low wages, undesirable working conditions, and the reputation of many small operators for cheating employees combined to cause difficulty attracting sufficient labor during the war. During the late 1940s and 1950s industry officials perfected the wood dealer system. A pulp or paper mill would contract with a prominent person in a county—usually a sheriff, probate judge, or powerful businessman—to deliver a certain number of cords of wood. The local person would recruit rural poor whites and blacks, furnish them money to buy a secondhand truck, power saws, and other equipment, and contract each to deliver a stipulated amount of timber. These local "wood dealers" furnished wood to mills but were not company employees. They typically did not report earnings to the Internal Revenue Service, thus avoiding taxes, and the timber companies avoided insurance, retirement, and liability for accidents. Customers got cheap goods, and Alabama recruited yet more low-wage industry for its unskilled labor force.

Huntsville charted the most unusual economic course thanks to cheap TVA power and assistance from the federal government. In 1950 the army transferred 500 military personnel, 130 German rocket scientists, 180 General Electric employees, and 120 civil service workers from Fort Bliss to Redstone Arsenal. In 1956 the army established at Redstone the Army Ballistic Missile Agency, which developed the Explorer and Pioneer rocket programs and the Jupiter family of rocket engines. The development marked the beginning of an incredible change in Huntsville that would not be fully realized until the 1960s.

Such economic activity tended to create an irregular pattern of prosperity and poverty. In 1950 the ten counties with the highest per capita incomes were all industrialized; the twenty-one poorest counties were all in the Black Belt or other rural areas.

A major factor in the growth of urban per capita income was union-

Riveters at Alabama Dry Docks and Shipbuilding Company (ADDSCO), 1943. The Second World War opened up a world of new economic activity to women. (Courtesy of the ADDSCO Collection, University of South Alabama Photographic Archives)

ism. Alabama contained a disproportionately large share of unionized manufacturing (iron and steel, tire factories, auto parts, and coal mining). In 1939 the state had 64,000 union members and by 1953 it had 168,000. The portion of union members among all nonagricultural workers increased from 16.1 percent in 1939 to 24.9 percent in 1953—the highest percentage of any southeastern state. Thanks to the UMW, coal miners became the highest-paid production workers in the United States after 1945. Antiunion companies struck back in 1953 by forcing a law through the legislature that prohibited making union membership a requirement for employment. Despite continuing strikes against textile mills, the industry successfully resisted unionism, sometimes by closing mills and moving operations elsewhere. But unionism benefited the state's economy by substantially raising per capita income for many workers.

THIRTY

The Flowering
of Alabama Liberalism:
Politics and Society
during the 1940s and 1950s

B Y the 1960s Alabama had become a state that seemed to epitomize
opposition to the federal government. But in the 1940s and 1950s
no state congressional delegation did more to expand federal powers to
assist the nation's weakest and most vulnerable people. Alabama's U.S.
senators Lister Hill and John Sparkman sponsored federal programs
to construct public housing, build hospitals, support medical research,
and provide free Salk antipolio vaccine. Four congressmen from north
Alabama in the 1940s—Bob Jones, Carl Elliott, Kenneth Roberts, and
Albert Rains—represented constituencies of small farmers who had
been helped by TVA and of industrial workers who belonged to unions.
Hill's longtime campaign manager and chief political strategist, Marc
Ray ("Foots") Clement, was probably the shrewdest political operative
of the times. Jones, Elliott, and Roberts were all his protégés at the
University of Alabama. John Sparkman, like Hill, had served as president of the Student Government Association at the Tuscaloosa campus.
He served five terms in the House representing TVA's Eighth Congressional District before winning election to the U.S. Senate in 1946 after
the death of Senator John Bankhead, Jr. Clement helped organize his
campaign. Elliott and Sparkman came from sturdy sharecropper parents. Elliott worked for the WPA and lived in housing called "Poverty
Ridge" while attending the university. So when Elliott joined with Hill to
write the National Defense Education Act, which provided federal loans
to college students, he must have remembered how difficult it had been
to pay his own way through college during the depression. Several
informal polls of House members voted the Alabama delegation the best
of any state.

The state's congressional delegation was also one of the South's most
liberal. Helen Fuller, managing editor of the *New Republic,* inquired of
Alabama progressive Herman C. Nixon in August 1955: "Why is it that
Alabama in the last generation has produced so many more liberally
minded public men than any of her neighboring states?"[1] Fuller's question was an excellent one, which Nixon never answered. Part of the

524

answer lay in the long tradition of political dissent and populist protest, especially in north Alabama. The depression spotlighted the state's poverty and its lack of welfare and educational programs. The New Deal encouraged the formation of unionism and produced strong popular loyalties among small farmers, workers, and even small businessmen. Federal patronage and a strong New Deal governor, Bibb Graves, further solidified reformers. Many influential journalists helped publicize their causes. Finally, Lister Hill provided effective ideological leadership, and Foots Clement became the reformers' organizing genius. The class-based liberalism of the 1930s and 1940s united black and white unionists who were experiencing common economic problems. James E. Folsom successfully won with that coalition, as did reformist congressmen.

But when Northern liberals and Southern conservatives increasingly linked liberalism to race relations, the New Deal coalition in Alabama began to unravel. As union wage scales allowed working class whites to move into the middle class, they began to resent blacks who competed for their high-paying jobs and who threatened their social status. By the late 1950s liberalism had taken on a racial meaning in Alabama politics that made it unacceptable to most white voters. Alabama's conservatives by no means conceded the battlefield during the 1940s, but they retreated to lick their wounds and regroup. As it turned out, time was on their side.

Outgoing governor Frank Dixon became the focus of anti–New Dealers by the time his term ended in 1942. He warned Southern Democrats that it was "their own party which is dynamiting their social structure, which is arousing bitterness and recrimination, which is attempting to force crackpot reforms on them in a time of national crisis."[2] Unfortunately for defenders of the status quo, Dixon was limited to one term, and they now confronted the most popular politician in Alabama, New Dealer Bibb Graves.

Graves's decision to try for an unprecedented third term spread despondency through anti–New Deal ranks. Realistically they had no chance of defeating him. They generally backed Chauncey Sparks, "the Bourbon from Barbour" County, who had run second in 1938, but even Sparks had the good sense to avoid negative comments about FDR and the New Deal. Birmingham businessman Sydney Smyer urged Sparks to run against organized labor, and when he adopted the strategy, business money began to flow into his campaign. But Sparks was a poor speaker and a colorless politician, and his campaign floundered until Graves died in March 1942.

A number of candidates entered the race because of Graves's poor health, including Cullman insurance salesman James E. Folsom, but none attracted much attention until the leader's death. At that point the

Graves forces cast about for another candidate. Most of them reluctantly endorsed Sparks, although the CIO backed the little-known Folsom. Sparks beat Folsom without a runoff, although the Cullman salesman ran exceptionally well in the hill country and Wiregrass. Although Sparks won easily, New Dealers swept the congressional races, and Graves's death almost certainly kept a liberal from the governor's office.

Certainly Sparks's election was no reliable barometer of liberal strength in the state. As governor he disappointed many anti–New Dealers by sponsoring tax revision that placed more of the burden on corporations, particularly utilities, and expanded social services. Some liberals such as Charles Dobbins liked Sparks and considered him a genuine progressive.

In 1946 James Folsom continued the tradition of the previous second-place finisher winning the second time around (five consecutive governors, including Folsom, fit the pattern). New Dealers divided loyalties among a variety of candidates: many of the old Graves forces backed Lieutenant Governor Handy Ellis, who had flirted with the Klan during the 1920s; Gordon Persons, a consumer-oriented member of the Public Service Commission, won support from urban progressives; and Folsom expanded his base among labor and small farmers. Anti–New Dealers rallied around Commissioner of Agriculture and Industry Joe Poole, a Butler County cotton planter who also attracted Big Mule support from Birmingham (especially Alabama Power Company and TCI). Although the state's Cooperative Extension Service headquartered at Auburn was officially nonpolitical, Director P. O. Davis and his army of county agents plunged neck-deep into the campaign on behalf of Poole, aiding the Alabama Farm Bureau in its efforts to elect him.

Of all Alabama's twentieth-century governors, Jim Folsom was the most compelling and flamboyant. Born on a small farm near the Wiregrass town of Elba in October 1908, he attended both the University of Alabama and Howard College briefly but graduated from neither. His family had a long tradition of political involvement in Coffee County, usually on behalf of insurgency, such as Republicanism or populism. After dropping out of college, he served in the merchant marine, worked as a doorman in New York, and even trained as a boxer. In 1933 he became director of the WPA in Marshall County, where he encountered the massive poverty and problems of hill country farmers. He returned to Elba in 1936, married, and ran for Congress against New Deal congressman Henry B. Steagall. Folsom actually attacked Steagall from the left of the New Deal, arguing for the Townsend Plan of federal aid to the elderly, federal aid to education, and more money for farm relief. He lost in 1936 and again two years later and decided to move to Cullman in 1938 to sell insurance.

Knowing of Graves's poor health, he decided to run in 1942 despite lack of money and support from influential local politicians and businessmen. Because he had no base of support there anyway, Folsom ran against the "professional politicians" and as a candidate of the little people. His size, theatrics, and use of a country band endeared him to this rustic constituency. At six feet, eight inches tall, he was a distinctive figure in his white western-style hat and his huge brogans. Folsom was not a physical freak, but having seen him once, the tendency was to look again and keep on looking. As in the 1930s, he ran a campaign to the left of other candidates. His second-place finish surprised political analysts because he had little organization or money.

After his 1942 loss, his life gyrated through a series of triumphs and tragedies. Voters elected him a delegate to the 1944 Democratic convention where he broke with the Alabama delegation and supported left-winger Henry Wallace for vice-president over Alabama's favorite-son nominee, Senator John Bankhead, Jr. Folsom's wife died that same year, increasing his excessive use of alcohol. In 1946 he began a love affair with Christine Putman Johnston, a clerk at Birmingham's Tutwiler Hotel, that resulted in the birth of an illegitimate child.

Despite these involvements he launched his 1946 campaign in Oneonta, calling for reapportionment of the legislature, revision of the antiquated 1901 constitution, abolition of the sales tax, increased old-age pensions and teacher salaries, and paved farm-to-market roads. He began his campaign with less than two hundred dollars in expense money, so he passed a suds bucket through the crowd for contributions. The one hundred dollars a day he collected in mostly small contributions of dimes and quarters literally kept him on the road, buying gas, food, and paying for hotel rooms. He also carried a corn-shuck mop to symbolize his pledge to scour the capitol, open up the windows, and allow a fresh breeze to flow through state government. Folsom had no campaign manager, no headquarters, no money, and no respect from his opponents. Ellis attacked Poole as the lackey of the Big Mules; Poole responded that Ellis represented wets, the Klan, and organized labor. Folsom commented that both Poole and Ellis were right about each other. In Mobile his backers gathered at a local barbershop because they had no other meeting place. In rural areas Big Jim, as he was now inevitably called, would often remove his shoes to rest his huge feet and demonstrate that he, like his supporters, could not afford the luxury of socks.

Gradually he attracted a following of fellow reformers. Gould Beech, editor of the *Southern Farmer*, became a key Folsom operative, speech writer, and the closest thing Big Jim had to a campaign manager. Longtime New Dealer Aubrey Williams—who had been denounced by

"Big Jim" (James E.) Folsom, the "Strawberry Pickers" Band, and his famous "Suds Bucket," 1946. Folsom financed his campaign partly by passing this "suds and scrubbing" bucket and promising audiences, "You furnish the suds and I'll do the scrubbing." (Courtesy of the Alabama Department of Archives and History)

anti–New Dealers as an atheist, a Communist, a "nigger-lover," and the "most dangerous man in America"—returned to Alabama from Washington in 1945 to publish the journal Beech edited. It circulated nationally to 1 million, but more importantly 80,000 Alabama farmers received the journal, the very audience Folsom sought to reach. Tucked between advertisements for John Deere tractors and trusses that promised relief from hernia pain were articles that championed social and racial justice.

Folsom's strategy paid off. He led the May 7 primary field with 28.5 percent of the vote to Ellis's 24.2 percent. In the runoff Ellis tried to link Folsom to the CIO and a Communist conspiracy, but Folsom blunted the issue with wisecracks. Before the primary, he noted, all the candidates had ignored him as harmless and unimportant. But now he was a "b-ig, ba-ad booger!" He complained that Ellis even accused him of wearing size-sixteen shoes. Then he would hold up his monstrous foot and confide that the charge was an outrageous lie: he only wore a fifteen and a half. Roars of laughter drowned out the charges of dangerous radicalism. Ellis tried to reach Folsom's rural constituency by having himself photographed behind a plow mule. But Folsom spotted a mistake in the harness and had the photo enlarged. He then delighted rural audiences by exhibiting the photograph and calling attention to the mistake. In the runoff Folsom won by a vote of 205,000 to 144,000, carrying north Alabama and the Wiregrass, his "friends and neighbors." New voters, many of them veterans, also elected 100 freshman members to the 135-person state legislature.

Big Jim's inauguration was a haberdasher's delight. He wore a size seven-and-five-eighths-inch silk hat, which made his huge size seem even larger, and a shirt with a seventeen-and-one-half-inch neckband and thirty-seven-inch sleeves. More than 100,000 people crowded the streets of the capital to watch his inaugural parade. Blacks were especially prominent in the crowds, which surged into the capitol following his swearing-in ceremony. The Strawberry Pickers provided music for the inaugural ball, which attracted an audience nearly as egalitarian as the parade.

Folsom provided more than merely a Jacksonian inauguration designed for the common folk. He had shattered both the anti–New Deal faction and the older progressive Thomas Kilby–Bibb Graves tradition. Journalist Grover Hall, Jr., attributed his victory to the "outcasts of Poker Flats in Alabama," and to some degree his triumph was a victory for the state's peripheral people. The poll tax still kept poor whites and blacks largely disfranchised, so the triumph required further explanation. The banners of important power brokers from earlier times—the Farm Bureau, Alabama Power Company, the Alabama League of Municipalities, and the Association of County Commissioners—were temporarily furled. New forces—the CIO, politicized small dirt farmers, the Alabama Education Association, returning veterans—had gained the ascendancy. The legislature contained more new faces than at any time during the century. Folsom stood poised to lead the state in a significantly different direction—toward reform and modernization. He squandered the opportunity.

The root cause of his failure was Big Jim himself. His massive frame contained a complex mixture of idealism, naiveté, racial tolerance, ignorance, and personal foibles sufficient to derail any size engine of reform. As one early adviser evaluated the governor: "On any given day you wouldn't know if he was going to be a genius or a fool."[3] Central to that equation of genius and buffoonery were his elemental populism, his racial tolerance, his love of power, his alcoholism, and his personal eccentricity.

No sooner had Folsom taken office than rumors began to circulate about his illegitimate child and of payoffs to Christine Johnston. He did pay her $10,000 to keep quiet, although she filed a paternity suit against him anyway in March 1948. Preoccupied with his personal problems and desperately stonewalling the stories that snooping journalists sought to confirm, he managed to alienate the press and failed to organize his forces in the legislature. The virtually all-new state legislature gave him an unprecedented opportunity to forge a new coalition. Instead, Folsom procrastinated until he finally had to rely heavily on patronage and favors to have his nominee elected speaker of the house, and the men selected as president pro tempore of the senate and chairman of the State Democratic Executive Committee opposed most of his agenda.

As his initial legislative battle Folsom tried to pack the Auburn board of trustees with allies committed to removing the Cooperative Extension Service from politics. Unlike the University of Alabama board of trustees, which was made self-perpetuating by the 1901 constitution, Auburn's board was politically appointed by the governor and confirmed by the senate. The University of Alabama board generally avoided the rowdier and seamier side of Alabama politics, but the Auburn board often swirled with controversy. The Cooperative Extension Service, the Farm Bureau, and Black Belt planters and politicians mobilized to defeat Folsom by blocking his nominees in the senate. This they successfully accomplished, bloodying the new governor in his first test of strength. The senate's new trustees promptly passed a resolution commending Auburn's extension agents.

Folsom had more success with legislative committees and used their reports on various state problems to craft a legislative agenda. Given his opponents' control of the upper house, he accomplished a remarkable amount of reform. With the help of a key legislator in the lower house, George C. Wallace of Barbour County, he won passage of an income tax and biennial budgets, repeal of some sales-tax exemptions on special interests, an increase in funds for old-age pensions and education, and the creation of four new regional trade schools. When the senate blocked his poll-tax reforms, Folsom used his power to appoint county registrars to place in office people who would register qualified blacks. As a result, the number of black registered voters during his two terms in office increased substantially. In 1947 only 1 percent of Alabama blacks were registered; by 1952 that percentage had increased to 5 and by 1958 to 15, compared to comparable figures for all Southern blacks of 12 percent in 1947, 20 percent in 1952, and 28 percent in 1958. Folsom also appointed the first woman to the Alabama Court of Appeals at a time when women could not even serve on Alabama juries.

Despite the limited successes, Folsom's attempt to change the political power balance in Alabama failed. The senate defeated his attempts at constitutional revision and reapportionment. Opponents of black voting passed the Boswell Amendment in the fall of 1946. The amendment allowed county registrars broad latitude in questioning would-be voters in order to exclude poor whites and blacks. Folsom stirred class issues within the state, and the 1949–50 legislature passed none of his programs. Frustrated by the legislative recalcitrance and nearing the end of his term, Big Jim maneuvered for best advantage in the 1954 gubernatorial election toward which he was already looking.

Folsom's 1946 victory provided only part of the evidence for Alabama's liberal resurgence. In 1944 the Farm Bureau, P. O. Davis and the Auburn Cooperative Extension Service, the Associated Industries of Alabama, and others in the big business/big agriculture coalition persuaded influential state senator James A. Simpson to oppose U.S. senator Lister Hill. The campaign was a classic test of pro– and anti–New Deal sentiment in the state. Hill defended the New Deal. Simpson campaigned against higher taxes for education, free textbooks, and rural electrification while favoring lower taxes on corporations. Simpson also interjected race in the campaign's later stages, attacking Hill for favoring a federal administration that threatened to abolish the poll tax and to enforce rulings forbidding racial discrimination in jobs involving federal contracts. Hill retaliated with his own form of race baiting. The nasty race ended with Hill taking a hard-fought 55 percent victory. Hill emerged from the 1944 campaign with his political position strengthened so that he publicly urged allies in the state legislature to abolish the poll tax and even more vigorously defended TVA from challenges to its authority by Alabama Power Company.

The next skirmish came two years later in a special election to fill the seat of Senator John Bankhead, Jr., who died in May 1946. Both ideological camps of Democrats put forward a candidate. Congressman John Sparkman, representing the strongly New Deal Tennessee Valley, won labor backing. Mobile's congressman Frank Boykin and state senator James A. Simpson divided the anti–New Deal vote. Sparkman, whose tenant farm family had been so poor that creditors had taken even their cow for debt payment, put himself through the University of Alabama by shoveling coal. He also made Phi Beta Kappa, took a master's degree in history with a thesis on Populist leader Reuben F. Kolb, and then completed his law degree. Having watched closely Folsom's victorious spring campaign, he ran on a similar platform. Governor-elect Folsom endorsed Sparkman, as did Senator Lister Hill. Boykin advanced the now-familiar charges that "radicals" from Washington and New York—with close ties to Communists, the CIO, and Birmingham's Negro Progressive Council—sponsored Sparkman's candidacy. The rhetoric, which would prove so compelling with Alabama voters during the next half century, convinced few in 1946 when Washington Democrats were associated with popular social programs, such as Social Security and TVA. Sparkman smashed his two opponents with 50.1 percent of the vote to 27.5 percent for Simpson and 21.2 percent for Boykin.

The trio of victories by Hill, Folsom, and Sparkman—augmented by the congressional victories of Albert Rains, Carl Elliott, Kenneth Roberts, and Bob Jones—provided evidence that New Deal forces were firmly in charge. Defenders of the status quo railed against Communist and CIO domination and began to raise the specter of race, but voters shoved such issues aside in favor of a class-based politics that united small farmers, unionists, and blacks in a winning combination. New Dealer Aubrey Williams could return to Montgomery and publish a journal, liberal by the standards of any region. In July 1948 he declared segregation to be the central evil of Southern society. That same year he became director of the Southern Educational Fund. Within that organization he pushed for racial integration and earned it a designation as a "Communist front organization" by the right-wing House Un-American Activities Committee. The NAACP praised the Alabamian in 1945 as a person "absolutely straight on our [race] question."[4] Ironically, one of the nation's most articulate advocates of blacks, the poor, and the common person during the 1940s lived and worked in Montgomery, Alabama.

Within Williams's circle of friends in the capital were attorney Clifford Durr and Virginia Foster Durr and newspaper editor Charles Dobbins. The Montgomery *Advertiser* fired Dobbins because of his refusal to blame the Soviet Union entirely for the origins of the cold war and for his support of the Rural Electrification Administration. But he began to publish the Montgomery *Examiner* and continued his political activism. Clifford and Virginia Durr spent much of the decade in Washington but formed fast friendships with the state's New Dealers. They supported left-wing Henry Wallace for president in 1948 over Harry Truman, a decision contrary to Aubrey Williams's policy of reluctant support for Truman. Reflecting upon the recent history of Alabama politics, journalist Grover Hall, Jr., compared the state favorably to its Southern neighbors at least in the area of race relations. He wrote: "Alabama has had incompetent governors, greedy governors, good, bad and indifferent governors. But it has been spared the shame of having a vicious governor or one willing to exploit the Negro issue."[5]

However true that might have been when Hall wrote it in 1942, his qualified praise did not apply by the later 1940s when race became central to state politics. More typical of the era was the comment of Charles Dobbins's father, who served a Baptist parish in the Black Belt: "We don't have politics in Alabama based on issues. All our politics is race."[6] By the early 1950s Williams, the Durrs, and Dobbins had either left the state or become pariahs, shunned by former Montgomery friends who made wild accusations of communism, atheism, and treason. The turning point in the ideological struggle came in the Dixiecrat movement of 1948.

Clifford and Virginia Durr and their daughters, 1940. The Durrs were New Dealers and leading civil rights and anti-poll tax activists from Montgomery. (Courtesy of the Alabama Department of Archives and History)

With FDR dead and the untrusted hand of Harry Truman guiding the Democratic party, Alabama's New Deal coalition began to unravel. The most telling evidence of division came in the 1948 presidential election.

The events of 1948 merely confirmed a pattern that developed throughout the decade. Those opposed to change increasingly focused on race. As early as 1943, then-governor Frank Dixon called for the formation of a Southern Democratic party to preserve segregation. Folsom's election, his appointment of voting officials willing to register poor whites and blacks, and the growth of anti–poll tax sentiment among Alabamians inspired the backlash of the 1946 Boswell Amendment (which sought to block court rulings making it easier for blacks to vote) and further polarized the state. The Birmingham *Age-Herald* endorsed repeal of the poll tax, saying it blocked government "of the people." But the Montgomery *Advertiser* warned that repeal would arm poor whites "with a political power that the responsible citizens cannot afford to grant."[7] Ratification of the Boswell Amendment once again pitted north Alabama against south Alabama. The amendment narrowly passed in a public referendum that closely paralleled voting returns in the 1944 Hill–Simpson senatorial race. The culminating element of this conflict began in 1947 when President Truman endorsed a strong civil rights package that included repeal of the poll tax, enforcement of legislation forbidding job discrimination because of race, and making lynching a federal offense.

Alabamians opposed to Truman's Fair Deal immediately made his civil rights initiative the primary issue in the contest for presidential electors and delegates to the 1948 Democratic convention. The state's Democratic party split into three factions. Governor Folsom led the one most loyal to the national party, although the faction—which included Clifford and Virginia Durr, Charles Dobbins, Aubrey Williams, and Gould Beech—contained many supporters of Henry Wallace who criticized Truman from the left.

A second group of party loyalists reluctantly backed Truman but rejected his civil rights program. They endorsed his anti-Communist containment policy, warned against a party bolt, and included Senators Hill and Sparkman and most of the congressional delegation.

The third faction opposed Truman and the national party. Within it was one subgroup ready to break immediately with the party and form its own organization. It was led by two veterans of the 1928 bolt against Al Smith, former KKK leader Horace Wilkinson and Birmingham attorney Hugh Locke. Eugene ("Bull") Connor, who denounced Truman's civil rights program as part of a Communist conspiracy, joined them. A more moderate subgroup decided to attend the Democratic National Convention, try to block adoption of the civil rights program, then bolt the party if unsuccessful. Former governor Frank Dixon, former lieutenant governor Handy Ellis, Mobile attorney Gessner T. McCorvey, and state senator E. C. Boswell led this wing.

McCorvey led the states' righters, whose agenda now had more to do with race than historic constitutional issues. They controlled the State Democratic Executive Committee and endorsed a slate of delegates pledged to walk out of the Democratic convention if the civil rights platform gained approval. But they had to convince voters to elect their slate. In the May–June 1948 elections, voters selected a slate of eleven presidential electors pledged not to vote for Truman. But they also split delegates to the national convention, electing fourteen states' righters to twelve national loyalists. When one of the states' righters became ill, George C. Wallace of Barbour County filled his place, giving the loyalists a thirteen-to-thirteen tie. As good as their word, the thirteen states' righters stalked out of the convention hall when the controversial platform passed, their ears ringing to denunciation by a Wisconsin delegate who shouted "Good riddance!" as the Alabamians departed.

The party bolters called for a national gathering of states' righters to meet in Birmingham on July 17, 1948. The historic municipal auditorium, which had earlier given birth to the liberal Southern Conference for Human Welfare, now served as birthplace for the States' Rights or "Dixiecrat" party. Although five Southern governors mingled among the 7,500 delegates, the meeting was hardly the celebrity affair that its planners had envisioned. The Virginia delegation consisted of four University of Virginia students and a young woman who stopped off while completing a cross-country trip. An Alabama resident originally from Kentucky carried the banner of his native state. The audience was swelled by students from nearby colleges, bored with summer school and anxious to see a spectacle. Many of the delegates represented what one national journalist dubbed the "hate fringe": Gerald L. K. Smith, who had flirted with fascism and was founder of the Christian Nationalist Convention; J. E. Perkins, author of the anti-Semitic *The Jews Have Got the Atom Bomb;* J. B. Stoner, founder of the Anti-Jewish party, which proposed making Jewishness a capital offense; Jessie Welch Jenkins, president of the national Patrick Henry Organization, whose chief goal was to abolish both national parties. Former governor Frank Dixon gave the keynote address. With a flurry of Confederate flags and exuberant if off-key renderings of "Dixie," the new party nominated South Carolina governor J. Strom Thurmond for president and Mississippi governor Fielding L. Wright as his running mate.

States' righters who controlled the State Democratic Executive Committee and presidential electors decided not even to list Truman's name on the official ballot. With Truman's name absent, voters cast 80 percent of their ballots for the Dixiecrat ticket. But only three other Deep South states joined Alabama in bolting the Democratic party. The bolt fell far short of its goal to deadlock the decision and throw the election into the House of Representatives where Southern congressmen could negotiate concessions.

Although ensuing clashes soon clouded the meaning of the Dixiecrat revolt, the event held important portent for the future. It was more than merely a states' rights revolt within Alabama's Democratic party. It suggested the growing racial coalescence of whites and the beginnings of an independent party movement that would soon blossom into Wallacism. Beyond that, it propelled many long-disaffected Democrats into the Republican party.

Following Truman's reelection, Alabama Democrats waged a fratricidal struggle over control of the party machinery. Chief prize in the battle was control of the seventy-two-member State Democratic Executive Committee. States' righters launched their campaign for control at an April 1950 banquet in Dothan attended by five hundred, including Dothan banker Wallace D. Malone, McCorvey, Ellis, and Dixon. Birmingham journalist John Temple Graves II, former New Dealer turned states' righter, delivered a major address that clearly anticipated the future for many of those gathered: "And, gentlemen, let us not wince anymore when we hear the word 'Republican.' Hell trembled for us once at the hideous name. That was because of the race problem." In the future, he said, Alabamians must endorse any national party committed to "states' rights and Constitutional government."[8] Four days after the Dothan meeting, one thousand loyalist Democrats gathered in Birmingham to attack Dixiecrats and affirm their loyalty to the national party. Those who attended the Dothan meeting included few officeholders beyond the Black Belt. The Birmingham gathering attracted Senators Hill and Sparkman, most of the congressional delegation, Governor Folsom, and many state legislators and labor leaders.

These meetings kicked off the struggle for executive committee dominance that would be determined in the May 1950 Democratic primary elections. The campaign was titanic. Hill, Sparkman, Foots Clement, Congressmen Rains, Elliott, and Bob Jones, and Governor Folsom led the loyalists. Congressmen George Andrews and Sam F. Hobbs, both representing Black Belt constituencies, industrialist Donald Comer, Horace Wilkinson, and Talladega newspaper publisher Tom Abernethy led the states' righters. All fifteen gubernatorial candidates endorsed one side or the other, although eventual winner Gordon Persons dropped any reference to the issue after endorsing the national loyalists. Two notable Young Democrats who campaigned for the loyalist slate were Ryan deGraffenried and George Wallace. Once again race furnished states' righters their strongest weapon. Horace Wilkinson, the rawest of their speakers, vowed that he would "rather die fighting for states' rights than live on Truman Boulevard in a nigger heaven."[9] Newspapers that would long champion segregation and states' rights lent their editorial pages to the cause: the Mobile *Press Register*, the Dothan *Eagle*, Abernethy's Talladega *Daily Home*, and Hamner Cobbs's Greensboro *Watchman*. Loyalist papers included the Montgomery *Advertiser*, the Birmingham *News*, the Huntsville *Times*, the Tuscaloosa *News*, and the Anniston *Star*. The loyalists swept north Alabama to win forty-three members on the executive committee. Loyalist Gordon Persons also won the governorship, beating the largest field in state history. His tours of the state in a crowd-pleasing helicopter probably had as much to do with victory as his loyalist sentiments, but he had close ties to state reformers. Charles Dobbins wrote his inaugural address and earned appointment to the state Board of Education. Persons appointed Auburn's reform journalist Neil Davis to the Pardon and Parole Board. At his confirmation hearing before a legislative committee, Dobbins created a stir by refusing to endorse white supremacy, but the legislature bent to the governor's pressure and confirmed him anyway.

Many observers interpreted the 1950 election results as a clear liberal/ loyalist victory. The state's major black newspaper, the Birmingham *World*, rejoiced: "Alabama liberalism, let's call it, gets a new lease on life. A new kind of politics has triumphed." The Huntsville *Times* reacted more prudently: "The Dixiecrat movement is washed up, unless something else comes along in the next few years to revive it."[10]

Loyalists controlled the new executive committee and required all Democratic candidates for electors in 1952 to take an oath of loyalty to national party nominees. But when the supreme court temporarily blocked the rule, states' righters nominated a slate that included textile tycoon Donald Comer, Dothan banker Wallace Malone, insurance man and former head of the state Chamber of Commerce Frank P. Samford, Mobile attorney and 1948 bolter Gessner McCorvey, Horace Wilkinson, and Black Belt legislator Walter C. Givhan. Tom Abernethy could have had a place but he had already deserted the states' righters for the Republican party. The supreme court finally upheld the loyalty oath, and a slate pledged to the national nominees won in May 1952. McCorvey, Comer, Malone, Winton M. Blount, and many other former Democrats and industrialists endorsed Republican nominee Dwight D. Eisenhower against what one states' righter called the "Trumanistic-Communistic ticket." "Ike" Eisenhower received only 35 percent of Alabama's vote but ran best in the Black Belt where states' righters had been strongest. Ike also performed well in urban counties where the Republican vote increased significantly between 1936 and 1956. One reason for Alabama's support of the 1952 Democratic ticket was the presence of Alabama senator John Sparkman as the vice-presidential candidate.

The bland but mildly progressive Persons administration (1951–55) sent mixed ideological signals. In 1953 the legislature enacted a so-called right-to-work law that allowed companies to resist union pressure to make union membership a condition for employment. The act infuriated unionists and mobilized them for the 1954 gubernatorial race. Yet reformers, assisted by the state's women's clubs, also secured passage of the Meek bill, which limited cumulative poll taxes to a maximum of three dollars and exempted completely anyone over age forty-five. The law opened the way for an estimated 100,000 new voters. Gessner McCorvey complained bitterly to Frank Dixon: "We are not going to be able to do much in the way of preventing the registration of white citizens, even though they are of a type which has no business voting."[11]

Folsom's 1954 campaign was both more sedate and more organized than his 1946 race. He still featured a country band, this time called the "Corn Grinders," a suds bucket for donations, and a reform agenda of better schools, higher teacher salaries and old-age pensions, improved health care, reapportionment, constitutional revision, and creation of a state industrial board to recruit industry. His new wife, Jamelle Moore, somewhat blunted his earlier sexual indiscretions. Even so, Folsom boasted that if some enemy baited a trap for him with a pretty girl, he was likely to catch Big Jim every time. His campaign slogan was a populistic invitation to the common people to take control of the state. The simple phrase "Y'all come" (also set to music) had a compelling appeal. Organized labor reached its pinnacle of power in Alabama during the 1954 campaign and provided much of Folsom's money and organizational structure. Four of the five gubernatorial candidates, including Folsom and eventual runner-up Jimmy Faulkner of Bay Minette, sided with the national loyalist wing of the party. Only Black Belt planter J. Bruce Henderson, who had favored the Dixiecrats in 1948, represented the states' righters. Folsom became the first Alabama candidate to use television effectively by conducting a series of "talkathons" where viewers called in questions. He straddled the volatile race issue, refusing to engage in the race baiting that was increasingly popular in the South. Ten of Alabama's twenty-four daily papers endorsed him, and he rolled to an easy victory over Jimmy Faulkner, carrying sixty-one of sixty-seven counties. Between them they won 75 percent of the vote to Henderson's 8 percent. The black-owned Birmingham *World* mistakenly editorialized: "Race issue politics is becoming losing politics in Alabama."[12] Senator John Sparkman easily defeated the Big Mule candidate, Birmingham congressman Laurie C. Battle. Loyalists also elected sixty-one of the seventy-two-person State Democratic Executive Committee. But in south Alabama prominent businessmen Gessner McCorvey, W. O. Bellingrath, Alfred F. Delchamps, and James C. Van Antwerp formed the Mobile Committee of States' Rights Democrats as a sort of halfway house on their journey to the Republican party. Birmingham businessmen organized a similar group.

Three times since 1948 Alabama voters had chosen the liberal side of the state Democratic party. But fourteen days before the Democratic runoff election on May 31, 1954, the Supreme Court issued its historic decision in the case of *Brown* v. *Board of Education of Topeka, Kansas.* Nothing in Alabama politics would be the same again.

Race always played a major role in Alabama social relations, but seldom was that role as ambivalent as between 1940 and 1954. In Birmingham white businessmen and blacks tried to create a local chapter of the National Urban League. In 1950 whites formed an Interracial Committee of the Community Chest and tried to persuade the city to hire black policemen, a proposal blocked by police commissioner Bull Connor. By 1944 Alabama contained five local chapters of the Southwide Committee on Interracial Cooperation. These groups merged into the Alabama Division of the Southern Regional Council, changed its name to the Alabama Council on Human Relations, and by 1955 had seven associations with some three hundred members, many of them Methodist ministers and laywomen. Jesuit Spring Hill College in Mobile voluntarily admitted blacks in 1951.

The CIO formed interracial unions. Some locals of the Steelworkers Union elected black vice-presidents. Other unions encountered more difficulty. The Mine, Mill, and Smelter Workers Union experienced discord because of white complaints of black and Communist domination of the union. CIO regional director Noel Beddow used black ministers to try to reassure black rank-and-file members while he calmed white unionists. But racial friction continued in the mid-1940s until Beddow moved to exclude several alleged Communists from the Alabama State Industrial Union Council.

Elsewhere around the state black policemen served in Montgomery, Mobile, Talladega, and Dothan by 1954, and a new generation of black leaders challenged traditional racial views. Businessman A. G. Gaston, attorneys Arthur Shores, Orzell Billingsley, and Peter Hall, and Baptist minister Fred L. Shuttlesworth, Jr., assumed leadership roles among blacks in Birmingham. In Montgomery the Reverend Ralph D. Abernathy, labor leader E. D. Nixon, teacher Jo Ann Robinson, and J. E. Pierce organized blacks. Statewide the NAACP united this network.

Sports served as an opening wedge to integration in Birmingham. A city ordinance prohibited blacks and whites from competition against each other. As a result, professional baseball and football teams refused to play in the Steel City in the early 1950s. In 1953 the Birmingham Barons of the Southern Association made a pennant drive that threatened to put them in a playoff with the Texas League champion, which had a black player. Pressure from Birmingham fans forced the city commission to eliminate baseball and football from the ordinance. The step also made possible an exhibition game between the Milwaukee Braves and the Brooklyn Dodgers. Cards, dice, dominoes, checkers, and basketball would remain racially pure. But Judge Hugh Locke opposed even this reform and led a public drive to restore rigid segregation. He collected 10,000 signatures on a petition and warned that "allowing a few Negroes to play baseball here will wind up with Negroes and whites marrying."[13] Voters defeated the liberalized sports policy by a decisive three-to-one margin only weeks after the *Brown* decision.

Politically most attention focused on Tuskegee. In 1941 Tuskegee Institute professor C. G. Gomillion formed the Tuskegee Civic Association to assist blacks in registering to vote. Four years later he filed a suit against the Macon County Board of Registrars for refusing to register black voters. One of the plaintiffs in the case, a black veteran named Otis Pinkard, explained: "After having been overseas fighting for democracy, I thought that when we got back here we should enjoy a little of it." For a year and a half the board of registrars refused to meet to register any voters. Finally the registrars assembled secretly to enroll 200 white voters. A vacancy occurred, and in 1949 Governor Folsom appointed as chief registrar Herman Bentley, a small farmer and lay Methodist minister from Notasulga. Bentley had only a seventh-grade education, but he possessed an enlightened understanding of the Bible. He freely accepted black applicants, quadrupling the number of black voters in Macon County during 1949. Bentley explained to critics: "I know I'm right because of the way I was brought up, because of the Scripture I study. I know I'm right because all people are created equal."[14] By 1950, 600 black voters, 30 percent of the total registration, held the balance of power in Macon County.

A white backlash worked to the advantage of legislator Samuel M. Engelhardt, Jr., a Macon County farmer-merchant who entered politics to block the rise of black political power. Fearing election of a Negro tax assessor who might raise taxes on the thousands of acres owned by the Engelhardt family, his concerns were both racial and economic. He became a major opponent of the civil rights movement over the next two decades. Engelhardt persuaded the state Democratic party to adopt a racist motto to appear at the top of all Democratic party ballots: "White Supremacy for the Right." He threatened to have any black teachers fired who advocated integration or belonged to organizations that did so. And he gerrymandered the city limits of Tuskegee to place most black voters outside the town. As a member of the state senate, he also led the states' rights opposition to Governor Folsom between 1954 and 1958. But all his efforts could only delay the inevitable. By 1954 approximately 50,000 black voters had registered in Alabama.

However much political progress blacks might have made during the 1940s and 1950s, economic conditions still revealed dramatic contrasts between the races. In 1950 one-third of white families in Birmingham earned less than $2,500 annually while three-fourths of the black families earned less. As unionism raised salaries for industrial workers, whites entered these jobs, pressuring blacks out of the work force. Black coal miners constituted 62 percent of the industry in 1930, 47 percent in 1950, and 39 percent in 1960. Black ore miners numbered 70 percent of the work force in 1930 but only 49 percent ten years later. Black steelworkers declined from 47 percent of all workers in 1930 to 32 percent in 1960. The percentage of blacks among all Jefferson County's industrial workers fell from 54 percent in 1930 to 33 percent in 1960.

Changing race relations only mirrored social upheaval in many aspects of Alabama life. Returning veterans married, had children, and entered college on the GI Bill, almost all at the same time, or so it seemed to many of them. In fall 1947 Auburn University enrolled a total of 6,082, six times as many students as in fall 1944, and 4,353 of these students were veterans. Enrollment at the University of Alabama quadrupled to 9,846, most of them vets. Suddenly, quonset huts and prefabricated barracks became serviceable but unaesthetic additions to campuses. Although at the time the event seemed unimportant, another significant development in higher education occurred in 1944. Governor Chauncey Sparks recommended creation of a four-year medical school, and the legislature established the Medical College of Alabama in Birmingham as a division of the University of Alabama.

Communications tied people together in new ways. In 1940 thirteen radio stations broadcast programs to nearly half of Alabama's 674,000 families who had radios. In 1941 Central Bell introduced the telephone dial system to Alabama, replacing a cheery operator (known as "central") who inquired, "Hello, what can I do for you?" (or at the very least, "Number, please") with an impersonal dial tone. By the early 1950s television arrived, causing some ministers to protest that the newfangled gadget would reduce attendance at Sunday worship. WSFA-TV in Montgomery mollified the Montgomery ministerial association by broadcasting some worship services.

The urban landscape also began to change. In Montgomery real estate developers turned a three-mile-long strip along Norman Bridge Road into Normandale, an upper middle class residential area hinged to the city's first shopping mall. Cities received their first urban renewal grants, which led to the demolition of many historic buildings and construction of low-income housing projects. Although at the time urban renewal seemed a humane way to provide decent housing and to tear down dilapidated inner-city buildings, Mobile, Montgomery, and Birmingham lost irretrievable parts of their history.

The 1950s provided other forms of social change as well. The polio epidemic of 1953 paralyzed many communities with fear. Some schools closed early and churches canceled vacation Bible schools and youth camps. Pentecostal churches moved uptown from rural areas and impoverished back streets as lower income members entered the middle class. In 1931 white Pentecostal churches accounted for less than one of every four white Montgomery churches; by 1952 they constituted 40 percent of the total. Mainstream churches also profited from a new wave of religious enthusiasm personified by television evangelist Billy Graham. Montgomery had eleven white Southern Baptist churches in 1940 and nearly twice that many in 1952.

Women revived the long-somnolent League of Women Voters. The wife of an air force officer stationed at Montgomery's Maxwell Air Force Base restored the league to life in 1947. New leagues formed in Wetumpka, Anniston, Tuscaloosa, Huntsville, Mobile, Auburn, and Birmingham. They worked for abolition of the poll tax, reapportionment, and other electoral, educational, and tax reforms. The league's generally reformist position on racial change cost it members in the late 1950s but also made it a factor in the victories of the 1940s and 1950s. On the state level few women held office. When Sybil Pool left the legislature in 1944 for higher statewide office, no woman took her place until 1962.

In 1948 Auburn's Cooperative Extension Service employed 136 female home demonstration agents, 29 of them black. By 1958 the figure stood at 159, 35 of them black. Although the service still preferred single women, so many deserted home demonstration work for higher-paying jobs that the agency began hiring married women as well.

Sports continued to provide an outlet for Alabamians both as participants and as spectators. Although the 1945 University of Alabama football team won the Southeastern Conference championship and beat Southern California in the Rose Bowl, the team fell on hard times after Coach Frank Thomas retired. Auburn became the dominant team in the state after Governor Chauncey Sparks and the legislature forced Alabama to renew its rivalry with Auburn in 1944. Auburn won a Southeastern Conference crown in 1953 and the mythical national championship in 1957.

The most famous athletes of the era wore baseball spikes, not football cleats. One of the greatest baseball players of the postwar era, Willie Mays, was born in Fairfield in May 1931, the son of a steelworker. Mays inherited good athletic genes. His mother had been a track star, his paternal grandfather and father, baseball players. His parents divorced when he was young, and the financial pressure of ten half-brothers and sisters forced him to live with an aunt in Fairfield. Although he participated in both football and baseball in high school, pro scouts who watched him play with the Birmingham Black Barons as a teenager considered him even then the greatest talent they had ever seen. He signed with the New York Giants and left the poverty of Birmingham for the bright lights of the Big Apple in May 1951. His first hit was a home run, but the Korean War soon drew him into another career. After two years in the army, he returned to the Giants in 1954 and led them to a World Series championship with 110 runs scored, forty-one home runs, and the highest batting average in either league. Writers chose him the Most Valuable Player in the National League and the Major League Player of the Year. In subsequent years his famous basket catches and his "Say hey!" verve and gusto made him a crowd favorite. *Time* magazine best captured his personality when it wrote that Willie Mays had a "boy's glee, a pro's sureness, a champion's flair." For many poor black Alabama boys, he also furnished a powerful role model.

What Mays was to poor blacks Hank Williams was to poor whites. Williams was born in Mount Olive (Butler County) in September 1923 into the family of a disabled First World War veteran. His father made a bare living sawing logs, driving oxen, running a locomotive, or tending a small store and strawberry patch. His church-organist mother taught him gospel songs and bought him a guitar, and a black man in nearby Georgiana taught him blues. During the Second World War Williams's band played honky-tonks in Mobile, where he worked in the shipyards, and in Montgomery. He achieved enough local fame to convince him he could make it in Nashville, so he caught a bus to Music City and tried to sell himself and his songs. Members of the Oklahoma Wranglers who knew him in those early days considered his technical skills terrible, his singing unprofessional, and his songs amateurish. Even by the rustic standards of country music, Williams was a rube. Vic McAlpin, another acquaintance, described him as an outsider:

He was a country hick like me. The kind of hick that comes from so far back in the country you're like a damn whipped dog people kick around in this business. You don't make friends too easy because you got your own thing, and you don't trust nobody very much, and to hell with 'em. A backwoods cat, that's what I call 'em. That's kinda the way he was.[15]

Williams's initial break came in 1947 when he signed a contract with Acuff-Rose as a fifty-dollar-a-month songwriter. In 1949 he joined the Grand Ole Opry and was an immediate hit. The man that *Time* magazine called the "King of the Hillbillies" and that others referred to as the "hillbilly Shakespeare" had a way of writing lyrics that probed the deepest emotions of rootless migrants driven off the land by agricultural change. Likely as not they wound up in Detroit, Akron, Dayton, or some other big city far from home and family. Williams was not an accomplished musician, so he placed little emphasis on melodic subtleties. It was the words he wrote and the nasal, lonely sound of his voice that mesmerized millions of displaced country people. Both the lyrics and the voice conveyed sadness, loneliness, unhappiness, and a strong sense of fatalism. His mixture of country and blues merged white and black musical traditions into a new kind of honky-tonk music, a white man's blues rooted in family crises, migration, hard times, and romantic failure.

Offstage his life matched his songs. His life disintegrated into alcoholism, drug abuse, and marital infidelity. His erratic behavior caused the Opry to fire him, his wife to divorce him, and some adoring fans to boo his drunken performances. But he seemed always to recover, moving to a new wife and a new job with the Louisiana Hayride, where he added Cajun elements ("Jambalaya") to his musical repertoire.

At the peak of his career, on New Year's Day 1953, Williams died at age twenty-nine of ailments related to alcohol and drug abuse. His funeral in Montgomery drew 20,000 people. Behind him he left one of the greatest legacies in the history of country music. In 1949 five of his songs made the country music top ten: "Lovesick Blues," "Mind Your Own Business," "You're Gonna Change," "My Bucket's Got a Hole in It," and "Wedding Bells." Four more won gold records the next year: "I Just Don't Like This Kind of Livin'," "Long Gone Lonesome Blues," "Moaning the Blues," and "Why Don't You Love Me?" Seven more made the top ten in 1951, including "Dear John," "Cold, Cold Heart," and "Hey, Good Lookin'." In 1952 he wrote "Jambalaya" and "Honky-Tonk Blues," among others. Even after his death in 1953 his songs—"Kawliga" and "Your Cheatin' Heart"—topped the musical popularity charts. No country singer ever dominated a half decade of music as Williams did between 1949 and 1953. Perhaps more than any person of his time he spoke for uprooted rural people. And the message came directly from the upheaval experienced by Alabama's poor whites between 1930 and 1950.

THIRTY-ONE

A Time to Hate:
Racial Confrontation,
1955–1970

HISTORIC changes already under way gained momentum during the years from 1955 to 1970. The 1960 census was the first depicting Alabama as an urban state: nearly 52 percent of the population lived in incorporated communities of 2,500 or more. The number of farms plunged from 212,000 in 1950 to only 116,000 in 1960. The out-migration of both blacks and whites dropped the rate of population growth to the lowest levels since the 1860s. During the nine decades between 1860 and 1950, Alabama's average rate of population gain over the preceding census had been 13.9 percent. During the 1950s growth slowed to 6.7 percent, and during the 1960s it dropped to 5.4. Poverty, poor schools, lack of good jobs, racial violence, political chaos and lack of leadership, decline in farming, Alabama's terrible public image—all of these factors and more contributed to the high out-migration of people.

Of the state's major cities only Huntsville and Mobile experienced significant growth. The population of Huntsville jumped from 16,400 in 1950 to 137,800 twenty years later; Mobile's increased from 129,000 to 190,000 during the same period. But Anniston and Montgomery experienced no growth, and Birmingham's population actually declined from 326,000 in 1950 to 301,000 in 1970. At last Atlanta won its long rivalry for supremacy in the Southeast. In 1950 the Georgia capital had a population of 331,000, only 5,000 more than Birmingham. But while Birmingham polarized racially, tolerated violence, and fractured into dozens of competing suburban communities, Atlanta profited from skillful political leadership and relatively peaceful social change. By 1970 the self-proclaimed "city too busy to hate" numbered 497,000, a staggering margin of nearly 200,000 over Alabama's largest metropolitan area.

Birmingham's leaders demonstrated little insight into changing economic patterns. While Atlanta's mayor William Hartsfield busily lobbied to bring a new southeastern regional airport to his city, Birmingham's leadership adopted a bunker mentality designed to exclude new elements that might upset traditional racial and social mores. This decision alone cost Birmingham the most important single element in the economic life of the region: the incredible transportation and business complex that became Hartsfield International Airport. Alabama maintained its traditional white racial and political traditions longer than any Southern state other than Mississippi. But its people paid an enormous price for this delaying action against the future.

The political liberalism that seemed so vibrant during the 1940s fell casualty to the racial polarization of the 1950s. Well-meaning attempts to persuade businessmen, educators, union officials, civic groups, media, and ministers to take stands on behalf of racial moderation failed for a number of reasons. Differences in attitudes toward race alienated friends, divided families, and split churches. They subjected moderates to vilification and even to violence. Advocates of racial justice often lost their jobs as well as their friends. Many whites feared economic competition from blacks, despised school busing of their children to achieve racial integration, and denounced affirmative action job hiring.

Neither did all blacks or whites agree upon the efficacy of racial change. Some blacks had profited from a segregated society, carving out spheres for themselves unthreatened by white competition. They cooperated with whites, sometimes for financial considerations but more often in order to survive in a society that could quickly turn violent when a black forgot his or her subordinate place.

During racial struggles in Montgomery, Birmingham, and Selma, whites also divided into many groups. A small radical fringe engaged in violence. Other intractable segregationists rejected violence but were prepared to take any action short of that, including closing all public schools. Moderate segregationists preferred racial separation but accepted the necessity of change; they merely tried to delay the inevitable as long as possible. Every community contained a small, usually silent and powerless minority of whites who favored integration but were too terrified by their isolation and the possibility of losing their jobs or suffering from acts of violence to speak or act. As Martin Luther King, Jr., was to write, the tragedy of Alabama was not the evil people who did dreadful acts of violence but the good people who did nothing.

Initial reaction to the 1954 *Brown* desegregation decision was vociferous but cautious. Governor Gordon Persons termed public school integration "unthinkable" but also warned against "hasty legislative action for any 'half-baked plan.'" Liberal congressman Carl Elliott hoped the state could preserve its traditions but added that the times required "cool heads and clear thinking." Dr. Ira F. Simmons, superintendent of Jefferson County schools, warned that it was "no time for hotheaded decisions or comments. We must be calm and collected about this and know what we are doing before we do anything." Most newspapers denounced the decision but appealed for calm. One outspoken white minister criticized fellow clergymen for their reluctance to endorse racial justice and predicted accurately that the "Country Club and the Christian Church" would be the last institutions "to acknowledge the rights of the Negro." The Birmingham *World*, the city's black newspaper, naively predicted there would be "no strong determined resistance" to execution of the *Brown* decision, "although some time will pass before its full implementation." Dr. W. H. Jernigan, president of the Negro Baptist Convention that met in Birmingham the month after the *Brown* decision, warned more realistically that blacks "must not expect segregationists to meekly surrender."[1]

As if to confirm this judgment, arsonists tried to burn the home of Birmingham NAACP leader Dr. John W. Nixon the week after the Supreme Court rendered its decision. The first public reaction in Alabama came when Birmingham voters overwhelmingly rejected a referendum to repeal a ban on integrated professional baseball and football in the city.

Some farsighted Alabama politicians and educators had already seen the likely pattern of events and had begun to make education for blacks truly separate and equal. In 1950–51 white teachers earned an average of $232 more per year than blacks. By 1955–56 administrators had narrowed the gap to only $6. Black teacher salaries had increased 212 percent between 1939 and 1951, and funding for black students had increased 310 percent during the 1940s alone.

Segregationists in the legislature approached the crisis in a different way. In 1953 they had created a Joint Interim Legislative Committee under Senator Albert Boutwell of Jefferson County to draft legislation designed to preserve segregation. Isolated attempts to integrate schools in September 1954 in Montgomery, Anniston, and Brewton failed, but the interim committee drafted an Alabama School Placement Law in 1955 just to be on the safe side. It allowed superintendents to assign students based on academic preparation, kinds of academic programs, availability of transportation, and other considerations.

A law the following year allowed a local school board to close any school faced with integration and denied that the state had responsibility to provide public education at all. Only Jefferson County representative Charles Nice, Jr., voted against this bill, and voters ratified it 104,000 to 68,000 (opposition came from white public school teachers and the mostly white hill counties). Senator Boutwell also devised a "freedom of choice" plan that allowed students to select their own segregated schools.

Not until September 1963 did blacks integrate Alabama public schools. So successful were the legal devices crafted by Boutwell and his allies that by the end of the 1964 school year only 4 of the state's 114 previously white school districts contained any blacks, and the total number of these Negro students amounted to only twenty-one.

Some of Alabama's liberal whites organized into groups such as the Fellowship of the Concerned (mainly women), the Alabama Council of Churches, and the Alabama Council on Human Relations (which affiliated with the Atlanta-based Southern Regional Council). The most active of these, the ACHR, helped establish a biracial committee in Mobile during 1956. The mayor appointed a committee of fifteen whites and thirteen blacks to advise him on all phases of city government. But the rapid growth of the KKK and instances of cross burning ended this hopeful initiative. Membership in the ACHR declined during the Montgomery bus boycott (1955–56) before rebounding to more than a thousand in 1966. When Governors George and Lurleen Wallace refused to allow their state to accept federal poverty grants during the 1960s, the ACHR became the conduit for them in Alabama, and its members also organized the state's first Head Start program for impoverished preschoolers in Lee County. Much of the state's ACHR membership came from active white churchgoers.

Die-hard segregationists organized as well. They formed the first Alabama White Citizens' Council in Dallas County in 1956, shortly after the Montgomery bus boycott began. The founder of the council spoke at the first meeting and outlined a simple strategy. Whites controlled the money in Dallas County and could make it difficult for a black integrationist to find a job, obtain credit, or renew a mortgage. Events proved him correct. By fall 1955, sixteen of twenty-nine black parents who had petitioned for admission of their children into white schools in three Black Belt counties had been fired from their jobs.

For large farmers and businessmen who renounced secrecy and violence and therefore found Klan membership unacceptable, the council operated as an upscale version of the Klan. Most of its early leaders were Black Belt politicians, notably Walter C. Givhan of Dallas County and Samuel Engelhardt, Jr., of Macon County. They organized a State Association of Citizens' Councils in 1956 with headquarters in Montgomery. At its peak the councils claimed 80,000 members in Alabama. They counted among their sympathizers some of the brightest legal minds in the state, including Montgomery judge Walter B. Jones, who founded and edited the *Alabama Lawyer*, the official journal of the Alabama Bar Association. Jones made the journal a forum for segregationists.

Citizens' Council spokesmen focused much of their rhetoric on a powerful if subterranean white fear of black sexual aggression. State senator Givhan told a Marengo County council meeting that the goal of the NAACP was "to open the bedroom door of our white women to the Negro." A leader of the Perry County council warned that only the council could keep blacks "out of the bedrooms of our white women."[2]

The most violent racists seldom advertised their deeds, but Kenneth L. Adams of Anniston was a notable exception. Adams owned five service stations, which he bedecked with signs proclaiming, "We Serve Whites Only." An official of the Klan and of J. B. Stoner's national States' Rights party, Adams was first indicted by a grand jury for setting fire to a bus carrying Freedom Riders and on charges of receiving explosives stolen from the Fort McClellan army base. Although the jury acquitted him on both charges, twelve of his peers did convict him of shooting an eighteen-year-old black male who had the temerity to try to flag Adams down to help fix his stalled car. Adams was sentenced to two years in prison for that crime. Another jury convicted him of firing shotgun blasts into the homes of two blacks and into a black church, crimes for which he drew nearly two more years in jail. But his most publicized exploit was an assault on singer Nat King Cole in 1956. Cole was performing before a white audience in Birmingham's municipal auditorium when Adams and two associates ran down the aisle, jumped onto the stage, and attacked the popular singer. Cole, paradoxically, was a native of Montgomery.

By such violence racists sought to deter a growing black militancy that traced its roots to the 1955–56 Montgomery bus boycott. That event not only began the modern civil rights movement in the United States and pioneered most of its strategies, but it also produced the movement's most important leader, Dr. Martin Luther King, Jr.

Although popular sentiment identifies the boycott with King, Montgomery had produced a vigorous indigenous black leadership before he arrived in the capital. Alabama State College furnished many of these leaders. Its 200 faculty members and 2,000 students provided leadership for a black community that had no newspaper or radio station and only two lawyers. The college served as a base for Jo Ann Robinson, an English professor and organizer of the Women's Political Council, which she founded in 1949. Another key leader, E. D. Nixon, headed the sleeping-car porters union and served as president of the state NAACP.

Despite the presence of Alabama State, the key to the successful bus boycott was ministerial leadership. Black theology carried a strong tradition of liberation and social uplift. Black ministers also constituted one of the few groups in the community not dependent upon whites for their jobs. Historically many black ministers had accommodated existing racial mores and even cooperated with white leaders. But the assertiveness of returning black veterans, better-educated lay people, and rising expectations fostered by the New Deal, Truman's racial policies, and the Supreme Court began to change ministerial roles. Although E. D. Nixon could mobilize the NAACP and Jo Ann Robinson could count on clubwomen, only the black church provided an effective vehicle for organizing a mass movement.

Throughout the boycott drama black Baptist ministers in their twenties played key leadership roles. When state officials harassed the NAACP, it transformed itself into the Alabama Christian Movement for Human Rights led mostly by Baptist ministers. Most had graduated from Atlanta's Morehouse College or Alabama State, and they formed an influential "old boy" network within the civil rights movement. Within the Southern Christian Leadership Conference formed in Montgomery during the boycott, Alabama Baptist preachers predominated. The Reverend Martin Luther King, Jr., and the Reverend Ralph D. Abernathy of Montgomery, the Reverend Fred L. Shuttlesworth, Jr., in Birmingham, and the Reverend Joseph E. Lowry of Mobile emerged as central figures in the SCLC.

Three black Baptist ministers dominated the Montgomery movement. The Reverend Ralph D. Abernathy, twenty-nine-year-old pastor of the black First Baptist Church, first suggested formation of the Montgomery Improvement Association as a vehicle for the boycott. He led the largest black congregation in the city. The emotional worship at Abernathy's church contrasted dramatically with the sedate services of Dexter Avenue Baptist Church. There the small congregation of three hundred drew a number of its members from Alabama State's faculty. Located just a block down Dexter Avenue from the capitol, it seemed symbolically as well as physically under the constant scrutiny of the white establishment.

The Reverend Vernon Johns conducted a stormy pastorate at Dexter Avenue Baptist for five years after 1948. As abrasive as he was brilliant, Johns offended some by his secularism and frightened others with his demand that they take seriously the ethical imperatives of the gospel. A native of Virginia, he had largely educated himself. When Oberlin College rejected his admission application, he appeared before the dean of the renowned Ohio college demanding to be admitted. The unimpressed administrator gave him a book in German to translate, then listened in astonishment as Johns read it to him in English. The dean of Oberlin's seminary conducted the next exam, and Johns proved as skillful translating Greek scripture as German poetry. Although he put aside his Latin and Hebrew as the years passed, the scholarly Baptist preacher collected history and poetry in Greek all his life. After enrolling in the seminary, he soon displaced as top scholar a white student who would later become president of the University of Chicago, where Johns did his graduate work in theology. The university had long been the leader in the application of religion to ethics, and he took from it a deep commitment to the social gospel. At Dexter Avenue Baptist Church he organized a cooperative supermarket in 1953, preached sermons demanding racial equality, and was ordered off a bus for sitting in a front seat reserved for whites. Johns's successor in September 1954 came from the same tradition, though he was less strident. Son of a prominent Atlanta pastor, Martin Luther King, Jr., attended Morehouse College and Crozier Theological Seminary and completed his doctorate at Boston University.

The city these ministers confronted in 1955 was not the old Montgomery of patrician William A. Gunter, Jr. As its mayor from 1910 to 1940, Gunter had earned the respect of rich and poor alike. But the Evangelical, prohibitionist, conservative middle class despised his anti-KKK fervor, his Episcopalianism, his easygoing tolerance of drinking and prostitution, and his welfare schemes directed toward the poor. After Gunter's death in 1940 his political machine steadily deteriorated, influenced as much by the decline of his power base among Cloverdale aristocrats and poor blacks and whites as by the growing population of lower middle class whites.

The victory of David Birmingham for a city commission spot demonstrated the point. Birmingham won because of lower middle class support. An ally of Governor Folsom, the new commissioner also opened government to blacks. He hired black policemen and appointed blacks to city boards. During his term many blacks registered to vote. By 1955 some 2,000 could vote, constituting 7.5 percent of Montgomery's registered voters. But when he ran for reelection in 1955 his opponent used Birmingham's racial liberalism against him, defeating the incumbent because of his concessions to black pressure. The new commission contained one bitter segregationist, one scion of the Gunter machine, and one representative of Birmingham's lower middle class coalition.

In March 1955, during the political campaign, police arrested a fifteen-year-old girl for refusing to vacate her seat when ordered to do so by a bus driver. The white driver acted within authority given him to enforce the city's segregation ordinance. The private bus company franchised by the city usually maintained the first ten seats for whites and the rear twenty-six for blacks. In order to expand seating for whites, the driver could move back and forth between rows a small metal placard with an arrow. If whites filled their allotted seats, the driver could order black patrons to move to the rear to provide additional places. Sometimes on a full bus whites chose to stand rather than displace blacks. But others demanded a seat and forced blacks to get up and stand while whites took their places. This situation infuriated blacks, as did the sometimes brusque shouts of drivers to surrender their seats. Black leaders met with white officials in March about the bus situation but decided not to press the issue.

On December 1, 1955, Rosa Parks rode a bus with twelve whites and twenty-six blacks, some of them standing. She occupied a seat in the center of the bus, glad to rest after a busy day as a seamstress at the

Rosa Parks, ca. 1990/91. She was arrested in Montgomery in 1955 for refusing to give up her seat on a bus to a white person. The courage she showed made her a symbol of the civil rights movement. (Courtesy of the Alabama Department of Archives and History)

Montgomery Fair department store. Her relaxation did not last long. When more whites boarded the bus, the driver instructed four blacks to stand up so the new patrons could take their seats. Three of the blacks did as they were instructed. Rosa Parks did not budge. Her inaction resulted from a spontaneous decision but one informed by a strong racial consciousness. She had belonged to the NAACP for fifteen years.

Police arrested her for violating the city's segregation ordinance. Attorney Clifford Durr, member of a prominent Montgomery family, was the only white attorney willing to help, so E. D. Nixon and Durr paid her bail. They had the perfect plaintiff to challenge the city's segregationist legal structure. Parks was a well-known and respected member of Montgomery's black community. She and her husband, a barber at Maxwell Air Force Base and thus immune to job threats, had lived in the city for a quarter century. She agreed to challenge the city's law, demonstrating courage that earned her a place in history.

The strategy for the movement evolved slowly. Nixon asked several ministers to help organize a boycott of the bus company, which received an estimated 70 percent of its revenue from black patrons. King asked for time to think about the proposal but finally endorsed the boycott, which began on December 5 and was 90 percent effective. That night more than 3,000 blacks met at Holt Street Baptist Church. The song that would become the anthem of the civil rights movement, "We Shall Overcome," waited in the future. They drew strength from a different, more traditional source. They prayed. They read Scripture. They sang "Onward Christian Soldiers" and "What a Fellowship, What a Joy Divine, Leaning On the Everlasting Arms." And they told each other that the boycott could not fail because God was with them. Then King spoke, demonstrating his firm but moderate philosophy as well as his oratorical power to mesmerize an audience:

> If you will protest courageously and yet with dignity and Christian love, when the history books are written in future generations, the historians will have to pause and say, "There lived a great people—a black people—who injected new meaning and dignity into the views of civilization." This is our challenge and our overwhelming responsibility.[3]

Because whites so distrusted the NAACP, Abernathy proposed formation of an organization he called the Montgomery Improvement Association (MIA). This group, which King served as president, and the Southern Christian Leadership Conference, which they organized a bit later, provided structure to the movement. The MIA organized the bus boycott. Black leaders fashioned a masterful plan complete with forty-eight dispatch locations and forty-two pickup stations. Volunteers who owned cars ferried blacks to work. Fortunately Montgomery was small enough that many blacks could walk to their jobs. Leaders used mass rallies at churches to keep enthusiasm high and raise money for the boycott.

Initially white leaders willingly negotiated, but as the boycott continued, tempers flared. The bus company lost $600 a day, whites had to pick up their own maids and yardmen, and blacks threatened the racial order. By late January 1956, local membership in the White Citizens' Council had reached 9,000. On the night of January 30, terrorists bombed King's home and two nights later blasted E. D. Nixon's house. Police began arresting boycott leaders who were easier to identify than the bombers. The city's political leadership polarized against concessions or even negotiations. Lawyers proved intractable foes of compromise, but businessmen presented a confused front. Montgomery's business community had divided between older, more conservative chamber of commerce members, who opposed new industry that might bring unionization to the city, and younger, more progressive leaders who organized into the Men of Montgomery. Their city lost a new DuPont plant and four other facilities in 1954 and 1955, and the bus boycott stymied growth. This younger group recognized what other cities would soon learn: racial violence provided a nasty public image and retarded economic development.

The legal challenge to the city's segregated buses, the case of *Browder* v. *Gayle,* proceeded slowly through the court system while the 382-day boycott paralyzed Montgomery. Finally in November 1956, the U.S. Supreme Court upheld a lower court finding that overruled the city's segregation ordinance and on December 17 ordered the desegregation of Montgomery buses. On December 21 King, Abernathy, and Nixon received early Christmas presents. They boarded a desegregated city bus and rode it downtown. The boycott ended and King shortly left Alabama's capital for Atlanta and the leadership of the SCLC. Those left behind had to endure sniper fire on buses in 1957 and the bombing of four black churches and Ralph Abernathy's home. Even though earlier bus boycotts had occurred in Harlem in 1941 and in Baton Rouge in 1953, it was the Montgomery affair that effectively launched the nation's modern civil rights movement.

After 1956 the epicenter of the movement moved to Nashville and Albany, Georgia, returning to Alabama only briefly in 1961 when mobs in Anniston, Birmingham, and Montgomery attacked Freedom Riders crossing the state on integrated buses. But in 1962 international attention focused on Birmingham.

As in Montgomery the context of the crisis contributed significantly to its outcome. Long before King arrived for the "children's crusade" in spring 1963, the Reverend Fred L. Shuttlesworth, Jr., had been agitating for change. The graduate of Selma University and Alabama State was a social activist. At Bethel Baptist Church where he pastored, he tried to persuade every adult member to register to vote, explaining: "I didn't want any deacon wearing out the carpet on the floor praying to the Lord who couldn't get up and walk to the polls."[4] He considered the NAACP too conservative and in 1956 helped organize the activist Alabama Christian Movement for Human Rights. For his trouble terrorists bombed his house on Christmas night 1956. Within the following year bombers struck seven more times in the Fountain Heights area, providing a new name for the neighborhood: "Dynamite Hill."

Attempts to integrate schools in 1957 also led to the kidnapping of Judge Aaron, a black man who happened to be at the wrong place at the wrong time. Klansmen picked Aaron at random on a road near Tarrant City, castrated him, then poured gasoline on his wounds, unintentionally cauterizing them and probably saving his life. That night Klansmen burned ten crosses at public schools in western Jefferson County. But such violence did not deter Shuttlesworth, who organized the integration of Birmingham buses and sit-ins at the lunch counters of local department stores. He filed so many suits that reached the Supreme Court (eleven) that he became the most litigious person in the history of the high court.

Shuttlesworth's chief antagonist was Eugene ("Bull") Connor. Although Connor's nickname owed nothing to "bulldog," his short, hefty, swaggering physique and his defiant, loud, aggressive manner made the nickname appropriate. He obtained that designation for the "bull" he supposedly dispensed during delays in Birmingham Baron baseball games during his years as a sports announcer. First elected police commissioner in 1937, Connor had served four terms in that office and had made the police department his personal fiefdom. The department was the last all-white police force in an American city of more than 50,000. Characterized by corruption, cronyism, low morale, and lack of discipline, the department has been described by a careful student as one divided into three parts: those who took payoffs, those receptive to them but not yet on the take, and those who refused bribes. He estimated the percentages of the three factions as 45/45/10. In 1951 Connor's reputation received a blow when detectives arrested him with his secretary locked in a room at the Tutwiler Hotel. Convicted of joint occupancy of a room with a member of the opposite sex and of extramarital intercourse, both of which were crimes in Birmingham at the time, he did not stand for reelection despite an Alabama Supreme Court ruling that overturned his conviction. Heightened racial tension in 1957 led to his political comeback. By 1960 he had become the leader of resistance to integration in Birmingham and a favorite Citizens' Council speaker statewide. Particularly fond of athletic metaphors (he cast his presidential vote as a delegate to the 1968 Democratic National Convention for University of Alabama football coach Bear Bryant), Connor told the Selma Citizen's Council in 1960: "Yes, we are on the one-yard line. Our backs are to the wall. Do we let them go over for a touchdown, or do we raise the Confederate flag as did our forefathers and tell them . . . 'You shall not pass'?"[5]

That same year New York *Times* reporter Harrison Salisbury reported from Birmingham that "every inch of middle ground has been fragmented by the emotional dynamite of racism," and the city allowed—

even participated in—violence. In light of subsequent evidence tying policemen to the Klan and the tardy arrival of officers to protect Freedom Riders, who were attacked in the Trailways bus station in the heart of downtown in 1961, the charge appears plausible. But in 1960 the Birmingham *News*, the chamber of commerce, and civic leaders blasted the newspaper, claiming New York contained more racism than Birmingham. The following year Connor closed city parks and golf courses rather than integrate them, a move that alienated business leaders and caused the Young Men's Business Club, a leading voice for racial moderation, to form Citizens for Progress and demand a change in the form of city government.

The following spring (1962), students at black Miles College began a selective buying campaign against Birmingham stores. City commissioners retaliated by cutting appropriations for food to needy families, a move that divided whites further and united blacks in anger.

Moderate attorney David Vann led a petition drive to change the form of government in November 1962, and advocates of the effort won a narrow victory. Some business leaders such as Sidney Smyer backed the change, as did some labor leaders. Smyer also worked out a compromise to end some symbols of segregation in downtown stores. But Connor and Commissioner Arthur Hanes ignored the agreement and restored segregation signs in stores. At that point the SCLC decided to make Birmingham the site of a massive demonstration. Having failed in Albany, the movement came to Birmingham looking for a villain. In Bull Connor it found just the right man.

Planning for "Project C," the movement's designation for demonstrations in Birmingham, began in December 1962. King dispatched associates to the city to devise preliminary strategies and recruit volunteers willing to go to jail in demonstrations. Aware of Birmingham's reputation for racism and violence, he wired President John F. Kennedy that it was "by far the worst big city in race relations in the United States. Much of what has gone on has had the tacit consent of high public officials."[6] Events during the course of the next year confirmed King's analysis, but he won little support from Kennedy. In fact the FBI had bugged King's phones and reported his plans for demonstrations to Birmingham city officials.

On April 2, 1963, Birmingham held runoff elections to fill positions in the new city government. Connor contested the runoff against moderate segregationist Albert Boutwell and pitched his mayoral campaign to racist appeals. The election would determine whether the city's two "foreign-owned newspapers" and the "bloc vote" would run the city or whether the "people of Birmingham are going to rule themselves."[7] The business community and newspapers backed Boutwell in the runoff, which drew a phenomenal 75 percent of the registered voters and resulted in a 39,600 to 21,600 Boutwell victory. King slipped into town on election day to supervise SCLC demonstrations scheduled to begin the following day. Boutwell and his new council took their oaths of office on April 15, but Connor and the other two lame-duck commissioners entered legal proceedings against them and refused to resign. So until the Alabama Supreme Court ruled in Boutwell's favor on May 23, each city government took turns meeting, voting on issues, and conducting city business. Wits proclaimed Birmingham the only city in the world with two mayors, a King, and a parade every day. Connor in his role as police commissioner proved especially disruptive during this critical interval. Moderate whites who had favored the change of government and privately worked for limited desegregation denounced King's timing when demonstrations began on April 3.

During April everything went badly for King and the SCLC. Few blacks proved willing to demonstrate when such action resulted in a term in the Birmingham jail. The national news media occupied themselves with other issues and ignored the demonstrations. The local press, even the black Birmingham *World*, buried demonstration stories on the back pages. On April 12, King began a nine-day jail sentence as white moderate ministers condemned the demonstrations and pleaded for time to change racial restrictions once the moderate Boutwell administration took office. King brooded in solitary confinement and answered his critics in one of his most famous essays, "Letter from the Birmingham Jail."

Drawing heavily upon his Christian heritage, King reminded them that the church had often proclaimed its boldest message from behind prison walls. To critics' call for restraint and patience, he replied that blacks had already waited 340 years for justice. To claims that he should obey the government, he pledged to honor laws he considered just but vowed to disobey ones he believed to be unjust.

When freed from jail King turned to the Reverend James Bevel for a new strategy. Bevel reminded King that in the Baptist tradition anyone old enough to declare faith in Jesus Christ was old enough to become a church member. If a child could cast off the shackles of spiritual bondage, that same child could act to break the chains of economic and political servitude.

On May 2, 1963, the second phase of Project C began, the children's crusade. Police arrested some 600 youngsters that day and thousands more on May 3. With jails packed, Connor faced a crisis. He had no more room for prisoners, so he stationed firemen and policemen at the exit of Kelly Ingram Park. Across from the demonstrators' staging area at Sixteenth Street Baptist Church, firemen positioned special monitor guns that forced water from two hoses through a single opening. The resultant water force could rip loose mortar from bricks and strip bark off trees. In fact, during ensuing days one stream accidentally directed on a policeman broke his rib. When the children emerged from Sixteenth Street Church on May 3, fire hoses swept many of them off their feet and sent them tumbling across the park.

Black Republican businessman A. G. Gaston sat in his office above Ingram Park speaking on the telephone with his moderate white friend David Vann. Together they had orchestrated the change of government and both deplored King's mistimed demonstrations. Gaston heard cries from his window and left his phone long enough to stare out at the scene unfolding beneath his office. When he returned to the phone he gasped: "Lawyer Vann, they've turned the fire hoses on a little black girl. And they're rolling that girl right down the middle of the street."[8] Children who tried to walk downtown from the other end of the park met attacks from German shepherd police dogs whose bites sent three to the hospital. An Associated Press photograph of a policeman holding a teenage black boy while a dog attacked him made headlines around the world and riveted attention on the city. The attacks also galvanized the previously disunited black community and brought thousands of furious parents into the demonstrations.

The Kennedy administration, fearing violence even beyond the magnitude of the University of Mississippi crisis of the previous fall, sent emissaries who met privately with the semisecret Senior Citizens Committee, a chamber of commerce blue ribbon group of white businessmen. Sidney Smyer and Birmingham *News* publisher Clarence B. Hanson, who had previously spent much of their time denouncing King and alleged Communist links to the SCLC, sought desperately to reach some sort of accommodation with King before the city's economy collapsed entirely. Plagued by a decade of racial violence and economic decline, the city's Big Mules now faced a crisis of pocketbook far more threatening than any crisis of conscience they might have felt. It was from these businessmen—not from the city's more enlightened but timid ministers, white college professors, or professionals—that resolution came.

But just as white businessmen and SCLC leaders hammered out compromises to desegregate downtown stores, terrorists retaliated with a series of bombings. The Ku Klux Klan attracted a thousand whites to a gathering at Moose Club Park on the outskirts of the city. Imperial Wizard Robert Shelton of Tuscaloosa denounced betrayal by "professional businessmen." Police Chief Jamie Moore recommended posting a police guard outside A. G. Gaston's motel, where King had established his headquarters. But Connor vetoed the recommendation, vowing to do nothing to "guard that nigger son-of-a-bitch."[9]

That night terrorists bombed Gaston's motel and the home of the Reverend A. D. King. Thousands of blacks rushed to Kelly Ingram Park and began to shower cars with rocks. Governor George Wallace dispatched Colonel Al Lingo, head of the Alabama state troopers. The state police stormed into the park, beating anyone in sight with clubs and shotguns and triggering a riot that lasted all night. Rioters burned six businesses, an apartment building, and several homes and cars. Club-swinging state troopers sent seventy people to area hospitals. Civil rights leaders struggled desperately to return the mobs to nonviolence and defuse what could easily have become the worst racial riot in American history. White businessmen now bore the brunt of racist criticism, as Art Hanes, Connor, Shelton, and others condemned their role in the compromise to desegregate Birmingham stores. President Kennedy publicly endorsed the settlement and ordered the army to preserve order in Birmingham if necessary. Some believed Birmingham's racial nightmare had ended. But the worst was yet to come.

In June 1963 Governor Wallace conducted his carefully rehearsed "stand in the schoolhouse door," a symbolic protest against the integration of the University of Alabama. Wallace would declare his belief that the federal government had exceeded its powers, then step aside so federal marshals could escort Vivian Malone and James Hood through registration.

The following September schools in Birmingham and Huntsville prepared to implement court orders to accept black students for the first time in Alabama public schools. Integration began routinely in Huntsville, but Birmingham once again became the center of a fire storm.

This time local ministers, businessmen, PTA leaders, teachers, and news media had prepared the city thoroughly. Moderate leaders, long subdued by their own fears and community pressure, did everything they could to assure peaceful compliance. Mayor Albert Boutwell, Police Chief Jamie Moore, Sheriff Melvin Bailey, and a biracial Community Affairs Committee worked all summer to avoid repetition of the ugly events of springtime. Unfortunately, they were not the only forces organizing in Birmingham.

All through the summer and with escalating frequency during August and early September, bitter-end segregationists met also. Led by militant racists such as Bob Creel, J. B. Stoner, Edward Fields, and Robert Shelton, former city politicians Art Hanes and Bull Connor, and ministers such as George Fisher and Ferrell Griswold (an orator for the right-wing John Birch Society), they were aided by state officials such as Governor Wallace and former attorney general MacDonald Gallion. Although Wallace and Gallion warned against violence, their speeches rang with denunciations of communism, the Kennedys, the leftist news media, intermarriage, and other calamities they predicted would result from school integration. Reporters for both state and national papers warned that Wallace's speeches tended to reenforce the violence-prone lunatic fringe of racists who had long sought to protect Birmingham's social order with bombs and guns, but such warnings fell on deaf ears. Forewarned of potential trouble by the events of the spring, President Kennedy federalized Alabama National Guardsmen to preserve order. Then on Sunday, September 15, Birmingham reached its nadir.

That Sunday the Sixteenth Street Baptist Church conducted its annual Youth Day. The church, which had sent so many of its young streaming downtown during May, prepared to turn over its eleven o'clock worship service to the next generation of Baptists. Four young girls talked with mounting excitement in the basement ladies' room as their hour of responsibility approached. Dressed in their nicest white dresses, both in acknowledgement of the way summer heat lingers into September in Alabama and in preparation for their coming responsibilities, the girls had left their Sunday school class a bit early. Above them on the next floor some of their mothers engaged in an animated discussion of the day's Sunday school lesson, which was entitled "The Love that Forgives." As they talked, a loud blast shook the church. Schoolteacher Maxine McNair made her way downstairs, where she encountered her sobbing father, who held a white shoe that had belonged to her only child Denise. It was her father who broke the news to her that the child was dead, together with her three companions. Chris McNair—a teacher and free-lance photographer—was worshiping in his own Lutheran church blocks away when he heard the explosion. He grabbed his camera and raced to the scene, only to learn there of his daughter's death. Firemen and ambulance drivers who sifted through the wreckage of the church found a kindergarten leaflet with the day's prayer: "Dear God, we are sorry for the times we were so unkind."[10]

That afternoon two thousand whites assembled at Midfield to listen to the Reverend Ferrell Griswold condemn the bombers, then the throng immediately cheered lustily as a teenager strung up an effigy labeled "Kennedy." Following the rally two sixteen-year-old Eagle Scouts who had gone to hear Griswold "talk about integrating the schools around here" were returning home when they saw two young blacks riding double on a bicycle. One of the Scouts, described later to police as a "model student," pulled out a pistol he had carried to school during the previous week's demonstrations, and he shot thirteen-year-old Virgil Ware, who was perched on the handlebars of his brother's bike. Sheriff's deputies who interrogated the killer explained that the teenager had been "inspired" at Griswold's rally.[11] That evening Wallace sent Al Lingo and his state troopers back into Birmingham, and one of them shot a fleeing black man in the back of the head.

Birmingham whites reacted to the events of September 15, in a variety of ways. Charles Morgan, Jr., a politically ambitious young attorney and active member of the liberal wing of the Democratic party, spoke to the Young Men's Business Club the morning after the bombing. He urged a collective sense of guilt; he anguished that "we all did it." For his candor he received death threats on his own life and those of his wife and child. Finally he left Birmingham to live in Washington. Boutwell believed that all Birmingham residents were victims of such terrorist acts. Many conscientious whites, perhaps finally understanding the meaning of King's words that the tragedy of Birmingham was not the evil of bad people but the silence of the good ones, made their way to Chris McNair's house. For many it was their first journey into the city's black neighborhoods. They knocked on the door, expressed tearful condolences, then retreated into their all-white neighborhoods. Later some of these same guilt-ridden residents would elect Chris McNair to the legislature, the only black to hold such office in Jefferson County's at-large election system. Among the mourners at the funeral service for three of the four girls were eight hundred Birmingham ministers, many of them white and listening to Martin Luther King, Jr., for the first time.

One of Denise McNair's acquaintances, a young Birmingham girl named Angela Davis, would not forget September 15, 1963, either. She began a long intellectual journey that would carry her into the Communist party. A young army officer named Colin Powell also worried over events in the city. Although a native of Harlem, he had married a young woman from Birmingham. While he served in Vietnam, his wife and baby daughter lived in the city with her parents. Years later, while he served as chairman of the Joint Chiefs of Staff, he recalled 1963 vividly: "When Bull Connor and his damn dogs were running up and down the street . . . my father-in-law was guarding the house with a shotgun."[12]

Like Montgomery and Birmingham, Selma had its own black leadership long before Martin Luther King, Jr., and SCLC galvanized it into action. Chief among black activists was J. L. Chestnut, Jr. Born in a house on a dirt street in east Selma, Chestnut spent a good deal of his time on "the drag," a street of black-owned stores, bars, and a movie theater. His father worked as a butcher in a meat market serving black customers. Everything in Selma divided according to race. A white butcher had his own block where he cut meat for whites and earned nearly twice as much as Chestnut. Even his name came from whites: Chestnut coming from his white great-grandfather and J. L. from the local white banker. For his education Chestnut entered Talladega College, then widely regarded as the best academic institution for blacks in the state. But he discovered that racial stereotypes were not exclusive to whites. The light-skinned students from Northern cities who constituted most of the Talladega student body shunned the darker-skinned, unsophisticated Selma boy, who preferred playing jazz on his saxophone to attending class and preferred the local Baptist church to the sedate Sunday chapel service. After a brief stay in Talladega, Chestnut transferred to Dillard University in New Orleans, where he could supplement his income playing jazz and where the students came from a background similar to his own. After graduating from Dillard, he took a law degree from Howard University in Washington, then in 1958 he returned to Selma to become the sixth black lawyer practicing in the state.

Civil rights activity in Selma predated Chestnut. In the 1930s blacks had organized the Dallas County Voters' League. The presence of Baptist-supported Selma University and the return of black veterans in the 1940s heightened attention to inequality. But Chestnut's return in 1958 brought a committed activist to town to begin agitating and organizing.

The setting was less than ideal. The White Citizens' Council of Alabama had begun in Selma, and Dallas County sheriff James G. Clark was a rural version of Bull Connor: racist, high-strung, and violent, with none of the training or restraint of a professional lawman.

When Chestnut and local officials invited the national Student Nonviolent Coordinating Committee (SNCC) to come to Selma in 1962 to launch a voter registration drive, 57 percent of Dallas County's population was black, but only 2 percent of them were registered to vote. More than 65 percent of eligible whites were registered. County registrars insisted they did not discriminate, but in fact they opened the registrar's office only thirty-seven days a year and processed only thirty applications a day. A voter already registered had to vouch for each applicant. Then registrants had to prove literacy in a test that gave wide latitude to the registrar. Some of the questions used to test black literacy in 1964 included: "Where do presidential electors cast ballots for President: their home state, the District of Columbia, or their home county?" A true-false question read: "Ambassadors may be named by the President without the approval of the United States Senate." Even blacks who passed six of the eight questions could fail because of minor spelling errors. Registrars rejected one Selma high school graduate and air force veteran because he mispronounced "construe, prejudice, convention, constitution, and electors."[13] The pastor of Tabernacle Baptist Church, a graduate of the University of Pittsburgh, failed the test numerous times.

John Lewis led SNCC voter registration drives in 1963 despite harassment by Sheriff Clark and violence by some Selma whites. Lewis was an Alabama native, born six miles from Troy. He entered the Baptist ministry and became an activist during his seminary days in Nashville. His efforts in Selma continued through 1963 and 1964, though the work went slowly. Clark forced black applicants to line up in an alley behind the courthouse and enter the building through a back loading entrance. He also required them to stand in line through rainstorms, refusing them access to the building while registrars took lunch breaks.

King and the SCLC arrived in Selma in January 1965. The two civil rights leaders and their organizations did not get along well, and new mayor Joseph T. Smitherman awaited them. More moderate than earlier leaders, Smitherman tried to replace Sheriff Clark's forces with more professionally trained city police. Unfortunately new police chief Wilson Baker got along with Clark no better than King did with John Lewis, so both white and black leaders struggled not only with each other but with their peers as well. The federal court intervened in February 1965 to speed registration of black voters, and Clark became increasingly irrational. When one black leader called the sheriff "a Hitler with his Gestapo," a deputy hit him in the face with his fist while cameras recorded the episode. Then the sheriff, oblivious to the media implications for Selma, boasted: "If I hit him, I don't know it. One of the first things I ever learned was not to hit a nigger with your fist, because his head is too hard."[14]

King planned a march from Selma to Montgomery to attract national attention, but Governor Wallace and Al Lingo decided to stop it at the Edmund Pettus Bridge, which crossed the Alabama River on the outskirts of Selma. When the marchers crossed the bridge, Lingo and Clark led mounted deputies and club-wielding state troopers in a senseless attack on the demonstrators. The Rebel Yell of Dallas County deputies while they charged into defenseless demonstrators evoked applause from white bystanders but outrage from Americans who witnessed the film that evening on network news. As Selma's hospital filled with demonstrators who had broken ribs and fractured skulls, arms, and legs, King called on the nation's religious leaders to come to Selma to reinforce his depleted forces.

Hundreds of clergymen, labor leaders, Hollywood personalities, and others swelled King's ranks. One of them, the Reverend James Reeb, was beaten on a Selma street by four white men and later died from his injuries. Sympathetic protest marches in Chicago, Kansas City, and New Haven, in Wisconsin, New York, and California, swelled the number of Selma recruits into the thousands.

Governor Wallace flew to Washington to confer with President Lyndon B. Johnson. The president appeared on television after the fruitless meeting, calling for an end to racial discrimination, announcing major legislation to extend voting rights to all Americans, and ending his speech by a paraphrase of the movement's slogan: "And we *shall* overcome."

Back in Selma civil rights activists who watched the speech on televi-

On the road during the Selma-to-Montgomery march for voting rights, March 1965 (Courtesy of the Alabama Department of Archives and History)

sion could hardly believe their ears. Here was the president of the United States endorsing their aims virtually in their own words. They immediately laid plans for their belated march. Wallace denounced the demonstrators as mobs using Communist tactics and said the state could not afford to provide them protection. This blunder allowed President Johnson to federalize the Alabama National Guard. In a parody of Wallace, LBJ said he could not understand why Wallace, an advocate of states' rights, had abrogated the responsibility of protecting the state's own citizens, forcing the federal government to do so.

The Selma to Montgomery march began on March 21, 1965, with 3,200 marchers. King sent them on their way with a ringing address: "Walk together, children, don't you get weary, and it will lead us to the promised land. And Alabama will be a new Alabama, and America will be a new America."[15] The speech captured the central theological message of King's Baptist faith: suffering was redemptive, and the anguish of blacks could create a new, more just Alabama and a restored vision of justice in the nation. Four days later King led 25,000 demonstrators up Dexter Avenue to Alabama's capitol. State police barred capitol grounds to the demonstrators. But from inside the capitol Wallace borrowed a pair of binoculars and read aloud one demonstrator's sign to associates gathered in the governor's office: "God is the answer." One of his bitter associates quipped, "That will make Lyndon mad."[16]

As his part in the three hours of speech making, King delivered one of his most memorable addresses: "They told us we wouldn't get here . . . , but all the world knows that we are here and that we are standing before the forces of power in Alabama, saying, 'We ain't gonna let nobody turn us around.'" Civil rights advocates "must see that the end we seek is a society at peace with itself, a society that can live with its conscience. That will be the day not of the white man, not of the black man. That will be the day of man as man." Ending his speech by quoting the "Battle Hymn of the Republic," he thundered, "Glory, hallelujah . . . Glory . . . hallelujah . . . Glory, hallelujah" as 25,000 electrified listeners thundered their approval.[17] That night Klansmen murdered a white Detroit housewife, Viola Liuzzo, as she transported marchers back to Selma. On August 6, 1965, President Johnson signed the Voting Rights Act into law. It provided for federal examiners to register voters in counties where less than 50 percent of adults were registered in 1964. Within a year after passage of the act, Dallas County had 6,000 new black voters. Adjacent Perry County went from 289 black voters to 2,460. Black registration in Lowndes and Wilcox counties increased from none to 1,496 in Lowndes and from none to 3,201 in Wilcox.

Alabama's black registration between 1960 and 1965 increased from 66,000 to 113,000; by 1969 it had more than doubled to 295,000. In 1965, 23.5 percent of Alabama's eligible blacks were registered; by 1970 the figure was 65.4 percent. The percentage of eligible whites raced up as well, from 78.7 percent in 1965 to 96.9 percent in 1970. These events constituted certainly the most important political transformation in the history of Alabama—and arguably within the nation. As one black Selma woman explained to a New York *Times* reporter: "Selma did something. It did something that's hard to explain, but it's inside where you can't see it. . . . I mean, you remember when Jim Clark said there wasn't going to be no march except over his dead body? Well we marched didn't we?"[18]

THIRTY-TWO

Racial Politics
and Economic Stagnation

FROM 1958 to 1980 the Supreme Court rendered decisions in fourteen cases involving racial issues in Alabama. Each became a landmark. They dealt with First Amendment rights of free press and public assembly, service by blacks on juries, voting rights, single-unit districts versus at-large elections, one man—one vote, and discrimination in public accommodations. From his position as federal judge of the District Court for the Middle District of Alabama from 1955 until 1979, Judge Frank M. Johnson, Jr., originated many of these cases and contributed importantly to the judicial assault on segregation, Alabama's inequitable tax structure, its unjustly apportioned legislature, and its inhumane treatment of prisoners and mental patients. It is fair to say that the bitter resistance of Alabama whites played a major role in the success of the civil rights agenda on a broad front. Subtle, less violent resistance had largely thwarted the movement. But the often violent and uniformly inept policies of Wallace, Lingo, Clark, Connor, Hanes, and others provided the movement with martyrs, publicity, recruits, and, most important of all, the moral high ground in virtually every confrontation. The long-range consequence was a state deeply polarized along racial lines, one of the highest numbers of elected black officials of any state, and a lingering residue of negative national stereotypes that proved that history is never over, history is never past, and generations unborn carry the burdens of their parents.

The very same momentum that drove Alabama blacks into the civil rights movement drove Alabama whites into Wallacism. In all of the South, Alabama was the only state that failed to elect any of the progressive reformers known as "New South governors" between the 1960s and the 1990s. One central reason was the bitter resentment of the state's white voters against any reformer who sought black support. As the tide of black voter registration rose, a white progressive candidate needed to carry only slightly more than 40 percent of the white vote to win. But so polarized and angry had whites become that no gubernatorial candidate endorsed by blacks could gain such a white following. When poor whites began to enter the middle class, they sought to protect their newly gained prosperity from black competition. And when their earning power failed to keep pace with inflation during the 1960s, they acted, not in rational ways—such as economic organization, unionism, joining political movements—but in nonrational ways—through scapegoating, fatalism, or blind rage. For their champion they chose George C. Wallace.

It became fashionable in the 1960s and 1970s for the national media to depict Wallace as a mean-spirited racist, a demagogue who appealed mainly to ignorant Southerners who shared his prejudices, a fanatic allied to the John Birch Society, the Minutemen, and other well-financed and eccentric right-wing groups. Actually none of these characterizations was correct. He was in fact an opportunist with populist instincts, who could be racially moderate by the standards of his time and culture, who appealed to many voters outside the South, and who derived most of his support from blue-collar working class whites.

Wallace was born in 1919 and grew up in Barbour County. Although his father and grandfather belonged to the "courthouse gang" that ran most south Alabama counties at the time, they were not well-to-do, and Wallace helped pay for his education with a National Youth Administration job during the depression. After finishing law school at the University of Alabama, he served with the air force during the Second World War. Following Wallace's release from service, Governor Chauncey Sparks appointed him an assistant attorney general. He won election to the state legislature as a candidate who advocated improved veterans', old-age, and welfare benefits and more money for mental hospitals and schools. One opponent attacked him as the "number one do-gooder in the legislature."[1] In 1948 he refused to join the States' Rights party, remaining loyal to national Democrats. Frustrated by conservative control of the legislature, Wallace defeated an ally of these interests to become the state's youngest circuit judge for Barbour, Bullock, and Dale counties.

As a judge he earned a reputation for treating blacks fairly. When attorney J. L. Chestnut, Jr., came before Judge Wallace representing a group of poor black farmers who had been fleeced by large processing companies, corporate attorneys from Birmingham insisted on referring to the black plaintiffs as "these people." Every time they used the phrase, Wallace's face grew redder until finally he interjected in an ice-cold voice: "Please refer to Mr. Hall's and Mr. Chestnut's clients as 'the plaintiff' or don't refer to them at all."[2] Judge Wallace awarded the plaintiffs more damages than they had requested.

During Jim Folsom's 1954 gubernatorial race, Wallace directed his south Alabama campaign and later helped the new governor organize the legislature. Folsom learned from his 1947 experience and carefully selected legislative allies such as Albert P. Brewer, Charles Nice, Jr., Rankin Fite, and George Hawkins for key committee and leadership posts. They easily controlled the house, but a bloc of some eighteen anti-administration senators allied to Attorney General John Patterson blocked Folsom in the senate. One of the "anti" senators, Sam Englehardt, Jr., sponsored a series of anti-integration bills. Groups resisting desegregation sprouted across the state: the States' Rights Association (which enrolled Sidney Smyer, Hugh Locke, and Englehardt), the Southerners (Mobile), the National Association for the Advancement of White People, and of course the White Citizens' Councils (which a Sylacauga paper called the "Ku Klux Klan in top hats and tails").[3] Business groups opposed Folsom's proposals to increase taxes in order to provide for the elderly and poor, warning that such taxes would prevent businesses from locating in Alabama. The Farm Bureau, Associated Industries of Alabama, Alabama Power Company, and other powerful interests lobbied senators to resist most of Folsom's initiatives, although a compromise tax reform did pass that provided an additional $10 million for old-age pensions.

Race completely dominated Folsom's second administration. Early in the term Folsom allowed antidesegregation acts to become law without his signature because they passed by veto-proof majorities. For instance, Senator Albert Boutwell's freedom-of-choice bill, which would have virtually closed down public education in Alabama, passed the house 99 to 1, with only Folsom's ally Charles Nice of Birmingham in opposition. But during the 1957 legislative session seven anti-integration bills passed, and Folsom vetoed all seven. Most passed over his veto.

Much of the segregationist pressure focused on public education. Never well funded, public schools became particularly vulnerable when faced with racial integration. In 1955 the average county provided only 20 percent of school expenditures while the state paid 80 percent. Local resistance to property taxes created this imbalance. Although the 1901 constitution limited property assessment to 60 percent of true value, some Black Belt counties assessed at only 5 percent. In fact in 1955 the fourteen most industrialized counties paid nearly 80 percent of the state's total ad valorem taxes. Folsom sought tax reform, and one of his urban allies told the legislature that fairer taxes would result in better schools for blacks and thus reduce pressure for integration. One legislator muffled his microphone and grumbled: "We don't want the black bastards to learn to read and write."[4] George Wallace spoke in favor of the tax package, denouncing opponents of the bill as people who had no interest in education and who only wanted to keep their taxes low. Although business interests finally agreed to a compromise because of the wretched condition of public schools, voters defeated the tax proposal, with 41,000 for the proposal and 186,000 against. The legislature also cut $30,000 from the appropriations for state teachers' colleges after one legislator revealed that some instructors at Alabama State College in Montgomery made as much as $4,900 annually. Congressman George Andrews announced his support of the Boutwell freedom-of-choice plan by stating, "I'd rather have no school system at all than an integrated system."[5] Voters approved the Boutwell plan 132,000 to 66,000. After Autherine Lucy's unsuccessful effort to integrate the University of Alabama in 1956, thirty faculty members left within the following year. And Auburn University's trustees dismissed an untenured economics professor for writing a letter to the student newspaper supporting school busing as a method to achieve desegregation, causing the university the first of many censures by the American Association of University Professors.

Attorney General John Patterson not only used his office to try to break a boycott of Tuskegee businesses by black citizens organized by C. G. Gomillion but he also obtained a legal ruling requiring the state chapter of the NAACP to reveal its membership list. Refusing to jeopardize the safety of its members, the organization refused the order. As a result Patterson virtually closed down the NAACP in Alabama for eight years, although blacks simply reorganized under other names.

Folsom's New Deal coalition, which had functioned so effectively to elect him in 1954, disintegrated two years later. Many secondary labor leaders became members of the Citizens' Councils. One AFL-CIO investigator estimated that 90 percent of the members of Birmingham's West End Citizens' Council belonged to labor unions. The head of that council, who served as secretary of the typesetters' local, estimated that 75 percent of Birmingham-area council members belonged to labor unions. The AFL-CIO decided to ban discussions of race at union meetings in order to retain white members but succeeded instead in driving away black unionists. So fractured did labor become that its membership declined from 24 percent of Alabama's manufacturing workers in 1956 to under 19 percent in 1964.

The result of such conflict was an unparalleled era of violence throughout the state. Alabama did not lack for demagogues to fan the smoldering ashes of racial discord. Baptist preacher Alvin Horn addressed a 1956 KKK rally in Montgomery where he denounced Jews, Catholics, "burr-headed niggers," and "garlic-eating Wops." Blacks, he assured his audience, "don't want an education, they want a funeral." State senator Albert Davis adopted a slightly revised revolutionary war slogan at another Klan rally: "Give me segregation or give me death."[6] Between 1956 and 1958, Alabama experienced more racial bombings (twenty-two churches and homes) than any other state. In Maplesville twenty-two carloads of Klansmen selected a house at random where six blacks were watching television. They broke in, beat all six, and shot at them when they ran.

As if racial discord were not enough to destroy the effectiveness of the administration, journalists reported tales of Folsom's womanizing, alcohol abuse, nepotism, cronyism, and misuse of the state airplane to fly to football games. So unpopular was Folsom by 1958 that no gubernatorial candidate sought his endorsement. One reason for Folsom's precipitous decline was George Wallace's desertion. Gearing up for his own 1958 gubernatorial campaign, Wallace found his one-time mentor a political liability, and he jettisoned him as quickly as he would soon abandon much of Folsom's populist ideology.

The 1958 field of gubernatorial candidates had someone for everybody. A wealthy Selma resident named Shearen Elebash dressed in Ivy League suits, spoke precise English, and exuded charm, education, and sophistication. The press dubbed him Alabama's Adlai Stevenson. But Elebash made the fatal mistake of addressing serious issues. He warned that public schools were incapable of meeting the challenges of an economic world increasingly dependent on technology. What few scientists and first-rate minds Alabama contained, he argued, were mainly imported from fine schools in other states. Alabama voters much preferred the fulminations of the three leading candidates, John Patterson, George Wallace, and Folsom ally Jimmy Faulkner of Baldwin County.

The field of frivolous candidates produced an especially eccentric array in that chaotic year. The Reverend Billy Lander Wilder had begun preaching at the age of thirteen and presently managed the evangelistic career of his fourteen-year-old son. He announced that God intended him to win, but apparently the Deity failed to communicate this message to Alabama voters, and Wilder was never a factor in the race. Navy veteran John Crommelin threw his former-admiral's hat in the ring with the announcement that the three leading candidates were all either secretly Jewish or dominated by a Jewish conspiracy. Voters happily also ignored him.

Faulkner took the early lead among what remained of Folsom's constituency, but their close association and the governor's quiet support hurt him. Gradually the contest turned into a two-man race between Patterson and Wallace.

Wallace in 1958 conducted the most issue-oriented of all his campaigns. Leaning heavily on his populist instincts, he promised to modernize the state's economy, recruit new industry, build trade schools, raise teacher salaries, improve medical care, and provide higher pensions for the elderly. But Patterson made race the central issue of the campaign. He reminded voters that as a circuit judge Wallace had halted a purge of black voters and had sentenced a white man to death for murdering a black. Patterson portrayed himself as the premier segregationist in the race who had fought the Tuskegee boycott and dismantled the state's NAACP. Folsom backers, blacks, and labor split between Faulkner and Wallace, allowing Patterson to lead the primary with 32 percent of the vote.

In the runoff Wallace tried to depict Patterson as an extremist on race and as a tool of the Big Mules who would threaten TVA. In a time of racial polarization, he tried to emphasize traditional economic issues and lost the initiative on race even though he proclaimed himself a segregationist. The Klan, which endorsed Patterson, denounced Wallace as "NAACP-loving George Wallace." Despite the support of labor, blacks, Jewish organizations, Democratic loyalists, well-educated people, and eight of the eleven large daily newspapers, Wallace lost to Patterson by a vote of 250,000 to 365,000. Wallace attributed his loss to being "outsegged" and vowed that it would never happen again. Nor did it.

After a lackluster Patterson administration that produced little except bombastic oratory against integration and a continued avalanche of bills to prevent it, an impressive array of politicians jockeyed for position in the 1962 governor's race. Wallace, Folsom, Bull Connor, and young Tuscaloosa attorney Ryan deGraffenried entered the field, with Connor and Wallace leading the race baiting, Folsom trying to rebuild his rural north Alabama base, and deGraffenried seeking to build a coalition of the middle class, the educated, and progressive business people. The first polls showed Folsom ahead. But he appeared on television in a daze (some claimed he was intoxicated, others that he had been drugged or was suffering the first symptoms of a blood clot) and could not remember his children's names when he tried to introduce them. Wallace inspired crowds most successfully with his bellicose attacks on federal judge Frank M. Johnson, a Republican native of Winston County and a former classmate of Wallace at the University of Alabama. President Eisenhower had appointed Johnson to the bench, and his civil rights opinions soon became classic documents in the legal history of the movement. Wallace, having learned his lesson well four years earlier, called his former friend "a low-down, carpet-bagging, scalawagging, race-mixing liar."[7] His new strategy played well at the branch heads, and Wallace led deGraffenried into the runoff by a vote of 207,000 to 161,000; Folsom came in a close third with 160,000 votes. Wallace easily defeated the more moderate deGraffenried in the runoff.

For the next twenty-five years Wallace would preside over Alabama in one way or another. Or at least his cronies would caretake while their mentor pursued loftier ambitions. The governor enjoyed elections more than holding office. If one includes his presidential campaigns, Wallace ran for public office directly or indirectly seven times between 1962 and 1974 (for governor in 1962, president in 1964, managed his wife's campaign for governor in 1966, ran for president in 1968, governor in 1970, president in 1972, and governor in 1974). He briefly entered the 1976 presidential race, and he won another term as governor in 1982. For better or worse, Wallacism and the reaction to it dominated public policy and political discourse for more than a quarter of the twentieth century.

During his first term as governor, Wallace implemented his Folsom-like 1962 platform, which had promised improvements in highways, education, and industrial recruitment. Although he used highway funds as a political weapon against legislative opponents, he did enlarge the interstate system. He also sponsored a system of junior, community, and trade colleges based on the notion that educational opportunities should be available within easy commuting distance of every Alabama student. Unfortunately he staffed the administration of many of these new schools with political friends and located them in counties represented by administration backers. Although the state advertised the system as the nation's third largest behind California and Florida, educators considered the quality of the system suspect. Without a statewide system of administrative oversight or coordination, higher education institutions battled each other in the capitol, where legislators were influenced by the political firepower of a school's senator or representative rather than by the merits of its educational vision. Wallace did attract a continuing stream of low-wage industry, but the state became an economic revolving door, bringing industry in with promises of low wages and tax benefits and then losing the industry when lower-wage foreign competition undersold markets. Thanks to a burgeoning national economy during the 1960s, Wallace could point to a record of sustained economic growth without resorting to significant tax increases. But Wallace's policies had little to do with Alabama's prosperity because the state usually tracked national economic patterns. The state relied little on stable property taxes and heavily on volatile sales, franchise, and income taxes, all of which quickly reflected general economic conditions.

Ironically Wallace first emerged as a national figure during the carefully orchestrated 1963 stand in the schoolhouse door. After the ill-fated attempt by Autherine Lucy to integrate the University of Alabama, blacks made several unsuccessful efforts to enter the school. Vivian Malone of Mobile, Sandy English of Birmingham, and James Hood of Gadsden filed suit for admission during the turbulent spring of 1963. After much conferring among Wallace, President Kennedy, and the Justice Department, the governor played out the charade on the steps of the administrative building at the university on June 11, 1963. He delivered a speech containing the obligatory references to states' rights, federal tyranny, and other by-then familiar topics, then stepped aside while federal marshals registered the first black students. Television news networks carried the tape on the evening's broadcasts, and Wallace received some 100,000 telegrams and letters of support within the next week, most of them from outside the state.

In January 1964 Harold A. Franklin entered the history graduate program at Auburn, but when the 1964 school year ended only a handful of black students attended formerly white schools and universities. Wallace had not prevented integration, but he had slowed it to a snail's pace. His success won him friends well beyond the borders of Alabama.

The legal vehicle through which Wallace directed his defense of segregation was the Committee on Constitutional Law and State Sovereignty (usually referred to simply as the Sovereignty Commission), created by the legislature at Wallace's urging. This committee drafted legislation designed to prevent integration, harass liberal organizations within Alabama, and serve as a political agency to publicize Wallace's views outside the state. The committee hired a firm to make a movie depicting Wallace's view of the Selma-to-Montgomery march ironically entitled "We Shall Overcome."[8] The film alleged that Communists played major roles in the Selma affair, that they and not Alabama whites perpetrated the violence that the media blamed on native Alabamians, and that sexual indecencies characterized all stages of the march. The forty-minute film became a favorite at White Citizens' Council meetings but reached an audience far broader than Southern racists. In fact the film ended with an upbeat testimony to the Wallace administration's record of educational and economic growth.

Wallace participated actively in the committee's proceedings and used it for his own political ambitions. It also established a research organization, the Legal Economic Cultural Research Association—In Defense of Principles of Constitutional Government (LECRA). As early as 1967 LECRA's director, Eli Howell, revealed Wallace's national political strategy to his directors, denouncing the nation's two-party system as a "revolutionary device which by the nature of its function, cannot but advance egalitarian objectives." Because the "vital center" of American politics was closely divided between the two parties, "minority bloc votes" held the balance of power.[9]

Many non-Alabama residents, first attracted to Wallace by his 1963 "stand" at the university, entered his organization files through the Sovereignty Commission. Literally thousands of letters from out of state demonstrated the popularity of the governor's views. A leader of the South Carolina Baptist Layman's Association wrote that his group enrolled 1,100 members in forty-six South Carolina counties. They had formed their organization to preserve the Baptist heritage as taught in the King James version of the Bible, to support the free enterprise system, to reject literature advocating ecumenical and one-world churches or governments, and to combat a subversive movement "cloaked under long robes of education and religion, foreign to our beliefs as Baptists."[10] A Kentucky resident wrote that his extensive travels throughout the South had convinced him that the vast majority of Southerners considered Wallace the George Washington of the region: "God has given you super strength for this mission. He has ordained you to carry on."[11]

By no means were the letter writers limited to Southerners. In fact they reveal Wallace's growing popularity among right-wing fringe groups who little understood his liberal ties to unionism or his populist heritage. A John Birch Society member from Iowa wrote that the "only real patriots left in America . . . come from the South." John H. Rousselot, director of public relations for the John Birch Society, requested a copy of "We Shall Overcome" to show at Birch Society meetings on the West Coast. The executive director of the Indiana Committee for Captive Nations saw Wallace on "Face the Nation," an appearance, he said, that "brought pride and joy to the hearts of millions of Americans." "Anti-Christ forces masquerading behind Communism" caused problems both in Alabama and the nation. A right-wing activist who headed the Anti-Communist Committee of Western New York and ran a "patriotic bookstore" watched Wallace each time he appeared on television and sought Sovereignty Commission materials to use among clergymen in the Buffalo area. Commission director Eli Howell won considerable support among non-Southern businessmen by attacking what he viewed as the leftist drift of American society "along the lines of syndicalist theory," "nationalization of education," and the destructive power of trade unionism, which he believed was poised to seize control of the nation's economy.[12]

Using this network of sympathizers, Wallace ventured outside state politics in 1964. He entered Democratic primaries in Wisconsin, Indiana, and Maryland to the general scorn of the national press and the bemusement of national Democratic party officials. But his performance (43 percent of the vote in Maryland and a third of the vote in the other two states) quickly turned their ridicule into alarm. Although he withdrew when the Republican party nominated conservative Barry Goldwater, Wallace returned to the national scene in 1968. He had become the first national candidate in the mid-twentieth century to tap the frustrations, alienation, sense of rejection, and latent racism of millions of working class American whites.

Lurleen and George Wallace, who dominated Alabama politics
from 1962 until 1986 (Courtesy of the Alabama Department of
Archives and History)

Having secured his Alabama base by having his wife elected governor
in 1966 (the state constitution barred Wallace from succeeding himself),
he launched his 1968 campaign under the banner of the American
Independent party with a series of short, memorable epithets: there was
"not a dime's worth of difference between the major parties"; if elected
he would throw the briefcases of "pointy-headed bureaucrats and intellectuals" into the Potomac River and restore government to the plain
people. The declining purchasing power of blue-collar and lower middle
class workers, the hated antiwar movement, and the spread of school
busing and neighborhood integration all helped create an atmosphere
receptive to the governor's message. Wallace's core Alabama constituency of farmers, union members, small businessmen, and aggrieved
Evangelical Christians prepared him well to communicate with such
"forgotten Americans" in other regions. It turned out that huge numbers
of Democratic voters in the industrial North and Midwest shared the
same fears, troubles, and prejudices as Alabamians. Financed both by
wealthy right-wingers and by grass-roots union members, Wallace appealed to Democrats fed up with their liberal leaders but not yet ready to
vote Republican. Polls showed him winning 20 percent of the vote
against Hubert H. Humphrey and Richard M. Nixon and perhaps throwing the election into the House of Representatives. But many voters who
sympathized with his message ultimately deserted him for one of the
viable candidates. Although Wallace virtually tied the other two candidates in the South with 34.3 percent of the vote (compared to 34.7 for
Nixon and 31.0 percent for Humphrey), he carried only Georgia, Ala-

575

bama, Mississippi, Louisiana, and Arkansas. His vote correlated closely to the 1964 Goldwater vote in the South and demonstrated the complex mix of political, racial, economic, and patriotic elements at work in those chaotic times.

After Wallace's wife Lurleen died of cancer midway through her term, Lieutenant Governor Albert P. Brewer became governor. In two years Brewer gave Alabama a reform program of increased funding for education, creation of the Alabama Commission on Higher Education, the state's first ethics commission, and a constitutional revision commission. He challenged Wallace in 1970 with a progressive, New South campaign amazingly devoid of racial overtones. By then the Voting Rights Act had registered tens of thousands of black voters, and Brewer tried to form a coalition of educated middle class whites, traditional New Deal north Alabama working class whites, and blacks. He nearly succeeded, taking a substantial lead in the first vote. But a third candidate took enough votes to deny Brewer a majority, and in the runoff Wallace ran one of the nastiest campaigns in state history. Combining racism with innuendos about Brewer and his family, Wallace barely won.

His campaign slogan, "Stand Up for Alabama," spoke more of his national aspirations than his vision for the state's future. The year 1972 found him again on the presidential trail, winning an early primary in Florida. An attempted assassination in Maryland ended this campaign but not before he swept primaries in Tennessee, North Carolina, Maryland, and Michigan on the same day and barely lost in Indiana. Riding a wave of home-state sympathy, he finally succeeded in changing the constitution to allow the governor to serve consecutive terms, and he easily won the governorship for the third time in 1974.

Despite his physical incapacity, resulting from the assassination attempt, he flirted with another presidential race in 1976 before eventually endorsing Georgia governor Jimmy Carter. Undoubtedly Wallace's national success in 1964, 1968, and 1972 played a role in Carter's narrow 1976 victory by attracting support for a Southern candidate. And his vigorous national campaigns presented merely a cruder, more proletarian version of a political agenda adopted by Richard Nixon and then developed fully by Ronald Reagan. They cleaned up Wallace's message and made it more suave and sophisticated, but in many ways the raw nerve that Alabama's governor exposed gave both parties' political leaders a two-decade-long toothache and sent American politics tumbling in a rightward direction. Although Wallace would win a fourth term in 1982, he was a gentler, crippled man by then who publicly apologized to black voters for his earlier rhetoric and won a substantial portion of their votes.

Wallace's long domination of state politics delayed the development both of the Republican party in the state and of a more moderate Democratic party. Although national party loyalists such as Judge Roy Mayhall and Robert S. Vance maintained control of the State Democratic Executive Committee from 1962 to 1977 and began to involve black politicians in party affairs, they had to expend much energy battling the Wallace forces who sought to make the state Democratic party a personal vehicle for the governor's national ambitions.

So great was the magnitude of Wallace's presence that it overshadowed all of the state's political traditions. The importance of the "friends' and neighbors' vote" declined rapidly in the 1960s partly because of growing black registration, especially in the Black Belt, and partly because of the ascendancy of race as an issue in traditionally liberal north Alabama. Wallace's declining vote in his native Barbour County and adjacent Bullock and Pike counties almost exactly matched increasing black registration. Conversely Albert Brewer lost white hill counties to Wallace in 1970. North-south sectionalism also gave way to racial politics. Historic differences in voting patterns changed rapidly as black voting majorities in many Black Belt counties transformed them from the most anti-national Democratic party to the most loyal national party Alabama counties, while many overwhelmingly white hill counties became Wallace strongholds. In 1970 Brewer, a native of Decatur in the Tennessee Valley, won 48 percent of the Black Belt vote to only 46 percent in north Alabama and 32 percent in the south. Regional differences still existed but were blurred by the politics of race.

Nor did the Big Mule–planter alliance survive the new racial politics. The 1960 census revealed Alabama's slowing population growth, which cost the state a congressional seat. The legislature had to redraw legislative boundaries or permit a statewide at-large election in 1962. Because more than half the population lived in north Alabama, a statewide ballot might give that region all eight congressional seats; so incumbent congressmen and their legislative allies worked feverishly to devise a solution. Legislators also confronted the implications of a reapportionment case, *Baker* v. *Carr* (then before the Supreme Court), which would shortly require them to do what they had studiously avoided for sixty-one years in violation of their own constitution: reapportion the state legislature. In 1960 Jefferson County, which contained 600,000 people, elected one state senator. So did Wilcox County, which contained 16,000 people. Many congressional redistricting proposals came before the legislature, but the most controversial one split populous Jefferson County into four separate congressional districts. Rural legislators from the Black Belt and from north Alabama voted for the "Jefferson chop-up" bill, whereas urban legislators from north Alabama generally opposed it and mounted a ninety-six-hour filibuster to block it. Perhaps more than any other action, the support of the Jefferson chop-up by white Black Belt legislators ended what Albert Brewer called the "sixty-year marriage of the Imperial Queen [Jefferson] and a scoundrel [the Black Belt]."[13] Henceforth, Jefferson County usually aligned with the political interests of north Alabama rather than with those of the Black Belt.

Perhaps the most lasting impact of Wallacism was the drawing of Alabama Democrats away from their national party, first toward an independent third party led by Wallace, then ultimately into the Republican party. Ever since Reconstruction many Alabama whites had visualized the Republican party as a vehicle of radical social change tainted by black influence and the Democratic party as the party of tradition, stability, and social order. But in the 1960s and 1970s the roles of the two parties completed a historic reversal begun during the New Deal. For Alabama whites the Republican party slowly became the party of traditional white values and social stability threatened by the iconoclasm and radicalism of the national Democratic party.

The 1962 senatorial election demonstrated the changes under way. That year Lister Hill defended his Senate seat against two fringe Democrats who conducted racist campaigns, Admiral John Crommelin and engineer Donald G. Hallmark. Hallmark belonged to the White Citizens' Council and Crommelin tried to tie Hill to the "communist-Jewish conspiracy," leading the Montgomery *Advertiser* to describe them as one "well-meaning, but misplaced" candidate and the other as just "misplaced."[14]

Previously Hill's sound thrashing of these two peripheral candidates would have guaranteed his election. But 1962 was not a typical year. John Grenier, a thirty-two-year-old New Orleans native, marine veteran, and Tulane and New York University graduate, had reorganized the Alabama Republican party. Working through the Young Republicans, he had gained control of the state party, swept aside an aging generation more concerned with administering federal patronage than winning elections, and installed an entirely new leadership under forty years of age.

Grenier recruited James D. Martin, a Gadsden oil distributor and president of the powerful Associated Industries of Alabama, to oppose Hill. Martin won the support of that organization as well as of the Farm Bureau, the chamber of commerce, and many south Alabama and Black Belt newspapers. So well funded was his campaign that Martin outspent the powerful incumbent senator. Hill only slowly realized his peril and returned to the state with barely three weeks left in the campaign. Rated as one of the six most liberal senators on issues other than race, Hill had every advantage of a distinguished career during which he had written or co-written the TVA Act, the Rural Telephone Act, the Rural Housing Act, Vocational Education Act, the GI Bill of Rights, the Rural Library Services Act, the National Defense Education Act of 1958, and the Hill-Burton Hospital Construction Act of 1946. This distinguished record did him little good in 1962 under Martin's relentless pounding on issues of states' rights, Southern pride, fiscal conservatism, and patriotism.

Borrowing from George Wallace's rhetoric, Martin began to sound like a Republican version of the "little judge from Barbour County." Grenier played the role of "heavy," savaging Hill as "the waterboy for the Bobby-and-Jack [Kennedy] touch football team" and telling pollsters that if they queried Alabamians they would find that only "Khruschev and Castro would finish lower than the Kennedy brothers."[15] Hill struck back by depicting Martin as a typical Big Mule with ties to Wall Street, big bankers, and the rich. But populist rhetoric won few votes in 1962. Hill even relied on a football analogy, reminding audiences that "Bear Bryant doesn't break up his great winning team at the University of Alabama and Alabama Democrats aren't going to break up their winning team either."[16] Wallace belatedly campaigned for Hill and helped to save him from a humiliating defeat. Martin led the early returns, carrying even Hill's native Montgomery County; but late returns from rural north Alabama gave Hill a razor-thin 6,800-vote victory out of 400,000 ballots cast. Hill's 1962 win in north Alabama was the last hurrah for the New Deal alliance that had prevailed for nearly three decades. Although Hill narrowly survived the 1962 challenge, he chose to retire in 1968 rather than face almost certain defeat from Lieutenant Governor James B. Allen, a Wallace protégé.

Grenier and Martin went on to play key roles in the 1964 draft-Goldwater movement, Grenier serving as Southern regional chairman of the presidential effort and later as Goldwater's executive director of the Republican National Committee. Goldwater won 69.5 percent of Alabama's vote in November 1964 and carried five Republican congressmen and ninety-four local GOP candidates into office on his coattails. Curiously, traditional hill county Republican strongholds like Winston County were becoming less Republican, while Black Belt counties still under white dominance gave Goldwater huge majorities. Martin decided to contest the governorship against Lurleen Wallace in 1966, but this contest pitting a "rich man's segregationist" against a "poor man's segregationist" ended Martin's career in a two-to-one drubbing.

That same year the combative Grenier lost by a 40-to-60 percent margin to incumbent senator John Sparkman, and two of the seats captured by Republicans in 1964 succumbed to a sobered and serious Democratic counterattack. In the late 1960s Alabama's Republican party was splintered and blunted by Wallace's racial politics and by its image as a rich man's club. It began to grow again when Wallace declined as a political force after 1972. As Alabama's Democratic party absorbed black voters, becoming both more biracial and more racially moderate, the party once again surrendered the isssue of racial politics to Republicans, who used it to good effect in the 1970s and 1980s. Republicans made gains not only in the affluent suburbs of all Alabama cities but especially among south Alabama rural whites. Of course neither Democrats nor Republicans held a monopoly on racism. Both Republican and Democratic factions used racist arguments against groups within their own camps, then turned such appeals against the opposition party in general elections.

The economic demography of the state contributed substantially to its changing politics. By 1970 cotton production had dipped to barely 500,000 bales from 824,000 twenty years earlier. Many fields previously devoted to cotton grew pine trees to feed the voracious national and international appetite for lumber. The loss of rural population allowed two-thirds of Alabama's land to return to forests. By the 1960s Alabama produced more lumber than any other Southern state.

Alabama also became a major center for the poultry industry. Before World War II Americans consumed little poultry except on special occasions, and the major commercial producers were located in New England, the Middle Atlantic states, and the Midwest. But changes in diet and technology altered this situation after the war. Feed dealers supplied chicks and feed on credit; and cheap, convenient TVA transportation and power encouraged north Alabama farmers to enter the commercial poultry industry. Frozen chickens appeared in supermarkets and attracted consumers interested in a nutritious, cheap meat. By 1970 revenue from the sale of broilers and eggs contributed 33 percent of Alabama's farm income, and the state ranked in the top three producers nationally.

The Rockefeller Foundation also awarded Auburn University's fisheries program $500,000 between 1965 and 1970 to double research on high-protein fish production designed to help impoverished countries. The program also received U.S. Agency for International Development grants. In 1970 USAID and Auburn created the International Center for Aquaculture. Between 1967 and 1975 forty-nine nations sent 250 teams to study at the center. A program historically devoted to providing alternative sources of income to Alabama farmers by encouraging catfish production gradually became a major resource for developing nations seeking high-protein foods.

Alabama's business development received a severe blow from the state's racial turmoil, despite Wallace's constant boasts of new industries and politically contrived statistics about how many new jobs the economy had generated. Birmingham lost virtually two decades of economic growth during the 1950s and 1960s. Gradually many leading businessmen became advocates of racial moderation, not necessarily out of social conviction so much as from economic self-interest. Whatever their motivation, they often played the key roles in resolving racial conflict through private conversations with civil rights leaders and through creation of organizations such as Operation New Birmingham. Although economists found it difficult to measure the effect of racial turmoil on Alabama's economy, two patterns seem clear. During the 1960s the state's reputation for conflict and violence placed added pressure on industrial recruitment. For example, when Hammermill Paper Company announced a 1965 decision to locate in Selma, national civil rights activists threatened to boycott the company's products. Although Alabama's rate of industrial growth continued on a steady course, the economies of more moderate Southern states such as Georgia, Florida, Texas, North Carolina, Virginia, and Tennessee grew faster.

As if racial turmoil were not problem enough, Alabama's manufacturing sector also entered the postindustrial world. The United States faced growing foreign competition, especially from German and Japanese steel- and automakers. Textile imports from Europe and Asia threatened another critical market. Suddenly Alabama's status as the South's premier industrial state became a mixed blessing. In 1962 the state contained some 125 textile plants employing 40,000. In fact one of every five employed persons in Alabama industry worked in some phase of textiles, and the industry paid one in every eight dollars in manufacturing wages. It consumed more cotton than Alabama farmers grew.

But many traditional industries began a steady decline. Dwight Mills in Gadsden closed, as did the historic Avondale Mills in Birmingham. Between 1950 and 1970 Birmingham also lost 25,000 steel-related jobs and the cornerstone of the city's historic economic structure. Republic Steel in Gadsden followed the same pattern. The new long-life steel-belted tires produced by Michelin and other foreign companies also undercut the profitability of Gadsden's Goodyear plant, which manufactured bias-ply tires. On top of everything else, the air force closed Selma's Craig Air Force Base in 1977, further deflating an economy already hard hit by racial upheaval and economic shifts. A tough new antipollution act passed by the legislature in 1971 levied the highest fines on polluters of water by any southeastern state, although state agencies chose to administer the law selectively. Nevertheless, national standards for pollution control proved the last straw for some of Alabama's aging plants.

At the same time that certain sectors of the economy seemed to be dying, others thrived. The Alabama Development Office vigorously recruited industry. A typical advertisement in the March 1966 issue of *Business Week* read: "Alabama has got what industry looks for. Our Cater and Wallace Acts finance $50 million plants as easily as $50 thousand plants."[17] Governor Wallace even gave prospective industrialists his office phone number to help resolve possible problems. The development office maintained a fleet of mobile classrooms ready to travel to a plant site to train workers. Between 1958 and 1961 Alabama and four other Southern states granted tax exemptions to new industry valued at $143 million. In addition, the state issued revenue bonds to build factories for the companies. As a result many new capital-intensive firms took advantage of Alabama's favorable tax benefits to locate in the state.

One study of development bond financing in Alabama indicated that of 212 firms that came to the state, 44 (20.8 percent) were national corporations listed on the major stock exchanges. Between 1952 and 1960 the average investment per job created amounted to $2,448. Between 1961 and 1968 this average increased to $20,473, nearly a 740 percent increase. These firms might have located in Alabama anyway, but the state's subsidy probably played a significant role. Unfortunately revenue bonds seemed to have been especially important in attracting low-wage, labor-intensive industries, and exempting industry from taxes for long periods starved local communities of revenue essential for upgrading education and public welfare.

Some of the new industry was homegrown and some depended heavily on federal expenditures. Diversified Products began in Opelika as an idea to encase iron barbells in plastic in order to minimize damage to floors and furniture. Ampex in the same community thrived as a manufacturer of magnetic tape. Winton M. Blount built his Blount Brothers corporation into one of the largest high-tech engineering firms in the world. While he served as president of the U.S. Chamber of Commerce in 1968, Blount was selected by President Richard M. Nixon to become postmaster general of the United States. Blount thus became the first Alabamian to hold a cabinet post in the twentieth century and only the second in history. In 1972 he ran a losing campaign for the U.S. Senate from Alabama, but he helped to invigorate the Republican party in the state.

The most notable economic change occurred in Huntsville, where the National Aeronautics and Space Administration created the George C. Marshall Space Flight Center in 1960 with Dr. Wernher Von Braun as director. NASA planned, directed, and conducted the nonmilitary space activities of the United States and charged the Marshall Center with the design and development of launch vehicle systems. Operating from a $100 million complex formally dedicated in fall 1960, the Marshall Center was the largest of NASA's ten installations. German and American scientists and engineers combined to provide the United States with one generation after another of successful rocket engines: Redstone, Jupiter, Saturn, and Centaur.

Unfortunately NASA contracts operated in a boom-and-bust cycle that brought frantic unplanned growth to Huntsville, followed by collapse. The Marshall Center's 1962 budget produced $30 million in local contracts, and NASA employees spent an additional $100 million in the Huntsville area that year. By 1964 the center's budget topped $1.7 billion, and Huntsville derived 90 percent of its income from the aerospace industry. Companies such as Boeing, Chrysler, General Electric, Hayes International, Lockheed, Northrop, and RCA located research/engineering facilities in the city. Other firms began locally. Brown Engineering started in 1953 when five businessmen borrowed $50,000 and formed a company specializing in engineering research related to aerospace technology. By 1964 Brown employed 3,000, paid a weekly payroll of $422,500, and had branches in Houston and Boca Raton. But after the moon exploration program ended in the mid-1960s, the city lost 17,400 NASA-related jobs, and entire neighborhoods looked like ghost towns. Huntsville seemed to be repeating a historic mistake, replacing one exclusive industry (textiles) with another (aerospace).

But city planners learned from their problems. Between 1965 and 1978 they concentrated on diversifying the economy, especially in the area of light industry, attracting tire, chemical, machinery, and metal companies. Fortunately the government's other facility, Redstone Arsenal, maintained a steady work force of about 10,000 as the cold war required munitions, rockets, and other ordnance developed and tested there.

Rapid economic development created tension between citizens who grieved over the destruction of historic buildings and threats to traditional values on one hand and real estate developers and modernizers who profited from such growth on the other. Entire sections of historic Mobile, Montgomery, Birmingham, Anniston, Auburn, and Huntsville disappeared. Main arteries leading into towns took on the appearance of a new kind of slum: metal buildings appeared overnight to dispense a variety of fast foods and transformed unique urban environments into bland, ugly patterns indistinguishable from Newark, New Jersey, or San Diego, California.

The economic shifts experienced during the 1950s and 1960s left lasting impressions. Thirty-five of Alabama's sixty-seven counties lost population. Every one of these counties lost agricultural employment, from a total of 133,100 in 1950 to 51,600 in 1960. Commuting by vehicle to an urban job became critical in stabilizing north Alabama's economy. Employment within this region underwent profound and lasting changes. Mining jobs declined by 59 percent and agriculture and forestry jobs by 61 percent, but construction jobs increased 35 percent, manufacturing (mainly textiles, auto parts, and tire/rubber products) 28 percent, and services 27 percent.

The national respect Alabama lost by racial violence and political mediocrity it regained by football. Perhaps it was no coincidence that the same blue-collar voters nationally who supported George Wallace for president also venerated Paul ("Bear") Bryant, who carried University of Alabama football to unprecedented heights. Bryant became the winningest coach in collegiate football history and led Alabama to a football dynasty rivaled only by Notre Dame in the history of the sport. At the age of forty-four, Bryant returned in 1958 to his alma mater, which had fallen on hard times. Not only was the University's football team at a low ebb, but the state's white society was under siege in a way unprecedented since the 1920s. Virtually all white Alabamians were digging in their heels and saying "never." That is precisely what the Bear asked his "skinny little boys" to do. They played bigger teams and better teams but they played no teams with greater pride or tenacity. And mostly they won. Bear and the university won national championships in 1961, 1964, 1965, 1973, 1978, and 1979 to add to four earlier titles.

By 1990 there were at least twelve books about Bear Bryant and ten more on Alabama football, not counting individual books by or about particular players such as Joe Namath, Kenny Stabler, or Steve Sloan. For children, *Young Bear: The Legend of Bear Bryant's Boyhood* dispensed values of overcoming poverty and adversity by persistence and resolution. For posterity, *Bryant: The Man . . . The Myth* (which spent most of its space on the myth) allocated all profits to the "We Believe Trust as a living memorial in honor of Coach Bryant's players." For those truly consumed, *The Road to No. 1* provided a game-by-game account of the 1978 championship season. One Alabama doctoral student even wrote a dissertation on "The Effects of the University of Alabama Football Training Program on Reaction Time and Speed of Movement."

If all this attention makes Alabama football seem like a religion, it is! In his book on *The Joy of Sports,* author Michael Novak discussed Alabama football in a chapter entitled "Regional Religions." The sport honored the state, the university, and the spirit of the South during difficult days when the Ku Klux Klan provided the main alternative vision of what Alabamians were like. Attending games became a religious ritual requiring a tithe of income for travel homes or hotel rooms, tickets, meals, and bowl games.

Race loomed large in Alabama football as in all else during these decades. Bryant was never an innovator, despite his great success. His genius consisted of adopting the ideas of others, refining them, and applying them within a system of pride and discipline. Whether the famous "wishbone" offense, which he borrowed from Texas and Oklahoma, or racial integration, which he borrowed from Kentucky and Tennessee, his adaptations worked better for him than for their originators. At first Bear worked well within Alabama's lily-white social system, turning football games into miniversions of the Civil War. The state might lose every time its lawyers appeared before the Supreme Court, but Bear's warriors hardly ever lost.

The classic example came in the 1963 Orange Bowl, where Alabama's defense pulverized Oklahoma 17 to 0. Bear attributed the victory to what he interpreted as a snub of the team by President Kennedy, who visited the Oklahoma locker room before the game but not Alabama's dressing quarters. Linebacker Lee Roy Jordan also believed the incident provided the team extra incentive. The game was also one of the first against a team with black players. Alabama's scouting reports had revealed that an Oklahoma halfback gave away some plays by his stance. Two Alabama players named Pell and O'Dell developed a key to these plays. Charlie Pell would shout, "Look out, Digger! Look out, Digger!" to warn O'Dell (whose nickname was Digger) whenever the play was headed his way. Oklahoma positioned a black player opposite Pell and when he began shouting, the referee, aware of the state's racial reputation, warned Pell to stop his racist shouts or be ejected from the game. Jordan explained to Bryant at halftime that the referee believed Pell was yelling, "Look out, nigger! Look out, nigger!" Bryant explained to the referee what had happened and the game proceeded without further incident.

In 1961 Southeastern Conference universities in the border South concluded that the time had come to recruit black athletes, but conference schools in Alabama and Mississippi warned of riots on campus and disintegration of the conference should its members take such action. Finally in 1965 the University of Kentucky signed a black player, followed the next year by Vanderbilt. Auburn signed a black basketball player, Henry Harris, during the 1967–68 season, breaking the athletic color barrier at the major college level in Alabama. But progress was so slow that only Harris and one other black basketball player competed during the 1969–70 season. Bryant and Auburn's Ralph ("Shug") Jordan declined to throw their considerable prestige behind this social experiment, though Alabama's head basketball coach, C. M. Newton, signed forward Wendell Hudson to a scholarship in April 1969. Not until Southern California's gifted running back Sam ("Bam") Cunningham ran over and around and by Bear's "skinny white boys" at Birmingham's Legion Field in 1970 did the Bear decide a new era had dawned in college athletics. Coach Bryant's stopwatch had expanded his social conscience.

At a more profound level the success of Alabama athletics left a mixed legacy. The football success of two otherwise undistinguished state universities during the 1950s and 1960s provided an athletic equivalent to Governor Wallace's contempt for "pointy-headed intellectuals" and "cerebral wimps." This overemphasis on football made it harder to recruit talented faculty or academically gifted students, many of whom left the state for schools with better-equipped laboratories and more challenging curricula even if their football programs struggled to break even.

Although football clearly stole the spotlight from other sports, Mobile's Henry Aaron did not perform in obscurity. Born in 1934, his life paralleled those of many earlier black Alabama athletes. Aaron's father worked as a boilermaker's helper at Alabama Drydock and Shipbuilding Company. Because of their own limited educations, his parents determined that their children would at least finish high school. But Central High School held few attractions for sixteen-year-old Henry, who began to play semipro ball because his school could not afford baseball equipment for a team. He told his father he was quitting school, but his father ended the conversation by reminding Henry that every day he left fifty cents for each child to use to buy nourishing school lunches, which left only a quarter for his own meal at work. If he could sacrifice his meals, Henry could postpone his pro baseball career until after high school graduation. The shamed boy got the message. He compromised with his parents by finishing high school but gaining their permission to delay college until after his baseball career ended. College had a long wait. After joining the Milwaukee Braves in 1954, Aaron became one of the premier power hitters in the history of the sport.

Although his idol Jackie Robinson had broken the color barrier a decade earlier, the intensely personal Aaron experienced his own problems. Never close to teammates or talkative to reporters, he earned a nickname not only for his power hitting ("hammering Hank") but also for his introspective personality ("the quiet superstar"). As he approached Babe Ruth's all-time home run record in 1973, some older white fans began taunting him and sending hate mail. Aaron concluded that in those racially tense years they simply did not want a black player to break Ruth's record. But on April 8, 1974, Aaron cracked home run number 715 to eclipse the Babe's forty-year-old record. Despite mediocre years for the Atlanta Braves and Milwaukee Brewers in the mid-1970s, his retirement at age forty-two left him the towering giant in his sport, although he never received the sort of adulation Ruth had. He played in 3,298 games, collected 3,771 hits (second only to Ty Cobb at that time), and broke the major league record for most career home runs (755) and most runs batted in (2,297). Aaron fulfilled his promise to his parents by completing his college education and later assumed a front-office job with the Atlanta Braves.

Few Alabama women excelled at athletics and they participated only peripherally in the 1960s women's movement. One exception was Leah Rawls Atkins, who won the world water skiing championship and became the first woman inducted into the Alabama Sports Hall of Fame. Many of the state's colleges and universities experienced feminist activity during the decade, and small groups formed in larger cities. Although part of a larger social iconoclasm that challenged traditional views on race, political conservatism, and the war in Vietnam, feminism proceeded under a more conservative banner in Alabama. Women entered professions and the job market in ever increasing numbers. Clara Stone Fields of Mobile, an honors chemistry graduate of the University of Alabama, won a seat in the legislature in 1962. She was selected as one of three outstanding legislators that year and ran for Congress unsuccessfully two years later. She lost her state seat in 1970. Several women took her place, though they turned out to be bitter opponents of the Equal Rights Amendment and other feminist causes. The resurrected League of Women Voters lost eight local chapters during the 1960s because of its generally favorable stance on the United Nations, federal antipoverty programs, and civil rights. It enrolled its first black members during the decade, although its mainly white upper and middle class membership had consistently supported reforms in the state. By the early 1970s the league became more involved with environmental, welfare, constitutional, and equal rights reforms.

Just as race permeated politics, sports, and even the agenda of the League of Women Voters, it dominated the state's literature. Monroeville novelist Harper Lee won the 1961 Pulitzer Prize for her novel *To Kill a Mockingbird*. The story of lawyer Atticus Finch and his daughter, Scout, and son, Jem, described the courageous effort of a right-thinking Alabama attorney to defend a black man accused of raping a white woman. As late as 1990 Lee's novel was still among the top ten works of fiction required by public and private high school teachers throughout the United States and had sold millions of copies in many languages. Shirley Ann Grau, a Louisiana native who lived in Montgomery during her early years, won a Pulitzer Prize in 1964 for *The Keepers of the House*, a daring novel about the effects of miscegenation on a gubernatorial race.

Black writers had long translated their racial experiences into literary energy, and Tuskegee Institute served as a primary incubator for their talent. George Wylie Henderson left his ministerial home for Tuskegee, and from there moved to New York, where he contributed to the Harlem renaissance with the publication of *Ollie Miss* in 1934. This frank and honest portrayal of an uncomplicated black woman in the rural South is one of the most compelling fictional accounts written during the decade. Oklahoma native Ralph W. Ellison followed Henderson to Tuskegee, studied music, and developed his initial interest in literature. In 1952 he completed *Invisible Man*, a memorable account of a young black man's attempt to gain recognition in the new American mass society. The novel earned Ellison a National Book Award in 1953. Critical acclaim pronounced it the finest novel written by a black novelist. Albert Murray, a Mobile native, also attended Tuskegee Institute, where he later taught literature. His *South to a Very Old Place* (1972) and *Train Whistle Guitar* (1974) established him as a significant essayist drawing deeply on the black experience in Alabama.

So the same racial forces ripping the state apart fueled its creative energy, providing subject matter for its novelists as well as a challenge to its athletic teams.

THIRTY-THREE

A Time to Heal:
Struggling to Find a New Vision,
1970–1990

THE prominence of race as a political issue steadily receded after 1972. George Wallace remained the dominant figure in state politics, continued to influence public discourse, and drove national politics to the right. But Wallace, ever the opportunist, moderated his racial views as increasing numbers of blacks registered to vote.

Birmingham, so long the national symbol of unyielding resistance to integration, experienced perhaps the most profound racial transition of any American city during the 1970s and 1980s. On June 25, 1973, the Birmingham *News* published a special magazine insert that analyzed the city ten years after the bloody confrontations of 1963. Although the articles were predictably upbeat, emphasizing how much the city and state had changed in a decade, they did not ignore problems either. In 1963 not a single black elected official had served the state; a decade later more than 120 constituted the largest number of any state in the Union. In May 1973 Chris McNair, the commercial photographer whose daughter had died in the September 1963 bombing of Sixteenth Street Baptist Church, won election to the state legislature in a countywide election. Several thousand of his votes came from whites, although the real key to his election was a low white turnout and a substantial black vote. The Jefferson County Progressive Democratic Council, organized just before the beginning of the Second World War, mobilized new black voters in forty-two units. The organization also elected attorney Arthur Shores and Miles College professor Richard Arrington, Jr., to the city council. The black voter organization became sophisticated in its endorsements. In 1970 the JCPDC refused to endorse the right-wing Democrat who challenged incumbent congressman John Buchanan, who had won election in the 1964 Goldwater sweep. Buchanan, a Southern Baptist minister with conservative fiscal policies who was remarkably liberal on race, received 35 percent of the black vote. But in 1972 Ben Erdreich, a progressive Jewish Democrat, won 97.5 percent of the black vote in a losing contest against Buchanan. In 1971 the JCPDC helped elect progressive Republican George Seibels mayor.

In 1973 West End High School contained a dramatically different student body than it had ten years earlier. The tree-shaded campus on Pearson Avenue had been the scene of major trouble when a thousand enraged white students surged into the streets to protest the presence of two new black students. By 1973 the 35 percent white student body passively accepted the nearly two-to-one black majority. In the job market the number of blacks in professional and technical jobs had nearly doubled between 1960 and 1970.

But bad news coexisted with the good. Despite the doubling of blacks in higher-paying jobs, they held only 7 percent of such positions. And the number of white students at West End declined precipitously every year as whites fled the city for the suburbs. Blacks numbered only 62 of the city's 1,200 policemen and firemen.

Older blacks accepted the slow pace of change. But younger ones chafed at the continuation of so many problems: limited access to professional jobs, the decline in the manufacturing sector that cost blacks thousands of high-paying union jobs, poor housing and health, resegregated education because of white flight, and continued police harassment. Richard Arrington, Jr., became the primary beneficiary of this resentment.

Born into a tenant farm family in rural Sumter County in October 1934, Arrington benefited from his parents' strong Primitive Baptist values and their emphasis on education. His father moved the family in 1940 to Fairfield where he took a job in the TCI steel mills so his children could attend Fairfield Industrial School. Richard Arrington attended Miles College after graduation, then took a Ph.D. in biology at the University of Oklahoma before returning to his alma mater to teach. In 1975 he played a key role in electing Democrat David Vann mayor. Vann had been one of the leading catalysts for change in Birmingham for more than a decade. He had been a leader of the Young Men's Business Club, a negotiator during the 1963 crises, the leading proponent of suburban merger with the city, and a chief advocate of legislative reapportionment. At the end of Vann's first term, Arrington broke with his old friend over the mayor's handling of the police shooting of a black woman and declared his own candidacy for mayor. In a heated election runoff Arrington narrowly beat Frank Parsons 44,800 to 42,800 by attracting 73 percent of registered blacks to the polls and picking up an estimated 10 percent of the white vote.

Arrington's 1979 inauguration was one part installation of a new mayor and nine parts black jubilee. Nationally his election was a powerful symbol of racial accommodation in a city that, due to white flight to the suburbs, was then more than 50 percent black. The new mayor's appointments were a mixture of competent young administrators and self-serving opportunists, of blacks and whites, of males and females. He presided over city government with considerable skill during a critical transition in the economy between 1979 and 1983. The development of the University of Alabama in Birmingham (UAB) Medical Center and undergraduate college, downtown renewal, and the further decline of the steel industry posed enormous challenges. Arrington attempted to diversify the economy with a creative mix of public and private funds and to enhance private development (with construction of a horse-racing track, a water theme park, and rebuilding downtown, for example). Many of his more ambitious projects failed, but he succeeded in stabilizing the economy, shifting it toward the service sector, stimulating significant downtown construction projects, and winning support of the Big Mules. He also organized a new political force in 1977, the Jefferson County Citizens Coalition, sometimes called "the Machine" because of its support of Arrington and his allies. He pushed aside older, more conservative black leaders, such as Arthur Shores and A. G. Gaston, but also increased his share of the white vote to 12 percent in his 1983 reelection triumph (70 percent of city voters went to the polls, but 77 percent of black registrants did so).

In January 1986 Arrington extended his influence statewide by forming the Alabama New South Coalition. This act culminated in a long power struggle at the state level that paralleled what had happened in Birmingham. State representative Joe Reed of Montgomery had dominated the Alabama Democratic Conference whose center of power had been the Black Belt. But ambitious urban black leaders—Arrington from Birmingham, Senator Hank Sanders, his wife Rose, and J. L. Chestnut, Jr., of Selma, and Michael Figures of Mobile—challenged Reed at a meeting of more than a thousand people at Birmingham's Boutwell Auditorium. In 1987 Arrington easily won a third term as mayor but carried only 10 percent of the white vote in a city still polarized by race.

Beyond politics perhaps the most dramatic change in Birmingham race relations was a new style of leadership. By the 1990s nearly a dozen organizations formally worked for racial harmony. Some of these—the Community Affairs Committee of Operation New Birmingham, Leadership Birmingham, and Greater Birmingham Ministries—reached major segments of both white and black communities and registered impressive service records. Others such as Police Athletic Teams and Youth Leadership Forum targeted specific audiences.

Despite all such efforts by people of goodwill, Birmingham's racial past often came back to haunt the city. During June 1990 Hall Thompson, a local businessman, made an offhand comment about the right of private country clubs to restrict membership to whomever they pleased. Unfortunately the Shoal Creek Country Club, which he founded, was about to host the 1990 Professional Golfers' Association tournament. A storm of controversy descended on Shoal Creek, the SCLC threatened demonstrations, television sponsors withdrew, and the entire event nearly collapsed. At the last minute the city's network of business and civil rights leaders, who had defused many such crises since 1972, once again prevailed. Louis Willie, respected president of Booker T. Washington Insurance Company, agreed to accept an honorary membership in Shoal Creek. The son of a Texas Pullman car porter, Willie had attended Wiley College in Marshall, Texas, and earned an MBA at the University of Michigan. A. G. Gaston had brought Willie to Birmingham in 1952, and the quiet-spoken Texan had become a racial pioneer as the first black member of the Kiwanis Club, the Downtown Club, and the Club.

Although not so well publicized, an event of even greater moral import may have been Mike Warren's resignation from the all-white Birmingham Country Club. Warren, president of Alabama Gas Company, explained: "I've been struggling with my membership in a club that did not have black members, did not have Jewish members for a while, and all the events of the last several weeks helped me make my decision."[1]

Other cities changed more slowly than Birmingham and with less media attention. In October 1974 the Council of Municipal Performance listed Montgomery as one of six cities with the most racially segregated housing in the nation. But not even the capital of the Confederacy could preserve the past inviolate. A portion of interstate highway 85 became Martin Luther King, Jr., Highway. Local attorney Morris Dees founded the Southern Poverty Law Center. After completing his undergraduate and law degrees at the University of Alabama, Dees made millions in direct mail solicitation. Early involvement in the civil rights movement led finally to his establishment of the poverty center. It became renowned for its work on behalf of black prisoners facing the death sentence, litigation to help the poor, and its damage suits on behalf of victims of violence by Ku Klux Klan and other white extremist organizations. In 1989 Dees funded a $700,000 memorial in Montgomery to forty Americans slain in the struggle for civil rights. Thirteen of them had died in Alabama, a total second only to the seventeen murdered in Mississippi.

In 1986 the late Supreme Court justice Hugo Black received belated tribute from a state in which the majority of white citizens had long considered him a traitor to its traditional views on religion and race. That year Black's alma mater hosted a symposium in honor of the 100th anniversary of his birth. University of Alabama president Joab L. Thomas commented upon the justice who probably had influenced American legal history as much as any other single person in the

Hugo L. Black, United States Senator and Associate Justice of the United States Supreme Court, was one of the most influential justices of the twentieth century. (Courtesy of the Alabama Department of Archives and History)

twentieth century: "If the South is to rise again this is the form it should take."[2] Regrettably Black, who always urged expatriate Alabama law students to return to their home state and try to make it better, did not live to see his vindication.

In southwestern Alabama the MOWA Band of Choctaws and the Poarch Band of Creeks sought to reestablish their historic rights to tribal land. Following decades of discrimination and racial segregation that had forced them to seek assimilation into the dominant white culture, they reasserted their pride as Indians during the 1970s and 1980s. In 1991 a U.S. Senate committee formally recognized the MOWA Choctaw community of 5,000 persons in Mobile and Washington counties. The Poarch Creeks had won such recognition earlier.

The pace of demographic change matched Alabama's racial transition. Black population declined 8.1 percent in the 1960s, the steepest decline in state history. By 1990 blacks constituted only one-fourth of the state's inhabitants. North Alabama grew while south Alabama's population continued to decline, and the state's rural population dropped by 2.9 percent. In 1970, 58.4 percent of Alabamians lived in towns and cities and only 41.6 percent in rural areas. Although the rural population was still large by comparison with other states, it was irreversibly declining, and more than half of Alabama's counties lost population during the 1980s. The number of farms mirrored this demography, dropping from 115,800 in 1960 to 86,000 in 1970 and to 47,000 in 1990. Farm acreage dropped just as rapidly. The total farm population had numbered 1.34

million in 1940; in 1990 it totaled only 85,600. The farms remaining were large and produced mainly for a commercial market. The average farm amounted to only 83 acres in 1940; by 1990 it contained 226 acres.

The 1980s passed into history as the worst agricultural decade since the Great Depression. Total farm acreage declined by 50 percent and land prices dropped by 25 percent, driven by the 1980 grain embargo to Russia and the worst drought in Alabama history. Only fruit and poultry farmers survived relatively unshaken. By 1989 the state's largest cash crop was an illegal one: marijuana earned an estimated $327 million, far exceeding earnings for traditional crops such as peanuts ($157 million), cotton ($119 million), and soybeans ($67 million). Although poultry producers lost chicks because of abnormally hot summers, their earnings doubled during the 1980s. Alabama followed only Arkansas and Georgia in poultry production and stood in position to take second place as the nation's appetite for healthier foods raised consumer demand. Cattle and calves trailed in second place as agricultural revenue producers. Greenhouse and nursery stock and catfish production also grew rapidly during the decade. Forest products led all agricultural products, most of them produced on small woodlots by private landowners.

Industry and business absorbed some of the displaced rural population. Much industrial growth during the 1970s occurred in rural areas or small towns, although by the 1980s this pattern had reversed.

Textile and apparel factories had led manufacturing employment for many years. The industry was especially important to rural Alabama. Its 350 mills and plants were located in all sixty-seven counties and employed 87,000 people by 1970, but that figure fell by 25,000 during the 1980s. Such industry leaders as Avondale Mills and West Point Pepperell became victims of leveraged buy-outs or outright purchase during the decade. But Russell Corporation continued to thrive on its specialty lines of sportswear and athletic uniforms. In 1990 it ranked as one of the most successful companies in the state and employed half of Alexander City's 14,000 people.

Coal mining experienced a similar decline. Although the state's two major producers, Jim Walter Resources and Drummond Corporation, mined a large amount of low-sulfur coal, production suffered from demands for cleaner fuels and fear of acid rain. Improved technology also cost jobs. During the 1980s employment in the industry dropped more than 40 percent, from 12,800 to 7,500. Although Alabama still ranked twelfth among all states in coal production, its slow growth rate was influenced heavily by international crises and growing environmental concerns.

Another industrial leader, automobile tires, also depended heavily on international market patterns. By 1990 Alabama led the nation in tire production. Plants experienced fewer labor-management confrontations than during earlier decades as foreign competition threatened the industry. By 1990 foreign companies had purchased four of the five tire manufacturing facilities in the state (Michelin in Dothan, Uniroyal Goodrich in Tuscaloosa and Opelika, which Michelin purchased, and Dunlop in Huntsville, which Sumitono bought). Only Goodyear in Gadsden remained under U.S. ownership.

The 1980s depression in the primary metals, automobile, and construction industries, which represented a disproportionately large share of the state's industrial base, worsened conditions in north Alabama. Woodward Iron Company closed the state's last iron mine in the 1970s as part of a process of replacing Alabama ore with a higher grade Venezuelan product. Nor did Birmingham's declining steel industry need the ore. By 1982 both UAB and South Central Bell employed more workers than U.S. Steel. Union labor lost high-paying jobs, which were replaced by lower-paying positions in the service and retail sectors. Businessmen generally rejoiced at the decline of unions, but they conceded that unions had raised per capita income in the city higher than that of any other metropolitan area of the Southeast and had laid the foundation for a black middle class. Even with this decline Alabama trailed only Kentucky in union membership in 1982, and the chances of a company being unionized in Birmingham stood at 50-50, the highest in the region. But Alabama's future clearly belonged to different kinds of industries such as insurance and construction.

Frank Samford, Jr., and Ronald K. Richey transformed Liberty National Insurance Company from a regional life insurance firm into the widely diversified national Torchmark Corporation, which sold financial services as well as insurance. The company won awards as one of the best managed in the industry, and its string of consecutive earnings and dividend increases after 1952 was unparalleled by any other company listed on the New York Stock Exchange.

Five Alabama construction companies ranked among the 100 largest contractors in the nation by 1989. Rust International led the way as the sixth largest, followed by BE&K (nineteenth), Harbert International (thirty-sixth), Blount Construction (fifty-fourth), and Brasfield and Gorrie, Incorporated (ninety-seventh). Although Rust and Blount experienced substantial problems during part of the 1980s, all emerged from the decade in strong condition.

By the mid-1980s Huntsville's economy was considered one of the most technologically sophisticated in the country. Although Alabama did not make a government list of twenty-four high-technology states (a categorization determined by the density of engineers, science technicians, mathematicians, natural scientists, and computer specialists), 35 percent of Alabama's engineers worked in the city. Huntsville profited from Reagan-era expenditures on the space shuttle, manned space station, and Strategic Defense Initiative ("Star Wars"). NASA budgeted 40 percent of the $8 billion budget for the space station to the Marshall Center, and Huntsville also received huge expenditures for SDI research. The state located its $22 million supercomputer in the city in the 1980s. Among five high-tech areas studied during the mid-1980s, only "Silicon Valley" in California contained a higher concentration of high-tech population than Huntsville, and such workers earned higher salaries in the "Rocket City" than in the other four.

Huntsville profited from progressive business leadership that coordinated industrial recruitment. By spending more than Birmingham or Mobile on attracting industry, and without competing efforts by numerous municipalities, Huntsville outstripped other Alabama cities. It even turned tourism to its benefit, boasting the state's largest tourist attraction, the Alabama Space and Rocket Center.

The state Department of Tourism began to promote effectively Alabama's magnificent resources during the 1980s. Birmingham turned a rusty iron mill, Sloss Furnace, into one of the nation's most significant industrial parks. The USS *Alabama* allowed visitors to examine a World War II battleship, and the Alabama Gulf Coast enjoyed unprecedented growth. Offshore from Mobile natural gas platforms dotted the Gulf of Mexico and Mobile Bay. Oil wells disgorged their treasures inland from Mobile.

Unfortunately all this regionalized prosperity masked abiding economic woes. In 1977 state leaders boasted that Alabama's unemployment rate had trailed the national average for six consecutive years, that its gross state product had grown faster than the nation's, and that its per capita income had also outpaced the national average. But the next year the economy began a nosedive that continued for a half decade, culminating in November 1982 reports that the state's unemployment rate of 15 percent led the nation. The state's 1981 per capita income was the third lowest in a twelve-state survey. The growth both in jobs and in population between 1970 and 1980 trailed all southeastern states.

Alabama's economic difficulties continued through the 1980s. The historic transition from manufacturing to service jobs—what one imaginative report called the "shift from mills to malls"—accelerated. Most of the new jobs created in the South during the decade occurred in services and trades. Whereas Alabama manufacturing accounted for one of every three nonfarm workers in 1969, that proportion declined to one in four twenty years later. Trade and service industries added 178,000 workers during the 1980s. Government jobs helped also. Such employment accounted for nearly 20 percent of Alabama's work force, the fourth

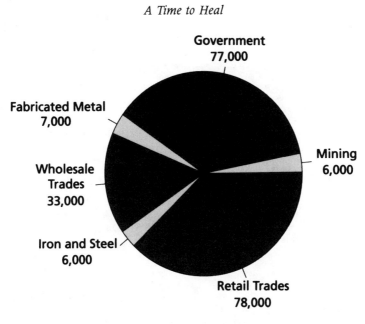

Government
77,000

Fabricated Metal
7,000

Mining
6,000

Wholesale
Trades
33,000

Iron and Steel
6,000

Retail Trades
78,000

Employment in the Birmingham Metropolitan Area, 1990

highest of any Southern state. The Birmingham metropolitan area demonstrated this pattern perfectly.

Racial and gender patterns changed also. Women held 44 percent of Alabama's jobs in 1989, up from 31 percent in 1969. Conversely, black men actually occupied a smaller percentage of jobs than twenty years before. And though black women constituted 12 percent of the work force, they filled one-third of the service jobs and only 3 percent of the managerial positions.

Alabama's economic ranking among ten Southern states remained near the bottom. The state did move up in per capita income rankings during the 1980s but remained ranked in the midforties among all states. In 1987 Alabamians took home 77.1 percent of the average U.S. income; in 1988 their share slipped to 76.6 percent.

As a new century neared, Alabama's economy remained sharply divided, with one-fifth of its people poor, one-third of its babies born into poverty, one-fifth of its population uninsured, and one-eighth of its people functionally illiterate. In 1980 Alabama was the third-poorest state in the nation, having slipped one spot from fourth in 1970. In 1990, twenty-nine Alabama counties contained no obstetrician/

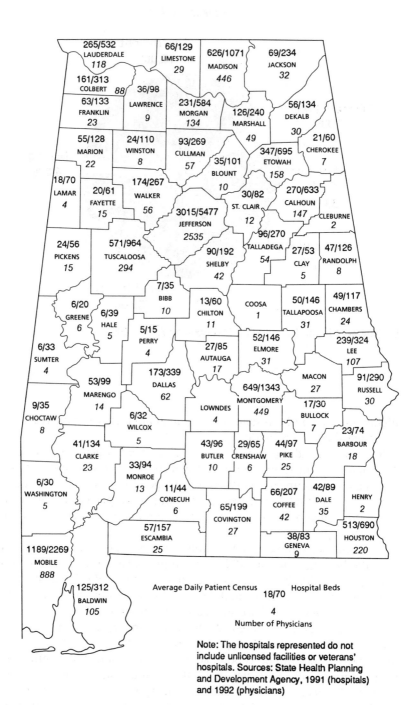

265/532 LAUDERDALE 118	66/129 LIMESTONE 29	626/1071 MADISON 446	69/234 JACKSON 32

161/313 COLBERT 88

36/98 LAWRENCE 9

63/133 FRANKLIN 23

231/584 MORGAN 134

126/240 MARSHALL 49

56/134 DEKALB 30

55/128 MARION 22

24/110 WINSTON 8

93/269 CULLMAN 57

35/101 BLOUNT 10

347/695 ETOWAH 158

21/60 CHEROKEE 7

18/70 LAMAR 4

20/61 FAYETTE 15

174/267 WALKER 56

3015/5477 JEFFERSON 2535

30/82 ST. CLAIR 12

270/633 CALHOUN 147

CLEBURNE 2

24/56 PICKENS 15

571/964 TUSCALOOSA 294

90/192 SHELBY 42

96/270 TALLADEGA 54

27/53 CLAY 5

47/126 RANDOLPH 8

7/35 BIBB 10

13/60 CHILTON 11

COOSA 1

50/146 TALLAPOOSA 31

49/117 CHAMBERS 24

6/20 GREENE 6

6/39 HALE 5

5/15 PERRY 4

27/85 AUTAUGA 17

52/146 ELMORE 31

239/324 LEE 107

6/33 SUMTER 4

53/99 MARENGO 14

173/339 DALLAS 62

MACON 27

649/1343 MONTGOMERY 449

91/290 RUSSELL 30

9/35 CHOCTAW 8

6/32 WILCOX 5

LOWNDES 4

17/30 BULLOCK 7

23/74 BARBOUR 18

41/134 CLARKE 23

33/94 MONROE 13

43/96 BUTLER 10

29/65 CRENSHAW 6

44/97 PIKE 25

6/30 WASHINGTON 5

11/44 CONECUH 6

65/199 COVINGTON 27

66/207 COFFEE 42

42/89 DALE 35

HENRY 2

57/157 ESCAMBIA 25

38/83 GENEVA 9

513/690 HOUSTON 220

1189/2269 MOBILE 888

125/312 BALDWIN 105

Average Daily Patient Census 18/70 Hospital Beds

4

Number of Physicians

Note: The hospitals represented do not include unlicensed facilities or veterans' hospitals. Sources: State Health Planning and Development Agency, 1991 (hospitals) and 1992 (physicians)

Health Care in Alabama, 1991/92

gynecologist. The private Center on Budget and Policy Priorities announced in 1988 that Alabama was one of only four states that met none of its ten adequacy standards measuring the effectiveness of government aid programs for the poor. And Alabama's infant mortality rate led the nation during the mid-1980s before improving slightly at the end of the decade.

Contrasting economic conditions revealed shocking inequities. Per capita income in the wealthy Birmingham suburb of Mountain Brook in 1987 reached $33,135; that same year per capita income in the Lowndes County town of Mosses amounted to only $1,473. In Birmingham in 1979, 22.0 percent of the population lived in poverty; in Mobile the poverty rate was 18.6 percent; in Montgomery, 19.4 percent; in Huntsville, 12.8 percent; in Mountain Brook, 2.6 percent.

A question that often puzzled state leaders involved a basic assumption that had long prevailed among Alabama businessmen. They believed that assiduous recruiting, low taxes, various tax exemptions and state bonds for factory construction, anti-union policies, and cheap labor would draw new industry into Alabama. This infusion would build the economic infrastructure and slowly but surely improve the state's standing compared to other less probusiness states. Thus it was a shock when another privately funded study by the Corporation for Enterprise Development in 1987 gave Alabama F's in all four of its economic categories, while extending A's to such states as Massachusetts, New York, New Jersey, Maryland, and Pennsylvania. Even worse news came from the report's summary: "Except for Florida, the Southeast suffers the legacy of poverty and smokestack-chasing. Almost uniformly, state economies are performing poorly; decades of underdevelopment have left them with little capacity on which to build." Only Tennessee among Southern states shared Alabama's straight F's. The same organization raised Alabama's score to two D's, a C, and a B in 1990. But when evaluating development capacity, the report summarized: "Held back by inadequate educational resources, a below average financial sector, and an uneven technological infrastructure, Alabama faces a serious investment challenge when it comes to critical development resources."[3]

The low taxes designed to attract business had strangled Alabama's schools, crippled its public health programs, and limited development of its cultural resources. In 1988 Alabama ranked fiftieth in property taxes, forty-first in corporate income taxes, fiftieth in expenditures for elementary and secondary education, and fiftieth in spending for public welfare. A low-skill manufacturing economy depended on none of these elements, but a high-tech, information-based economy required all of them. So, in an ironic twist of history, the very policies Alabama businessmen and politicians had cultivated for a century to attract business had in fact prevented the best and most stable companies from locating there. By the 1990s much of the state's business leadership complained about the state's cultural and educational environment, which was often cited as the reason high-technology businesses located plants in other Southern states.

In 1991–92 Alabama spent $3,600 per pupil for elementary and high school education, compared to a regional average of $5,100. Alabama ranked forty-third in teacher salaries in 1992. Between 1985 and 1987 four of Birmingham's ten high schools produced no student who scored at or above the national average in reading, language, or science. Of the six remaining high schools, 17 percent was the highest percentage of students scoring at or above the national average. Employers across the state complained that high school graduates could not perform high school–level work. One obvious reason for this anomaly was that the Alabama high school exit examination used in 1988 tested at a level of late fifth grade rather than late twelfth grade, and it allowed students to retest repeatedly. Although 99 percent of the students ultimately passed the exam, they often exhibited reading and computational skills at a grammar school level. And nearly one-third of Alabama's students dropped out before completing high school.

By 1990 state newspapers conducted numerous detailed studies of tax rates as one source of educational and welfare deficiencies. In 1972 the state had adopted a three-layered assessment of property. Most individual property owners were assessed at 15 percent of value, but huge tracts of forest and agricultural lands were appraised in a similar manner thanks to aggressive lobbying by the Farm Bureau and the Forestry Association. In 1978 these same interests pushed through a "current use" concept that allowed assessment of land to be based on how it was used rather than on its real market value. Tracts of timberland in the middle of a city could be assessed at the same rate as a remote plot in a swamp. While the tax burden on large landowners declined, state and local sales taxes levied without regard for ability to pay increased.

So Alabama entered the last decade of the century with some of the most regressive taxes in the United States, a system that taxed heaviest those least able to pay. By the 1990s even many progressive businessmen clamored for tax reform.

The 1990 reelection bid by a Republican chief executive demonstrated how fundamentally politics had changed. In 1920 Alabama was the domain of "yellow dog Democrats," so called because they would have voted for a canine had it appeared on the party's ballot. But by 1990 the state contained not a few "yellow dog Republicans" who were just as loyal to their party and who voted a straight ticket regardless of candidate. The rise of a viable Republican party in many counties forced a higher level of discipline on Democrats. Black voting patterns also changed dramatically, splitting along class, gender, and personality lines.

Despite his physical confinement to a wheelchair, George Wallace towered above Alabama's political landscape. No man since Huey Long of Louisiana had so completely dominated a Southern state. Wallace governed through an inner cabinet composed of close associates—his brother Gerald, Henry B. Steagall, Billy Joe Camp, Elvin Stanton, and Bill Rushton. While other Southern states elected a succession of so-called New South governors, Alabama remained mesmerized by Wallace.

Although commentators disagreed over what constituted a "New South" governor, two characteristics predominated: a break with racial politics (Georgia's Jimmy Carter, Arkansas's Dale Bumpers, and Florida's Reuben Askew were examples) and emphasis on educational reform (North Carolina's Jim Hunt, Mississippi's William Winter, Tennessee's Lamar Alexander, and South Carolina's Dick Riley, for example). Alabama voters did not lack candidates for this distinction. In fact a number ran against the Wallaces: Ryan deGraffenried before his untimely death in a plane crash during the 1966 governor's race; Albert Brewer, who had perhaps the best reform credentials and barely lost to Wallace in 1970; Lieutenant Governor George McMillan, who narrowly lost to Wallace in 1982 when Wallace received 30 percent of the black vote after a tearful apology for his earlier career of race baiting.

In between Wallace's 1974 and 1982 victories, businessman Forrest ("Fob") James traveled the state in a yellow school bus promising educational reform and progressive government. He won because he was perceived as an outsider, a businessman who offered professionalism and vision after the Wallace era of cronyism and confrontation. But in office James was inept and contradictory. After campaigning as a take-charge activist governor, he refused to use the governor's prerogatives to organize the legislature or influence its proceedings. Although James promised businesslike efficiency, in fact disorganization and indecision characterized his four-year term. After running a campaign as a progressive advocate of improving the quality of life in Alabama, he refused to support tax reforms that would have funded such change. Unfortunately James served during a time of sharp economic downturn and national depression, which might have thwarted an even more adroit reformer.

One of the few positive elements in the state's political life at the time was a sweeping judicial reform program begun by Alabama Supreme Court chief justice Howell Heflin. The plan, when enacted during the 1970s, made Alabama a leader in judicial reform and led to Heflin's election to the U.S. Senate.

601

In 1986 Lieutenant Governor Bill Baxley tried to recombine the old New Deal coalition, minus its racism. Rallying blacks, unionists, and north Alabama farmers, Baxley locked in a photo-finish runoff with Attorney General Charles Graddick in the Democratic primary election. Although Graddick won by a few thousand votes, the supreme court threw out the results because Graddick had actively solicited Republicans to vote in the Democratic primary. In a state where citizens were not only unaccustomed to party primaries but, in fact, did not know what they were, voters expressed their fury in the November general election by selecting an obscure farmer as governor. Guy Hunt smashed Baxley with a vote of 696,000 to 537,000 to become the first Republican governor of Alabama since Reconstruction.

Graddick's decision to withdraw as a write-in candidate just before the general election may have sealed Hunt's victory. Some wealthy businessmen and lobbyists helped Graddick reach his decision by contributing $250,000 to pay off his campaign debts. Subsequently Graddick switched his affiliation to the Republican party and campaigned for Hunt's reelection in 1990.

Governor Hunt turned the Wallace crowd out of state government, named some worthy replacements to his cabinet, boosted tourism, improved the state's shabby national image, aggressively recruited industry, and strengthened the Republican party statewide by appointing members of his own party to vacancies at the local level. But he fell far short of the New South standard. He faced an uncooperative Democratic legislature despite steady gains made by Republicans. In 1983 only three Republicans served in the senate and only eight in the house. By 1989, eight of thirty-five senators and 22 of 105 members in the house represented the GOP. Hunt led a move to depose Wallace's speaker of the house, Tom Drake of Cullman, whom businessmen disliked, and supported Eufaula's Jimmy Clark. Historically, Alabama governors had chosen the speaker and decided who would chair key committees, but in 1975 Lieutenant Governor Jere Beasley had begun the practice of organizing the senate himself. In 1987 Clark did the same, charting an independent legislative agenda for the lower house. Together with Taylor Harper of Grand Bay, who chaired the house Ways and Means Committee, they frustrated Hunt's legislative agenda at every turn.

Even had Hunt enjoyed a cooperative relationship with house Democrats, his own party contained substantial internal division. Hunt represented the older hill country Republican tradition that traced its origins back to differences between north and south Alabama over secession, slavery, and planter domination. Confined mainly to a tier of counties adjacent to Winston and Cullman counties this wing of the party had few members and little influence. In 1986 the Republicans had pretty much conceded the governor's office before Democratic infighting opened the door for Hunt.

Larger and more influential elements of the GOP came from other sources. White-flight Democrats switched parties out of disgust over integration, school busing, and various other racial grievances. Special interests, especially the forest products interests and the Farmers Federation (as the old Farm Bureau was called, now identified as ALFA), desired whichever candidate would best protect the current-use tax law and Alabama-based insurance companies (which had become a chief concern of the Farm Bureau because of its Farm Bureau Insurance Company). Well-educated urban businessmen desired to reform education, bring order to the state's chaotic and outmoded tax structure, and move beyond racial politics. Within the state GOP all these elements vied for influence. Winton M. Blount III (Red Blount's son), Alabama Power chief executive officer Elmer Harris, and other progressive businessmen sought meaningful tax and educational reform. But Hunt's legislative liaison, Joe McCorquodale, owned large timber tracts himself and attentively represented the interests of the Farmers Federation and the Forestry Association.

Hunt, overwhelmed by the office, vacillated between wings of his party and ended his first term with claims of extensive economic modernization not supported by figures on per capita income and poverty rates. Republican maverick representative William Slaughter of Mountain Brook left the legislature in frustration in 1990, blasting both parties and all recent chief executives: "We haven't had in my lifetime the dynamic and effective leadership that's truly needed to transform the state, to give people a real sense of their lost opportunities and the vision necessary to make them ready to reclaim their lost opportunities."[4]

Slaughter could have added that most Alabama voters refused to pay the price to create a New South state even had they elected such a leader. Like most voters, Alabamians wanted progress in education, health, and jobs and higher per capita incomes. But they desired all these at no sacrifice to themselves. They routinely defeated local referenda to raise tax revenues for schools, arguing that existing funds could do the job except for waste, mismanagement, and incompetent teachers. Vital improvements in cultural resources depended almost entirely on private philanthropy.

In 1990 Guy Hunt began his reelection bid with a strong public approval rating, all the advantages of incumbency, and a nearly twenty-point lead in the polls. Former governor Fob James, Congressman Ronnie Flippo, Attorney General Don Siegelman, and AEA lobbyist Paul Hubbert led the hotly contested Democratic field. Black political organizations and leaders, reflecting their growing maturity and strength, gave

Siegelman and Hubbert most of their backing but offered some support to Flippo and James as well. Hunt branded runoff opponents Siegelman and Hubbert as liberals who would raise taxes and expressed delight when Hubbert won the runoff.

Although Hubbert did represent organized educators, appealed to unionists for support, and won the endorsement of black organizations, he tried to take the political middle ground by condemning the coddling of prisoners and the parole of criminals convicted of violent crimes, attacking welfare, and opposing abortion and gun control. He also supported retired banker Willard L. ("Jack") Hurley as chairman of the State Democratic Executive Committee to try to win the support of business.

Both campaigns were well financed by special interests. Wealthy business people, the Farmers Federation, the Forestry Association, the Business Council of Alabama, and others contributed more than $5 million to Hunt. Unions, blacks, trial lawyers, teachers, dog-racing interests, and others contributed about the same amount to Hubbert. Although Hubbert pulled even in the last days of the campaign, a last-minute Hunt media blitz identifying Hubbert with a black education lobbyist and the National Education Association's support for the rights of homosexual teachers, combined with the defection by some 10 to 20 percent of black voters, cost Hubbert the election.

Hunt's victory was entirely personal, as the entire slate of Republican candidates for state office lost badly. High Republican hopes in legislative races, where an unprecedented twenty-four Republicans ran for the senate and fifty-eight for the house, evaporated when the party balance in the legislature remained the same as in the previous session. In his loss Hubbert had united his party and instilled discipline, underscoring the fact that one effect of the gains made by the GOP during the 1980s was the increasing pressure it applied on Democrats.

Republican Bill Cabaniss ran a proenvironmental campaign against incumbent Democrat U.S. senator Howell Heflin. Although the senator was himself a millionaire, he ridiculed Cabaniss, who lived in the state's wealthiest community of Mountain Brook, as a "Gucci-clothed, Mercedes-driving, polo-playing, Jacuzzi-soaking, Perrier-drinking, Aspen-skiing, Grey Poupon, richie rich, high society Republican who has a summer home at Kennebunkport, but who eats broccoli."[5] It was not a cerebral issue, but it brought gales of laughter from populistic Democratic audiences.

Reformers received little encouragement from governor or legislature. In 1973 the nationally constituted Citizens Conference on State Legislatures rated the Alabama legislature the poorest in the nation in terms of equipment needed to function properly. Although subsequent legislatures created a fiscal office and a reference service, the state's law-making entity continued to rank near the bottom nationally in the size of staff available to assist legislators. Because most part-time legislators had no secretaries and little access to research staffs, they turned to lobbyists for information. Well-funded special interests thus gained a disproportionate influence in legislative proceedings by providing data quickly on any issue affecting them. Even lobbyists began to refer to themselves as "Alabama's third house" in tribute to their influence. Funded by political action committees, lobbyists tended to shape the political process to a greater extent than elected representatives.

Lax, ineffective, or poorly designed ethics laws allowed state officials to take money from these interests as campaign contributions even as matters affecting their interests awaited action. Scandals involving such payoffs became increasingly frequent, as did the defense that such practices were common among officeholders. In fact Governor Hunt's second term was punctuated by charges of ethics violations, including use of state aircraft to fly to preaching engagements where he received "love offerings" and illegal diversion of campaign and inaugural funds to pay personal debts. On April 22, 1993, a Montgomery circuit court jury convicted the governor of illegally transferring funds from an inaugural account to his personal account. He thus became Alabama's first sitting governor to be convicted of a felony and removed from office. Jim Folsom, son and namesake of the former governor and lieutenant governor at the time, acceded to the governorship that same day.

Meanwhile urban legislators, finally given a proportional share of seats because of court rulings, feuded among themselves. In 1990 Jefferson County's eighteen-member house delegation, the state's largest, included nine Republicans and nine Democrats: ten whites, and eight blacks. All of the blacks were Democrats, and nine of the ten whites were Republicans. Members from the suburbs opposed a chairman from the city, and city representatives resented suburbanites. Often the bitterness of clashes within Jefferson County's delegation exceeded that of party clashes and racial divisions in the legislature itself.

So as the century neared its end, economic and political conditions in Alabama had not changed much. In fact, the 1918 Russell Sage Foundation report, which chided Alabamians for strangling their schools and mental institutions with low taxes, appeared as valid an indictment in 1990 as it had nearly three-quarters of a century earlier. Change tended to come as it usually had—when an outraged citizen initiated litigation that resulted in judicial intervention. White Alabamians prided themselves on maintaining states' rights. Yet their century-long shirking of leadership capable of solving their own problems created a familiar pattern: in 1915 and 1919 the legislature refused to enfranchise women, so finally Congress did so; the 1901 constitution required the legislature to reapportion itself every ten years, something it never did until the U.S. Supreme Court compelled such action in the 1960s; the state discriminated against blacks in education, public accommodations, and hiring policies until the courts intervened; the Democratic party denied blacks and Republicans fair representation through at-large elections until the Supreme Court mandated single-unit districts; federal judges assumed control of the state's prison and mental health systems because citizens would not tax themselves to provide humane treatment for prisoners or the mentally ill; and in the 1990s underfunded school districts in poor counties once again sought judicial redress for educational funding that favored wealthy communities. On March 31, 1993, Montgomery judge Eugene Reese declared Alabama's system of funding education to be unconstitutional because it discriminated against rural and handicapped students. Once again, as so many times in the past, judicial leadership forced Alabamians to face problems long ignored by their elected officials.

THIRTY-FOUR

Gender, "Jocks," and Shakespeare: Alabama Society and Culture, 1970–1993

ALABAMA'S society and culture as the twentieth century came to a close reflected the glacial pace of economic and political change. The status of women demonstrated both the tenacious hold of tradition and the slow inroads of modernity. Only a handful of women served in the legislature before the late 1970s. After the 1976 elections, for the first time in history, two women served as state lawmakers at the same time. Three more joined them in 1978, including Louphenia Thomas of Birmingham, the first black woman legislator. The 1978 delegation also included two Mobile women who would serve ably into the 1990s.

Republican Ann Bedsole and Democrat Mary Stephen Zoghby won acclaim for their efforts on behalf of historic preservation and women's issues. Bedsole broke with Governor Hunt and many members of her party in the 1990s by opposing a stringent antiabortion law proposed by her colleagues. She also became the first Republican woman elected to both the house and the senate. Bedsole received some female company in February 1993 when Sandra Escott-Russell won a special election in Jefferson County and became the first black woman to take a seat in the upper chamber. Democrat Pat Davis from Birmingham proved that women could also exemplify the seamy side of Alabama politics when she was indicted and convicted of extorting bribes.

Women won political posts in cities throughout the state. Female mayors served Anniston, Auburn, and many smaller communities. In 1971 Nina Miglionico won reelection and Angie Proctor won a first term to the Birmingham city council, where they generally voted with two blacks in favor of progressive legislation. In 1975 the first black woman, Bessie Estelle, won a council seat.

These victories reflected a more profound change in Birmingham's leadership patterns. Women had always exercised influence within spheres traditionally reserved for them, but during these decades they broadened their circle of influence. A 1988 Birmingham *Post-Herald* survey to determine the city's leading women discovered some interesting patterns. Many were wives and mothers who had begun their careers late. Family court judge Sandra H. Ross earned a bachelor's degree in English from Birmingham-Southern College, taught high school for two years, then quit to become a full-time mother. At age twenty-nine she enrolled in Samford University's Cumberland School of Law, which afforded many nontraditional women students a new career. Active in many aspects of child welfare reform statewide, Ross also participated in a wide range of civic activities.

Sheila Blair was an outsider who earned influence by her own efficiency, industry, and vision. Blair brought a sociology degree from Vassar College and a distinctive Northern accent to Birmingham. Following twenty years of full-time work as a mother, wife, and civic volunteer, she took a master's degree in education from UAB and in 1982 became executive director of Leadership Birmingham. Known for her empathy and efficiency, she helped turn Leadership Birmingham into one of the city's most important resources. Its year-long leadership classes brought together blacks and whites, labor unionists and CEOs, Jews, Catholics, and Protestants where they could confidentially and frankly discuss community problems. They learned to respect different opinions and to appreciate each other despite ideological and policy differences. Between 1984 and 1989, 222 people participated in the program, including 50 women. From these classes came many of the leaders who defused the 1990 Shoal Creek controversy and other potential fire storms. Other cities copied the Leadership Birmingham pattern, and in 1990 it became the prototype of Leadership Alabama, which sought to build a problem-solving network statewide to provide the leadership and vision so long missing from the state's political discourse. Leadership Alabama's founders came from the more progressive junior ranks of Alabama business: Bill Smith (CEO, Royal Cup Coffee, Birmingham), Mike Jenkins (CEO, Jenkins Brick Company, Montgomery), and Winton M. Blount III (CEO, Blount and Associates, Montgomery).

One of the chief participants in both leadership programs was a remarkable black woman, Odessa Woolfolk. Of all the women nominated in the *Post-Herald* poll, Woolfolk received the most votes. A native of the city's Titusville community, she earned a bachelor's degree in history and political science from Talladega College and went on to graduate school in California. After earning a master's degree in urban studies from Occidental College in Los Angeles, she did additional graduate work at the University of Chicago and Yale. She became director of the Center for Urban Affairs at UAB in 1980 and special assistant to the president for community relations in 1988. An energetic problem solver as popular in the white community as in the black, she received frequent mention in the 1990s as a possible successor to Richard Arrington as mayor of Birmingham.

Although religious and family values mandated a traditional maternal and housewifely role for women, economic reality dictated that nearly half of Alabama's labor force consist of females in 1990, with the percentage growing every year. In Birmingham Dr. Judy Merritt presided over Jefferson State Junior College so professionally that she was named as one of the top community college administrators in the nation. In 1988 Mary Richards came to Auburn University as dean of the College of Liberal Arts, largest academic division of the university and the largest liberal arts program in the state. Montgomery's June M. Collier headed National Industries, one of the ten largest producers of automotive wiring systems in the world.

Such success did not come without resistance. When Laurie Thrasher brought her art degree to Birmingham from the University of Wisconsin, she hoped to open a small pottery shop. Instead she gained employment as an assembly line worker at U.S. Pipe. After being laid off, she went to work as one of sixteen female coal miners among 600 male U.S. Steel miners. She encountered resentment from male miners who refused to help women lift fifty-five-gallon 200-pound oil drums or set timber supports. So women learned to help each other with such tasks. Two women who worked at the Jim Walter Resources coal mine in Brookwood encountered more bellicose opposition in 1979 when they began distributing the Socialist Workers party newspaper. In a throwback to the 1930s, someone burned their cars during a work shift. The fact that all three women were militant unionists may have had as much to do with male harassment as the fact that they were women. Despite much progress, only 5.7 percent of state legislators were women in 1991. That figure put the state ahead only of Kentucky and Louisiana. Nationwide, women constituted 17 percent of state legislators. Nonetheless, Alabama women slowly obtained recognition long denied them. When American historians in 1993 selected the most distinguished women of the twentieth century, two of the top ten were Alabamians: Rosa Parks (number three) and Helen Keller (number nine).

Education changed less dramatically during the 1980s than other aspects of public life. Alabama ranked at or near the bottom of all states in the proportion of its citizens who had graduated from high school and college. In 1980, 500,000 people aged twenty-five or older had completed less than eight years of school, and 142,000 of these people had finished less than four years. Almost all Alabamians agreed that education was in deep trouble, but they divided almost evenly about the cause of the trouble and its remedy. Information surveys confirmed what low standardized scores already had suggested: many Alabamians were woefully ignorant about the world in which they lived. Only 18 percent knew the name of the state's lieutenant governor in 1989 and only 23 percent could name at least one U.S. congressman from Alabama. A 1990 survey of 1,033 high school students in twelve schools revealed that 66 percent could not explain capitalism, only 49 percent knew that Karl Marx wrote the *Communist Manifesto*, 86 percent did not know when the Civil War occurred, and 55 percent could not correctly identify the Holocaust. Only 24 percent knew that Martin Luther led the sixteenth-century Protestant Reformation. Many students identified the leading Protestant reformer as the pope or as Jim Bakker of the PTL Club.

When Southern Opinion Research pollsters asked in 1989 whether the major problems facing public schools consisted of lack of money or unwise use of existing funds, 37 percent of the respondents said lack of money and 45 percent cited unwise expenditures. Although a slight majority expressed willingness to pay higher taxes for school improvement, poll data demonstrated convincingly that educational reform and funding increases went hand in hand.

Actually Alabama had always spent an above-average share of total state revenue on education, but the state's poverty combined with waste and duplication to cripple the system. During the integration crisis of the 1950s state legislators had officially renounced the state's responsibility to provide a system of public schools. As a consequence educators had pushed for a system that would earmark specified taxes solely for education. They succeeded in having most growth revenue sources such as sales taxes reserved for education. Because Alabama's property taxes were the lowest in the United States, this stable funding base contributed less than in other states. By 1982 Alabama earmarked a higher percentage of state revenue (an estimated 88 percent) for education than any other state. As a result of its funding structure, revenues for schools expanded rapidly during boom times only to collapse during economic recessions.

The growth period of the mid-1960s produced huge revenue increases that were earmarked for education and could not be used to meet desperate problems in other sectors. Educators and legislators sought ways to expend funds, and although representatives of higher education and kindergarten through twelfth grade initially fought over distribution of the money, they finally agreed to a proportional split.

Legislators freely admitted that public schools in the districts of powerful committee chairmen flourished while schools elsewhere languished. Supporters argued that such specially designated funds were necessary to pass education budgets. The cochairman of the powerful senate Finance and Taxation Committee explained in 1990: "All of this special money or pork money has a purpose. In order to get the budgets passed you've got to give these people a reason to vote for it or else we'd wallow around down there [in Montgomery] for days as we have in the past."

Many educators opposed the system but few (if any) refused to accept the money when offered. Reform senator Mac Parsons of Hueytown believed the system would not change so long as influential legislators believed pork greased the levers of the budget machine. As he analyzed: "It's a hell of a notion that you've got to put a bribe in the budget to get legislators to support something."[1]

Colleges participate in the same process. In 1963 Representative Rankin Fite of Hamilton suggested to Governor Wallace the creation of five junior colleges and five trade schools funded by a two-cent beer tax. Wallace agreed to the proposal, which expanded during the following quarter century into a forty-two-school organization. By 1989 these schools enrolled 64,000 students in a network larger than both major state university systems and claiming one-fifth the state's total budget for higher education.

In 1989 the Birmingham *News* assigned a four-person team of reporters to study the junior college/trade school system, and the resulting six-part series leveled a multitude of charges. The far-flung system had developed the strongest political constituency of any part of education. Seven two-year college educators served in the legislature, where they often voted on matters affecting their own schools and jobs. Two of the legislators, neither of whom possessed a college degree, became college presidents after they became legislators. Wasteful duplication reigned supreme, with three schools each in Birmingham, Mobile, and Gadsden and two in a number of other towns. Legislative horse trading had produced a bizarre salary structure: one barber who taught his skill to state prison inmates earned $46,073 for the 1988–89 school year. That was $17,204 more than a physics professor earned after four years of teaching experience at Jefferson State Junior College and more than the average salary paid to full professors at Auburn University. Because the presidents of two-year schools usually came from secondary educational backgrounds and encountered competition for funding from the four-year system, they became more closely aligned to high schools than to colleges. Fred Gainous, the first black chancellor of the junior college system, tried to reshape it in 1989, merging campuses, modernizing curricula, and curtailing extravagant salaries paid to poorly educated trade school faculty. He sought to coordinate a system where every campus had operated as a private fiefdom.

Lack of coordination also existed in the four-year colleges despite the creation of the Alabama Commission on Higher Education during the Brewer administration. The agency had little real authority, and one chancellor after another suffered the ignominy of being ignored by college presidents who took their funding requests directly to local legislators.

Eliminating politics from higher education proved an impossible task. For example, in April 1990 the legislature approved a controversial bill sought by Wallace State Community College in Cullman County to establish a new physical therapy program. The program duplicated one at nearby UAB. But powerful Wallace State president James Bailey won support from the lieutenant governor and governor, both of whom came from Cullman County, and from powerful legislators Tom Drake of Cullman and Bill Bowling of Hanceville.

Joseph Sutton, director of the Alabama Commission on Higher Education, opposed the program. Sutton decried the academic standards of a college that aspired to four-year status so that it could offer a baccalaureate degree in shirt painting. Representative Bowling responded that Wallace State was the only two-year college offering three levels of T-shirt painting courses that trained workers for three north Alabama industries: "You stood up there and made a mockery of shirt painting," he chided Sutton.[2] The legislature approved the new program despite state financial problems that resulted in a 6.5 percent proration of the education budget for the 1990–91 year.

Nor were four-year colleges blameless. Governor Wallace manipulated political friends into the presidencies of several of these institutions. Troy State president Ralph Adams used his friendship with Governor George Wallace to build one of the most far-flung college empires in the United States, with campuses in Dothan and Montgomery as well as on military bases at Fort Rucker, Fort Benning in Georgia, and in various foreign countries. Auburn University administrators allowed duplicate nursing schools to exist forty-five miles apart and a duplicate agricultural research facility on Interstate 85, only twenty miles away from one on the main campus. Administrators of the three-campus University of Alabama system permitted engineering schools at all three. In fact, Alabama entered the 1990s with seven engineering programs in a state that was smaller both in population and in square miles than Georgia, which had only a single engineering program at Georgia Tech.

Surveys during the 1980s of the best "category one" research universities in the nation included none of Alabama's institutions in its listings, and except for some programs at the UAB medical school, virtually no national peer ratings included distinguished departments or programs from Alabama universities.

Despite the lack of institution-wide strength, individual pockets of distinction existed in many universities. The absence of a major research focus hurt the national reputations of both major state universities, but the emphasis on teaching and state problem solving compensated somewhat for the deficiency in primary research. Methodist-affiliated Birmingham-Southern College continued a century-long tradition of excellence that brought recognition in virtually every survey of undergraduate liberal arts education. Talladega College and Tuskegee University also provided some excellent programs. Samford University developed into a respected private regional university. In 1990 Presbyterian layman Ralph Beeson, who had already given Samford millions of dollars for its schools of education and theology, left the Baptist university a bequest of nearly $39 million, the largest private contribution to a college in Alabama history. Samford's Cumberland School of Law provided a valuable resource for the state, as did its Beeson Divinity School. Many divisions of UAB's medical college excelled. In 1989 medical college faculty won five grants totaling $17 million for AIDS research. The University of Alabama in Huntsville attracted comparable support for aerophysics research. In 1990 the army and NASA projected contracts and grants to UAH over a two-decade period estimated at $100 million. During one ten-day period of 1990 UAH received contracts in excess of $22 million. Auburn equaled these feats with grants to agriculture, fisheries, engineering, and physics, relying especially heavily on Strategic Defense Initiative grants. Regional universities such as South Alabama, Troy State, Jacksonville State, Livingston, and North Alabama continued to provide low-cost quality undergraduate teaching programs.

All the research universities provided an important multiplier effect for local economies. In 1988 UAB ranked forty-third among American universities in acquiring federal research monies and twentieth in biomedical research funds obtained from the National Institutes of Health. It generated an estimated $818 million for Birmingham's economy. By 1990 UAB accounted directly or indirectly for 43,500 jobs, making it by far the area's largest employer. Like many new downtown campuses, UAB became deeply involved in urban problem solving. Perhaps more than any other single institution in Birmingham, UAB restored a sense of pride and accomplishment to the Magic City and stabilized its economy. Auburn, UAB, and the University of Alabama's Tuscaloosa campus all sponsored successful "incubator" programs for small businesses and produced spin-off companies from university research.

National surveys of the leading factors that attract high-tech firms to locate in an area mention good public schools, respected research universities, and strong cultural programs. Although many Alabamians considered stock car racing, country music, and the annual Alabama-Auburn football game all the culture they needed, well-educated scientists and engineers often looked for more. Outside the major cities in Alabama they found little, and many believed even metropolitan areas were lacking. Nevertheless, the emergence of a substantial number of wealthy, native-born business people during the decades after the Second World War began to change the cultural landscape.

Long rich in folk culture, Alabama finally began to produce comparable excellence in elite culture. Charles Ireland, CEO of Vulcan Materials Company, contributed generously to the Birmingham Museum of Art. Montgomery businessman Winton ("Red") Blount and his wife Carolyn donated 100 acres of land and $21 million in 1984 to construct a theater complex to house the Alabama Shakespeare Festival. The professional repertory company attracted critical acclaim and a faithful following as a fine regional theater. Blount's gift was the second largest contribution to the arts made by any American during that year. The Shakespeare Festival demonstrated that the arts could change a society, however grudgingly. When fundamentalist religious groups and others attacked the National Endowment for the Arts, which provided support for the theater, festival patrons filled up petitions deploring this politicizing of the arts. A 1990 festival production of Molière's *Tartuffe* featured a love affair between a black Valere and a white Mariane. Some in the audience sensed the irony of an interracial kiss onstage before an audience of Alabamians where, only a generation earlier, Citizens' Council toughs had beaten native son Nat King Cole for having the audacity to sing and play the piano before a white audience.

Such respect for the fine arts did not diminish the enormous appreciation for popular and folk culture rooted so deeply in ordinary citizens of both races. Lionel Richie began life in Tuskegee as the son of a teacher mother and an army captain father. While attending Tuskegee Institute, he formed a band called "the Commodores." In 1969 the band played a gig in Small's Paradise Club in Harlem and two years later won its first recording contract with Motown Records. That began a career in which Richie matched the popular success of Nat King Cole and other musical predecessors. In 1986 he won an Oscar for the best song in a movie, which also won Best Song of the Year. His hit tunes "Three Times a Lady," "Lady," and "Endless Love" all topped the pop charts, and his album "We Are the World" raised $50 million for African famine relief in 1985.

White folk musicians continued a tradition that began in fiddle festivals and barn dances long before Hank Williams, though he was its most famous practitioner. Arlen Moon began making fiddles and banjos when he was a boy growing up poor on Turkey Hop Hill near Holly Pond. Lacking the money to buy instruments and yearning to play old-time music and bluegrass, he solved his dilemma by learning to build beautiful instruments, one of which—a solid walnut five-string banjo— earned its way into a Smithsonian Institution folk art exhibition in Washington. The Louvin and Delmore brothers from near Fort Payne perfected close duet harmony and reached a huge country music audience.

Randy Owen and two of his cousins were influenced by such musical traditions while growing up on small farms near Fort Payne in the 1950s. Owen read no music but wrote wonderful lyrics. His cousin Teddy Wayne Gentry began a band called the "Sand Mountain Chicken Pluckers" in honor of the area's most successful agricultural enterprise, but the name happily underwent a series of transitions until the group arrived at the descriptive title "Alabama." In 1979 the band recorded "My Home's in Alabama," which became its first major hit. The Academy of Country Music voted "Alabama" as Vocal Group of the Year in 1981 and 1982. In 1983 the band produced the top three country single recordings, a feat it repeated in 1984. By 1986, when "Alabama" won the Entertainer of the Year award for the fifth consecutive time, the band's albums had sold sixteen million copies. In 1993 the group received a People's Choice Award as favorite music group. The three cousins do not forget their simple roots: each year their "June Jam" in Fort Payne raises thousands of dollars for various philanthropies.

Other Alabama country singers reached a more limited audience. Tammy Wynette, though born in Mississippi, claimed the northwestern Alabama town of Red Bay as her adopted home. She won a Grammy for her 1970 hit "Stand By Your Man," although her numerous marriages made the advice confusing.

Alabama writers also kept alive the state's reputation for fine literature. Mobile novelist Eugene Walter won the 1953 Lippincott Fiction Prize contest for young novelists. Mary Ward Brown, who began her writing career as a grandmother in the 1980s, won acclaim for *Tongues of Flame*, an anthology of her short stories. Walker Percy, a native of Birmingham, established a reputation during the 1960s and 1970s as one of the nation's most distinguished novelists. His anguished, Catholic critique of the collapse of American moral values produced a stream of incisive novels: *The Moviegoer* (1961), *The Last Gentleman* (1967), *Love in the Ruins* (1971), *Lancelot* (1977), and *The Second Coming* (1980). Youthful novelist Vicki Covington utilized the conflict between fundamentalist and moderate religion and her warm memories of her grandmother in two provocative novels about contemporary Alabama society, *Gathering Home* and *Bird of Paradise*.

It came as no surprise that religion played such a large role in the fiction of Percy and Covington. Christianity was a primary force shaping Alabama culture. But the state's religious life was much more complex than many casual observers recognized.

Differences among Southern Baptists, the state's largest denomination, which enrolled one-fourth of Alabama's four million people, demonstrate this religious diversity. In 1964 the Reverend John Buchanan, whose father had served a distinguished pastorate at Birmingham's Southside Baptist Church, won a seat to Congress representing the Sixth

Congressional District. A moderate Republican with strong feelings about separation of church and state, the Baptist minister won considerable backing from Jewish and black voters as well as from whites.

But by 1980 Buchanan's politics seemed tepid to a white constituency caught up in the "moral majority" movement. Politicized Fundamentalists and Evangelicals endorsed his fellow parishioner at Southside Baptist, insurance agent Albert Lee Smith. Smith beat Buchanan in a nasty Republican primary, then held the seat against a Democratic candidate in the November general election. Beaten by Ben Erdreich in 1982, Smith retired from Congress determined to purge "liberal" Baptists from the Southern Baptist Convention. In June 1990 Smith sent letters to state Baptist leaders urging the election of a Fundamentalist Birmingham pastor as president of the state convention. But state Baptists followed a decade-long pattern of resisting presidents prominently identified with either camp and elected a nonpolitical pastor. Although Baptists at their conventions regularly passed resolutions condemning abortion, such resolutions were not binding on any individual or congregation. In fact, in 1990 the pastor of Birmingham's Baptist Church of the Covenant became president of a group of Alabama clergymen in favor of choice for women in the matter.

Although mainstream churches in Alabama (Methodist, Presbyterian, Episcopal, Lutheran) experienced the same steady decline typical of these denominations nationwide, Pentecostal congregations multiplied rapidly. Led by the Assemblies of God and the Church of God, such congregations supplanted the cooler and more rational religion of the mind with a warm and stirring religion of the heart. Alabamians had always preferred a religion they could feel to one they had to understand, and the new faiths featured popular music with a beat, validation of newly won middle class prosperity, and charismatic pulpit orators. The Cathedral of the Cross (Assemblies of God), begun in 1958, soon dwarfed other Birmingham congregations and numbered more than 4,300 members. Located in the mainly white suburb of Huffman, the congregation included an estimated 75 to 100 black members by 1990.

Alabama's popular culture reflected the profound conditioning of evangelical religion. When the "lifestyle market analyst" queried Americans about their favorite leisure-time activity, most in San Francisco preferred sipping wine, most Washingtonians picked foreign travel, and most Bostonians favored skiing. But in Birmingham, a majority of respondents listed reading the Bible. A 1989 state poll discovered that the average Alabama adult attended church more than three times a month and nearly a third attended once a week. Those figures also differed substantially by race and gender (only 10 percent of blacks compared to 25 percent of whites never attended church; 14 percent of women did not attend compared to 36 percent of Alabama's males). Two-thirds of adult Alabamians did not drink beer or liquor. But secularism had made some inroads. Nearly two-thirds of Alabamians favored a state lottery as a way of raising additional money, and 64 percent believed abortion should be legal under some circumstances (rape, to protect the health of the mother, or if there were a strong chance of a severe birth defect). But a majority favored making abortions harder to obtain if a married woman simply did not want more children or if an unmarried woman did not want to marry the father. Alabamians split almost equally about the morality of abortions for poor women who could not afford more children. For many citizens churches still provided the most profound bonding, the deepest source of community belonging, and the strongest sense of personal worth and meaning to be found in society. But they differed sharply over the political implications of religious faith.

Citizens also maintained their historic affection for region and country. Alabamians strongly identified with Southern tradition. Polls in 1989 revealed 91 percent of the respondents did not believe that the First Amendment protected those who burned the American flag as part of a political protest; but nearly the same number felt the same way about anyone burning the state flag (89 percent) or even the Confederate flag (87 percent). Citizens also remained nature's children; one in three adults hunted or fished during a typical month. But 52 percent of Alabamians also favored stricter gun control laws. And half the population admitted to eating grits at least once a week, while 5 percent ate grits at least once a day.[3]

Alabama also kept its military tradition strong. Native son Admiral Thomas M. Moorer served both as chief of Naval Operations and as chairman of the Joint Chiefs of Staff. Citizens elected former Vietnam War POW Jeremiah Denton to a U.S. Senate term in 1980. And during the 1990–91 Iraq crisis, the Alabama National Guard provided one of the highest percentages of guardsmen to total population. This information came as no surprise to the state that had operated the largest National Guard program in the United States (21,500 men and women compared to 21,200 in the second-place Texas National Guard).

Violence channeled into military activity may well be necessary in a dangerous world. But Alabamians also showed a preference for less disciplined and restrained forms. Cascading rates of domestic violence, murders between relatives and acquaintances, and random shootings interrupted the state's tranquillity. On a hazy November day in 1989 the Cincinnati-based yacht *Mary L* turned a bend in the Mobile River some forty miles above the port city. Two Chickasaw residents, Quiller Ragan and his wife Lillian, continued their bream fishing from a skiff anchored in the river. Someone fired a gun and the yacht moved quickly down-river, turned around, then returned upriver where someone fired a shotgun. Lillian Ragan lost an eye and a finger in the exchange of gunfire. Stories about what happened conflicted. The yacht owners charged that Quiller Ragan stood up in his skiff and fired two shotgun blasts at the left side of the yacht. When the yacht returned to get the skiff's registration number, Ragan fired again, and crew members on the yacht returned the fire, hitting Mrs. Ragan. Ragan described the confrontation as beginning when the *Mary L* threatened to swamp his skiff. After running a flag up a pole to warn the yacht, he fired a rifle in the air to announce his presence. The yacht went by, then returned upriver when a crewman fired a shotgun, hitting his wife. Ragan then fired a rifle and a pistol at the "fleeing yacht." The episode was only the worst of many confrontations between midwestern yacht owners and Mobile River fishermen after the Tennessee-Tombigbee Waterway provided the Tennessee and Ohio rivers access to the Gulf in 1985.

Alabama society did sanction a milder form of violence called football. A 1989 poll that asked "what Alabamian, living or dead, do you admire the most?" offered insight into the values of citizens. With so many prominent and laudable people from whom to select (names frequently mentioned included Helen Keller, Martin Luther King, Jr., Hugo Black, Rosa Parks, Julia Tutwiler, and Booker T. Washington), Alabamians chose George Wallace and Bear Bryant by a landslide. Asked to choose a favorite football team in 1989, 37 percent of the citizens preferred the University of Alabama Crimson Tide to 21 percent for the Auburn Tigers; 9 percent favored both equally, 8 percent selected another school, and a quarter of the population expressed no interest in the state's unofficial religion. Surprisingly, although 65 percent could identify the coach at Auburn, only 43 percent knew that Bill Curry coached at Alabama. Nonetheless, more people knew the coaches at both major universities than knew the name of their lieutenant governor. And named behind Wallace and Bryant as most admired Alabamians were Auburn's Heisman Trophy winner Bo Jackson and Mobile's baseball star Hank Aaron.

Bryant's popularity was not confined to Alabama. His dominance of college football during the 1960s and 1970s had made him a Southern icon. Fans of other Southern football schools might detest the Crimson Tide, but as one Mississippi sportswriter expressed it: "When 'Bama went north and east and west, it wasn't going to play just a football game, it was going on a crusade, and Bear was our Richard the Lion-Hearted. Bear was our best, and our best could and did beat the best of anywhere else, and that was important to all of us below the Mason-Dixon Line."[4] During a time of racial conflict, external criticism from every part of the civilized world, and dreary self-image, Bear Bryant's boys went out and "kicked Yankee butt." Becoming the winningest coach in football history—with 323 victories before his retirement at the end of the 1982 season—sealed his reputation nationally. Restoring a sense of state and regional pride established his image back home.

Bryant represented more than just victory on the field. He proved that people could win in life. The youngest of eleven children, his father had been a semi-invalid. His mother had supported the family by selling homegrown produce with young Paul's help. He had always been a self-described "mama's boy," a fact that helped him enormously when he began to recruit hulking youngsters from matriarchal black families. When he abandoned bear wrestling to play football for the Fordyce (Arkansas) High School Red Bugs, he found self-esteem and success. The offer of a football scholarship to Alabama promised a way out of poverty. According to legend his mother had taken his only pair of shoes to a cobbler and had had cleats attached to them; after that he had worn them everywhere from the turf of the football stadium to church. Bryant explained his commitment to the sport in negative terms: "For years, the one thing that motivated me was the fear of going back to plowing and driving those mules in Arkansas and chopping cotton for 50 cents an hour."[5]

The Bryant myth became one of the South's great success stories, a tale of rags to riches capable of inspiring a people mired in poverty. He taught that outmanned, undersized, disadvantaged people could claw and scrap and fight their way to the top if only they had the will and tenacity to prevail.

Like many of the people who admired him, he had to make compromises on the road to success. Early in his career recruiting scandals sullied his reputation. Rumors described the training of his young recruits as bordering on brutality. One Jackson, Mississippi, sports journalist recalled: "He was meaner than hell when he was young and kind-hearted as they come as an old man."[6] Just as Southern Baptist and Pentecostal churches affirmed the newly prosperous middle class, Bryant's career symbolized the way in which education and indomitable will could transform poor outcasts into respectable middle class people. Popular imagery had always depicted Auburn as the college of choice for the sons and daughters of hayseeds and drivers of secondhand Fords and the University of Alabama as the party school for well-healed fraternity boys and sorority girls. But Bryant gave the university a new image. A 1989 poll revealed that Alabama fans predominated among families with incomes of less than $40,000 a year. Families with incomes higher than that split their loyalties evenly. Democrats favored Alabama over Auburn by 36 to 16 percent. The margin of Republicans favoring Alabama dropped to only 10 percentage points (37 to 27).

As white families became prosperous, fewer white males were willing to subject themselves to the bodily abuse required by football. Education offered them a safer and more certain road to the good life. But the lives of many black youngsters closely paralleled the depression-scarred childhood of Paul Bryant. When Bryant began to recruit black players, he became a master at it. During the 1970s and 1980s impoverished blacks from inner-city housing projects and rural shacks entertained middle and upper class whites in Legion Field as once upon a time Christian gladiators had amused wealthy Romans.

In 1990 Willie Wyatt starred as a five-foot, ten-inch 262-pound nose guard for the university. Journalists voted him the most valuable player in the 1990 Senior Bowl in Mobile, and he then took his degree in criminal justice on to pro football. Wyatt grew up like the young Bryant. His house stood at the end of an old dirt road near Gardendale. It had no running water, no indoor plumbing, and no central heat. Bare light bulbs hung from exposed rafters. When he was older he and other male relatives moved to a lean-to shed without a floor, heat, or insulation so that the women and children could have more room. When a coach from Alabama came to offer him a scholarship, Wyatt invited him to look around: "Coach, this is my incentive." Later he told an interviewer:

I'm not ashamed to say I had it rough growing up. But having it rough is not always bad. What I've learned and what I've seen, I'll never forget. Those are vital experiences in my life that helped set my values. I didn't have the things a lot of others take for granted. But maybe that's the reason I worked so hard. The credit goes to my mother. She raised six kids without a father in the house. She kept us out of trouble and reminded us to always be thankful for what we did have.[7]

In this way Alabama differed little from Auburn. Pat Dye coached the Tigers to dominance in the Southeastern Conference in the late 1980s just as Alabama had dominated it in the previous two decades. During the decade Auburn won or shared four conference championships and regularly won poll rankings among the top ten teams nationally. During the 1970s and 1980s the school produced two Heisman Trophy winners, symbolic of the nation's finest college football player.

Dye's premier player came from a background much like Wyatt's. Born the son of a steelworker in Bessemer in 1962, Vincent ("Bo") Jackson was only a child when his parents separated. His mother and maternal grandparents raised him as one of ten children in a three-room house. Poverty and uncommon strength turned Jackson into a bully who dominated classmates as well as track, baseball, and football teams at McAdory High School. His mother persuaded him to turn down a $250,000 bonus to play baseball directly out of high school because she wanted him to go to college and earn a degree. Pat Dye pursued and won him by allowing Jackson to compete in track and baseball as well as football. He became one of the few modern college athletes to excel in three sports. In 1986 he won the celebrated Heisman Trophy, then went on to star for the Kansas City Royals in professional baseball and the Oakland Raiders in football. Many sportswriters pronounced him to be the greatest American athlete of the twentieth century.

Unfortunately the positive lessons taught by football had a down side. For many Alabamians the spirit became a religion and Bear Bryant was its prophet. They related only half in jest tales of Bryant walking on water. How could one disbelieve when the Bear pulled out so many miraculous victories? When Bryant died in January 1983 his funeral became a sacred ritual combining sports, education, and religion. Three Tuscaloosa churches filled with 1,300 people, but another 10,000 mourned on downtown streets. His funeral was the first for a Southern celebrity to include blacks in prominent roles. Black players from his 1982 team served as pallbearers, and legendary Grambling coach Eddie Robinson, who finally broke Bryant's victory record, spoke, praising Bryant's humility and his role in removing Southern racial barriers. No matter that Bryant was a latecomer to racial equality. As the funeral cortege left for burial at Birmingham's Elmwood Cemetery, the 300-car motorcade stretched for five miles and took two hours to pass. Along the way to Interstate 59 mourners read signs that bade farewell, like the one that said: "God needs an offensive coordinator."[8] Between 500,000 and 700,000 people waited along the interstate to offer their farewells, and 10,000 more awaited the body at Elmwood. Most of the mourners were working class people who had made Bryant their hero.

Overemphasis on football plagued the state's universities. Auburn experienced one crisis after another during the 1980s over star players who did not attend class or were caught cheating or plagiarizing. Faculty accused trustees of resisting a strong curriculum reform because of their fear that it would jeopardize the recruiting of gifted athletes. Both major universities led conference schools in recruiting marginal academic players, and neither could boast of graduation rates. Between 1978 and 1990 only 23 percent of the basketball players and 39 percent of the football players at the University of Alabama graduated. Auburn's figures were distressingly similar. Frustrated university presidents admitted that the situation had gotten out of hand.

Football at Alabama and Auburn were not the only games in the state, although 'Bama added another national championship in 1992. Teams at Jacksonville State, Troy State, and the University of North Alabama also won conference and national championships in their division during the 1970s, '80s, and '90s. Birmingham-Southern College and Jacksonville State won national titles in basketball and baseball. Both

Auburn and the University of Alabama won tournament and conference titles in basketball. Women's basketball at Auburn and women's gymnastics at the University of Alabama regularly competed for national championships. And Alabama stock car drivers Davey Allison, Donnie Allison, Bobby Allison, Neil Bonnett, and Red Farmer became known as the "Alabama gang" because of their dominance of the sport. The track at Talladega boasted the fastest times in racing history, and its premier races attracted hundreds of thousands of fans to the rural Alabama site. Southerners exported stock car racing to the rest of the nation just as they had Pentecostal religion and Bear Bryant's Alabama teams. The life-and-death earnestness of stock car racing, the opportunity it afforded poorly educated "good old boys" to make good, would have made Bear proud.

Many Alabamians considered sports frivolous and overemphasized. Perhaps they were right. But football especially provided a window through which one could peer inside a culture to determine what made it tick and what constituted its values.

National recognition for its superb athletes continued a long Alabama tradition. So did racial conflict and poverty. As Alabama approached a new century it did so with major problems: continuing racial polarization, lack of political vision, and short-sighted leadership in many aspects of public and private life. But it also brought tenacious folk culture, a strong work ethic, a sense of individual responsibility, an increasingly visionary younger business community, broader opportunities for women, and a physical environment incredibly beautiful and diverse, even if often neglected and polluted. Perhaps for the people of Alabama the best was still to come.

Alabama: Past and Future

IN 1835 the Cherokees—the last of the native Americans in Alabama—set out for the western reservations along their "Trail of Tears." On the old Cherokee and other tribal lands live the descendants of the white settlers and the black slaves who, in coercive alliance, built the burgeoning cotton economy of antebellum Alabama.

This history has chronicled the journey through time of these whites and blacks. Constant hope and expectation were sometimes waylaid by false leaders who called for changes in the route and by those who extracted exorbitant tolls for every painful mile of travel. And there were always those of truer vision to remind the errant and recall the travelers to a happier future. What do the historical mileposts and the maps reveal?

The Alabama progression may be viewed from two vantage points. From far above only the toiling column can be observed; only the twists and turns of collective action and group policy come into focus. From this stance the little groups that surge ahead and scout the flanks and search for new directions are lost to view. There were two separate routes to the present, and two very different pictures emerge.

Alabama did not begin its life with a clean slate. The settlers brought their customs and their earlier experience, their concepts of law, society, and religion into a huge domain where distance and dispersion quickly modified values. Survival on a raw frontier often looked more like the violent world of Thomas Hobbes than the more mannered inconveniences of John Locke.

It is interesting—if ultimately futile—to speculate on the possibilities for Alabama if the cotton textile industry in England and then New England had not developed when it did. Would Alabama's economy and therefore much of its culture have more closely mirrored the cohesiveness and tighter social control of New England and the Middle States? Most probably not, although an entire state of small farmers would have produced a different future. In fact, more than half the state barely shared in the cotton/slave revolution, and those small farmer areas

623

cultivated an independence within a localism that bred suspicion of the world outside. Overlaid with poverty, they were rarely receptive to new ideas or changing times, nor did they always immediately see education as a vehicle toward salvation. They were often men and women of strong pride, a fierce independence, and the solid values of those who are reminded that life is hard and often short and that only the fundamental questions are worth consideration.

What there was of "culture" and higher aspiration and awareness and reaction to a bigger world was centered in the rising planter class. A minority, they were the people who could soon afford fine homes and who inevitably pursued the social and cultural graces as a hallmark of their financial status. The sons of wealthy planters sought the higher education of their day—a classical foundation capped by legal training. Imagination, innovation, and reform receive little reinforcement from a discipline that preaches the virtues of continuity and the wisdom of the prior decision. The argument from precedent rather than the argument from morality has often marked the official Southern response to the crises of change from that day to the present.

Planters and small farmers met in uneasy association in their state government. In its structure the government followed the democratic precepts of the day, including the penchant for a powerful legislature and a weak executive. It was not an efficient government. It lacked the expertise and therefore the control to manage its few institutional endeavors. The civic ideal of selfless service was not broadly shared, and the state bank failed in a welter of political favoritism. The progressive idea of a penitentiary and the enlightened decision to abandon the bloody punishments of the past floundered in a scandal of unpunished and almost unpublicized fraud and corruption.

The winds of progress and change, the whispers of new ideas and new directions, came to Alabama during the 1830s and early 1840s. Gifted and thoughtful men sat in the legislature and spoke their minds on a host of democratic issues. The egalitarian aspects of Jacksonian democracy scorned appointments to public office and demanded that the people choose their public servants. Alabamians who read their newspapers heard the rustle of change as they turned the pages, and for at least a brief time there was talk of a new age in which even women might be given greater legal protection and some political rights.

As Northern reformers and the rise of antislavery sentiment tried to lend substance to the idea of a new democracy, the reaction of many Southern leaders was to reject that troubling road and deny democracy itself. Fundamental economic change was shifting the standards of New England while leaving the South almost untouched. So there was no compromise and no accommodation. The debate was no dry and arcane argument over labor economics. It was a passionate fight over ways of living and thinking. Alabama planters might declaim on the glories of Greece and Rome (where slavery flourished) and see themselves symbolically assembling in a new forum in Montgomery. Yet their theories were so irrelevant to the modern world as to make the South an exhibit in the Museum of Anachronisms.

Perhaps all virtues have their defects. Few groups have freely moved to change their practices by being told what evil people they are. Southerners and Alabamians were not inclined to welcome moral lectures. The New England conscience (and there were a few Southern consciences that joined it) was a standing example of how thoroughly disagreeable even righteousness can be. In turn, the Southern virtue of loyalty to place and position too often precluded a critical spirit to ask whom and what they really served. Between 30,000 and 40,000 Alabamians died to set a price on the fact that their legalistic leaders were wrong: slavery was antidemocratic and a state cannot secede from the Union.

As a belated codicil to the rationale—preserving the Union—slavery was added to the Northern agenda of why the Civil War was fought. A few Alabamians still insisted that slavery should not go, pending a decision by the Supreme Court. But a majority reluctantly bid adieu to the "peculiar institution." So black women and men were no longer slaves. Now, as of 1865, they were free and, as of 1868, they were citizens. Or were they? That was the question Radical Republicans and Southern Democrats fought over for the next decade.

If one accepts the thought that the voluntary relinquishment of slavery was too much to expect of white Alabamians in the 1850s, it is more difficult to accept that even defeat made so little difference in 1865. Some had learned, but many had not. The hobgoblin of "outside influence" was abroad in the land and was presented as reason in plenty to oppose the Reconstruction government and the hopes for black equality. Reform sponsored by the victors and applied to the vanquished was not a perfect formula for acceptance and support.

Whatever the motives for accommodation—and economic order and justice should have been strong ones—what if white Alabama in 1865 had set out to make the great change work? What if those racial judgments of black ignorance and inferiority had led to the determination to end that ignorance and lessen that supposed inferiority by mustering all the effort and the meager means at hand? What if goodwill had set the pace and written the agenda? It was a road not taken. The consequences of the war were evaded and repulsed and refused and rejected. The costs of that decision were enormous. White Alabamians denied democratic progress for themselves as they denied it to Alabama blacks. Would it have been better to start the process of racial accommodation in 1865 rather than in 1955? Another ninety years of segregation and injustice did not make it any easier.

In a flurry of faults and narrow interests, broadly shared by Radical Republicans and Bourbon Democrats, Reconstruction failed in its larger aims. A broader tax base, a reorganized judicial system, public education, and social welfare programs were weakened or rejected in the wake of the Bourbon victory in 1874. In the place of Radical Reconstruction came Bourbon Reconstruction with fraud at the ballot box and economic exploitation. The Alabama Bourbons were not the original authors of poverty; they had not directly created a suffocating credit stringency and a deflationary monetary policy. But they profited handsomely from the system, and they failed to produce a creative response to the ills that affected their fellow citizens, black and white. For the Bourbons it was enough to guard their economic interests with the cry of race and Reconstruction at election time.

Out of the ever-growing economic crisis of the 1880s and 1890s a sharper class interest began to emerge. In Alabama it was a farmer-labor alliance—a surprising Southern embryo of the much later New Deal. Populism challenged Bourbon philosophy at every point—including its views on race—and at none more strongly than in the premise that government should be used to reshape the economic rules for the benefit of all the people. While manipulating the law and the legal system for their own purposes, the Bourbons had publicly subscribed to a vision of society as divinely made and thus immune to the blasphemy of change.

Here was another chance to take a higher road and perhaps the closest that Alabamians came to gaining control of their social and political direction. The Populist movement failed, but the organized impulse for reform remained alive and surprisingly strong in the hill counties. Populists joined the Republicans, whose percentage of the vote increased after 1900. These were not votes for a Republican status quo. Time, of course, did not stop, nor did growth wither and die. In the last half of the nineteenth century Alabama had its own industrial revolution with coal, iron, and steel. Parts of the state and many of its citizens moved toward the mainstream of American life. Railroads crisscrossed the state and cities rose. The ideas of "outside influence" brought industrialization to Alabama, and if it did not produce a better life for everyone, at least for some it brought a different one. Industrialization began to shift the balance of state power away from the Black Belt. There is a direct line of development from the Alabama Coal Mining Company in Montevallo in 1856 to the establishment of the George C. Marshall Space Flight Center in Huntsville in 1958.

At the time and later, Alabama's relative poverty slowed the pace of progress. Alabamians were not poor because their state was poor. It was a rich state full of poor people. Who shared in the fortunes made in growing cotton? Who profited and raised their standard of living from the riches made in mining coal and making iron and steel? How many Alabamians fared better from the proceeds and profits of railroad traffic or the turpentine industry or timber or cattle operations or from the textile industry?

For the blacks of Alabama the turn of the century marked the nadir of their journey and their aspirations. It was a time of bitter retrogression in almost every statistic of the black experience. The final symbolism was bestowed when the constitution of 1901 removed their votes so that white men could not steal them. The black population figures tell a part of the story: a small increase from 1900 to 1910, a decline from 1910 to 1920.

When the faint whispers of the Progressive movement reached Alabama they already spoke of muddled aims and mixed methods. It was a pleasing thought to clean up the existing system, and Alabamians surely profited from the rising discussion of social problems. The educational system gained a little ground, but the net effect was disappointing. Lower freight rates did not change the direction of Alabama life, nor did an unabashed antilabor policy signal a new day.

The First World War was a spasmodic tremor in Alabama affairs. The augmentation of federal power suggested that the old and the new were incompatible—and that centralized democracy had little in accord with what many perceived as Southern values. Both the energy and the attitudes of the war were only fleeting heralds of the future, and Alabama life entered the 1920s essentially unchanged.

Always ambivalent on the liquor issue, Alabamians took Prohibition in their stride. Staunch drys boasted that less whiskey was available, while wets replied that at least some was. In spite of feminist hopes it was difficult to discern fundamental effects of the long overdue extension of the suffrage, although the League of Women Voters was a force of influence until 1928. Yet the most basic tenet of democracy was reason enough to double the size of the electorate. The revived Ku Klux Klan of native Alabamian William Joseph Simmons received a warm welcome. Side by side with the Klan's prejudice and its violence was a sharp edge of anticorporate, antiestablishment sentiment. And with all the imagery of the Jazz Age to obscure the greater reality, the Alabama sharecropper went on following his mule down a row of cotton as the boll weevil ate its way through the field. Even nature's crop reduction system could not raise the falling price of cotton. The Alabama coal miner was no better off. He worked in a depressed industry, trying to support a family on a wage that denied even marginal improvement in his way of life. The little pay that textile workers earned was augmented by pooling the salaries of family-unit labor, but it was at the cost of regimentation and low class esteem.

Nationwide depression laid its heavy hand on Alabama and stretched and strained society in a hundred ways. The old practices, the old principles, the old relationships were bombarded by all those outside influences and new ideas that had been shut out for so long. The Great Depression was a major culture shock. It produced a tenant farmers union and communists agitating among the blacks (or even more alarming, black communists agitating among the blacks). Above all there was the federal government that brought some help in one hand and control and requirements and more than a hint of democracy in the other. The mighty light cast across an entire region of Alabama by the Tennessee Valley Authority had psychological as well as material benefits. Still, Alabamians often sought to accept one proffered hand and reject the other, and to some extent the method succeeded. Even in the throes of economic dissolution the old order survived.

In 1941 another war to preserve democracy came. Of much longer duration and greater magnitude than World War I, the conflict stirred Alabama life in all directions. Perhaps most of all it brought a measure of prosperity with a major growth of economic opportunities. Prosperity, in turn, had ramifications in unleashing a groundswell of upward mobility—most notably displayed in the expansion of higher education in the state. Money more equitably distributed was a new and powerful cure for the ills of society. Yet the old sore of racial discrimination still infected Alabama society, still stifled its energies and held it back.

A massive force of unskilled labor, white and black, had always set limits on Alabama endeavors and had always directed them to the most exploitive industries. Now came yet another chance to change the script and learn new lines and produce a new itinerary. The civil rights policies of the Truman administration ending segregation in the armed forces, the rising civil rights movement, and *Brown* v. *Board of Education*—those outside influences at work again—signaled a new determination by the federal government. It meant that white Southerners could no longer remain as Americans on their own terms. They could not pick the rights and freedoms that they liked and reject the rest. They could no longer decide who shared in freedom's bounty.

With their Southern neighbors, Alabama's politicians tried the old artifices of defiance. From White Citizens' councils to the violence that produced martyrs, to the Dixiecrats and posturing in schoolhouse doors, a majority of Alabama politicians (there was no constructive leadership here) failed their citizens. The arguments that antisegregationists preached what they often did not practice, that white Southerners had no monopoly on prejudice and discrimination, were sometimes true and always specious. Choosing to wait for a seamless web of perfection is to wait forever. What was worth saving in the South that equal rights would overthrow? These were the poorest states in the nation, the lowest on the indices of education and income, the highest in the areas of illiteracy and mortality.

Finally, the federal government overthrew legal segregation and brought another New South, far newer than the past can show. That Newest South is in the ferment of creation. It will come in fits and starts, with impasses and resolutions, with arguments and acrimony. Calm and rational discussion may well be best, and that will follow crisis and protest. Even the latter is better than the silence of the past.

To encapsulate almost 175 years of Alabama history in some tidy package of interpretation is a formidable task, complex and elusive. Yet one aspect, full of contradictions and ambiguities, deserves consideration. Since the 1850s the government of Alabama has seemed to bar the road to change and reform. Its political leaders have refused to face all but the smallest of its people's problems. At the same time there is a rich story of the activities and ideas of dissenters, endlessly protesting the rigors and restrictions of the status quo and painting their own pictures of a better life. So it is fair to ask if Alabama is a "conservative" state or a "liberal" state—and to inquire as to its character and direction.

After the brief "reform spirit" of the 1840s the Alabama lords of property and wealth were handed a potent weapon to protect their interests and their position from the circling crowds of a much poorer white majority. The planter and the later industrialist became adept at playing the game of white supremacy and racial politics that kept them from being isolated as a minority interest group. By rallying a majority of white men to their side they were able to reduce change to a trickle while keeping their own interests inviolate. Alabama society was cut off from normal growth and from the thrust and parry of contending social forces. That was why populism was a genuine attack on the status quo— it attacked the center of the problem—and why progressivism fell lamentably short of true reform.

As the legal apparatus of segregation and inequality was dismantled, as blacks gained the right to vote and speak with a political voice, the heirs to the old entrenched interests began to lose some of their privileges and their power. There has been change and there will be more, but legal racial equality solved only the problems caused by its absence. All the others were left untouched and undisturbed. Racial politics, sired by black or white, is an agent of misdirection that hides the real issues that confront society.

With exceptions of degree, Alabama political leadership has disappointed its people too often. It is interesting to imagine an Alabama legislature drawn from the full spectrum of life in the state. Its purview and vision would inevitably transcend the width of the local courthouse. But images and concepts of politics and public life must change before it becomes clear that the trouble with "good old boys" in politics is that they are always so good to themselves.

What of that other vantage point from which to view the past? There is a sharper angle that shows life in its bits and pieces, illuminating the individuals and groups that follow different routes. For every self-serving politician who sought his own protection in the status quo or who sought to legalize injustice, there have been dissenters and reformers who tried to change the system. The supposedly granite face of a privileged and reactionary Alabama was always a porous facade that protest threatened to dissolve. Alabamians have a rich heritage of seeking the better way. They have been blessed with a remarkable number of political leaders, judges, attorneys, teachers, ministers, intellectuals, creative artists, businessmen, farmers, and workers who have taken a stand in troubled times. This spread and shape of things is the other view, and its vitality and its promise are illustrated by modern Alabama with all its growth and broadening prospects.

Alabamians have passed their time in a favored land. They have always deserved the most efficient and caring government, the most equitable society, and the finest educational system in the world. To the extent that they have been denied these things, everybody has suffered. To the extent that they have been granted, everyone has profited, and the state has grown and flourished.

Alabama's citizens are in the process of becoming the people of a new century. They have the honesty, the insight, and the compassion to examine their past. They have the ability to purge the bad and retain the good. They have the imagination to ask for more and the judgment to know if it has been granted.

The past is a lesson. The present is a time for action. A better future beckons.

APPENDIX A

Governors of Alabama

The Mississippi Territory (1799–1817)

Name	Place of Birth	Party	Dates in Office
Winthrop Sargent of Massachusetts	Massachusetts	Federalist	1799–1801
William C. C. Claiborne of Tennessee	Virginia	Democratic	1801–1805
Robert Williams of North Carolina	Virginia	Democratic	1805–1809
David Holmes of Virginia	Pennsylvania	Democratic	1809–1817

The Alabama Territory (1817–1819)

Name	Place of Birth	Party	Dates in Office
William Wyatt Bibb of Georgia	Virginia	Democratic	1817–1819

The State of Alabama

Name	Place of Birth	Party	Dates in Office
William Wyatt Bibb of Autauga County	Virginia	Democratic	1819–1820
Thomas Bibb of Limestone County	Virginia	Democratic	1820–1821
Israel Pickens of Greene County	North Carolina	Democratic	1821–1825
John Murphy of Monroe County	North Carolina	Democratic	1825–1829
Gabriel Moore of Madison County	North Carolina	Democratic	1829–March 1831
Samuel B. Moore of Jackson County	Tennessee	Democratic	March 1831–Nov. 1831
John Gayle of Greene County	South Carolina	Democratic	1831–1835
Clement Comer Clay of Madison County	Virginia	Democratic	1835–July 1837
Hugh McVay of Lauderdale County	South Carolina	Democratic	July 1837–Nov. 1837
Arthur P. Bagby of Monroe County	Virginia	Democratic	1837–1841

631

Governors of Alabama

Name	Place of Birth	Party	Dates in Office
Benjamin Fitzpatrick of Autauga County	Georgia	Democratic	1841–1845
Joshua L. Martin of Limestone County	Tennessee	Democratic	1845–1847
Reuben Chapman of Madison County	Virginia	Democratic	1847–1849
Henry W. Collier of Tuscaloosa County	Virginia	Democratic	1849–1853
John A. Winston of Sumter County	Madison County	Democratic	1853–1857
Andrew B. Moore of Perry County	South Carolina	Democratic	1857–1861
John Gill Shorter of Barbour County	Georgia	Democratic	1861–1863
Thomas H. Watts of Montgomery County	Butler County	Democratic	1863–April 1865
Lewis E. Parons of Talladega County (Provisional Governor)	New York	Democratic	June 1865–Dec. 1865
Robert M. Patton of Lauderdale County	Virginia	Republican	Dec. 1865–July 1867
Wager Swayne of Montgomery County (Military Governor)	Ohio		July 1867–July 1868
William Hugh Smith of Randolph County	Georgia	Republican	July 1868–Nov. 1870
Robert B. Lindsay of Colbert County	Scotland	Democratic	1870–1872
David P. Lewis of Madison County	Virginia	Republican	1872–1874
George S. Houston of Limestone County	Tennessee	Democratic	1874–1878
Rufus W. Cobb of Shelby County	St. Clair County	Democratic	1878–1882
Edward A. O'Neal of Lauderdale County	Madison County	Democratic	1882–1886
Thomas Seay of Hale County	Hale County	Democratic	1886–1890
Thomas G. Jones of Montgomery County	Georgia	Democratic	1890–1894

Governors of Alabama

Name	Place of Birth	Party	Dates in Office
William C. Oates of Henry County	Pike County	Democratic	1894–1896
Joseph F. Johnston of Jefferson County	North Carolina	Democratic	1896–1900
William J. Samford of Lee County	Georgia	Democratic	1900–June 1901
William D. Jelks of Barbour County	Macon County	Democratic	June 1901–1907
Russell M. Cunningham of Jefferson County (acting governor while Governor Jelks was ill)	Lawrence County	Democratic	1904–1905
Braxton Bragg Comer of Jefferson County	Barbour County	Democratic	1907–1911
Emmet O'Neal of Lauderdale County	Lauderdale County	Democratic	1911–1915
Charles Henderson of Pike County	Pike County	Democratic	1915–1919
Thomas E. Kilby of Calhoun County	Tennessee	Democratic	1919–1923
William W. Brandon of Tuscaloosa County	Talladega County	Democratic	1923–1927
Bibb Graves of Montgomery County	Montgomery County	Democratic	1927–1931
Benjamin M. Miller of Wilcox County	Wilcox County	Democratic	1931–1935
Bibb Graves of Montgomery County	Montgomery County	Democratic	1935–1939
Frank M. Dixon of Jefferson County	California	Democratic	1939–1943
Chauncey M. Sparks of Barbour County	Barbour County	Democratic	1943–1947
James E. Folsom of Cullman County	Coffee County	Democratic	1947–1951
Gordon Persons of Montgomery County	Montgomery County	Democratic	1951–1955
James E. Folsom of Cullman County	Coffee County	Democratic	1955–1959
John Patterson of Russell County	Tallapoosa County	Democratic	1959–1963

Governors of Alabama

Name	Place of Birth	Party	Dates in Office
George C. Wallace of Barbour County	Barbour County	Democratic	1963–1967
Lurleen B. Wallace of Barbour County	Tuscaloosa County	Democratic	1967–May 7, 1968
Albert P. Brewer of Morgan County	Tennessee	Democratic	May 7, 1968–1971
George C. Wallace of Barbour County	Barbour County	Democratic	1971–1979
Jere Beasley of Barbour County (acting governor)	Barbour County	Democratic	June 5–July 7, 1972
Forrest ("Fob") James, Jr. of Lee County	Chambers County	Democratic	1979–1983
George C. Wallace of Barbour County	Barbour County	Democratic	1983–1987
Guy Hunt of Cullman County	Cullman County	Republican	1987–1993
James E. Folsom, Jr.	Cullman County	Democratic	1993–

APPENDIX B

Counties of Alabama

In Order of Organization

County	Date of Organization	Origin of the Name	County Seat
Washington	June 4, 1800	President George Washington	Chatom
Madison	Dec. 13, 1808	President James Madison	Huntsville
Baldwin	Dec. 21, 1809	Senator Abraham Baldwin of Georgia	Bay Minette
Clarke	Dec. 10, 1812	General John Clarke of Georgia	Grove Hill
Mobile	Dec. 18, 1812	Maubila Indians	Mobile
Monroe	June 29, 1815	President James Monroe	Monroeville
Montgomery	Dec. 6, 1816	Major Lemuel P. Montgomery of Tennessee	Montgomery
Franklin	Feb. 6, 1818	Benjamin Franklin	Russellville
Lauderdale	Feb. 6, 1818	Colonel James Lauderdale of Tennessee	Florence
Lawrence	Feb. 6, 1818	Captain James Lawrence of U.S. Navy	Moulton
Limestone	Feb. 6, 1818	Limestone Creek	Athens
Marengo	Feb. 6, 1818	Napoleonic battle in Europe	Linden
Morgan	Feb. 6, 1818	General Daniel Morgan of Virginia	Decatur
Blount	Feb. 6, 1818	Governor Willie Blount of Tennessee	Oneonta
Tuscaloosa	Feb. 6, 1818	Chief Tuscaloosa (Tascaluza)	Tuscaloosa
Bibb	Feb. 7, 1818	Governor William Wyatt Bibb	Centreville
Shelby	Feb. 7, 1818	Governor Isaac Shelby of Kentucky	Columbiana
Dallas	Feb. 9, 1818	A. J. Dallas, U.S. Secretary of the Treasury	Selma
Conecuh	Feb. 13, 1818	An Indian word, Conecuh River	Evergreen
Marion	Feb. 13, 1818	General Francis Marion of South Carolina	Hamilton
St. Clair	Nov. 20, 1818	General Arthur St. Clair of Pennsylvania	Ashville
Autauga	Nov. 21, 1818	Indian village of Atagi	Prattville
Butler	Dec. 13, 1819	Captain William Butler of Creek Wars	Greenville

635

Counties of Alabama

County	Date of Organization	Origin of the Name	County Seat
Greene	Dec. 13, 1819	General Nathaniel Greene of Georgia	Eutaw
Henry	Dec. 13, 1819	Governor Patrick Henry of Virginia	Abbeville
Jackson	Dec. 13, 1819	General Andrew Jackson	Scottsboro
Jefferson	Dec. 13, 1819	President Thomas Jefferson	Birmingham
Perry	Dec. 13, 1819	Commodore Oliver H. Perry, naval hero	Marion
Wilcox	Dec. 13, 1819	Lieutenant Joseph M. Wilcox of the Creek Wars	Camden
Pickens	Dec. 20, 1820	General Andrew Pickens of South Carolina	Carrollton
Covington	Dec. 17, 1821	Brigadier General Leonard W. Covington of Maryland	Andalusia
Pike	Dec. 17, 1821	General Zebulon M. Pike	Troy
Walker	Dec. 26, 1823	Senator John Williams Walker	Jasper
Fayette	Dec. 20, 1824	Marquis de Lafayette	Fayette
Dale	Dec. 22, 1824	General Sam Dale	Ozark
Lowndes	Jan. 20, 1830	Congressman William Lowndes of South Carolina	Hayneville
Barbour	Dec. 18, 1832	Governor James Barbour of Virginia	Clayton
Calhoun	Dec. 18, 1832	Senator John C. Calhoun	Anniston
Chambers	Dec. 18, 1832	Senator Henry Chambers of Alabama	Lafayette
Coosa	Dec. 18, 1832	Town of Alabama Indians	Rockford
Macon	Dec. 18, 1832	Senator Nathaniel Macon of North Carolina	Tuskegee
Randolph	Dec. 18, 1832	Senator John Randolph of Virginia	Wedowee
Russell	Dec. 18, 1832	Colonel Gilbert C. Russell of Creek Wars	Phenix City
Sumter	Dec. 18, 1832	General Thomas Sumter of South Carolina	Livingston
Talladega	Dec. 18, 1832	From Creek town	Talladega
Tallapoosa	Dec. 18, 1832	An Indian name	Dadeville
Cherokee	Jan. 9, 1836	The Indian tribe	Centre
DeKalb	Jan. 9, 1836	Major General Baron DeKalb of Poland	Fort Payne
Marshall	Jan. 9, 1836	Chief Justice John Marshall	Guntersville
Coffee	Dec. 29, 1841	General John Coffee	Elba
Choctaw	Dec. 29, 1847	The Indian tribe	Butler

Counties of Alabama

County	Date of Organization	Origin of the Name	County Seat
Winston	Feb. 12, 1850	Governor John A. Winston	Double Springs
Elmore	Feb. 15, 1866	General John A. Elmore	Wetumpka
Crenshaw	Nov. 30, 1866	Judge Anderson Crenshaw	Luverne
Bullock	Dec. 5, 1866	Colonel Edward C. Bullock	Union Springs
Lee	Dec. 5, 1866	General Robert E. Lee	Opelika
Cleburne	Dec. 6, 1866	Major General Patrick R. Cleburne of Arkansas	Heflin
Clay	Dec. 7, 1866	Senator Henry Clay of Kentucky	Ashland
Etowah	Dec. 7, 1866	A Cherokee Indian name	Gadsden
Hale	Jan. 30, 1867	Colonel Stephen F. Hale	Greensboro
Lamar	Feb. 4, 1867	Senator L. Q. C. Lamar of Mississippi	Vernon
Colbert	Feb. 6, 1867	Chiefs George and Levi Colbert of Chickasaw nation	Tuscumbia
Escambia	Dec. 10, 1868	An Indian name, Escambia River	Brewton
Geneva	Dec. 26, 1868	Geneva, Switzerland	Geneva
Chilton	Dec. 30, 1868	Confederate congressman William P. Chilton	Clanton
Cullman	Jan. 24, 1877	Johann G. Cullman	Cullman
Houston	Feb. 9, 1903	Governor George S. Houston	Dothan

Notes

1. Native Peoples of Alabama

1. The Spaniard's name is Hernando of the province of Soto, and he should be properly referred to as Soto, but traditionally he has been called De Soto and sometimes, incorrectly, Desoto.

2. Edward Gaylord Bourne, ed., *Narratives of the Career of Hernando de Soto*, 2 vols. (New York: Allerton Book Co., 1904), 2:20.

3. John A. Walthall, *Prehistoric Indians of the Southeast: Archaeology of Alabama and the Middle South* (University: University of Alabama Press, 1980), 40–47.

4. Ned J. Jenkins and Richard A. Krause, *The Tombigbee Watershed in Southern Prehistory* (University: University of Alabama Press, 1986), 52, 67.

5. Paul D. Welch, *Moundville's Economy* (Tuscaloosa: University of Alabama Press, 1991), 6, 185–90.

6. See Emma Lila Fundaburk and Mary Douglass Fundaburk Foreman, *Sun Circles and Human Hands: The Southern Indians—Art and Industries* (Luverne, Ala.: Privately Printed, 1957), 55–57, 68–77.

7. Quoted in John C. Hall, "The Search for Hernando de Soto," *Alabama Heritage*, no. 4 (Spring 1987): 19.

8. Grace Steele Woodward, *The Cherokees* (Norman: University of Oklahoma Press, 1963), 18.

9. James Adair, *The History of the American Indians* (1775; reprint, New York: Johnson Reprint, 1968), 227–29.

10. William Fyffe to [his brother] John, February 3, 1761, quoted in Woodward, *Cherokees*, 33–35.

11. Quoted in John R. Swanton, *The Indians of the Southeastern United States* (Washington, D.C.: Government Printing Office, 1946; reprint, Washington, D.C.: Smithsonian Institution Press, 1984), 691.

12. *Alabama* comes from the Choctaw *àlba* meaning plants or weeds and *àmo* meaning to cut, trim, or gather or "those who clear the land." *Alabama*

does not mean "here we rest," as some early histories of the state supposed. See William A. Read, *Indian Place Names in Alabama* (University: University of Alabama Press, 1984), 4.

13. *The Travels of William Bartram,* ed. Mark Van Doren (New York: Dover Publications, 1928), 403–04.

14. Quoted in Charles Wayne Goss, "The French and the Choctaw Indians, 1700–1763" (Ph.D. diss., Texas Tech University, 1977), 50–51.

15. Bourne, *Narratives of de Soto,* 2:134.

16. Bartram, *Travels,* 313.

17. David H. Corkran, *The Creek Frontier, 1540–1783* (Norman: University of Oklahoma Press, 1967), 16–17.

18. Adair, *American Indians,* 401–02.

19. Joseph B. Oxendine, *American Indian Sports Heritage* (Champaign, Ill.: Human Kinetics Books, 1988), xx.

20. Charles Hudson, *The Southeastern Indians* (Knoxville: University of Tennessee Press, 1976), 122–37.

21. Albert James Pickett, *History of Alabama* (1851; reprint, Birmingham: Birmingham Book and Magazine Co., 1962), 81–83.

2. European Exploration and Colonization in Alabama

1. Robert H. Fuson, trans., *The Log of Christopher Columbus* (Camden, Me.: International Marine Publishing Co., 1987), 71.

2. Oliver Dunn and James E. Kelley, Jr., trans., *The Diario of Christopher Columbus's First Voyage to America, 1492–1493* (Norman: University of Oklahoma Press, 1989), 63, 65; and Lawrence A. Clayton, "The Spanish Heritage of the Southeast," *Alabama Heritage,* no. 4 (Spring 1987): 4.

3. Morris Bishop, *The Odyssey of Cabeza de Vaca* (New York: Century Co., 1933), 57.

4. Charles Hudson, Chester B. DePratter, and Marvin T. Smith, "Hernando de Soto's Expedition through the Southern United States," in *First Encounters: Spanish Explorations in the Caribbean and the United States, 1492–1570,* ed. Jerald T. Milanich and Susan Milbrath (Gainesville: University of Florida Press, 1989), 87.

5. All quotes for de Soto's travels in Alabama are from Bourne, *Narratives of de Soto,* specifically, Elvas, 1:78–101; Biedma, 2:15–26; and Ranjel, 2:112–32, and from John Grier Varner and Jeannette Johnson Varner, trans. and eds., *The Florida of the Inca* (Austin: University of Texas Press, 1962), 379, the account of Inca Garcilaso de la Vega.

6. Peter J. Hamilton, *Colonial Mobile* (1897, 1910; reprint, edited with intro-

duction and annotations by Charles G. Summersell, University: University of Alabama Press, 1976), 31–32.

7. Quoted in Herbert I. Priestley, *Tristán de Luna* (Glendale, Calif.: Arthur H. Clark Co., 1936), 138.

8. Richebourg Gaillard McWilliams, trans., *Iberville's Gulf Journals* (University: University of Alabama Press, 1981), 35–39.

9. André Pénicaut, *Fleur de Lys and Calumet: Being the Pénicaut Narrative of French Adventure in Louisiana,* trans. and ed. Richebourg Gaillard McWilliams (1953; reprint, Tuscaloosa: University of Alabama Press, 1988), 57–58.

10. Census of Louisiana by Nicholas de La Salle, in Dunbar Rowland and Albert Godfrey Sanders, eds., *Mississippi Provincial Archives, 1701–1729, French Dominion,* 5 vols. (Jackson: Mississippi Department of Archives and History, 1929), 2:18–20.

11. Quoted in Goss, "French and the Choctaw Indians," 50.

12. Hamilton, *Colonial Mobile,* 66.

13. Jay Higginbotham, *Old Mobile: Fort Louis de la Louisiane, 1702–1711* (1977; reprint, Tuscaloosa: University of Alabama Press, 1991), 132–42, 161–77.

14. Minutes of the Council of Marine, Paris, September 8, 1716, quoted in Daniel H. Thomas, *Fort Toulouse: The French Outpost at the Alabamas on the Coosa* (1960; reprint, Tuscaloosa: University of Alabama Press, 1989), 6.

15. Adair, *American Indians,* 267.

16. Jean-Bernard Bossu to Marquis de l'Estrade, May 2, 1759, in Seymour Feiler, trans. and ed., *Jean-Bernard Bossu's Travels in the Interior of North America, 1751–1762* (Norman: University of Oklahoma Press, 1962), 144.

17. Letter of Captain Thomas Robinson, June 22, 1763, in William Roberts, *An Account of the First Discovery and Natural History of Florida* (1763; reprint, Gainesville: University Presses of Florida, 1976), 95.

18. Quoted in Robert R. Rea, *Major Robert Farmar of Mobile* (Tuscaloosa: University of Alabama Press, 1990), 44.

19. Captain Lieutenant James Campbell, Thirty-fourth Regiment of Foot, to John Campbell, Fourth Earl of Loudoun, December 15, 1763, in Robert R. Rea, "A Letter from Mobile, 1763," *Alabama Review* 22 (July 1969): 234–35.

20. Quoted in Rea, *Major Robert Farmar,* 37.

21. Quoted in Robert R. Rea, "'Graveyard for Britons,' West Florida, 1763–1781," *Florida Historical Quarterly* 47 (April 1969): 346.

22. Quoted in Robin F. A. Fabel, *Bombast and Broadsides: The Lives of George Johnstone* (Tuscaloosa: University of Alabama Press, 1987), 33–46.

23. This document may be found in Milo B. Howard, Jr., and Robert R. Rea, trans., *The Memoire Justificatif of the Chevalier Montault de Monberaut, Indian Diplomacy in British West Florida, 1763–1765* (University: University of Alabama Press, 1965), 32.

24. Fabel, *Bombast and Broadsides,* 56.

25. Robert R. Rea, "John Eliot, Second Governor of British West Florida," *Alabama Review* 30 (October 1977): 264.

26. Quoted in Lucille Griffith, "Peter Chester and the End of the British Empire in West Florida," *Alabama Review* 30 (January 1977): 19.

27. Robin F. A. Fabel, *The Economy of British West Florida, 1763–1783* (Tuscaloosa: University of Alabama Press, 1988), 198–210.

3. Creeks and Americans at War

1. Quoted in J. Barton Starr, *Tories, Dons, and Rebels: The American Revolution in British West Florida* (Gainesville: University Presses of Florida, 1976), 133–34.

2. Quoted in Jack D. L. Holmes, "Alabama's Forgotten Settlers: Notes on the Spanish Mobile District, 1780–1813," *Alabama Historical Quarterly* 33 (Summer 1971): 88.

3. Pickett, *History of Alabama,* 342–43.

4. Edward J. Cashin, *Lachlan McGillivray, Indian Trader: The Shaping of the Southern Colonial Frontier* (Athens: University of Georgia Press, 1992), 19.

5. Kathryn E. Holland Braund, *Deerskins & Duffels: The Creek Indian Trade with Anglo-America, 1685–1815,* (Lincoln: University of Nebraska Press, 1993), 50–55, 90–92.

6. Cashin, *Lachlan McGillivray,* 77.

7. John Pope, *A Tour Through the Southern and Western Territories of the United States of North-America* (1792; reprint, Gainesville: University Presses of Florida, 1979), 46–51.

8. Arturo O'Neill to Don José de Ezpeleta, October 19, 1783, in John W. Caughey, *McGillivray of the Creeks* (Norman: University of Oklahoma Press, 1938), 62–63.

9. Corkran, *Creek Frontier,* 324.

10. Quoted in Randolph C. Downes, "Creek-American Relations, 1790–1795," *Journal of Southern History* 8 (August 1942): 352–53.

11. Pickett, *History of Alabama,* 414, 432.

12. Quoted in Downes, "Creek-American Relations," 363.

13. Andrew Ellicott, *The Journal of Andrew Ellicott* (1803; reprint, Chicago: Quadrangle Books, 1962), 204–05.

14. Quoted in Merritt B. Pound, *Benjamin Hawkins—Indian Agent* (Athens: University of Georgia Press, 1951), 135–36.

15. Quoted in Henry DeLeon Southerland, Jr., and Jerry Elijah Brown, *The Federal Road through Georgia, the Creek Nation and Alabama, 1806–1836* (Tuscaloosa: University of Alabama Press, 1989), 20.

16. Quoted in Benjamin W. Griffith, Jr., *McIntosh and Weatherford, Creek Indian Leaders* (Tuscaloosa: University of Alabama Press, 1988), 66.

17. Quoted in Frank L. Owsley, Jr., *Struggle for the Gulf Borderlands: The Creek War and the Battle of New Orleans, 1812–1815* (Gainesville: University Presses of Florida, 1981), 42.

18. Quoted in H. S. Halbert and T. H. Ball, *The Creek War of 1813 and 1814* (1895; reprint, with introduction by Frank L. Owsley, Jr., University: University of Alabama Press, 1969), 42.

19. John Francis Hamtramck Claiborne, *Life and Times of Gen. Sam Dale, the Mississippi Partisan* (New York: Harper and Brothers, 1860), 53.

20. They also may have been called Red Sticks for the red ceremonial wooden *atasas* and red wands Tecumseh's party waved during their war dances. See James Leitch Wright, Jr., *Creeks and Seminoles: The Destruction and Regeneration of the Muscogulge People* (Lincoln: University of Nebraska Press, 1986), 171.

21. Theron A. Nunez, Jr., "Creek Nativism and the Creek War of 1813–1814," *Ethnohistory* 5 (1958): 147.

22. Joel W. Martin, *Sacred Revolt: The Muskogees' Struggle for a New World* (Boston: Beacon Press, 1991), 147.

23. Brigadier General Ferdinand L. Claiborne to Major D. Beasley, Mimms's Station, August 7, 1813, in "Letters Relating to the Tragedy of Fort Mims: August–September, 1813," ed. James F. Doster, *Alabama Review* 14 (October 1961): 272–73.

24. Major Daniel Beasley to General Claiborne, August 30, 1813, in ibid., 281–82.

25. Harry Toulmin to General Flournoy, Mount Vernon, August 30, 1813, in ibid., 283–84.

26. Quoted in Martin, *Sacred Revolt,* 157.

27. Quoted in Griffith, *McIntosh and Weatherford,* 112.

28. Andrew Jackson to John Coffee, September 29, 1813, in *The Papers of Andrew Jackson, 1804–1813,* vol. 2, ed. Harold D. Moser and Sharon MacPherson (Knoxville: University of Tennessee Press, 1984), 431–32.

29. George Stiggins manuscript quoted in Nunez, "Creek Nativism," 299.

30. *The Autobiography of Sam Houston,* ed. Donald Day and Harry Herbert Ullom (Norman: University of Oklahoma Press, 1954), 11–12.

31. Alexander McCulloch to Frances F. McCulloch, April 1, 1813, in Thomas W. Cutrer, "'The Tallapoosa Might Truly Be Called the River of Blood': Major Alexander McCulloch and the Battle of Horseshoe Bend, March 27, 1813," *Alabama Review* 43 (January 1990): 38.

32. Houston, *Autobiography*, 13–14.

4. Land in the Alabama Wilderness Beckons

1. James Graham to Thomas Ruffin, November 9, 1817, in *The Papers of Thomas Ruffin*, 4 vols., ed. J. D. deRoulhac Hamilton (Raleigh: North Carolina Historical Commission, 1918), 1:198; Southerland and Brown, *Federal Road*, 102.

2. James Graham to Thomas Ruffin, August 10, 1817, in Ruffin, *Papers*, 1:194.

3. John L. Androit, ed., *Population Abstract of the United States* (McLean, Va.: Androit Associates, 1983), 4, 40, 139, 120, 316, 424.

4. D. R. Williams to Bolling Hall, January 26, 1824, Hall Family Papers, Alabama Department of Archives and History, Montgomery.

5. See Virginia Van der Veer Hamilton, *Alabama: A Bicentennial History* (New York: W. W. Norton, 1977), 3–6.

6. Quoted in Southerland and Brown, *Federal Road*, 91.

7. Richard Breckenridge, "Diary, 1816," *Transactions of the Alabama Historical Society*, 3 (1898–99): 143–49.

8. Gideon Lincecum, "Autobiography," *Publications of the Mississippi Historical Society* 8 (1904): 464–65, 468.

9. Peter J. Hamilton, "Indian Trails and Early Roads," in *Report of the Alabama Historical Commission to the Governor of Alabama, December 1, 1900*, 3 vols., ed. Thomas McAdory Owen (Montgomery: Brown Printing Co., 1901), 1:428.

10. P. M. Goode to James Asbury Tait, December 27, 1817, Tait Family Papers, Alabama Department of Archives and History.

11. Quoted in Peter J. Hamilton, "Early Roads of Alabama," *Transactions of the Alabama Historical Society* 2 (1898): 52.

12. *Niles' Weekly Register*, April 5, 1817, 96.

13. Quotes from Malcolm J. Rohrbough, *The Land Office Business* (New York: Oxford University Press, 1968), 110–11.

14. *Jones Valley Times*, May 13, 1854.

15. Quoted in Ray Mathis, *John Horry Dent: South Carolina Aristocrat on the Alabama Frontier* (University: University of Alabama Press, 1979), 23.

16. Quoted in Sally G. McMillen, *Motherhood in the Old South: Pregnancy, Childbirth, and Infant Rearing* (Baton Rouge: Louisiana State University Press, 1990), 65.

17. J. Wayne Flynt, "Alabama," in *Religion in the Southern States: A Historical Study,* ed. Samuel S. Hill (Macon: Mercer University Press, 1983), 5–6.

18. Frances C. Roberts, "Politics and Public Land Disposal in Alabama's Formative Period," *Alabama Review* 22 (July 1969): 167–72; Hugh C. Bailey, *John Williams Walker: A Study in the Political, Social, and Cultural Life of the Old Southwest* (University: University of Alabama Press, 1964), 23, 43, 68, 80–81.

19. Clarence Edwin Carter, *The Territorial Papers of the United States,* 28 vols. (Washington, D.C.: Government Printing Office, 1952), 5:290.

20. John Williams Walker to Charles Tait, January 18, 1817, Tait Family Papers; Malcolm Cook McMillan, *Constitutional Development in Alabama, 1798–1901: A Study in Politics, the Negro, and Sectionalism* (1955; reprint, Spartanburg, S.C.: Reprint Co., 1978), 18–19.

21. *Journal of the House of Representatives of the Alabama Territory,* 1st sess., 1818, 57, 114; Bailey, *Walker,* 84–85.

22. *Acts of the Alabama Territory,* 1818, 57.

23. John Williams Walker to Charles Tait, February 1, 1818, Tait Family Papers.

24. John Williams Walker to Charles Tait, November 25, 1818, ibid.

5. The Early Years: Defining the Issues

1. Anne Royall to Matt [a friend in Virginia], Huntsville, January 1, 1818, in Anne Newport Royall, *Letters from Alabama, 1817–1822,* ed. Lucille Griffith (University: University of Alabama Press, 1969), 119.

2. Ibid., 10, 118–19.

3. Huntsville *Alabama Republican,* June 5, 1819. John Williams Walker to Charles Tait, June 17, July 6, 1819, Tait Family Papers.

4. John Williams Walker to Charles Tait, November 18, December 3, 1818, February 8, 1819, Tait Family Papers. Huntsville *Alabama Republican,* January 16, 1819.

5. McMillan, *Constitutional Development,* 42–43.

6. Israel Pickens to John Williams Walker, January 5, 1820, John Williams Walker Papers, Alabama Department of Archives and History.

7. Thomas G. Percy to John Williams Walker, November 17, 1819; and Israel Pickens to John Williams Walker, January 27, 1820, ibid.

8. John McKinley to John Williams Walker, December 20, 1819; John M. Taylor to John Williams Walker, December 8, 1819, ibid.

9. Huntsville *Alabama Republican*, October 30, 1819.

10. William Wyatt Bibb to John Williams Walker, February 21, April 13, 1820; Thomas Bibb to John Williams Walker, February 22, 1820, Walker Papers; William Wyatt Bibb to Charles Tait, April 15, 1820, Tait Family Papers.

11. Bailey, *Walker,* 104–05.

12. Henry Hitchcock to John Williams Walker, January 2, 1821, Walker Papers.

13. "Israel Pickens biographical essay," in Israel Pickens Papers, Alabama Department of Archives and History; William H. Brantley, *Banking in Alabama, 1816–1860,* 2 vols. (Birmingham: Birmingham Printing Co., 1961), 1:37.

14. Quoted in Brantley, *Banking in Alabama,* 1:46–47.

15. Emma Lila Fundaburk, "Business Corporations in Alabama in the Nineteenth Century" (Ph.D. diss., Ohio State University, 1963), 15–17.

16. Henry Hitchcock to John Williams Walker, January 2, 1821, Walker Papers.

17. Hugh C. Bailey, "Israel Pickens, Peoples' Politician," *Alabama Review* 13 (April 1964): 86–87.

18. Jabez Wiggins Heustis, *History of the Bilious Fever of Alabama as it Appeared in Cahawba and its Vicinity in the Summers and Autumns of 1821 and 1822* (Cahawba: William B. Allen, 1825), 371, 373, 420.

19. William H. Brantley, *Three Capitals: A Book About the First Three Capitals of Alabama, St. Stephens, Huntsville, & Cahawba, 1818–1826* (1947; reprint, University: University of Alabama Press, 1976), 90–92; Brantley, *Banking in Alabama,* 1:67–71.

6. The Early Years: Confronting the Issues

1. Israel Pickens to Major William B. Lenoir, March 3, 1822, Pickens Papers.

2. William Kelly to Israel Pickens, cited in Bailey, "Israel Pickens," 90–91.

3. J. Mills Thornton III, *Politics and Power in a Slave Society: Alabama, 1800–1860* (Baton Rouge: Louisiana State University Press, 1978), notes that although the faction continued its "entrepreneurial endeavors" and certainly was active in local politics, "in the state at large, the Broad River group abandoned political life forever shortly after Governor Pickens' decisive triumph" in 1823; see 14–16.

4. Thomas Perkins Abernethy, *The Formative Period in Alabama, 1815–1828* (University: University of Alabama Press, 1965), 117–19; Albert Burton Moore, *History of Alabama* (1934; reprint, Tuscaloosa: Alabama Book Store, 1951), 214–15.

5. Moore, *History of Alabama,* 117.

6. Thomas S. Woodward, *Woodward's Reminiscences of the Creek, or Muscogee Indians* (Montgomery: Barrett and Wimbish, 1859; reprint, Mobile: Southern University Press, 1965), 59.

7. Ibid., 62.

8. Doy L. McCall, "LaFayette's Visit to Alabama," *Alabama Historical Quarterly* 17 (Spring/Summer 1955): 75.

9. Woodward, *Reminiscences,* 62.

10. See Southerland and Brown, *Federal Road,* 69, 75–76; Tennant S. McWilliams, "The Marquis and the Myth: Lafayette's Visit to Alabama, 1825," *Alabama Review* 22 (April 1969): 135–40.

11. Auguste Levasseur, *LaFayette in America in 1824 and 1825; or Journal of a Voyage to the United States,* 2 vols., trans. John D. Godman (Philadelphia: Carey and Lee, 1929), 2:84.

12. *Journal of the Senate of the State of Alabama,* 1825, 27–28.

13. Breckenridge, "Diary, 1816," 151.

14. Lincecum, "Autobiography," 465.

15. Quoted in G. Ward Hubbs, *Tuscaloosa: Portrait of an Alabama County* (Northridge, Calif.: Windsor Publications, 1987), 20–21.

16. John Murphy to President and Directors of the Bank of the United States, September 5, 1826; Nicholas Biddle to Governor John Murphy, October 6, 1826, Governor John Murphy Papers, Alabama Department of Archives and History.

17. Mobile *Commercial-Register,* September 5, 1826.

18. Anne Newport Royall to Matt, [Florence,] July 15, 1821, in Royall, *Letters from Alabama,* 229–30.

19. Ruth Ketring Nuermberger, *The Clays of Alabama: A Planter-Lawyer-Politician Family* (Lexington: University of Kentucky Press, 1958), 5–6, 24–27.

20. William McKinley to Henry Clay, June 3, September 29, 1823, in *The Papers of Henry Clay,* 8 vols. to date, ed. James F. Hopkins (Lexington: University of Kentucky Press, 1963), 3:427–28, 490.

21. Huntsville *Democrat,* May 26, 1831.

22. Mobile *Commercial-Register,* July 6, 1832. King's letter was dated June 13, 1832.

23. Griffith, *McIntosh and Weatherford,* 237–40, 248–52.

24. Quoted in Peter A. Brannon, "Removal of Indians from Alabama," *Alabama Historical Quarterly* 12 (1950): 96.

25. Quotes from Marvin L. Ellis III, "The Indian Fires Go Out: Removing the

Creeks from Georgia and Alabama, 1825–1837" (Master's thesis, Auburn University, 1982), 71–72.

26. Jeremiah Austill to Lewis Cass, July 31, 1833, Creek records, Roll 223, cited in Frank L. Owsley, Jr., "Francis Scott Key's Mission to Alabama in 1833," *Alabama Review* 23 (July 1970): 185.

27. Thornton, *Politics and Power,* 27–29.

28. Nuermberger, *Clays of Alabama,* 42.

29. Thornton, *Politics and Power,* 19.

7. The Cotton Kingdom

1. Hiram Fuller, *Belle Brittan on a Tour at Newport and Here and There* (New York: Derby and Jackson, 1858), 112.

2. Captain Basil Hall, *Travels in America in the Years 1827 and 1828,* 3 vols. (Edinburgh: Cadell and Company, 1829), 3:308–10.

3. [Joseph Holt Ingraham,] *The South-West, By A Yankee,* 2 vols. (New York: Harper and Brothers, 1835), 2:91.

4. Harriet Martineau, *Society in America,* 2 vols. (New York: Sanders and Otley, 1837), 2:302.

5. B. A. Botkin, ed., *Lay My Burden Down: A Folk History of Slavery* (Chicago: University of Chicago Press, 1945), 89.

6. Philip Henry Gosse, *Letters from Alabama* (1859; reprint, Tuscaloosa: University of Alabama Press, 1993), 40.

7. Quoted in Jacqueline Jones, *Labor of Love, Labor of Sorrow: Black Women, Work, and the Family, from Slavery to the Present* (New York: Basic Books, 1985; reprint, New York: Vintage Books, 1986), 23.

8. Botkin, *Lay My Burden Down,* 85.

9. Ibid., 84.

10. Herbert G. Gutman, *The Black Family in Slavery and Freedom, 1750–1925* (New York: Random House, 1976; reprint, New York: Vintage Books, 1977), 160–68.

11. George P. Rawick, ed., *The American Slave: A Composite Autobiography,* vol. 6, *Alabama and Indiana Narratives* (Westport, Conn.: Greenwood Publishing Co., 1972), 7, 10.

12. Harold Courlander, *The African* (New York: Bantam Books, 1969), 128.

13. John W. Blassingame, ed., *Slave Testimony: Two Centuries of Letters, Speeches, Interviews, and Autobiographies* (Baton Rouge: Louisiana State University Press, 1977), 643.

14. "Caesar Blackwell," *South West Baptist,* November 13, 1850, in *Alabama Baptist Historian* 27 (July 1991): 19.

15. Blassingame, *Slave Testimony,* 534.

16. Rawick, *American Slave,* supplement, 1:56.

17. Quoted in Bruce Collins, *White Society in the Antebellum South* (London: Longman, 1985), 178.

18. Rawick, *American Slave,* 6:10.

19. John Williams Walker to Chapley R. Wellborn, September 20, 1818, Walker Papers.

20. Hutson Lee to Bolling Hall, October 17, November 3, 25, 1858, Hall Family Papers.

21. Huntsville *Democrat,* June 4, 1824.

22. Journal of James Asbury Tait, Tait Family Papers.

23. Quoted in Weymouth T. Jordan, "Plantation Medicine in the Old South," *Alabama Review* 3 (April 1950): 86.

24. William Wyatt Bibb to Charles Tait, September 19, 1818, Tait Family Papers.

25. Tait Journal.

26. James B. Sellers, *Slavery in Alabama* (University: University of Alabama Press, 1950), 224.

27. Quoted in James Oakes, *Slavery and Freedom: An Interpretation of the Old South* (New York: Vintage Books, 1991), 69.

28. Frances C. Roberts, "An Experiment in Emancipation of Slaves by an Alabama Planter" (Master's thesis, University of Alabama, 1940), discusses the entire legal history of the Townsends' estates.

29. Blassingame, *Slave Testimony,* 234.

30. Rawick, *American Slave,* 6:7, 124.

31. Herbert Aptheker, *American Negro Slave Revolts* (New York: Columbia University Press, 1943; reprint, New York: International Publishers, 1978), 341.

32. Marshall Rachleff, "Big Joe, Little Joe, Bill and Jack: An Example of Slave-Resistance in Alabama," *Alabama Review* 32 (April 1979): 141–46.

33. James B. Sellers, *History of the University of Alabama, 1818–1902* (University: University of Alabama Press, 1953), 236.

34. *Travels in the Southland, 1822–1823: The Journal of Lucius Verus Bierce,* ed. George W. Knepper (Columbus: Ohio State University Press, 1966), 99–100.

35. Sarah Haynsworth Gayle Diary, quoted in Elizabeth Fox-Genovese, *Within the Plantation Household: Black and White Women of the Old South* (Chapel Hill: University of North Carolina Press, 1988), 9.

36. Quoted in Sellers, *Slavery in Alabama*, 133.

37. Ibid., 372.

38. Quoted in Harriet E. Amos [Doss], *Cotton City: Urban Development in Antebellum Mobile* (University: University of Alabama Press, 1985), 91.

39. Rawick, *American Slave*, 6:129.

8. Antebellum Society

1. W. J. Cash, *The Mind of the South* (New York: Vintage Books, 1941), ix–x, 4–14, 20–22; Harvey H. Jackson, "Time, Frontier, and the Alabama Black Belt: Searching for W. J. Cash's Planter," *Alabama Review* 44 (October 1991): 243–68.

2. Daniel R. Hundley, *Social Relations in Our Southern States* (New York: Henry B. Price, 1860), 72.

3. Quoted in Elizabeth Bowles Warbasse, *Changing Legal Rights of Married Women, 1800–1861* (New York: Garland, 1987), 92.

4. Ibid., 77–78; *Journal of the House of the State of Alabama,* 1828, 210.

5. January 2, 1830, quoted in ibid., 93–94.

6. *Acts of Alabama*, 1848, March 1, 1848, 79; ibid., 1850, February 13, 1850, 63.

7. Quoted in Kenneth R. Johnson, "White Married Women in Antebellum Alabama," *Alabama Review* 43 (January 1990): 7.

8. Quoted in Frances Gibson Satterfield, *Madame Le Vert: A Biography of Octavia Walton Le Vert* (Edisto Island, S.C.: Edisto Press, 1987), 67.

9. Sarah Gayle to John Gayle, January 10, 1832, in Josiah Gorgas Papers, W. S. Hoole Special Collections, University of Alabama.

10. Sophy [Sophia Peck] Watson to Henry Watson, July 24, 1848, in Hugh C. Bailey and William Pratt Dale II, "Missus Alone in de 'Big House,'" *Alabama Review* 8 (January 1955): 46.

11. Israel Pickens to Colonel Thomas Lenoir, August 23, 1824, in Pickens Papers.

12. Quoted in J. Wayne Flynt, *Montgomery: An Illustrated History* (Woodland Hills, Calif.: Windsor Publications, 1980), 7.

13. Quoted in Anne Firor Scott, *The Southern Lady from Pedestal to Politics, 1830–1930* (Chicago: University of Chicago Press, 1970), 68–69.

14. Israel Pickens to Major William B. Lenoir, March 3, 1822, Pickens Papers.

15. Gosse, *Letters from Alabama*, 43–44.

16. Quoted in Robert Eno Hunt, "Organizing a New South: Education Reformers in Antebellum Alabama, 1840–1860" (Ph.D. diss., University of Missouri–Columbia, 1988), 54–55.

17. Israel Pickens to William B. Lenoir, January 15, 1823, Pickens Papers.

18. Clay letter quoted in Sellers, *History of the University of Alabama*, 59–60.

19. Huntsville *Democrat*, November 23, 1824.

20. Samuel S. Lewis to Domestic and Foreign Missionary Society, June 22, 1833, in Edgar Legare Pennington, "The Episcopal Church in the Alabama Black Belt, 1822–1836," *Alabama Review* 4 (April 1951): 121.

21. Virginia Clay-Clopton, *A Belle of the Fifties: Memoirs of Mrs. Clay of Alabama* (New York: Doubleday, Page and Co., 1905), 9–10; Fox-Genovese, *Within the Plantation Household*, 14.

22. Mark Twain, *Life on the Mississippi* (New York: Harper and Row, 1917), 332–33, 370–71, 375–78.

23. Hundley, *Social Relations*, 127.

24. Rollin G. Osterweis, *Romanticism and Nationalism in the Old South* (Baton Rouge: Louisiana State University Press, 1971), 46–49.

25. Howard Winston Smith, "An Annotated Edition of Hooper's *Some Adventures of Captain Simon Suggs*" (Ph.D. diss., Vanderbilt University, 1965), 13.

26. Ibid., 83.

27. Quoted in Harriet E. Amos [Doss], "'City Belles': Images and Realities of the Lives of White Women in Antebellum Mobile," *Alabama Review* 34 (January 1981): 17.

28. Tyrone Power, *Impressions of America, During the Years 1833, 1834, and 1835*, 2 vols. (London: Richard Bentley, 1836), 2:211, 218.

29. Joseph Holt Ingraham, *The Sunny South; or, The Southerner at Home* (Philadelphia: G. G. Evans, 1860), 504.

30. Emily Moore to Barbara Simmons, April 11, 1858, Simmons Family Papers, W. S. Hoole Special Collections, University of Alabama.

31. F. N. Boney, ed., "Southern Sojourn: A Yankee Salesman in Ante-bellum Alabama," *Alabama Review* 20 (April 1967): 151.

32. Mary Betts Lewis to Mary F. Lewis, October (no date), 1842, Clay Family Papers, Huntsville Public Library.

9. Party Politics and States' Rights

1. *Journal of the Senate of the State of Alabama*, called sess., 1832, 14.

2. Thornton, *Politics and Power*, 31.

3. Quoted in ibid., 33.

4. Larry Schweikart, "Alabama's Antebellum Banks: New Interpretations, New Evidence," *Alabama Review* 38 (July 1985): 206–07.

5. Quoted in Larry Schweikart, *Banking in the American South from the Age of Jackson to Reconstruction* (Baton Rouge: Louisiana State University Press, 1987), 68.

6. Quoted in John Michael Dollar, "John McKinley: Enigmatic Trimmer" (Master's thesis, Samford University, 1981), 189–90.

7. Quoted in ibid., 185–86.

8. Joseph Glover Baldwin, *The Flush Times of Alabama and Mississippi* (1853; reprint, New York: Hill and Wang, 1957), 60, 63.

9. Theodore Henley Jack, *Sectionalism and Party Politics in Alabama, 1819–1842* (Menasha, Wis.: Collegiate Press, 1919), 70.

10. Huntsville *Democrat,* October 31, 1840.

11. Tuscaloosa *Independent Monitor,* June 11, 1841.

12. Thomas B. Alexander, et al., "The Basis of Alabama's Ante-Bellum Two-Party System," *Alabama Review* 19 (October 1966): 255, 266, 276; and Thomas B. Alexander, et al., "Who Were the Alabama Whigs?" *Alabama Review* 16 (January 1963): 6, 13.

13. Tuscaloosa *Independent Monitor,* June 16, 1841.

14. Ibid., August 25, 1841.

15. Quoted in Thornton, *Politics and Power,* 49.

16. Huntsville *Democrat,* December 4, 1841.

17. Thornton, *Politics and Power,* 46–47.

18. Report from the Bank Committee, December 19, 1842, in William Garrett, *Reminiscences of Public Men in Alabama for Thirty Years* (Atlanta: Plantation Publishing, 1872), 252.

19. Ibid., 411–12.

20. Baldwin, *Flush Times,* 192.

21. *Journal of the Senate of the State of Alabama,* 1842, 250.

22. *Congressional Globe,* 28th Cong., 1st sess., 1843–44, 80.

23. John W. Vandiver, "History of Talladega County" (typescript, Samford University Library, n.d.), 155.

24. Thornton, *Politics and Power,* 5–7.

25. Quoted in Flynt, *Montgomery,* 16.

26. Ibid., 5; Robert Gamble, *The Alabama Catalog, Historic Buildings Survey: A Guide to the Early Architecture of the State* (Tuscaloosa: University of Alabama Press, 1987), 67.

27. Garrett, *Reminiscences,* 460–61.

10. Yancey and the Alabama Platform

1. Dwight Lowell Dumond, *Anti-Slavery Origins of the Civil War* (Ann Arbor: University of Michigan Press, 1939), 98–99.

2. Ralph B. Draughon, Jr., "The Young Manhood of William L. Yancey," *Alabama Review* 19 (January 1966): 35–36.

3. Quoted in Eric H. Walther, *The Fire-Eaters* (Baton Rouge: Louisiana State University Press, 1992), 49.

4. John Witherspoon DuBose, *The Life and Times of William Lowndes Yancey* (Birmingham: Roberts and Son, 1892), 83.

5. Quoted in Frederick McKee Beatty, "William Lowndes Yancey and Alabama Secession" (Master's thesis, University of Alabama, 1990), 37.

6. Quoted in Malcolm Cook McMillan, "William L. Yancey and the Historians: One Hundred Years," *Alabama Review* 20 (July 1967): 175–76.

7. Quoted in Thomas M. Williams, *Dixon Hall Lewis* (Auburn: Alabama Polytechnic Institute Historical Studies, 4th series, 1910), 20, 24.

8. James E. Sanders to George S. Houston, February 26, 1848, in Thornton, *Politics and Power,* 123–24.

9. Quoted in Williams, *Dixon Hall Lewis,* 32.

10. Quoted in ibid., 33.

11. Quoted in Ralph B. Draughon, Jr., "George Smith Houston and Southern Unity, 1846–1849," *Alabama Review* 19 (July 1966): 201.

12. George S. Houston to Howell Cobb, March 14, 1849, in "The Correspondence of Robert Toombs, Alexander H. Stephens, and Howell Cobb," ed. Ulrich B. Phillips, *Annual Report of the American Historical Association* (Washington, D.C.: Government Printing Office, 1911), 157.

13. George S. Houston to Howell Cobb, June 26, 1849, in ibid., 166.

14. George S. Houston to Howell Cobb, August 10, 1849, in ibid., 173.

15. Quoted in Beatty, "William Lowndes Yancey," 64.

16. Walther, *Fire-Eaters,* 60.

17. Garrett, *Reminiscences,* 545.

18. Montgomery *Advertiser,* September 23, 1851.

19. Quoted in Moore, *History of Alabama,* 251.

20. Quoted in Lewy Dorman, *Party Politics in Alabama from 1850 through 1860* (Montgomery: Alabama State Department of Archives and History, Historical and Patriotic Series no. 13, 1935), 61.

21. Clay-Clopton, *Belle of the Fifties,* 21–23.

22. C. C. Clay, Jr., to Bolling Hall, September 30, 1853, C. C. Clay Papers, Alabama Department of Archives and History.

23. Thornton, *Politics and Power,* 322.

24. Quoted in Clay-Clopton, *Belle of the Fifties,* 23.

25. Quoted in Dorman, *Party Politics in Alabama,* 97.

26. Victoria V. Clayton, *White and Black Under the Old Regime* (1899; reprint, New York: Books for Libraries, 1970), 74.

11. The Secession Crisis

1. Mathis, *John Horry Dent,* 193–94.

2. *The Journals of Thomas Hubbard Hobbs,* ed. Faye Acton Axford (University: University of Alabama Press, 1976), 192.

3. Quoted in Thornton, *Politics and Power,* 327.

4. Montgomery *Advertiser,* June 29, 1853, February 14, 1855, quoted in ibid., 329.

5. Garrett, *Reminiscences,* 650.

6. See Thornton, *Politics and Power,* chap. 5, "Fear and Favor," especially 341–42.

7. William Kauffman Scarborough, ed., *The Diary of Edmund Ruffin,* vol. 1 (Baton Rouge: Louisiana State University Press, 1972), 186–88, 220–21.

8. Thornton, *Politics and Power,* 285–87.

9. Quoted in Ethel Armes, *The Story of Coal and Iron in Alabama* (1910; reprint, Birmingham: Book-keepers Press, 1972), 119.

10. Quoted in Randall M. Miller, "Daniel Pratt's Industrial Urbanism: The Cotton Mill Town in Ante-Bellum Alabama," *Alabama Historical Quarterly* 34 (Spring 1972): 11.

11. Quoted in Armes, *Coal and Iron,* 105.

12. Robert J. Norrell, "Distant Prosperity: Modernization in Nineteenth-Century Alabama," typescript, 1991, in possession of author.

13. Dorman, *Party Politics in Alabama,* 144.

14. Clarence Phillips Denman, *The Secession Movement in Alabama* (Montgomery: Alabama State Department of Archives and History, 1933), 76–79.

15. Quoted in William L. Barney, *The Secessionist Impulse: Alabama and Mississippi in 1860* (Princeton, N.J.: Princeton University Press, 1974), 243.

16. Ibid., 92–98.

17. Ralph A. Wooster, *The Secession Conventions of the South* (Princeton, N.J.: Princeton University Press, 1962), 53–56, 65–66.

18. William R. Smith, *The History and Debates of the Convention of the People of Alabama, January 1861* (Atlanta: Rice and Co., 1861), 119.

19. Quoted in Malcolm Cook McMillan, *The Alabama Confederate Reader* (University: University of Alabama Press, 1963; reprint, 1993), 36–37.

20. See Thornton, *Politics and Power,* 442–61.

21. Both quotations from Denman, *Secession,* 88.

22. Quoted in Smith, *History and Debates,* 267–68.

12. At War with the Union

1. Quoted in McMillan, *Confederate Reader,* 23–24.

2. *"The Pioneer Banner:* A Confederate Camp Newspaper," *Alabama Historical Quarterly* 23 (Fall and Winter 1961): 211–19; Edward Young McMorris, *History of the First Regiment Alabama Volunteer Infantry, C.S.A.,* Alabama Department of Archives and History, Bulletin no. 2 (Montgomery: Brown Printing, 1904), 16–25.

3. McMillan, *Constitutional Development,* 76–85; Smith, *Debates,* 363–65.

4. *Congressional Globe,* 36th Cong., 2d sess., 1860–61, 645; and David Ritchey, "Williamson R. W. Cobb: Rattler of Tinware and Crockery for Peace," *Alabama Historical Quarterly* 36 (Summer 1974): 118–19.

5. Chriss Doss presentation to Civil War Conference, Auburn University, September 5, 1991.

6. Quoted in McMillan, *Confederate Reader,* 55–57.

7. Barbara Leigh Smith Bodichon, *An American Diary, 1857–8,* ed. Joseph W. Reed, Jr. (London: Routledge and Kegan Paul, 1972), 113.

8. Thomas Cooper DeLeon, *Four Years in Rebel Capitals* (Mobile: Gossip Printing Co., 1890), 26.

9. William Howard Russell, *My Diary North and South* (Boston: T.O.H.P. Burnham, 1863), 164–71.

10. C. Vann Woodward, ed., *Mary Chesnut's Civil War* (New Haven: Yale University Press, 1981), 18, 93–94.

11. Quoted in McMillan, *Confederate Reader,* 79.

12. Quoted in ibid., 85–87.

13. Quoted in ibid., 88.

14. DeLeon, *Four Years in Rebel Capitals,* 35.

15. Walter L. Fleming, *Civil War and Reconstruction* (New York: Columbia University Press, 1905), 78–80; Thomas Leonard Livermore, *Numbers and Losses in the Civil War in America, 1861–1865* (Boston: Houghton Mifflin, 1901), 20–21.

16. Rawick, *American Slave,* 6:350–51.

17. McMorris, *First Regiment Alabama*, 23.

18. Mary A. H. Gay, *Life in Dixie During the War* (Atlanta: Charles P. Byrd, 1897), 18.

19. Benjamin Franklin Jackson to [Matilda] Jackson, December 3, 1863, in *So Mourns the Dove*, ed. Alto Loftin Jackson (New York: Exposition Press, 1965), 73–75.

20. Ray Mathis, *In the Land of the Living: Wartime Letters by Confederates from the Chattahoochee Valley of Alabama and Georgia* (Troy, Ala.: Troy State University Press, 1981), 77.

21. Harriet Fitts Ryan, ed., "The Letters of Harden Perkins Cochrane, 1862–1864," *Alabama Review* 8 (January 1955): 56, 65, 69.

22. William Jemison Mims to Kate Mims, October 27, 1862, in Mims Letters, Birmingham Public Library, Birmingham; Benjamin [Franklin] Jackson to Matilda Jackson, October 11, 1863, in Jackson, *So Mourns the Dove*, 68; and Turner Vaughan to Dr. Samuel Watkins Vaughan, May 8, 1863, in *A Civil War Diary and Letters to "Pa,"* ed. William W. Vaughan (Selma: Old Depot Museum, n.d.), no page numbers.

23. Quoted in Harry Vollie Barnard, *Tattered Volunteers: The Twenty-Seventh Alabama Infantry Regiment, C.S.A.* (Northport, Ala.: Hermitage Press, 1965), 52–53.

24. Quoted in L. B. Williams, *A Sketch of the 33rd Alabama Volunteer Infantry Regiment* (Auburn: privately published, 1990), 24.

25. William Jemison Mims to Kate Mims, March 5, 1865, Mims Letters.

26. Samuel King Vann to Nancy Elizabeth Neel, August 25, 1864, in "Most Lovely Lizzie: Love Letters of a Young Confederate Soldier," arranged by William Young Elliott, in Samuel King Vann Papers, Alabama Department of Archives and History.

27. Samuel King Vann to Nancy Elizabeth Neel, October 3, 1864, in ibid.

28. [Andrew] B. Moore to [Juliet Opie] Hopkins, September 10, 1861, in Lucille Griffith, "Mrs. Juliet Opie Hopkins and Alabama Military Hospitals," *Alabama Review* 6 (April 1953): 119.

29. Kate Cumming, *A Journal of Hospital Life in the Confederate Army of Tennessee* (Louisville: J. P. Morton, 1866), 12.

30. Quoted in Flynt, "Alabama," 14.

13. The Home Front

1. Sarah Espy Diary, March 19, 1861, Alabama Department of Archives and History.

2. Parthenia Antoinette Hague, *A Blockaded Family: Life in Southern Alabama During the Civil War* (Boston: Houghton Mifflin, 1888), 39.

3. Quoted in Malcolm Cook McMillan, *The Disintegration of a Confederate State: Three Governors and Alabama's Wartime Home Front, 1861–1865* (Macon: Mercer University Press, 1986), 33.

4. William Edmund Crane, *Bugle Blast* (Cincinnati: P. G. Thomson, 1884), 9; and Bessie Russell, ed., "Rowena Webster's Recollections of Huntsville during the 1862 Occupation," *Huntsville Historical Review* 2 (April 1972): 38.

5. Mary Cook Chadick, "Civil War Days in Huntsville: A Diary of Mrs. W. D. Chadick," *Alabama Historical Quarterly* 9 (Summer 1947): 203–04, 209.

6. Sarah Espy Diary, December 7, 1863.

7. Nancy E. Barrow to James H. Barrow, April 8, 1864, in William H. Davidson, *Word From Camp Pollard, C.S.A.* (West Point, Ga.: Hester Printing Co., 1978), 235–39.

8. Quoted in Henry Eugene Sterkx, *Partners in Rebellion: Alabama Women in the Civil War* (Rutherford, N.J.: Fairleigh Dickinson University Press, 1970), 133.

9. Quoted in George C. Rable, *Civil Wars: Women and the Crisis of Southern Nationalism* (Urbana: University of Illinois Press, 1989), 84.

10. Quoted in Bell Irvin Wiley, *Confederate Women* (Westport, Conn.: Greenwood Press, 1975), 56.

11. J. W. Hill to Governor John Gill Shorter, January 1, 1862, in John Gill Shorter Papers, Alabama Department of Archives and History.

12. Laurence M. Jones to John Gill Shorter, March 17, 1862, ibid.

13. M. L. Stansel to John Gill Shorter, March 27, 1862, ibid.

14. James B. Daniel to Martha Ann [Mattie] Daniel, January 5, 1863, in "The Civil War Correspondence of James B. Daniel," ed. Hubert J. Thompson (Senior honors thesis, Samford University, 1980), 77.

15. Elias Davis to John T. Lathem, September 2, 1861, Elias Davis Papers, Southern Historical Collection, University of North Carolina, Chapel Hill.

16. H. B. Wood to Sarah Wood, January 9, 1862, in *The Marble Valley Boys*, ed. Wayne B. Wood (Hoover, Ala.: Interface Printing Co., 1986), 24.

17. Quoted in Leah Rawls Atkins, *The Valley and the Hills: An Illustrated History of Birmingham and Jefferson County* (Woodland Hills, Calif.: Windsor Publications, 1981), 36.

18. Quoted in Bessie Martin, *Desertion of Alabama Troops from the Confederate Army: A Study in Sectionalism* (1932; reprint, New York: AMS Press, 1966), 146.

19. Quoted in ibid., 31.

20. Bush Jones to John Gill Shorter, July 12, 1863; and Company B, Fifty-fourth Regiment, especially H. H. Moreland to Shorter, July 20, 1863, Shorter Papers.

21. John Allan Wyeth, *That Devil Forrest: Life of Lieutenant-General Nathan Bedford Forrest* (1899; reprint, Baton Rouge: Louisiana State University Press, 1989), 175.

22. Streight's report in McMillan, *Confederate Reader,* 199.

23. Sarah Espy Diary, May 2–3, 1863.

24. Streight's report in McMillan, *Confederate Reader,* 199–200.

25. Quoted in Beatty, "William Lowndes Yancey," 124.

26. Quoted in McMillan, *Disintegration,* 70.

27. Quoted in ibid., 83.

28. General [William] T. Sherman to Major General [Lovell] H. Rousseau, July 7, 1864, in McMillan, *Confederate Reader,* 261.

29. Quoted in Charles G. Summersell, *CSS* Alabama: *Builder, Captain, and Plans* (University: University of Alabama Press, 1985), 84–85.

30. Quoted in William N. Still, Jr., *Iron Afloat: The Story of the Confederate Armorclads* (Nashville: Vanderbilt University Press, 1971), 201.

31. Quoted in McMillan, *Confederate Reader,* 315.

32. Quoted in James Pickett Jones, *Yankee Blitzkrieg: Wilson's Raid through Alabama and Georgia* (Athens: University of Georgia Press, 1976), 49.

14. Reconstruction: The Second Beginning

1. Quoted in Robert H. McKenzie, "The Economic Impact of Federal Operations in Alabama During the Civil War," *Alabama Historical Quarterly* 38 (Spring 1976): 57.

2. Opelika *Era and Whig,* September 29, 1871.

3. William Garrett, *Reminiscences of Public Men in Alabama for Thirty Years* (Atlanta: Plantation Publishing, 1872), 735.

4. Quoted in Walter L. Fleming, *Civil War and Reconstruction in Alabama* (1905; reprint, Gloucester, Mass.: Peter Smith, 1949), 364.

5. Quoted in Richard N. Current, ed., *Reconstruction* (Englewood Cliffs, N.J.: Prentice-Hall, 1965), 15.

6. Quoted in John B. Myers, "The Freedmen and the Law in Post-Bellum Alabama, 1865–1867," *Alabama Review* 23 (January 1970): 57.

7. Quoted in Michael L. Lanza, *Agrarianism and Reconstruction Politics: The Southern Homestead Act* (Baton Rouge: Louisiana State University Press, 1990), 27.

8. Quoted in Loren Schweninger, "James Rapier and the Negro Labor Movement, 1869–1872," *Alabama Review* 28 (July 1975): 186.

9. Quoted in John B. Myers, "The Alabama Freedmen and the Economic Adjustments During Presidential Reconstruction, 1865–1867," *Alabama Review* 26 (October 1973): 260.

10. Quoted in Myers, "Freedmen and the Law," 60.

11. Quoted in ibid., 59.

15. Radical Reconstruction

1. Loren Schweninger, "Alabama Blacks and the Congressional Reconstruction Acts of 1867," *Alabama Review* 31 (July 1978): 183.

2. Quoted in ibid., 190.

3. General George G. Meade to General [Ulysses] S. Grant, March 23, 1868, in William Letford and Henry Eugene Sterkx, eds., "Military Reconstruction in Alabama; A Selected List of Documents from 1867–1869," Alabama Department of Archives and History, Montgomery.

4. Fleming, *Civil War and Reconstruction,* 735–36; Willis Brewer, *Alabama: Her History, Resources, War Record and Public Men From 1540 to 1872* (1872; reprint, Spartanburg, S.C.: Reprint Co., 1975), 509.

5. Fleming, *Civil War and Reconstruction,* 599.

6. Quoted in Stephen B. Weeks, *History of Public School Education in Alabama* (Washington, D.C.: Government Printing Office, 1915), 81.

7. Fleming, *Civil War and Reconstruction,* 626.

8. *Acts of Alabama,* 1890–91, 554–55.

9. Fleming, *Civil War and Reconstruction,* 609.

10. Howard N. Rabinowitz, "Half a Loaf: The Shift from White to Black Teachers in the Negro Schools of the Urban South, 1865–1890," *Journal of Southern History* 40 (November 1974): 578.

11. Weeks, *Public Education,* 106.

16. The Bourbon Oligarchy and the New Old South

1. Florence *Times Journal,* September 30, 1874.

2. Grove Hill *Clarke County Democrat,* November 10, 1874.

3. Garrett, *Reminiscences,* 625.

4. Ibid., 732.

5. Montgomery *Alabama State Journal,* July 23, 1875, as quoted in Malcolm Cook McMillan, *Constitutional Development in Alabama, 1798–1901: A Study in Politics, the Negro, and Sectionalism* (Chapel Hill: University of North Carolina Press, 1955), 185.

6. Seale *Russell Register,* January 20, 1876.

7. William Warren Rogers, *The One-Gallused Rebellion; Agrarianism in Alabama, 1865–1896* (Baton Rouge: Louisiana State University Press, 1970), 17.

8. Jonathan M. Wiener, *Social Origins of the New South; Alabama, 1860–1885* (Baton Rouge: Louisiana State University Press, 1978), 83–84.

9. Ibid., 93.

17. The Agricultural Alternative and the Rise of Industry

1. Joseph Squire, *Geological Survey of Alabama; Report on the Cahaba Coal Field* (Montgomery: Brown Printing Co., 1890), 18.

2. Ethel Armes, *The Story of Coal and Iron in Alabama* (Birmingham: Chamber of Commerce, 1910), 257.

3. Ibid., 253.

4. Montgomery *Advertiser,* January 23, 1869, quoting Wetumpka *Gazette.*

5. Greenville *Advocate,* March 11, 1880.

6. Bessemer *Pig,* April 25, 1892.

7. Montgomery *Advertiser,* July 29, 1865.

8. Birmingham *Sunday Chronicle,* August 23, 1885.

9. C. Vann Woodward, *Origins of the New South, 1877–1913* (Baton Rouge: Louisiana State University Press, 1951), 133.

18. New Winds and Old Voices

1. Union Springs *Herald,* July 14, 1875, quoting Demopolis *News Journal.*

2. Centreville *Bibb Blade,* July 8, 1880.

3. James L. Pugh to Edward A. O'Neal, illegible date, 1882, in Edward A. O'Neal Papers, Southern Historical Collection, University of North Carolina at Chapel Hill.

4. Birmingham *Evening Chronicle,* July 19, 1885.

5. *Second Annual Session of the State Grange, 1874,* 11. The Grange published the proceedings of its annual meetings, and the documents are on file at the Alabama Department of Archives and History.

6. Selma *Southern Argus,* November 21, 1873.

7. Butler *Choctaw Herald,* January 22, 1874.

8. Moulton *Advertiser,* January 12, 1888.

9. Ibid., June 23, 1887.

10. Ibid., October 6, 1887.

11. Ibid., September 29, 1887.

12. Ibid., May 24, 1888.

13. Centreville *Bibb Blade,* April 7, 1887.

14. Montgomery *Advertiser,* December 31, 1889, quoting Montgomery *Alliance Advocate.*

15. Newton *Messenger,* March 2, 1889.

16. Grove Hill *Clark County Democrat,* August 1, 1889.

17. Troy *Enquirer,* August 13, 1887.

18. Union Springs *Bullock County Reporter,* February 1, 1889.

19. Montgomery *Advertiser,* August 7, 1889.

20. Ibid., August 9, 1889.

19. The Defeat of Reform

1. Montgomery *Advertiser,* December 12, 1889.

2. Ibid., February 13, 1890, quoting Centre *Cherokee Advertiser.*

3. Montgomery *Alliance Herald,* April 16, 1894.

4. Butler *Choctaw Advocate,* April 27, 1892, quoting Selma *Mirror.*

5. Reuben F. Kolb to T. A. Street, April 22, 1892, in O. D. Street Papers, W. S. Hoole Special Collections, University of Alabama.

6. Montgomery *Advertiser,* June 9, 1892.

7. Butler *Choctaw Advocate,* July 13, 1892.

8. *Official Proceedings of the Democratic State Convention,* June 8, 1892 (N.p., n.d.), 10.

9. Union Springs *Herald,* June 15, 1892.

10. Eufaula *Times and News,* July 21, 1892.

11. Robert McKee to Frank Baltzell, August 7, 1892, in Robert McKee Papers, Alabama Department of Archives and History.

12. Chappell Cory to Thomas G. Jones, August 14, 1892, in Thomas G. Jones Papers, Alabama Department of Archives and History.

13. Butler *Choctaw Alliance,* December 14, 1892.

14. Evergreen *Star,* September 21, 1891.

15. "Eureka" to Montgomery *Alliance Herald,* May 4, 1893.

16. Anniston *Weekly Times,* May 25, 1893, quoting Montgomery *Alliance Herald.*

17. Eufaula *Times and News,* May 18, 1893, quoting Tuscumbia *North Alabamian.*

18. Eufaula *Times and News,* August 17, 1893, quoting Montgomery *Alliance Herald.*

19. Centre *Cherokee Sentinel,* November 30, 1893.

20. Union Springs *Herald,* May 23, 1894.

21. Butler *Choctaw Alliance,* June 20, 1894.

22. Marion *Star,* July 12, 1894.

23. Anniston *Alabama Leader,* July 25, 1895.

24. Union Springs *Herald,* January 29, 1896.

25. Eufaula *Times and News,* April 30, 1896; Prattville *Progress,* May 15, 1896.

26. Greenville *Living Truth,* July 2, 1896.

27. Tuscaloosa *Journal,* July 29, 1896.

28. Butler *Choctaw Alliance,* October 27, 1896.

29. Sheldon Hackney, *Populism to Progressivism in Alabama* (Princeton, N.J.: Princeton University Press, 1969), 326.

20. Politics, Education, and the "Splendid Little War"

1. Hackney, *Populism to Progressivism,* 144.

2. Alabama *House Journal,* 1896–97, 375–76, as quoted in David Alan Harris, "Racists and Reformers: A Study of Progressivism in Alabama, 1896–1911" (Ph.D. diss., University of North Carolina at Chapel Hill, 1967), 83.

3. *Report of the Joint Committee of the General Assembly of Alabama upon the Convict System of Alabama* (Montgomery: Brown Printing Co., 1901), 18.

4. Harris, "Racists and Reformers," 65.

5. George W. Prewett, "Unequal Funding of Alabama's Public Schools: An Historical Perspective," revised address given at the annual meeting of the Alabama Association of Historians, Birmingham, February 1, 1991, 3.

6. Joseph H. Parks and Oliver C. Weaver, Jr., *Birmingham-Southern College, 1856–1956* (Nashville: Parthenon Press, 1957).

7. *Acts of Alabama,* 1873, 177.

8. Saffold Berney, *Hand-Book of Alabama* (Birmingham: Roberts and Son, 1892), 201.

9. See, for example, Albert Burton Moore, *History of Alabama* (University, Ala.: University Supply Store, 1934), 651.

10. Alabama *House Journal,* 1896–97, 386.

11. Minutes of the Democratic State Convention, March 29, 1899, 25–27, Alabama Department of Archives and History, as quoted in Harris, "Racists and Reformers," 134.

12. Columbiana *Shelby Sentinel,* May 5, 1898. Our thanks to Professor Charlton Moseley, Georgia Southern University, for material on the First and Second Alabama.

13. Quoted in Willard B. Gatewood, Jr., "Alabama's 'Negro Soldier Experiment,' 1898–1899," *Journal of Negro History* 57 (October 1971): 345.

14. Robert Lee Bullard Diary, quoted in ibid., 346.

15. Quoted in ibid., 348.

16. Quoted in ibid., 350.

17. Beth Taylor Muskat, "The Last March: The Demise of the Black Militia in Alabama," *Alabama Review* 43 (January 1990): 30.

18. Ibid., 32.

21. The Constitution of 1901

1. Quoted in Harris, "Racists and Reformers," 149.

2. Quoted in McMillan, *Constitutional Development,* 262.

3. Hackney, *Populism to Progressivism,* 209.

4. Quoted in McMillan, *Constitutional Development,* 279.

5. Quoted in ibid., 269.

6. Quoted in ibid., 281.

7. Quoted in ibid., 282.

8. Quoted in ibid., 319.

9. Woodward, *Origins of the New South,* 323.

10. Quoted in McMillan, *Constitutional Development,* 303.

11. Quoted in ibid.

12. Quoted in ibid., 342.

13. Quoted in ibid., 343.

14. Quoted in ibid., 349n.

15. Ibid., 351.

22. The Chimerical Impulse of Progressivism

1. Montgomery *Journal,* April 13, 1904, quoted in James F. Doster, *Railroads in Alabama Politics, 1875–1914* (University: University of Alabama Press, 1957), 140; Hackney, *Populism to Progressivism,* 260.

2. Quoted in Harris, "Racists and Reformers," 312.

3. Hackney, *Populism to Progressivism,* 287.

4. Ibid., 291.

5. Harris, "Racists and Reformers," 378.

6. Hackney, *Populism to Progressivism,* 302.

7. Quoted in Harris, "Racists and Reformers," 390.

8. Ibid., 360.

9. David E. Alsobrook, "Mobile v. Birmingham: The Alabama Medical College Controversy, 1912–1920," *Alabama Review* 36 (January 1983): 44.

10. Ibid., 55.

11. Richard A. Straw, "The Collapse of Biracial Unionism: The Alabama Coal Strike of 1908," *Alabama Historical Quarterly* 37 (Summer 1975): 108.

12. Ibid., 109.

13. Ibid.

14. Ibid., 112.

15. Ibid.

16. Ibid.

17. James B. Sellers, *The Prohibition Movement in Alabama, 1702–1943* (Chapel Hill: University of North Carolina Press, 1943), 101.

18. Ibid., 81.

19. Ibid., 95.

20. Ibid., 104.

21. Ibid., 122.

22. Harris, "Racists and Reformers," 412.

23. Women in Alabama from 1865 to 1920

1. Laura Harris Craighead, *History of the Alabama Federation of Women's Clubs, 1895–1918* (Montgomery: Paragon Press, 1936), 14–15.

2. Ibid., 178.

3. Anne Gary Panell and Dorothea E. Wyatt, *Julia Strudwick Tutwiler and Social Progress in Alabama* (University: University of Alabama Press, 1961), 98.

4. John Hitz, "Helen Keller," *American Anthropologist* 8 (April–June 1906): 311.

24. Domestic Issues, the Creative State, and the Great War

1. The authors are especially indebted to Dr. Benjamin Buford Williams for his information and his insights on Alabama literature. His study is cited in the bibliography.

2. William J. Breen, "Black Women and the Great War: Mobilization and

Reform in the South," *Journal of Southern History* 44 (August 1978): 421–40.

3. Huntsville *Times,* November 11, 1918.

4. Birmingham *Age-Herald,* November 12, 1918.

25. The Politics of Reform and Stability during the 1920s

1. Hastings H. Hart, *Social Problems of Alabama: A Study of the Social Institutions and Agencies of the State of Alabama As Related to Its War Activities* (New York: Russell Sage Foundation, 1918), 15.

2. Quoted in Emily Owen, "The Career of Thomas E. Kilby in Local and State Politics," Master's thesis, University of Alabama, 1942, 130.

3. Quoted in Jimmie Frank Gross, "Strikes in the Coal, Steel, and Railroad Industries in Birmingham from 1918 to 1922," Master's thesis, Auburn University, 1962, 48.

4. Quoted in ibid., 112.

5. Quoted in Elizabeth B. Clark, "The Abolition of the Convict Lease System in Alabama, 1913–1928," Master's thesis, University of Alabama, 1949, 95.

6. Ibid., 96.

7. Quoted in William E. Gilbert, "Bibb Graves as a Progressive, 1927–1930," *Alabama Review* 10 (January 1957): 30.

8. Alabama, State Department of Education, *Report on Illiteracy by Division of Exceptional Education, 1927* (Birmingham: N.p., 1927), 14–15.

9. Alabama, State Department of Education, *Annual Report for the Scholastic Year Ending September 30, 1920, Part I* (N.p., n.d.), 11.

10. Daniel W. Hollis III, "The Hall Family and Twentieth-Century Journalism in Alabama," *Alabama Review* 32 (April 1979): 125–26.

11. Quoted in Ellin Sterne, "Prostitution in Birmingham, Alabama, 1890–1925," Master's thesis, Samford University, 1977, 121.

12. Quoted in J. Wayne Flynt, "Organized Labor, Reform, and Alabama Politics, 1920," *Alabama Review* 23 (July 1970): 172.

13. Quoted in Ralph M. Tanner, "James Thomas Heflin: United States Senator, 1920–1931," Ph.D. diss., University of Alabama, 1967, 6, 100.

14. Ibid., 113–17.

15. Jimmy R. McLeod, "Methodist and Baptist Reaction to the 1928 Presidential Campaign in Alabama," Master's thesis, Samford University, 1972, 130–31, 135, 141, 146.

16. Hugh D. Reagan, "The Presidential Campaign of 1928 in Alabama," Ph.D. diss., University of Texas, 1961, 411, 443, 449.

17. Ralph N. Brannen, "John McDuffie: State Legislator, Congressman, Federal Judge, 1883–1950," Ph.D. diss., Auburn University, 1975, 123, 125, 137.

18. Tanner, "James Thomas Heflin," 147.

19. Vincent J. Dooley, "United States Senator James Thomas Heflin and the Democratic Party Revolt in Alabama," Master's thesis, Auburn University, 1963, 16, 164.

26.   Change and Stability during the Roaring Twenties

1. Quoted in Sterne, "Prostitution in Birmingham," 127.

2. Quoted in Carole Marks, *Farewell—We're Good and Gone: The Great Black Migration* (Bloomington: Indiana University Press, 1989), 24.

3. Birmingham *News*, December 8, 10, and 27, 1925.

4. Ibid., January 1, 1926.

5. Ibid., December 29 and 30, 1925.

6. Ibid., January 2, 1926; and Al Browning, *Bowl, Bama, Bowl: A Crimson Tide Football Tradition* (Huntsville: Strode Publishers, 1977), 13.

7. Zipp Newman, *The Impact of Southern Football* (Montgomery: MB Publishing, 1969), 171.

27.   Hard Times, 1930–1940

1. Edith Foster, "Field Report," January 9–14, 1934, FERA State Series, Alabama, box 3, Record Group 69, National Archives, Washington, D.C.

2. Joseph G. Kohlenberg to Harry L. Hopkins, December 18, 1934, ibid., box 7.

3. Quoted in Marlene Hunt Rikard, "An Experiment in Welfare Capitalism: The Health Care Services of the Tennessee Coal, Iron, and Railroad Company," Ph.D. diss., University of Alabama, 1983, 284.

4. H. W. Stephenson to Harry L. Hopkins, April 15, 1934, FERA State Series, Alabama, box 5.

5. Belle Ogle to Harry L. Hopkins, May 31, 1934, ibid., box 6.

6. Lorena Hickok to Harry L. Hopkins, April 2, 1934, Lorena Hickok Papers, Franklin D. Roosevelt Library, Hyde Park, New York.

7. Grover Hall to Major [Clark] Howell, November 29, 1936, Grover Hall Papers, Alabama Department of Archives and History, Montgomery.

8. Kenneth E. Barnhart, "Supplement to a Study of the Transient Homeless in

Birmingham, Alabama, January–July, 1933," copy in FERA State Series, Alabama, box 3.

9. "Alabama Transient Bureau Monthly Statistical Report," in ibid.

10. Quoted in J. Wayne Flynt, *Mine, Mill, and Microchip: A Chronicle of Alabama Enterprise* (Northridge, Calif.: Windsor Publications, 1987), 166.

11. Bryant Sanders to FDR, undated, President's Personal Library File 21-A, Clergy Letters, Alabama, box 4, Roosevelt Library; F. J. Jacobs to FDR, November 6, 1935, ibid., box 3; Rev. E. A. Scott to FDR, October 21, 1934, ibid.; Rev. S. D. McCormick to FDR, September 30, 1935, ibid.; Rev. W. H. Pettus to FDR, September 27, 1935, ibid., box 4.

12. Rev. Jirden Frye to FDR, March 8, 1936, ibid., box 3.

13. Rev. Charles W. Smith to FDR, September 26, 1935, ibid., box 4; Rev. T. B. Hurst to FDR, September 27, 1935, ibid.; Rev. E. W. Butler to FDR, October 3, 1935, ibid., box 3; Rev. Adger Moore to FDR, September 27, 1935, ibid.

14. R. M. Hunter to FDR, September 28, 1935, ibid., box 4.

15. Quoted in James H. Jones, *Bad Blood: The Tuskegee Syphilis Experiment—A Tragedy of Race and Medicine* (New York: Free Press, 1981), 62–63.

16. Hattie Freeman to FDR, June 2, 1934, FERA State Series, Alabama, box 8.

17. Quoted in J. Wayne Flynt, *Poor But Proud: Alabama's Poor Whites* (Tuscaloosa: University of Alabama Press, 1989), 291.

18. Montgomery *Advertiser,* January 21 and 22, 1933.

19. Marie Bankhead Owen to Tallulah Bankhead, May 13, 1931, Marie Bankhead Owen Papers, Alabama Department of Archives and History.

20. Dr. Harris P. Dawson, "Fifty-Eight Years of Pediatric Practice in Montgomery, Alabama," Dawson Diary, Alabama Department of Archives and History.

21. Nancy Milford, *Zelda: A Biography* (New York: Harper and Row, 1970), 192–93.

22. Ovader Foster and Addie Moates to FDR, August 21, 1935, FERA State Series, Alabama, box 2.

23. "Instructions to Rehabilitation Subscribers in Group I," Alabama Relief Administration, FERA-WPA, box 56, Harry L. Hopkins Papers, Roosevelt Library.

24. Lorena Hickok to Harry L. Hopkins, April 7, 1934, FERA Hickok Reports, March–April, 1934, box 11, Hickok Papers.

25. Paul E. Mertz, *New Deal Policy and Southern Rural Poverty* (Baton Rouge: Louisiana State University Press, 1978), 52; [Loraine Bedsole] Tunstall to Thad Holt, July 28, 1933, FERA State Series, Alabama, box 1.

26. Confidential Report on Birmingham, Alabama (1934), box 68, Hopkins Papers.

28. How New a Deal in Alabama?

1. Brannen, "John McDuffie," 192–93, 218–19.

2. Owen Dees, "A General Review of the Miller Administration, 1931–1935," Master's thesis, Auburn University, 1936, 9.

3. Ibid., 60.

4. Ibid., 83.

5. Ibid., 106.

6. William A. Nunnelly, *Bull Connor* (Tuscaloosa: University of Alabama Press, 1991), 30.

7. Mary Edna Carlisle to [Eleanor] Roosevelt, August 7, 1934, FERA State Series, Alabama, box 6.

8. Nell Irvin Painter, *The Narrative of Hosea Hudson: His Life as a Negro Communist in the South* (Cambridge: Harvard University Press, 1979), 76.

9. William J. Baker, *Jesse Owens: An American Life* (New York: Free Press, 1986), 13.

29. A State Forged by War, 1940–1954

1. Quoted in Clinton W. Whitten, "Alabama Editorial Opinion on American Entry into World War II (1939–1942)," Master's thesis, Auburn University, 1961, 69.

2. Mary Martha Thomas, "Rosie the Alabama Riveter," *Alabama Review* 39 (July 1986): 201, 204.

3. Flynt, *Mine, Mill, and Microchip*, p. 174.

4. Robert J. Norrell, *Reaping the Whirlwind: The Civil Rights Movement in Tuskegee* (New York: Alfred A. Knopf, 1985), 52.

5. Ralph B. Draughon, "General Holland M. Smith, U.S.M.C.," *Alabama Review* 21 (January 1968): 71–72.

30. The Flowering of Alabama Liberalism: Politics and Society during the 1940s and 1950s

1. Sarah Newman Shouse, *Hillbilly Realist: Herman Clarence Nixon of Possum Trot* (University: University of Alabama Press, 1986), 168.

2. William D. Barnard, *Dixiecrats and Democrats: Alabama Politics, 1942–1950* (University: University of Alabama Press, 1974), 3.

3. Carl Grafton, "James E. Folsom and Civil Liberties in Alabama," *Alabama Review* 32 (January 1979): 5.

4. Leonard Dinnerstein, "The Senate's Rejection of Aubrey Williams as Rural Electrification Administrator," *Alabama Review* 21 (April 1968): 136.

5. Barnard, *Dixiecrats and Democrats*, 58.

6. Charles G. Dobbins, "Alabama Governors and Editors, 1930–1955: A Memoir," *Alabama Review* 29 (April 1976): 154.

7. Delores Ann Hobbs, "The States' Rights Movement of 1948," Master's thesis, Samford University, 1968, 16.

8. Paul Maxwell Smith, Jr., "Loyalists and States' Righters in the Democratic Party of Alabama, 1949–1954," Master's thesis, Auburn University, 1966, 21.

9. Ibid., 44.

10. Ibid., 62.

11. Thomas J. Gilliam, "The Second Folsom Administration: The Destruction of Alabama Liberalism, 1954–1958," Ph.D. diss., Auburn University, 1975, 30.

12. Ibid., 73.

13. Ibid., 20.

14. Norrell, *Reaping the Whirlwind*, 61, 74.

15. Jack Hurst, *Nashville's Grand Ole Opry* (New York: Harry N. Abrams, 1975), 176–77.

31. A Time to Hate: Racial Confrontation, 1955–1970

1. George R. Stewart, "Birmingham's Reaction to the 1954 Desegregation Decision," Master's thesis, Samford University, 1967, 17–19, 26, 28, 63, 68.

2. Timothy H. Briles, "The *Brown* Decision in Alabama: Rationale Behind the Reaction, 1954–1957," Master's thesis, Auburn University, 1984, 34–35.

3. Janet Stevenson, *The Montgomery Bus Boycott, December, 1955* (New York: Franklin Watts, 1971), 26.

4. Nunnelly, *Bull Connor*, 130–31.

5. Ibid., 89.

6. Taylor Branch, *Parting the Waters: America in the King Years, 1954–1963* (New York: Simon and Schuster, 1988), 684.

7. Nunnelly, *Bull Connor*, 135.

8. Branch, *Parting the Waters*, 759.

9. Ibid., 793.

10. Charles Morgan, Jr., *A Time to Speak* (New York: Harper and Row, 1964), 162.

11. J. Wayne Flynt, "The Ethics of Democratic Persuasion and the Birmingham Crisis," *Southern Speech Journal* 35 (Fall 1969): 46–47.

12. *Newsweek,* September 3, 1990, 38.

13. John R. Snow, "The Selma Campaign: A Chronicle of the Civil Rights Movement," Master's thesis, Auburn University, 1974, 10–12.

14. Ibid., 58.

15. Ibid., 116–17.

16. Ibid., 125.

17. Ibid., 126.

18. Ibid., 132.

32. Racial Politics and Economic Stagnation

1. Gilliam, "Second Folsom Administration," 59.

2. J. L. Chestnut, Jr., and Julia Cass, *Black in Selma: The Uncommon Life of J. L. Chestnut, Jr.* (New York: Farrar, Straus and Giroux, 1990), 126.

3. Gilliam, "Second Folsom Administration," 132.

4. Ibid., 202.

5. Ibid., 378.

6. Ibid., 510.

7. Nunnelly, *Bull Connor,* 124.

8. Film script of "We Shall Overcome," Administration Files, box 5, State Sovereignty Commission Papers, Alabama Department of Archives and History.

9. Eli Howell to Board of Directors, LECRA, September 6, 1967, box 1, ibid.

10. J. M. Bell to George Wallace, September 19, 1965, box 5, ibid.

11. Boyd Powell to George Wallace, May 16, 1965, box 5, ibid.

12. Mrs. William F. Keppy to George Wallace, April 28, 1965; John Rousselot to George Wallace, May 14, 1965; George O. McMillin to George Wallace, March 15, 1965; Homer F. Swihart to George Wallace, May 10, 1965, all in box 5, ibid., Eli Howell to Dr. John A. Howard, box 1, ibid.

13. Anne Permaloff and Carl Grafton, "The Chop-Up Bill and the Big Mule Alliance," *Alabama Review* 43 (October 1990): 265.

14. Julia Marks Young, "A Republican Challenge to Democratic Progressivism in the Deep South: Alabama's 1962 United States Senatorial Contest," Master's thesis, Auburn University, 1978, 31.

15. Ibid., 145–46.

16. Ibid., 168.

17. James C. Cobb, *The Selling of the South: The Southern Crusade for Industrial Development, 1936–1980* (Baton Rouge: Louisiana State University Press, 1982), 93.

33. A Time to Heal: Struggling to Find a New Vision, 1970–1990

1. Birmingham *Post-Herald*, July 20, 1990.

2. New York *Times*, March 20, 1986.

3. Opelika-Auburn *News*, March 19, 1987, and Birmingham *Post-Herald*, April 6, 1990.

4. Birmingham *News*, November 15, 1989.

5. Quoted in Birmingham *News*, July 12, 1992.

34. Gender, "Jocks," and Shakespeare: Alabama Society and Culture, 1970–1993

1. Birmingham *News*, August 4, 1990.

2. Birmingham *Post-Herald*, April 6, 1990.

3. *The Annual Report of Southern Opinion Research, 1989* (N.p.: Southern Opinion Research, 1990), 7–14.

4. Charles Reagan Wilson, "The Death of Bear Bryant: Myth and Ritual in the Modern South," *South Atlantic Quarterly* 86 (Summer 1987): 292.

5. Ibid., 288.

6. Ibid., 291.

7. Birmingham *Post-Herald*, November 27, 1989.

8. Wilson, "Death of Bear Bryant," 285.

Bibliography

Books, articles, and theses and dissertations are the only works cited in the bibliography, which is divided into three parts to conform with the book's time divisions. The materials are arranged in this manner to make sources easier to find, particularly for students. Primary materials—published and unpublished federal, state, county, and local government documents, newspapers, manuscripts, and similar sources—are cited only in Part III for a period with fewer secondary sources. Nor was it possible or considered desirable to attempt an exhaustive accounting of secondary sources. Specific quotations are listed in the notes at the end of the chapters.

Alabama is fortunate in having a wide variety of historical materials on deposit at the Alabama Department of Archives and History in Montgomery; the libraries at the University of Alabama and Auburn University are important research centers; holdings at Tuskegee University are a rich source for black history. Other colleges and universities, state and private, also have research data relevant to the state.

Special mention should be made of the outstanding collections at the Birmingham Public Library. The Mobile Public Library has historical sources for south Alabama that are not available elsewhere. Regional libraries and archives and the Library of Congress and the National Archives in Washington, D.C., have much valuable material on Alabama.

Part I. From Early Times to the End of the Civil War: Chapters 1–13

BOOKS

Abernethy, Thomas Perkins. *The Formative Period in Alabama, 1815–1828.* University: University of Alabama Press, 1965.

Adair, James. *The History of the American Indians.* 1775. Reprint. New York: Johnson Reprint, 1968.

Amos [Doss], Harriet E. *Cotton City: Urban Development in Antebellum Mobile.* University: University of Alabama Press, 1985.

Armes, Ethel. *The Story of Coal and Iron in Alabama.* 1910. Reprint. Birmingham: Book-keepers Press, 1972.

Atkins, Leah Rawls. *The Valley and the Hills: An Illustrated History of Birmingham and Jefferson County.* Woodland Hills, Calif.: Windsor Publications, 1981.

Badger, R. Reid, and Lawrence A. Clayton, eds. *Alabama and the Borderlands: From Prehistory to Statehood.* University: University of Alabama Press, 1985.

Bailey, Hugh C. *John Williams Walker: A Study in the Political, Social, and Cultural Life of the Old Southwest.* University: University of Alabama Press, 1964.

Baldwin, Joseph Glover. *The Flush Times of Alabama and Mississippi.* 1853. Reprint. New York: Hill and Wang, 1957.

Barney, William L. *The Secessionist Impulse: Alabama and Mississippi in 1860.* Princeton, N.J.: Princeton University Press, 1974.

Bartram, William. *The Travels of William Bartram.* Edited by Mark Van Doren. New York: Dover Publications, 1928.

Bergeron, Arthur W. *Confederate Mobile.* Jackson: University of Mississippi Press, 1991.

Betts, Edward Chambers. *Historic Huntsville from Early History of Huntsville, Alabama, 1804–1870.* 1909. Reprint. Birmingham: Southern University Press, 1966.

Blassingame, John W., ed. *Slave Testimony: Two Centuries of Letters, Speeches, Interviews, and Autobiographies.* Baton Rouge: Louisiana State University Press, 1977.

Blesser, Carol. *In Joy and in Sorrow: Women, Family, and Marriage in the Victorian South, 1830–1900.* New York: Oxford University Press, 1991.

Bourne, Edward Gaylord, ed. *Narratives of the Career of Hernando de Soto.* 2 vols. New York: Allerton Book Co., 1904.

Boyd, Minnie Clare. *Alabama in the Fifties: A Social Study.* New York: Columbia University Press, 1931.

Brantley, William H. *Banking in Alabama, 1816–1860.* 2 vols. Birmingham: Birmingham Printing Co., 1961.

———. *Three Capitals, A Book About the First Three Capitals of Alabama: St. Stephens, Huntsville & Cahawba, 1818–1826.* 1947. Reprint. University: University of Alabama Press, 1976.

Braund, Kathryn E. Holland. *Deerskins and Duffels: The Creek Indian Trade with Anglo-America, 1685–1815.* Lincoln: University of Nebraska Press, 1993.

Brewer, Willis. *Alabama: Her History, Resources, War Record, and Public Men, From 1540 to 1872.* Montgomery: Barrett and Brown, 1872.

Bryant, William O. *Cahaba Prison and the* Sultana *Disaster.* Tuscaloosa: University of Alabama Press, 1990.

Cashin, Edward J. *Lachlan McGillivray, Indian Trader: The Shaping of the Southern Colonial Frontier.* Athens: University of Georgia Press, 1992.

Cashin, Joan E. *A Family Venture: Men and Women on the Southern Frontier.* New York: Oxford University Press, 1991.

Caughey, John W. *McGillivray of the Creeks.* Norman: University of Oklahoma Press, 1938.

Claiborne, John Francis Hamtramck. *Life and Times of Gen. Sam Dale, the Mississippi Partisan.* New York: Harper and Brothers, 1860.

———. *Mississippi as a Province, Territory and State, with Biographical Notices of Eminent Citizens.* 1880. Reprint. Baton Rouge: Louisiana State University Press, 1964.

Clark, Willis G. *History of Education in Alabama, 1702–1889.* Bureau of Education, Circular no. 3. Washington, D.C.: Government Printing Office, 1889.

Clay-Clopton, Virginia. *A Belle of the Fifties: Memoirs of Mrs. Clay of Alabama.* New York: Doubleday, Page and Co., 1905.

Clayton, Lawrence A., Vernon James Knight, Jr., and Edward C. Moore, eds. *The De Soto Chronicles: The Expedition of Hernando De Soto to North America in 1539–1543.* 2 vols. Tuscaloosa: University of Alabama Press, 1993.

Clayton, Victoria V. *White and Black Under the Old Regime.* 1899. Reprint. New York: Books for Libraries, 1970.

Connor, Henry G. *John Archibald Campbell: Associate Justice of the United States Supreme Court.* 1920. Reprint. New York: Da Capo Press, 1971.

Corkran, David H. *The Creek Frontier, 1540–1783.* Norman: University of Oklahoma Press, 1967.

Cotterill, R. S. *The Southern Indians: The Story of the Civilized Tribes Before Removal.* Norman: University of Oklahoma Press, 1954.

Cumming, Kate. *A Journal of Hospital Life in the Confederate Army of Tennessee.* Louisville: J. P. Morton, 1866.

Davis, Charles S. *The Cotton Kingdom in Alabama.* 1939. Reprint. Philadelphia: Porcupine Press, 1974.

Delaney, Caldwell. *Confederate Mobile.* Mobile: Haunted Book Shop, 1971.

———. *Remember Mobile.* Mobile: Gill Printing and Stationery Co., 1948.

Delaney, Norman C. *John McIntosh Kell of the Raider Alabama.* University: University of Alabama Press, 1973.

DeLeon, Thomas Cooper. *Belles, Beaux and Brains of the 60's.* New York: G. W. Dillingham, 1909.

———. *Four Years in Rebel Capitals.* Mobile: Gossip Printing Co., 1890.

Denman, Clarence Phillips. *The Secession Movement in Alabama.* Montgomery: Alabama State Department of Archives and History, 1933.

Dodd, Donald B., and Wynelle S. Dodd. *Historical Statistics of the South, 1790–1970.* University: University of Alabama Press, 1973.

———. *Winston: An Antebellum and Civil War History of a Hill County of North Alabama.* Vol. 4 of *Annals of Northwest Alabama,* compiled by Carl Elliott. Birmingham: Oxmoor Press, 1972.

Dorman, Lewy. *Party Politics in Alabama from 1850 through 1860.* Montgomery: Alabama State Department of Archives and History, Historical and Patriotic Series no. 13, 1935.

DuBose, John Witherspoon. *The Life and Times of William Lowndes Yancey.* Birmingham: Roberts and Son, 1892.

Eccles, W. J. *France in America*. 1972. Reprint. East Lansing: Michigan State University Press, 1990.

Fabel, Robin F. A. *Bombast and Broadsides: The Lives of George Johnstone*. Tuscaloosa: University of Alabama Press, 1987.

————. *The Economy of British West Florida, 1763–1783*. Tuscaloosa: University of Alabama Press, 1988.

Fitts, Alston, III. *Selma: Queen City of the Black Belt*. Selma: Clairmont Press, 1989.

Fleming, Walter L. *Civil War and Reconstruction in Alabama*. New York: Columbia University Press, 1905.

Flynt, J. Wayne. *Montgomery: An Illustrated History.* Woodland Hills, Calif.: Windsor Publications, 1980.

————. *Poor But Proud: Alabama's Poor Whites*. Tuscaloosa: University of Alabama Press, 1989.

Folmar, John Kent, ed. *From That Terrible Field: Civil War Letters of James M. Williams, Twenty-First Alabama Infantry Volunteers*. University: University of Alabama Press, 1981.

Fox-Genovese, Elizabeth. *Within the Plantation Household: Black and White Women of the Old South*. Chapel Hill: University of North Carolina Press, 1988.

Fretwell, Mark E. *This So Remote Frontier: The Chattahoochee Country of Alabama and Georgia*. Eufaula, Ala.: Historic Chattahoochee Commission, 1980.

Fundaburk, Emma Lila, and Mary Douglass Fundaburk Foreman. *Sun Circles and Human Hands: The Southern Indians—Art and Industries*. Luverne, Ala.: Privately Printed, 1957.

Gamble, Robert. *The Alabama Catalog, Historic Buildings Survey: A Guide to the Early Architecture of the State*. Tuscaloosa: University of Alabama Press, 1987.

Garrett, William. *Reminiscences of Public Men in Alabama for Thirty Years.* Atlanta: Plantation Publishing, 1872.

Gibson, Arrell Morgan. *The Chickasaws*. Norman: University of Oklahoma Press, 1971.

Gosse, Philip Henry. *Letters from Alabama*. 1859. Reprint. Tuscaloosa: University of Alabama Press, 1993.

Griffith, Benjamin W., Jr. *McIntosh and Weatherford, Creek Indian Leaders*. Tuscaloosa: University of Alabama Press, 1988.

Griffith, Lucille, ed. *Alabama: A Documentary History to 1900*. University: University of Alabama Press, 1968.

Gutman, Herbert G. *The Black Family in Slavery and Freedom, 1750–1925*. New York: Random House, 1976. Reprint. New York: Vintage Books, 1977.

Hague, Parthenia Antoinette. *A Blockaded Family: Life in Southern Alabama During the Civil War*. Boston: Houghton Mifflin, 1888.

Halbert, H. S., and T. H. Ball. *The Creek War of 1813 and 1814*. 1895. Reprint, with introduction by Frank L. Owsley, Jr. University: University of Alabama Press, 1969.

Hamilton, Peter J. *Colonial Mobile.* 1897. 1910. Reprint. Edited with introduction and annotations by Charles G. Summersell. University: University of Alabama Press, 1976.

Hawkins, Benjamin. *Letters, Journals and Writings of Benjamin Hawkins.* 2 vols. Savannah: Beehive Press, 1980.

———. *A Sketch of the Creek Country, In the Years 1798 and 1799 and Letters from Benjamin Hawkins, 1796–1806.* Originally published in the *Collections of the Georgia Historical Society.* Spartanburg, S.C.: Reprint Co., 1982.

Henry, Robert Selph. *"First With the Most" Forrest.* Jackson, Tenn.: McCowat-Mercer Press, 1944.

Heustis, Jabez Wiggins. *History of the Bilious Fever of Alabama as it Appeared in Cahawba and its Vicinity in the Summers and Autumns of 1821 and 1822.* Cahawba: William B. Allen, 1825.

Higginbotham, Jay. *Old Mobile: Fort Louis de la Louisiane, 1702–1711.* 1977. Reprint. Tuscaloosa: University of Alabama Press, 1991.

Hobbs, Thomas Hubbard. *The Journals of Thomas Hubbard.* Edited by Faye Acton Axford. University: University of Alabama Press, 1976.

Hoole, William Stanley. *According to Hoole: Collected Essays and Tales.* University: University of Alabama Press, 1973.

———. *Alabama Tories: The First Alabama Cavalry, U.S.A., 1862–1865.* Tuscaloosa: Confederate Publishing Co., 1960.

Horseman, Reginald. *Josiah Nott of Mobile: Southerner, Physician, and Racial Theorist.* Baton Rouge: Louisiana State University Press, 1987.

Hubbs, G. Ward. *Tuscaloosa: Portrait of an Alabama County.* Northridge, Calif.: Windsor Publications, 1987.

Hudson, Charles. *The Southeastern Indians.* Knoxville: University of Tennessee Press, 1976.

Hundley, Daniel R. *Social Relations in Our Southern States.* New York: Henry B. Price, 1860.

Jack, Theodore Henley. *Sectionalism and Party Politics in Alabama, 1819–1842.* Menasha, Wis.: Collegiate Press, 1919.

Jackson, Alto Loftin, ed. *So Mourns the Dove: Letters of a Confederate Infantryman and His Family.* New York: Exposition Press, 1965.

Jenkins, Ned J., and Richard A. Krause. *The Tombigbee Watershed in Southern Prehistory.* University: University of Alabama Press, 1986.

Jones, Jacqueline. *Labor of Love, Labor of Sorrow: Black Women, Work, and the Family, from Slavery to the Present.* New York: Basic Books, 1985. Reprint. New York: Vintage Books, 1986.

Jones, James Pickett. *Yankee Blitzkrieg: Wilson's Raid Through Alabama and Georgia.* Athens: University of Georgia Press, 1976.

Jones, Katherine M. *Heroines of Dixie: Confederate Women Tell Their Story of the War.* New York: Bobbs-Merrill, 1955.

Jordan, Thomas, and J. P. Pryor. *The Campaigns of Lieut.-Gen. N. B. Forrest and of Forrest's Cavalry.* 1868. Reprint. Dayton: Morningside Press, 1988.

Jordan, Weymouth T. *Ante-Bellum Alabama: Town and Country.* 1957. Reprint. Tuscaloosa: University of Alabama Press, 1987.

Levasseur, Auguste. *LaFayette in America in 1824 and 1825; or Journal of a Voyage to the United States.* Translated by John D. Godman. 2 vols. Philadelphia: Carey and Lee, 1929.

Lonn, Ella. *Desertion During the Civil War.* New York: Century, 1928.

——. *Salt as a Factor in the Confederacy.* New York: Walter Neale, 1933.

Lyell, Charles. *A Second Visit to the United States of North America.* 2 vols. New York: Harper and Brothers, 1849.

McGee, Val. *Claybank Memories: A History of Dale County, Alabama.* Ozark, Ala.: Dale County Historical Society, 1989.

McLaurin, Melton, and Michael Thomason. *Mobile: The Life and Times of a Great Southern City.* Woodland Hills, Calif.: Windsor Publications, 1981.

McMillan, Malcolm Cook. *The Alabama Confederate Reader.* University: University of Alabama Press, 1963.

——. *Constitutional Development in Alabama, 1798–1901: A Study in Politics, the Negro, and Sectionalism.* 1955. Reprint. Spartanburg, S.C.: Reprint Co., 1978.

——. *The Disintegration of a Confederate State: Three Governors and Alabama's Wartime Home Front, 1861–1865.* Macon: Mercer University Press, 1986.

McMillen, Sally G. *Motherhood in the Old South: Pregnancy, Childbirth, and Infant Rearing.* Baton Rouge: Louisiana State University Press, 1990.

McWhiney, Grady. *Cracker Culture: Celtic Ways in the Old South.* Tuscaloosa: University of Alabama Press, 1988.

McWilliams, Richebourg Gaillard, trans. *Iberville's Gulf Journals.* University: University of Alabama Press, 1981.

Marshall, James William. *The Presbyterian Church in Alabama.* Montgomery: Presbyterian Historical Society of Alabama, 1977.

Martin, Bessie. *Desertion of Alabama Troops from the Confederate Army: A Study in Sectionalism.* 1932. Reprint. New York: AMS Press, 1966.

Martin, Joel W. *Sacred Revolt: The Muskogees' Struggle for a New World.* Boston: Beacon Press, 1991.

Martineau, Harriet. *Society in America.* 2 vols. New York: Sanders and Otley, 1837.

Mathis, Ray. *In the Land of the Living: Wartime Letters by Confederates from the Chattahoochee Valley of Alabama and Georgia.* Troy, Ala.: Troy State University Press, 1981.

——. *John Horry Dent: South Carolina Aristocrat on the Alabama Frontier.* University: University of Alabama Press, 1979.

Matte, Jacqueline Anderson. *The History of Washington County, First County in Alabama.* Chatom, Ala.: Washington County Historical Society, 1982.

Milanich, Jerald T., and Susan Milbrath, eds. *First Encounters: Spanish Explora-*

tions in the Caribbean and the United States, 1492–1570. Gainesville: University of Florida Press, 1989.

Milham, Charles G. *Gallant Pelham: American Extraordinary.* Washington, D.C.: Public Affairs Press, 1959.

Miller, Randall M., ed. *"Dear Master": Letters of a Slave Family.* Ithaca, N.Y.: Cornell University Press, 1978.

Moore, Albert Burton. *Conscription and Conflict in the Confederacy.* New York: Macmillan, 1924.

———. *History of Alabama.* 1934. Reprint. Tuscaloosa: Alabama Book Store, 1951.

Moore, Glover. *William Jemison Mims, Soldier and Squire.* Birmingham: Birmingham Printing Co., 1966.

Nuermberger, Ruth Ketring. *The Clays of Alabama: A Planter-Lawyer-Politician Family.* Lexington: University of Kentucky Press, 1958.

Oakes, James. *Slavery and Freedom: An Interpretation of the Old South.* New York: Vintage Books, 1991.

Olmsted, Fredrick Law. *The Cotton Kingdom.* Edited by Arthur M. Schlesinger. New York: Alfred A. Knopf, 1970.

Osterweis, Rollin G. *Romanticism and Nationalism in the Old South.* Baton Rouge: Louisiana State University Press, 1971.

Owen, Thomas M. *History of Alabama and Dictionary of Alabama Biography.* 4 vols. Chicago: S. J. Clarke, 1921.

Owsley, Frank L. *King Cotton Diplomacy: Foreign Relations of the Confederate States of America.* Chicago: University of Chicago Press, 1931.

———. *Plain Folk of the Old South.* Baton Rouge: Louisiana State University Press, 1949.

Owsley, Frank L., Jr. *The C.S.S. Florida: Her Building and Operations.* Tuscaloosa: University of Alabama Press, 1987.

———. *Struggle for the Gulf Borderlands: The Creek War and the Battle of New Orleans, 1812–1815.* Gainesville: University Presses of Florida, 1981.

Pénicaut, André. *Fleur de Lys and Calumet: Being the Narrative of French Adventure in Louisiana.* Translated and edited by Richebourg Gaillard McWilliams. 1953. Reprint. Tuscaloosa: University of Alabama Press, 1988.

Pickett, Albert James. *History of Alabama, and Incidentally of Georgia and Mississippi, from the Earliest Period.* 1851. Reprint. Birmingham: Birmingham Book and Magazine Co., 1962.

Posey, Walter Brownlow. *Alabama in the 1830's As Recorded by British Travellers.* Birmingham: Birmingham-Southern College Bulletin, vol. 21, 1938.

Pound, Merritt B. *Benjamin Hawkins—Indian Agent.* Athens: University of Georgia Press, 1951.

Powell, Mary Lucas, ed. *What Mean These Bones: Studies in Southeastern Bioarchaeology.* Tuscaloosa: University of Alabama Press, 1991.

Priestley, Herbert I. *Tristán de Luna.* Glendale, Calif.: Arthur H. Clark, 1936.

Rable, George C. *Civil Wars: Women and the Crisis of Southern Nationalism.* Urbana: University of Illinois Press, 1989.

Ramsdell, Charles William. *Behind the Lines in the Southern Confederacy.* Baton Rouge: Louisiana State University Press, 1944.

Rawick, George P., ed. *The American Slave: A Composite Autobiography.* Vol. 6, *Alabama and Indiana Narratives,* and Supplement, Series 1, vol. 1, *Alabama Narratives.* Westport, Conn.: Greenwood Publishing Co., 1972.

Rea, Robert R. *Major Robert Farmar of Mobile.* Tuscaloosa: University of Alabama Press, 1990.

Read, William A. *Indian Place Names in Alabama.* University: University of Alabama Press, 1984.

Riley, Benjamin F. *Makers and Romance of Alabama History.* N.p., 1915[?].

Rowland, Dunbar, and Albert Godfrey Sanders, eds. *Mississippi Provincial Archives, 1701–1729, French Dominion.* 5 vols. Jackson: Mississippi Department of Archives and History, 1929.

Royall, Anne Newport. *Letters from Alabama, 1817–1822.* Edited by Lucille Griffith. University: University of Alabama Press, 1969.

Russell, William Howard. *My Diary North and South.* Boston: T.O.H.P. Burnham, 1863.

Satterfield, Frances Gibson. *Madame Le Vert: A Biography of Octavia Walton Le Vert.* Edisto Island, S.C.: Edisto Press, 1987.

Schweikart, Larry. *Banking in the American South from the Age of Jackson to Reconstruction.* Baton Rouge: Louisiana State University Press, 1987.

Scott, Anne Firor. *The Southern Lady from Pedestal to Politics, 1830–1930.* Chicago: University of Chicago Press, 1970.

Sellers, James B. *History of the University of Alabama, 1818–1902.* University: University of Alabama Press, 1953.

———. *Slavery in Alabama.* University: University of Alabama Press, 1950.

Semmes, [Admiral] Raphael. *The Confederate Raider Alabama.* Edited by Philip Van Doren Stern. Gloucester, Mass.: Peter Smith, 1969.

———. *Service Afloat: or, The Remarkable Career of the Confederate Cruisers Sumter and Alabama.* Baltimore: Baltimore Publishing Co., 1887.

Smith, William R. *The History and Debates of the Convention of the People of Alabama, January 1861.* Atlanta: Rice and Co., 1861.

Smith, Winston. *Days of Exile: The Story of the Vine and Olive Colony in Alabama.* Demopolis: Marengo County Historical Society, 1978.

Southerland, Henry DeLeon, Jr., and Jerry Elijah Brown. *The Federal Road through Georgia, the Creek Nation, and Alabama, 1806–1836.* Tuscaloosa: University of Alabama Press, 1989.

Starr, J. Barton. *Tories, Dons, and Rebels: The American Revolution in British West Florida.* Gainesville: University Presses of Florida, 1976.

Sterkx, Henry Eugene. *Partners in Rebellion: Alabama Women in the Civil War.* Rutherford, N.J.: Fairleigh Dickinson University Press, 1970.

Stuckey, Sterling. *Slave Culture: Nationalist Theory and the Foundations of Black America.* New York: Oxford University Press, 1987.

Summersell, Charles G. *CSS* Alabama: *Builder, Captain, and Plans.* University: University of Alabama Press, 1985.

Swanton, John R. *Final Report of the United States DeSoto Expedition Commission.* Washington D.C.: Smithsonian Institution Press, 1985.

————. *The Indians of the Southeastern United States.* Washington, D.C.: U.S. Government Printing Office, 1946. Reprint. Washington, D.C.: Smithsonian Institute Press, 1984.

Tatum, Georgia Lee. *Disloyalty in the Confederacy.* Chapel Hill: University of North Carolina Press, 1934.

Thomas, Daniel H. *Fort Toulouse: The French Outpost at the Alabamas on the Coosa.* 1960. Reprint. Tuscaloosa: University of Alabama Press, 1989.

Thornton, J. Mills, III. *Politics and Power in a Slave Society: Alabama, 1800–1860.* Baton Rouge: Louisiana State University Press, 1978.

Tompkins, Alma Cole. *Charles Tait.* Auburn: Alabama Polytechnic Institute Historical Studies, 4th series, 1910.

Turner, Maxine. *Navy Gray: A Story of the Confederate Navy on the Chattahoochee and Apalachicola Rivers.* Tuscaloosa: University of Alabama Press, 1988.

Vandiver, Frank E. *Ploughshares into Swords: Josiah Gorgas and Confederate Ordnance.* Austin: University of Texas Press, 1952.

————, ed. *The Civil War Diary of General Josiah Gorgas.* University: University of Alabama Press, 1947.

Varner, John Grier, and Jeannette Johnson Varner, trans. and eds. *The Florida of the Inca.* Austin: University of Texas Press, 1962.

Walker, Anne Kendrick. *Back Tracking in Barbour County.* Richmond: Diety Press, 1941.

Walthall, John A. *Moundville: An Introduction to the Archaeology of a Mississippian Chiefdom.* Tuscaloosa: Alabama Museum of Natural History, 1977.

————. *Prehistoric Indians of the Southeast: Archaeology of Alabama and the Middle South.* University: University of Alabama Press, 1980.

Walther, Eric H. *The Fire-Eaters.* Baton Rouge: Louisiana State University Press, 1992.

Welch, Paul D. *Moundville's Economy.* Tuscaloosa: University of Alabama Press, 1991.

Wiley, Bell Irvin. *Confederate Women.* Westport, Conn.: Greenwood Press, 1975.

————. *The Life of Johnny Reb: The Common Soldier of the Confederacy.* Garden City, N.Y.: Doubleday, 1971.

Williams, Benjamin Buford. *A Literary History of Alabama: The Nineteenth Century.* Rutherford, N.J.: Fairleigh Dickinson University Press, 1979.

Williams, Thomas M. *Dixon Hall Lewis.* Auburn: Alabama Polytechnic Institute Historical Studies, 4th series, 1910.

Willoughby, Lynn. *Fair to Middlin': The Antebellum Cotton Trade of the Apalachicola/ Chattahoochee River Valley.* Tuscaloosa: University of Alabama Press, 1993.

Woodman, Harold D. *King Cotton and His Retainers: Financing and Marketing the Cotton Crop of the South, 1800–1925.* 1968. Reprint. Columbia: University of South Carolina Press, 1990.

Woodward, Grace Steele. *The Cherokees.* Norman: University of Oklahoma Press, 1963.

Woodward, Thomas S. *Woodward's Reminiscences of the Creek, or Muscogee Indians.* Montgomery: Barrett and Wimbish, 1859. Reprint. Mobile: Southern University Press, 1965.

Wooster, Ralph A. *The People in Power: Courthouse and Statehouse in the Lower South, 1850–1860.* Knoxville: University of Tennessee Press, 1969.

———. *The Secession Conventions of the South.* Princeton, N.J.: Princeton University Press, 1962.

Wright, James Leitch, Jr. *Creeks and Seminoles: The Destruction and Regeneration of the Muscogulge People.* Lincoln: University of Nebraska Press, 1986.

———. *The Only Land They Knew: The Tragic Story of the American Indians in the Old South.* New York: Free Press, 1981.

ARTICLES

Alexander, Thomas B., and Peggy J. Duckworth. "Alabama Black Belt Whigs during Secession." *Alabama Review* 17 (July 1964): 181–97.

Alexander, Thomas B., Peggy Duckworth Elmore, Frank M. Lowrey, and Mary Jane Pickens Skinner. "The Basis of Alabama's Ante-Bellum Two-Party System." *Alabama Review* 19 (October 1966): 243–76.

Alexander, Thomas B., Kit C. Carter, Jack R. Lister, Jerry C. Oldshue, and Winfred G. Sandlin. "Who Were the Alabama Whigs?" *Alabama Review* 16 (January 1963): 5–19.

Amos [Doss], Harriet E. "'Birds of Passage' in a Cotton Port: Northerners and Foreigners Among the Urban Leaders of Mobile, 1820–1860." In *Class, Conflict, and Consensus: Antebellum Southern Community Studies,* edited by Orville Vernon Burton and Robert C. McMath, Jr. Westport, Conn.: Greenwood Press, 1982.

———. "'City Belles': Images and Realities of the Lives of White Women in Antebellum Mobile." *Alabama Review* 34 (January 1981): 3–19.

———. "Religious Reconstruction in Microcosm at Faunsdale Plantation." *Alabama Review* 42 (October 1989): 243–69.

Atkins, Leah Rawls. "Felix Grundy McConnell: Old South Demagogue." *Alabama Review* 30 (April 1977): 83–100.

———. "The First Legislative Session: The General Assembly of Alabama, Huntsville, 1819." *Alabama Review* 23 (January 1970): 30–44.

———. "Williamson R. W. Cobb and the Graduation Act of 1854." *Alabama Review* 28 (January 1975): 16–31.

Bibliography

Bailey, Hugh C. "Disloyalty in Early Confederate Alabama." *Journal of Southern History* 23 (1957): 522–28.

———. "Israel Pickens, Peoples' Politician." *Alabama Review* 17 (April 1964): 83–101.

Bailey, Hugh C., and William Pratt Dale II. "Missus Alone in de 'Big House.'" *Alabama Review* 8 (January 1955): 43–54.

Barber, Douglas. "Council Government and the Genesis of the Creek War." *Alabama Review* 38 (July 1985): 163–74.

Bearss, Edwin C. "Rousseau's Raid on the Montgomery and West Point Railroad." *Alabama Historical Quarterly* 25 (Spring-Summer 1963): 7–48.

Beerman, Eric. "José De Ezepeleta: Alabama's First Spanish Commandant during the American Revolution." *Alabama Review* 29 (October 1976): 249–60.

Beidler, Philip D. "Alabama at Gettysburg." *Alabama Heritage,* no. 10 (Fall 1988): 16–31.

Bigham, Darrel E. "From the Green Mountains to the Tombigbee: Henry Hitchcock in Territorial Alabama, 1817–1819." *Alabama Review* 26 (July 1973): 209–28.

Brannon, Peter A. "Removal of Indians from Alabama." *Alabama Historical Quarterly* 12 (1950): 91–117.

Braund, Kathryn E. Holland. "Guardians of Tradition and Handmaidens to Change: Women's Roles in Creek Economic and Social Life during the Eighteenth Century." *American Indian Quarterly* 14 (Summer 1990): 239–58.

Breckenridge, Richard. "Diary, 1816." *Transactions of the Alabama Historical Society* 3 (1898–99): 142–53.

Brooks, Daniel Fate. "Henry Stiles Atwood: Antebellum Eccentric of Wilcox County." *Alabama Review* 34 (January 1981): 20–30.

Chadick, Mary Cook. "Civil War Days in Huntsville: A Diary of Mrs. W. D. Chadick." *Alabama Historical Quarterly* 9 (Summer 1947): 199–333.

Chappell, Gordon T. "John Coffee: Land Speculator and Planter." *Alabama Review* 22 (January 1969): 24–43.

———. "John Coffee: Surveyor and Land Agent." *Alabama Review* 14 (October 1961): 243–50.

Childress, David T. "Mount Vernon Barracks: The Blue, The Gray, and The Red." *Alabama Review* 42 (April 1989): 125–35.

Clayton, Lawrence A. "The Spanish Heritage of the Southeast." *Alabama Heritage,* no. 4 (Spring 1987): 2–11.

Cook, James F. "The 1863 Raid of Abel D. Streight: Why It Failed." *Alabama Review* 22 (October 1969): 254–69.

Cozart, Toccoa. "Henry W. Hilliard." *Transactions of the Alabama Historical Society* 4 (1902): 277–99.

Current-Garcia, Eugene. "Joseph Glover Baldwin: Antebellum Wit." *Alabama Heritage,* no. 13 (Summer 1989): 32–43.

683

———. "Mr. Spirit and His Alabama Wits." *Alabama Heritage,* no. 4 (Spring 1987): 38–51.

Cutrer, Thomas W. "'The Tallapoosa Might Truly Be Called the River of Blood': Major Alexander McCulloch and the Battle of Horseshoe Bend, March 27, 1813." *Alabama Review* 43 (January 1990): 35–39.

Dean, Lewis S. "Alabama Gold: Harvest of the Piedmont." *Alabama Heritage,* no. 21 (Summer 1991): 20–29.

———. "Michael Tuomey and the Pursuit of a Geological Survey of Alabama, 1847–1857." *Alabama Review* 44 (April 1991): 101–11.

Donald, W. J. "Alabama Confederate Hospitals." *Alabama Review* 15 (October 1962): 271–81; 16 (January 1963): 64–78.

Doster, James F. "Early Settlements on the Tombigbee and Tensaw Rivers." *Alabama Review* 12 (April 1959): 83–94.

———, ed. "Letters Relating to the Tragedy of Fort Mims: August–September, 1813." *Alabama Review* 14 (October 1961): 269–85.

Draughon, Ralph B., Jr. "George Smith Houston and Southern Unity, 1846–1849." *Alabama Review* 19 (July 1966): 186–207.

———. "The Young Manhood of William L. Yancey." *Alabama Review* 19 (January 1966): 28–40.

Dupre, Daniel. "Ambivalent Capitalists on the Cotton Frontier: Settlement and Development in the Tennessee Valley of Alabama." *Journal of Southern History* 56 (May 1990): 215–40.

Emerson, O. B. "The Bonapartist Exiles in Alabama." *Alabama Review* 11 (April 1958): 135–43.

Essler, Elizabeth McTyeire. "The Agricultural Reform Movement in Alabama, 1850–1860." *Alabama Review* 1 (October 1948): 243–60.

Fabel, Robin F. A. "George Johnstone and the 'Thoughts Concerning Florida'— A Case of Lobbying?" *Alabama Review* 29 (July 1976): 164–76.

Fabel, Robin F. A., and Robert R. Rea, "Lieutenant Thomas Campbell's Sojourn Among the Creeks, November 1764–May 1765." *Alabama Historical Quarterly* 36 (Summer 1974): 97–111.

Fleming, Mary Love [Edwards]. "Dale County and Its People During the Civil War." *Alabama Historical Quarterly* 19 (Spring 1957): 61–109.

Flynt, J. Wayne. "Alabama." In *Religion in the Southern States: A Historical Study,* edited by Samuel S. Hill. Macon: Mercer University Press, 1983.

French, Thomas L., Jr., and Edward L. French. "Horace King, Bridge Builder." *Alabama Heritage,* no. 11 (Winter 1989): 34–47.

Fretwell, Mark E. "Rousseau's Alabama Raid." *Alabama Historical Quarterly* 18 (Winter 1956): 526–50.

Griffin, Richard W. "Cotton Manufacture in Alabama to 1865." *Alabama Historical Quarterly* 18 (Fall 1956): 289–307.

Griffith, Lucille. "Mrs. Juliet Opie Hopkins and Alabama Military Hospitals." *Alabama Review* 6 (April 1953): 99–120.

———. "Peter Chester and the End of the British Empire in West Florida." *Alabama Review* 30 (January 1977): 14–33.

Hall, John C. "The Search for Hernando de Soto." *Alabama Heritage,* no. 4 (Spring 1987): 12–27.

Helmbold, F. Wilbur. "Early Alabama Newspapermen, 1810–1820." *Alabama Review* 12 (January 1959): 53–68.

Holmes, Jack D. L. "Alabama's Forgotten Settlers: Notes on the Spanish Mobile District, 1780–1813." *Alabama Historical Quarterly* 33 (Summer 1971): 87–97.

———. "Notes on the Spanish Fort San Esteban de Tombecbé." *Alabama Review* 18 (October 1965): 281–90.

Hoole, William Stanley. "Jeremiah Clemens, Novelist." *Alabama Review* 18 (January 1965): 5–36.

Howard, Milo B., Jr. "Alabama State Currency, 1861–1865." *Alabama Historical Quarterly* 25 (Spring-Summer 1963): 70–98.

———. "The General Ticket." *Alabama Review* 19 (July 1966): 163–74.

———, ed. "A. B. Moore Correspondence Relating to Secession." *Alabama Historical Quarterly* 23 (Spring 1961): 1–27.

Jackson, Carlton Luther. "Alabama's Hilliard: A Nationalistic Rebel of the Old South." *Alabama Historical Quarterly* 31 (Fall-Winter 1969): 183–205.

———. "The White Basis System and the Decline of Alabama Whiggery." *Alabama Historical Quarterly* 25 (Fall-Winter 1963): 246–53.

Jackson, Harvey H. "Time, Frontier, and the Alabama Black Belt: Searching for W. J. Cash's Planter." *Alabama Review* 44 (October 1991): 243–68.

Johnson, Evans C. "Henry W. Hilliard and the Civil War Years." *Alabama Review* 17 (April 1964): 102–12.

Johnson, Kenneth R. "White Married Women in Antebellum Alabama." *Alabama Review* 43 (January 1990): 3–17.

Jones, Allen W. "A Federal Raid into Southeast Alabama." *Alabama Review* 14 (October 1961): 259–68.

———. "A Georgia Confederate Soldier Visits Montgomery, Alabama, 1862–1863." *Alabama Historical Quarterly* 25 (Spring-Summer 1963): 99–113.

Kloeppel, James E. "The Confederate Submarine *H. L. Hunley.*" *Alabama Heritage,* no. 18 (Fall 1990): 2–19.

Letford, William, and Allen W. Jones. "Military and Naval Activities in Alabama from 1861–1865." *Alabama Historical Quarterly* 23 (Spring 1961): 189–206.

Lincecum, Gideon. "Autobiography of Gideon Lincecum." *Publications of the Mississippi Historical Society* 8 (1904): 443–519.

Long, Melvin Durward. "Political Parties and Propaganda in Alabama in the Presidential Election of 1860." *Alabama Historical Quarterly* 25 (Spring-Summer 1963): 120–35.

———. "Unanimity and Disloyalty in Secessionist Alabama." *Civil War History* 11 (1965): 257–73.

Longacre, Edward G. "To Tuscaloosa and Beyond: A Union Cavalry Raider in

Alabama, March–April, 1865." *Alabama Historical Quarterly* 44 (Spring-Summer 1982): 109–22.

McMillan, Malcolm Cook. "The Alabama Constitution of 1819: A Study." *Alabama Lawyer* 12 (January 1951): 77–91.

———. "Alabama Constitution of 1819: A Study of Constitution-Making on the Frontier." *Alabama Review* 3 (October 1950): 263–85.

———. "The Original Draft of the Alabama Constitution of 1819 as Reported by the Committee of Fifteen, Clement Comer Clay, Chairman." *Alabama Lawyer* 20 (January 1959): 5–36.

———. "William L. Yancey and the Historians: One Hundred Years." *Alabama Review* 20 (July 1967): 163–86.

McWhiney, Grady. "Were the Whigs a Class Party in Alabama?" *Journal of Southern History* 23 (November 1957): 510–22.

McWilliams, Tennant S. "The Marquis and the Myth: Lafayette's Visit to Alabama, 1825." *Alabama Review* 22 (April 1969): 135–46.

Marks, Laurence H. "Fort Mims: A Challenge." *Alabama Review* 18 (October 1965): 275–80.

Martin, John Milton. "William R. King: A Jacksonian Senator." *Alabama Review* 18 (October 1965): 243–67.

———. "William R. King and the Vice Presidency." *Alabama Review* 16 (January 1963): 35–54.

Mellown, Robert O. "Alabama's Fourth Capital: The Construction of the State House in Tuscaloosa." *Alabama Review* 40 (October 1987): 259–83.

———. "Steamboat Travel in Early Alabama." *Alabama Heritage*, no. 2 (Fall 1986): 2–11.

Miller, Carl F. "Life 8,000 Years Ago Uncovered in an Alabama Cave." *National Geographic Magazine* 110 (October 1956): 542–58.

———. "Russell Cave: New Light on Stone Age Life." *National Geographic Magazine* 113 (March 1958): 426–38.

Miller, Grace Lewis. "The Mobile and Ohio Railroads in Antebellum Times." *Alabama Historical Quarterly* 7 (1945): 58–59.

Miller, Randall M. "Daniel Pratt's Industrial Urbanism: The Cotton Mill Town in Ante-Bellum Alabama." *Alabama Historical Quarterly* 34 (Spring 1972): 5–35.

Moffat, Charles H. "Charles Tait, Planter, Politician, and Scientist of the Old South." *Journal of Southern History* 14 (May 1948): 206–33.

Napier, John H., III. "Montgomery During the Civil War." *Alabama Review* 41 (April 1988): 103–31.

Neeley, Mary Ann. "Lachlan McGillivray: A Scot on the Alabama Frontier." *Alabama Historical Quarterly* 36 (Spring 1974): 5–14.

———. "Painful Circumstances: Glimpses of the Alabama Penitentiary, 1846–1852." *Alabama Review* 44 (January 1991): 3–16.

Norrell, Robert J. "Distant Prosperity: Modernization in Nineteenth-Century Alabama." Typescript, 1991. In possession of author.

Nuermberger, Ruth Ketring. "The Royal Party in Early Alabama Politics." *Alabama Review* 6 (April 1953): 81–98; 6 (July 1953): 198–212.

Nunez, Theron A., Jr. "Creek Nativism and the Creek War of 1813–1814." *Ethnohistory* 5 (1958): 1–47, 131–75, 292–301.

Owsley, Frank L. "The Clays in Early Alabama History." *Alabama Review* 2 (October 1949): 243–68.

Owsley, Frank L., Jr. "The C.S.S. *Florida's* Tour de Force at Mobile Bay." *Alabama Review* 15 (October 1962): 262–70.

———. "The Fort Mims Massacre." *Alabama Review* 24 (July 1971): 192–204.

———. "Francis Scott Key's Mission to Alabama in 1833." *Alabama Review* 23 (July 1970): 181–92.

———. "Jackson's Capture of Pensacola." *Alabama Review* 19 (July 1966): 175–85.

Patterson, Ernest F. "Alabama's First Railroad." *Alabama Review* 9 (January 1956): 33–45.

Pennington, Edgar Legare. "The Episcopal Church in the Alabama Black Belt, 1822–1836." *Alabama Review* 4 (April 1951): 117–26.

Rachleff, Marshall. "Big Joe, Little Joe, Bill and Jack: An Example of Slave-Resistance in Alabama." *Alabama Review* 32 (April 1979): 141–46.

Rea, Robert R. "'Graveyard for Britons,' West Florida, 1763–1781." *Florida Historical Quarterly* 47 (April 1969): 345–64.

———. "A Letter from Mobile, 1763." *Alabama Review* 22 (July 1969): 230–37.

———. "John Eliot, Second Governor of British West Florida." *Alabama Review* 30 (October 1977): 243–65.

———. "Planters and Plantations in British West Florida." *Alabama Review* 29 (July 1976): 220–35.

———. "The Trouble at Tombeckby." *Alabama Review* 21 (January 1968): 21–39.

Ritchey, David. "Williamson R. W. Cobb: Rattler of Tinware and Crockery for Peace." *Alabama Historical Quarterly* 36 (Summer 1974): 112–20.

Roberts, Barbara. "Sisters of Mercy: From Vicksburg to Shelby Springs." *Alabama Heritage*, no. 11 (Winter 1989): 2–17.

Roberts, Frances C. "Dr. David Moore, Urban Pioneer of the Old Southwest." *Alabama Review* 18 (January 1965): 37–46.

———. "Politics and Public Land Disposal in Alabama's Formative Period." *Alabama Review* 22 (July 1969): 163–74.

Rogers, William Warren. "Kossuth's Visit to Alabama." *Alabama Review* 17 (April 1964): 113–22.

Rogers, William Warren, and James Pickett Jones. "Montgomery as the Confederate Capital: View of a New Nation." *Alabama Historical Quarterly* 26 (Spring 1964): 1–125.

Russell, Bessie, ed. "Rowena Webster's Recollections of Huntsville during the 1862 Occupation." *Huntsville Historical Review* 2 (April 1972): 36–47.

Schweikart, Larry. "Alabama's Antebellum Banks: New Interpretations, New Evidence." *Alabama Review* 38 (July 1985): 202–21.

Scott, Sutton S. "Recollections of the Alabama Democratic State Convention of 1860." *Transactions of the Alabama Historical Society* 4 (1902): 313–20.

Sellers, James B. "Student Life at the University of Alabama Before 1860." *Alabama Review* 2 (October 1949): 269–93.

Shields, Johanna Nicol. "A Sadder Simon Suggs: Freedom and Slavery in the Humor of Johnson Hooper." *Journal of Southern History* 56 (November 1990): 641–64.

Starr, J. Barton. " 'The Spirit of What is There Called Liberty': The Stamp Act in British West Florida." *Alabama Review* 29 (October 1976): 261–72.

Steward, Luther N., Jr. "John Forsyth." *Alabama Review* 14 (April 1961): 98–123.

Thomson, Bailey. "John C. C. Sanders: Lee's 'Boy Brigadier.' " *Alabama Review* 32 (April 1979): 83–107.

Tucker, Phillip Thomas. "The First Missouri Confederate Brigade's Last Stand at Fort Blakeley in Mobile Bay." *Alabama Review* 42 (October 1989): 270–91.

Vandiver, Frank E. "The Shelby Iron Works in the Civil War: A Study of a Confederate Industry." *Alabama Review* 1 (January 1948): 12–26; 1 (April 1948): 111–27; 1 (July 1948): 203–17.

Venable, Austin L. "The Conflict Between the Douglas and Yancey Forces in the Charleston Convention." *Journal of Southern History* 8 (May 1942): 226–41.

Walton, Brian G. "Elections to the United States Senate in Alabama Before the Civil War." *Alabama Review* 27 (January 1974): 3–38.

Wiener, Jonathan M. "Female Planters and Planters' Wives in Civil War and Reconstruction: Alabama, 1850–1870." *Alabama Review* 30 (April 1977): 135–49.

Williams, Clanton W. "Conservatism in Old Montgomery, 1817–1861." *Alabama Review* 10 (April 1957): 96–110.

———. "Early Ante-Bellum Montgomery: A Black-Belt Constituency." *Journal of Southern History* 7 (November 1941): 495–525.

———. "Presidential Election Returns and Related Data for Ante-Bellum Alabama." *Alabama Review* 1 (October 1948): 279–93; 2 (January 1949): 63–73.

Williams, Jack K. "Crime and Punishment in Alabama, 1819–1840." *Alabama Review* 6 (January 1953): 14–30.

Wood, Wayne B. "From Montgomery to Gettysburg: War Letters from Alabama Soldier Henry B. Wood." *Alabama Heritage*, no. 15 (Winter 1990): 26–45.

Woodward, Joseph H. "Alabama Iron Manufacturing, 1860–1865." *Alabama Review* 7 (July 1954): 199–207.

Wooster, Ralph A. "The Alabama Secession Convention." *Alabama Review* 12 (January 1959): 69–75.

DISSERTATIONS AND THESES

Abrams, David L. "The State Bank of Alabama, 1841–1845." Master's thesis, Auburn University, 1965.

Bibliography

Amos [Doss], Harriet E. "Social Life in an Antebellum Cotton Port: Mobile, Alabama, 1820–1860." Ph.D. diss., Emory University, 1976.

Atkins, Leah Rawls. "Southern Congressmen and the Homestead Bill." Ph.D. diss., Auburn University, 1974.

Beatty, Frederick McKee. "William Lowndes Yancey and Alabama Secession." Master's thesis, University of Alabama, 1990.

Bjurberg, Richard H. "A Political and Economic Study of Alabama's Governors and Congressmen, 1831–1861." Master's thesis, Auburn University, 1947.

Boucher, Ann Williams. "Wealthy Planter Families in Nineteenth-Century Alabama." Ph.D. diss., University of Connecticut, 1978.

Brannen, Ralph N. "John Gill Shorter: War Governor of Alabama, 1861–1863." Master's thesis, Auburn University, 1956.

Brooks, Daniel Fate. "The Mind of Wilcox County: An Antebellum History, 1819–1861." Master's thesis, Samford University, 1984.

Buchanan, Robert P. "The Military Campaign for Mobile, 1864–1865." Master's thesis, Auburn University, 1963.

Carter, Kit Carson, Jr. "A Critical Analysis of the Basis of Party Alignment in Lowndes County, Alabama, 1836–1860." Master's thesis, University of Alabama, 1961.

Clark, James Harold. "History of the North East and South West Railroad to 1872." Master's thesis, University of Alabama, 1949.

Collins, Helen. "The Alabama Territory, 1817–1819." Master's thesis, Auburn University, 1941.

Crockett, Charles Elliott. "A History of Nullification in the State of Alabama from 1832–1852." Master's thesis, Auburn University, 1968.

Dodd, Donald B. "Unionism in Northwest Alabama Through 1865." Master's thesis, Auburn University, 1961.

Dollar, John Michael. "John McKinley: Enigmatic Trimmer." Master's thesis, Samford University, 1981.

Douglass, Susan Goode. "Canals and River Improvement in Alabama, 1819–1840." Master's thesis, Auburn University, 1970.

Draughon, Ralph B., Jr. "William Lowndes Yancey: From Unionist to Secessionist." Ph.D. diss., University of North Carolina, 1968.

Ellis, Marvin L., III. "The Indian Fires Go Out: Removing the Creeks from Georgia and Alabama, 1825–1837." Master's thesis, Auburn University, 1982.

Everse, Martin Lee. "The Iron Works at Brierfield: A History of Iron Making in Bibb County, Alabama." Master's thesis, Samford University, 1984.

Faircloth, Ronald W. "The Legislative Career of Dixon Hall Lewis, 1826–1848." Master's thesis, Auburn University, 1965.

Framer, Edward M. "Alabama Negroes, 1861–1865." Master's thesis, Auburn University, 1955.

Fundaburk, Emma Lila. "Business Corporations in Alabama in the Nineteenth Century." Ph.D. diss., Ohio State University, 1963.

Gilham, Leon Edward, Jr. "General John T. Croxton's Raid Upon Tuscaloosa County and the University of Alabama." Master's thesis, Samford University, 1980.

Goss, Charles Wayne. "The French and the Choctaw Indians, 1700–1763." Ph.D. diss., Texas Tech University, 1977.

Green, Michael D. "Federal-State Conflict in the Administration of Indian Policy: Georgia, Alabama, and the Creeks, 1824–1834." Ph.D. diss., University of Iowa, 1973.

Halperin, Rick. "Leroy Pope Walker and the Problems of the Confederate War Department, February–September, 1861." Ph.D. diss., Auburn University, 1978.

Harper, John H. "Rousseau's Alabama Raid." Master's thesis, Auburn University, 1965.

Holland, Kathryn E. "Mutual Convenience, Mutual Dependence: The Creek, Augusta, and the Deerskin Trade, 1733–1783." Ph.D. diss., Florida State University, 1986.

Hunt, Robert Eno. "Organizing a New South: Education Reformers in Antebellum Alabama, 1840–1860." Ph.D. diss., University of Missouri–Columbia, 1988.

Ikerman, William J. "The Role of the Steamboat in the Development of the Cotton Kingdom in Alabama, 1819–1860." Master's thesis, Auburn University, 1963.

Jackson, Carlton Luther. "A History of the Whig Party in Alabama, 1828–1860." Ph.D. diss., University of Georgia, 1962.

Johnson, Evans C. "A Political Life of Henry W. Hilliard." Master's thesis, University of Alabama, 1947.

LeGrand, Phyllis L. "Destitution and Relief of Indigent Soldiers' Families of Alabama during the Civil War." Master's thesis, Auburn University, 1964.

Long, Melvin Durward. "Alabama in Formation of the Confederacy." Ph.D. diss., University of Florida, 1959.

Lynch, Jeanne Hall. "Thomas H. Watts: War Governor of Alabama, 1863–1865." Master's thesis, Auburn University, 1957.

Manley, Frances Formby. "Activities of Women in Alabama before 1860." Master's thesis, Auburn University, 1932.

Martin, John Milton. "William Rufus King: Southern Moderate." Ph.D. diss., University of North Carolina, 1955.

Miller, Randall M. "The Cotton Mill Movement in Antebellum Alabama." Ph.D. diss., Ohio State University, 1971.

Reynolds, Donald Eugene. "Southern Newspapers in the Secession Crisis, 1860–1861." Ph.D. diss., Tulane University, 1965.

Roberts, Frances C. "An Experiment in Emancipation of Slaves by an Alabama Planter." Master's thesis, University of Alabama, 1940.

Robinson, Robert L. "Mobile in the 1850s: A Social, Cultural and Economic History." Master's thesis, University of Alabama, 1955.

Rogers, William Warren. "Alabama and the Compromise of 1850." Master's thesis, Auburn University, 1951.

Seale, Kathleen. "The Alabama Platform, 1848–1860." Master's thesis, Auburn University, 1937.

Smith, Thomas Alton. "Mobilization of the Army in Alabama, 1859–1865." Master's thesis, Auburn University, 1953.

Taylor, Paul Wayne. "Mobile: 1818–1859 as Her Newspapers Pictured Her." Master's thesis, University of Alabama, 1951.

Thompson, Alan Smith. "Mobile, Alabama, 1850–1861: Economic, Political, Physical, and Population Characteristics." Ph.D. diss., University of Alabama, 1979.

Part II. From 1865 through 1920: Chapters 14–24

BOOKS

Anderson, Robert Mapes. *Visions of the Disinherited: The Making of American Pentacostalism.* New York: Oxford University Press, 1979.

Armes, Ethel. *The Story of Coal and Iron in Alabama.* Birmingham: Chamber of Commerce, 1910.

Bailey, Hugh C. *Edgar Gardner Murphy; Gentle Progressive.* Miami: University of Miami Press, 1968.

Bailey, Kenneth K. *Southern White Protestantism in the Twentieth Century.* New York: Harper and Row, 1964.

Bennett, James R. *Old Tannehill; A History of the Pioneer Ironworks in Roupes Valley (1829–1865).* Birmingham: Birmingham Historical Commission, 1986.

Bond, Horace Mann. *Negro Education in Alabama: A Study in Cotton and Steel.* Washington, D.C.: Associated Publishers, 1939.

Braddy, Nella. *Anne Sullivan Macy: The Story Behind Helen Keller.* Garden City, N.Y.: Doubleday, Doran, 1933.

Brock, G. W. *Historical Sketches State Teachers College.* Livingston, Ala.: N.p., 1938.

Bureau of Educational Research, University of Alabama. *A Study of Stillman Institute A Junior College for Negroes.* Tuscaloosa: University of Alabama, 1946.

Clark, Willis G. *History of Education in Alabama, 1702–1889.* Bureau of Education, Circular no. 3. Washington D.C.: Government Printing Office, 1889.

Craighead, Laura Harris. *History of the Alabama Federation of Women's Clubs, 1895–1918.* Montgomery: Paragon Press, 1936.

Cruickshank, George M. *A History of Birmingham and Its Environs.* 2 vols. New York: Lewis, 1920.

Current, Richard N. *Those Terrible Carpetbaggers.* New York: Oxford University Press, 1988.

Doster, James F. *Railroads in Alabama Politics, 1875–1914.* University: University of Alabama Press, 1957.

DuBois, W. E. B. *Black Reconstruction in America, 1860–1880.* New York: Harcourt, Brace, 1935.

Bibliography

Ellison, Rhoda Coleman. *Bibb County, Alabama; The First Hundred Years, 1818–1918.* University: University of Alabama Press, 1984.

———. *History of Huntingdon College, 1854–1954.* University: University of Alabama Press, 1954.

Fitzgerald, Michael R. *The Union League Movement in the Deep South.* Baton Rouge: Louisiana State University Press, 1989.

Fleming, Walter L. *Civil War and Reconstruction in Alabama.* 1905. Reprint. Gloucester, Mass.: Peter Smith, 1949.

———. *The Freedmen's Savings Bank; A Chapter in the Economic History of the Negro Race.* Chapel Hill: University of North Carolina Press, 1927.

Foster, Gaines M. *Ghosts of the Confederacy: Defeat, the Lost Cause, and the Emergence of the New South, 1865–1913.* Baton Rouge: Louisiana State University Press, 1987.

Friedman, Jean E. *The Enclosed Garden: Women and Community in the Evangelical South, 1830–1900.* Chapel Hill: University of North Carolina Press, 1985.

Fry, Joseph A. *John Tyler Morgan and the Search for Southern Autonomy.* Knoxville: University of Tennessee Press, 1992.

Going, Allen J. *Bourbon Democracy in Alabama, 1874–1890.* University: University of Alabama Press, 1951.

Gray, Jerome A., Joe L. Reed, and Norman W. Walton. *History of the Alabama State Teachers Association.* Washington, D.C.: National Education Association, 1987.

Griffith, Lucille. *Alabama College, 1896–1969.* Montevallo: University of Montevallo, 1969.

Hackney, Sheldon. *Populism to Progressivism in Alabama.* Princeton, N.J.: Princeton University Press, 1969.

Hammett, Hugh B. *Hilary Abner Herbert: A Southerner Returns to the Union.* Philadelphia: American Philosophical Society, 1976.

Harlan, Louis R. *Booker T. Washington: The Making of a Black Leader.* New York: Oxford University Press, 1972.

———. *Booker T. Washington: The Wizard of Tuskegee.* New York: Oxford University Press, 1983.

Harris, Carl V. *Political Power in Birmingham, 1871–1921.* Knoxville: University of Tennessee Press, 1977.

Harvey, Ira. *A History of Educational Finance in Alabama, 1819–1986.* Auburn: Truman Pierce Institute for Advancement of Teacher Education, 1989.

Hill, Samuel S. *Southern Churches in Crisis.* New York: Holt, Rinehart, and Winston, 1967.

Holley, Howard L. *A History of Medicine in Alabama.* Birmingham: University of Alabama School of Medicine, 1982.

Hollifield, Mollie. *Auburn Loveliest Village of the Plains.* N.p., 1955.

Howard, Gene L. *Death at Cross Plains; An Alabama Reconstruction Tragedy.* University: University of Alabama Press, 1984.

Huey, Mattie McAdory. *History of the Alabama Division of the United Daughters of the Confederacy.* Opelika: N.p., 1937.

Hyman, Michael. *The Anti-Redeemers: Hill Country Political Dissenters in the Lower South from Redemption to Populism.* Baton Rouge: Louisiana State University Press, 1990.

Kenny, Michael. *Catholic Culture in Alabama; Centenary Story of Spring Hill College, 1830–1930.* New York: America Press, 1931.

Kerr, John Leeds. *The Louisville and Nashville; An Outline History.* New York: Young and Ottley, 1933.

Kerr, Norwood Allen. *History of the Alabama Experiment Station, 1883–1982.* Auburn: Alabama Agricultural Experiment Station, 1985.

Kolchin, Peter. *First Freedom: The Response of Alabama Blacks to Emancipation and Reconstruction.* Westport, Conn.: Greenwood Press, 1972.

Kraditor, Aileen S. *The Idea of the Woman Suffrage Movement, 1893–1924.* New York: Columbia University Press, 1965.

Lovett, Rose Gibbons. *The Catholic Church in the Deep South: The Diocese of Birmingham in Alabama, 1540–1976.* Birmingham: The Diocese, 1980.

McDowell, John Patrick. *The Social Gospel in the South, 1886–1939: The Women's Home Mission Movement in the Methodist Episcopal Church.* Baton Rouge: Louisiana State University Press, 1982.

McMillan, Malcolm Cook. *Constitutional Development in Alabama, 1798–1901: A Study in Politics, the Negro, and Sectionalism.* Chapel Hill: University of North Carolina Press, 1955.

McMillan, Malcolm Cook, and Allen Jones. *Auburn University Through the Years, 1856–1973.* Auburn: Auburn University Bulletin, 1973.

Manly, Louise. *History of Judson College.* Atlanta: Foote and Davis, 1913.

Millett, Allan R. *The General; Robert L. Bullard and Officership in the United States Army, 1881–1925.* Westport, Conn.: Greenwood Press, 1975.

Morris, Robert C. *Reading, 'Riting and Reconstruction; The Education of Freedmen in the South, 1861–1870.* Chicago: University of Chicago Press, 1981.

Norrell, Robert J. *The Autobiography of a New South Industrialist.* Chapel Hill: University of North Carolina Press, 1991.

Panell, Anne Gary, and Dorothea E. Wyatt. *Julia Strudwick Tutwiler and Social Progress in Alabama.* University: University of Alabama Press, 1961.

Parks, Joseph H., and Oliver C. Weaver, Jr. *Birmingham-Southern College, 1856–1956.* Nashville: Parthenon Press, 1957.

Perman, Michael. *The Road to Redemption, 1867–1879.* Chapel Hill: University of North Carolina Press, 1984.

Pruitt, Ruth, and William Warren Rogers. *Stephen S. Renfroe Alabama's Outlaw Sheriff.* Tallahassee: Sentry Press, 1972.

Rabinowitz, Howard N., ed. *Southern Black Leaders of the Reconstruction Era.* Urbana: University of Illinois Press, 1982.

Rable, George C. *"But There Was No Peace": The Role of Violence in the Politics of Reconstruction.* Athens: University of Georgia Press, 1984.

Reid, Whitelaw. *After the War; A Tour of the Southern States, 1865–1866.* 1866. Reprint, edited by C. Vann Woodward. New York: Harper and Row, 1965.

Richardson, Jesse Monroe. *The Contributions of John William Abercrombie to Public Education.* Nashville: George Peabody College, 1949.

Rogers, William Warren. *The One-Gallused Rebellion; Agrarianism in Alabama, 1865–1896.* Baton Rouge: Louisiana State University Press, 1970.

Rogers, William Warren, and Robert David Ward. *August Reckoning; Jack Turner and Racism in Post–Civil War Alabama.* Baton Rouge: Louisiana State University Press, 1973.

Rogers, William Warren, Jr. *Black Belt Scalawag; Charles Hays and Southern Republicans.* Athens: University of Georgia Press, 1993.

Sawyer, Eppie White. *The First Hundred Years: The History of Jacksonville State University, 1883–1983.* Jacksonville, Ala.: Jacksonville Centennial Committee, 1983.

Schweninger, Loren. *James T. Rapier and Reconstruction.* Chicago: University of Chicago Press, 1983.

Scott, Anne Firor. *The Southern Lady from Pedestal to Politics, 1830–1930.* Chicago: University of Chicago Press, 1970.

Sellers, James B. *History of the University of Alabama, 1818–1902.* University: University of Alabama Press, 1953.

———. *The Prohibition Movement in Alabama, 1702–1943.* Chapel Hill: University of North Carolina Press, 1943.

Sherer, Robert G. *Subordination or Liberation? The Development and Conflicting Theories of Black Education in Nineteenth Century Alabama.* University: University of Alabama Press, 1977.

Sheridan, Richard C. *Deshler Female Institute; An Example of Female Education in Alabama, 1874–1918.* Birmingham: Birmingham Printing and Publishing Co., 1986.

Stover, John F. *The Railroads of the South, 1865–1890.* Chapel Hill: University of North Carolina Press, 1955.

Thomas, Mary Martha. *The New Women in Alabama: Social Reform and Suffrage, 1890–1920.* Tuscaloosa: University of Alabama Press, 1992.

Trelease, Allen W. *White Terror: The Ku Klux Klan Conspiracy and Southern Reconstruction.* New York: Harper and Row, 1971.

Walker, Anne Kendrick. *Life and Achievements of Alfred Montgomery Shook.* Birmingham: Birmingham Publishing Co., 1952.

Ward, Robert David, and William Warren Rogers. *Convicts, Coal, and the Banner Mine Tragedy.* Tuscaloosa: University of Alabama Press, 1987.

———. *Labor Revolt in Alabama; The Great Strike of 1894.* University: University of Alabama Press, 1965.

Weeks, Stephen B. *History of Public School Education in Alabama.* Washington, D.C.: Government Printing Office, 1915.

Wiebel, Arthur V. *Biography of a Business.* N.p.: United States Steel Corporation, 1960.

Wiener, Jonathan M. *Social Origins of the New South; Alabama, 1860–1885.* Baton Rouge: Louisiana State University Press, 1978.

Wiggins, Sarah Woolfolk. *The Scalawag in Alabama Politics, 1865–1881.* University: University of Alabama Press, 1977.

Williams, Benjamin Buford. *A Literary History of Alabama: The Nineteenth Century.* Rutherford, N.J.: Fairleigh Dickinson University Press, 1979.

Wilson, Charles Reagan. *Baptized in Blood: The Religion of the Lost Cause.* Athens: University of Georgia Press, 1980.

Wolfe, Suzanne Rau. *The University of Alabama: A Pictorial History.* University: University of Alabama Press, 1983.

ARTICLES

Allen, Lee N. "The Women's Suffrage Movement in Alabama, 1910–1920." *Alabama Review* 11 (April 1958): 81–89.

Alsobrook, David E. "Mobile v. Birmingham: The Alabama Medical College Controversy, 1912–1920." *Alabama Review* 36 (January 1983): 37–56.

Anderson, George L. "The South and Problems of Post–Civil War Finance." *Journal of Southern History* 9 (May 1943): 181–95.

Berkin, Carol Ruth. "Women's Life." In *Encyclopedia of Southern Culture,* edited by Charles Reagan Wilson and Willis Ferris. Chapel Hill: University of North Carolina Press, 1989.

Bethel, Elizabeth. "The Freedmen's Bureau in Alabama." *Journal of Southern History* 14 (February 1948): 49–92.

Breen, William J. "Black Women and the Great War: Mobilization and Reform in the South." *Journal of Southern History* 44 (August 1978): 421–40.

Clark, Thomas D. "The Furnishing and Supply System in Southern Agriculture since 1865." *Journal of Southern History* 12 (February 1946): 24–44.

Cloyd, Daniel Lee. "Prelude to Reform: Political, Economic, and Social Thought of Alabama Baptists, 1877–1890." *Alabama Review* 31 (January 1978): 48–64.

Cohen, William. "Negro Involuntary Servitude in the South, 1865–1940: A Preliminary Analysis." *Journal of Southern History* 42 (February 1976): 32–60.

Cox, John, and LaWanda Cox. "General O. O. Howard and the 'Misrepresented Bureau.'" *Journal of Southern History* 19 (November 1953): 427–56.

Crumley, L. A., George S. Vann, and E. W. Patton. "History of Alabama Dentists Prior to 1941." Typescript, 1941[?]. Alabama Department of Archives and History, Montgomery.

Daniel, Mike. "The Arrest and Trial of Ryland Randolph, April–May, 1868." *Alabama Historical Quarterly* 40 (Fall and Winter 1978): 127–43.

Davis, Thomas J. "Alabama's Reconstruction Representatives in the U.S. Congress, 1868–1878: A Profile." *Alabama Historical Quarterly* 44 (Spring and Summer 1982): 32–49.

Delaney, Caldwell. "Mary McNeil Fenollosa, An Alabama Woman of Letters." *Alabama Review* 16 (July 1963): 163–73.

Figh, Margaret Gillis. "Bartow Lloyd, Humorist and Philosopher of the Alabama Back Country." *Alabama Review* 5 (April 1952): 83–99.

Fisk, Sara Huff. "Howard Weeden, Artist and Poet." *Alabama Review* 14 (April 1961): 124–37.

Fitzgerald, Michael R. "Radical Republicanism and the White Yeomanry During Alabama Reconstruction, 1865–1868." *Journal of Southern History* 54 (November 1988): 565–96.

Flynt, J. Wayne. "Alabama White Protestantism and Labor, 1900–1914." *Alabama Review* 25 (July 1972): 192–217.

———. "Southern Protestantism and Reform, 1890–1920." In *Varieties of Religious Experience,* edited by Samuel S. Hill. Baton Rouge: Louisiana State University Press, 1988.

Folmar, John Kent. "Reaction to Reconstruction: John Forsyth and the Mobile *Advertiser and Register,* 1865–1867." *Alabama Historical Quarterly* 37 (Winter 1975): 245–63.

Fuller, Justin. "Boomtowns and Blast Furnaces: Town Promotion in Alabama, 1865–1893." *Alabama Review* 29 (January 1976): 37–48.

———. "Henry F. DeBardeleben, Industrialist of the New South." *Alabama Review* 39 (January 1986): 3–18.

Garrett, Mitchell Bennett. "Sixty Years of Howard College." *Howard College Bulletin* 85 (October 1927): 1–67.

Gatewood, Willard B., Jr. "Alabama's 'Negro Soldier Experiment,' 1898–1899." *Journal of Negro History* 57 (October 1971): 333–51.

Gilbert, Abby L. "The Comptroller of the Currency and the Freedmen's Savings Bank." *Journal of Negro History* 57 (April 1972): 125–43.

Going, Allen J. "Historical Societies in Alabama." *Alabama Review* 1 (January 1948): 39–49.

Going, William T. "The Prose Fiction of Samuel Minturn Peck." *Alabama Review* 8 (January 1955): 36–42.

———. "Samuel Minturn Peck, Late Laureate of Alabama: A Fie de Siecle Study." *Georgia Review* 8 (Summer 1954): 190–200.

Goodrich, Gillian. "Romance and Reality, The Birmingham Suffragists, 1892–1920." *Journal of the Birmingham Historical Society* 5 (January 1978): 5–21.

Harris, Carl V. "Stability and Change in Discrimination Against Black Public Schools: Birmingham, Alabama, 1871–1931." *Journal of Southern History* 51 (August 1985): 375–416.

Hasson, Gail S. "Health and Welfare of Freedmen in Reconstruction Alabama." *Alabama Review* 35 (April 1982): 94–110.

Hennessey, Melinda Meek. "Political Terrorism in the Black Belt: The Eutaw Riot." *Alabama Review* 33 (January 1980): 35–48.

Horton, Paul. "Testing the Limits of Class Politics in Postbellum Alabama: Agrarian Radicalism in Lawrence County." *Journal of Southern History* 57 (February 1991): 63–84.

Howard, Milo B., Jr. "Histories of Alabama." *Alabama Review* 22 (October 1969): 243–53.

Howington, Arthur F. "John Barley Corn Subdued: The Enforcement of Prohibition in Alabama." *Alabama Review* 23 (July 1970): 212–25.

Hume, Richard L. "The Freedmen's Bureau and Freedmen's Vote in the Reconstruction of South Alabama: An Account by Agent Samuel S. Gardner." *Alabama Historical Quarterly* 37 (Fall 1975): 217–24.

James, Felix. "The Tuskegee Institute Movable School, 1906–1923." *Agricultural History* 45 (July 1971): 201–09.

Johnson, Kenneth R. "The Peabody Fund: Its Role and Influence in Alabama." *Alabama Review* 27 (April 1974): 101–26.

Jones, Allen W. "Political Reform and Party Factionalism in the Deep South: Alabama's 'Dead Shoes' Senatorial Primary of 1906." *Alabama Review* 26 (January 1973): 3–32.

Keeler, Rebecca T. "Alva Belmont: Exacting Benefactor for Women's Suffrage." *Alabama Review* 41 (April 1988): 132–45.

Keith, Jean E. "The Role of the Louisville and Nashville Railroad in the Early Development of Alabama Coal and Iron." *Business Historical Society Bulletin* 26 (September 1952): 165–74.

Kelley, Don Quinn. "Ideology and Education: Uplifting the Masses in Nineteenth Century Alabama." *Phylon* 40 (June 1979): 147–58.

Kendrick, Jack E. "Alabama's Congressmen in the Wilson Administration." *Alabama Review* 24 (October 1971): 243–60.

Knapp, Virginia. "William Phineas Brown, Business Man and Pioneer Mine Operator in Alabama." *Alabama Review* 3 (April 1950): 10–22; 3 (July 1950): 193–99.

Kolchin, Peter. "Scalawags, Carpetbaggers, and Reconstruction: A Quantitative Look at Southern Congressional Politics, 1868–1872." *Journal of Southern History* 45 (February 1979): 63–76.

Lennox, Tim. "Rosa Zinszer: Birmingham Entrepreneuse Extraordinary." *Journal of the Birmingham Historical Society* 6 (January 1980): 19–23.

Lincoln, C. Eric. "The Black Church in the Context of American Religion." In *Varieties of Religious Experience*, edited by Samuel S. Hill. Baton Rouge: Louisiana State University Press, 1988.

Link, William L. "Privies, Progressivism, and Public Schools: Health Reform and Education in the Rural South, 1909–1920." *Journal of Southern History* 54 (November 1980): 623–42.

Longacre, Edward G., ed. "To Tuscaloosa and Beyond: A Union Cavalry Raider in Alabama, March–April, 1865." *Alabama Historical Quarterly* 44 (Spring and Summer 1982): 109–22.

McKenzie, Robert H. "The Economic Impact of Federal Operations in Alabama During the Civil War." *Alabama Historical Quarterly* 38 (Spring 1976): 51–68.

———. "Farrah's Future: The First One Hundred Years of the University of Alabama School of Law, 1872–1972." *Alabama Law Review* 25 (Fall 1972): 121–64.

——. "Reconstruction of the Alabama Iron Industry, 1865–1880." *Alabama Review* 25 (July 1972): 178–91.

Meigs, Henry V. "Cotton Manufacturing in Alabama." In Saffold Berney, *Hand-Book of Alabama*. Birmingham: Roberts and Son, 1892.

Moore, James Tice. "Redeemers Reconsidered: Change and Continuity in the Democratic South, 1870–1900." *Journal of Southern History* 44 (August 1978): 357–78.

Muskat, Beth Taylor. "The Last March: The Demise of the Black Militia in Alabama." *Alabama Review* 43 (January 1990): 18–34.

Myers, John B. "The Alabama Freedmen and the Economic Adjustments During Presidential Reconstruction, 1865–1867." *Alabama Review* 26 (October 1973): 252–66.

——. "The Freedmen and the Law in Post-Bellum Alabama, 1865–1867." *Alabama Review* 23 (January 1970): 56–69.

Neal, Christine. "Daughters of the South." *Alabama Heritage,* no. 21 (Summer 1991): 6–19.

Nieman, Donald G. "Andrew Johnson, the Freedmen's Bureau, and the Problem of Equal Rights, 1865–1866." *Journal of Southern History* 44 (August 1978): 401–20.

Nolan, Paul T. "Alabama Drama, 1870–1916: A Checklist." *Alabama Review* 18 (January 1965): 65–72.

Oldshue, Jerry. "Remembering Education in Hale County During Reconstruction." *Alabama Review* 41 (October 1988): 289–98.

Perry, William F. "The Genesis of Public Education in Alabama." *Transactions of the Alabama Historical Society* 2 (1897–98): 14–27.

Preer, Jean. " 'Just and Equitable Division,' Jim Crow and the 1890 Land Grant College Act." *Prologue* 22 (Winter 1990): 323–37.

Prewett, George W. "Unequal Funding of Alabama's Public Schools: An Historical Perspective." Revised address given at the annual meeting of the Alabama Association of Historians, Birmingham, February 1, 1991.

Pruitt, Paul M., Jr. "Julia Tutwiler: Years of Experience." *Alabama Heritage,* no. 23 (Winter 1992): 31–36.

——. "Julia Tutwiler: Years of Innocence." *Alabama Heritage,* no. 22 (Fall 1991): 37–44.

Rabinowitz, Howard N. "Half a Loaf: The Shift from White to Black Teachers in the Negro Schools of the Urban South, 1865–1890." *Journal of Southern History* 40 (November 1974): 565–94.

Reid, Robert. "Changing Interpretations of the Reconstruction Period in Alabama History." *Alabama Review* 27 (October 1974): 263–81.

Rikard, Marlene Hunt. " 'Take Everything You Are . . . and Give It Away,' Pioneer Industrial Social Workers at TCI." *Journal of the Birmingham Historical Society* 7 (March 1981): 24–41.

Roberts, Frances W. "William Manning Lowe and the Greenback Party in Alabama." *Alabama Review* 5 (April 1952): 100–121.

Rodabaugh, Karl. "Congressman Henry D. Clayton, Patriarch in Politics: A Southern Congressman During the Progressive Era." *Alabama Review* 31 (April 1978): 110–20.

Rogers, William Warren. "The Alabama State Grange." *Alabama Review* 8 (April 1955): 104–18.

———. "The Founding of Alabama's Land Grant College at Auburn." *Alabama Review* 40 (January 1987): 14–37.

———. "James M. Whitehead: Agrarian Editor of the Deep South." *Alabama Historical Quarterly* 25 (Fall and Winter 1963): 280–86.

Rogers, William Warren, Jr. "The Eutaw Prisoners: Federal Confrontation with Violence in Reconstruction Alabama." *Alabama Review* 43 (April 1990): 98–121.

Schaffer, Daniel. "War Mobilization in Muscle Shoals, Alabama, 1917–1918." *Alabama Review* 39 (April 1986): 110–46.

Schoonover, Shirley G. "Alabama Public Health Campaign, 1900–1919." *Alabama Review* 28 (July 1975): 218–31.

Schweninger, Loren. "Alabama Blacks and the Congressional Reconstruction Acts of 1867." *Alabama Review* 31 (July 1978): 182–98.

———. "Black Citizenship and the Republican Party in Reconstruction Alabama." *Alabama Review* 29 (April 1976): 83–103.

———. "James Rapier and the Negro Labor Movement, 1869–1872." *Alabama Review* 28 (July 1975): 185–201.

Sherer, Robert G. "John William Beverly: Alabama's First Negro Historian." *Alabama Review* 26 (July 1973): 194–208.

Shofner, Jerrell H., and William Warren Rogers. "Joseph C. Manning: Militant Agrarian, Enduring Populist." *Alabama Historical Quarterly* 29 (Spring/Summer 1967): 7–37.

Sloan, John Z. "The Ku Klux Klan and the Alabama Election of 1872." *Alabama Review* 18 (April 1965): 113–32.

Stephenson, Wendell H. "Some Pioneer Alabama Historians: I. George Petrie." *Alabama Review* 1 (July 1948): 164–79.

———. "Some Pioneer Alabama Historians: II. Walter L. Fleming." *Alabama Review* 1 (October 1948): 261–78.

———. "Some Pioneer Alabama Historians: III. Thomas S. Owen." *Alabama Review* 2 (January 1949): 45–62.

Straw, Richard A. "The Collapse of Biracial Unionism: The Alabama Coal Strike of 1908." *Alabama Historical Quarterly* 37 (Summer 1975): 92–114.

———. "Soldiers and Miners in a Strike Zone: Birmingham, 1908." *Alabama Review* 38 (October 1985): 289–308.

Swenson, Mary. "To Uplift a State and Nation: The Formative Years of the Alabama League of Women Voters, 1920–1921." *Alabama Historical Quarterly* 37 (Summer 1975): 115–35.

Thigpen, Richard. "The Four Public Buildings of the University of Alabama to Survive the Civil War." *Alabama Review* 34 (July 1981): 50–58.

Thornton, J. Mills, III. "Fiscal Policy and the Failure of Radical Reconstruction in the Lower South." In *Region, Race, and Reconstruction: Essays in Honor of C. Vann Woodward,* edited by S. Morgan and James McPherson. Oxford: Oxford University Press, 1982.

Trelease, Allen W. "Who Were the Scalawags?" *Journal of Southern History* 29 (November 1963): 445–68.

Vance, Silas W. "The Teacher of Helen Keller." *Alabama Review* 24 (January 1971): 51–62.

Vandiver, Frank E. "Josiah Gorgas and the Brierfield Iron Works." *Alabama Review* 3 (January 1950): 6–21.

———. "The Shelby Iron Works in the Civil War: A Study of a Confederate Industry." *Alabama Review* 1 (January 1948): 12–26; 1 (April 1948): 111–27; 1 (July 1948): 203–17.

Ward, Robert David. "Stanley Hubert Dent and American Military Policy, 1916–1920." *Alabama Historical Quarterly* 33 (Fall and Winter 1971): 177–89.

Ward, Robert David, and Frederick W. Brogdon. "The Revolt Against Wilson: Southern Leadership and the Democratic Caucus of 1920." *Alabama Historical Quarterly* 38 (Summer 1976): 144–57.

Weaver, Bill L., and James A. Thompson. "Women in Medicine and the Issue in Late Nineteenth Century Alabama." *Alabama Historical Quarterly* 43 (Winter 1981): 292–314.

White, Kenneth B. "The Alabama Freedmen's Bureau and Black Education: The Myth of Opportunity." *Alabama Review* 34 (April 1981): 107–24.

———. "Black Lives, Red Tape: The Alabama Freedmen's Bureau." *Alabama Historical Quarterly* 43 (Winter 1981): 241–58.

———. "Wager Swayne: Racist or Realist?" *Alabama Review* 31 (April 1978): 92–109.

Wiggins, Sarah Woolfolk. "Alabama: Democratic Bulldozing and Republican Folly." In *Reconstruction and Redemption in the South,* edited by Otto H. Olson. Baton Rouge: Louisiana State University Press, 1980.

———. "Ostracism of White Republicans in Alabama During Reconstruction." *Alabama Review* 27 (January 1974): 52–64.

———. "Proposals for Women Suffrage in Alabama in 1867." *Alabama Historical Quarterly* 32 (Fall and Winter 1970): 181–85.

Williams, Benjamin Buford. "'Betsy Hamilton': Alabama Local Colorist." *Alabama Historical Quarterly* 26 (Summer 1964): 235–39.

Williamson, Edward N. "The Alabama Election of 1874." *Alabama Review* 17 (July 1964): 210–18.

Wood, Forrest G. "On Revising Reconstruction History: Negro Suffrage, White Disfranchisement, and Common Sense." *Journal of Negro History* 51 (April 1966): 98–113.

Woodward, Joseph H. "Alabama Iron Manufacturing, 1860–1865." *Alabama Review* 7 (July 1954): 199–207.

Woolfolk, Sarah Van. "George E. Spencer: A Carpetbagger in Alabama." *Alabama Review* 19 (January 1966): 41–52.

Zimmerman, Jane. "The Penal Reform Movement in the South during the Progressive Era, 1890–1917." *Journal of Southern History* 17 (November 1951): 462–92.

DISSERTATIONS AND THESES

Allen, Lee N. "The Woman Suffrage Movement in Alabama." Master's thesis, Auburn University, 1949.

Brittain, Joseph Matt. "Negro Suffrage and Politics in Alabama Since 1870." Ph.D. diss., Indiana University, 1958.

Crews, Elmer J., Jr. "Pentacostal Religion: The Social Origins of the Church of God." Master's thesis, Auburn University, 1983.

Day, Robert Williams. "Legal and Historical Development of Public Education in Alabama, 1901–1942." Ph.D. diss., University of North Carolina, 1951.

Dotson, James Ray. "The Historical Development of the State Normal School for White Teachers in Alabama." Ed.D. diss., University of Alabama, 1961.

Gershenberg, Irving. "Alabama: An Analysis of the Growth of White Public Education in a Southern State, 1880–1930." Ph.D. diss., University of California at Berkeley, 1967.

Gilman, Robert. "The Other Emancipation: Studies in the Society and Economy of Alabama Whites During Reconstruction." Ph.D. diss., Johns Hopkins University, 1972.

Gross, Jimmie Frank. "Alabama Politics and the Negro, 1874–1901." Ph.D. diss., University of Georgia, 1969.

Harris, David Alan. "Racists and Reformers: A Study of Progressivism in Alabama, 1896–1911." Ph.D. diss., University of North Carolina at Chapel Hill, 1967.

Head, Holman. "The Development of the Labor Movement in Alabama Prior to 1900." Master's thesis, University of Alabama, 1955.

Hoar, Peter Michael. "A History of Public Education in Alabama, 1865–1875." Master's thesis, Alabama Polytechnic Institute, 1956.

McKenzie, Robert H. "A History of the Shelby Iron Company, 1865–1881." Ph.D. diss., University of Alabama, 1971.

Massey, Richard, Jr. "A History of the Lumber Industry in Alabama and West Florida, 1880–1914." Ph.D. diss., Vanderbilt University, 1960.

Miller, Mary Swenson. "Lobbyist for the People: The League of Women Voters of Alabama, 1920–1975." Master's thesis, Auburn University, 1978.

Mitchell, Martha C. "Birmingham: Biography of a City of the New South." Ph.D. diss., University of Chicago, 1946.

Myers, John B. "Black Human Capital: The Freedmen and the Reconstruction of Labor in Alabama, 1860–1880." Ph.D. diss., Florida State University, 1974.

Perry, Robert Eugene. "Middle-Class Townsmen and Northern Capital: The Rise of the Alabama Cotton Textile Industry, 1865–1900." Ph.D. diss., Vanderbilt University, 1986.

Phillips, Alma Carmichael. "The Influence of J. L. M. Curry on the Origin and Development of the Public School System of Alabama." Master's thesis, Birmingham-Southern College, 1956.

Pruitt, Paul M., Jr. "Joseph C. Manning, Alabama Populist: A Rebel Against the Solid South." Ph.D. diss., College of William and Mary, 1980.

Rodabaugh, Karl. "The Turbulent Nineties: Agrarian Revolt and Alabama Politics." Ph.D. diss., University of North Carolina at Chapel Hill, 1981.

Roush, Gerald Lee. "Aftermath of Reconstruction: Race, Violence, and Politics in Alabama, 1874–1884." Master's thesis, Auburn University, 1973.

Stompler, Russell. "A History of the Financing of Public Schools in Alabama from Earliest Times." Ph.D. diss., University of Alabama, 1955.

Thompson, James Lee. "The Historical Development of the Congressional District Secondary Schools in Alabama." Ph.D. diss., University of Alabama, 1965.

Watson, Joel C. "Isaac Taylor Tichenor and the Administration of the Alabama Agricultural and Mechanical College." Master's thesis, Auburn University, 1968.

Webb, Samuel L. "Two-Party Politics in the One-Party South: Alabama Hill Country, 1880–1920." Ph.D. diss., University of Arkansas, 1991.

Part III. From the 1920s to the 1990s: Chapters 25–34

BOOKS

Agee, James, and Walker Evans. *Let Us Now Praise Famous Men.* Boston: Houghton Mifflin, 1941.

Akens, David S. *Historical Origins of the George C. Marshall Space Flight Center.* Huntsville: National Aeronautics and Space Administration, 1960.

Bain, Robert, Joseph M. Flora, and Louis D. Rubin, Jr. *Southern Writers: A Biographical Dictionary.* Baton Rouge: Louisiana State University Press, 1979.

Barnard, Hollinger F., ed. *Outside the Magic Circle: The Autobiography of Virginia Foster Durr.* University: University of Alabama Press, 1985.

Barnard, William D. *Dixiecrats and Democrats: Alabama Politics, 1942–1950.* University: University of Alabama Press, 1974.

Bartley, Numan V., and Hugh D. Graham. *Southern Politics and the Second Reconstruction.* Baltimore: Johns Hopkins University Press, 1975.

Bass, Jack, and Walter DeVries. *The Transformation of Southern Politics: Social Change and Political Consequence Since 1945.* New York: Basic Books, 1976.

Beidler, Philip D., ed. *The Art of Fiction in the Heart of Dixie: An Anthology of Alabama Writers.* University: University of Alabama Press, 1986.

Black, Earl, and Merle Black. *Politics and Society in the South.* Cambridge: Harvard University Press, 1987.

Bogie, Donald W. *Education in Alabama: A Demographic Perspective.* Montgomery:

Center for Demographic and Cultural Research, Auburn University at Montgomery, 1990.

Branch, Taylor. *Parting the Waters: America in the King Years, 1954–1963.* New York: Simon and Schuster, 1988.

Brown, Virginia Pounds, and Laurella Owens. *Toting the Lead Row: Ruby Pickens Tartt, Alabama Folklorist.* University: University of Alabama Press, 1981.

Carmer, Carl. *Stars Fell on Alabama.* New York: Farrar and Rinehart, 1934.

Carter, Dan J. *Scottsboro: A Tragedy of the American South.* Baton Rouge: Louisiana State University Press, 1969.

Cason, Clarence. *90° in the Shade.* Chapel Hill: University of North Carolina Press, 1935.

Cauthen, Joyce H. *With Fiddle and Well-Rosined Bow: Old-Time Fiddling in Alabama.* Tuscaloosa: University of Alabama Press, 1989.

Chapman, H. H. *The Iron and Steel Industries of the South.* University: University of Alabama Press, 1953.

Chestnut, J. L., Jr., and Julia Cass. *Black in Selma: The Uncommon Life of J. L. Chestnut, Jr.* New York: Farrar, Straus and Giroux, 1990.

Citizens Committee of the Jefferson County Coordinating Council of Social Forces. *The Jefferson County Survey of Health, Welfare, and Recreation Needs and Services.* University: University of Alabama Press, 1955.

Citizen's Conference on State Legislatures. *The Sometimes Governments.* 2d ed. New York: Bantam Books, 1973.

Cobb, James C. *Industrialization and Southern Society, 1877–1984.* Lexington: University Press of Kentucky, 1984.

———. *The Selling of the South: The Southern Crusade for Industrial Development, 1936–1980.* Baton Rouge: Louisiana State University Press, 1982.

Crelling, John K., ed. *Plain Southern Eating: From the Reminiscences of A. L. Tommie Bass, Herbalist.* Durham: Duke University Press, 1988.

Dees, Morris. *A Season for Justice: The Life and Times of Civil Rights Lawyer Morris Dees.* New York: Scribners, 1991.

Dodd, Donald B., and Wynelle S. Dodd. *Historical Statistics of the South, 1790–1970.* University: University of Alabama Press, 1973.

Education Activity and Its Relationship to Economic Growth. Jacksonville, Ala.: Center for Economic Research, Jacksonville State University, 1987.

Fite, Gilbert C. *Cotton Fields No More: Southern Agriculture, 1865–1980.* Lexington: University Press of Kentucky, 1984.

Fitzgerald, Zelda. *Save Me the Waltz.* London: Grey Wall Press, 1953.

Flynt, J. Wayne. *Poor But Proud: Alabama's Poor Whites.* Tuscaloosa: University of Alabama Press, 1989.

Franklin, Jimmie Lewis. *Back to Birmingham: Richard Arrington, Jr., and His Times.* Tuscaloosa: University of Alabama Press, 1989.

Garrow, David, ed. *The Montgomery Bus Boycott and the Women Who Started It: The Memoir of Jo Ann Robinson.* Knoxville: University of Tennessee Press, 1987.

Bibliography

Grafton, Carl, and Anne Permaloff. *Big Mules and Branchheads: James E. Folsom and Political Power in Alabama.* Athens: University of Georgia Press, 1985.

Grant, Nancy L. *TVA and the Black Americans: Planning for the Status Quo.* Philadelphia: Temple University Press, 1990.

Grantham, Dewey W. *The Life and Death of the Solid South: A Political History.* Lexington: University Press of Kentucky, 1988.

Hamilton, Virginia Van der Veer. *Hugo Black: The Alabama Years.* Baton Rouge: Louisiana State University Press, 1972.

———. *Lister Hill: Statesman from the South.* Chapel Hill: University of North Carolina Press, 1987.

Hart, Hastings H. *Social Problems of Alabama: A Study of the Social Institutions and Agencies of the State of Alabama As Related to Its War Activities.* New York: Russell Sage Foundation, 1918.

Havard, William C., ed. *The Changing Politics of the South.* Baton Rouge: Louisiana State University Press, 1972.

The Health of America's Southern Children. N.p.: Children's Defense Fund, 1989.

Hodes, Art, and Chadwick Hensen, eds. *Selections from the Guitar: Portraits from the Jazz Record.* Berkeley and Los Angeles: University of California Press, 1977.

Hollis, Daniel W., III. *An Alabama Newspaper Tradition: Grover C. Hall and the Hall Family.* University: University of Alabama Press, 1983.

Johnson, Charles S., Edwin R. Embree, and W. W. Alexander. *The Collapse of Farm Tenancy: Summary of Field Studies and Statistical Surveys, 1933–1935.* Chapel Hill: University of North Carolina Press, 1935.

Johnson, Evans C. *Oscar W. Underwood: A Political Biography.* Baton Rouge: Louisiana State University Press, 1980.

Jones, James H. *Bad Blood: The Tuskegee Syphilis Experiment—A Tragedy of Race and Medicine.* New York: Free Press, 1981.

Kelley, Robin D. *Hammer and Hoe: Alabama Communists During The Great Depression.* Chapel Hill: University of North Carolina Press, 1990.

Kennedy, Robert F., Jr. *Judge Frank M. Johnson, Jr.* New York: G. P. Putnam's Sons, 1978.

Key, V. O., Jr. *Southern Politics in State and Nation.* New York: Alfred A. Knopf, 1949.

King, Martin Luther, Jr. *Stride Toward Freedom: The Montgomery Story.* New York: Harper and Brothers, 1958.

Knopke, Harry J., Robert J. Norrell, and Ronald W. Rogers. *Opening Doors: Perspectives on Race Relations in Contemporary America.* Tuscaloosa: University of Alabama Press, 1991.

Knowlton, Evelyn H. *Pepperell's Progress: History of a Cotton Textile Company, 1844–1945.* Cambridge: Harvard University Press, 1948.

Lamis, Alexander P. *The Two-Party South.* New York: Oxford University Press, 1984.

Logan, Onnie Lee. *Mother Wit: An Alabama Midwife's Story.* New York: E. P. Dutton, 1989.

Maharidge, Dale, and Michael Williamson. *And Their Children After Them: The Legacy of Let Us Now Praise Famous Men.* New York: Pantheon Books, 1989.

Marks, Carole. *Farewell—We're Good and Gone: The Great Black Migration.* Bloomington: Indiana University Press, 1989.

Martin, Thomas W. *The Story of Electricity in Alabama Since the Turn of the Century: 1900–1952.* Birmingham: Thomas W. Martin, 1953.

Mayfield, Sara. *The Constant Circle: H. L. Mencken and His Friends.* New York: Delacorte Press, 1968.

———. *Exiles from Paradise: Zelda and Scott Fitzgerald.* New York: Delacorte Press, 1971.

Mertz, Paul E. *New Deal Policy and Southern Rural Poverty.* Baton Rouge: Louisiana State University Press, 1978.

Milford, Nancy. *Zelda: A Biography.* New York: Harper and Row, 1970.

Morgan, Charles, Jr. *A Time to Speak.* New York: Harper and Row, 1964.

Newman, Zipp. *The Impact of Southern Football.* Montgomery: MB Publishing, 1969.

Nixon, Herman C. *Lower Piedmont Country: The Uplands of the Deep South.* New York: Duell, Sloan and Pearce, 1946.

Norrell, Robert J. *Reaping the Whirlwind: The Civil Rights Movement in Tuskegee.* New York: Alfred A. Knopf, 1985.

Nunnelly, William A. *Bull Connor.* Tuscaloosa: University of Alabama Press, 1991.

Painter, Nell Irvin. *The Narrative of Hosea Hudson: His Life as a Negro Communist in the South.* Cambridge: Harvard University Press, 1979.

Rabinowitz, Howard N. *Race Relations in the Urban South, 1865–1900.* New York: Oxford University Press, 1978.

Raines, Howell. *My Soul Is Rested: Movement Days in the Deep South Remembered.* New York: G. P. Putnam's Sons, 1977.

Rosengarten, Theodore. *All God's Dangers: The Life of Nate Shaw.* New York: Alfred A. Knopf, 1975.

Salmond, John A. *The Conscience of a Lawyer: Clifford J. Durr and American Civil Liberties, 1899–1975.* Tuscaloosa: University of Alabama Press, 1990.

———. *A Southern Rebel: The Life and Times of Aubrey Willis Williams, 1890–1965.* Chapel Hill: University of North Carolina Press, 1983.

Shouse, Sarah Newman. *Hillbilly Realist: Herman Clarence Nixon of Possum Trot.* University: University of Alabama Press, 1986.

Silvester, Peter J. *A Left Hand Like God: A Study of Boogie-Woogie.* London: Quartet Books, 1988.

Sims, George. *The Little Man's Big Friend: James E. Folsom in Alabama Politics, 1946–1958.* University: University of Alabama Press, 1985.

Smith, Douglas L. *The New Deal in the Urban South.* Baton Rouge: Louisiana State University Press, 1988.

The South at Work: Employment in the South, 1969–1989. Durham: Institute for Southern Studies, 1989.

Bibliography

Taft, Philip. *Organizing Dixie: Alabama Workers in the Industrial Era.* Edited by Gary M. Fink. Westport, Conn.: Greenwood Press, 1981.

Terry, Paul W., and Verner M. Sims. *They Live on the Land: Life in an Open-Country Southern Community.* University: University of Alabama Press, Bureau of Education Research, 1940.

Wilhelm, Dwight M. *A History of the Cotton Textile Industry of Alabama, 1809–1950.* Montgomery: N.p., 1950.

Willard, William R. *Medical Education and Medical Care in Alabama, Some Inadequacies, Some Solutions.* N.p., 1983.

Williams, Roger M. *Sing a Sad Song: The Life of Hank Williams.* New York: Ballantine Books, 1970.

Wright, Gavin. *Old South, New South: Revolutions in the Southern Economy Since the Civil War.* New York: Basic Books, 1986.

Yarbrough, Tinsley E. *Judge Johnson and Human Rights in Alabama.* University: University of Alabama Press, 1981.

ARTICLES

Akenson, James E., and Harvey G. Neufeldt. "Alabama's Illiteracy Campaign for Black Adults, 1915–1930: An Analysis." *Journal of Negro Education* 54 (Spring 1985): 189–95.

Allen, Lee N. "The 1924 Underwood Campaign in Alabama." *Alabama Review* 9 (July 1956): 176–87.

———. "The Underwood Presidential Movement of 1924." *Alabama Review* 15 (April 1962): 83–99.

Alsobrook, David E. "Mobile v. Birmingham: The Alabama Medical College Controversy, 1912–1920." *Alabama Review* 36 (January 1983): 37–56.

Armbrester, Margaret E. "John Temple Graves, II: A Southern Liberal Views the New Deal." *Alabama Review* 32 (July 1979): 203–13.

"Articles on Air University." *Pegasus* (June 1948): 1–16.

Atkins, Leah Rawls. "Senator James A. Simpson and Birmingham Politics of the 1930s: His Fight Against the Spoilsmen and the Pie-Men." *Alabama Review* 41 (July 1988): 3–29.

Barnard, William D. "The Old Order Changes: Graves, Sparks, Folsom, and the Gubernatorial Election of 1942." *Alabama Review* 28 (July 1975): 163–84.

Biles, Roger. "The Urban South in the Great Depression." *Journal of Southern History* 56 (February 1990): 71–100.

Billington, Monroe. "The Alabama Clergy and the New Deal." *Alabama Review* 32 (July 1979): 214–25.

Blaser, Kent. "'Pictures from Life's Other Side': Hank Williams, Country Music, and Popular Culture in America." *South Atlantic Quarterly* 84 (Winter 1985): 12–26.

Bloomer, John W. "'The Loafers' in Birmingham in the Twenties." *Alabama Review* 30 (April 1977): 101–07.

Bibliography

Brewer, Albert P. "Famous Filibusters: High Drama in the Alabama Legislature." *Alabama Review* 43 (April 1990): 83–97.

Brownell, Blaine A. "Birmingham, Alabama: New South City in the 1920s." *Journal of Southern History* 38 (February 1972): 21–48.

———. "The Notorious Jitney and the Urban Transportation Crisis in Birmingham in the 1920s." *Alabama Review* 25 (April 1972): 105–18.

Cobbs, Nicholas H., Jr. "Hamner Cobbs as Editor of the Greensboro *Watchman*." *Alabama Review* 39 (October 1986): 261–70.

Cronenberg, Allen. "U-Boats in the Gulf: The Undersea War in 1942." *Gulf Coast Historical Review* 5 (Spring 1990): 163–78.

Crowther, Edward R. "Alabama's Fight to Maintain Segregated Schools, 1953–1956." *Alabama Review* 43 (July 1990): 206–25.

Daniel, Pete. "Black Power in the 1920s: The Case of Tuskegee Veterans Hospital." *Journal of Southern History* 36 (August 1970): 368–88.

Dinnerstein, Leonard. "The Senate's Rejection of Aubrey Williams as Rural Electrification Administrator." *Alabama Review* 21 (April 1968): 133–43.

Dobbins, Charles G. "Alabama Governors and Editors, 1930–1955: A Memoir." *Alabama Review* 29 (April 1976): 135–54.

Draughon, Ralph B. "General Holland M. Smith, U.S.M.C." *Alabama Review* 21 (January 1968): 64–76.

Erisman, Fred. "The Romantic Regionalism of Harper Lee." *Alabama Review* 24 (April 1973): 122–36.

Fairclough, Adam. "The Preachers and the People: The Origins and Early Years of the Southern Christian Leadership Conference, 1955–1959." *Journal of Southern History* 52 (August 1986): 403–40.

Flick, Warren A. "The Wood Dealer System in Mississippi: An Essay on Regional Economics and Culture." *Journal of Forest History* 29 (July 1985): 131–38.

Flynt, J. Wayne. "The Ethics of Democratic Persuasion and the Birmingham Crisis." *Southern Speech Journal* 35 (Fall 1969): 40–53.

———. "Growing Up Baptist in Anniston, Alabama: The Legacy of the Reverend Charles R. Bell, Jr." In *Clearings in the Thicket: An Alabama Humanities Reader*, edited by Jerry Elijah Brown. Macon: Mercer University Press, 1985.

———. "Organized Labor, Reform, and Alabama Politics, 1920." *Alabama Review* 23 (July 1970): 163–80.

———. "Religion in the Urban South: The Divided Religious Mind of Birmingham, 1900–1930." *Alabama Review* 30 (April 1977): 108–34.

"Football's Supercoach." *Time* 116 (September 29, 1980): 70–77.

Gilbert, William E. "Bibb Graves as a Progressive, 1927–1930." *Alabama Review* 10 (January 1957): 15–30.

Gittler, Joseph B., and Roscoe R. Giffin. "Changing Patterns of Employment in Five Southeastern States, 1930–1940." *Southern Economic Journal* 11 (October 1944): 169–82.

Going, William T. "Two Alabama Writers: Zelda Sayre Fitzgerald and Sara Haardt Mencken." *Alabama Review* 23 (January 1970): 3–29.

———. "William March's Alabama." *Alabama Review* 16 (October 1963): 243–59.

Harris, Carl V. "Stability and Change in Discrimination Against Black Public Schools: Birmingham, Alabama, 1871–1931." *Journal of Southern History* 51 (August 1985): 375–416.

Hawks, Joanne Varner. "A Select Few: Alabama's Women Legislators, 1922–1983." *Alabama Review* 38 (July 1985): 175–201.

Holley, Howard L. "Medical Education in Alabama." *Alabama Review* 7 (October 1954): 245–64.

Hollis, Daniel W., III. "The Hall Family and Twentieth-Century Journalism in Alabama." *Alabama Review* 32 (April 1979): 119–40.

Hoole, William Stanley. "Alabama's World War II Prisoner of War Camps." *Alabama Review* 20 (April 1967): 83–114.

Howington, Arthur F. "John Barley Corn Subdued: The Enforcement of Prohibition in Alabama." *Alabama Review* 23 (July 1970): 212–25.

Ingalls, Robert P. "Antiradical Violence in Birmingham During the 1930s." *Journal of Southern History* 47 (November 1981): 521–44.

Johnson, Edna Boone. "The Photographs of *Let Us Now Praise Famous Men*: Truths in Tandem." *Alabama Review* 44 (July 1991): 184–203.

Junod, Tom. "A New Head of State." *Sports Illustrated* 75 (October 7, 1991): 95–102.

Keeler, Rebecca T. "Alva Belmont: Exacting Benefactor for Women's Suffrage." *Alabama Review* 41 (April 1988): 132–45.

Key, Jack B. "Henry B. Steagall: The Conservative as a Reformer." *Alabama Review* 17 (July 1964): 198–209.

Lewis, John E. "Repeal in Alabama." *Alabama Review* 20 (October 1967): 263–71.

Martin, Charles H. "Southern Labor Relations in Transition: Gadsden, Alabama, 1930–1943." *Journal of Southern History* 47 (November 1981): 545–68.

Martin, David L. "Alabama: Personalities and Factionalism." In *Interest Group Politics in the Southern States*, edited by Ronald J. Hrebenar and Clive S. Thomas. Tuscaloosa: University of Alabama Press, 1992.

Matthews, John M. "Clarence Cason Among the Southern Liberals." *Alabama Review* 38 (January 1985): 3–18.

Morgan, Carl C., Jr. "Craig Air Force Base: Its Effect on Selma, 1940–1977." *Alabama Review* 42 (April 1989): 83–96.

Norrell, Robert J. "Caste in Steel: Jim Crow Careers in Birmingham, Alabama." *Journal of American History* 73 (December 1986): 669–94.

———. "Labor at the Ballot Box: Alabama Politics from the New Deal to the Dixiecrat Movement." *Journal of Southern History* 57 (May 1991): 201–34.

O'Toole, Laurence J., Jr. "Gubernatorial Transition in Alabama." In *Gubernatorial Transitions: The 1982 Election*, edited by Thad L. Beyle. Durham: Duke University Press, 1985.

Pearce, Juliette D. "Maxwell: The Man and the Base." *Aerospace Historian* 16 (Spring 1969): 6–9.

Permaloff, Anne, and Carl Grafton. "The Chop-Up Bill and the Big Mule Alliance." *Alabama Review* 43 (October 1990): 243–69.

Reiman, Richard A. "Aubrey Williams: A Southern New Dealer in the Civil Rights Movement." *Alabama Review* 43 (July 1990): 181–205.

Rieff, Burt M. "Browder v. Gayle: The Legal Vehicle of the Montgomery Bus Boycott." *Alabama Review* 41 (July 1988): 193–208.

Rikard, Marlene Hunt. "George Gordon Crawford: Man of the New South." *Alabama Review* 31 (July 1978): 163–81.

Salmond, John. "'Aubrey Williams Remembers': A Note on Franklin D. Roosevelt's Attitude Toward Negro Rights." *Alabama Review* 25 (January 1972): 62–77.

Saloutos, Theodore. "The Alabama Farm Bureau Federation: Early Beginnings." *Alabama Review* 13 (July 1960): 185–98.

Sandlin, Winfred G. "Lycurgus Breckenridge Musgrove." *Alabama Review* 20 (July 1967): 205–15.

Schwenning, G. T. "Prospects of Southern Textile Unionism." *Journal of Political Economy* 39 (December 1931): 738–810.

Sellers, James B. "Alabama's Losses in the Korean Conflict." *Alabama Review* 13 (July 1960): 210–15.

Smith, Dale C., and James Everett Voyles. "New Coalitions in Alabama Voting Patterns." *Alabama Review* 27 (July 1974): 197–212.

Snell, William R. "Fiery Crosses in the Roaring Twenties: Activities of the Revised Klan in Alabama, 1915–1930." *Alabama Review* 23 (October 1970): 256–76.

Straw, Richard A. "The United Mine Workers of America and the 1920 Coal Strike in Alabama." *Alabama Review* 28 (April 1975): 104–28.

Sweeney, Charles P. "Bigotry in the South." *Nation* 119 (November 24, 1924): 585–86.

———. "Bigotry Turns to Murder." *Nation* 113 (August 31, 1921): 232–33.

Tanner, Ralph. "The Wonderful World of Tom Heflin." *Alabama Review* 36 (July 1983): 163–74.

Taylor, James S. "John M. Patterson and the 1958 Alabama Gubernatorial Race." *Alabama Review* 23 (July 1970): 212–25.

Thomas, Mary Martha. "Rosie the Alabama Riveter." *Alabama Review* 39 (July 1986): 196–212.

Thornton, J. Mills, III. "Alabama Politics, J. Thomas Heflin, and the Expulsion Movement of 1929." *Alabama Review* 21 (April 1968): 83–112.

———. "Challenge and Response in the Montgomery Bus Boycott of 1955–1956." *Alabama Review* 33 (July 1980): 163–235.

———. "Selma's Smitherman Affair of 1955." *Alabama Review* 44 (April 1991): 112–31.

Walker, Chip. "German Creative Activities in Camp Aliceville, 1943–1946." *Alabama Review* 38 (January 1985): 19–37.

Walls, Peggy G. "Gold Mining at Hog Mountain in the 1930s." *Alabama Review* 37 (July 1984): 202–20.

Wilgus, D. K. "Country-Western Music and the Urban Hillbilly." *Journal of American Folklore* 53 (April–June 1970): 157–79.

Wilson, Charles Reagan. "The Death of Bear Bryant: Myth and Ritual in the Modern South." *South Atlantic Quarterly* 86 (Summer 1987): 283–94.

MANUSCRIPT COLLECTIONS

Alabama Cooperative Extension Service. Annual Reports, State Home Demonstration Work. Auburn University Archives.

Alabama State Sovereignty Commission Administrative Files. Alabama State Archives, Montgomery.

Annual Reports, 1920–1941, Cooperative Extension Papers. Auburn University Archives.

Carmichael, Mary Alice Beatty. "Donald Croom Beatty: Alabama's Aviator, Explorer, and Inventor." 1988. Unpublished ms. in author's possession.

Clergy Letters, Alabama. President's Personal File. Franklin D. Roosevelt Library, Hyde Park, New York.

Dawson, Harris P. "Fifty-Eight Years of Pediatric Practice in Montgomery, Alabama." Unpublished diary, Alabama State Archives, Montgomery.

Denison, George A. "The History of Public Health in Alabama." Unpublished ms., 1951. Alabama State Archives, Montgomery.

Eleanor Roosevelt Papers. Franklin D. Roosevelt Library, Hyde Park, New York.

Florence Charles Hall Pinkston Papers. Alabama State Archives, Montgomery.

Grover C. Hall, Sr. Papers. Alabama State Archives, Montgomery.

Harry L. Hopkins Papers. Franklin D. Roosevelt Library, Hyde Park, New York.

John A. Peterson Diaries. Alabama State Archives, Montgomery.

Lorena Hickok Papers. Franklin D. Roosevelt Library, Hyde Park, New York.

Marie Bankhead Owen Papers. Alabama State Archives, Montgomery.

Martin, Charles H. "The Integration of Southeastern Conference Athletics." Unpublished ms. presented to Southern Historical Association, November 30, 1990.

Philip Taft Research Notes. Birmingham Public Library and Archives.

Tallulah Bankhead Correspondence, 1931–1934. Alabama State Archives, Montgomery.

Thad Holt Papers. Alabama State Archives, Montgomery.

U.S. Federal Emergency Relief Administration State Series, Alabama. Record Group 69, National Archives, Washington, D.C.

DISSERTATIONS AND THESES

Anderson, Elizabeth Lynne. "Improving Rural Life in Alabama: The Home Demonstration Program, 1911–1972." Master's thesis, Auburn University, 1984.

Austin, Deborah Waldrop. "Thomas Monroe Campbell and the Development of Negro Agriculture Extension Work, 1883–1956." Master's thesis, Auburn University, 1975.

Autrey, Dorothy A. "The National Association for the Advancement of Colored People in Alabama, 1913–1952." Ph.D. diss., University of Notre Dame, 1985.

Bevis, John D. "Frank M. Dixon: Alabama's Reform Governor." Master's thesis, Samford University, 1968.

Brannen, Ralph N. "John McDuffie: State Legislator, Congressman, Federal Judge, 1883–1950." Ph.D. diss., Auburn University, 1975.

Briles, Timothy H. "The *Brown* Decision in Alabama: Rationale Behind the Reaction, 1954–1957." Master's thesis, Auburn University, 1984.

Buford, James A., Jr. "Some Aspects of Competition in the Southern Pine Industry of Alabama, 1967–1972." Ph.D. diss., University of Georgia, 1974.

Burns, Gladys King. "The Alabama Dixiecrat Revolt of 1948." Master's thesis, Auburn University, 1965.

Carmichael, Odelle. "A Decade of Aid to Dependent Children in Alabama." Master's thesis, Tulane University, 1946.

Clark, Elizabeth B. "The Abolition of the Convict Lease System in Alabama, 1913–1928." Master's thesis, University of Alabama, 1949.

Cooke, Leonard C. "The Development of the Road System of Alabama." Master's thesis, University of Alabama, 1935.

Corley, Robert G. "The Quest for Racial Harmony: Race Relations in Birmingham, Alabama, 1947–1963." Ph.D. diss., University of Virginia, 1979.

Crider, Robert F. "The Social Philosophy of L. L. Gwaltney, 1919–1950." Master's thesis, Samford University, 1969.

Dees, Owen. "A General Review of the Miller Administration, 1931–1935." Master's thesis, Auburn University, 1936.

Dooley, Vincent J. "United States Senator James Thomas Heflin and the Democratic Party Revolt in Alabama." Master's thesis, Auburn University, 1963.

Dysart, Mary Dixie. "'Us Poor Country People Need Help': The Impact of Federal Maternity and Infancy Legislation in Alabama, 1920–1935." Master's thesis, Auburn University, 1991.

Feldman, Glenn A. "Horace Wilkinson and Alabama Politics, 1887–1957." Master's thesis, Auburn University, 1992.

Gilbert, William E. "The First Administration of Governor Bibb Graves, 1927–1930." Master's thesis, University of Alabama, 1953.

Gilliam, Thomas J. "The Montgomery Bus Boycott of 1955–1956." Master's thesis, Auburn University, 1968.

———. "The Second Folsom Administration: The Destruction of Alabama Liberalism, 1954–1958." Ph.D. diss., Auburn University, 1975.

Gross, Jimmie Frank. "Strikes in the Coal, Steel, and Railroad Industries in Birmingham from 1918 to 1922." Master's thesis, Auburn University, 1962.

Gunnells, Robert D. "The Civilian Conservation Corps in Alabama." Master's thesis, Auburn University, 1990.

Hamner, Ned. "The Congressional Career of John Hollis Bankhead, Jr." Master's thesis, University of Alabama, 1951.

Heacock, Walter J. "William Brockman Bankhead, A Biography." Ph.D. diss., University of Wisconsin, 1952.

Hobbs, Delores Ann. "The States' Rights Movement of 1948." Master's thesis, Samford University, 1968.

Hudnall, Jarrett, Jr. "An Economic Analysis of Income and Employment in a Four-State Deep South Region: 1950–1960." Ph.D. diss., University of Alabama, 1966.

Huntley, Horace. "Iron Ore Miners and Mine Mill in Alabama: 1933–1952." Ph.D. diss., University of Pittsburgh, 1976.

Jakeman, Robert Jefferson. "Jim Crow Earns His Wings: The Establishment of Segregated Flight Training at Tuskegee, Alabama, 1934–1942." Ph.D. diss., Auburn University, 1988.

Kerr, Norwood A. "The Alabama Agricultural Experiment Station, 1872–1982." Ph.D. diss., Auburn University, 1982.

Key, Jack B. "John H. Bankhead, Jr. [2nd] of Alabama: The Conservative as Reformer." Ph.D. diss., Johns Hopkins University, 1966.

King, Gladys G. "History of the Alabama Convict Department." Master's thesis, Auburn University, 1937.

Lamonte, Edward S. "Politics and Welfare in Birmingham, Alabama, 1900–1975." Ph.D. diss., University of Chicago, 1976.

Lanier, Osmos, Jr. "The First Administration of James Elisha Folsom, Governor of Alabama, 1947–1950." Master's thesis, Auburn University, 1959.

Littleton, Dowe W. "Defending the Home Front: The Alabama State Council of Defense, 1917–1919." Master's thesis, Auburn University, 1991.

McConnell, Carese Brown. "Alabama's Attempts Through Legal Actions to Maintain Segregated Public Schools, 1954–1964." Master's thesis, Auburn University, 1968.

McKiven, Henry M., Jr. "Class, Race, and Community: Iron and Steel Workers in Birmingham, Alabama, 1875–1920." Ph.D. diss., Vanderbilt University, 1990.

McLeod, Jimmy R. "Methodist and Baptist Reaction to the 1928 Presidential Campaign in Alabama." Master's thesis, Samford University, 1972.

Madison, Mary Jo. "Shots in the Dark: Lynching in Tuscaloosa, Alabama, 1933." Master's thesis, Auburn University, 1991.

Miller, Mary Swenson. "Lobbyist for the People: The League of Women Voters of Alabama, 1920–1975." Master's thesis, Auburn University, 1978.

Moore, Kathleen L. "Dominant Themes in the Life of Neil Owen Davis, Editor of the *Lee County* (Alabama) *Bulletin* from 1937–1975." Master's thesis, Auburn University, 1982.

Morring, Thomas F. "The Impact of Space Age Spending on the Economy of Huntsville, Alabama." Master's thesis, Massachusetts Institute of Technology, 1964.

Murray, William D. "The Folsom Gubernatorial Campaign of 1946." Master's thesis, University of Alabama, 1949.

Nelson, Linda J. "To the Serving of Our Brethren: Origins and Early Social Ministry of the Independent Presbyterian Church of Birmingham, Alabama, 1915–1930." Master's thesis, University of Alabama in Birmingham, 1985.

Owen, Emily. "The Career of Thomas E. Kilby in Local and State Politics." Master's thesis, University of Alabama, 1942.

Pearce, John F. "Human Resources in Transition: Rural Alabama Since World War II." Ph.D. diss., University of Alabama, 1966.

Pendleton, Debbie. "New Deal Labor Policy and Alabama Textile Unionism." Master's thesis, Auburn University, 1988.

Reagan, Hugh D. "The Presidential Campaign of 1928 in Alabama." Ph.D. diss., University of Texas, 1961.

Rikard, Marlene Hunt. "An Experiment in Welfare Capitalism: The Health Care Services of the Tennessee Coal, Iron, and Railroad Company." Ph.D. diss., University of Alabama, 1983.

————. "George Gordon Crawford: Man of the New South." Master's thesis, Samford University, 1971.

Shell, Merlyn Pierce. "The 1932 Democratic Campaign in Alabama." Master's thesis, Auburn University, 1949.

Smith, Paul Maxwell, Jr. "Loyalists and States' Righters in the Democratic Party of Alabama, 1949–1954." Master's thesis, Auburn University, 1966.

Snell, William R. "The Ku Klux Klan in Jefferson County, Alabama, 1916–1930." Master's thesis, Samford University, 1967.

Snow, John R. "The Selma Campaign: A Chronicle of the Civil Rights Movement." Master's thesis, Auburn University, 1974.

Sterne, Ellin. "Prostitution in Birmingham, Alabama, 1890–1925." Master's thesis, Samford University, 1977.

Stewart, George R. "Birmingham's Reaction to the 1954 Desegregation Decision." Master's thesis, Samford University, 1967

Tankersley, Will Hill. "Developmental Forces in the Economy of Montgomery, Alabama." Master's thesis, Auburn University, 1970.

Tanner, Ralph M. "James Thomas Heflin: United States Senator, 1920–1931." Ph.D. diss., University of Alabama, 1967.

Thomas, Rebecca L. "The Narrow Path: John J. Eagan and the Social Gospel in the New South." Master's thesis, Samford University, 1988.

Thompson, Jan Gregory. "A History of the Alabama Council on Human Relations, From Roots to Redirection, 1920–1968." Ph.D. diss., Auburn University, 1983.

Underwood, Anthony P. "A Progressive History of the Young Men's Business Club of Birmingham, Alabama, 1946–1970." Master's thesis, Samford University, 1980.

Ward, Robert David. "The Political Career of Stanley Hubert Dent, Jr." Master's thesis, Auburn University, 1951.

Whitten, Clinton W. "Alabama Editorial Opinion on American Entry Into World War II (1939–1942)." Master's thesis, Auburn University, 1961.

Young, Julia Marks. "A Republican Challenge to Democratic Progressivism In the Deep South: Alabama's 1962 United States Senatorial Contest." Master's thesis, Auburn University, 1978.

GOVERNMENT DOCUMENTS / PUBLICATIONS

Alabama State Department of Education. *Annual Reports. 1920–1929.*

Alabama State Department of Education. *Report on Illiteracy By Division of Exceptional Education, 1927.* Birmingham: Birmingham Printing Company, 1927.

Alabama Department of Industrial Relations. *The Iron and Steel Industry in Alabama.* Montgomery: Alabama Department of Industrial Relations, 1950.

Alabama. *First Annual Report. State Child Welfare Department of Alabama. For Year Ending September 30, 1920.*

Alabama. Child Welfare Department. *Annual Report for the Fiscal Year Ending September 30, 1930.*

Alabama. State Department of Education. *Opportunity Schools for White Adults: Course of Study and Suggestions to Teachers.* Birmingham: Birmingham Printing Company, 1929.

Currie, R. D. Coal-Mine Safety Organizations in Alabama. Technical Paper, 489, Bureau of Mines, U.S. Department of Commerce. Washington: Government Printing Office, 1931.

Goss, Ernst P. "High Technology Employment in Huntsville and Selected U.S. Cities." Center for High Technology Management and Economic Research, University of Alabama at Huntsville, September 1985.

Hoffsommer, Harold. *Landlord-Tenant Relations and Relief in Alabama.* Research Bulletin, Series 2, No. 9, Division of Research, Statistics, and Finance, 1935.

Kilgrow, Adelaide, and Eugene Marvin Thomas, III. *History of Education in Alabama.* Bulletin 1975, No. 7. Alabama State Department of Education. 1975[?]

U.S. Bureau of the Census. *Population, 1920.* Washington: Government Printing Office, 1923.

U.S. Bureau of the Census. *Population, 1920, Vol. I.* Washington: Government Printing Office, 1921.

U.S. Bureau of the Census. *1940, Population.* Washington: Government Printing Office, 1942.

U.S. Bureau of the Census. *Population, 1950. Vol. I.* Washington: Government Printing Office, 1952.

U.S. Bureau of the Census. *1970, Characteristics of the Population, Vol. I, Part 2. Alabama.* Washington: Government Printing Office, 1973.

U.S. Bureau of the Census. *Religious Bodies, 1926. Vol. II. Separate Denominations.* Washington: Government Printing Office, 1929.

U.S. Bureau of the Census. *Religious Bodies, 1926. Vol. I. Summary and Detailed Tables.* Washington: Government Printing Office, 1930.

U.S. Department of Commerce. *Statistical Abstract of the United States, 1935.* Washington: 1935.

U.S. Department of Labor, Women's Bureau. *Women In Alabama Industries.* Washington: Government Printing Office, 1924.

Index

References to illustrations are printed in **boldface.**

About the Authors

LEAH RAWLS ATKINS is Director of the Center for Arts & Humanities at Auburn University and adjunct professor in the Department of History. A native of Birmingham, Alabama, she received her B.S., M.A., and Ph.D. from Auburn University. She has taught history at Auburn, the University of Alabama at Birmingham, and Samford University. Her publications include *The Valley and the Hills: An Illustrated History of Birmingham and Jefferson County* (1981), *The Romantic Ideal: Alabama's Plantation Eden* (1978), *A Manual for Writing Alabama State and Local History* (1976), and *A Century of Women at Auburn: Blossoms Amid the Deep Verdure* (1992).

WAYNE FLYNT is Distinguished University Professor at Auburn University. Although a native of Pontotoc, Mississippi, he grew up in Alabama. He received his A.B. from Howard College (now Samford University) and his M.S. and Ph.D. from Florida State University. From 1977 to 1985 he served as chairman of the Department of History, Auburn University. He is author of *Duncan Upshaw Fletcher: Dixie's Reluctant Progressive* (1971), *Cracker Messiah: Governor Sidney J. Catts of Florida* (1977), *Dixie's Forgotten People: The South's Poor Whites* (1979), *Montgomery: An Illustrated History* (1980), *Southern Poor Whites: A Selected Annotated Bibliography* (1981), *Mine, Mill and Microchip: A Chronicle of Alabama Enterprise* (1987), and *Poor but Proud: Alabama's Poor Whites* (1989).

WILLIAM WARREN ROGERS is Professor of History, The Florida State University. He received his B.S. and M.S. in history from Auburn University and his Ph.D. from The University of North Carolina at Chapel Hill. He is author of *The One-Gallused Rebellion: Agrarianism in Alabama* (1970) and co-author (with Robert David Ward) of *Labor Revolt in Alabama: The Great Strike of 1894* (1965), *August Reckoning: Jack Turner and Racism in Post-Civil War Alabama* (1973), and *Convicts, Coal, and the Banner Mine Tragedy* (1987). He is a native of Sandy Ridge, Alabama.

ROBERT DAVID WARD is Professor Emeritus of History, Georgia Southern University. He is a native of Montevallo, Alabama. He received his B.S. and M.S. in history from Auburn University and his Ph.D. from The University of North Carolina at Chapel Hill. He is co-author (with William Warren Rogers) of *Labor Revolt in Alabama: The Great Strike of 1894* (1965), *August Reckoning: Jack Turner and Racism in Post-Civil War Alabama* (1973), and *Convicts, Coal, and the Banner Mine Tragedy* (1987).